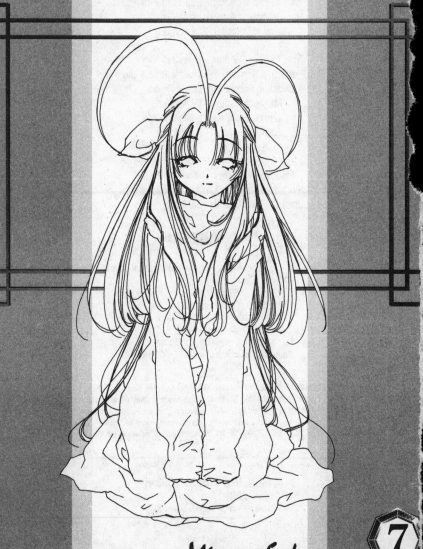

mamotte
shugogetten

7

Minene Sakurano

Mamotte Shugogetten Volume 4
Created by Minene Sakurano

Translation - Beni Axia Conrad
English Adaption - Liz Forbes
Retouch and Lettering - Star Print Brokers
Production Artist - Vince Rivera
Graphic Designer - James Lee

Editor - Hyun Joo Kim
Pre-Production Supervisor - Vicente Rivera, Jr.
Pre-Production Specialist - Lucas Rivera
Managing Editor - Vy Nguyen
Senior Designer - Louis Csontos
Senior Designer - James Lee
Senior Editor - Bryce P. Coleman
Senior Editor - Jenna Winterberg
Associate Publisher - Marco F. Pavia
President and C.O.O. - John Parker
C.E.O. and Chief Creative Officer - Stu Levy

A 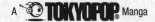 Manga

TOKYOPOP and 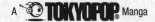 are trademarks or registered trademarks of TOKYOPOP Inc.

TOKYOPOP Inc.
5900 Wilshire Blvd. Suite 2000
Los Angeles, CA 90036

E-mail: info@TOKYOPOP.com
Come visit us online at www.TOKYOPOP.com

ISBN: 978-1-4278-0593-5

First TOKYOPOP printing: March 2009
10 9 8 7 6 5 4 3 2 1
Printed in the USA

mamotte
shugogetten™

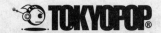

HAMBURG // LONDON // LOS ANGELES // TOKYO

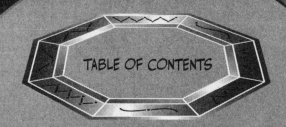

TABLE OF CONTENTS

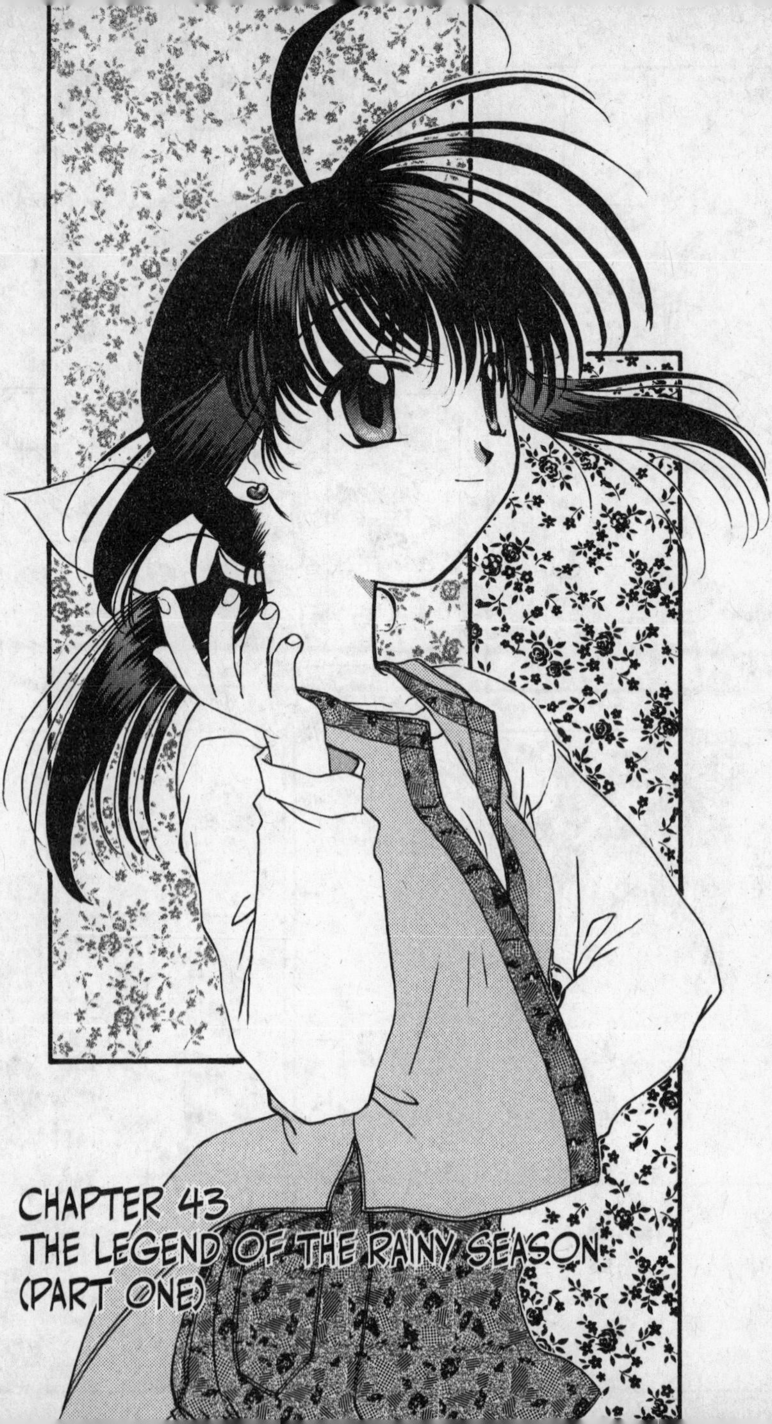
CHAPTER 43
THE LEGEND OF THE RAINY SEASON
(PART ONE)

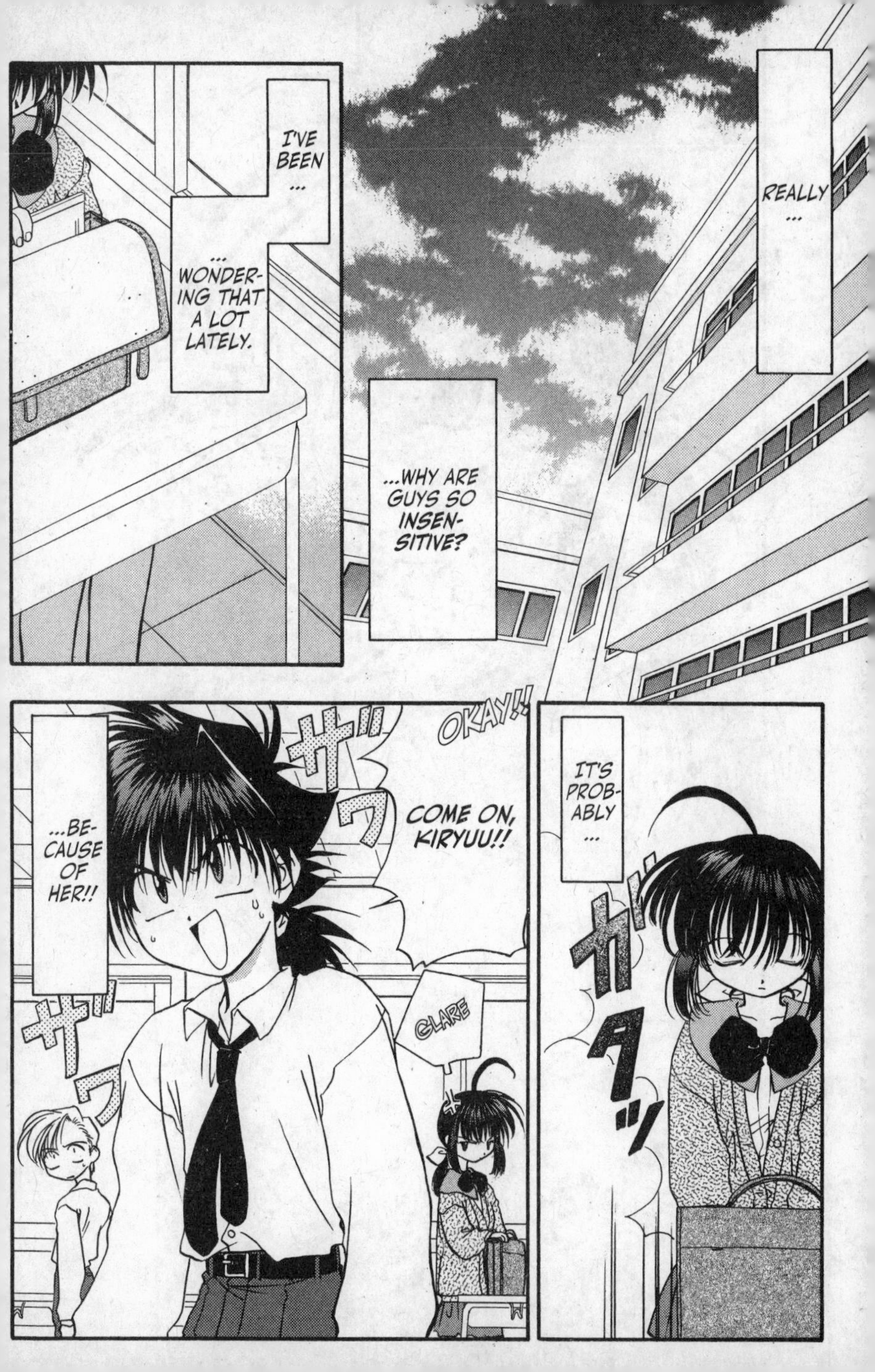
REALLY...
...WHY ARE GUYS SO INSEN-SITIVE?
I'VE BEEN...
...WONDER-ING THAT A LOT LATELY.
IT'S PROB-ABLY...
ガタッ
OKAY!!
ザワ
COME ON, KIRYUU!!
...BE-CAUSE OF HER!!
GLARE
ザワ

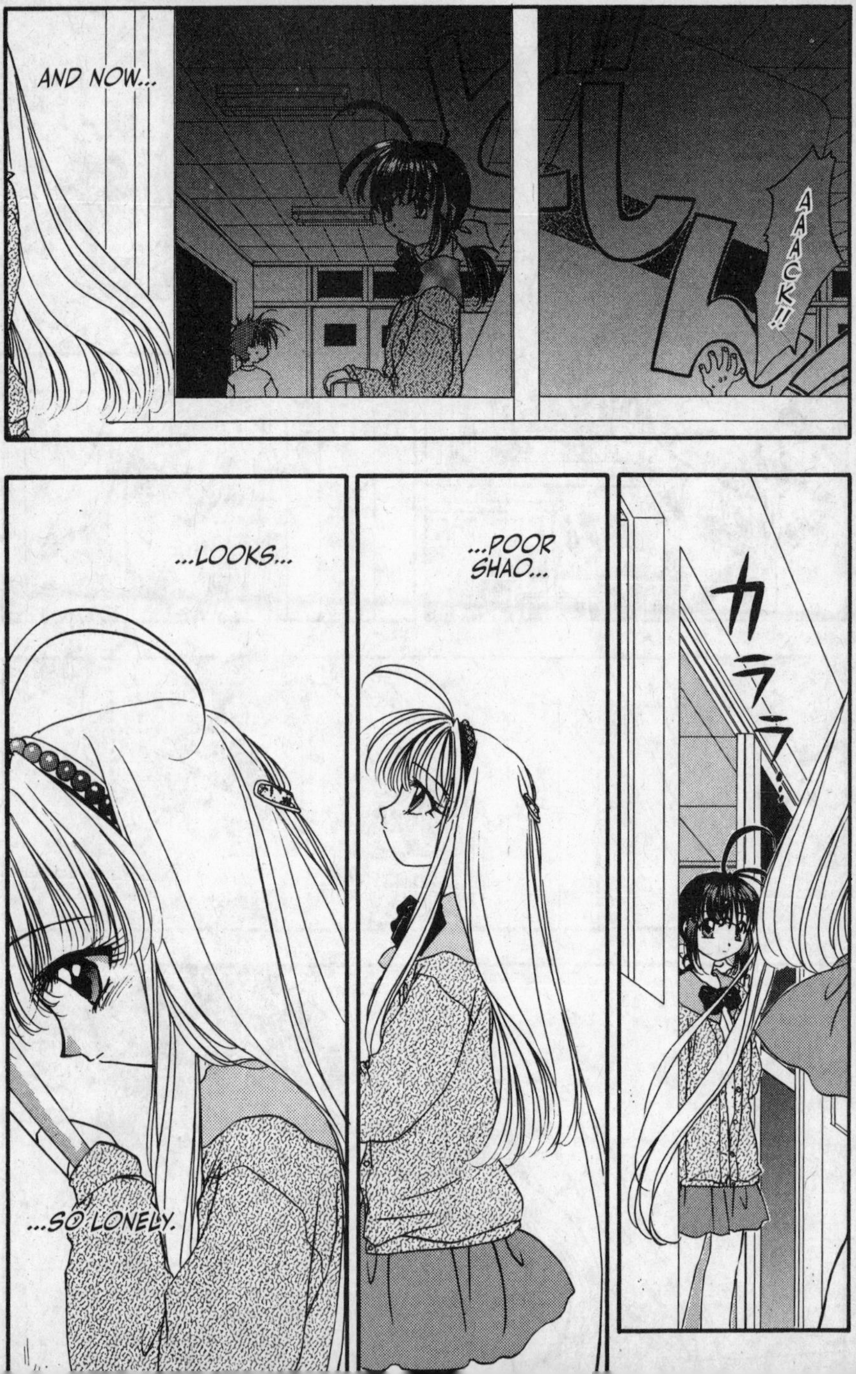
AAACK!!
AND NOW...
カラララ...
...POOR SHAO...
...LOOKS...
...SO LONELY.

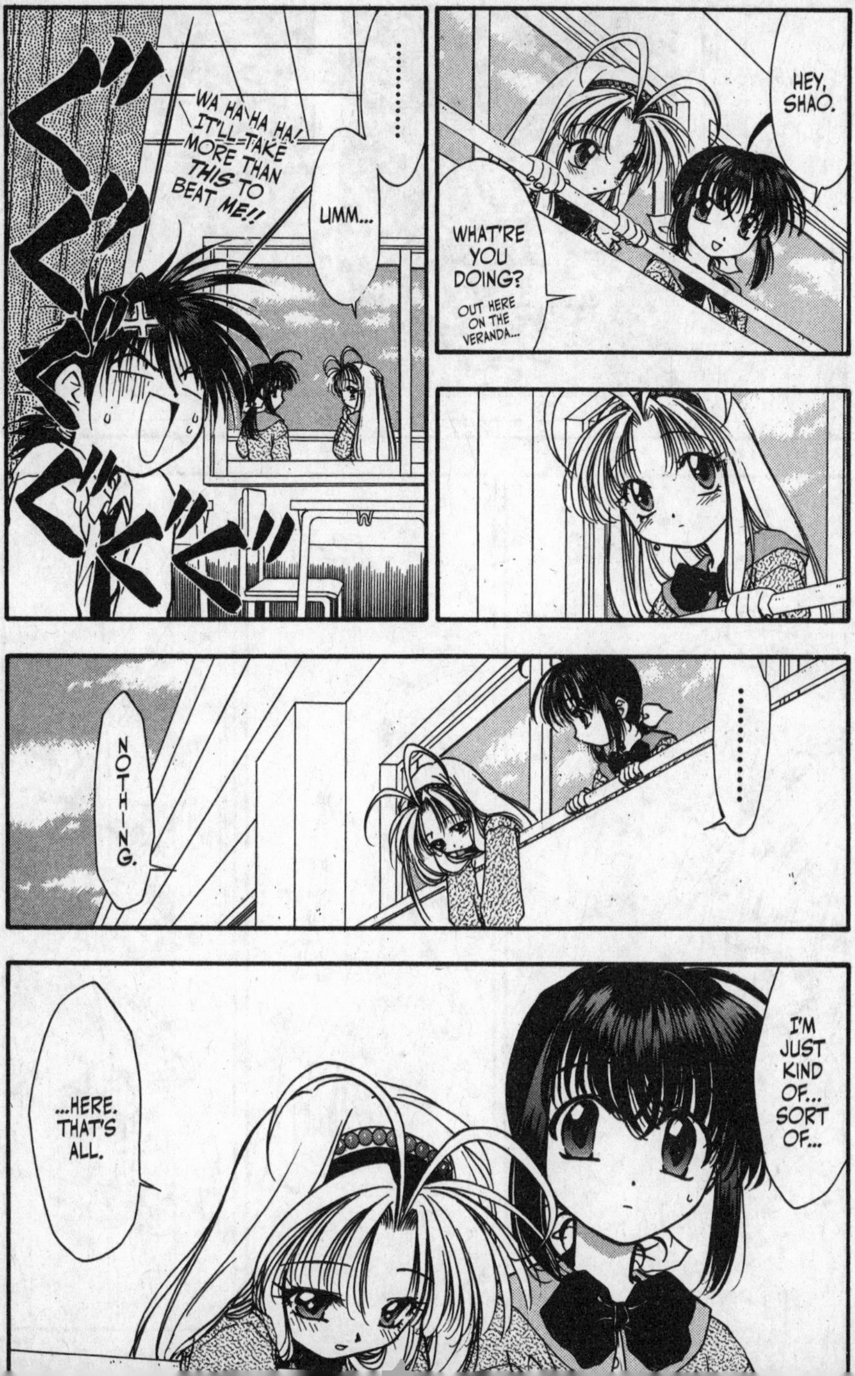
HEY, SHAO.
WHAT'RE YOU DOING?
OUT HERE ON THE VERANDA...
......
UMM...
WA HA HA HA! IT'LL TAKE MORE THAN THIS TO BEAT ME!!
......
NOTHING.
I'M JUST KIND OF... SORT OF...
...HERE. THAT'S ALL.

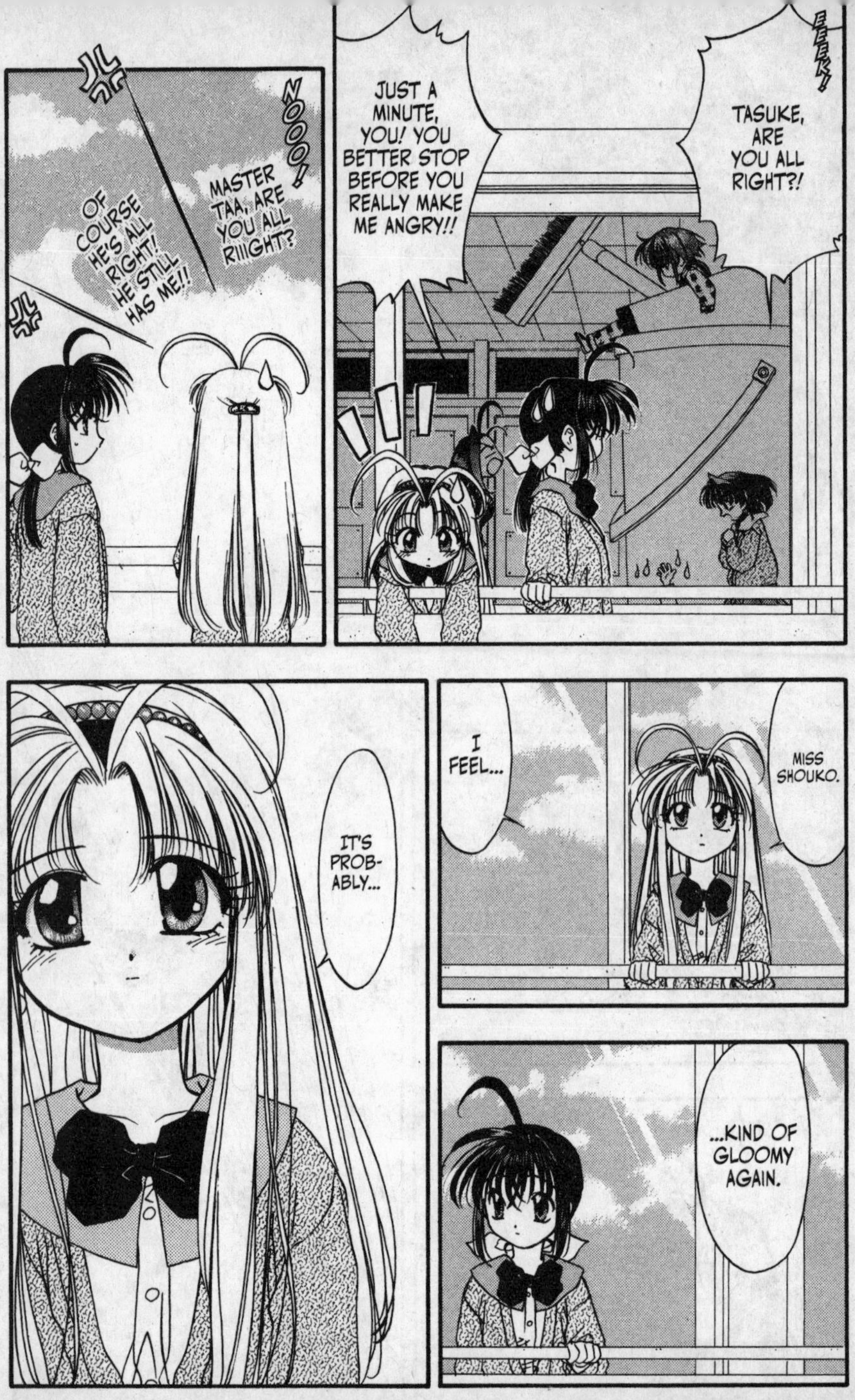
EEEK!
TASUKE, ARE YOU ALL RIGHT?!
JUST A MINUTE, YOU! YOU BETTER STOP BEFORE YOU REALLY MAKE ME ANGRY!!
NOOOO!
MASTER TAA, ARE YOU ALL RIIIGHT?
OF COURSE HE'S ALL RIGHT! HE STILL HAS ME!!
MISS SHOUKO.
I FEEL...
...KIND OF GLOOMY AGAIN.
IT'S PROB-ABLY...

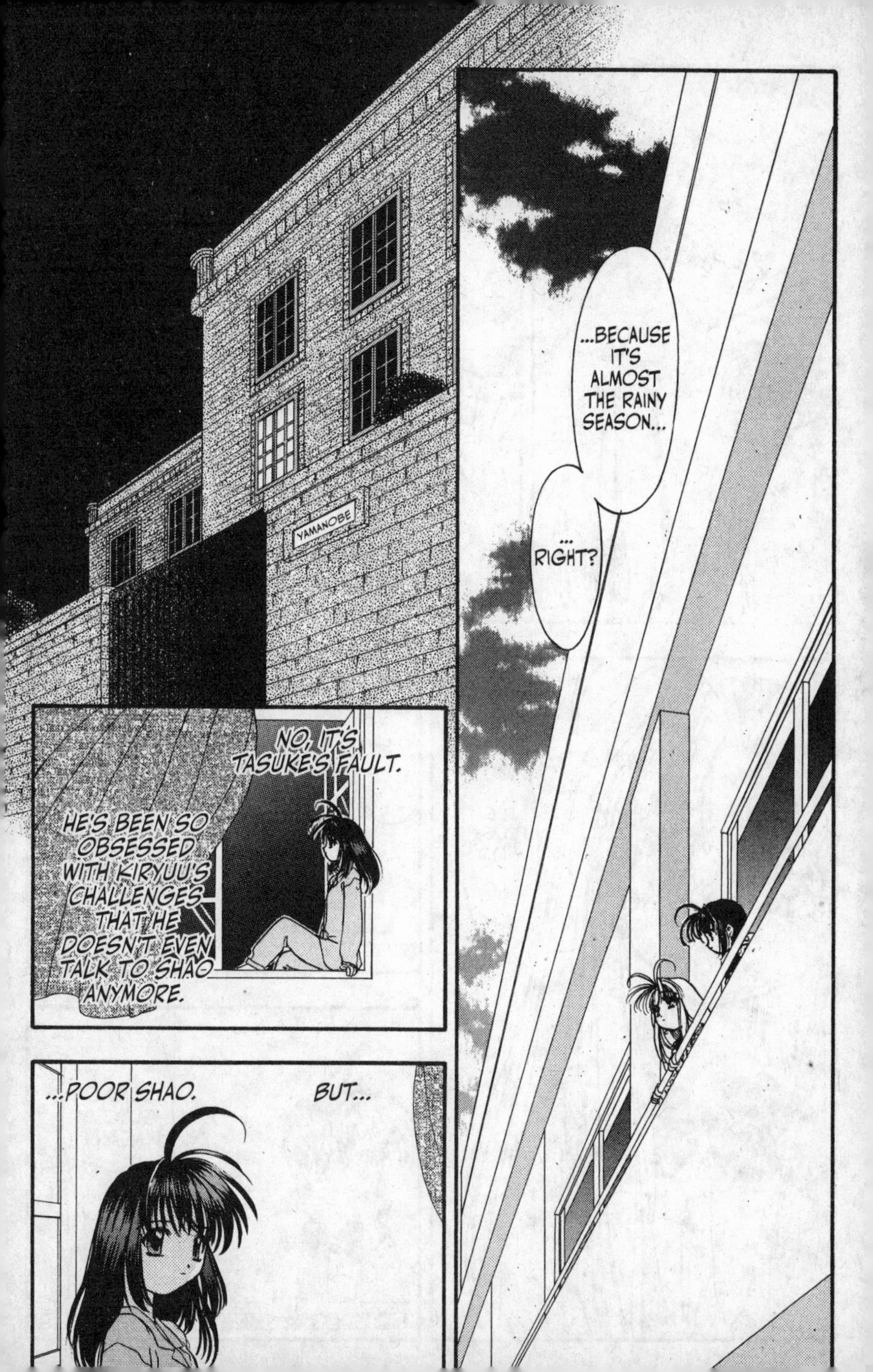
...BECAUSE IT'S ALMOST THE RAINY SEASON...
...RIGHT?
YAMANOBE
NO, IT'S TASUKE'S FAULT.
HE'S BEEN SO OBSESSED WITH KIRYUU'S CHALLENGES THAT HE DOESN'T EVEN TALK TO SHAO ANYMORE.
...POOR SHAO.
BUT...

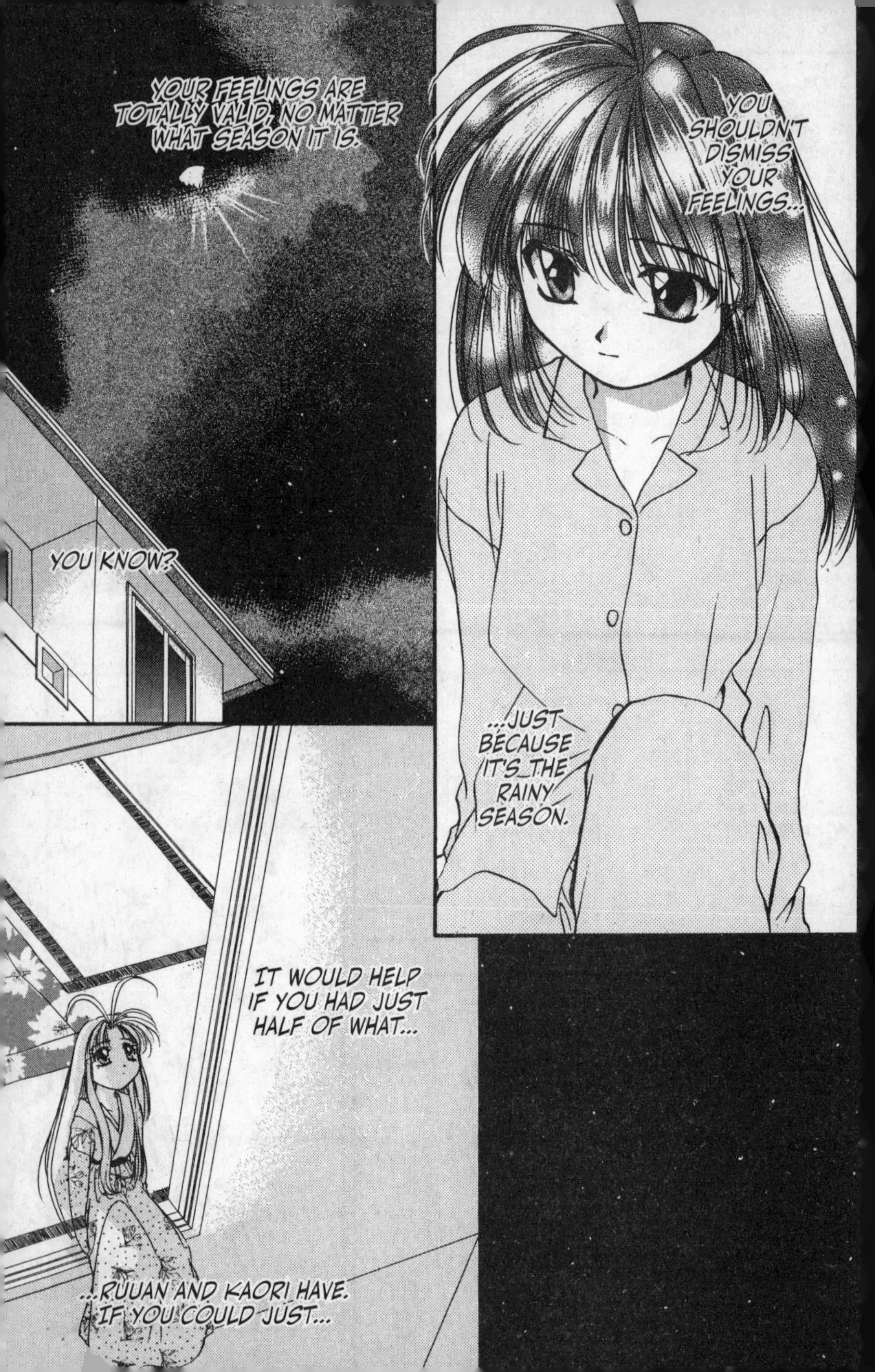
YOU SHOULDN'T DISMISS YOUR FEELINGS...
...JUST BECAUSE IT'S THE RAINY SEASON.
YOUR FEELINGS ARE TOTALLY VALID, NO MATTER WHAT SEASON IT IS.
YOU KNOW?
IT WOULD HELP IF YOU HAD JUST HALF OF WHAT...
...RUUAN AND KAORI HAVE. IF YOU COULD JUST...

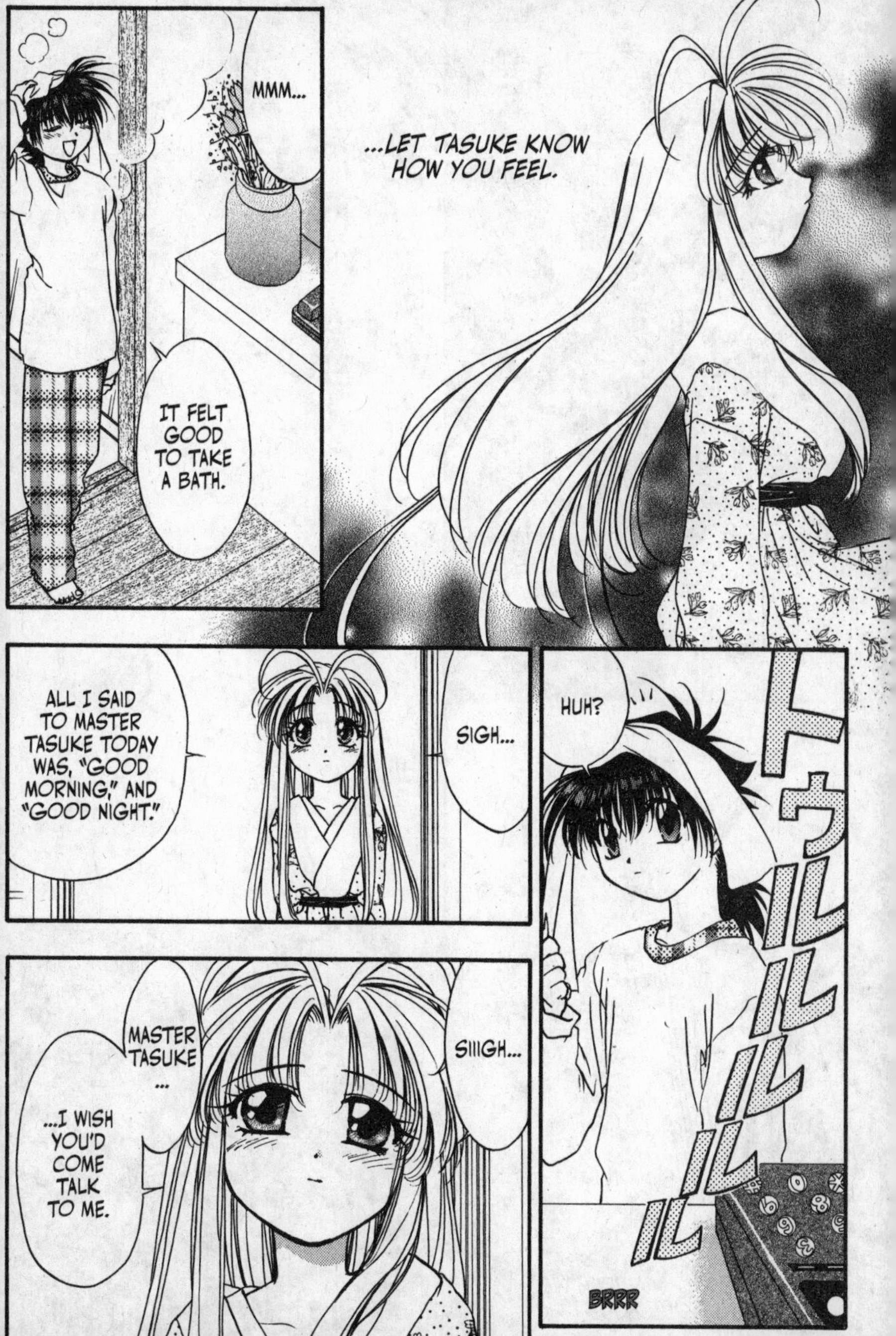
...LET TASUKE KNOW HOW YOU FEEL.
MMM...
IT FELT GOOD TO TAKE A BATH.
HUH?
トウルルルルル
BRRR
SIGH...
ALL I SAID TO MASTER TASUKE TODAY WAS, "GOOD MORNING," AND "GOOD NIGHT."
SIIIGH...
MASTER TASUKE ...
...I WISH YOU'D COME TALK TO ME.

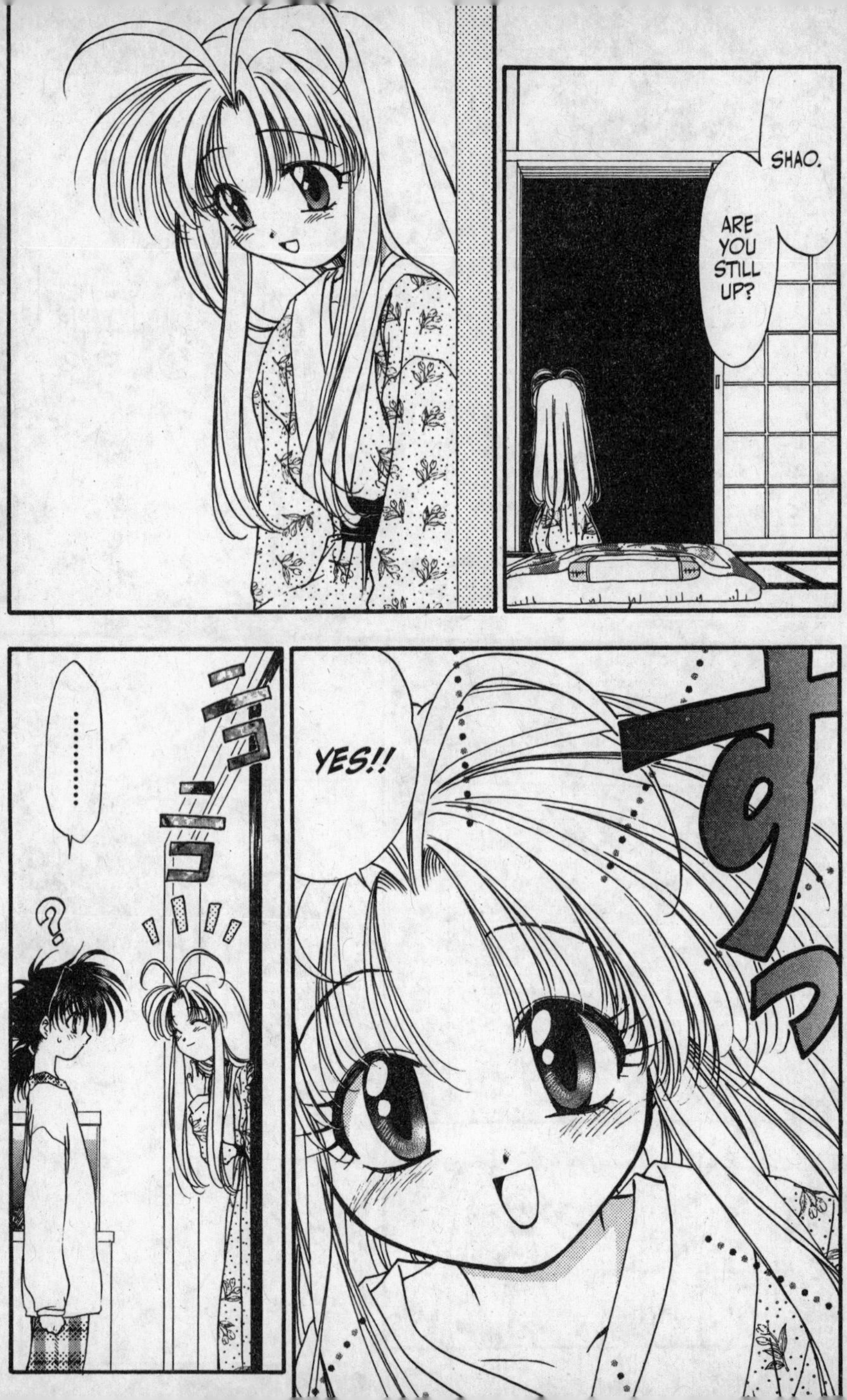
SHAO.
ARE YOU STILL UP?
YES!!
すっ
......
?

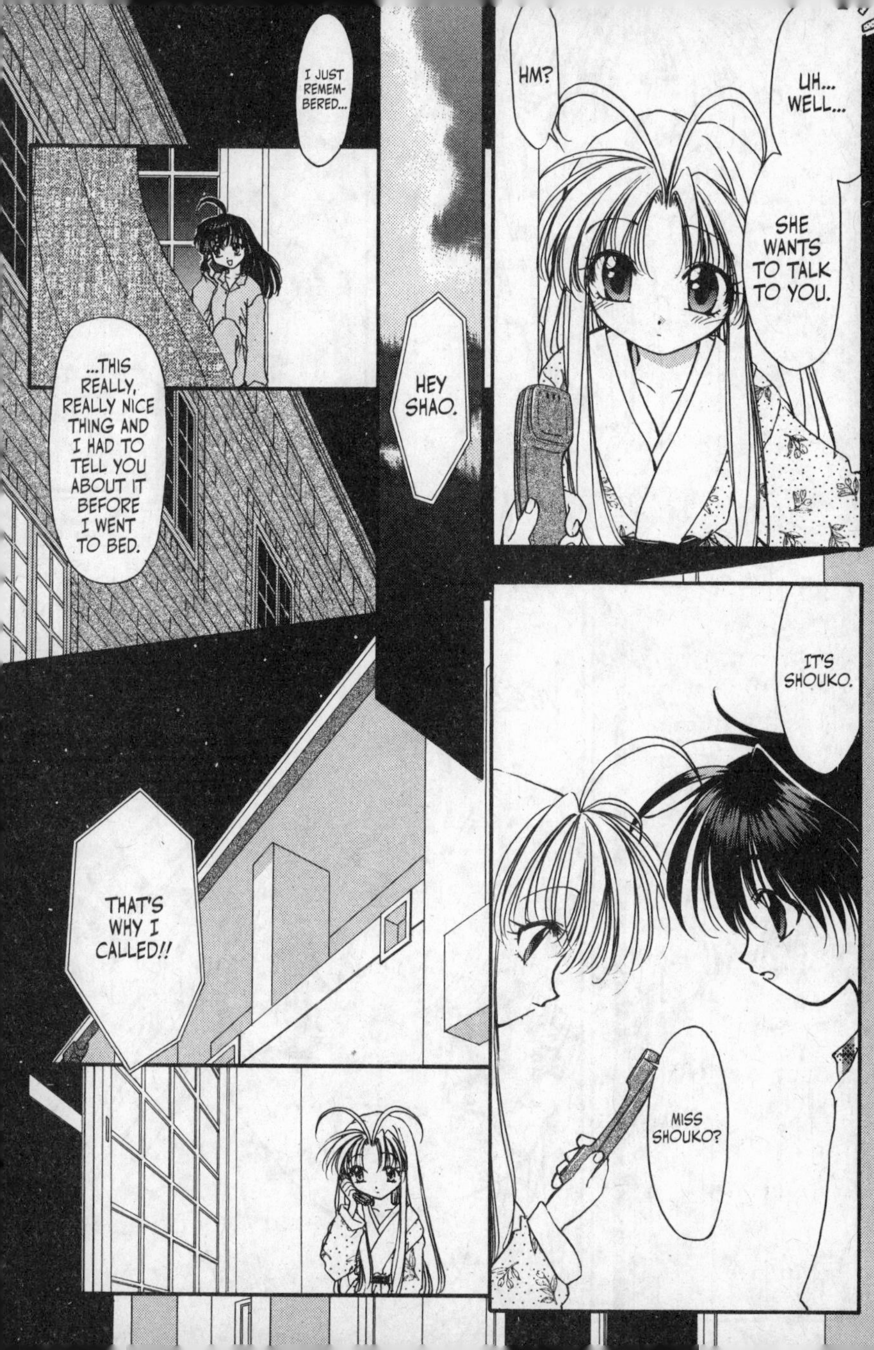
UH... WELL...
HM?
SHE WANTS TO TALK TO YOU.
IT'S SHOUKO.
MISS SHOUKO?
HEY SHAO.
I JUST REMEMBERED...
...THIS REALLY, REALLY NICE THING AND I HAD TO TELL YOU ABOUT IT BEFORE I WENT TO BED.
THAT'S WHY I CALLED!!

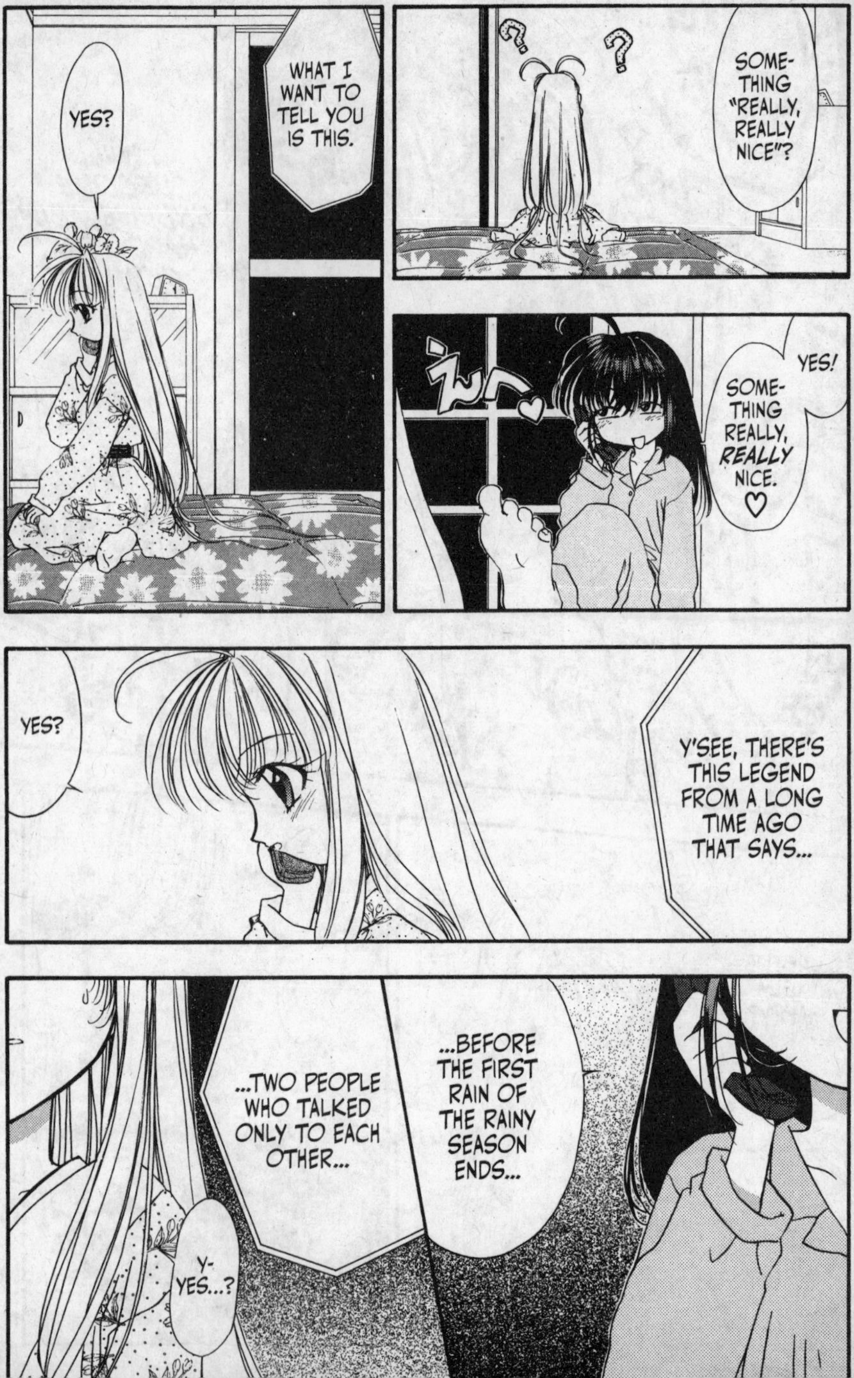
SOME-THING "REALLY, REALLY NICE"?
YES!
SOME-THING REALLY, REALLY NICE. ♡
WHAT I WANT TO TELL YOU IS THIS.
YES?
Y'SEE, THERE'S THIS LEGEND FROM A LONG TIME AGO THAT SAYS...
YES?
...BEFORE THE FIRST RAIN OF THE RAINY SEASON ENDS...
...TWO PEOPLE WHO TALKED ONLY TO EACH OTHER...
Y-YES...?

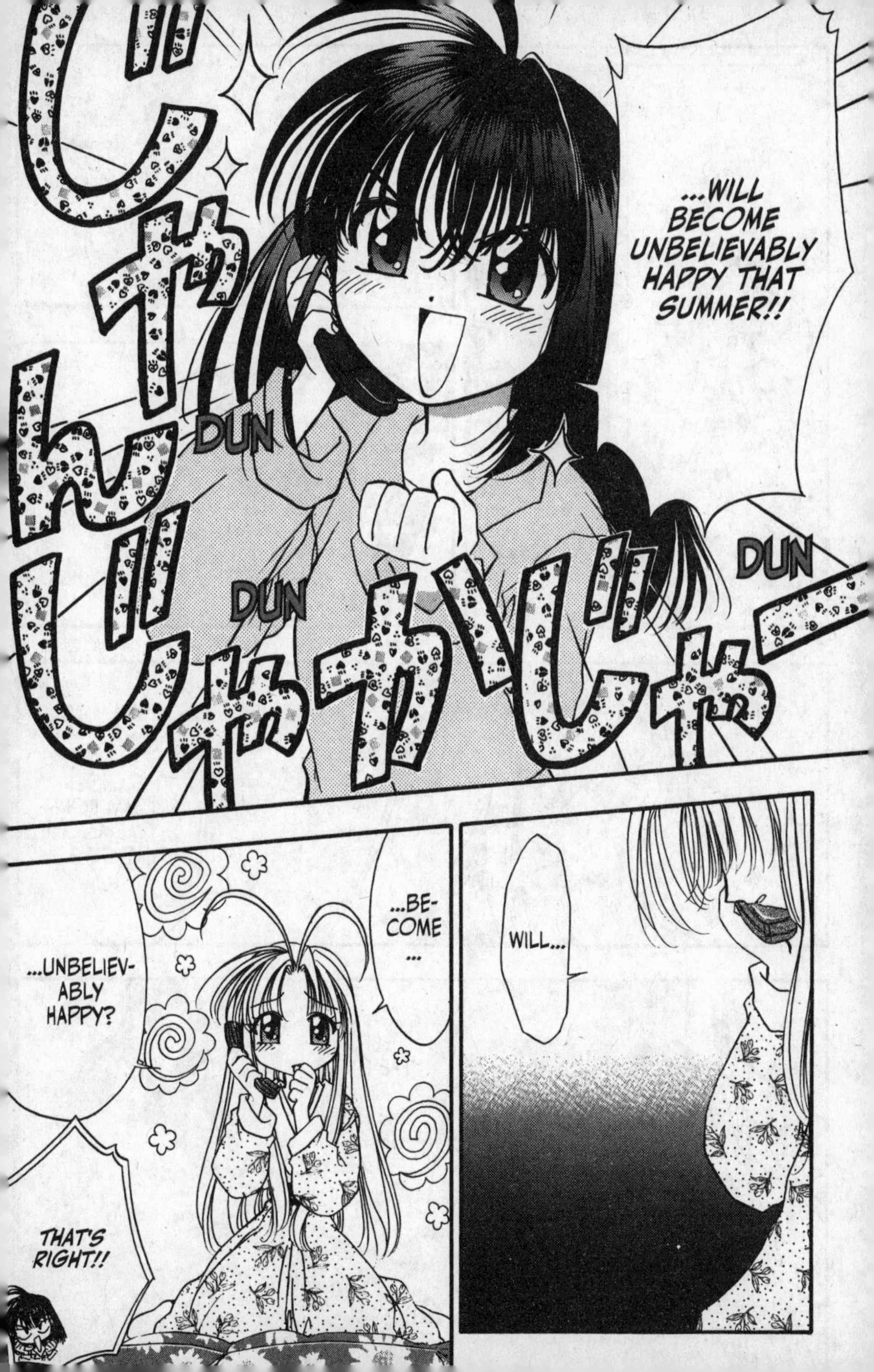
...WILL BECOME UNBELIEVABLY HAPPY THAT SUMMER!!
じゃんじゃかじゃー
DUN
DUN
DUN
WILL...
...BE-COME ...
...UNBELIEV-ABLY HAPPY?
THAT'S RIGHT!!

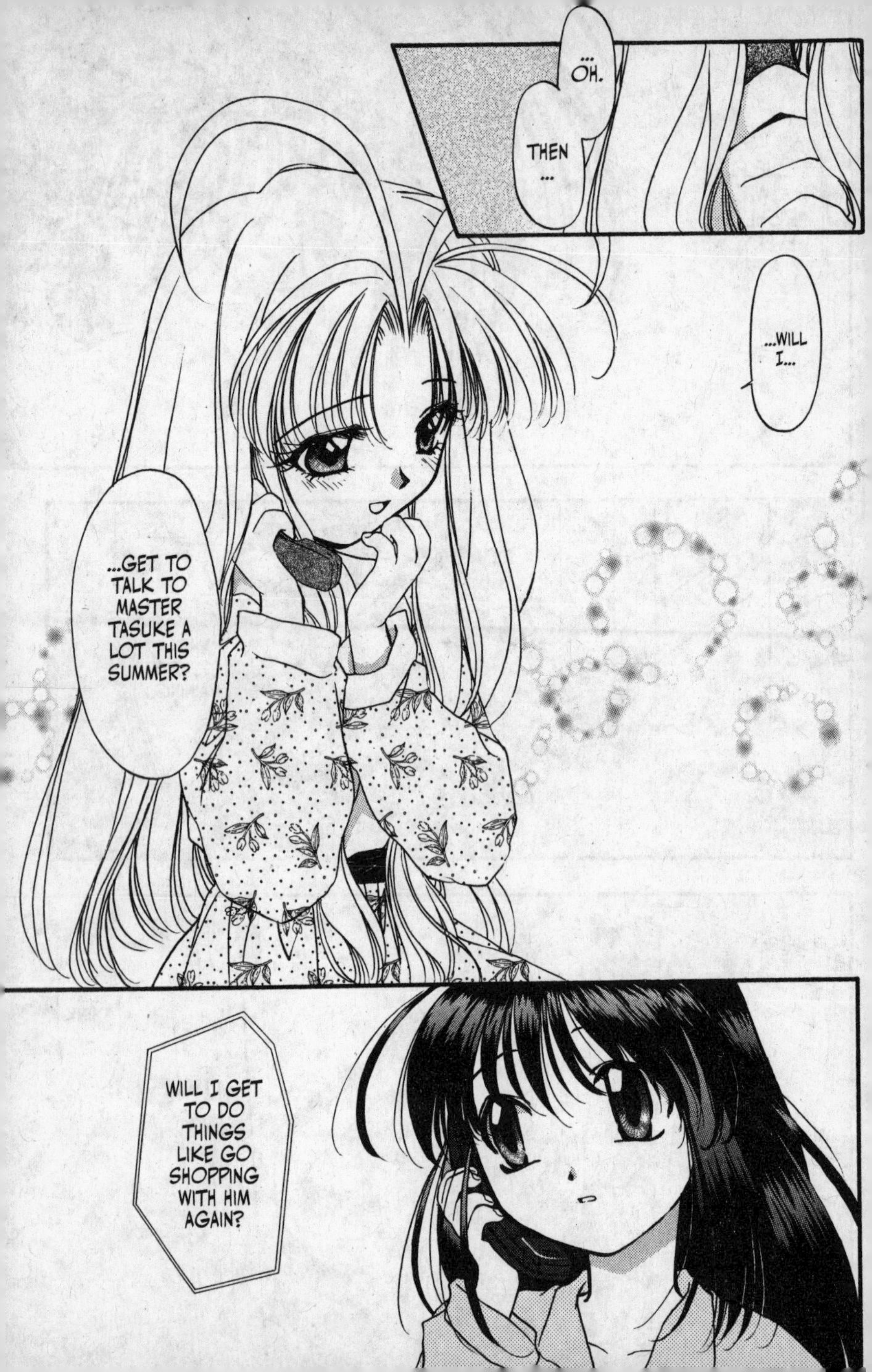
...OH.
THEN ...
...WILL I...
...GET TO TALK TO MASTER TASUKE A LOT THIS SUMMER?
WILL I GET TO DO THINGS LIKE GO SHOPPING WITH HIM AGAIN?

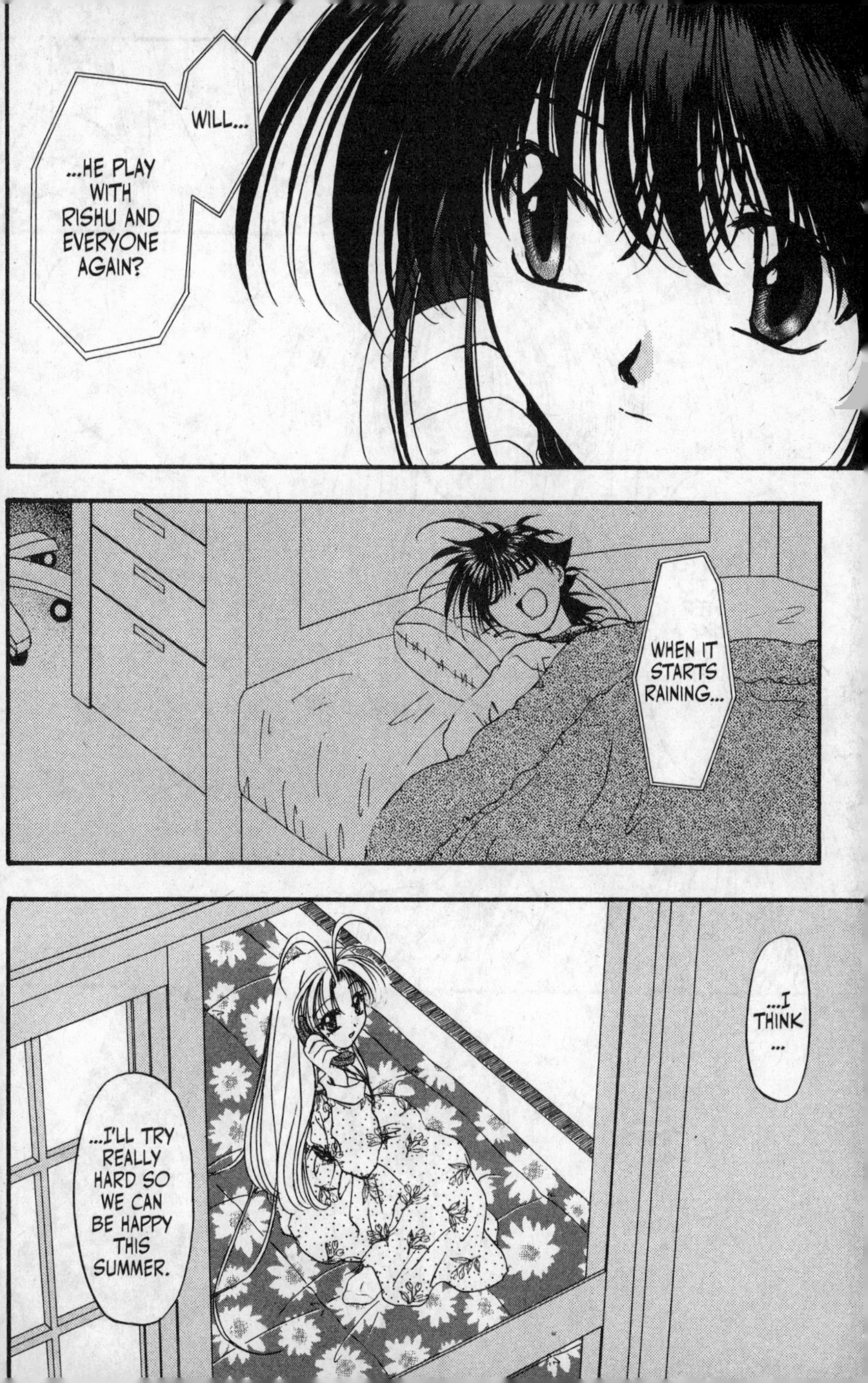
WILL...
...HE PLAY WITH RISHU AND EVERYONE AGAIN?
WHEN IT STARTS RAINING...
...I THINK...
...I'LL TRY REALLY HARD SO WE CAN BE HAPPY THIS SUMMER.

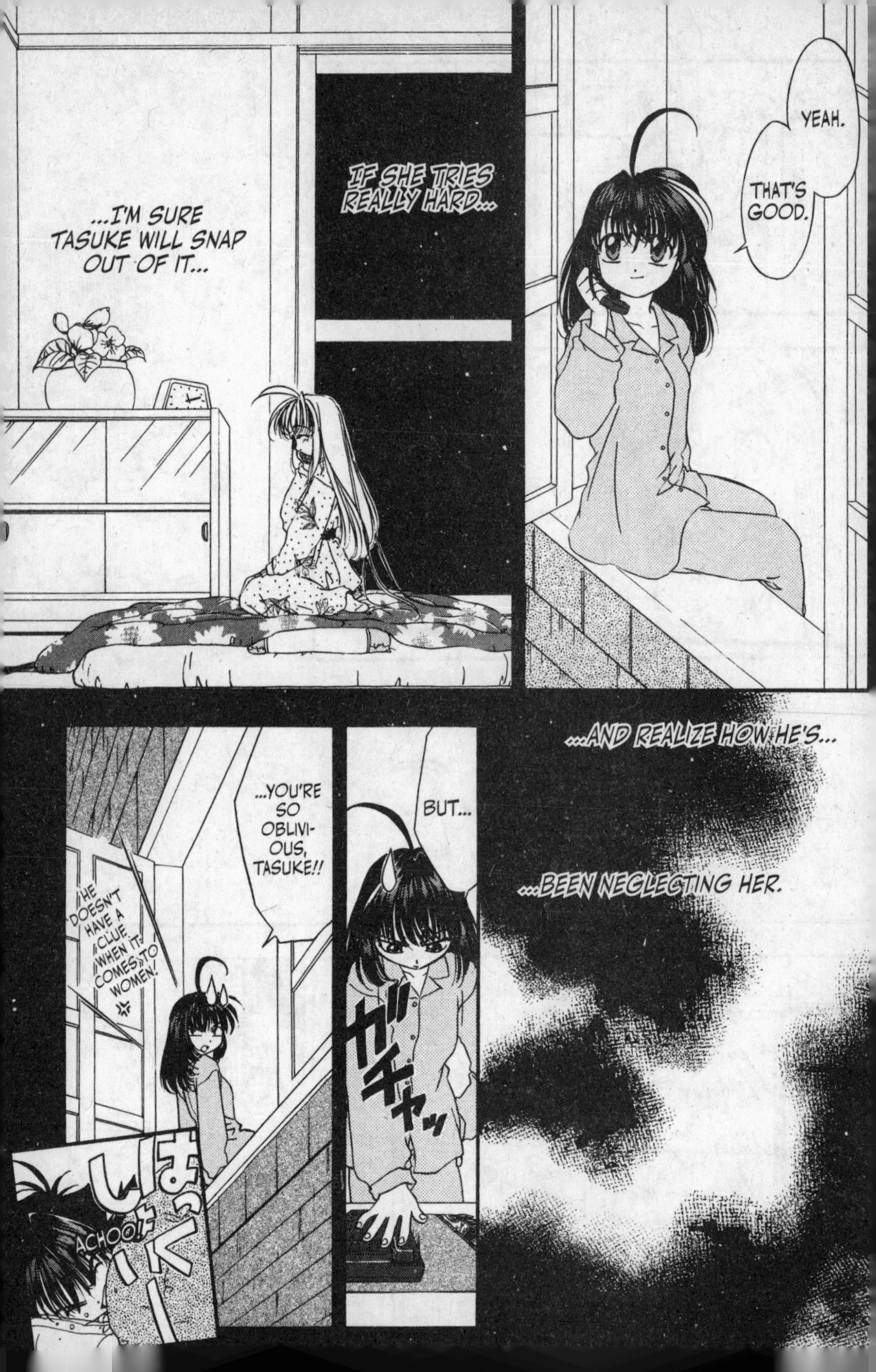
YEAH.
THAT'S GOOD.
IF SHE TRIES REALLY HARD...
...I'M SURE TASUKE WILL SNAP OUT OF IT...
...AND REALIZE HOW HE'S...
...BEEN NEGLECTING HER.
BUT...
ガチャッ
...YOU'RE SO OBLIVIOUS, TASUKE!!
HE DOESN'T HAVE A CLUE WHEN IT COMES TO WOMEN!
はっくしー
ACHOO!!

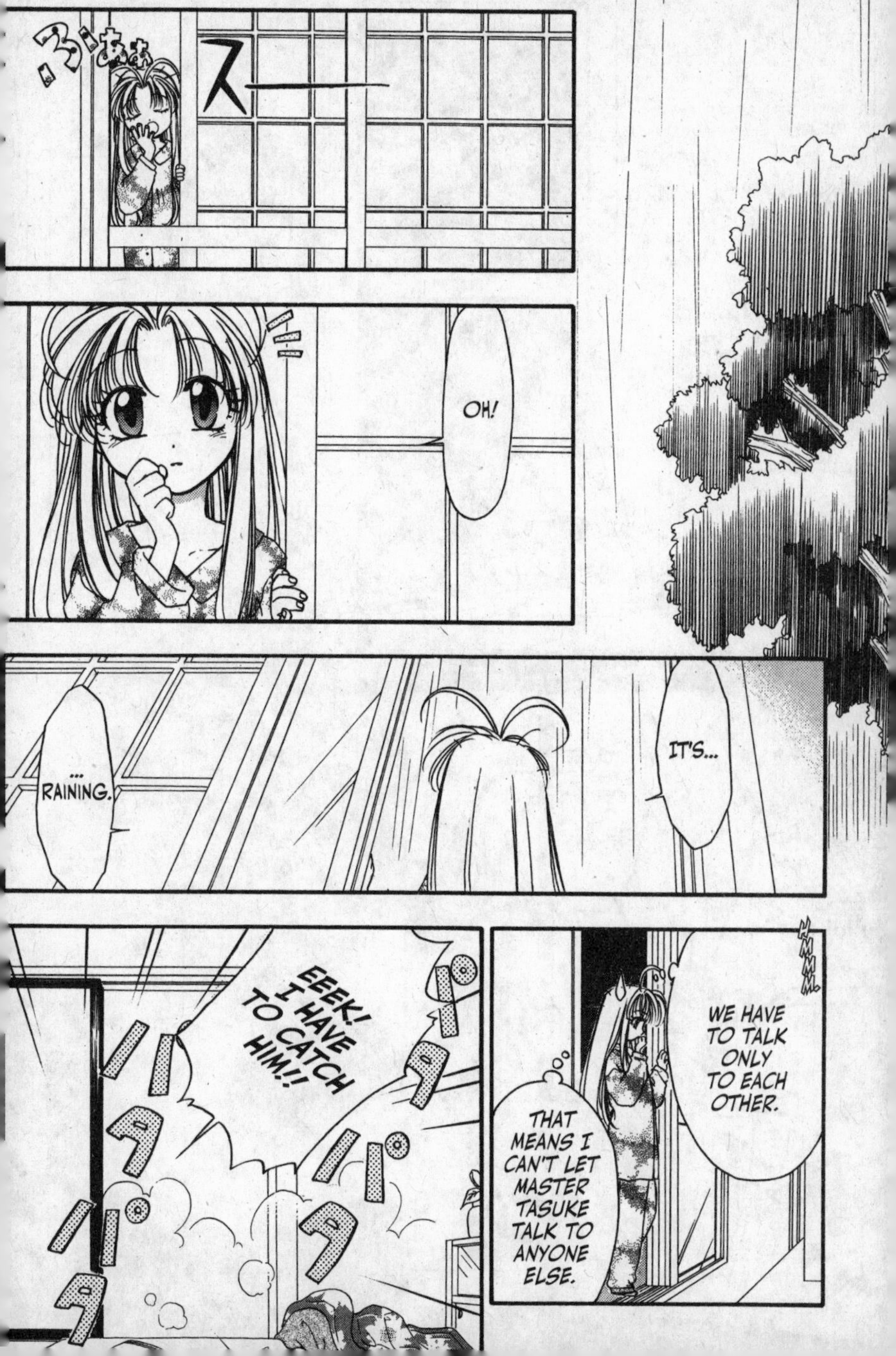
ふぁぁ
スー
OH!
IT'S...
... RAINING.
HMMM.
WE HAVE TO TALK ONLY TO EACH OTHER.
THAT MEANS I CAN'T LET MASTER TASUKE TALK TO ANYONE ELSE.
EEEK! I HAVE TO CATCH HIM!!
パタパタ
パタパタ

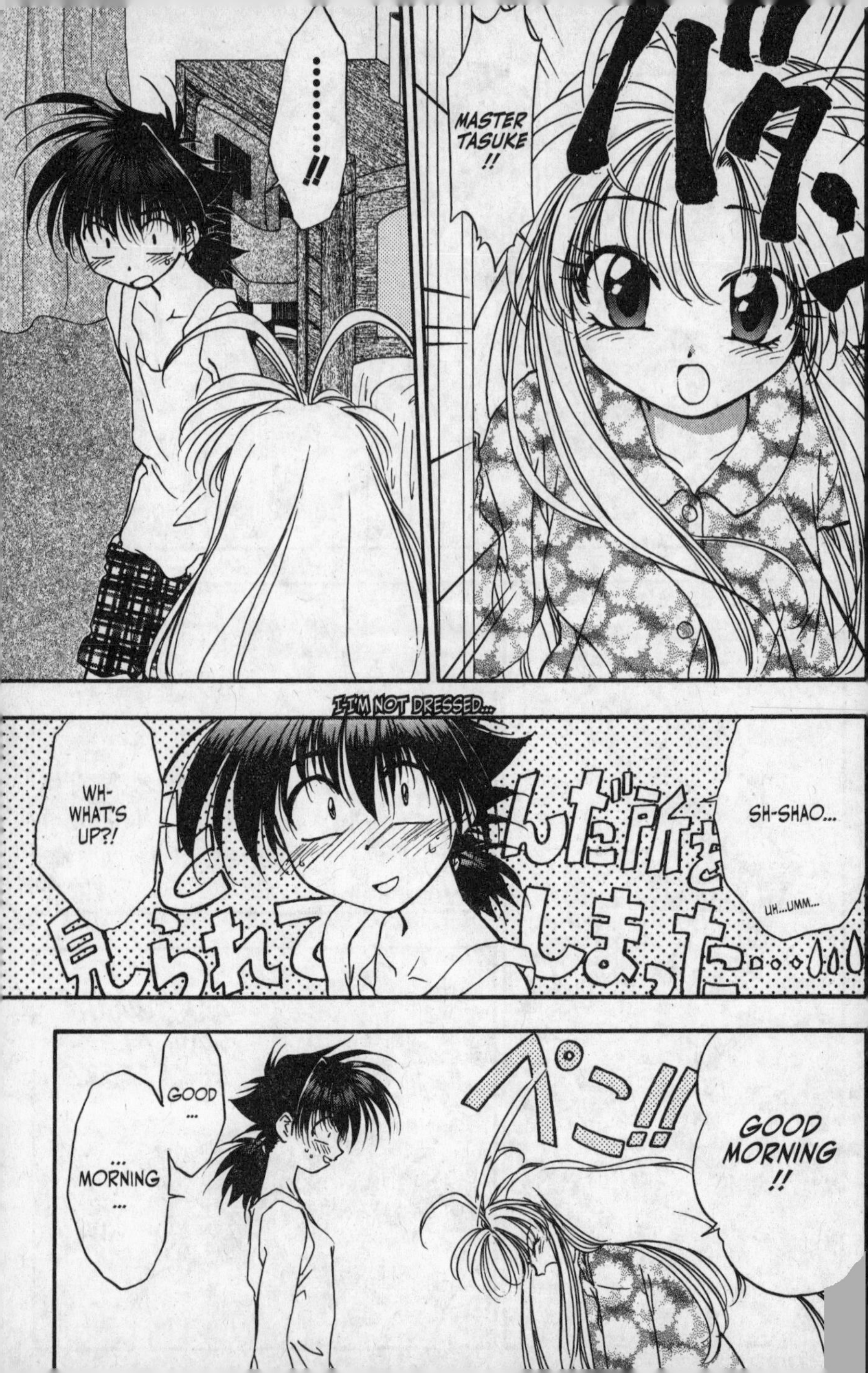
バタ
MASTER TASUKE !!
......!!
SH-SHAO...
I'M NOT DRESSED...
WH- WHAT'S UP?!
UH...UMM...
んだ所を
見られて
しまった
ペこ!!
GOOD MORNING !!
GOOD ... ... MORNING ...

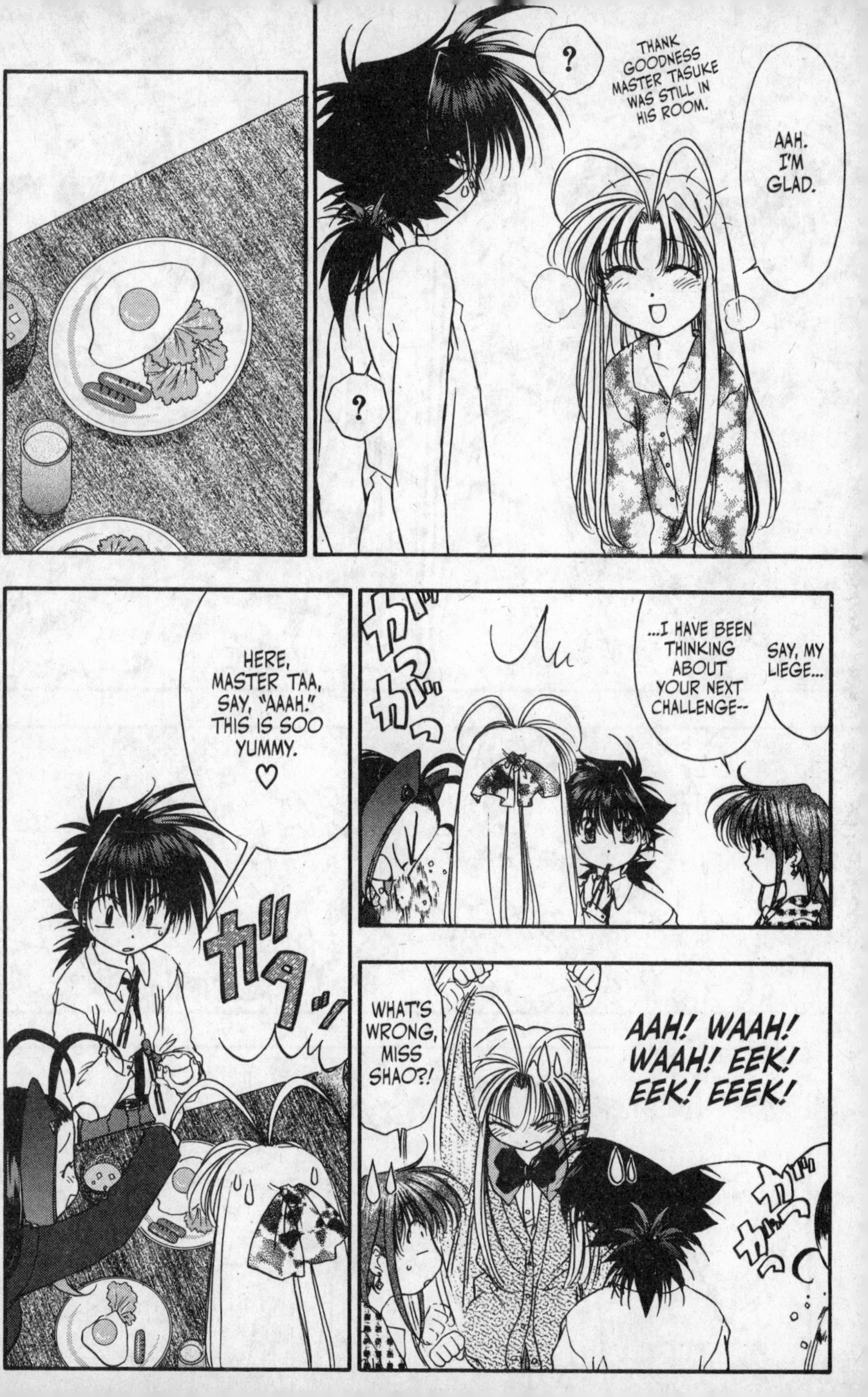
AAH. I'M GLAD.
THANK GOODNESS MASTER TASUKE WAS STILL IN HIS ROOM.
?
?
SAY, MY LIEGE...
...I HAVE BEEN THINKING ABOUT YOUR NEXT CHALLENGE--
AAH! WAAH! WAAH! EEK! EEK! EEEK!
WHAT'S WRONG, MISS SHAO?!
HERE, MASTER TAA, SAY, "AAAH." THIS IS SOO YUMMY. ♡
ガタッ

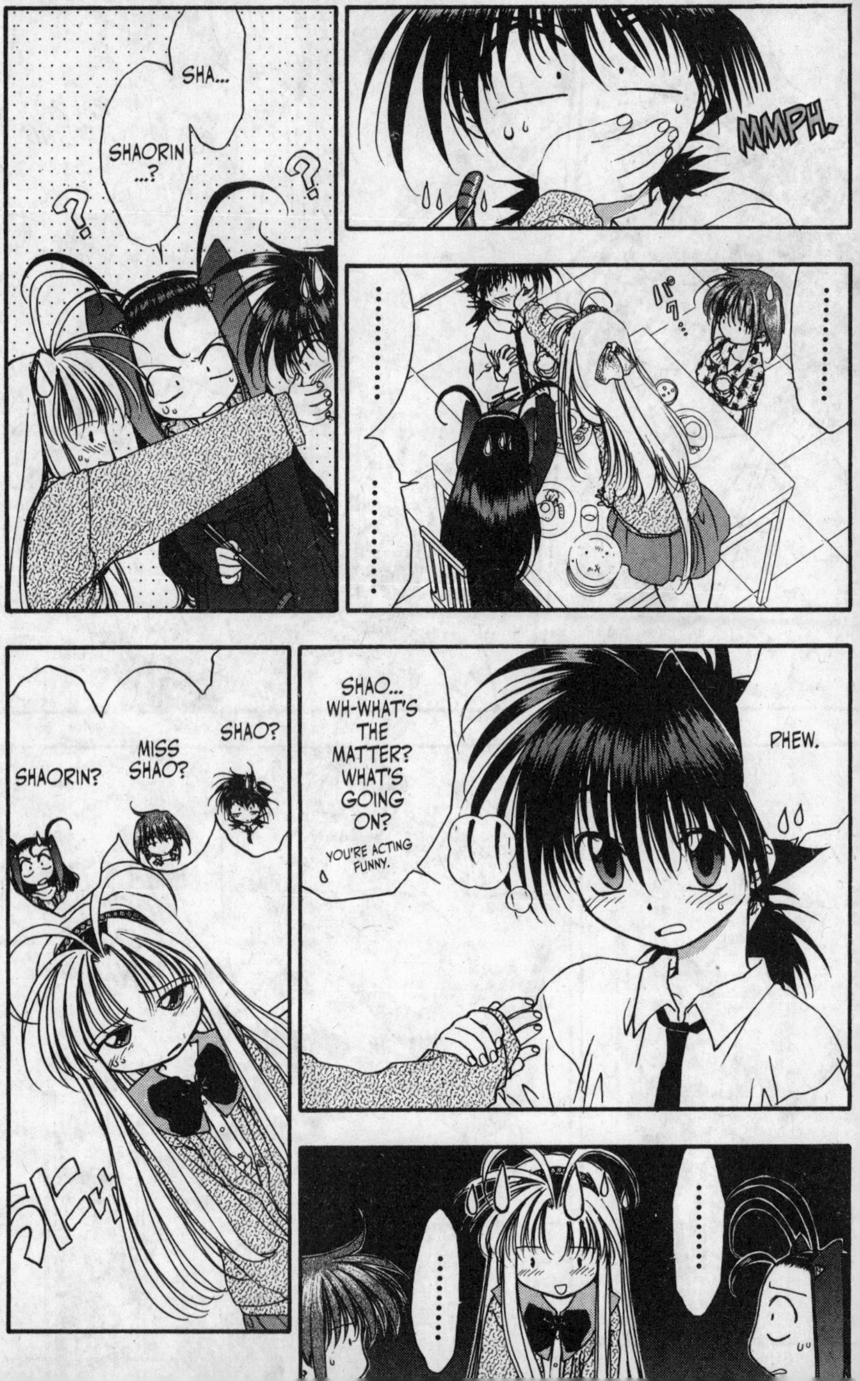
MMPH.
......
......
パク...
SHA...
SHAORIN ...?
PHEW.
SHAO... WH-WHAT'S THE MATTER? WHAT'S GOING ON?
YOU'RE ACTING FUNNY.
......
......
SHAO?
MISS SHAO?
SHAORIN?

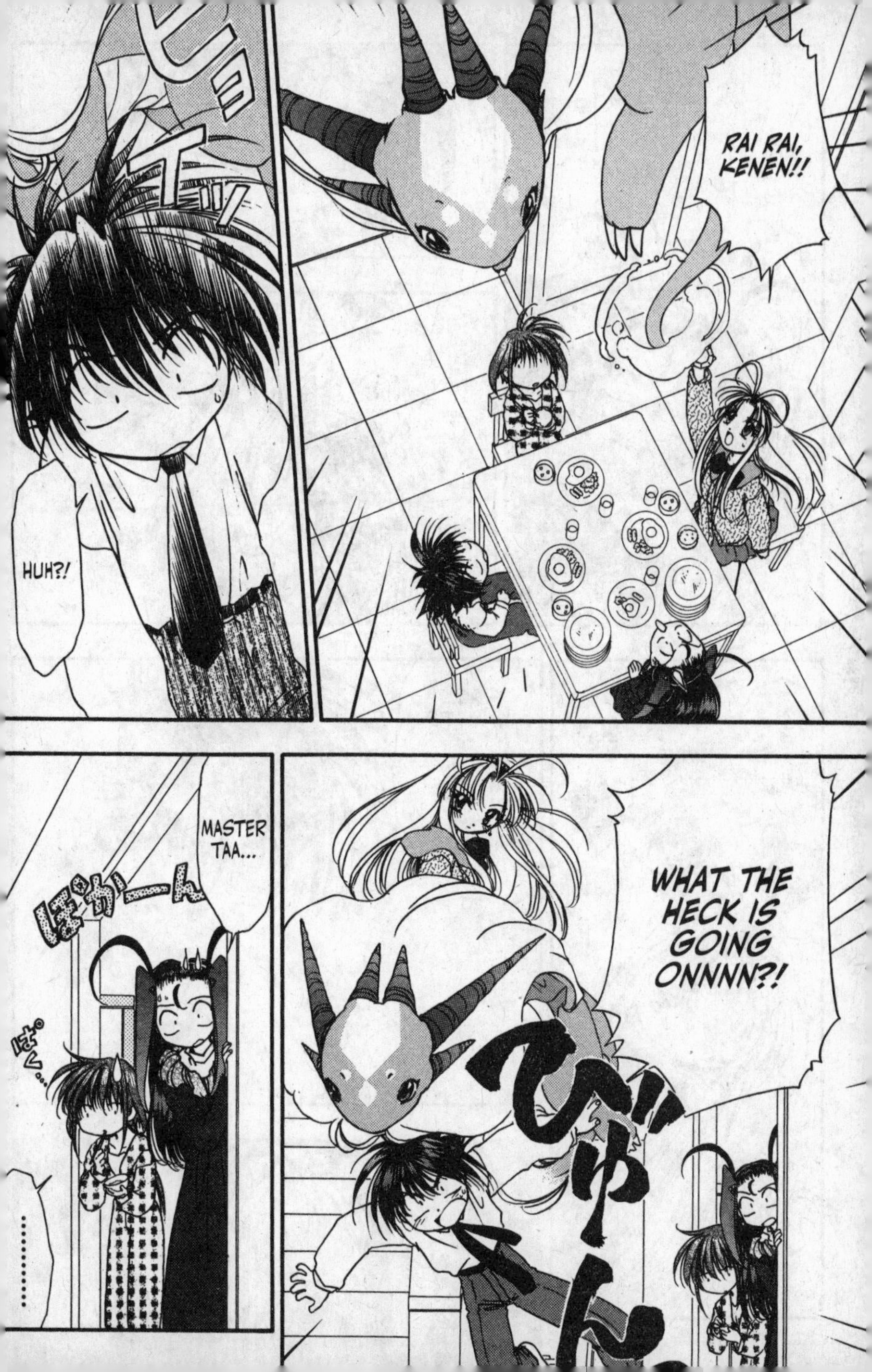
RAI RAI, KENEN!!
HUH?!
WHAT THE HECK IS GOING ONNNN?!
MASTER TAA...
....

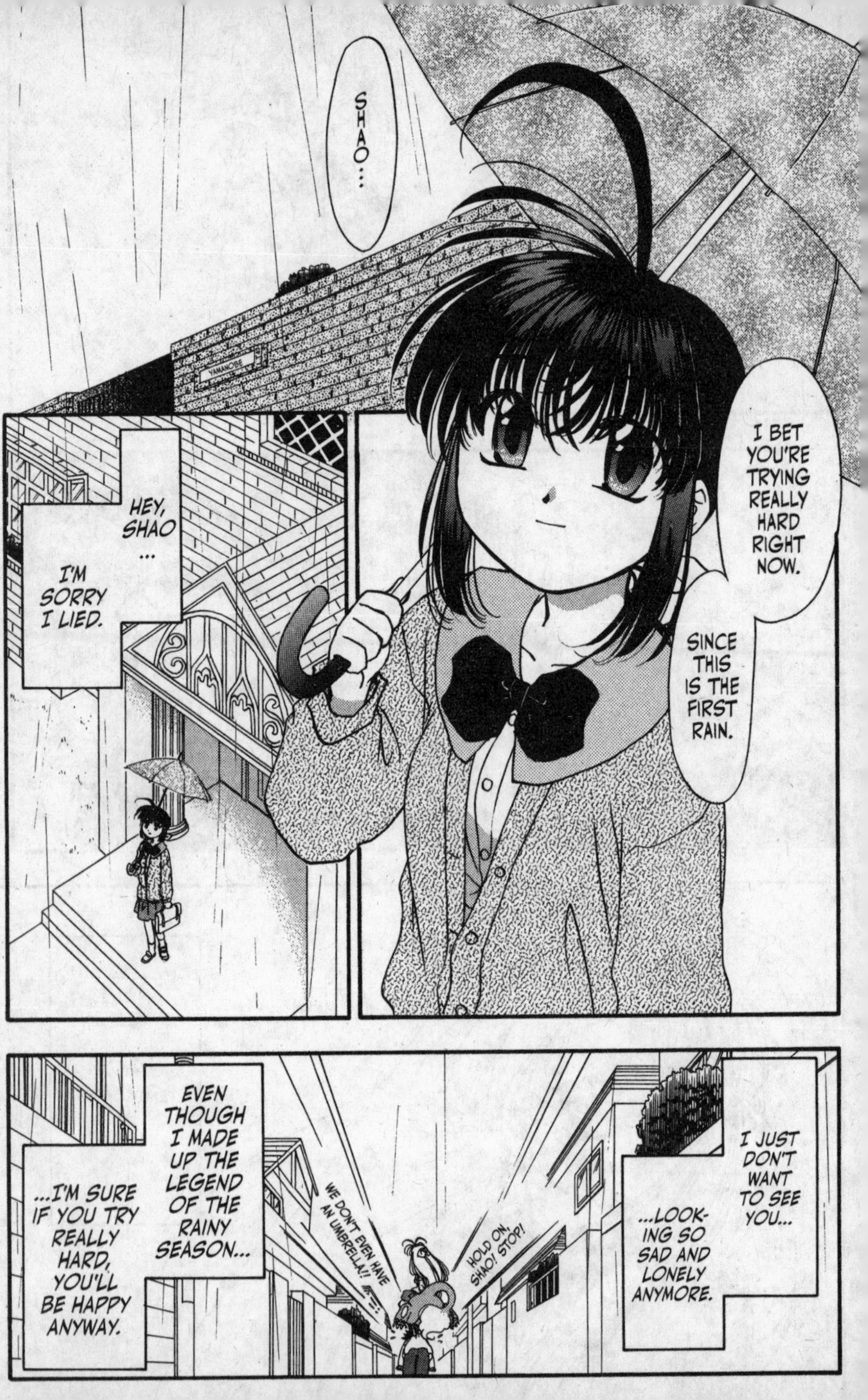

SHAO...
I BET YOU'RE TRYING REALLY HARD RIGHT NOW.
SINCE THIS IS THE FIRST RAIN.
HEY, SHAO...
I'M SORRY I LIED.
I JUST DON'T WANT TO SEE YOU...
...LOOKING SO SAD AND LONELY ANYMORE.
HOLD ON, SHAO! STOP!
WE DON'T EVEN HAVE AN UMBRELLA!!
EVEN THOUGH I MADE UP THE LEGEND OF THE RAINY SEASON...
...I'M SURE IF YOU TRY REALLY HARD, YOU'LL BE HAPPY ANYWAY.

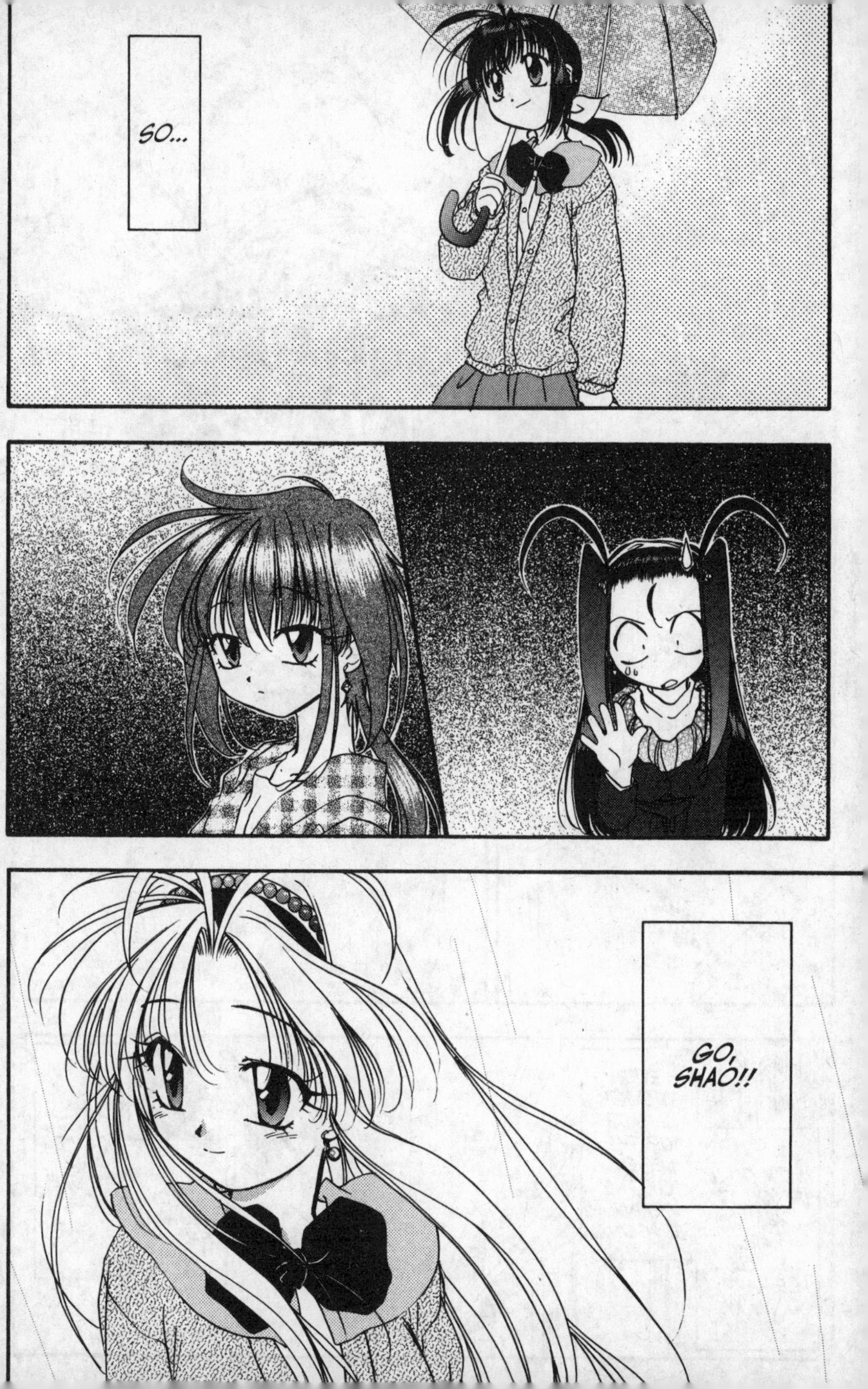
SO...
GO, SHAO!!

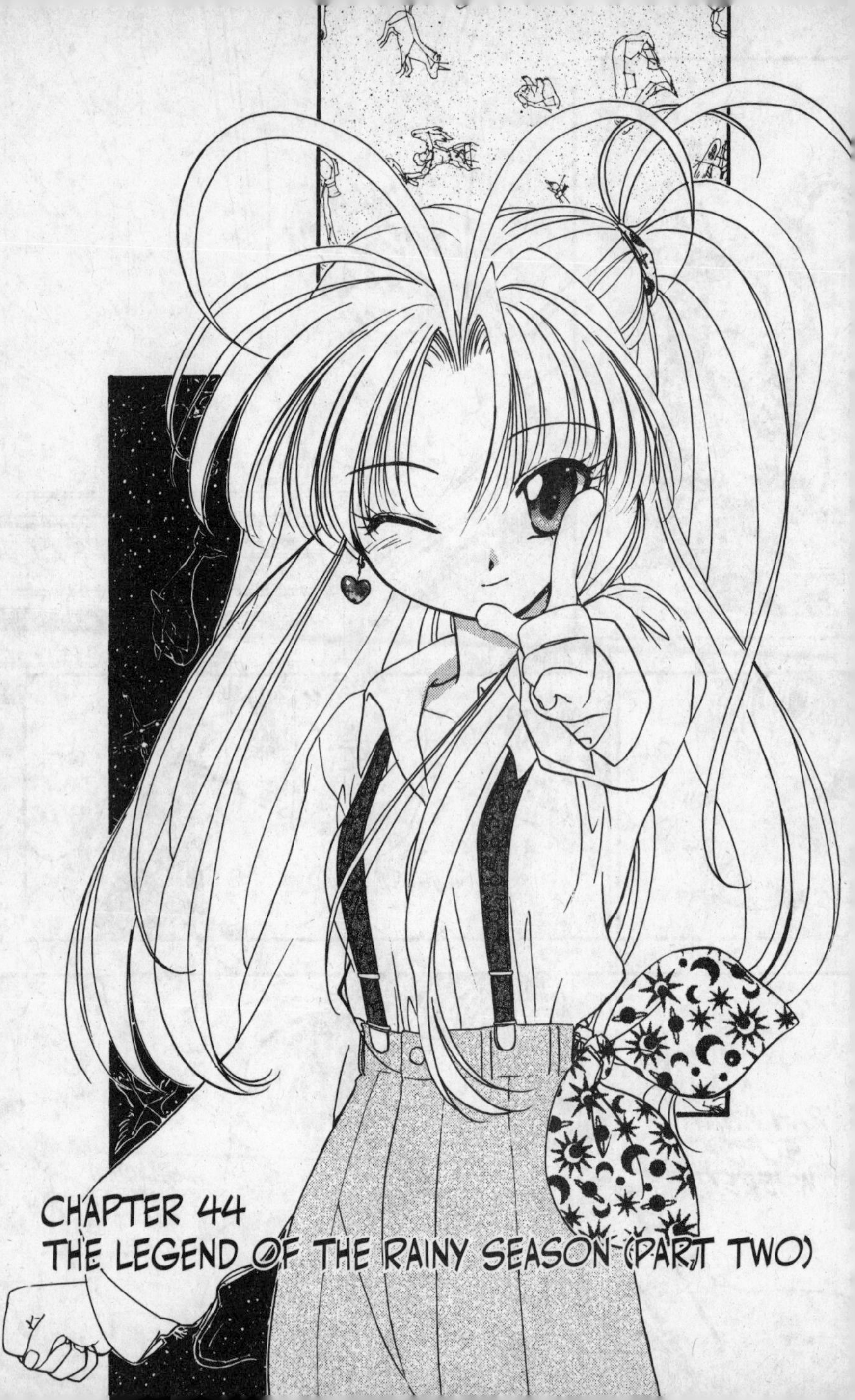

CHAPTER 44
THE LEGEND OF THE RAINY SEASON (PART TWO)

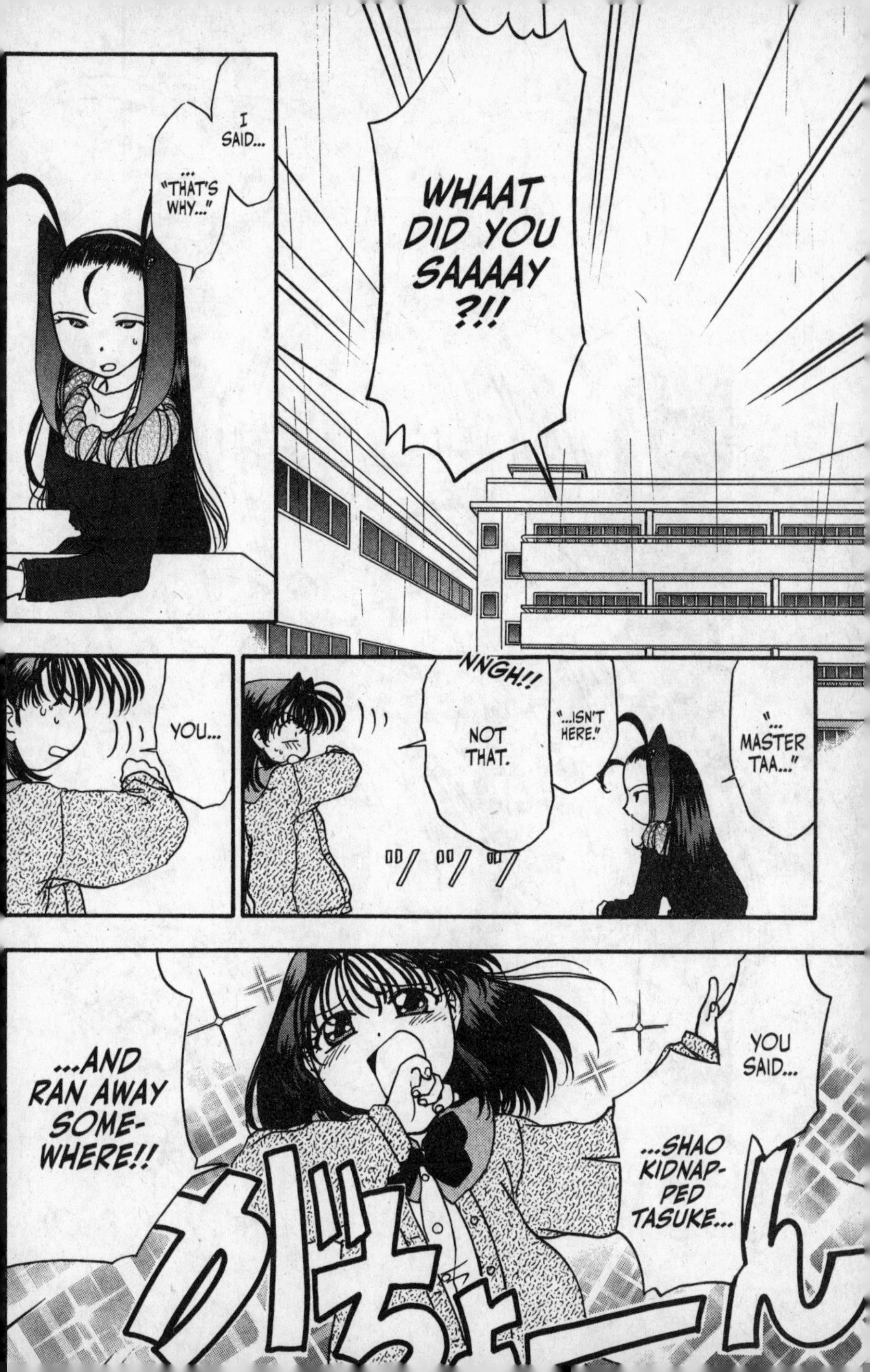
WHAAT DID YOU SAAAAY?!!
I SAID...
... "THAT'S WHY..."
"... MASTER TAA..."
"...ISN'T HERE."
NNGH!!
NOT THAT.
YOU...
YOU SAID...
...SHAO KIDNAPPED TASUKE...
...AND RAN AWAY SOMEWHERE!!

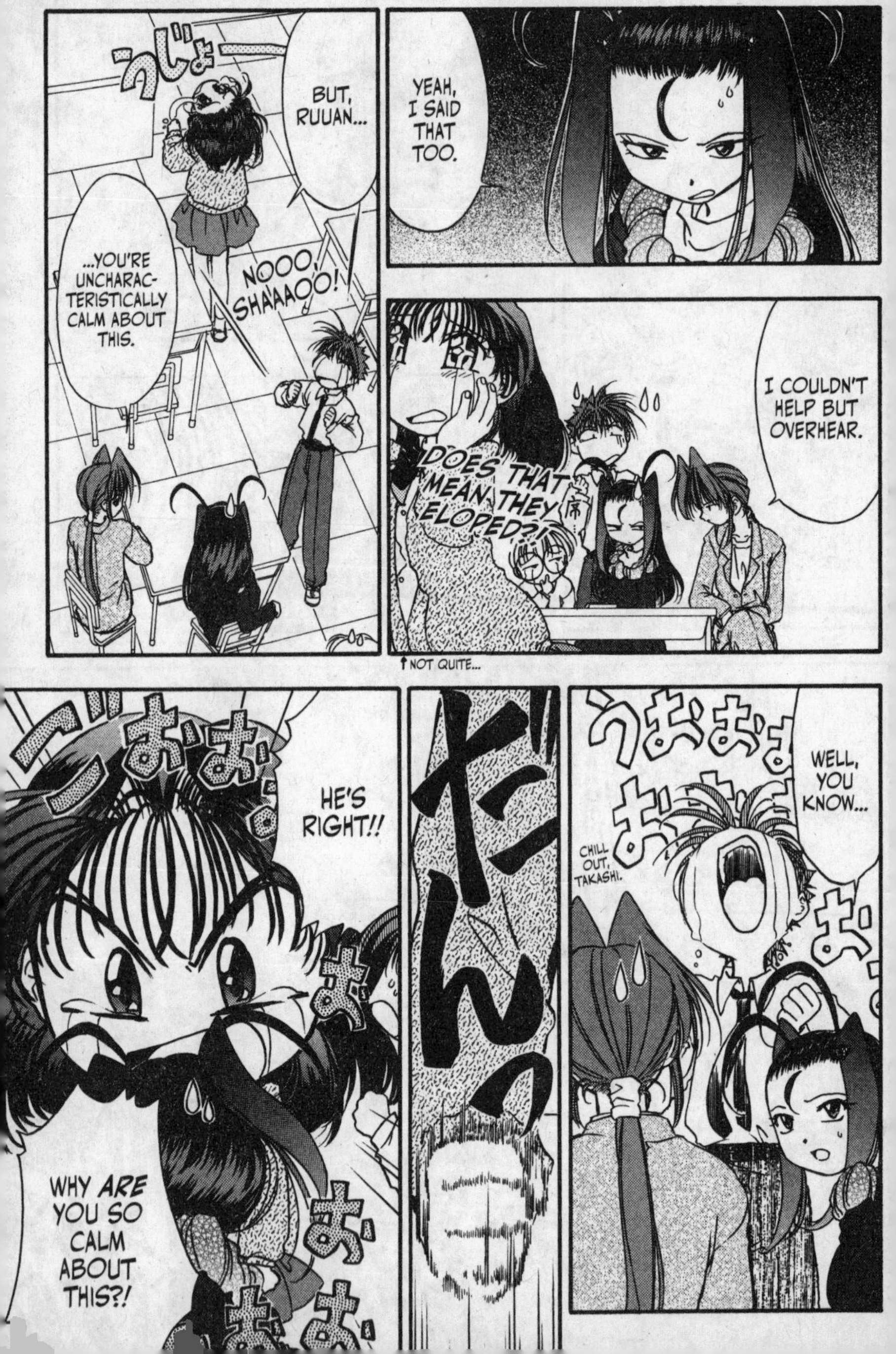
YEAH, I SAID THAT TOO.
I COULDN'T HELP BUT OVERHEAR.
DOES THAT MEAN THEY ELOPED?!
NOT QUITE...
うじょー
BUT, RUUAN...
...YOU'RE UNCHARAC-TERISTICALLY CALM ABOUT THIS.
NOOO, SHAAAOO!
WELL, YOU KNOW...
うおおお
CHILL OUT, TAKASHI.
だんっ
HE'S RIGHT!!
WHY ARE YOU SO CALM ABOUT THIS?!

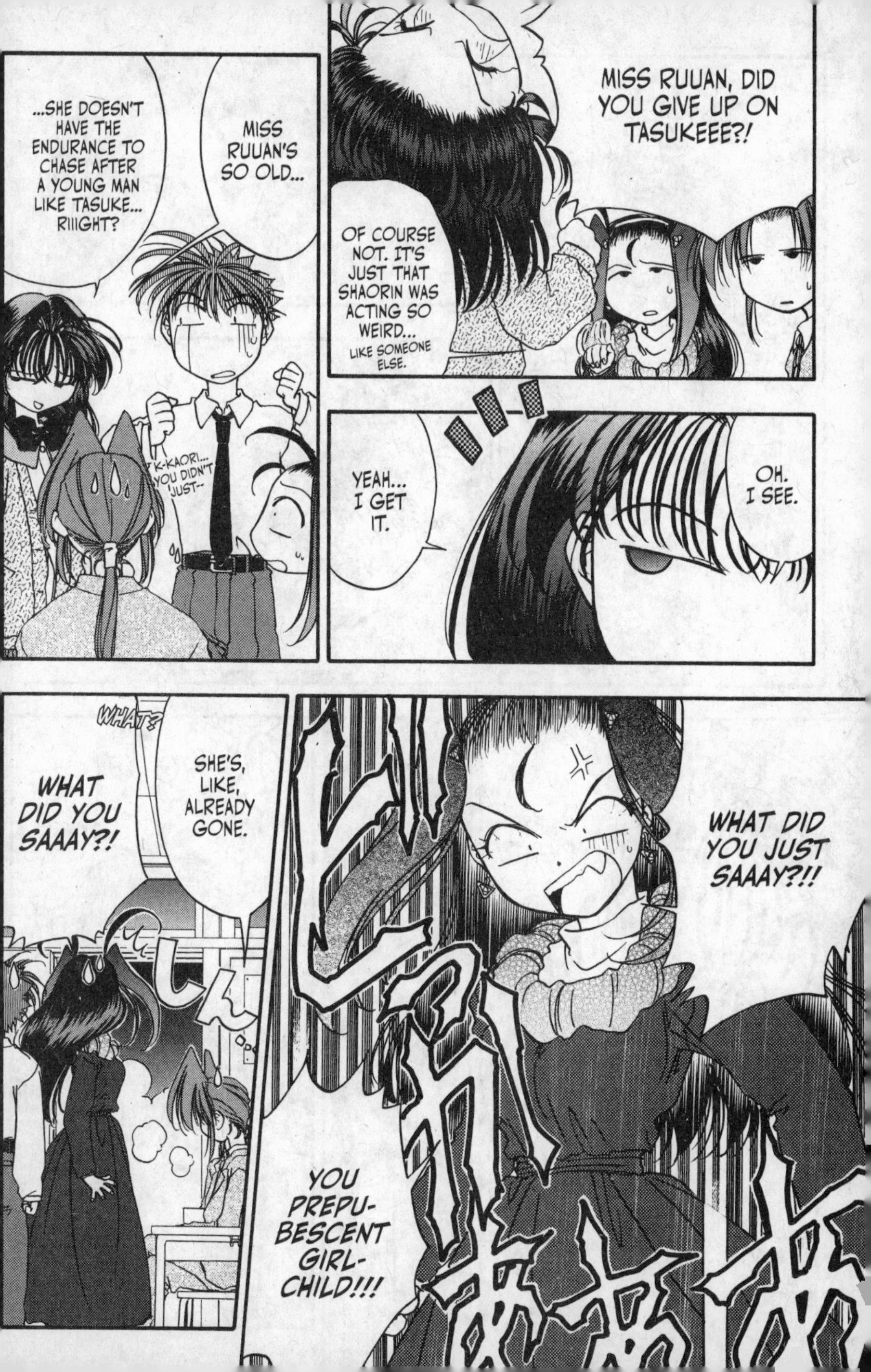
MISS RUUAN, DID YOU GIVE UP ON TASUKEEE?!
OF COURSE NOT. IT'S JUST THAT SHAORIN WAS ACTING SO WEIRD... LIKE SOMEONE ELSE.
OH. I SEE.
YEAH... I GET IT.
MISS RUUAN'S SO OLD...
...SHE DOESN'T HAVE THE ENDURANCE TO CHASE AFTER A YOUNG MAN LIKE TASUKE... RIIIGHT?
K-KAORI... YOU DIDN'T JUST--
WHAT DID YOU JUST SAAAY?!!
YOU PREPU-BESCENT GIRL-CHILD!!!
SHE'S, LIKE, ALREADY GONE.
WHAT?
WHAT DID YOU SAAAY?!

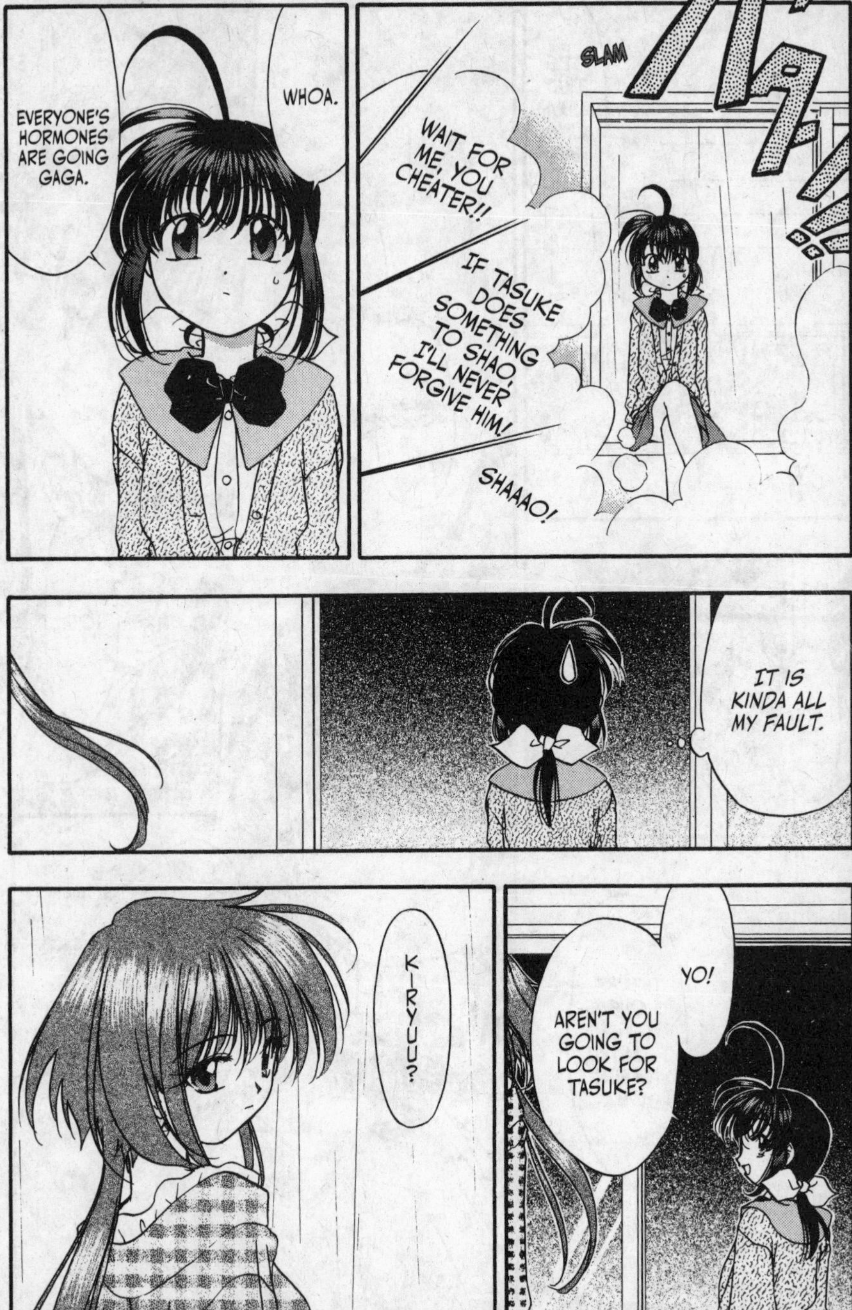
SLAM
WAIT FOR ME, YOU CHEATER!!
IF TASUKE DOES SOMETHING TO SHAO, I'LL NEVER FORGIVE HIM!
SHAAAO!
WHOA.
EVERYONE'S HORMONES ARE GOING GAGA.
IT IS KINDA ALL MY FAULT.
YO!
AREN'T YOU GOING TO LOOK FOR TASUKE?
KIRYUU?

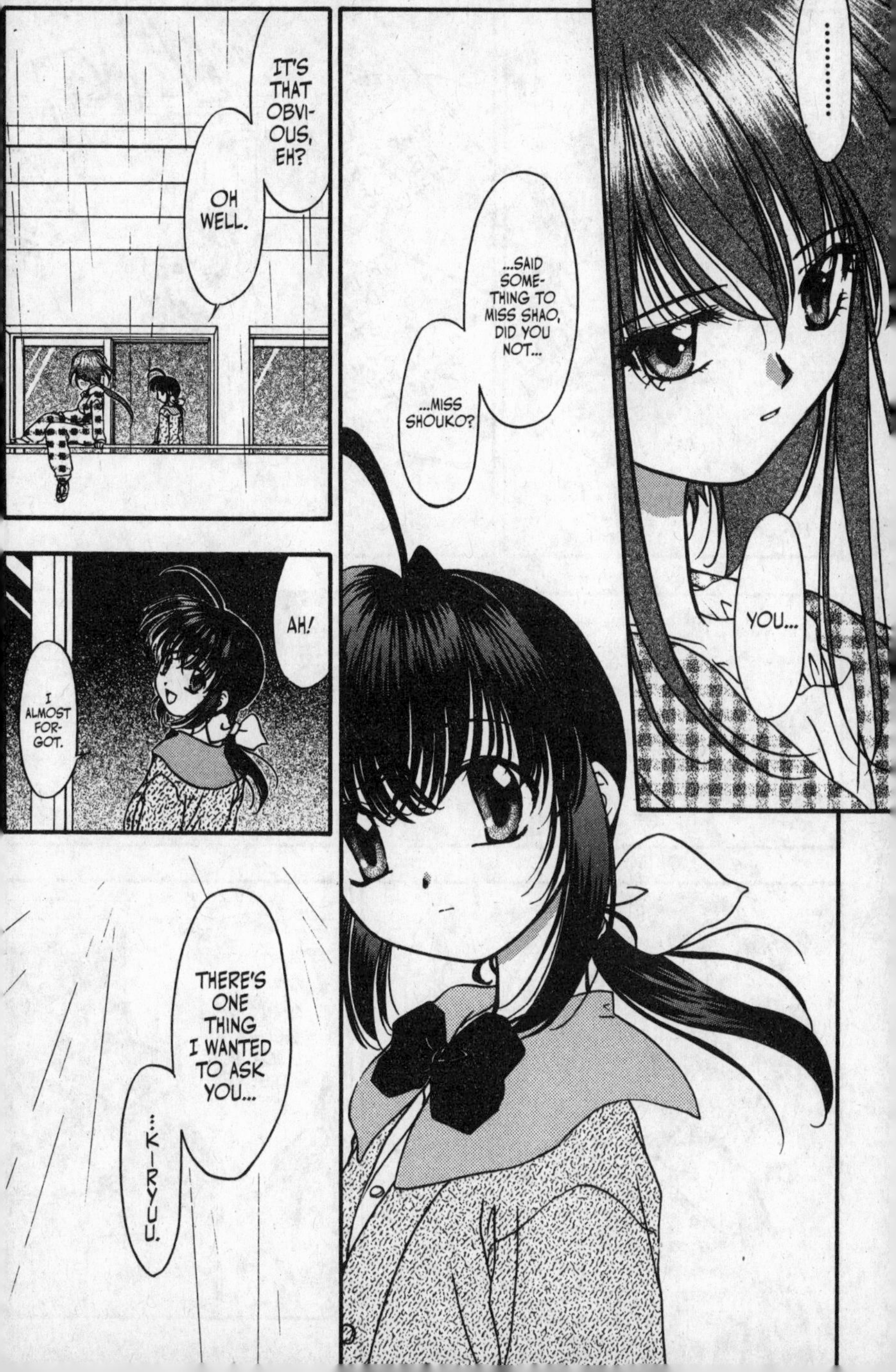
......
YOU...
...SAID SOMETHING TO MISS SHAO, DID YOU NOT...
...MISS SHOUKO?
IT'S THAT OBVIOUS, EH?
OH WELL.
AH!
I ALMOST FORGOT.
THERE'S ONE THING I WANTED TO ASK YOU...
...KIRYUU.

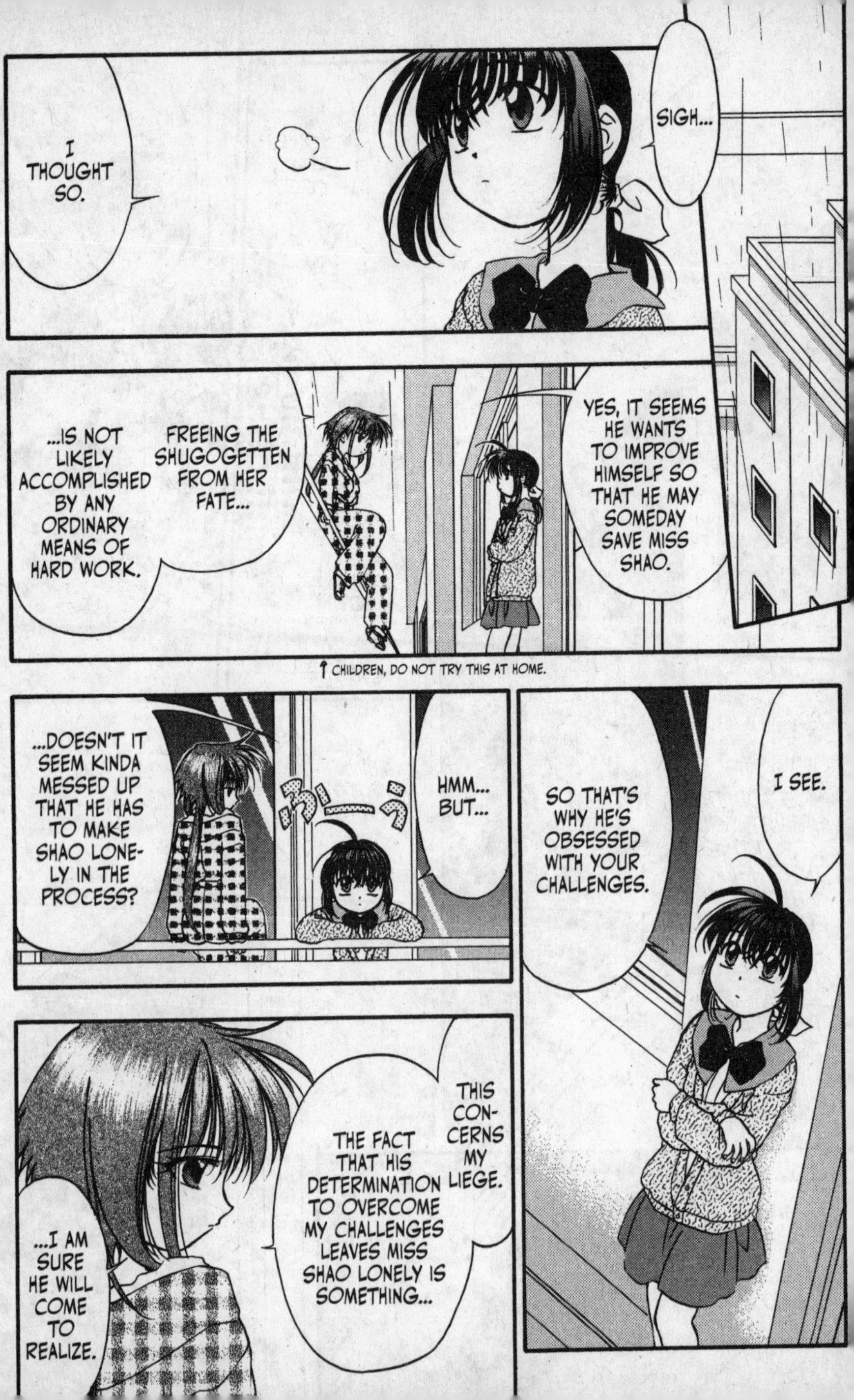
SIGH...
I THOUGHT SO.
YES, IT SEEMS HE WANTS TO IMPROVE HIMSELF SO THAT HE MAY SOMEDAY SAVE MISS SHAO.
FREEING THE SHUGOGETTEN FROM HER FATE...
...IS NOT LIKELY ACCOMPLISHED BY ANY ORDINARY MEANS OF HARD WORK.
CHILDREN, DO NOT TRY THIS AT HOME.
I SEE.
SO THAT'S WHY HE'S OBSESSED WITH YOUR CHALLENGES.
HMM... BUT...
...DOESN'T IT SEEM KINDA MESSED UP THAT HE HAS TO MAKE SHAO LONE-LY IN THE PROCESS?
THIS CON-CERNS MY LIEGE.
THE FACT THAT HIS DETERMINATION TO OVERCOME MY CHALLENGES LEAVES MISS SHAO LONELY IS SOMETHING...
...I AM SURE HE WILL COME TO REALIZE.

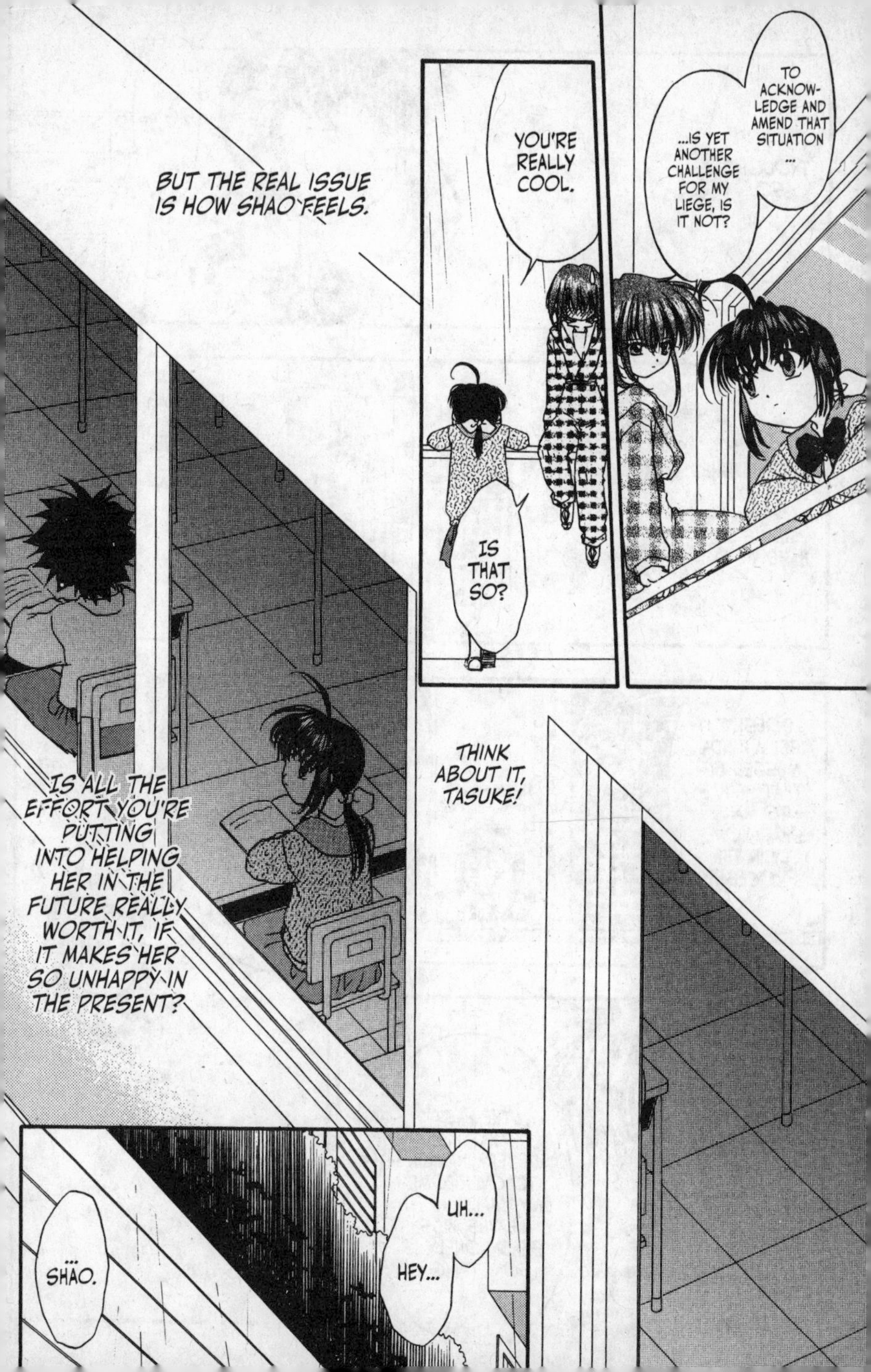
TO ACKNOWLEDGE AND AMEND THAT SITUATION...
...IS YET ANOTHER CHALLENGE FOR MY LIEGE, IS IT NOT?
YOU'RE REALLY COOL.
IS THAT SO?
BUT THE REAL ISSUE IS HOW SHAO FEELS.
THINK ABOUT IT, TASUKE!
IS ALL THE EFFORT YOU'RE PUTTING INTO HELPING HER IN THE FUTURE REALLY WORTH IT, IF IT MAKES HER SO UNHAPPY IN THE PRESENT?
UH...
HEY...
...SHAO.

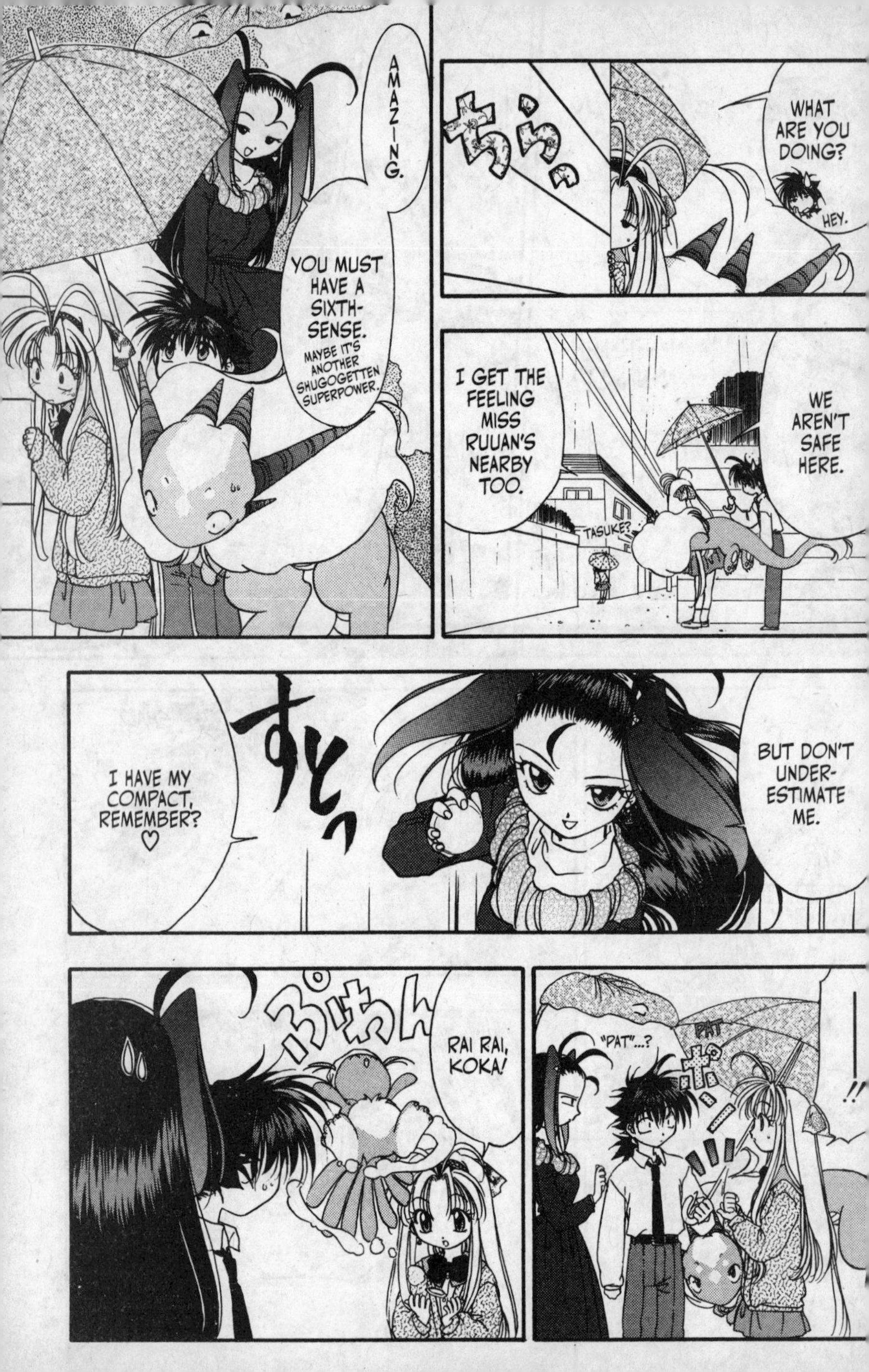
ちらっ
WHAT ARE YOU DOING?
HEY.
WE AREN'T SAFE HERE.
TASUKE?
I GET THE FEELING MISS RUUAN'S NEARBY TOO.
AMAZING.
YOU MUST HAVE A SIXTH-SENSE.
MAYBE IT'S ANOTHER SHUGOGETTEN SUPERPOWER.
BUT DON'T UNDER-ESTIMATE ME.
すとっ
I HAVE MY COMPACT, REMEMBER? ♡
—!!
PAT
ポッ
"PAT"...?
RAI RAI, KOKA!
ぷわん

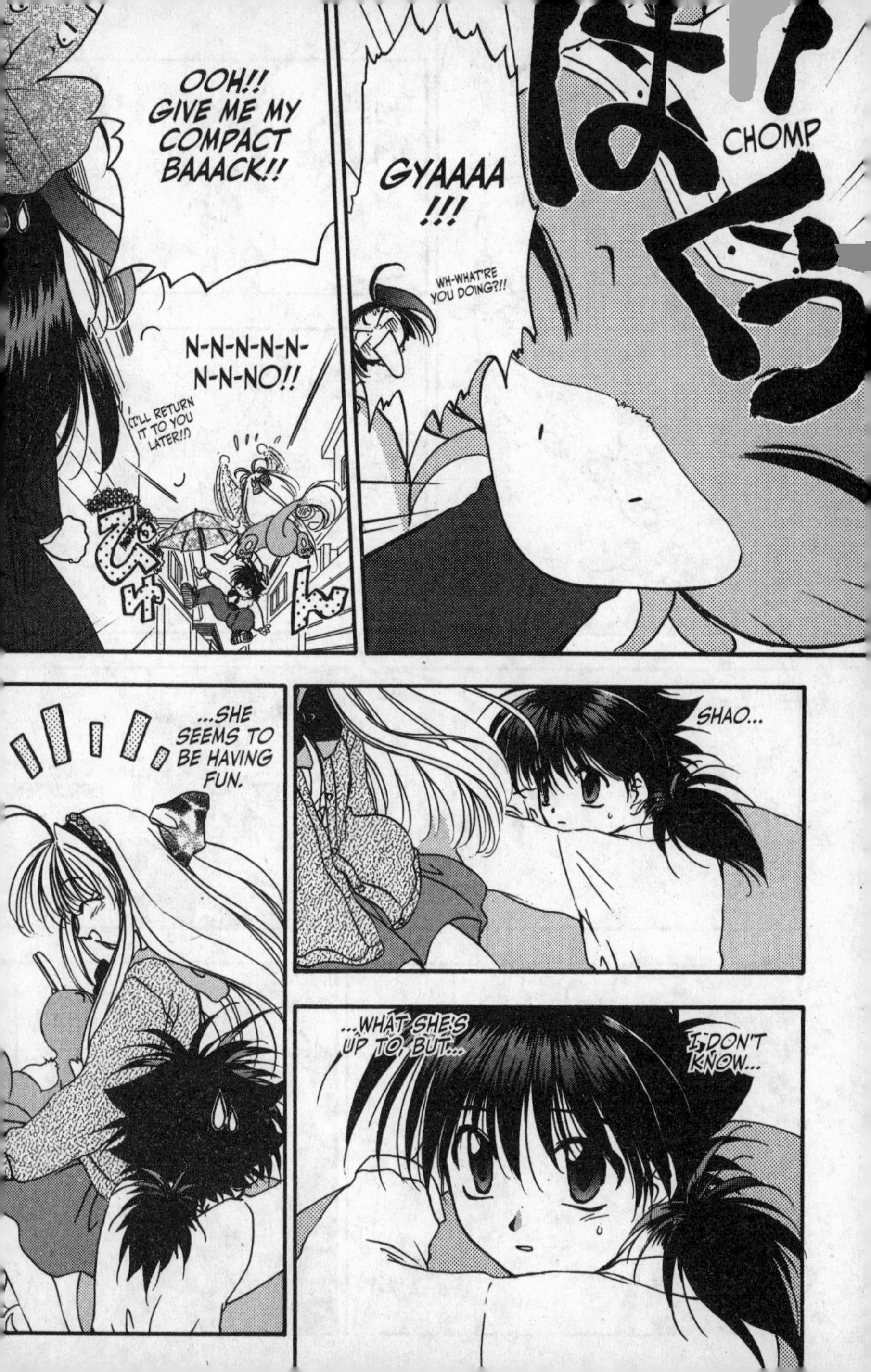
CHOMP
GYAAAA!!!
WH-WHAT'RE YOU DOING?!!
OOH!! GIVE ME MY COMPACT BAAACK!!
N-N-N-N-N-N-N-NO!!
(I'LL RETURN IT TO YOU LATER!!)
SHAO...
I DON'T KNOW...
...WHAT SHE'S UP TO, BUT...
...SHE SEEMS TO BE HAVING FUN.

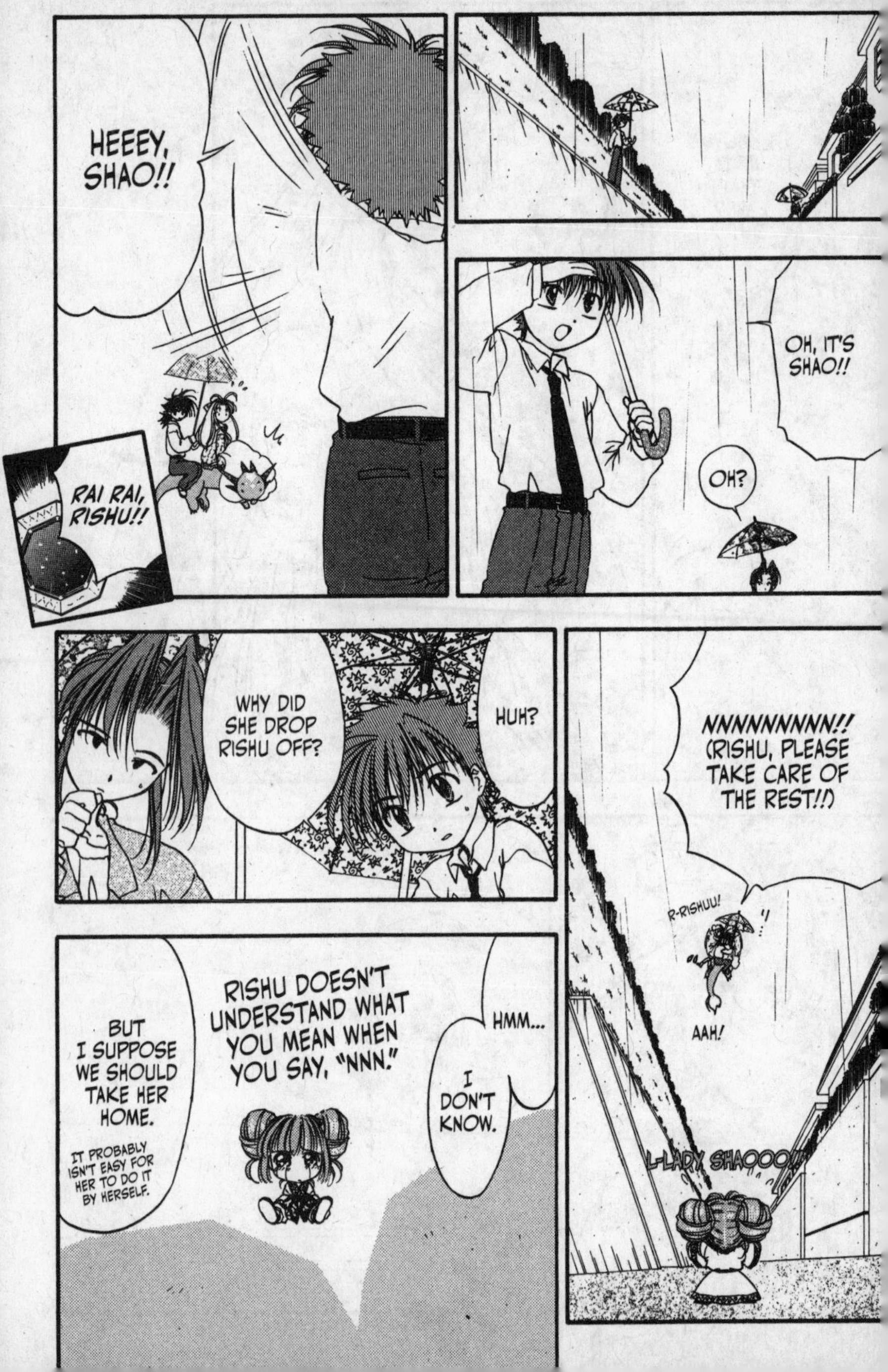
OH, IT'S SHAO!!
OH?
HEEEY, SHAO!!
RAI RAI, RISHU!!
NNNNNNNNN!! (RISHU, PLEASE TAKE CARE OF THE REST!!)
R-RISHUU!
AAH!
L-LADY SHAOOO!!
HUH?
WHY DID SHE DROP RISHU OFF?
HMM...
I DON'T KNOW.
RISHU DOESN'T UNDERSTAND WHAT YOU MEAN WHEN YOU SAY, "NNN."
BUT I SUPPOSE WE SHOULD TAKE HER HOME.
IT PROBABLY ISN'T EASY FOR HER TO DO IT BY HERSELF.

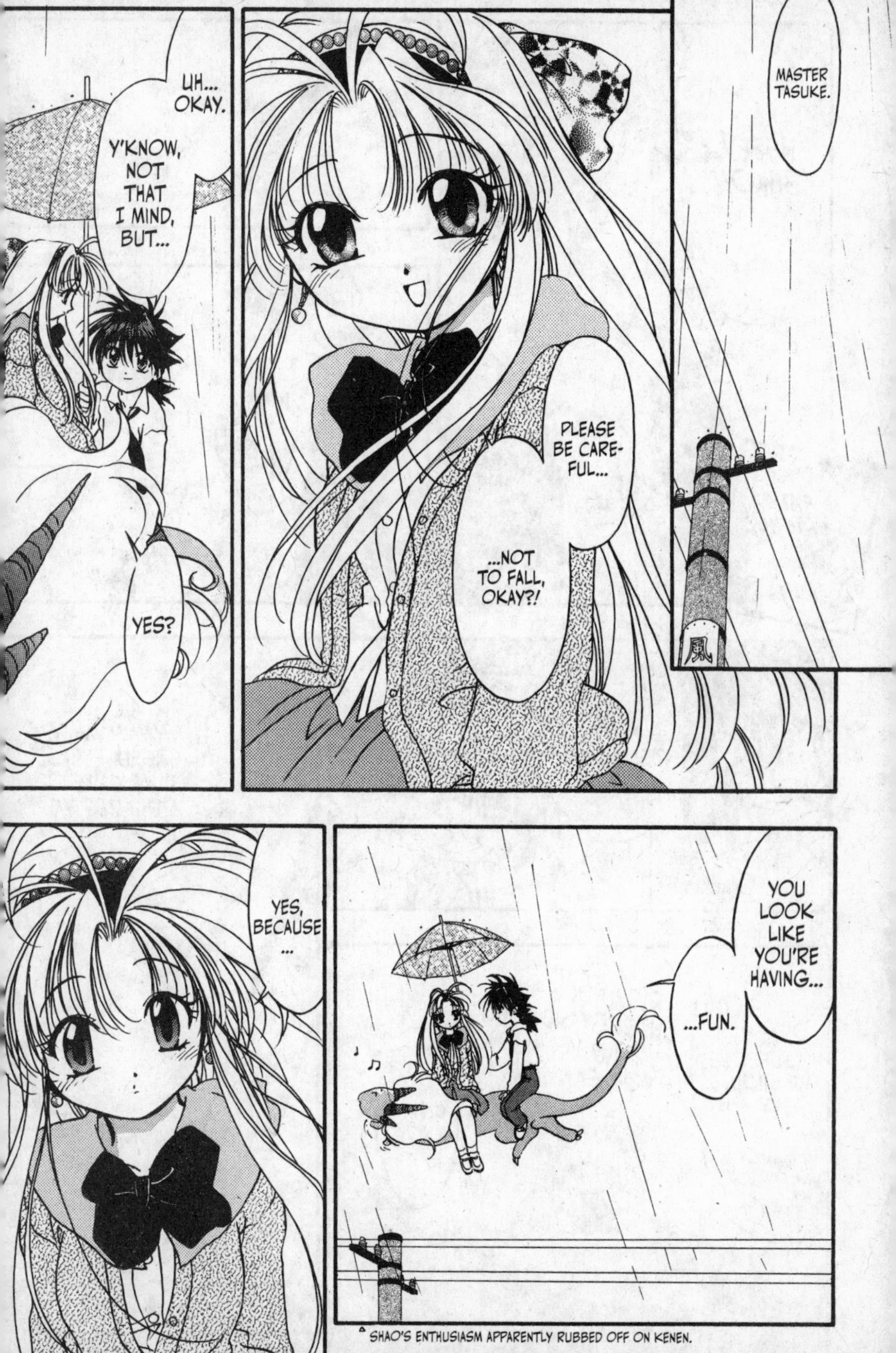
MASTER TASUKE.
PLEASE BE CARE-FUL...
...NOT TO FALL, OKAY?!
UH... OKAY.
Y'KNOW, NOT THAT I MIND, BUT...
YES?
YOU LOOK LIKE YOU'RE HAVING...
...FUN.
YES, BECAUSE ...

SHAO'S ENTHUSIASM APPARENTLY RUBBED OFF ON KENEN.

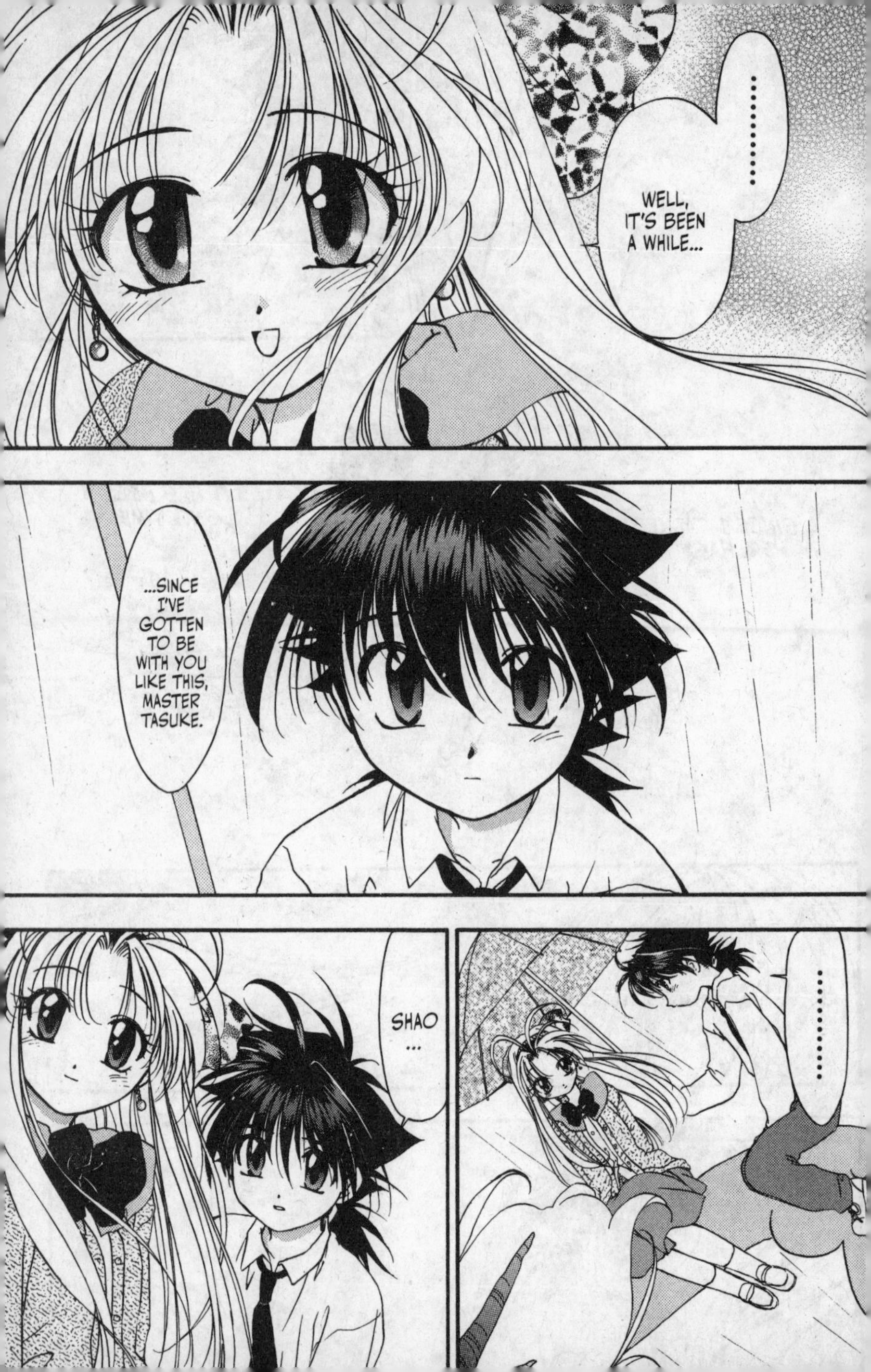
......
WELL, IT'S BEEN A WHILE...
...SINCE I'VE GOTTEN TO BE WITH YOU LIKE THIS, MASTER TASUKE.
......
SHAO ...

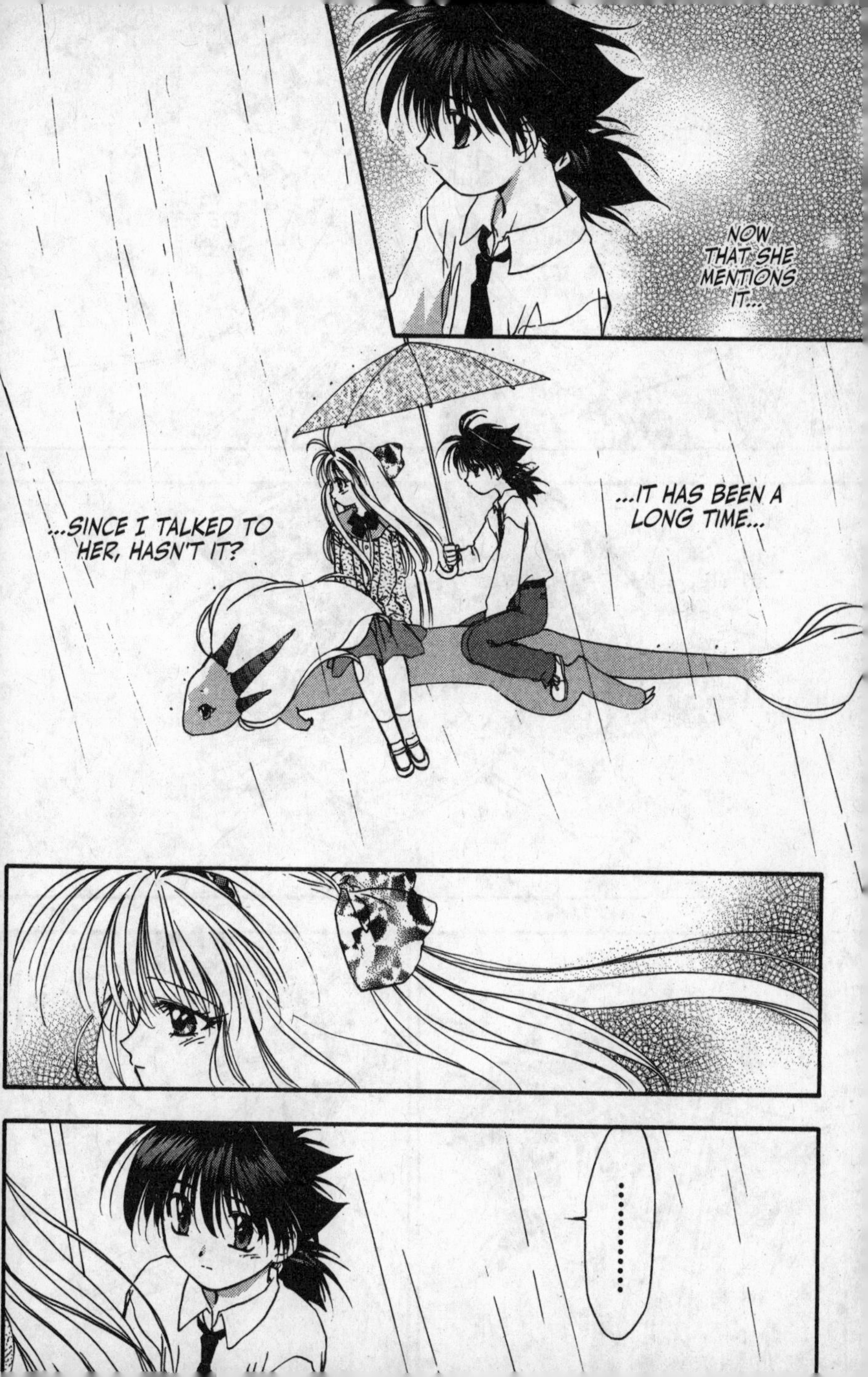
NOW THAT SHE MENTIONS IT...
...IT HAS BEEN A LONG TIME...
...SINCE I TALKED TO HER, HASN'T IT?
....

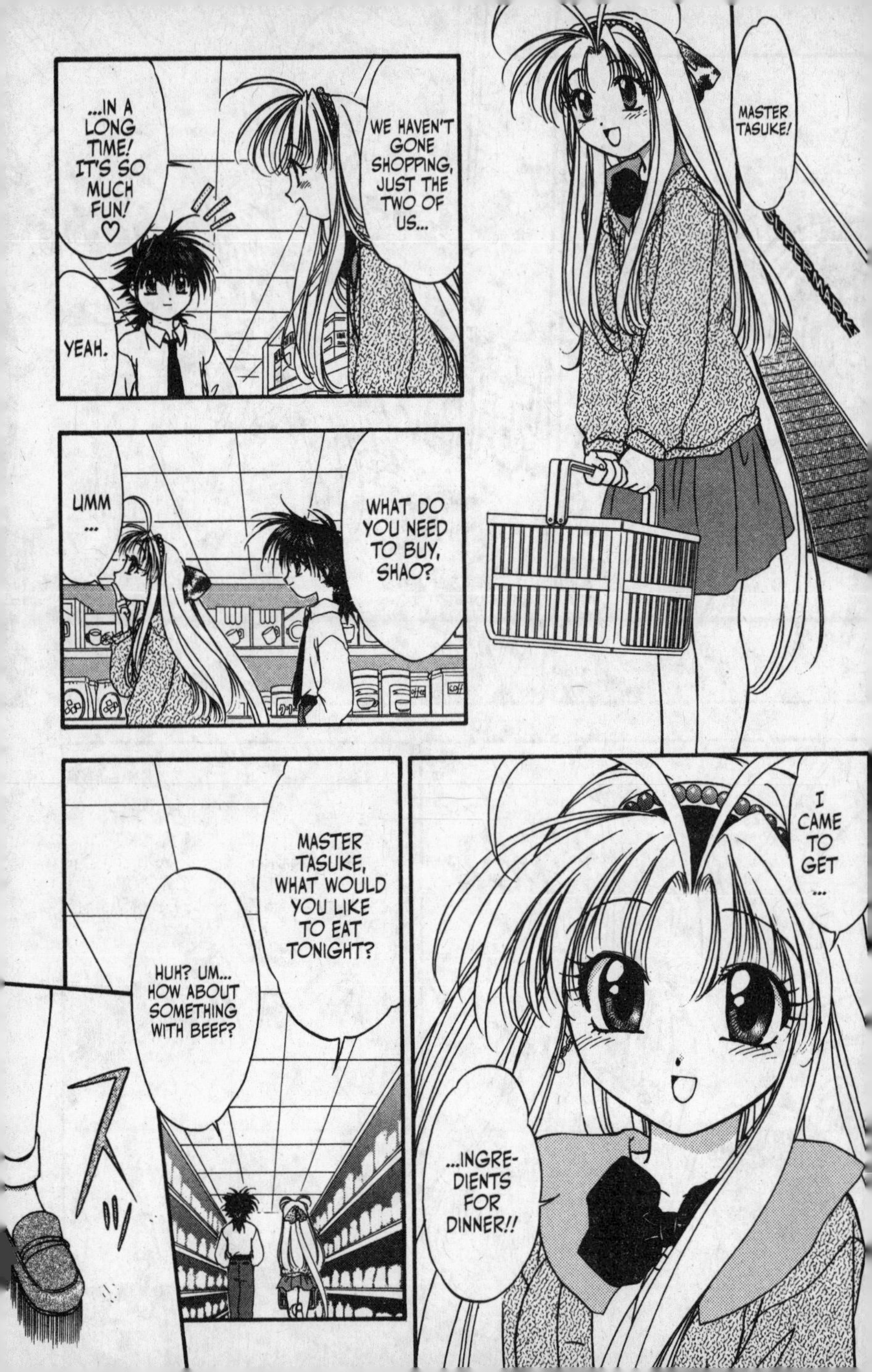
MASTER TASUKE!
WE HAVEN'T GONE SHOPPING, JUST THE TWO OF US...
...IN A LONG TIME! IT'S SO MUCH FUN! ♡
YEAH.
WHAT DO YOU NEED TO BUY, SHAO?
UMM ...
I CAME TO GET ...
...INGRE-DIENTS FOR DINNER!!
MASTER TASUKE, WHAT WOULD YOU LIKE TO EAT TONIGHT?
HUH? UM... HOW ABOUT SOMETHING WITH BEEF?

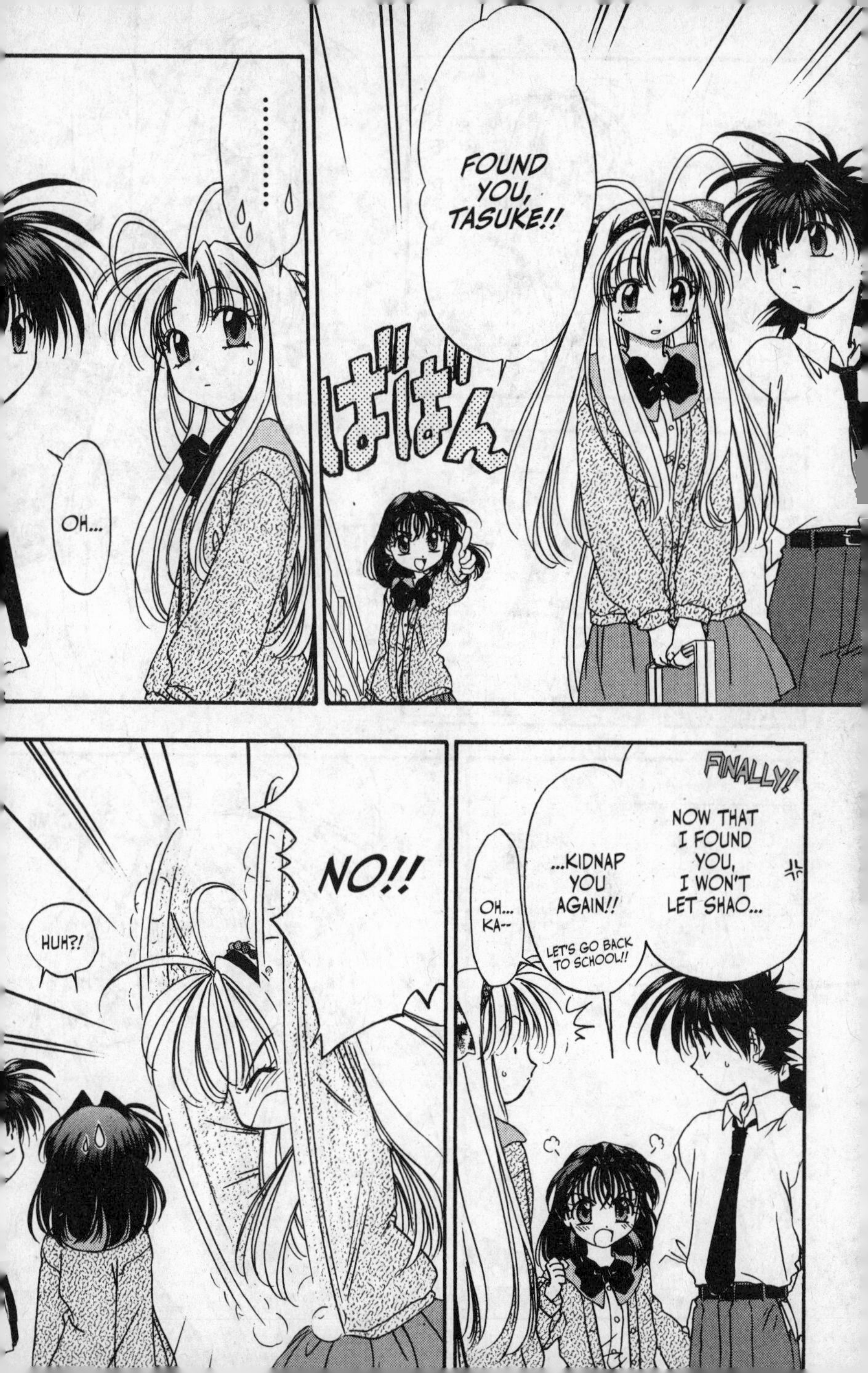

FOUND YOU, TASUKE!!
ばばん
......
OH...
FINALLY!
NOW THAT I FOUND YOU, I WON'T LET SHAO...
...KIDNAP YOU AGAIN!!
LET'S GO BACK TO SCHOOL!!
OH... KA--
NO!!
HUH?!

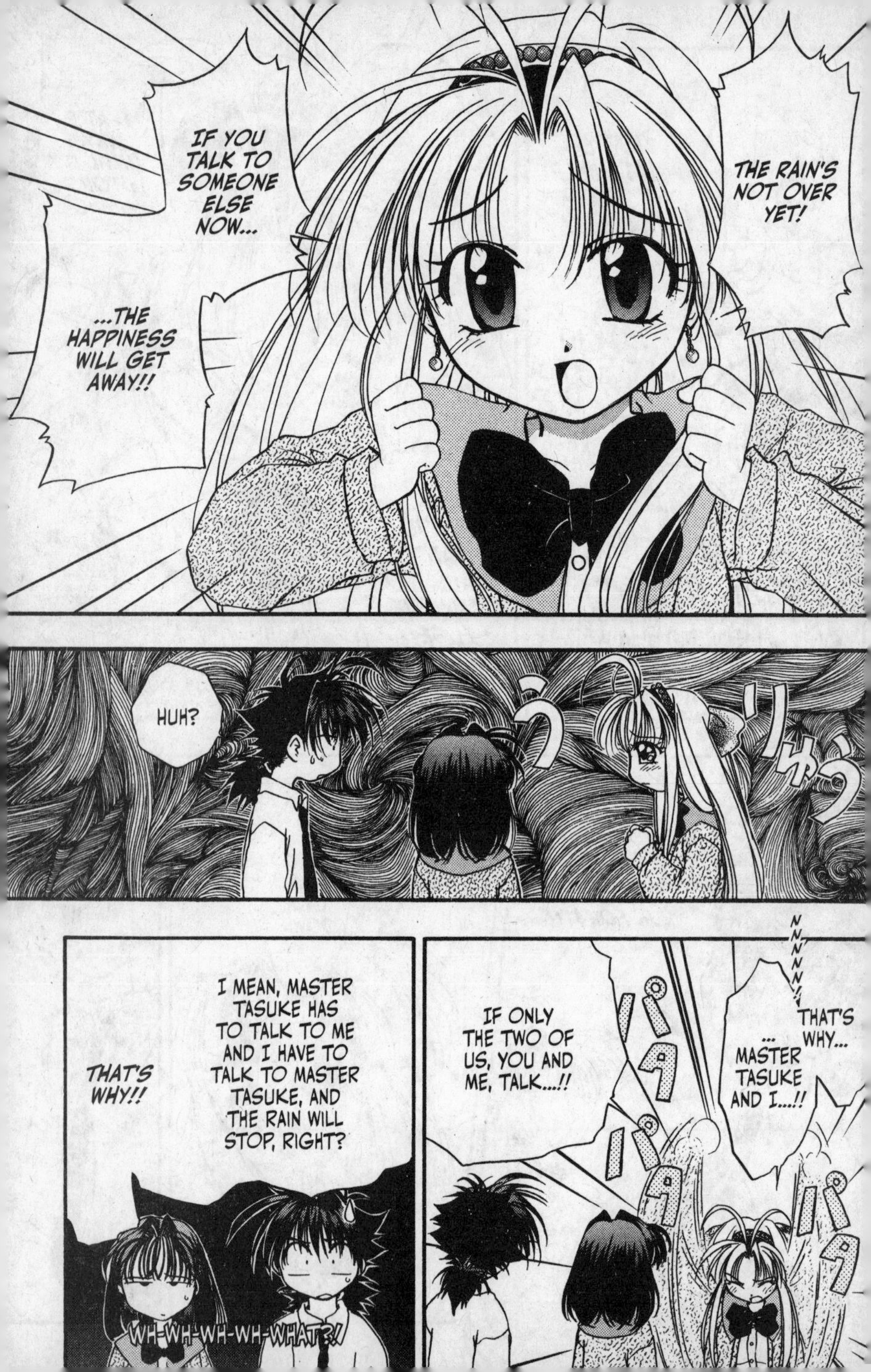
THE RAIN'S NOT OVER YET!
IF YOU TALK TO SOMEONE ELSE NOW...
...THE HAPPINESS WILL GET AWAY!!
HUH?
NNNNNN!!
THAT'S WHY...
...MASTER TASUKE AND I...!!
パタパタパタ
IF ONLY THE TWO OF US, YOU AND ME, TALK...!!
I MEAN, MASTER TASUKE HAS TO TALK TO ME AND I HAVE TO TALK TO MASTER TASUKE, AND THE RAIN WILL STOP, RIGHT?
THAT'S WHY!!
WH-WH-WH-WH-WHAT?!

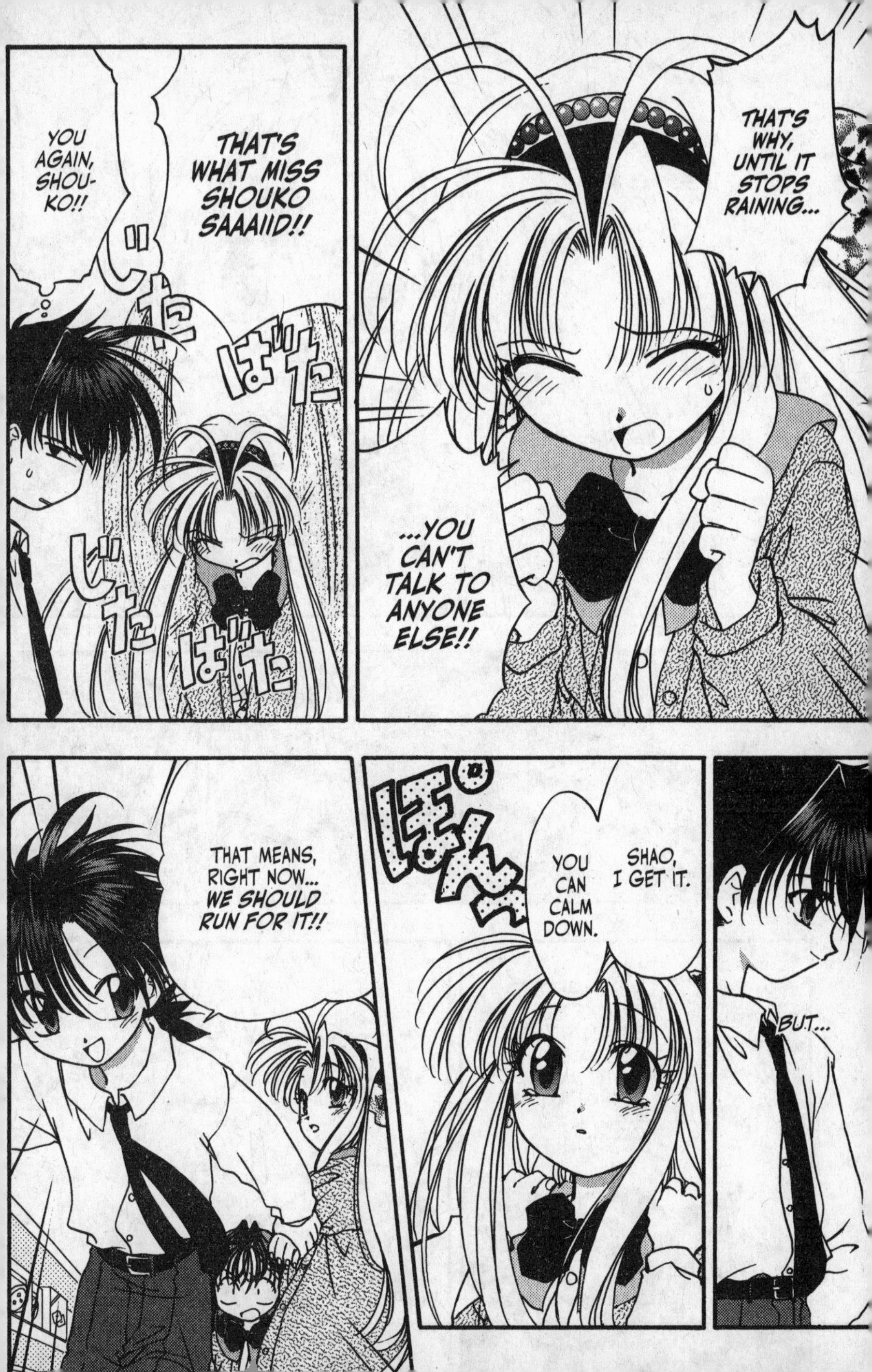
THAT'S WHY, UNTIL IT STOPS RAINING...
...YOU CAN'T TALK TO ANYONE ELSE!!
THAT'S WHAT MISS SHOUKO SAAAIID!!
YOU AGAIN, SHOUKO!!
じたばた
じたばた
BUT...
ぽん
SHAO, I GET IT.
YOU CAN CALM DOWN.
THAT MEANS, RIGHT NOW... WE SHOULD RUN FOR IT!!

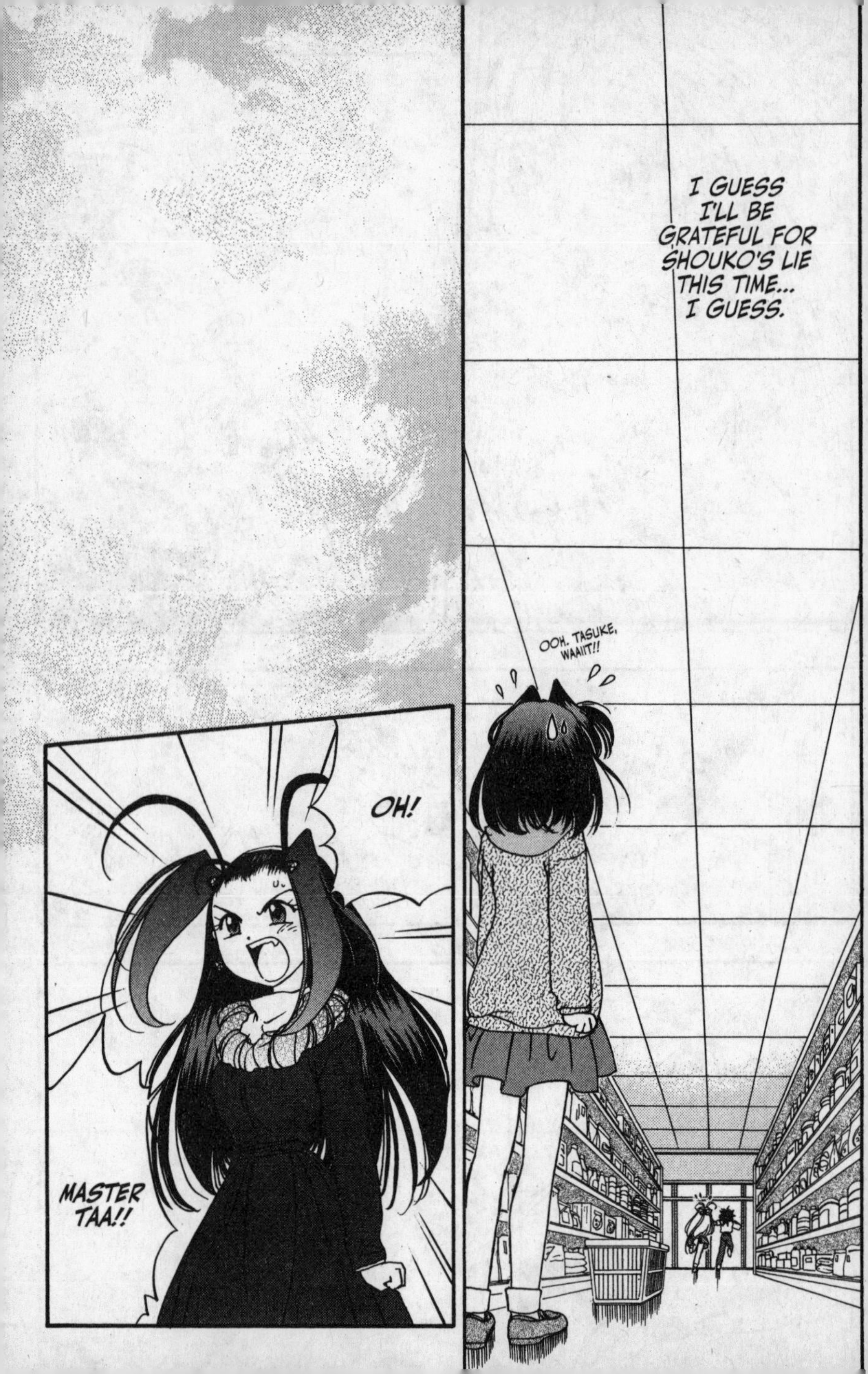
I GUESS I'LL BE GRATEFUL FOR SHOUKO'S LIE THIS TIME... I GUESS.
OOH. TASUKE, WAAIIT!!
OH!
MASTER TAA!!

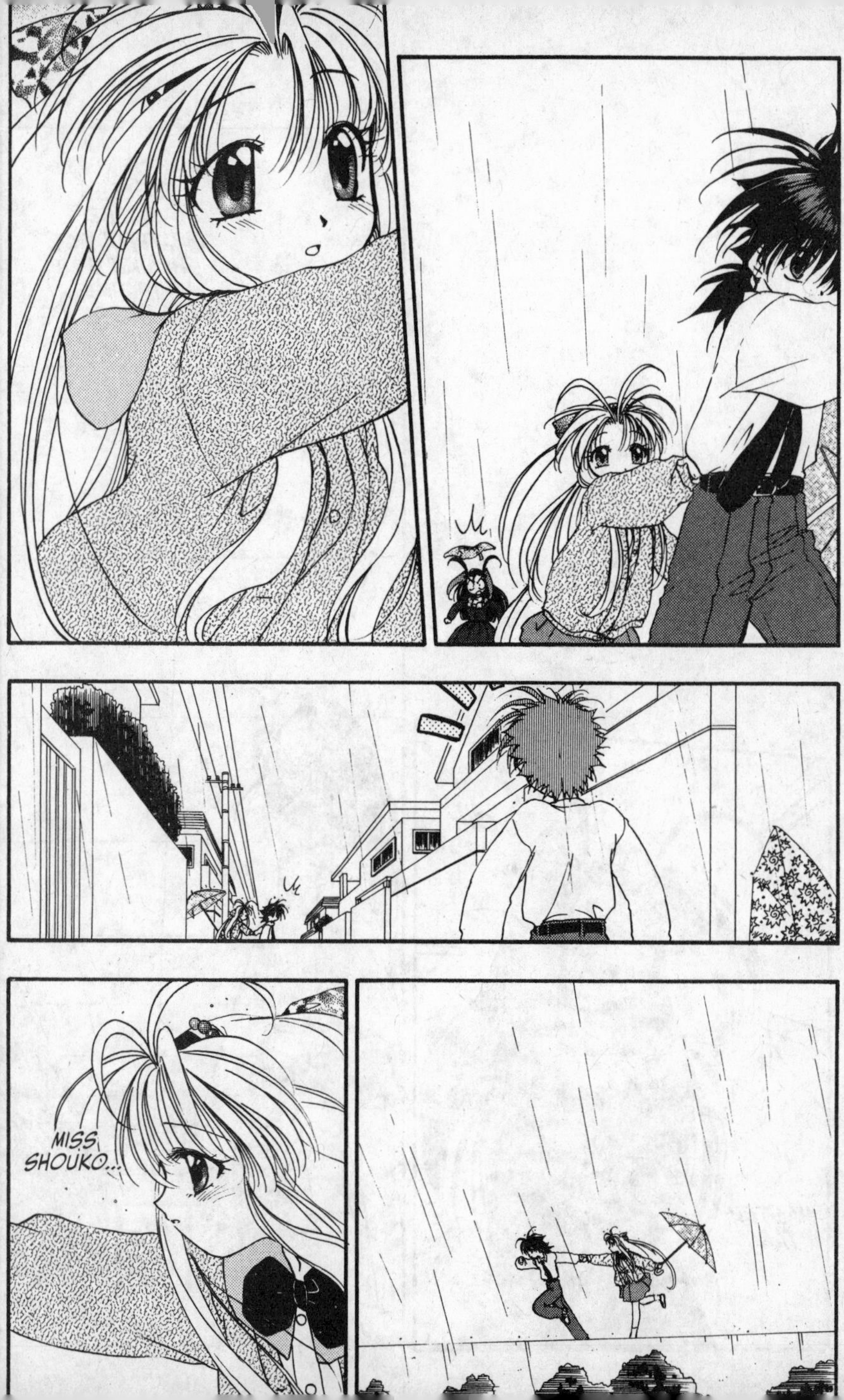
MISS SHOUKO...

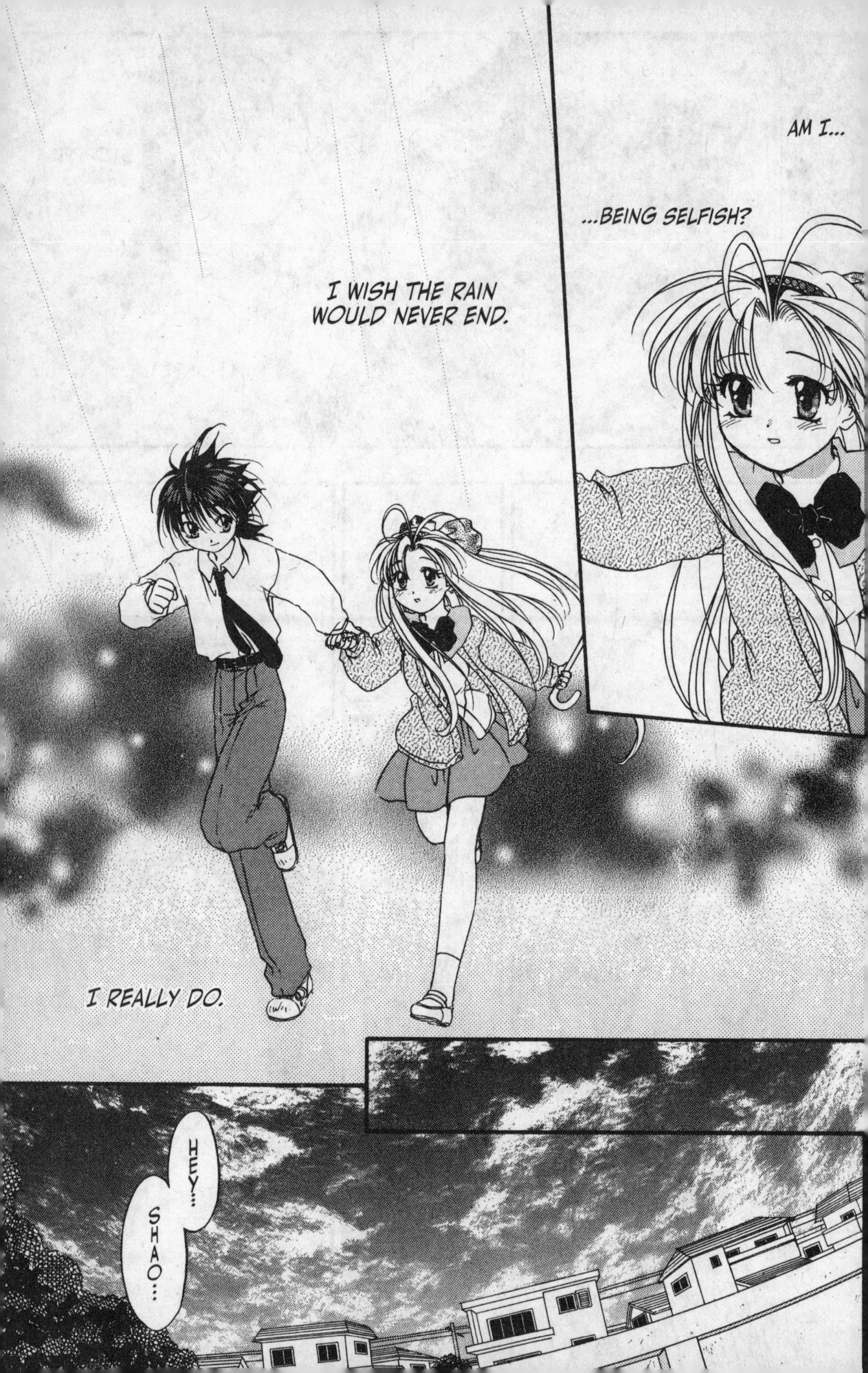
AM I...
...BEING SELFISH?
I WISH THE RAIN WOULD NEVER END.
I REALLY DO.
HEY...
SHAO...

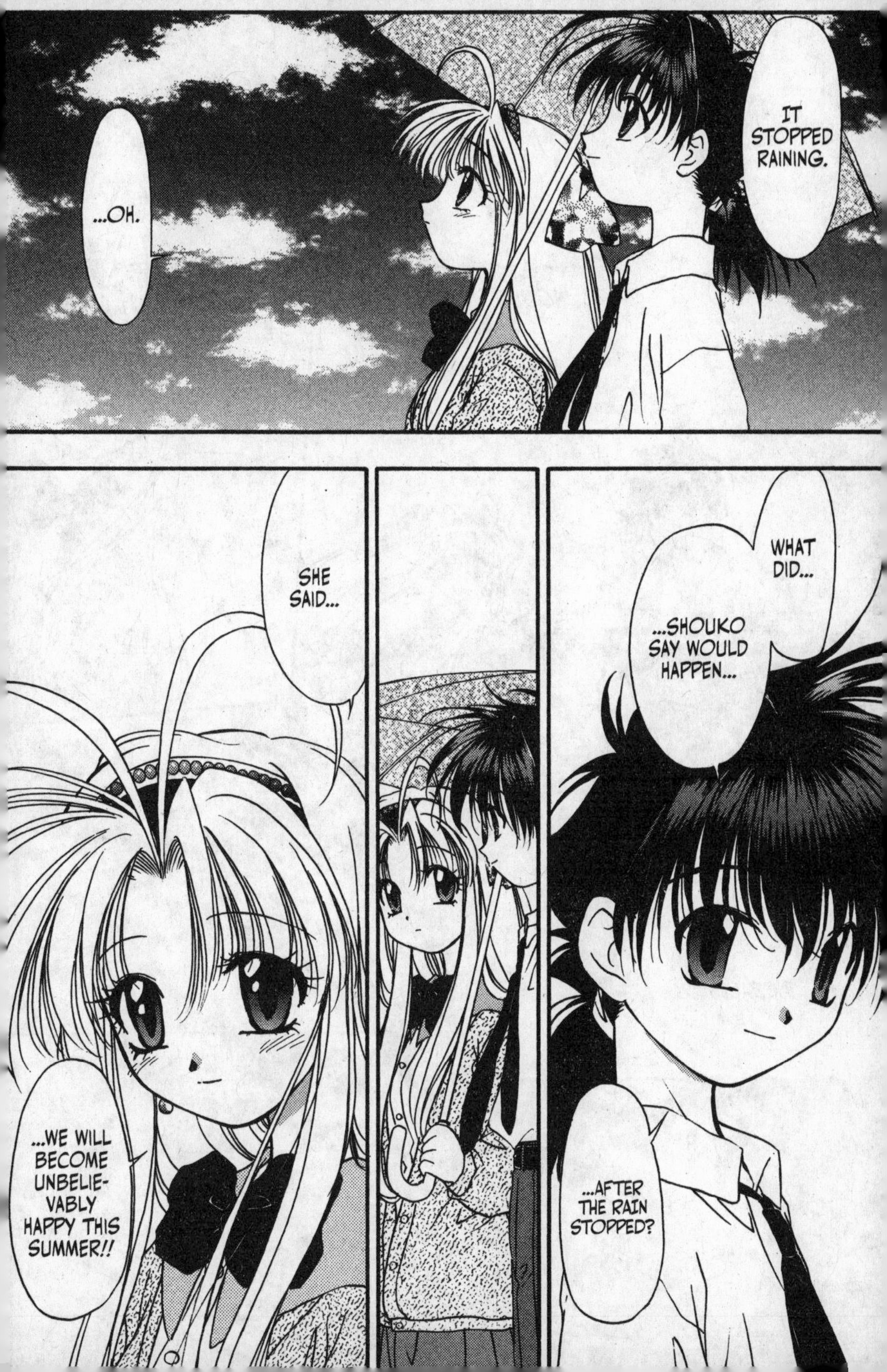
IT STOPPED RAINING.
...OH.
WHAT DID...
...SHOUKO SAY WOULD HAPPEN...
...AFTER THE RAIN STOPPED?
SHE SAID...
...WE WILL BECOME UNBELIE-VABLY HAPPY THIS SUMMER!!

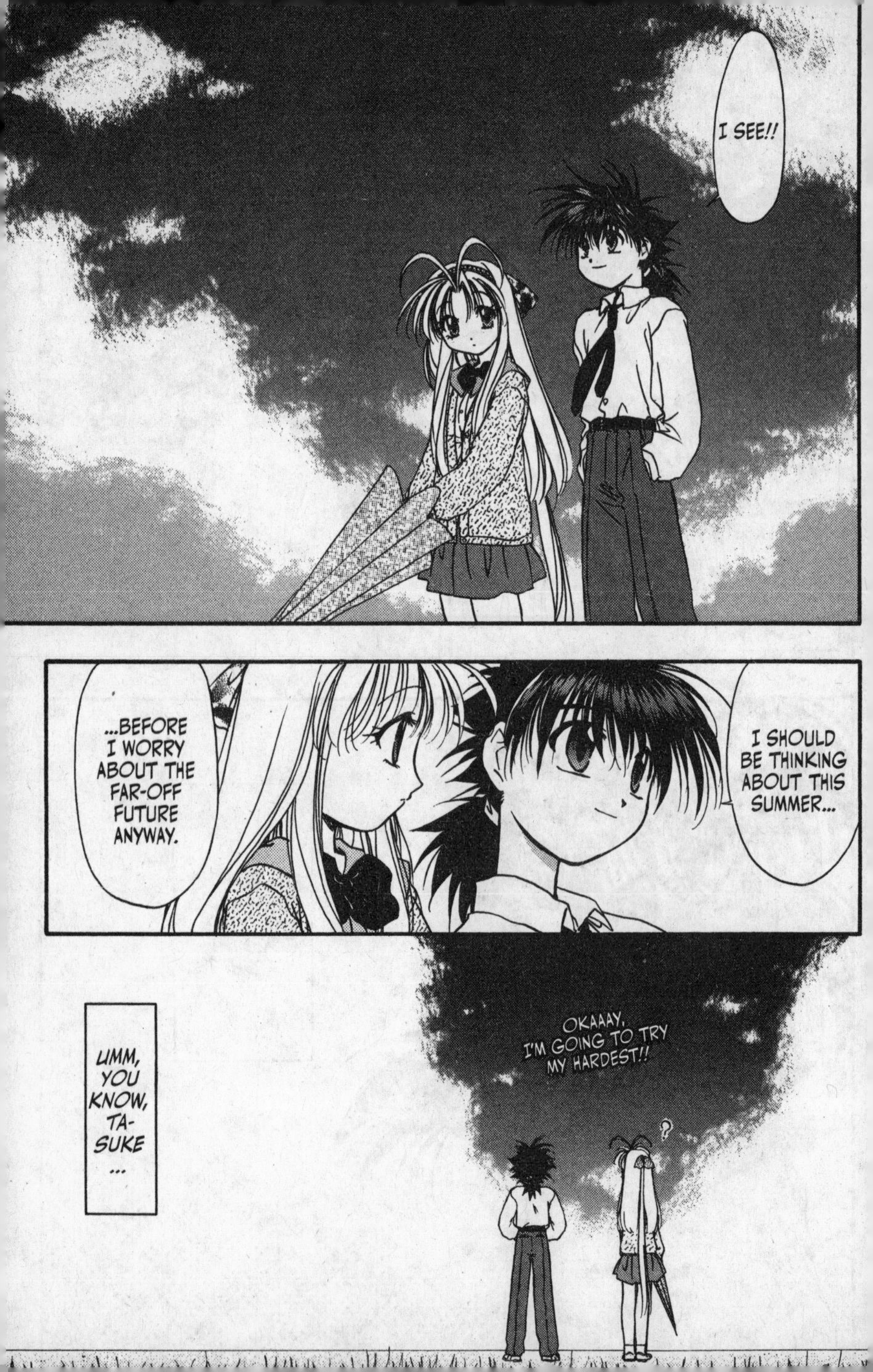
I SEE!!
I SHOULD BE THINKING ABOUT THIS SUMMER...
...BEFORE I WORRY ABOUT THE FAR-OFF FUTURE ANYWAY.
OKAAAY, I'M GOING TO TRY MY HARDEST!!
UMM, YOU KNOW, TA-SUKE ...

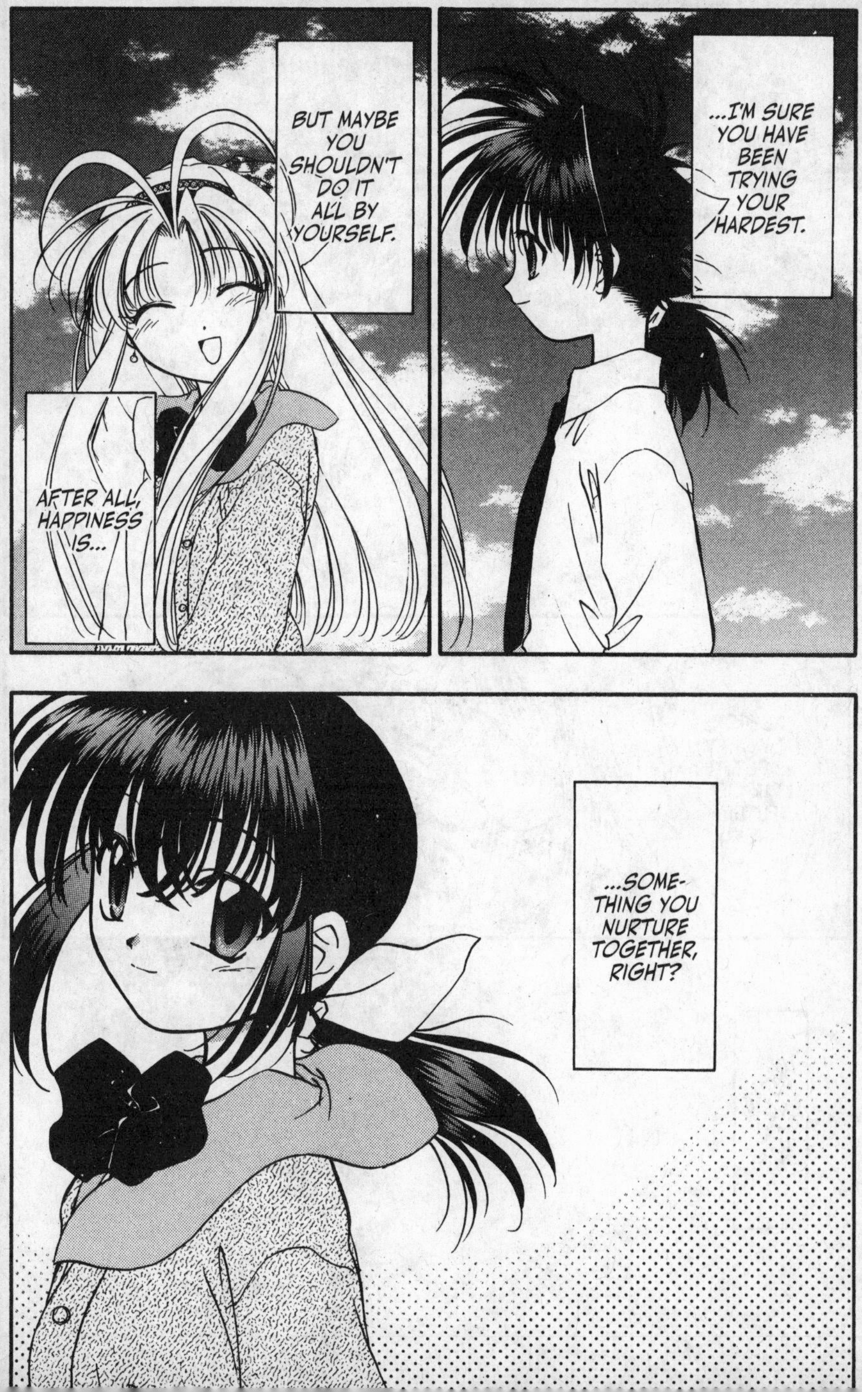
...I'M SURE YOU HAVE BEEN TRYING YOUR HARDEST.
BUT MAYBE YOU SHOULDN'T DO IT ALL BY YOURSELF.
AFTER ALL, HAPPINESS IS...
...SOME-THING YOU NURTURE TOGETHER, RIGHT?

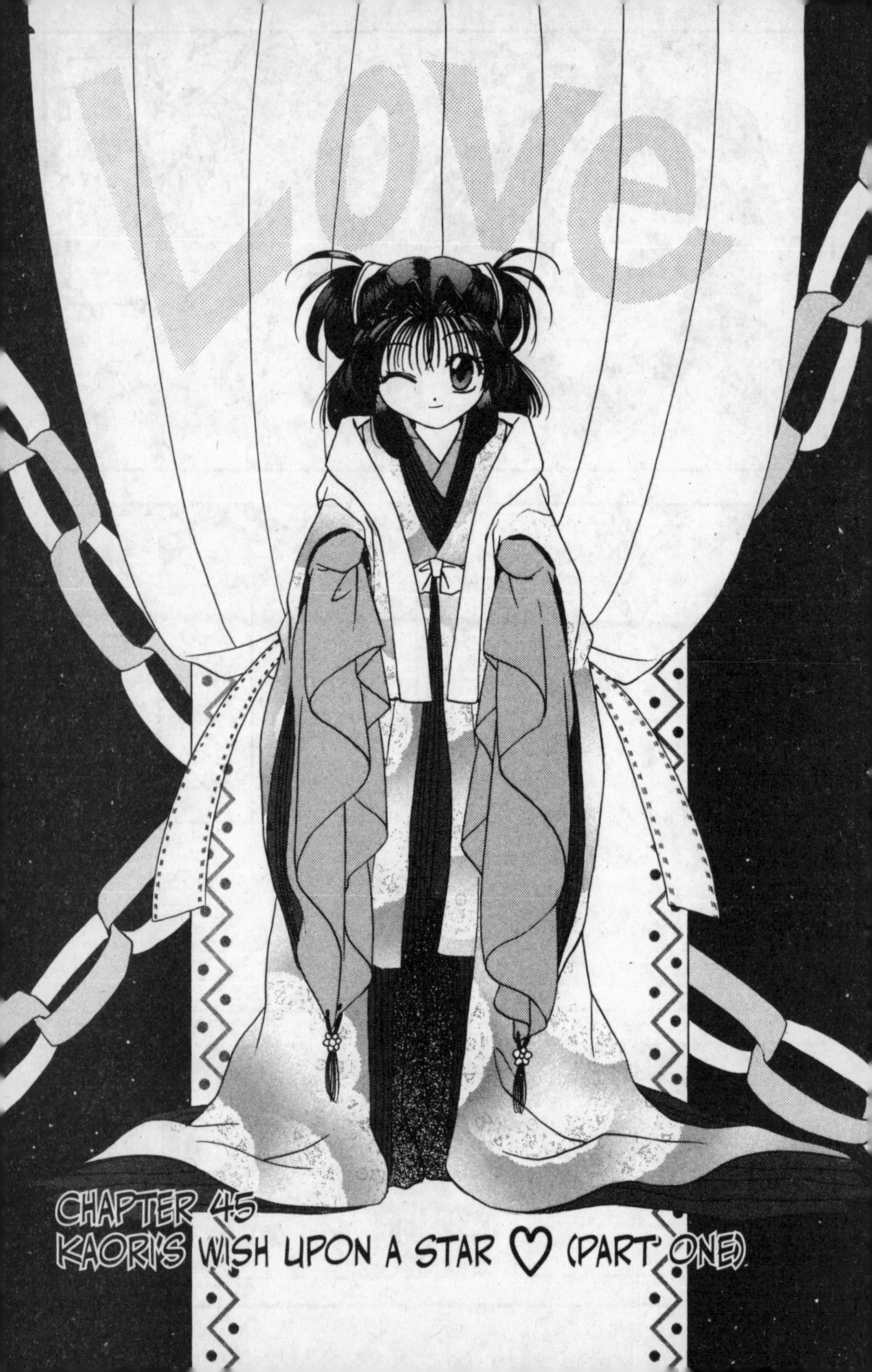
Love
CHAPTER 45
KAORI'S WISH UPON A STAR ♡ (PART ONE)

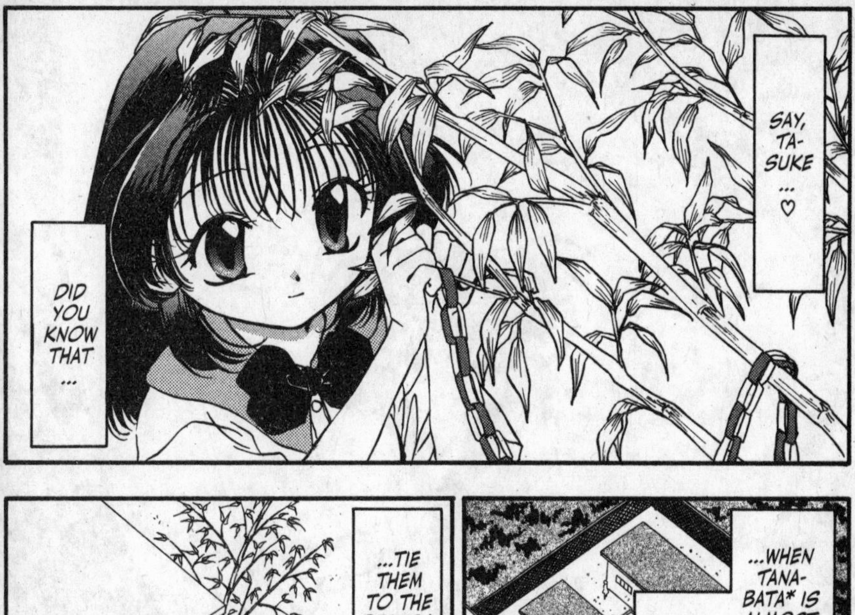
SAY, TA-SUKE ... ♡
DID YOU KNOW THAT ...
...WHEN TANA-BATA* IS ALMOST HERE...
...YOU CAN WRITE YOUR WISHES ON A PAPER AND...
...TIE THEM TO THE BRANCH-ES OF BAM-BOO?
IF YOU DO THAT, DO YOU KNOW WHAT HAP-PENS?

* FESTIVAL HELD ON THE SEVENTH DAY OF THE SEVENTH MONTH. IT IS SAID THAT THIS IS THE ONLY DAY THAT PRINCESS ORI (THE STAR, VEGA) CAN CROSS THE MILKY WAY TO MEET HER LOVE, HIKOBOSHI (ALTAIR).

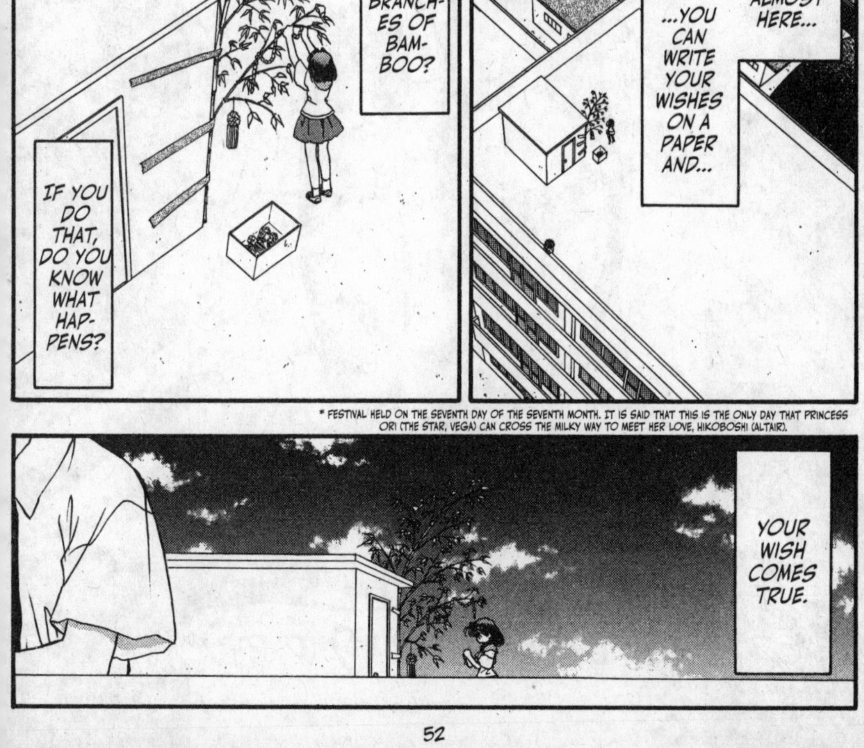
YOUR WISH COMES TRUE.

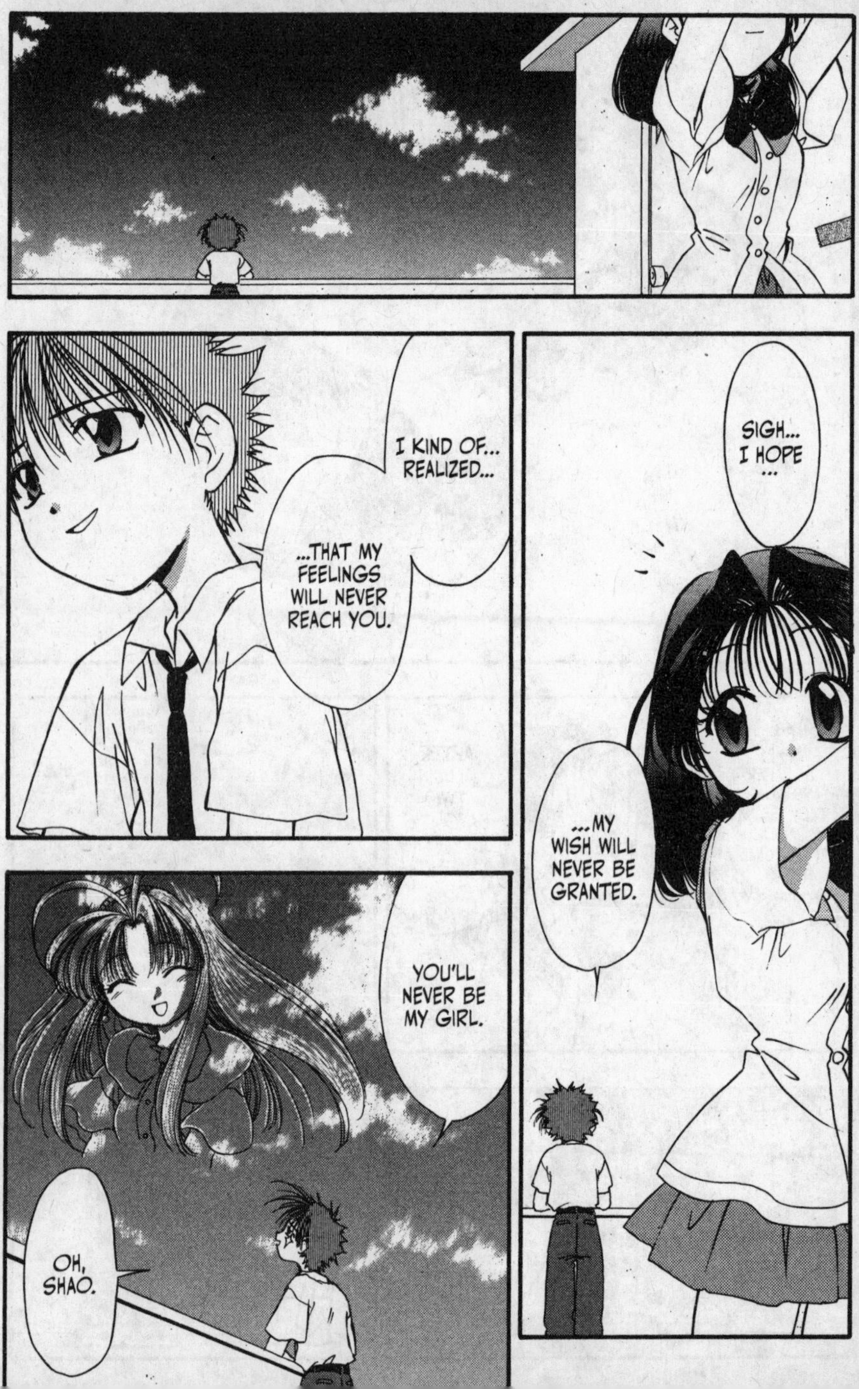
SIGH... I HOPE ...
...MY WISH WILL NEVER BE GRANTED.
I KIND OF... REALIZED...
...THAT MY FEELINGS WILL NEVER REACH YOU.
YOU'LL NEVER BE MY GIRL.
OH, SHAO.

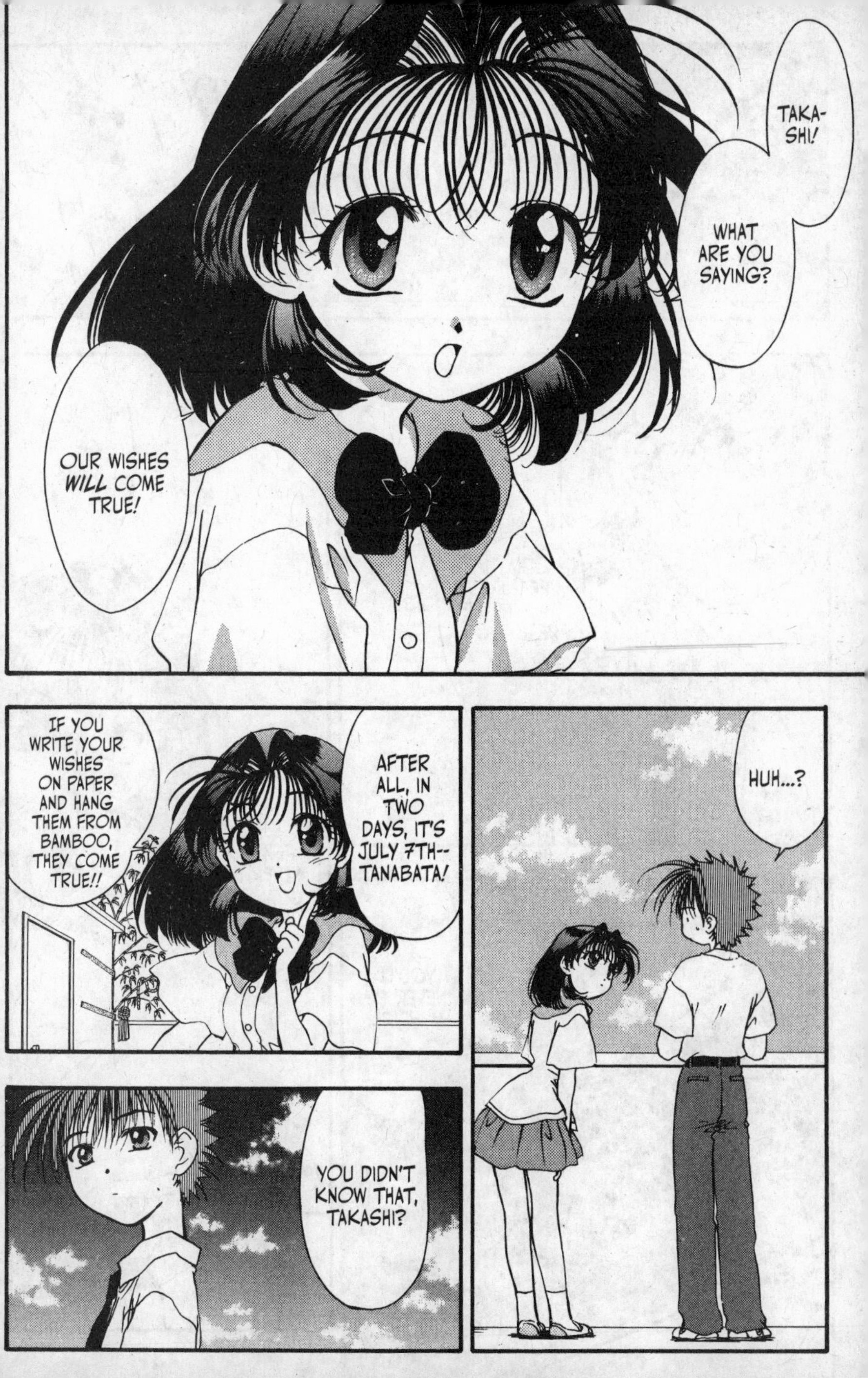
TAKA-SHI!
WHAT ARE YOU SAYING?
OUR WISHES *WILL* COME TRUE!
HUH...?
AFTER ALL, IN TWO DAYS, IT'S JULY 7TH-- TANABATA!
IF YOU WRITE YOUR WISHES ON PAPER AND HANG THEM FROM BAMBOO, THEY COME TRUE!!
YOU DIDN'T KNOW THAT, TAKASHI?

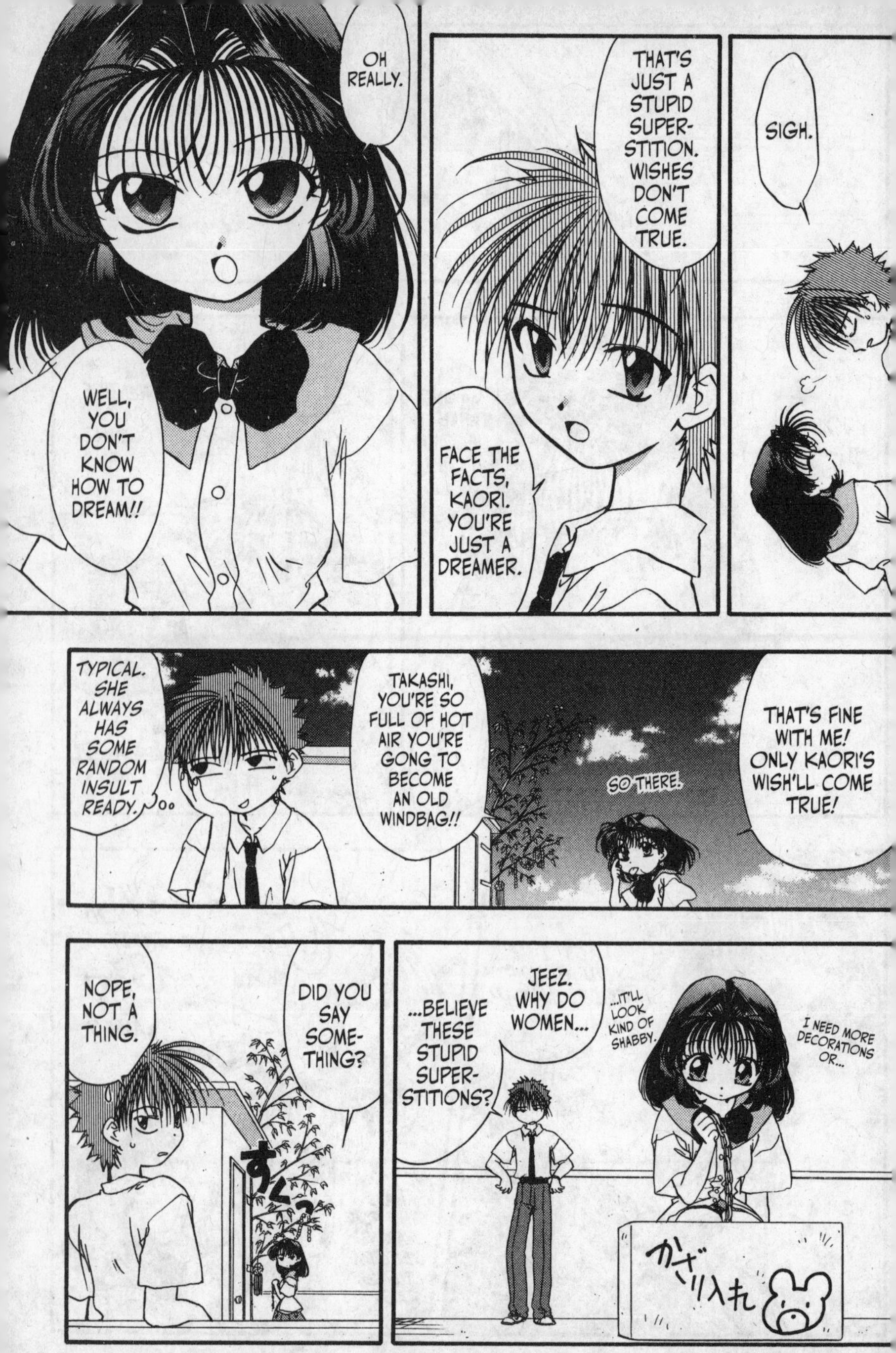
SIGH.
THAT'S JUST A STUPID SUPER-STITION. WISHES DON'T COME TRUE.
FACE THE FACTS, KAORI. YOU'RE JUST A DREAMER.
OH REALLY.
WELL, YOU DON'T KNOW HOW TO DREAM!!
THAT'S FINE WITH ME! ONLY KAORI'S WISH'LL COME TRUE!
SO THERE.
TAKASHI, YOU'RE SO FULL OF HOT AIR YOU'RE GONG TO BECOME AN OLD WINDBAG!!
TYPICAL. SHE ALWAYS HAS SOME RANDOM INSULT READY.
I NEED MORE DECORATIONS OR...
...IT'LL LOOK KIND OF SHABBY.
JEEZ. WHY DO WOMEN...
...BELIEVE THESE STUPID SUPER-STITIONS?
かざり入れ
DID YOU SAY SOME-THING?
すくっ
NOPE, NOT A THING.

BOX: DECORATIONS

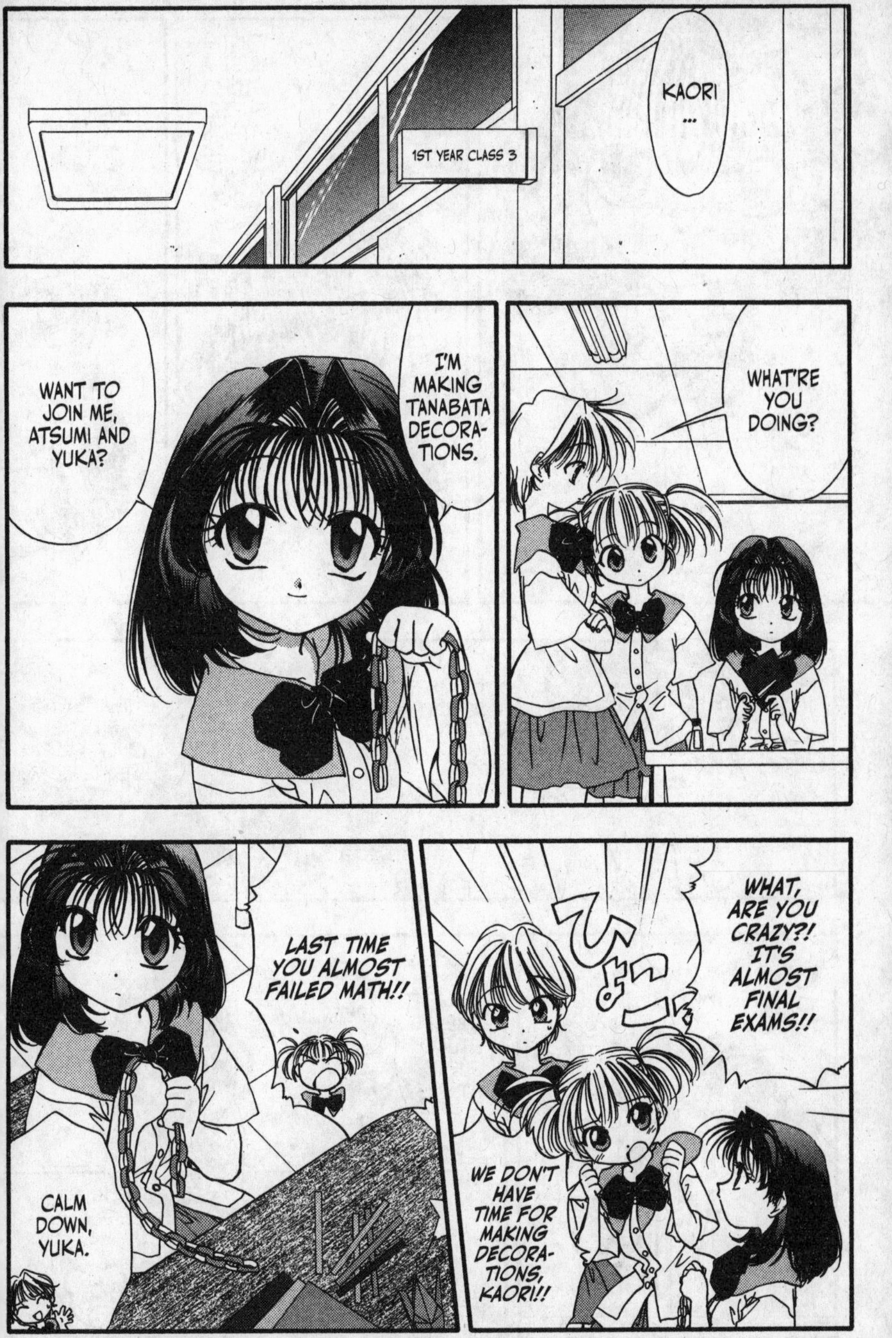
KAORI ...
1ST YEAR CLASS 3
WHAT'RE YOU DOING?
I'M MAKING TANABATA DECORATIONS.
WANT TO JOIN ME, ATSUMI AND YUKA?
WHAT, ARE YOU CRAZY?! IT'S ALMOST FINAL EXAMS!!
WE DON'T HAVE TIME FOR MAKING DECORATIONS, KAORI!!
LAST TIME YOU ALMOST FAILED MATH!!
CALM DOWN, YUKA.

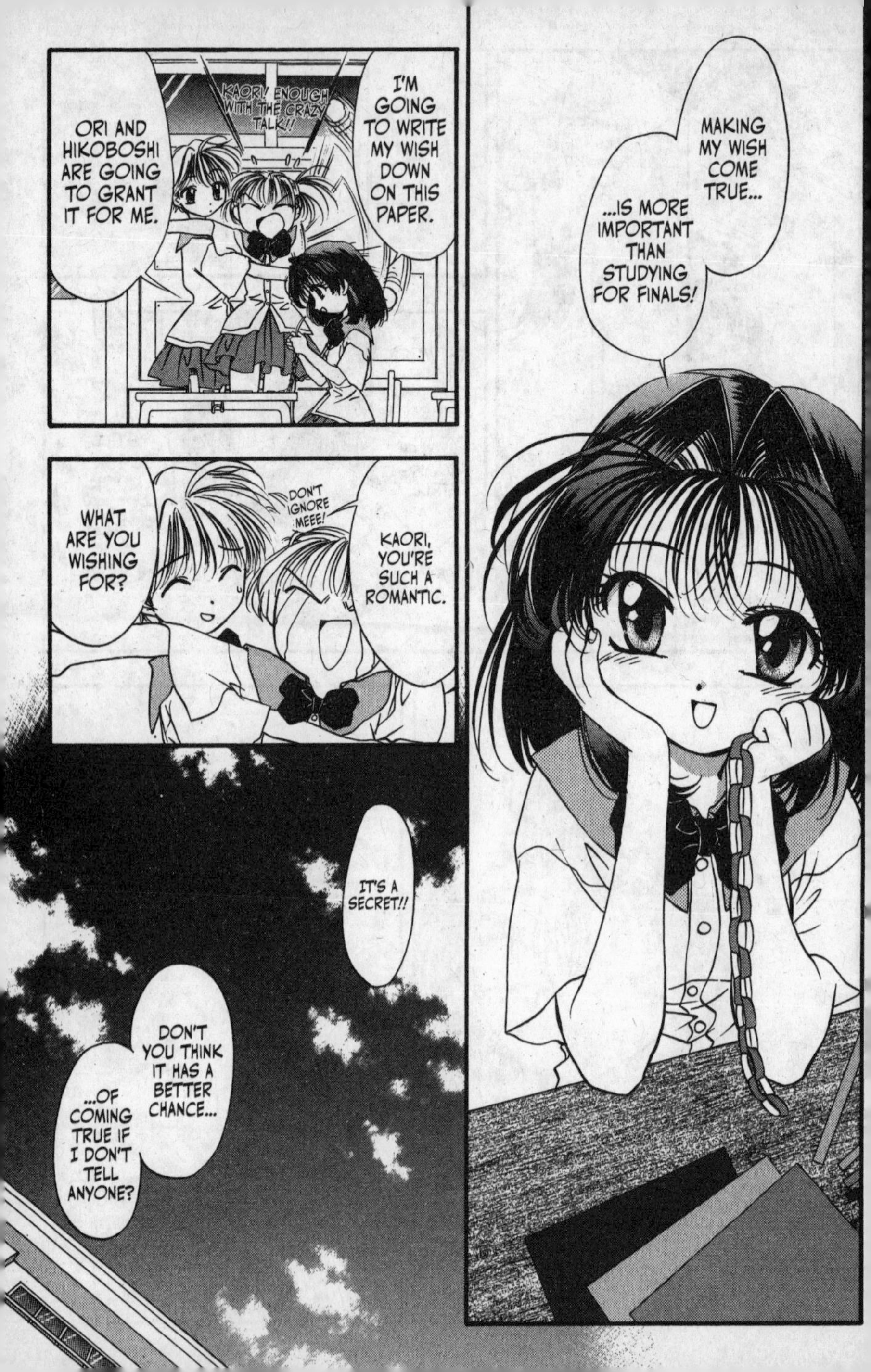
MAKING MY WISH COME TRUE...
...IS MORE IMPORTANT THAN STUDYING FOR FINALS!
I'M GOING TO WRITE MY WISH DOWN ON THIS PAPER.
KAORI! ENOUGH WITH THE CRAZY TALK!!
ORI AND HIKOBOSHI ARE GOING TO GRANT IT FOR ME.
KAORI, YOU'RE SUCH A ROMANTIC.
DON'T IGNORE MEEE!
WHAT ARE YOU WISHING FOR?
IT'S A SECRET!!
DON'T YOU THINK IT HAS A BETTER CHANCE...
...OF COMING TRUE IF I DON'T TELL ANYONE?

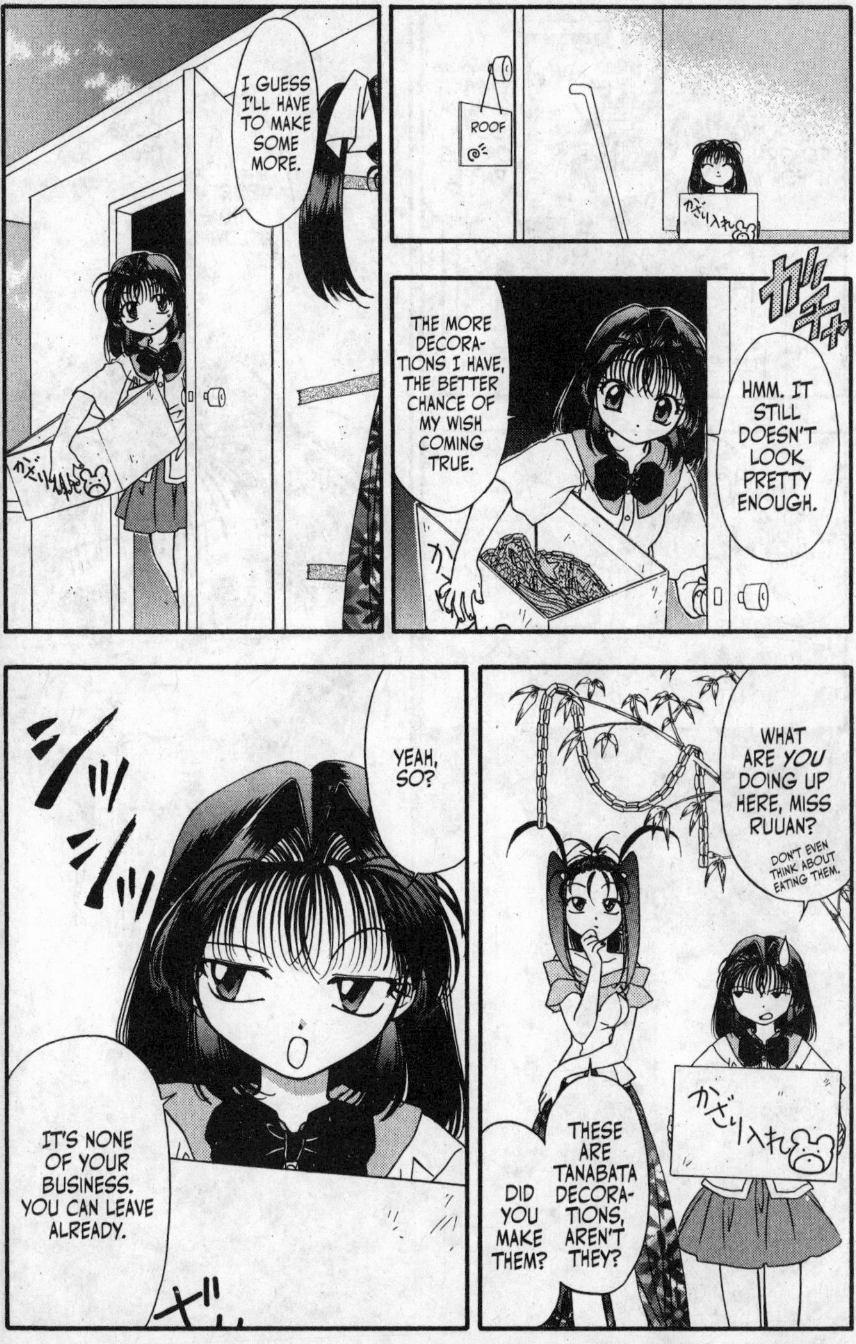
ROOF
かざり入れ
HMM. IT STILL DOESN'T LOOK PRETTY ENOUGH.
THE MORE DECORATIONS I HAVE, THE BETTER CHANCE OF MY WISH COMING TRUE.
I GUESS I'LL HAVE TO MAKE SOME MORE.
WHAT ARE YOU DOING UP HERE, MISS RUUAN?
DON'T EVEN THINK ABOUT EATING THEM.
THESE ARE TANABATA DECORATIONS, AREN'T THEY?
DID YOU MAKE THEM?
かざり入れ
YEAH, SO?
IT'S NONE OF YOUR BUSINESS. YOU CAN LEAVE ALREADY.

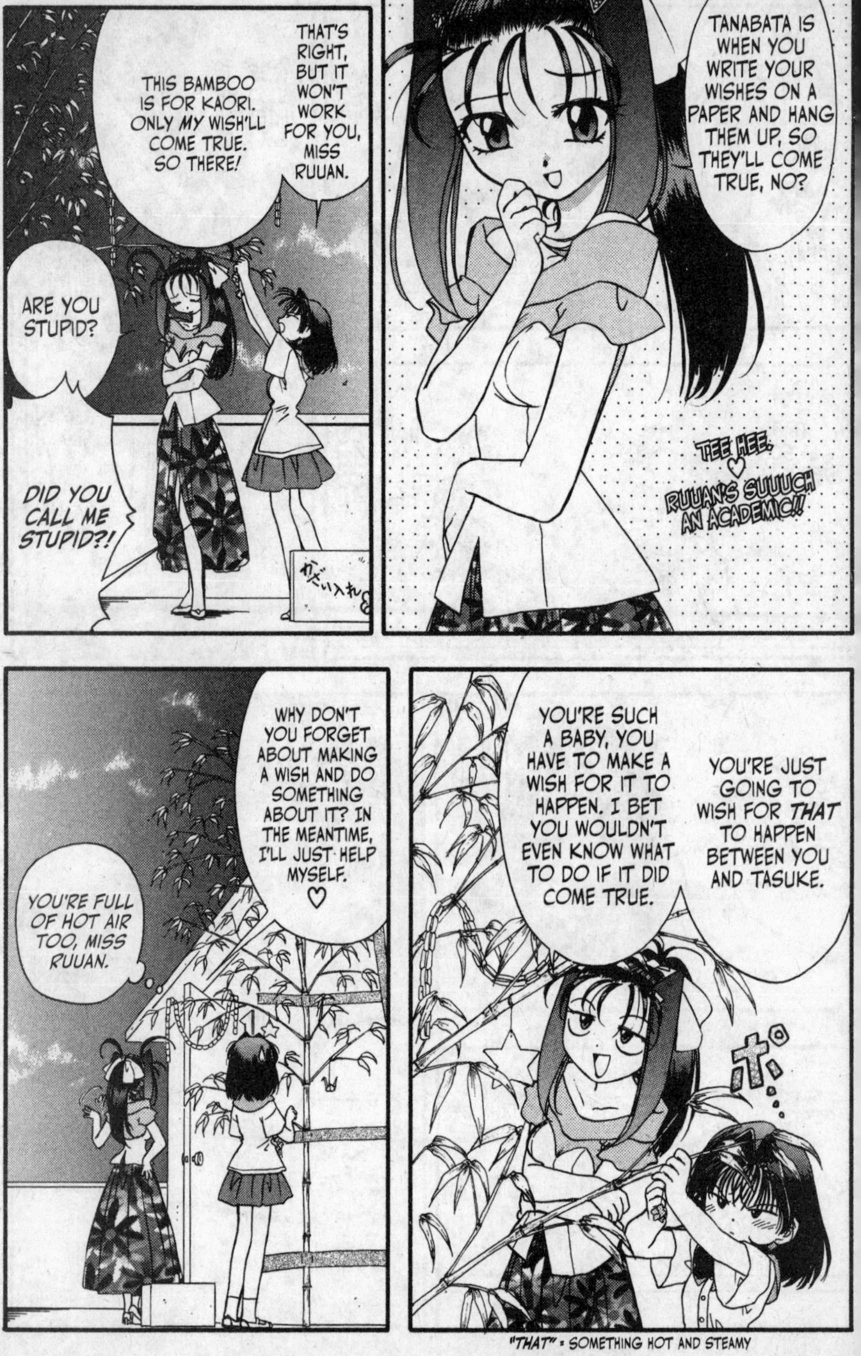
TANABATA IS WHEN YOU WRITE YOUR WISHES ON A PAPER AND HANG THEM UP, SO THEY'LL COME TRUE, NO?
TEE HEE. ♡ RUUAN'S SUUUCH AN ACADEMIC!!
THAT'S RIGHT, BUT IT WON'T WORK FOR YOU, MISS RUUAN.
THIS BAMBOO IS FOR KAORI. ONLY *MY* WISH'LL COME TRUE. SO THERE!
ARE YOU STUPID?
DID YOU CALL ME STUPID?!
YOU'RE JUST GOING TO WISH FOR *THAT* TO HAPPEN BETWEEN YOU AND TASUKE.
YOU'RE SUCH A BABY, YOU HAVE TO MAKE A WISH FOR IT TO HAPPEN. I BET YOU WOULDN'T EVEN KNOW WHAT TO DO IF IT DID COME TRUE.
ポ
WHY DON'T YOU FORGET ABOUT MAKING A WISH AND DO SOMETHING ABOUT IT? IN THE MEANTIME, I'LL JUST HELP MYSELF. ♡
YOU'RE FULL OF HOT AIR TOO, MISS RUUAN.

"THAT" = SOMETHING HOT AND STEAMY

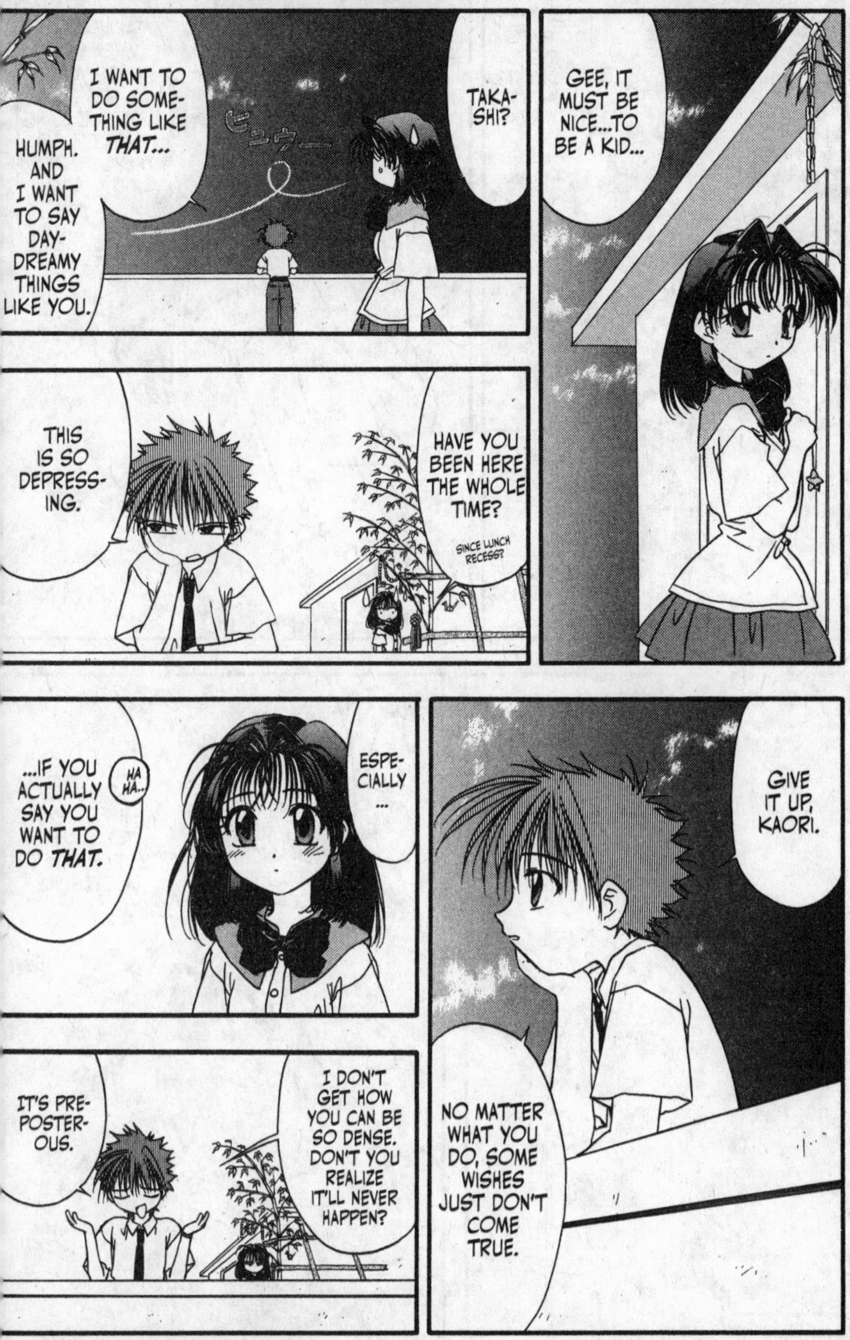
GEE, IT MUST BE NICE...TO BE A KID...
TAKA-SHI?
ヒュウー
I WANT TO DO SOME-THING LIKE *THAT*...
HUMPH. AND I WANT TO SAY DAY-DREAMY THINGS LIKE YOU.
HAVE YOU BEEN HERE THE WHOLE TIME?
SINCE LUNCH RECESS?
THIS IS SO DEPRESS-ING.
GIVE IT UP, KAORI.
NO MATTER WHAT YOU DO, SOME WISHES JUST DON'T COME TRUE.
ESPE-CIALLY ...
HA HA...
...IF YOU ACTUALLY SAY YOU WANT TO DO *THAT*.
I DON'T GET HOW YOU CAN BE SO DENSE. DON'T YOU REALIZE IT'LL NEVER HAPPEN?
IT'S PRE-POSTER-OUS.

WHAT KID SAYS "PREPOSTEROUS"...?

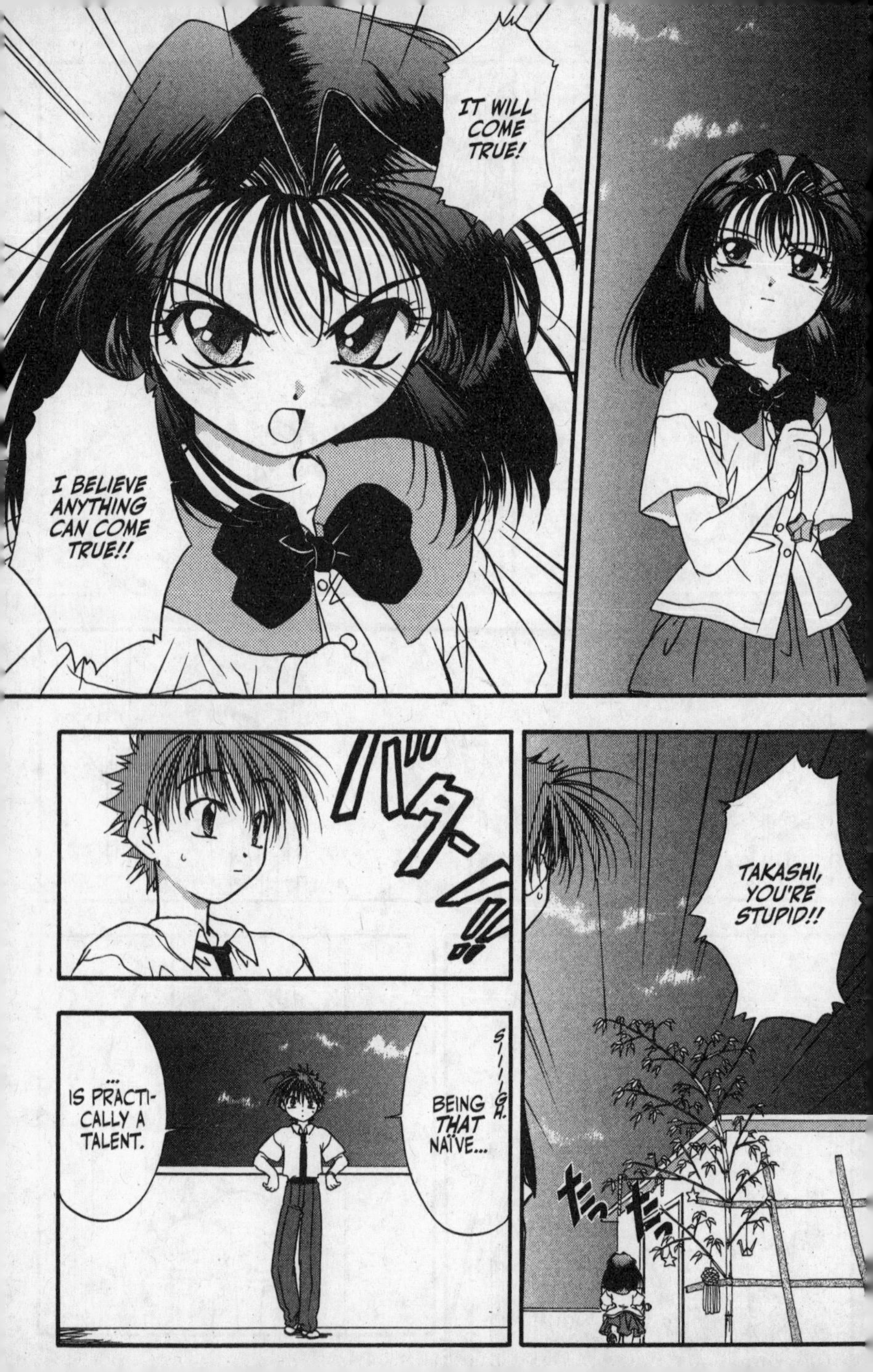
IT WILL COME TRUE!
I BELIEVE ANYTHING CAN COME TRUE!!
TAKASHI, YOU'RE STUPID!!
タッ
タッ
バタン!!
SIIIIGH.
BEING THAT NAÏVE...
... IS PRACTI-CALLY A TALENT.

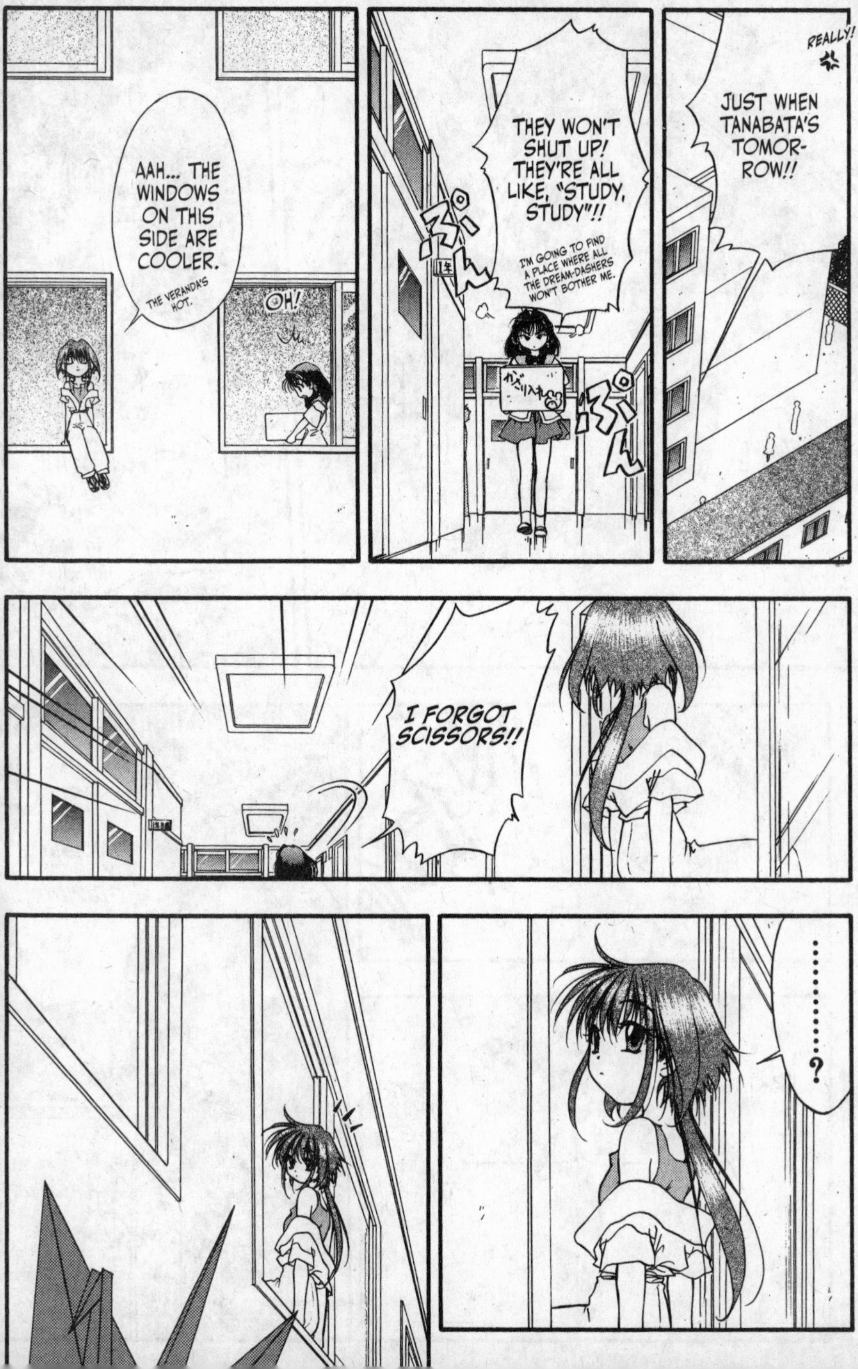
REALLY!
JUST WHEN TANABATA'S TOMORROW!!
THEY WON'T SHUT UP! THEY'RE ALL LIKE, "STUDY, STUDY"!!
I'M GOING TO FIND A PLACE WHERE ALL THE DREAM-DASHERS WON'T BOTHER ME.
AAH... THE WINDOWS ON THIS SIDE ARE COOLER.
THE VERANDA'S HOT.
OH!
I FORGOT SCISSORS!!
........?

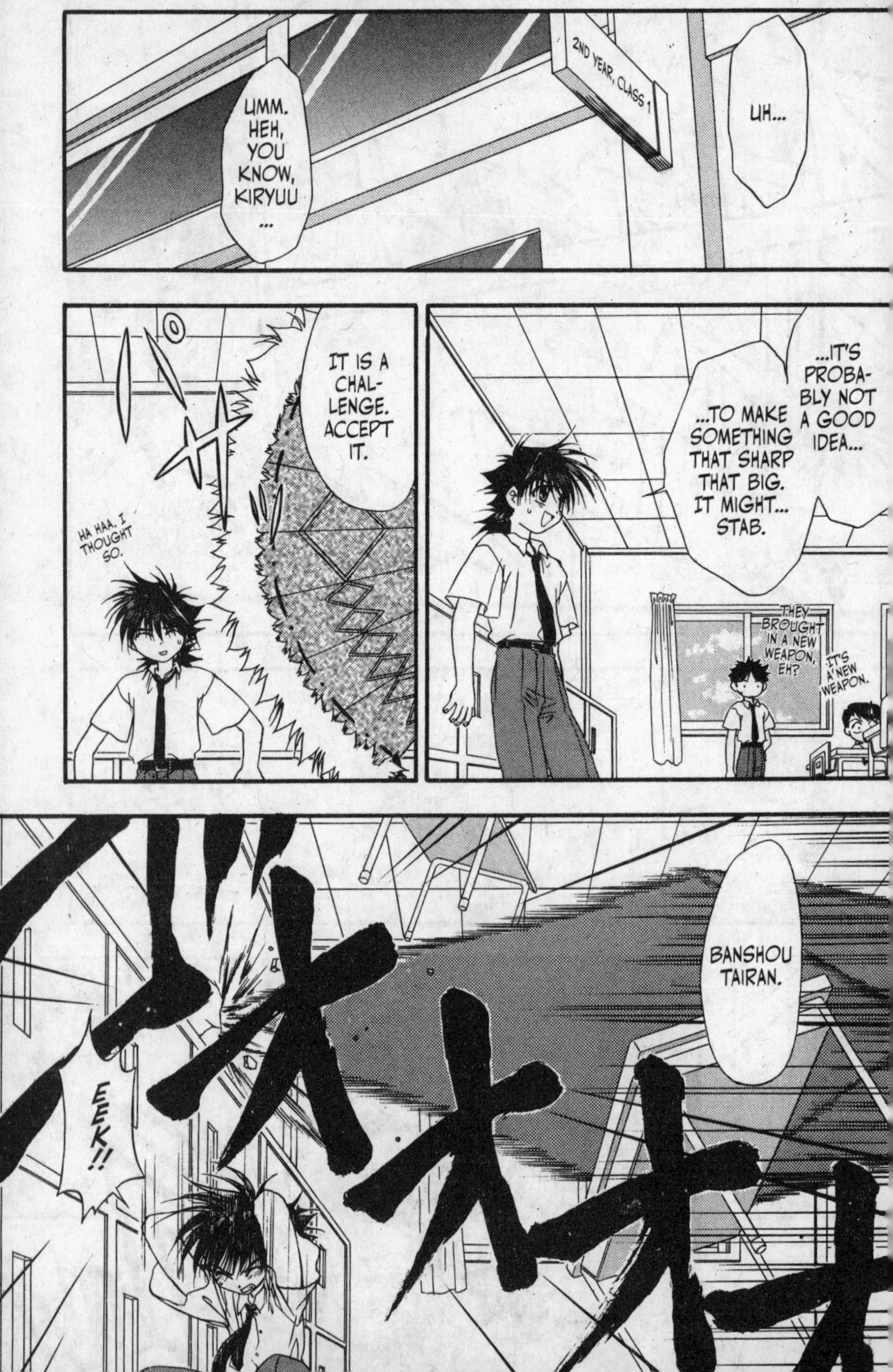
2ND YEAR, CLASS 1
UH...
UMM. HEH, YOU KNOW, KIRYUU ...
...IT'S PROBA-BLY NOT A GOOD IDEA...
...TO MAKE SOMETHING THAT SHARP THAT BIG. IT MIGHT... STAB.
THEY BROUGHT IN A NEW WEAPON, EH?
IT'S A NEW WEAPON.
IT IS A CHAL-LENGE. ACCEPT IT.
HA HAA. I THOUGHT SO.
BANSHOU TAIRAN.
EEK!!

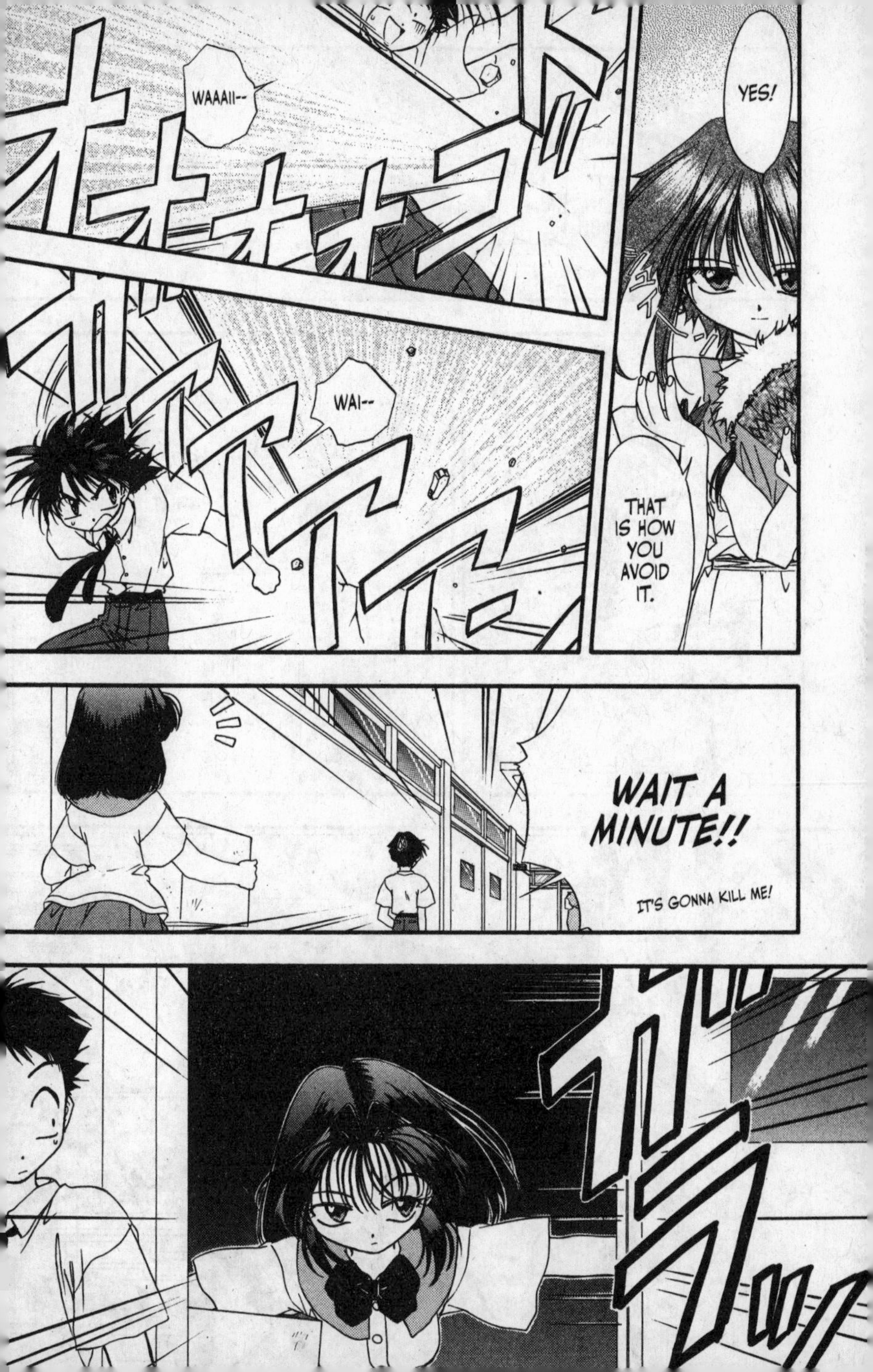
YES!
THAT IS HOW YOU AVOID IT.
WAAAII--
WAI--
WAIT A MINUTE!!
IT'S GONNA KILL ME!

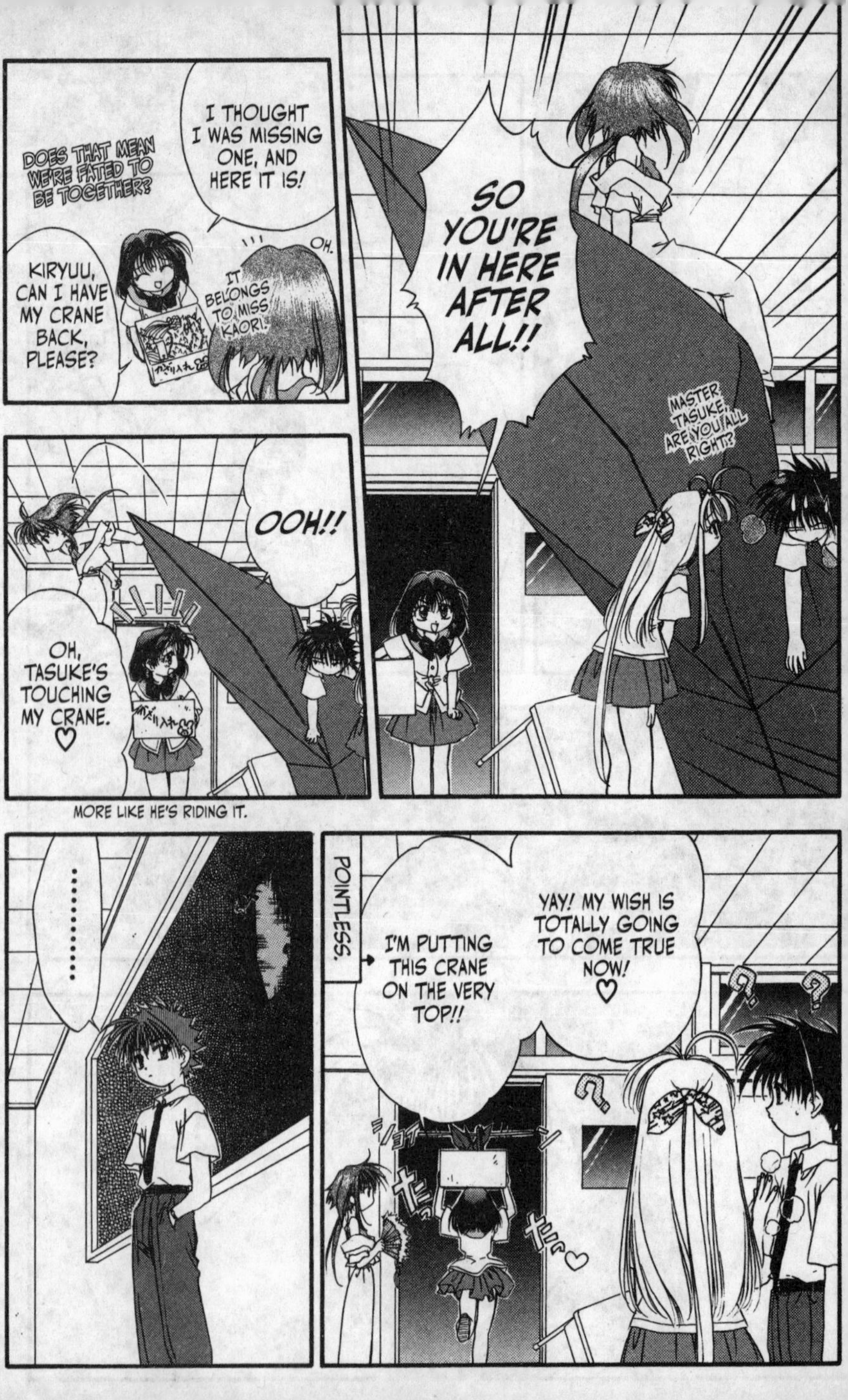
SO YOU'RE IN HERE AFTER ALL!!
MASTER TASUKE, ARE YOU ALL RIGHT?
I THOUGHT I WAS MISSING ONE, AND HERE IT IS!
OH.
IT BELONGS TO MISS KAORI.
DOES THAT MEAN WE'RE FATED TO BE TOGETHER?
KIRYUU, CAN I HAVE MY CRANE BACK, PLEASE?
OOH!!
OH, TASUKE'S TOUCHING MY CRANE. ♡
MORE LIKE HE'S RIDING IT.
YAY! MY WISH IS TOTALLY GOING TO COME TRUE NOW! ♡
I'M PUTTING THIS CRANE ON THE VERY TOP!!
POINTLESS.
......

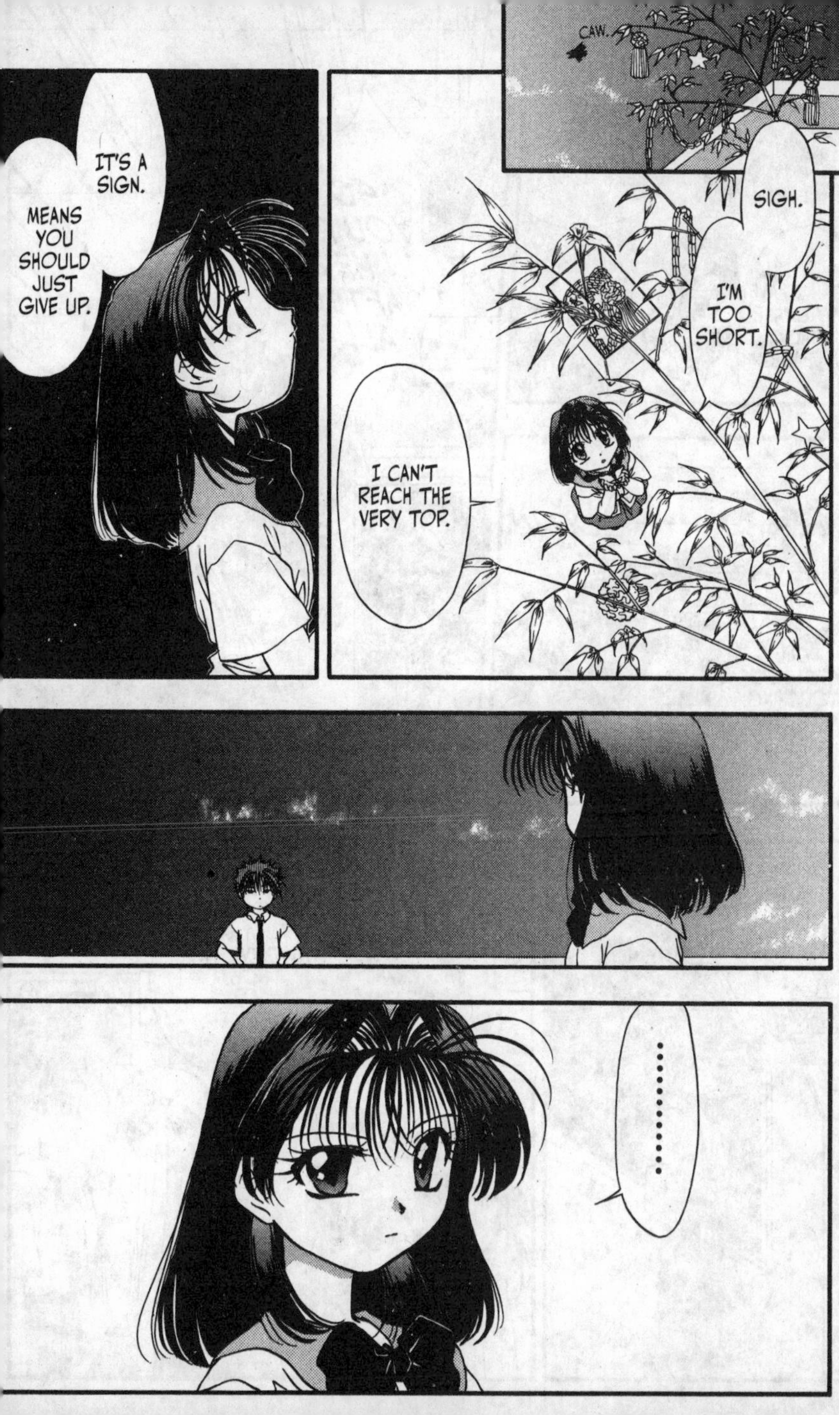
CAW.
SIGH.
I'M TOO SHORT.
I CAN'T REACH THE VERY TOP.
IT'S A SIGN.
MEANS YOU SHOULD JUST GIVE UP.
......

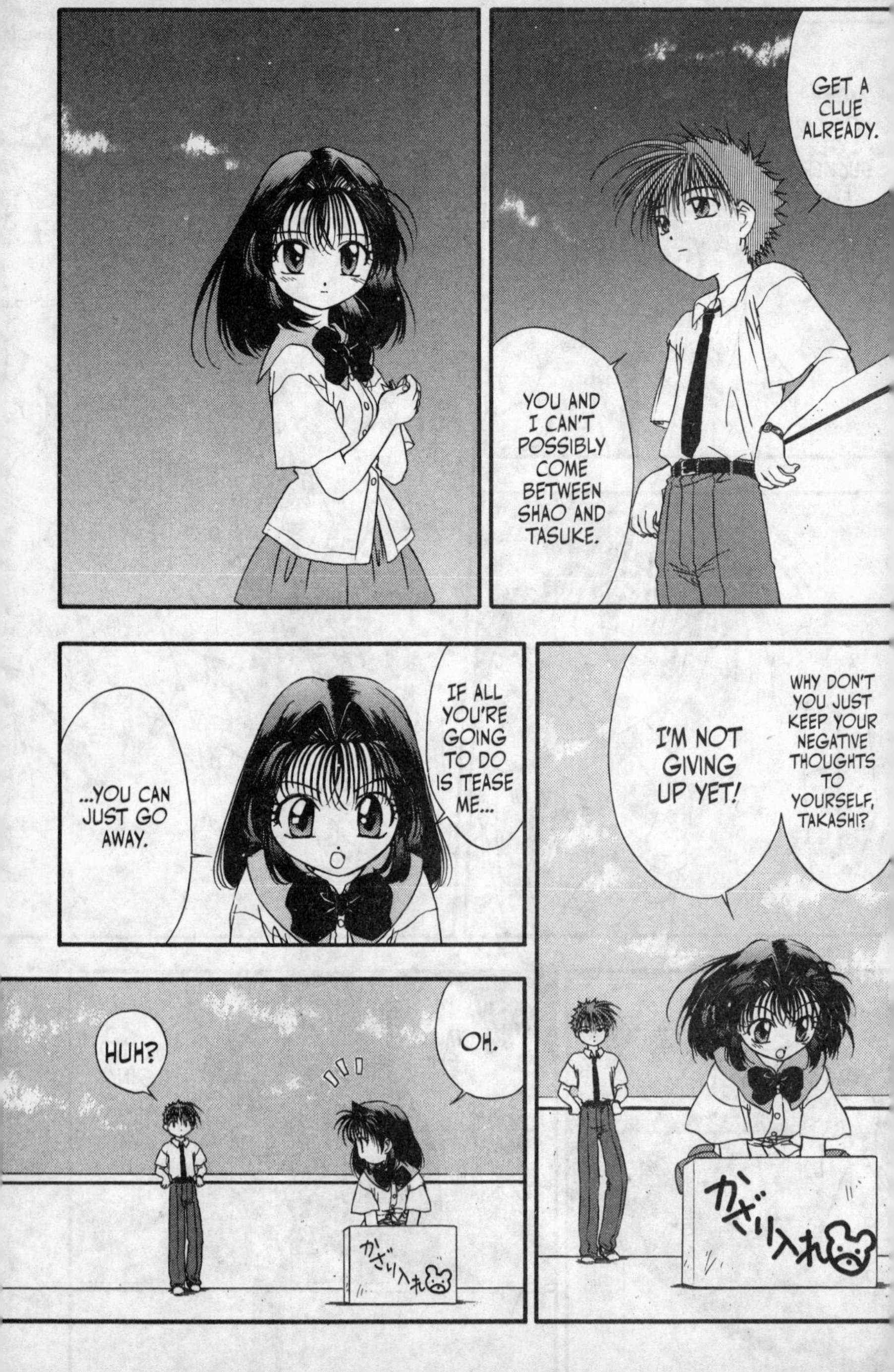
GET A CLUE ALREADY.
YOU AND I CAN'T POSSIBLY COME BETWEEN SHAO AND TASUKE.
WHY DON'T YOU JUST KEEP YOUR NEGATIVE THOUGHTS TO YOURSELF, TAKASHI?
I'M NOT GIVING UP YET!
かざり入れ
IF ALL YOU'RE GOING TO DO IS TEASE ME...
...YOU CAN JUST GO AWAY.
OH.
HUH?
かざり入れ

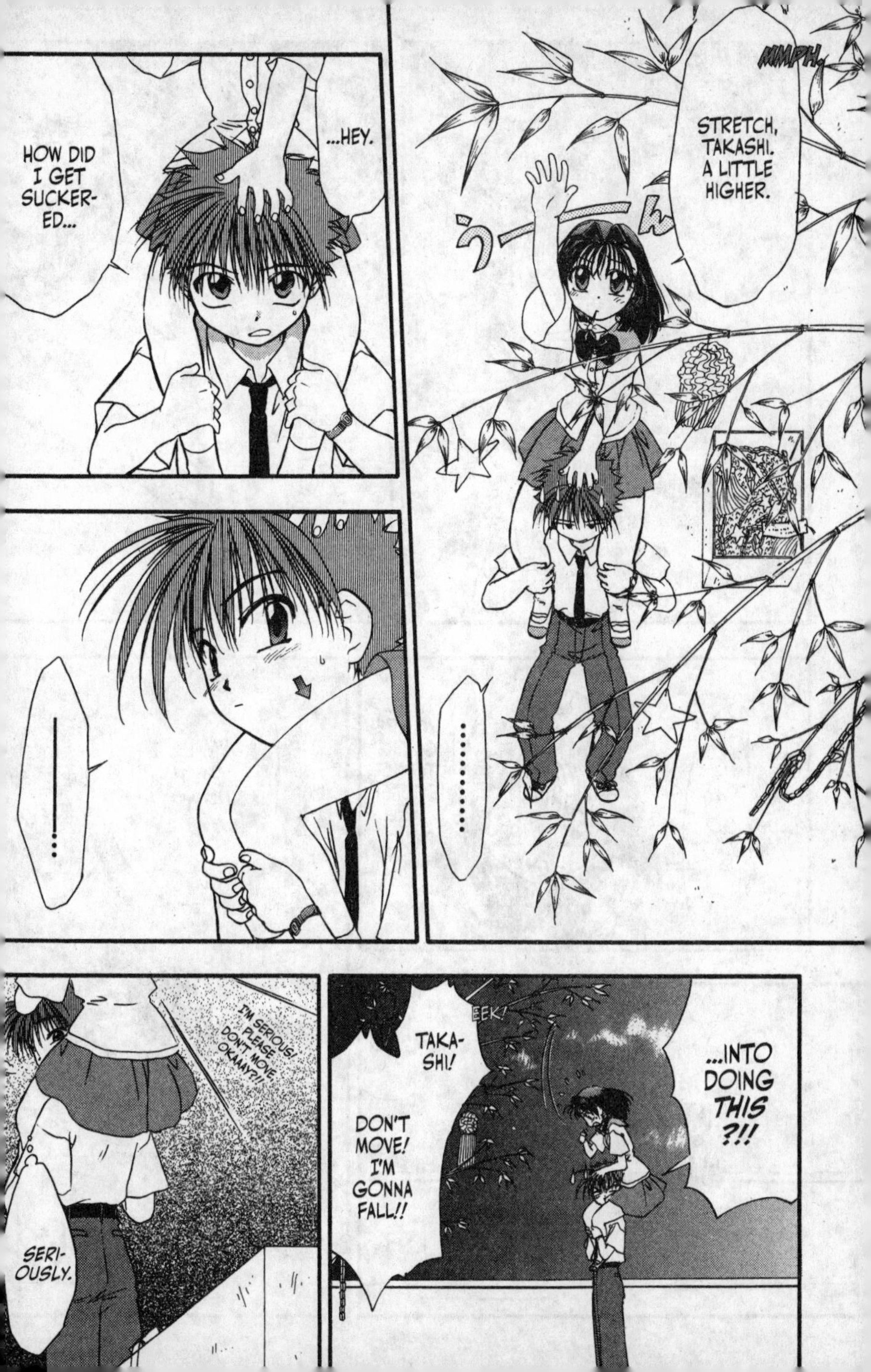
MMPH.
STRETCH, TAKASHI. A LITTLE HIGHER.
うーーん
......
...HEY.
HOW DID I GET SUCKER-ED...
......
...INTO DOING THIS?!!
EEK!
TAKA-SHI!
DON'T MOVE! I'M GONNA FALL!!
I'M SERIOUS! PLEASE DON'T MOVE, OKAAAY?!!
SERI-OUSLY.

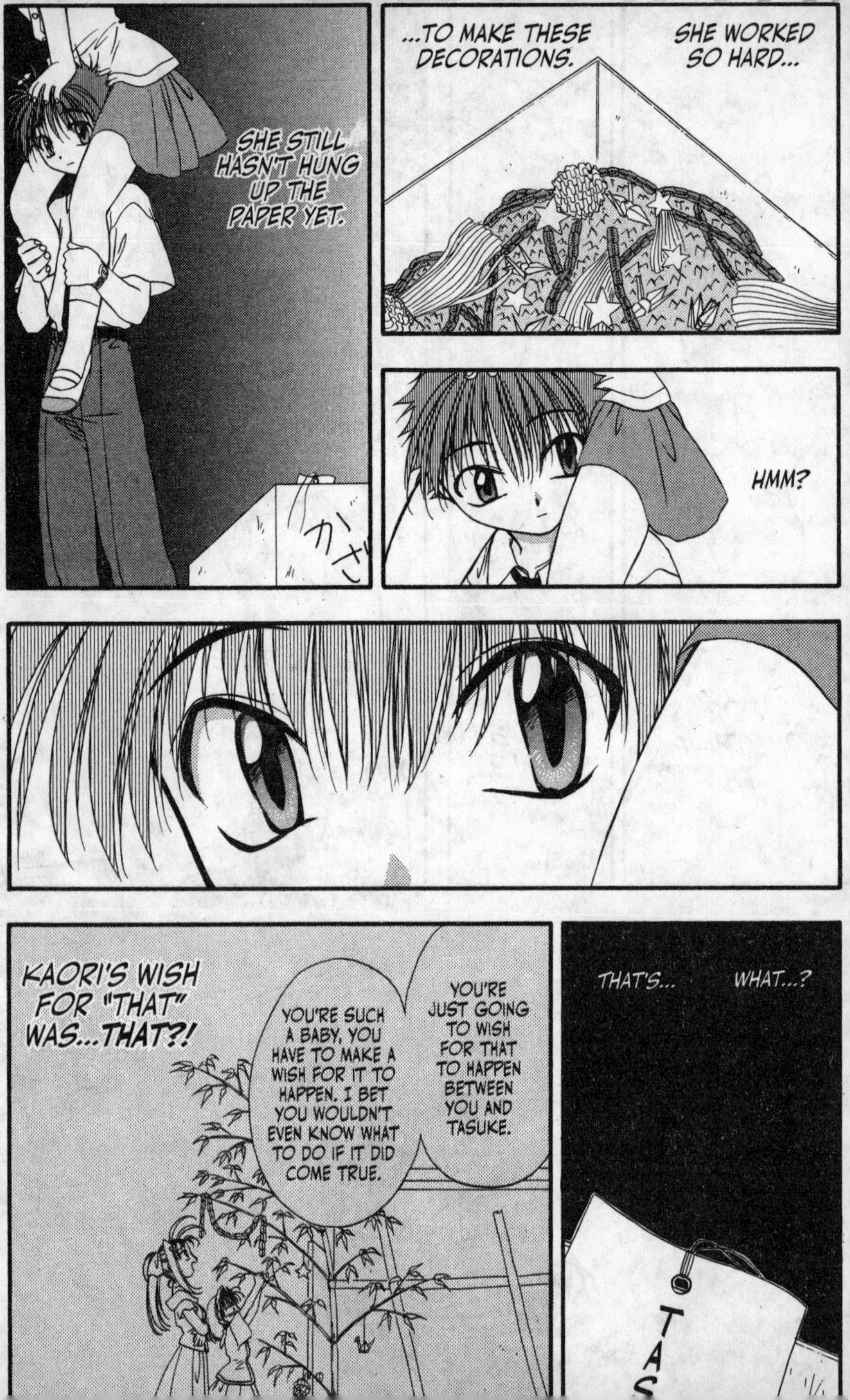
SHE WORKED SO HARD...
...TO MAKE THESE DECORATIONS.
HMM?
SHE STILL HASN'T HUNG UP THE PAPER YET.
かさ
THAT'S...
WHAT...?
TAS
YOU'RE JUST GOING TO WISH FOR THAT TO HAPPEN BETWEEN YOU AND TASUKE.
YOU'RE SUCH A BABY, YOU HAVE TO MAKE A WISH FOR IT TO HAPPEN. I BET YOU WOULDN'T EVEN KNOW WHAT TO DO IF IT DID COME TRUE.
KAORI'S WISH FOR "THAT" WAS...THAT?!

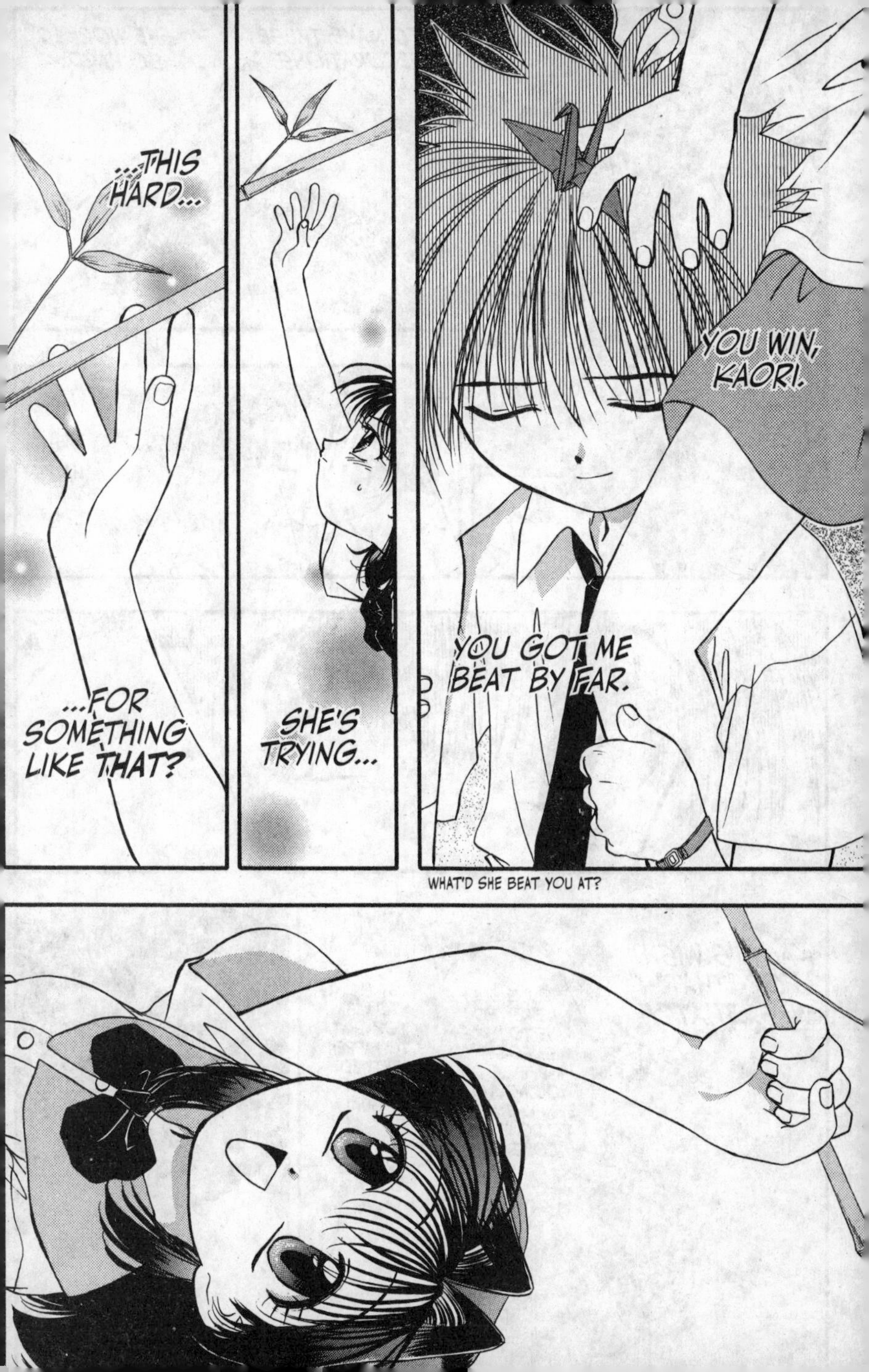
YOU WIN, KAORI.
YOU GOT ME BEAT BY FAR.
SHE'S TRYING...
...THIS HARD...
...FOR SOMETHING LIKE THAT?
WHAT'D SHE BEAT YOU AT?

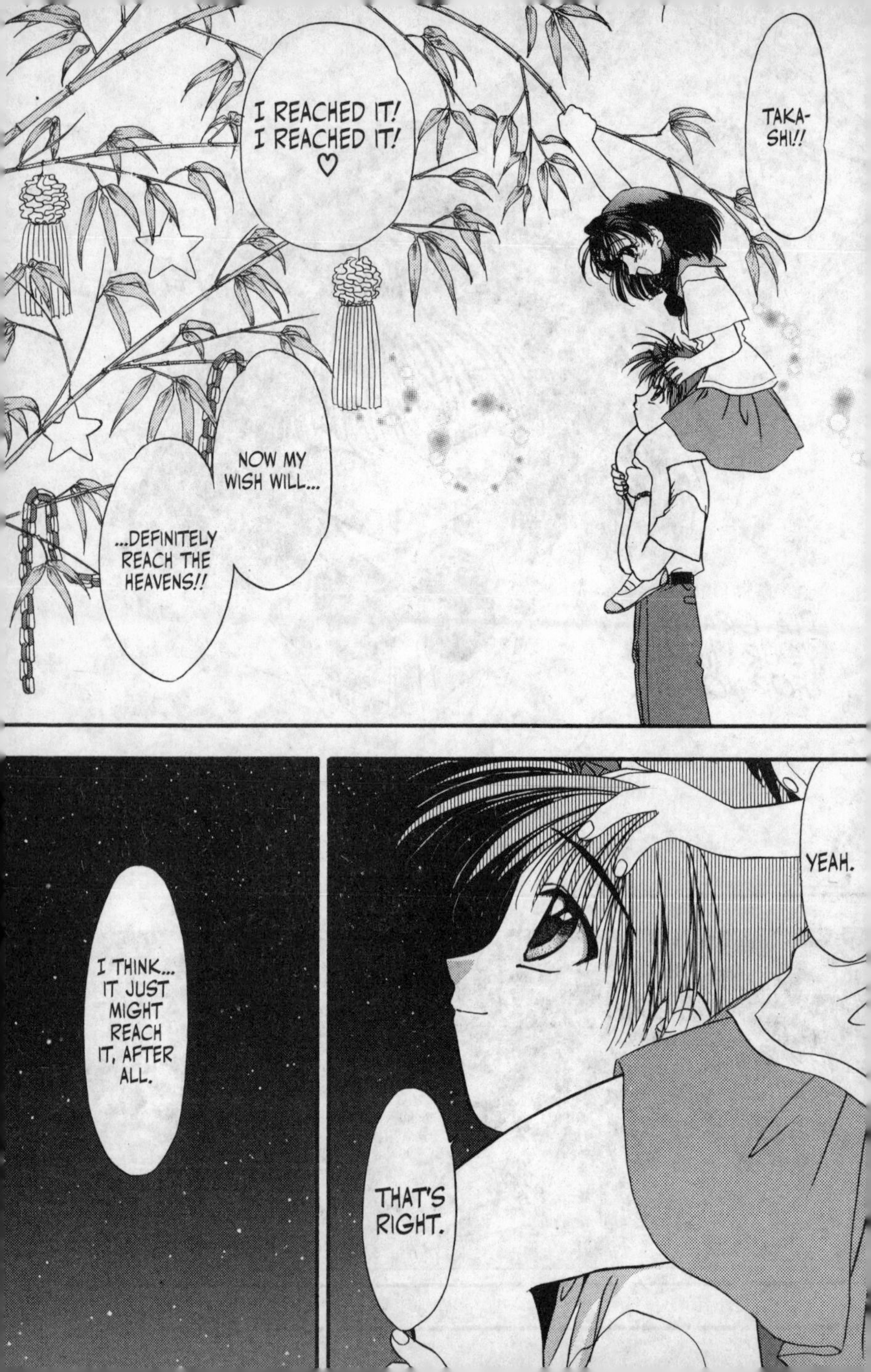
TAKA-SHI!!
I REACHED IT! I REACHED IT! ♡
NOW MY WISH WILL...
...DEFINITELY REACH THE HEAVENS!!
YEAH.
THAT'S RIGHT.
I THINK... IT JUST MIGHT REACH IT, AFTER ALL.

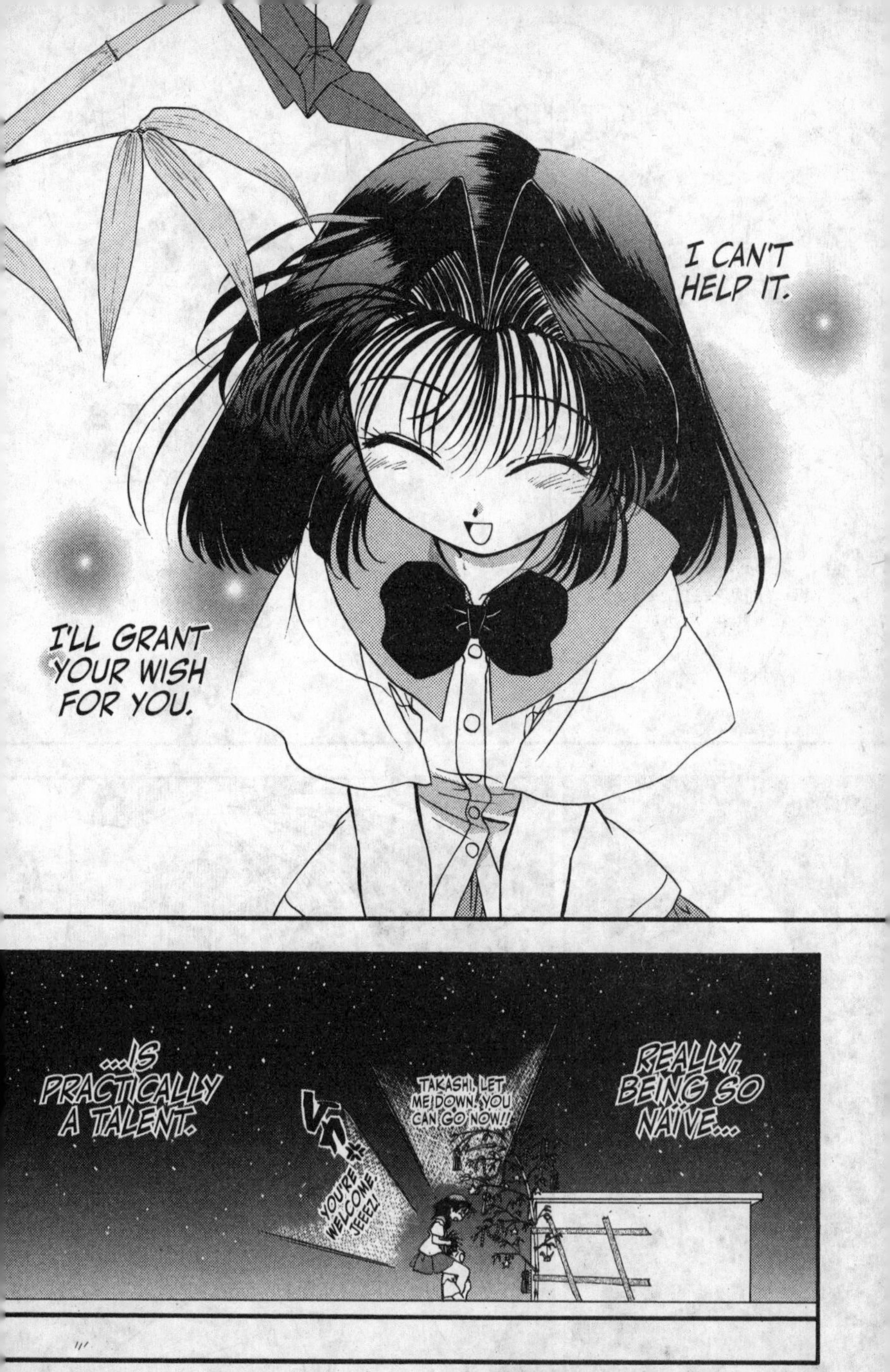
I CAN'T HELP IT.
I'LL GRANT YOUR WISH FOR YOU.
REALLY, BEING SO NAÏVE...
TAKASHI, LET ME DOWN. YOU CAN GO NOW!!
YOU'RE WELCOME. JEEEZ!
...IS PRACTICALLY A TALENT.

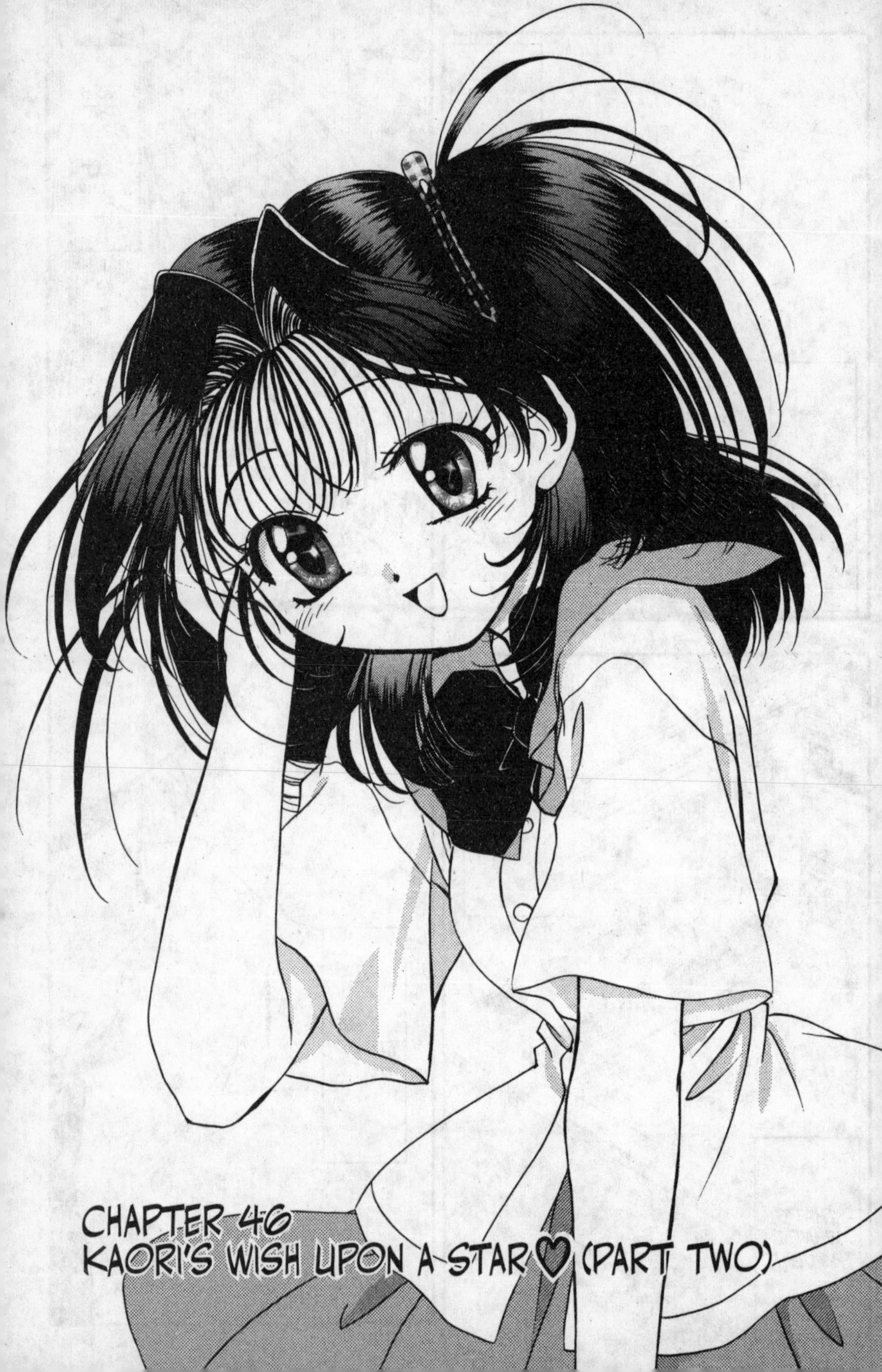

Chapter 46
Kaori's Wish upon a Star♡ (Part Two)

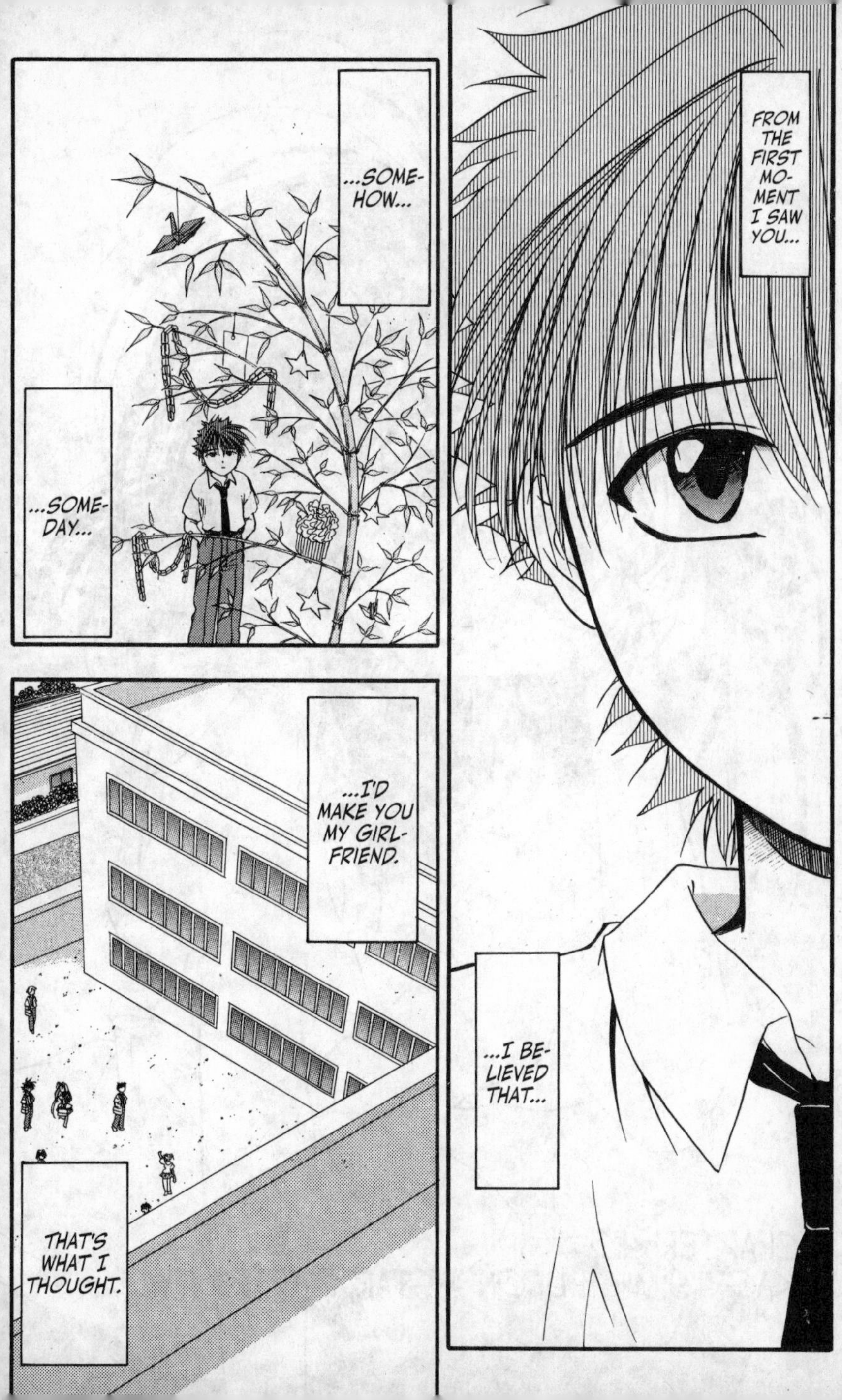
FROM THE FIRST MOMENT I SAW YOU...
...I BELIEVED THAT...
...SOMEHOW...
...SOMEDAY...
...I'D MAKE YOU MY GIRLFRIEND.
THAT'S WHAT I THOUGHT.

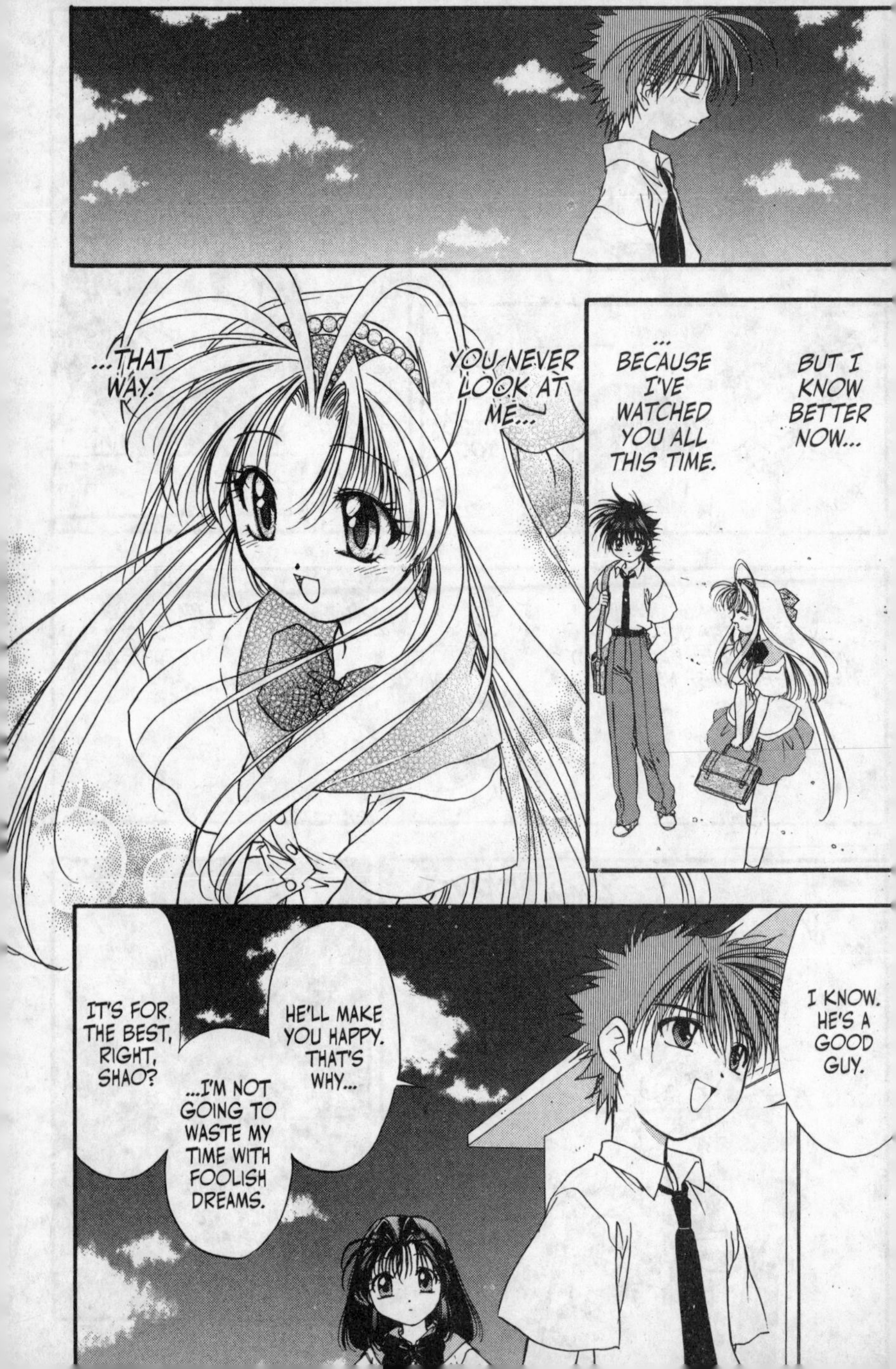
BUT I KNOW BETTER NOW...
...BECAUSE I'VE WATCHED YOU ALL THIS TIME.
YOU NEVER LOOK AT ME...
...THAT WAY.
I KNOW. HE'S A GOOD GUY.
HE'LL MAKE YOU HAPPY. THAT'S WHY...
...I'M NOT GOING TO WASTE MY TIME WITH FOOLISH DREAMS.
IT'S FOR THE BEST, RIGHT, SHAO?

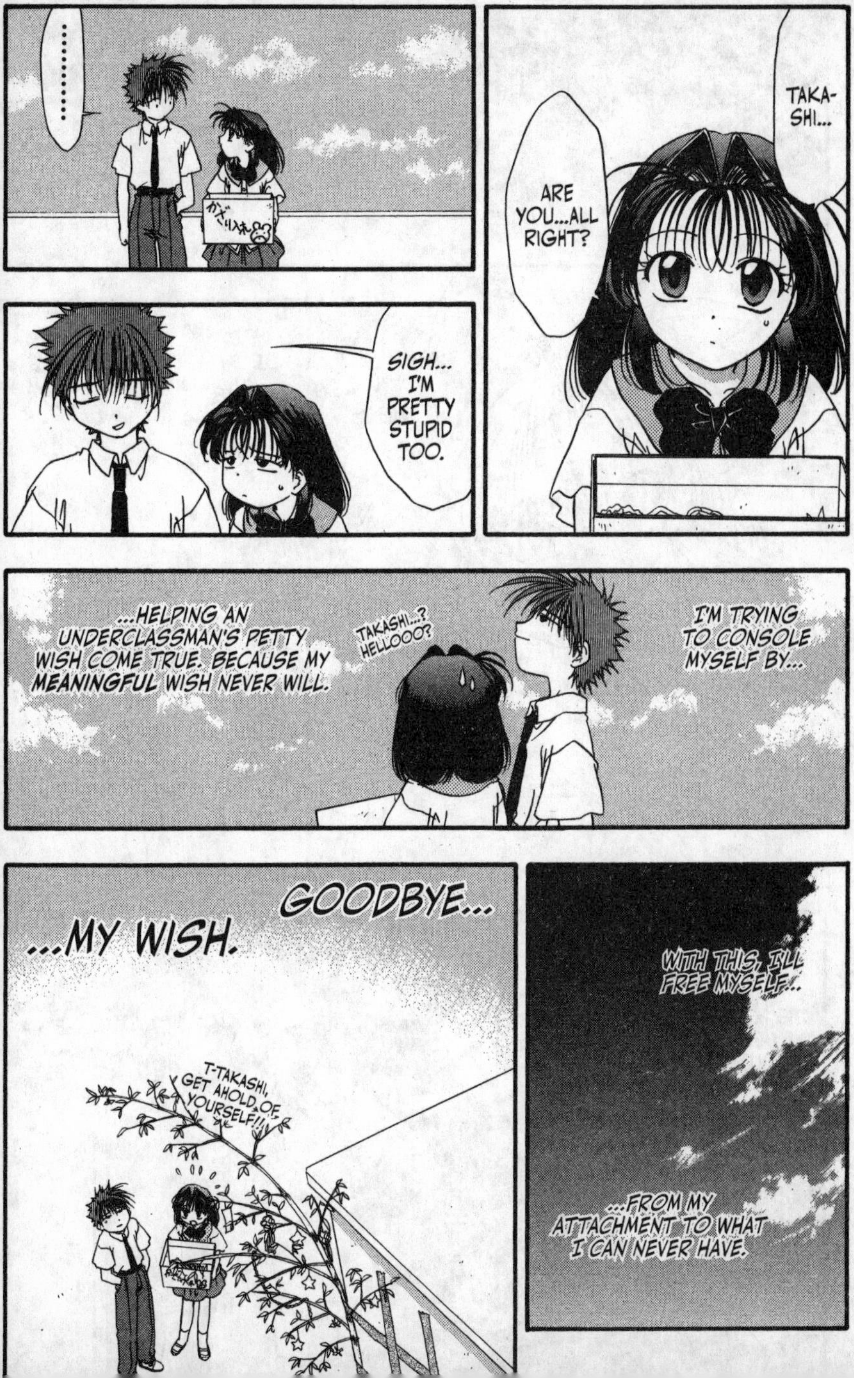
TAKA-SHI...
ARE YOU...ALL RIGHT?
......
SIGH... I'M PRETTY STUPID TOO.
I'M TRYING TO CONSOLE MYSELF BY...
TAKASHI...? HELLOOO?
...HELPING AN UNDERCLASSMAN'S PETTY WISH COME TRUE. BECAUSE MY MEANINGFUL WISH NEVER WILL.
WITH THIS, I'LL FREE MYSELF...
...FROM MY ATTACHMENT TO WHAT I CAN NEVER HAVE.
GOODBYE...
...MY WISH.
T-TAKASHI, GET AHOLD OF YOURSELF!!

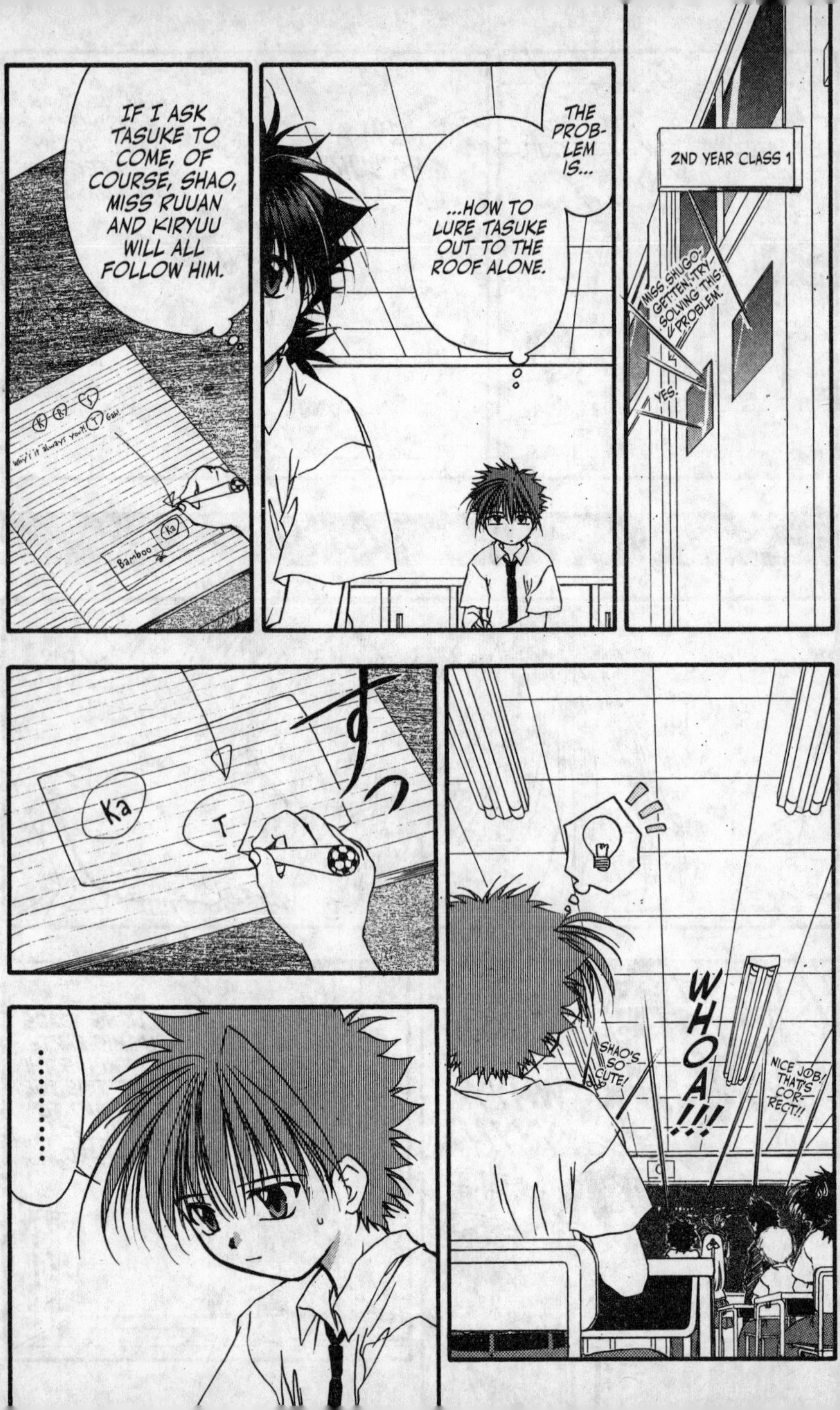
2ND YEAR CLASS 1
MISS SHUGOGETTEN, TRY SOLVING THIS PROBLEM.
YES.
THE PROBLEM IS...
...HOW TO LURE TASUKE OUT TO THE ROOF ALONE.
IF I ASK TASUKE TO COME, OF COURSE, SHAO, MISS RUUAN AND KIRYUU WILL ALL FOLLOW HIM.
K
R
S
Why's it always You?!
T
Gah!
Ka
Bamboo
WHOA!!!
NICE JOB! THAT'S CORRECT!!
SHAO'S SO CUTE!
すっ
Ka
T
....

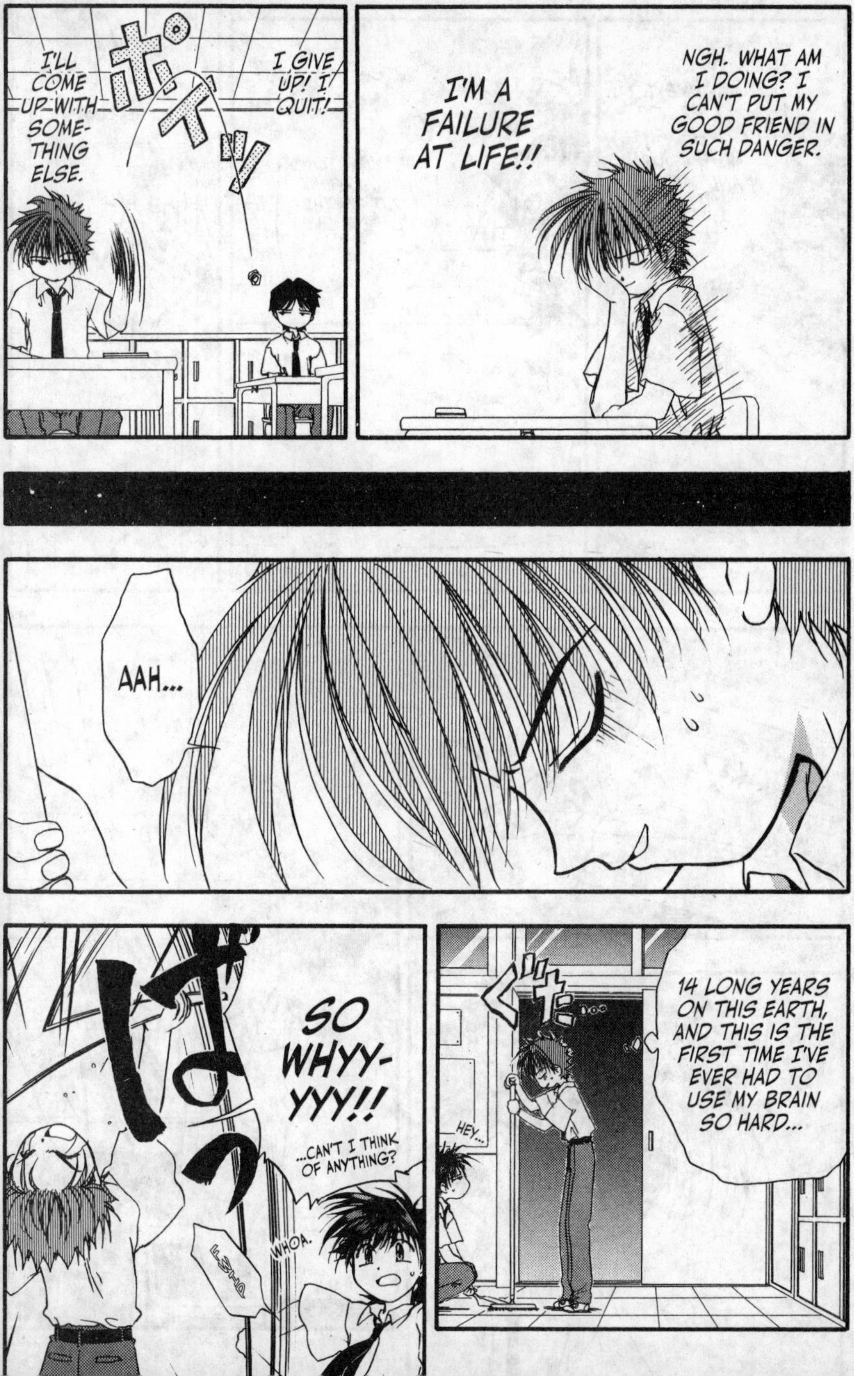
NGH. WHAT AM I DOING? I CAN'T PUT MY GOOD FRIEND IN SUCH DANGER.
I'M A FAILURE AT LIFE!!
I GIVE UP! I QUIT!
ポイッ
I'LL COME UP WITH SOME-THING ELSE.
AAH...
14 LONG YEARS ON THIS EARTH, AND THIS IS THE FIRST TIME I'VE EVER HAD TO USE MY BRAIN SO HARD...
ぐだ
HEY...
SO WHYY-YYY!!
...CAN'T I THINK OF ANYTHING?
ぱっ
WHOA.

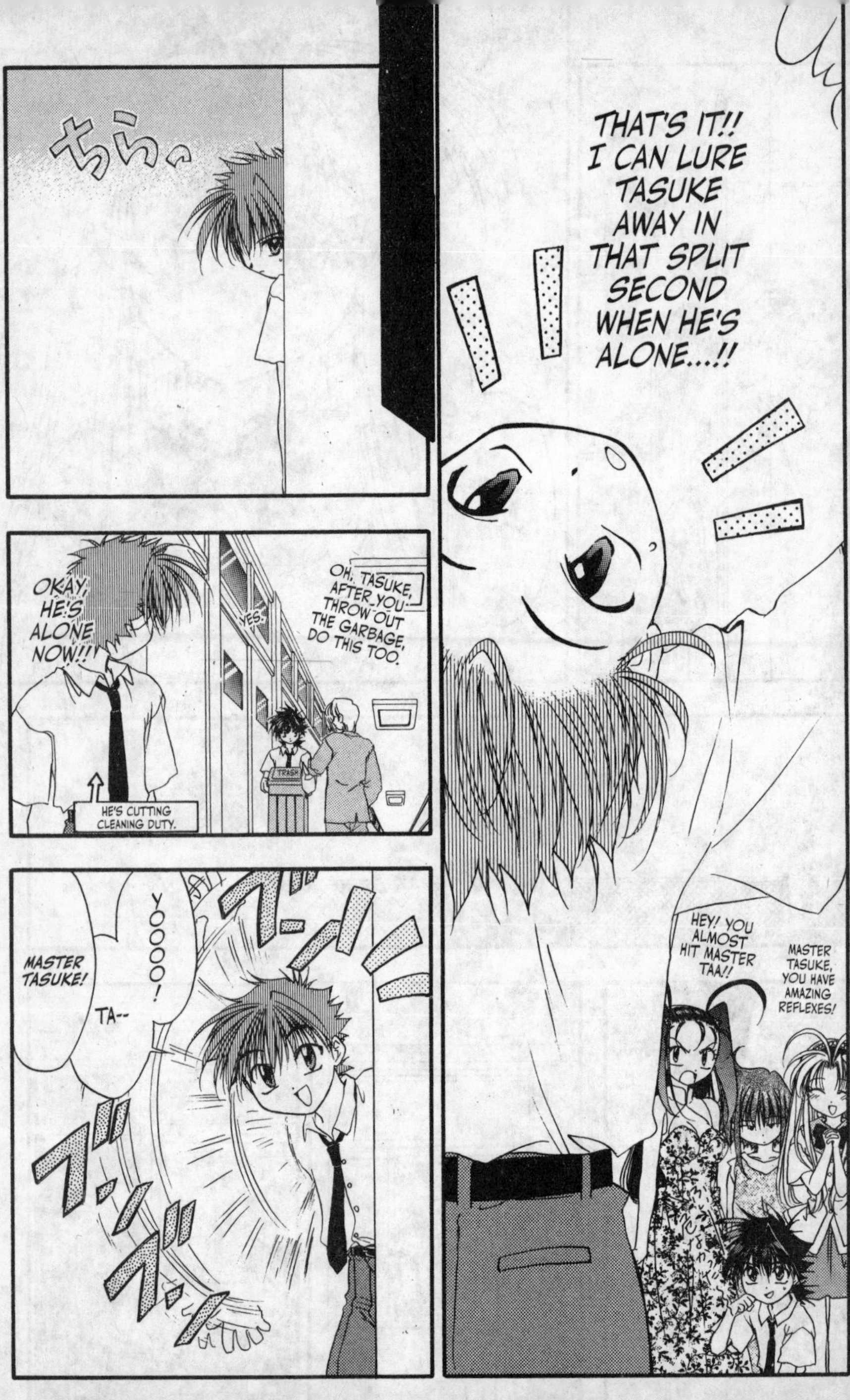

THAT'S IT!! I CAN LURE TASUKE AWAY IN THAT SPLIT SECOND WHEN HE'S ALONE...!!
HEY! YOU ALMOST HIT MASTER TAA!!
MASTER TASUKE, YOU HAVE AMAZING REFLEXES!
ちら
OKAY, HE'S ALONE NOW!!
OH, TASUKE, AFTER YOU THROW OUT THE GARBAGE, DO THIS TOO.
YES.
TRASH
HE'S CUTTING CLEANING DUTY.
MASTER TASUKE!
TA--
YOOOO!

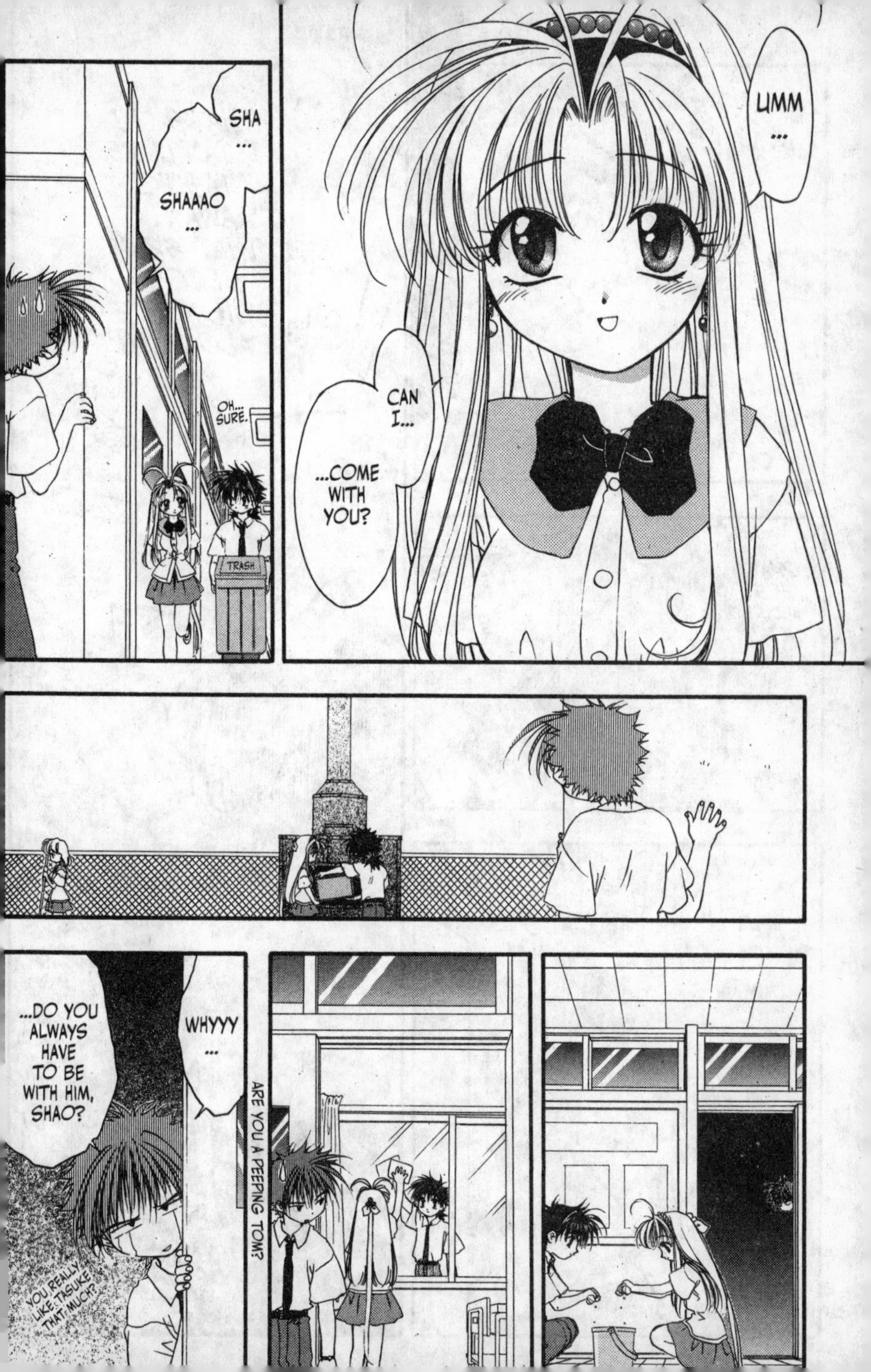
UMM ...
CAN I...
...COME WITH YOU?
SHA ...
SHAAAO ...
OH... SURE.
TRASH
ARE YOU A PEEPING TOM?
WHYYY ...
...DO YOU ALWAYS HAVE TO BE WITH HIM, SHAO?
YOU REALLY LIKE TASUKE THAT MUCH?

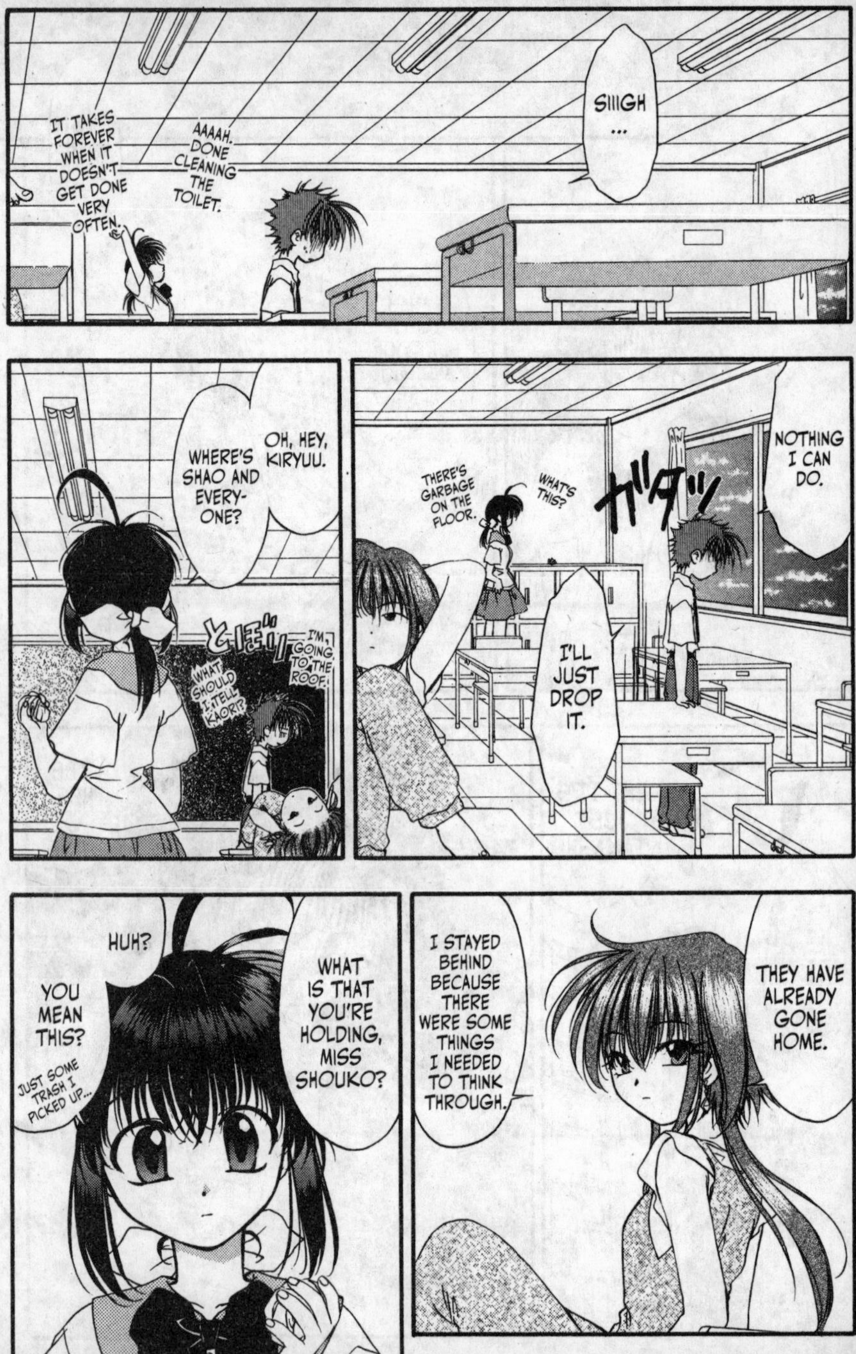
SIIIGH ...
AAAAH. DONE CLEANING THE TOILET.
IT TAKES FOREVER WHEN IT DOESN'T GET DONE VERY OFTEN.
NOTHING I CAN DO.
ガタッ
WHAT'S THIS?
THERE'S GARBAGE ON THE FLOOR.
I'LL JUST DROP IT.
OH, HEY, KIRYUU.
WHERE'S SHAO AND EVERYONE?
I'M GOING TO THE ROOF.
WHAT SHOULD I TELL KAORI?
THEY HAVE ALREADY GONE HOME.
I STAYED BEHIND BECAUSE THERE WERE SOME THINGS I NEEDED TO THINK THROUGH.
WHAT IS THAT YOU'RE HOLDING, MISS SHOUKO?
HUH?
YOU MEAN THIS?
JUST SOME TRASH I PICKED UP...

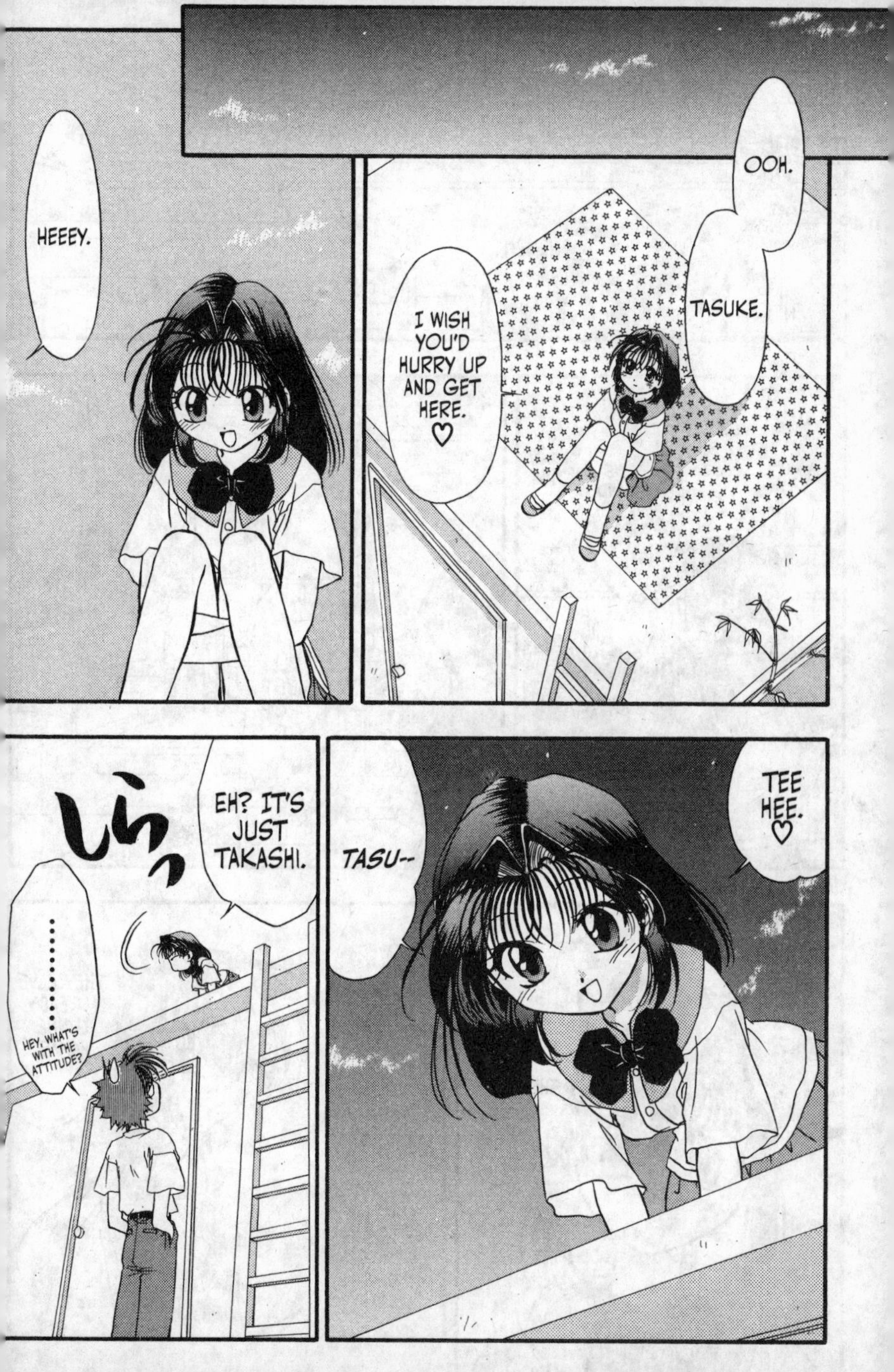
OOH.
TASUKE.
I WISH YOU'D HURRY UP AND GET HERE. ♡
HEEEY.
TEE HEE. ♡
TASU--
EH? IT'S JUST TAKASHI.
しらっ
......
HEY, WHAT'S WITH THE ATTITUDE?

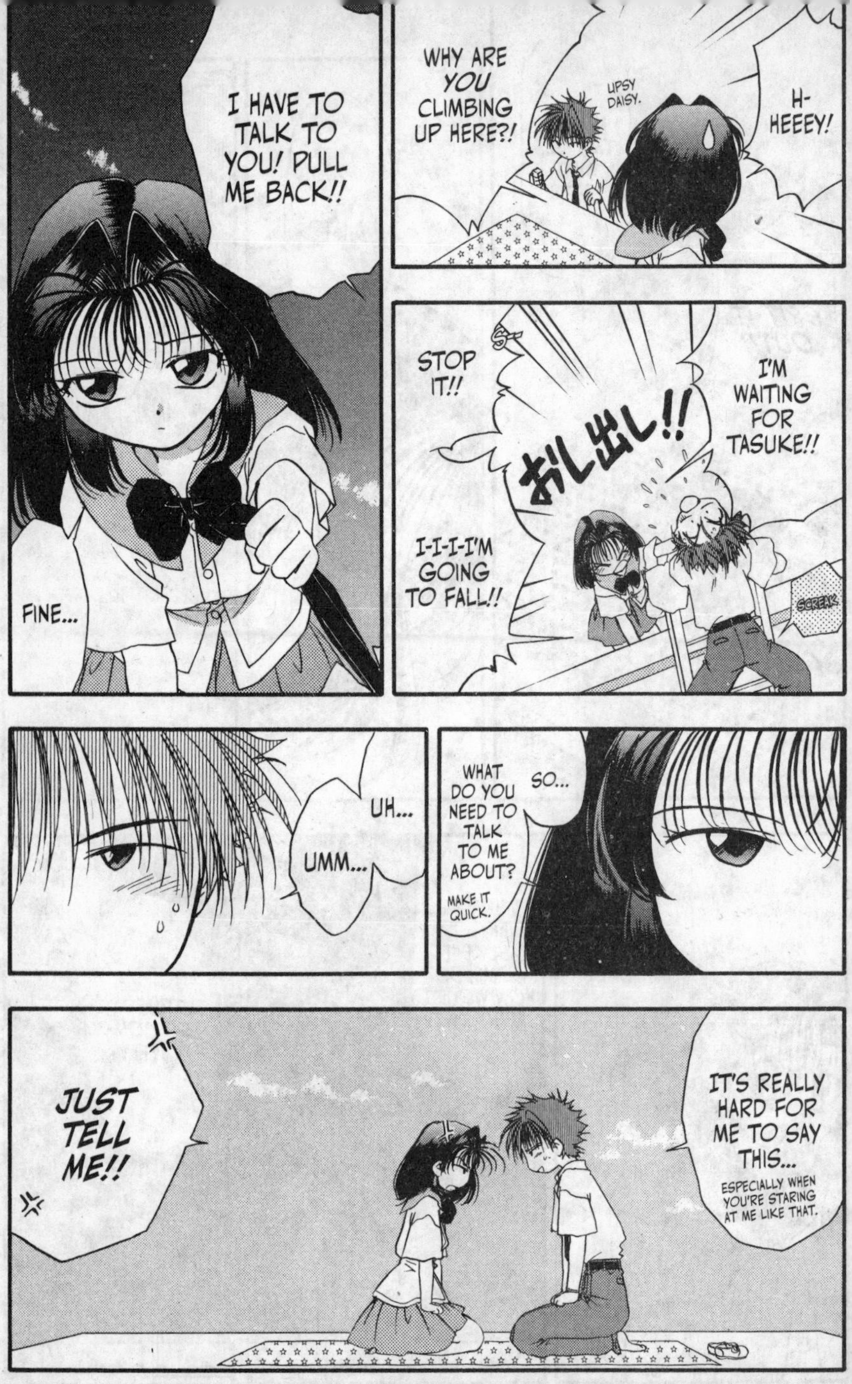
H-HEEEY!
UPSY DAISY.
WHY ARE YOU CLIMBING UP HERE?!
I'M WAITING FOR TASUKE!!
おし出し!!
STOP IT!!
I-I-I-I'M GOING TO FALL!!
SCREAK
I HAVE TO TALK TO YOU! PULL ME BACK!!
FINE...
SO...
WHAT DO YOU NEED TO TALK TO ME ABOUT?
MAKE IT QUICK.
UH...
UMM...
IT'S REALLY HARD FOR ME TO SAY THIS...
ESPECIALLY WHEN YOU'RE STARING AT ME LIKE THAT.
JUST TELL ME!!

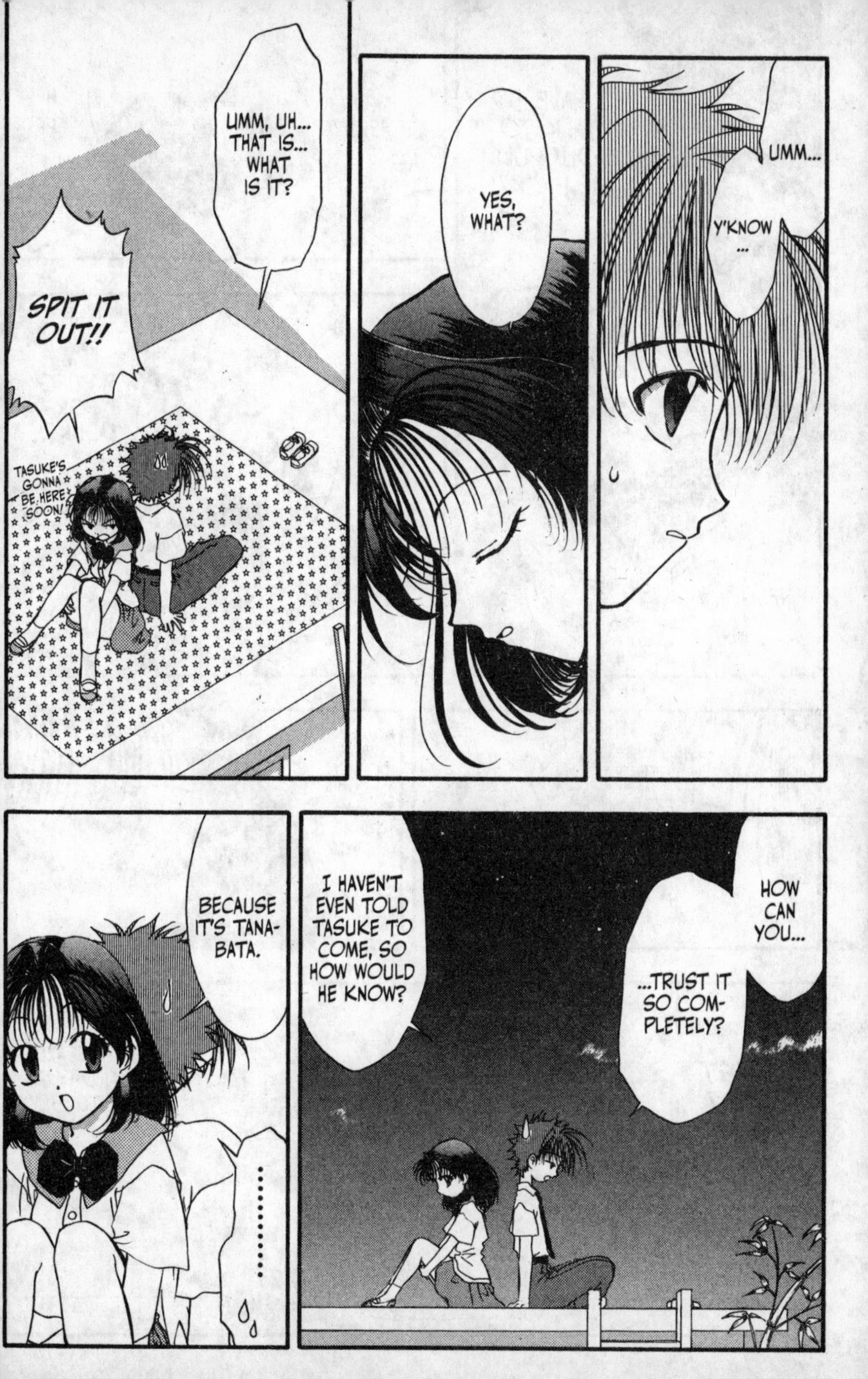
UMM...
Y'KNOW ...
YES, WHAT?
UMM, UH... THAT IS... WHAT IS IT?
SPIT IT OUT!!
TASUKE'S GONNA BE HERE SOON!
HOW CAN YOU...
...TRUST IT SO COM-PLETELY?
I HAVEN'T EVEN TOLD TASUKE TO COME, SO HOW WOULD HE KNOW?
BECAUSE IT'S TANA-BATA.
....

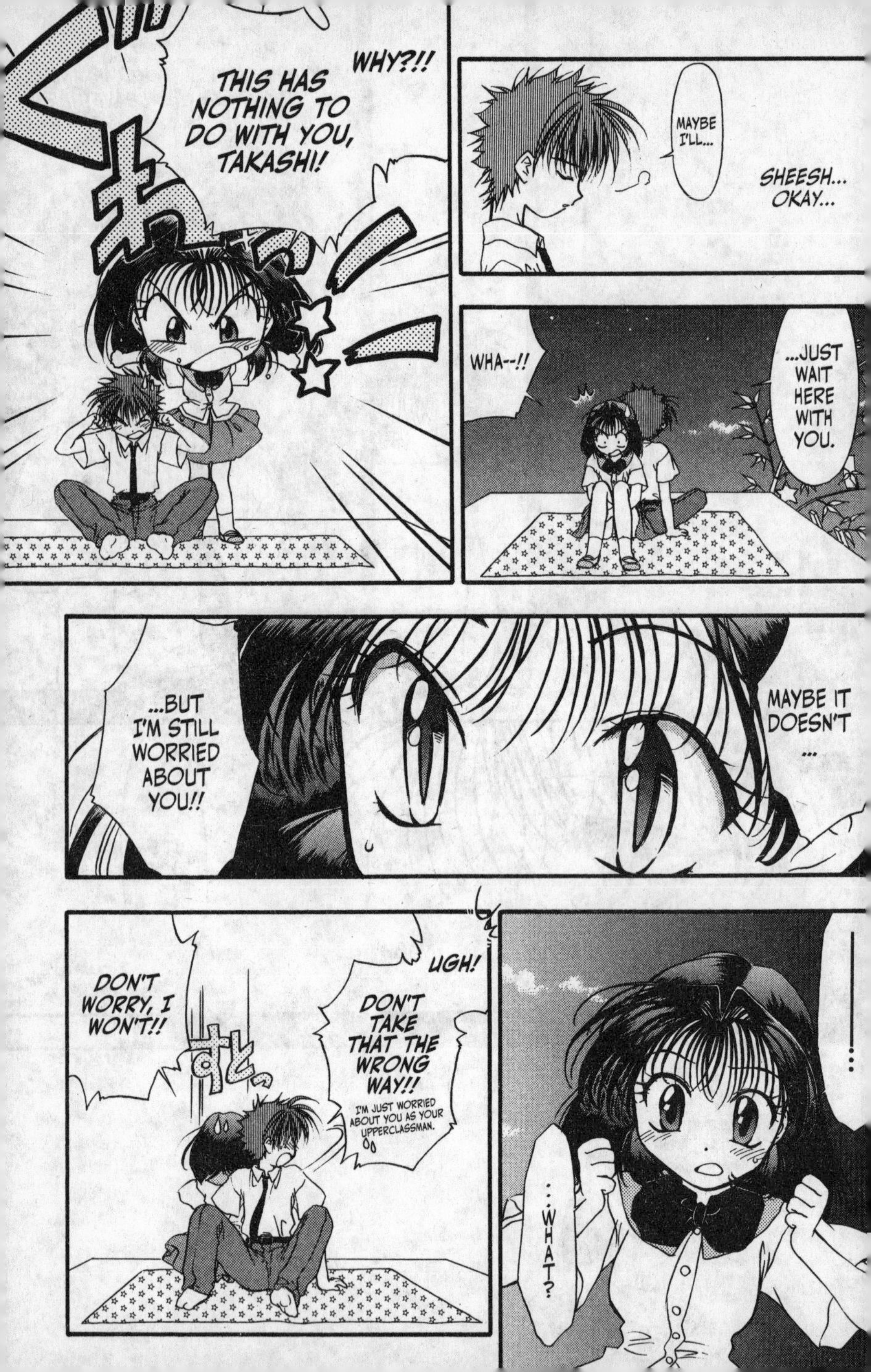

SHEESH... OKAY...
MAYBE I'LL...
...JUST WAIT HERE WITH YOU.
WHA--!!
WHY?!!
THIS HAS NOTHING TO DO WITH YOU, TAKASHI!
MAYBE IT DOESN'T ...
...BUT I'M STILL WORRIED ABOUT YOU!!
...
...WHAT?
UGH!
DON'T TAKE THAT THE WRONG WAY!!
I'M JUST WORRIED ABOUT YOU AS YOUR UPPERCLASSMAN.
DON'T WORRY, I WON'T!!

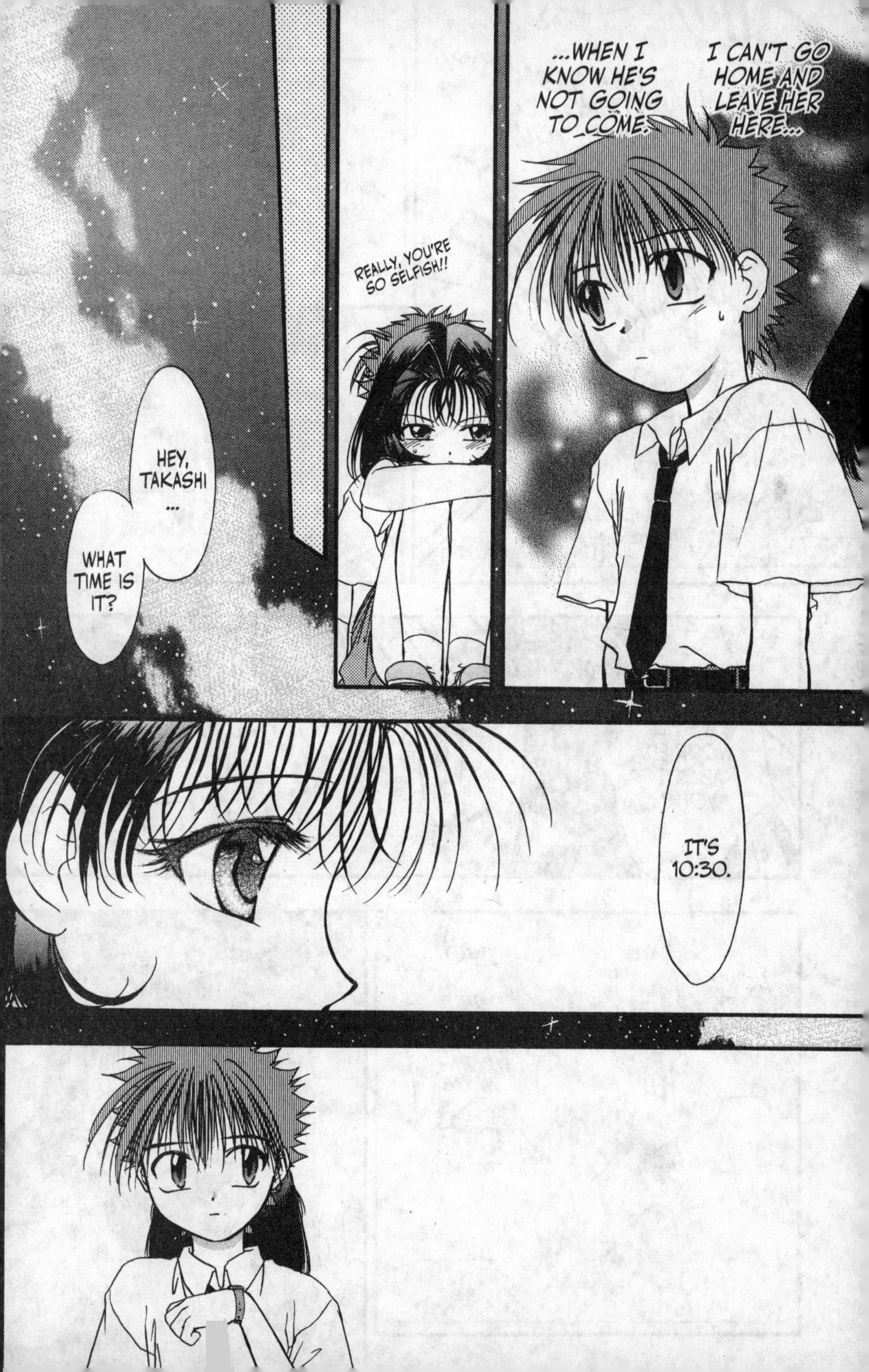
I CAN'T GO HOME AND LEAVE HER HERE...
...WHEN I KNOW HE'S NOT GOING TO COME.
REALLY, YOU'RE SO SELFISH!!
HEY, TAKASHI ...
WHAT TIME IS IT?
IT'S 10:30.

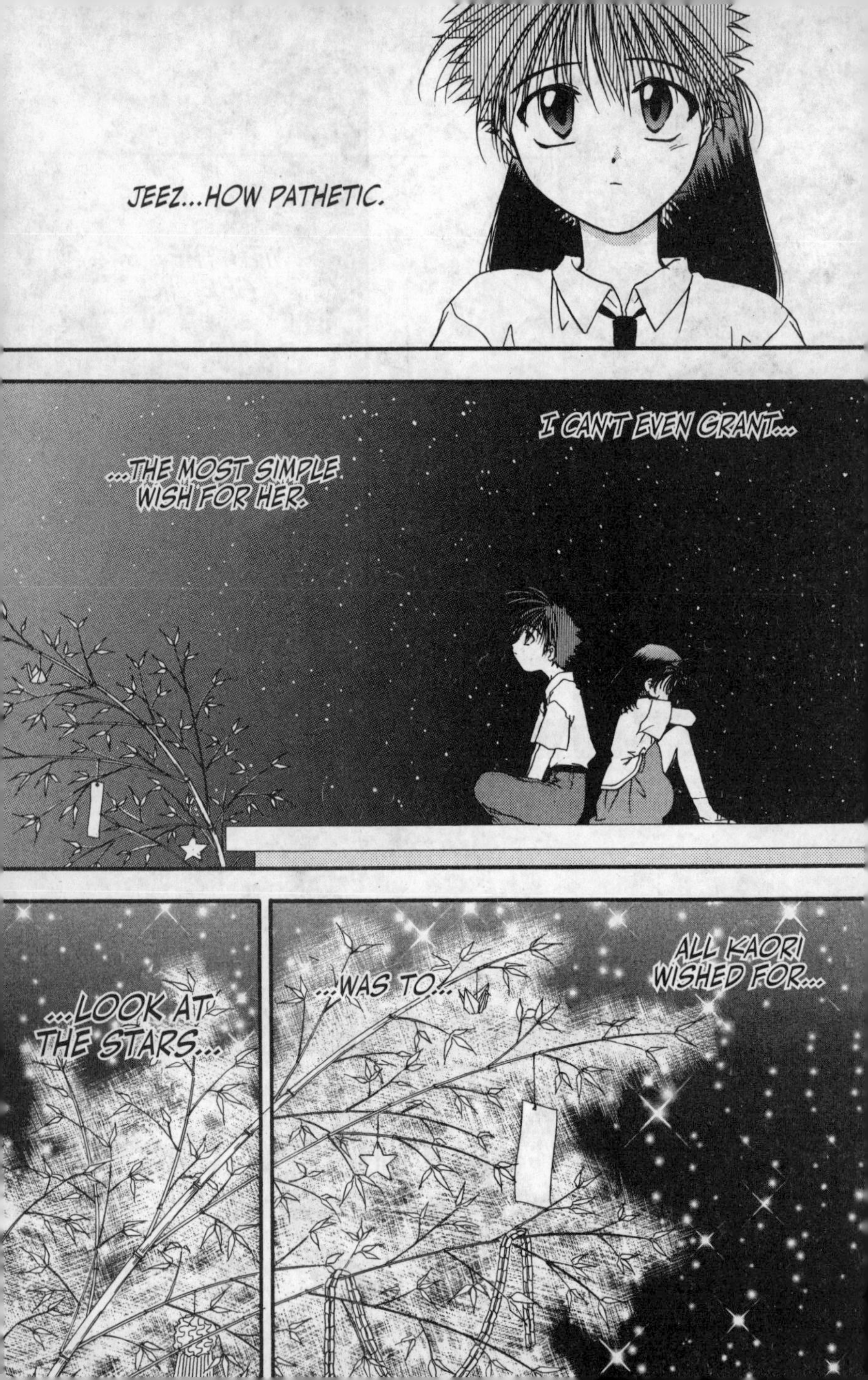
JEEZ...HOW PATHETIC.
I CAN'T EVEN GRANT...
...THE MOST SIMPLE WISH FOR HER.
ALL KAORI WISHED FOR...
...WAS TO...
...LOOK AT THE STARS...

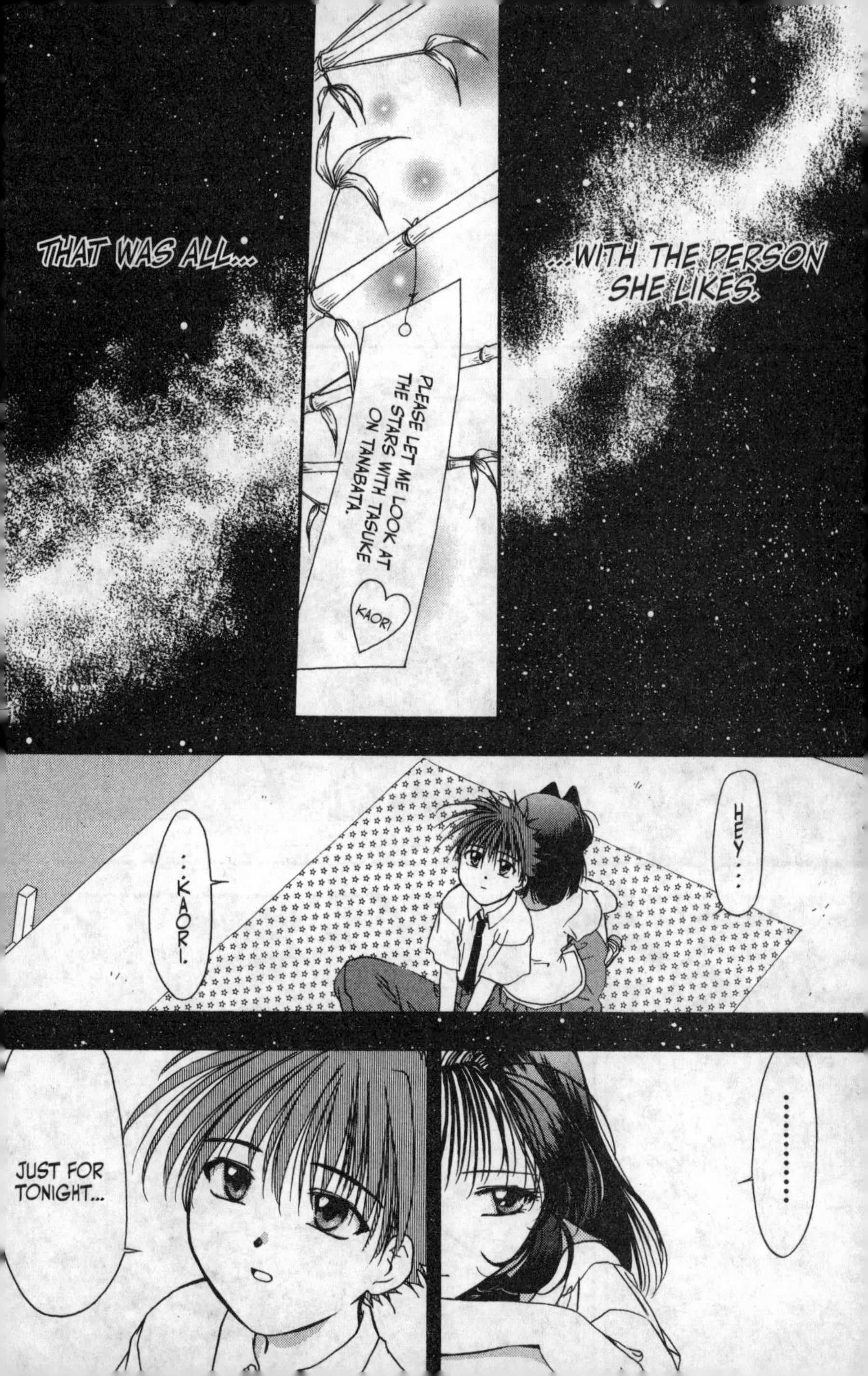
THAT WAS ALL...
...WITH THE PERSON SHE LIKES.
PLEASE LET ME LOOK AT THE STARS WITH TASUKE ON TANABATA.
KAORI
HEY...
...KAORI.
....
JUST FOR TONIGHT...

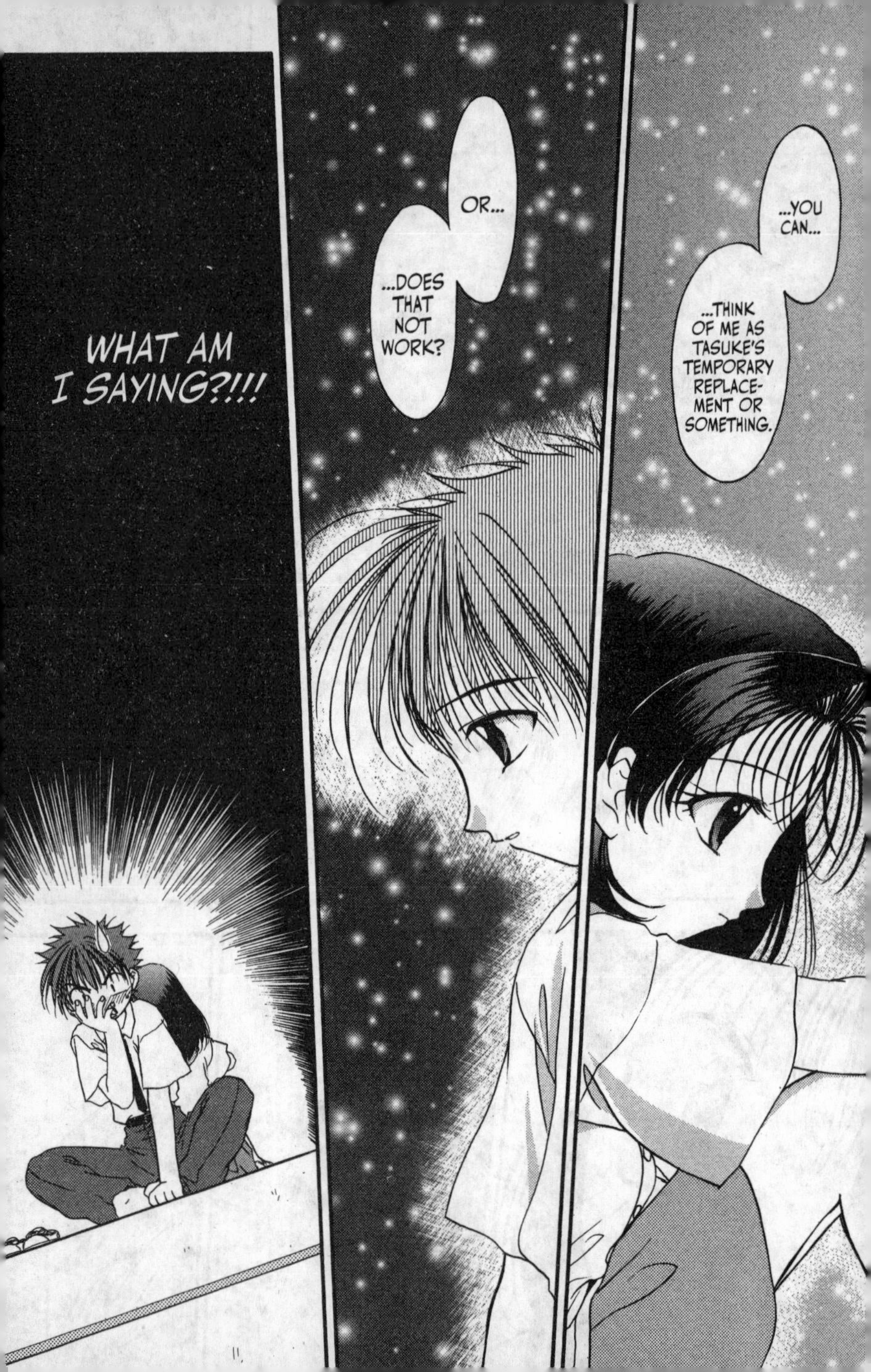
...YOU CAN...
...THINK OF ME AS TASUKE'S TEMPORARY REPLACE-MENT OR SOMETHING.
OR...
...DOES THAT NOT WORK?
WHAT AM I SAYING?!!!

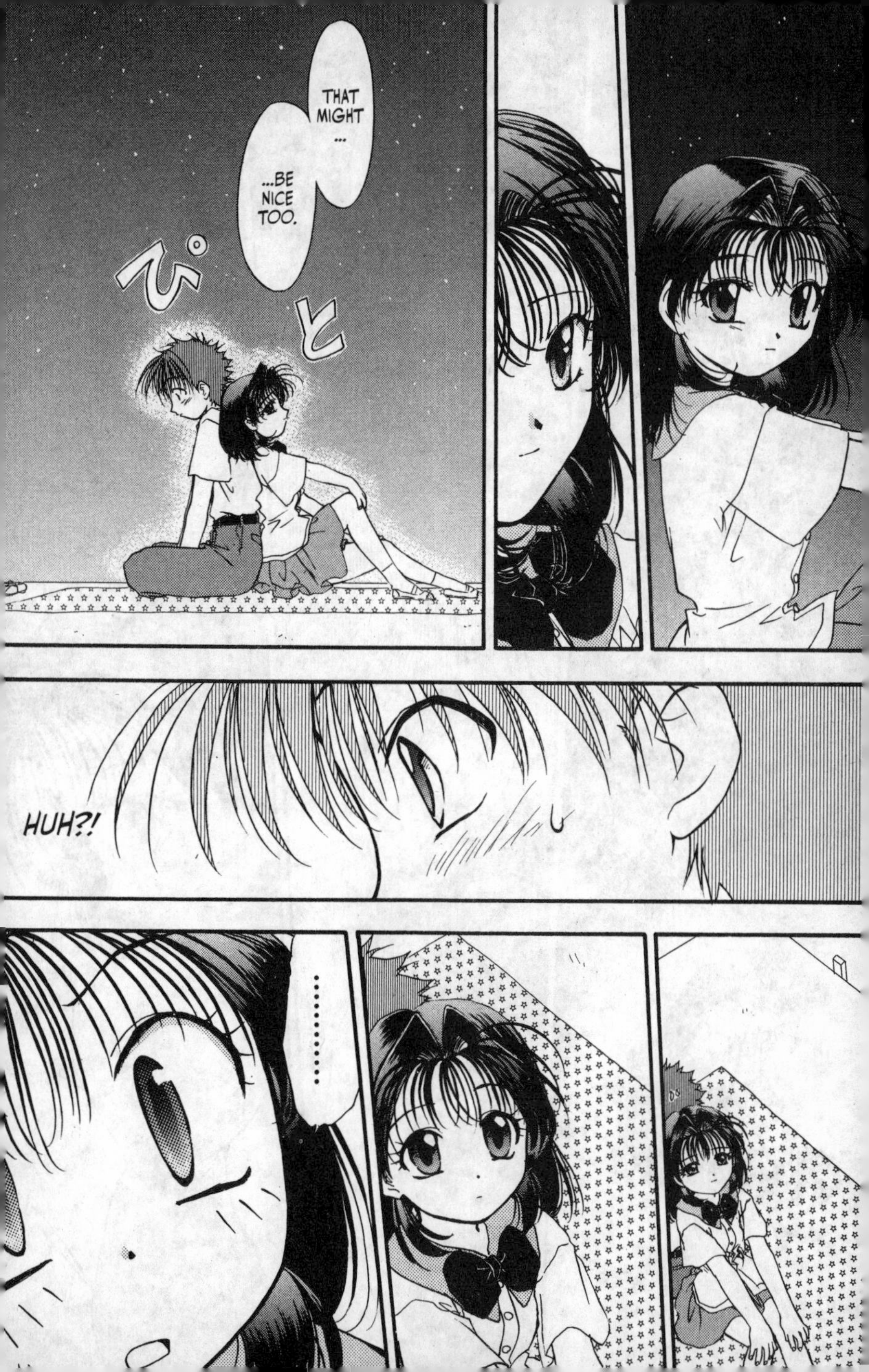
THAT MIGHT ...
...BE NICE TOO.
ぴと
HUH?!
....

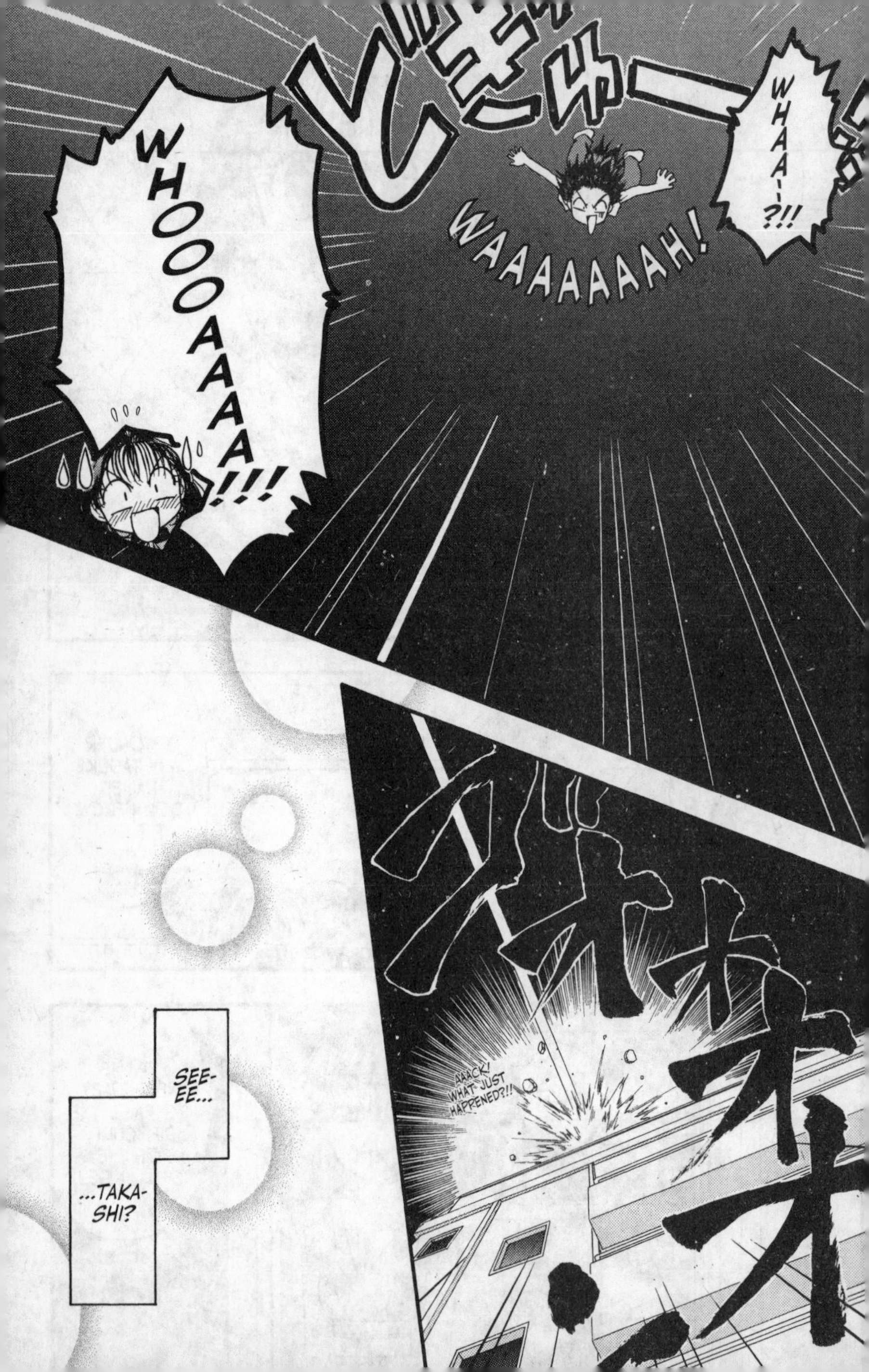
WHAAA-?!!
WAAAAAAAAH!
WHOOOAAAAA!!!
AAACK! WHAT JUST HAPPENED?!!
SEE-EE...
...TAKA-SHI?

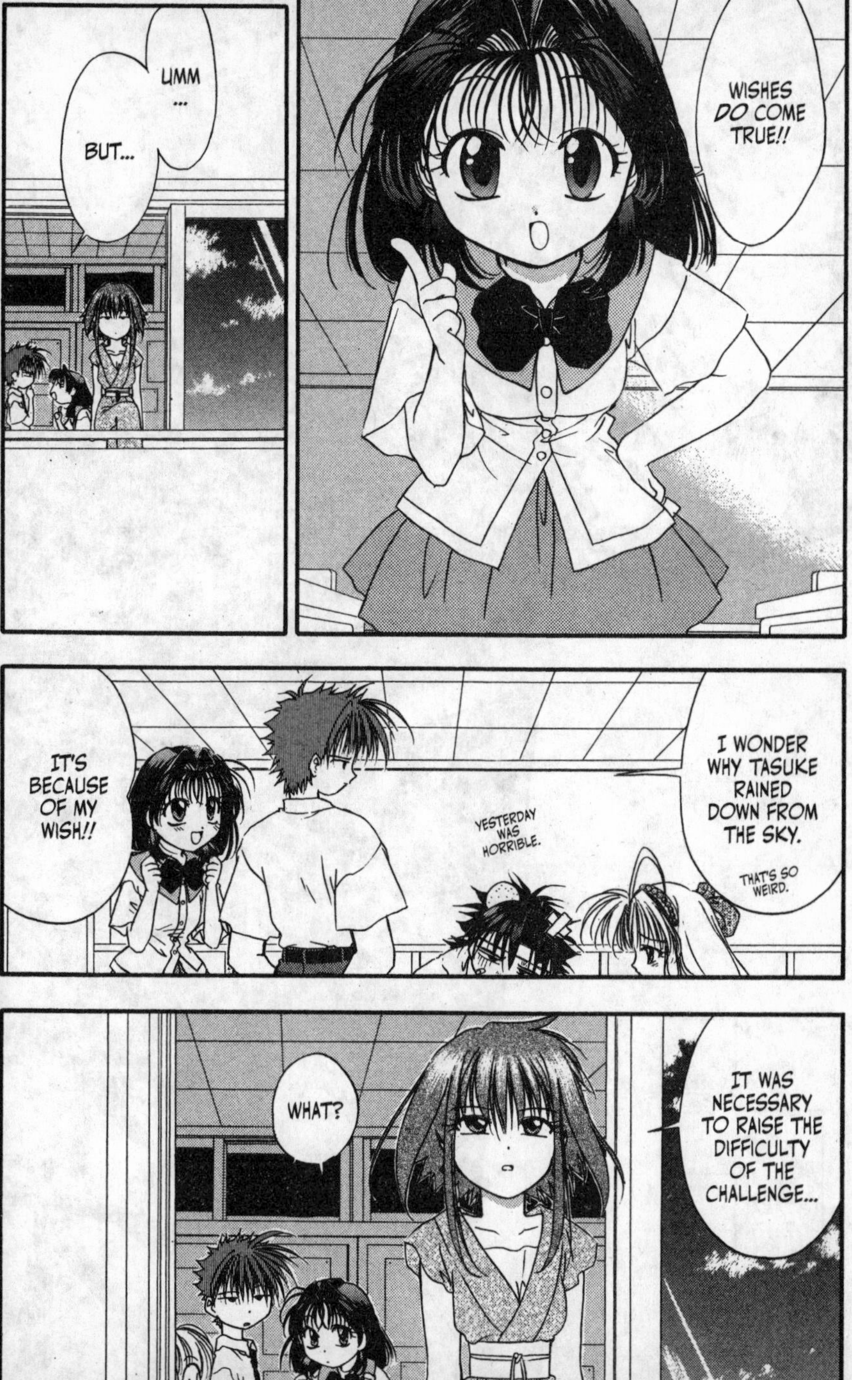
WISHES DO COME TRUE!!
UMM ... BUT...
I WONDER WHY TASUKE RAINED DOWN FROM THE SKY.
THAT'S SO WEIRD.
YESTERDAY WAS HORRIBLE.
IT'S BECAUSE OF MY WISH!!
IT WAS NECESSARY TO RAISE THE DIFFICULTY OF THE CHALLENGE...
WHAT?

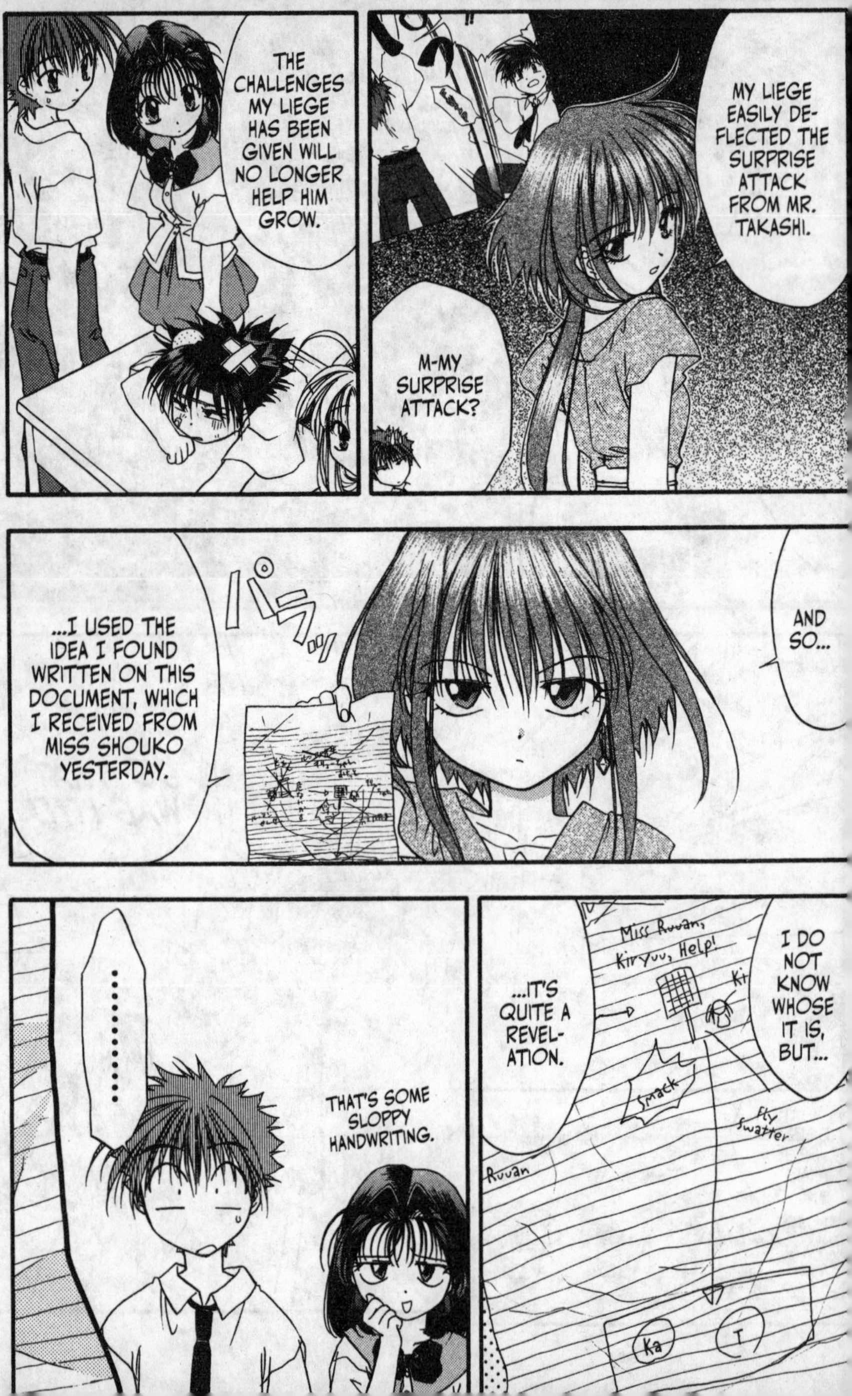
MY LIEGE EASILY DEFLECTED THE SURPRISE ATTACK FROM MR. TAKASHI.
M-MY SURPRISE ATTACK?
THE CHALLENGES MY LIEGE HAS BEEN GIVEN WILL NO LONGER HELP HIM GROW.
AND SO...
パラッ
...I USED THE IDEA I FOUND WRITTEN ON THIS DOCUMENT, WHICH I RECEIVED FROM MISS SHOUKO YESTERDAY.
I DO NOT KNOW WHOSE IT IS, BUT...
Miss Ruuan, Kiryuu, Help!
Ki
Smack
Fly Swatter
Ruuan
Ka
T
...IT'S QUITE A REVELATION.
THAT'S SOME SLOPPY HANDWRITING.
....

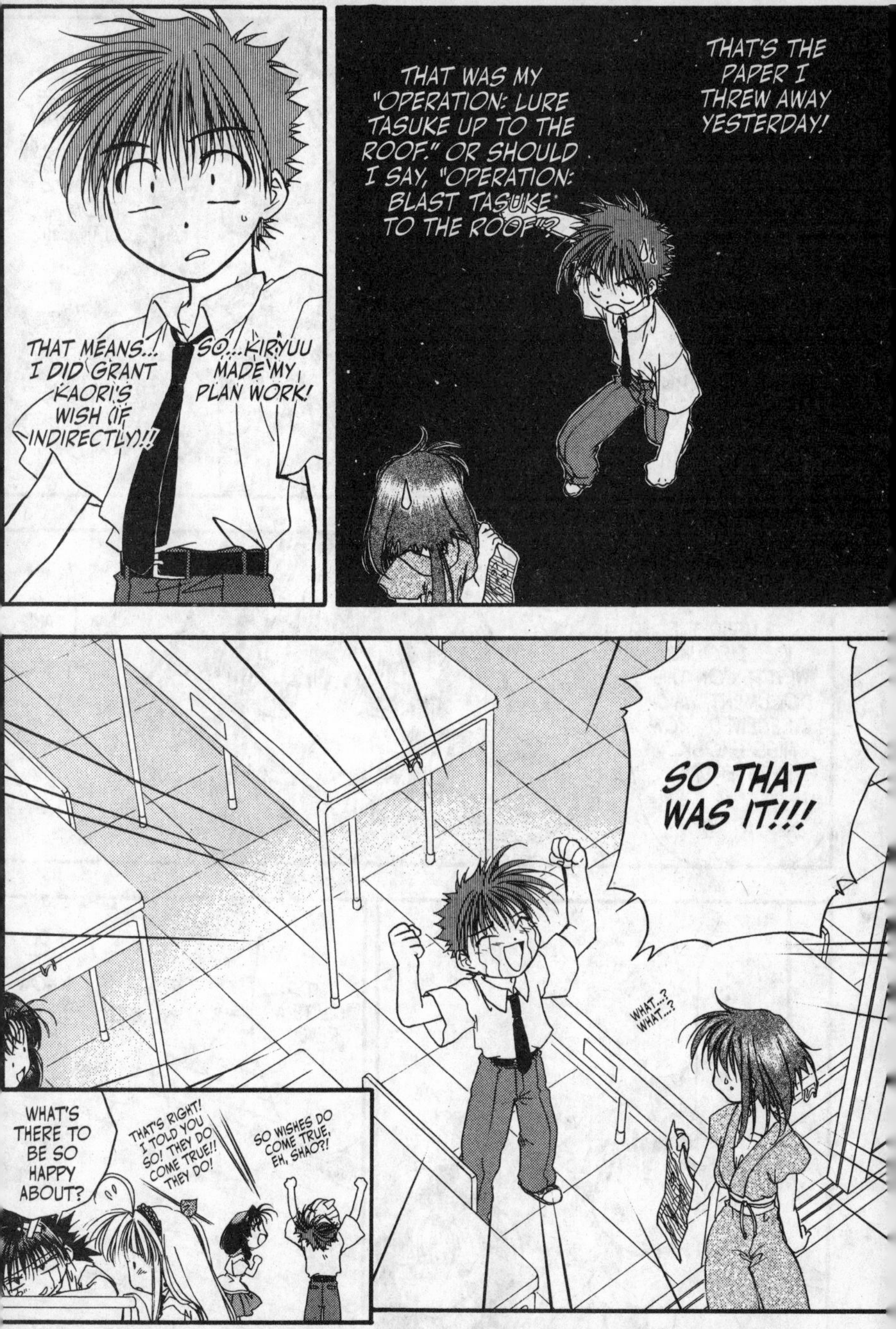
THAT'S THE PAPER I THREW AWAY YESTERDAY!
THAT WAS MY "OPERATION: LURE TASUKE UP TO THE ROOF." OR SHOULD I SAY, "OPERATION: BLAST TASUKE TO THE ROOF"!?
SO...KIRYUU MADE MY PLAN WORK!
THAT MEANS... I DID GRANT KAORI'S WISH (IF INDIRECTLY)!!
SO THAT WAS IT!!!
WHAT...? WHAT...?
SO WISHES DO COME TRUE, EH, SHAO?!
THAT'S RIGHT! I TOLD YOU SO! THEY DO COME TRUE!! THEY DO!
WHAT'S THERE TO BE SO HAPPY ABOUT?

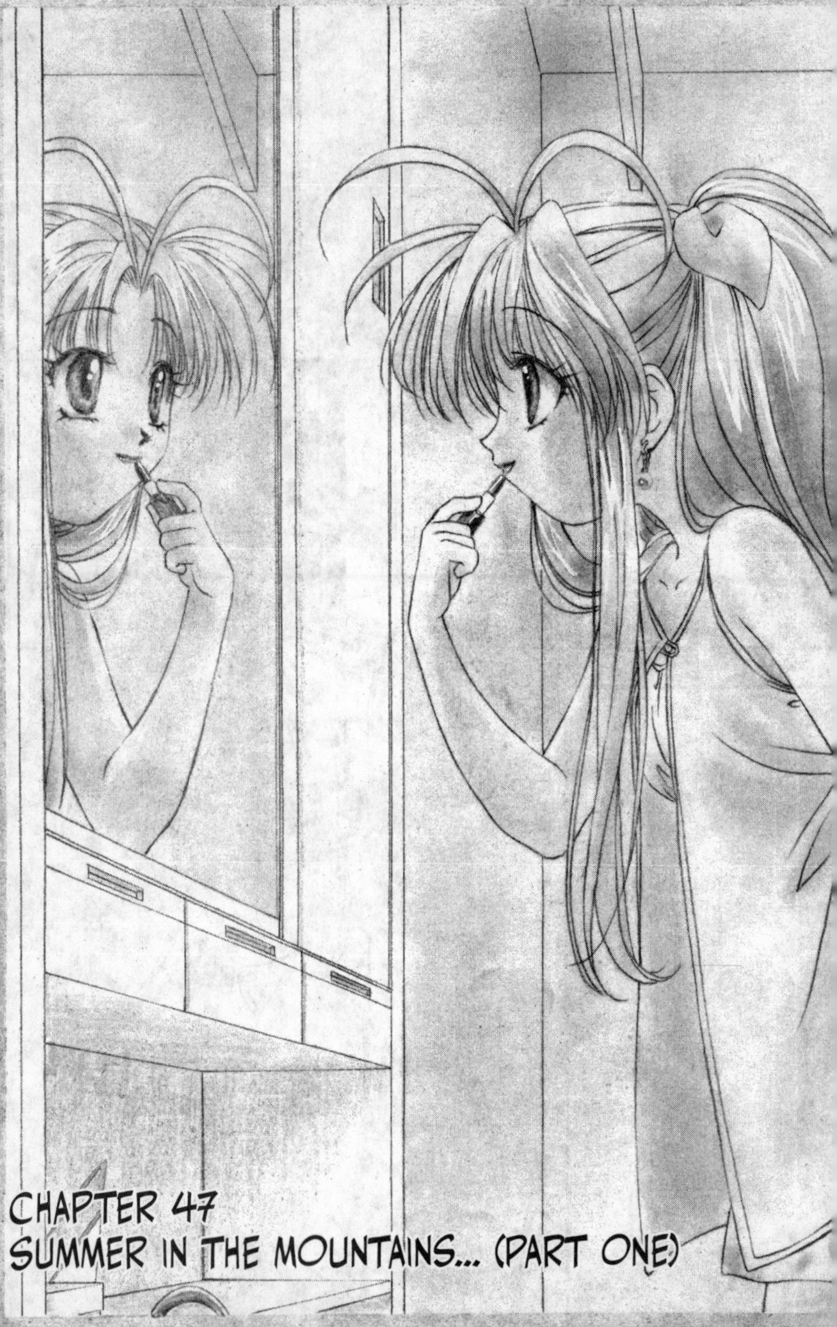

CHAPTER 47
SUMMER IN THE MOUNTAINS... (PART ONE)

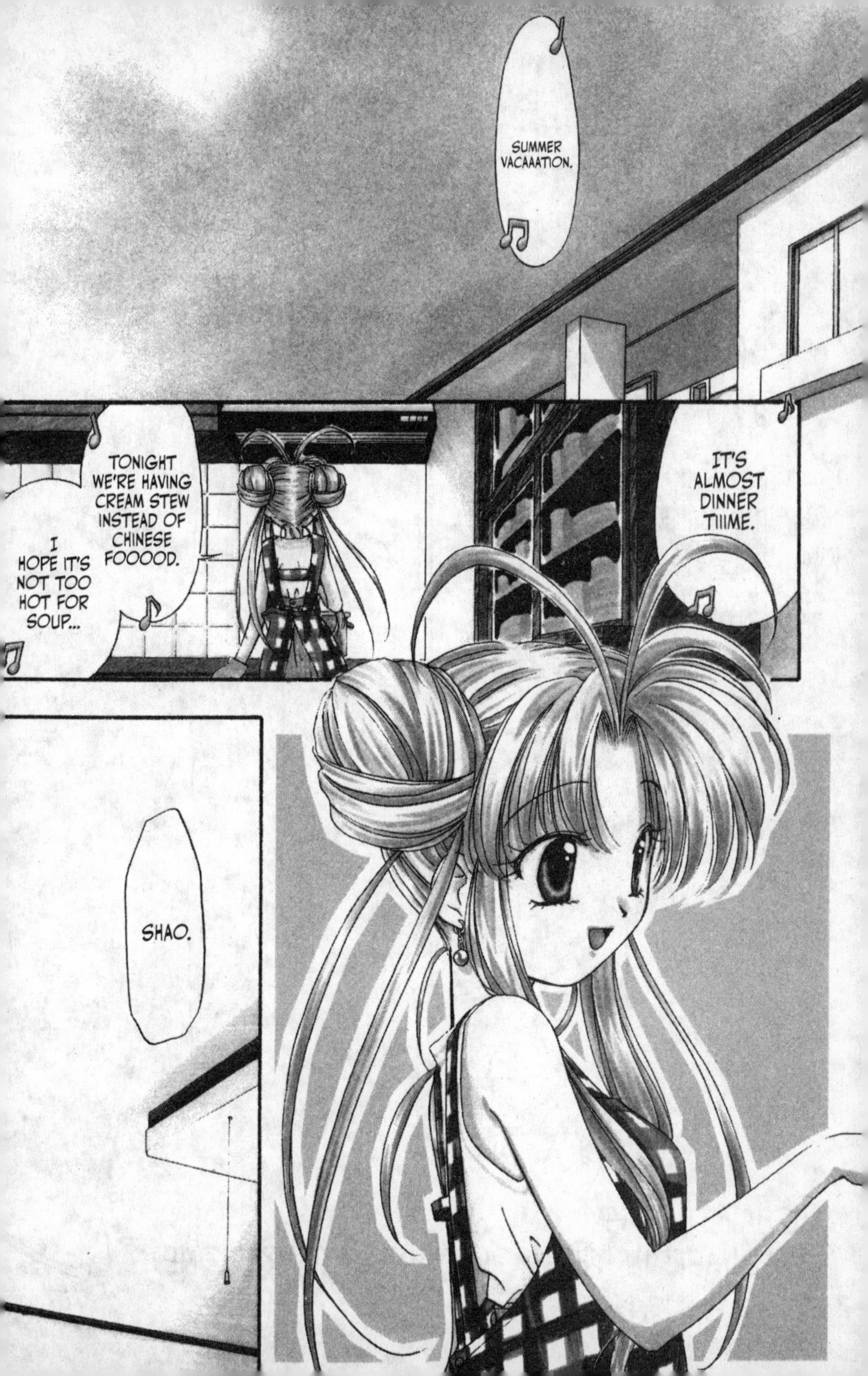
SUMMER VACAAATION.
IT'S ALMOST DINNER TIIIME.
TONIGHT WE'RE HAVING CREAM STEW INSTEAD OF CHINESE FOOOOD.
I HOPE IT'S NOT TOO HOT FOR SOUP...
SHAO.

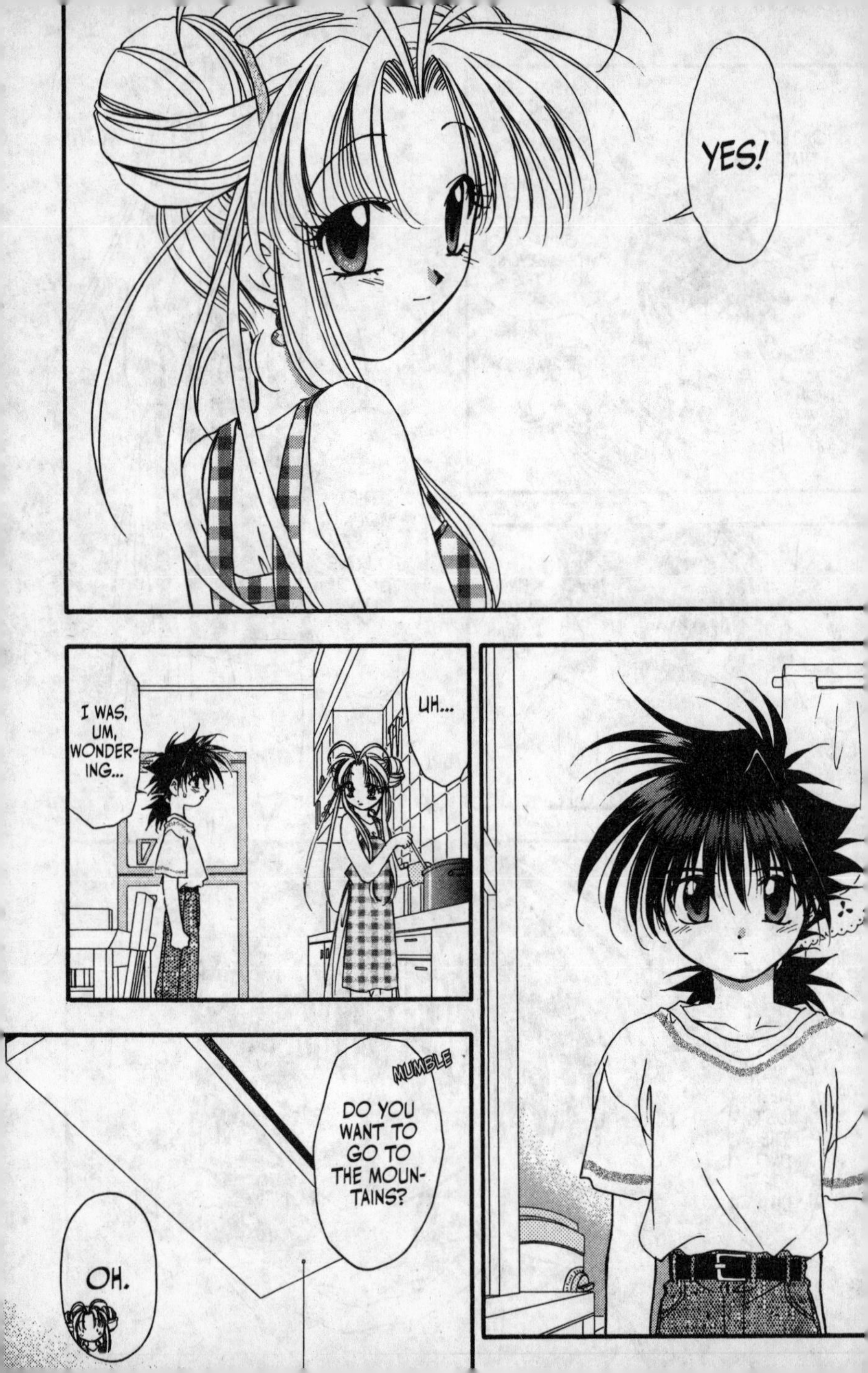
YES!
UH...
I WAS, UM, WONDER-ING...
MUMBLE
DO YOU WANT TO GO TO THE MOUN-TAINS?
OH.

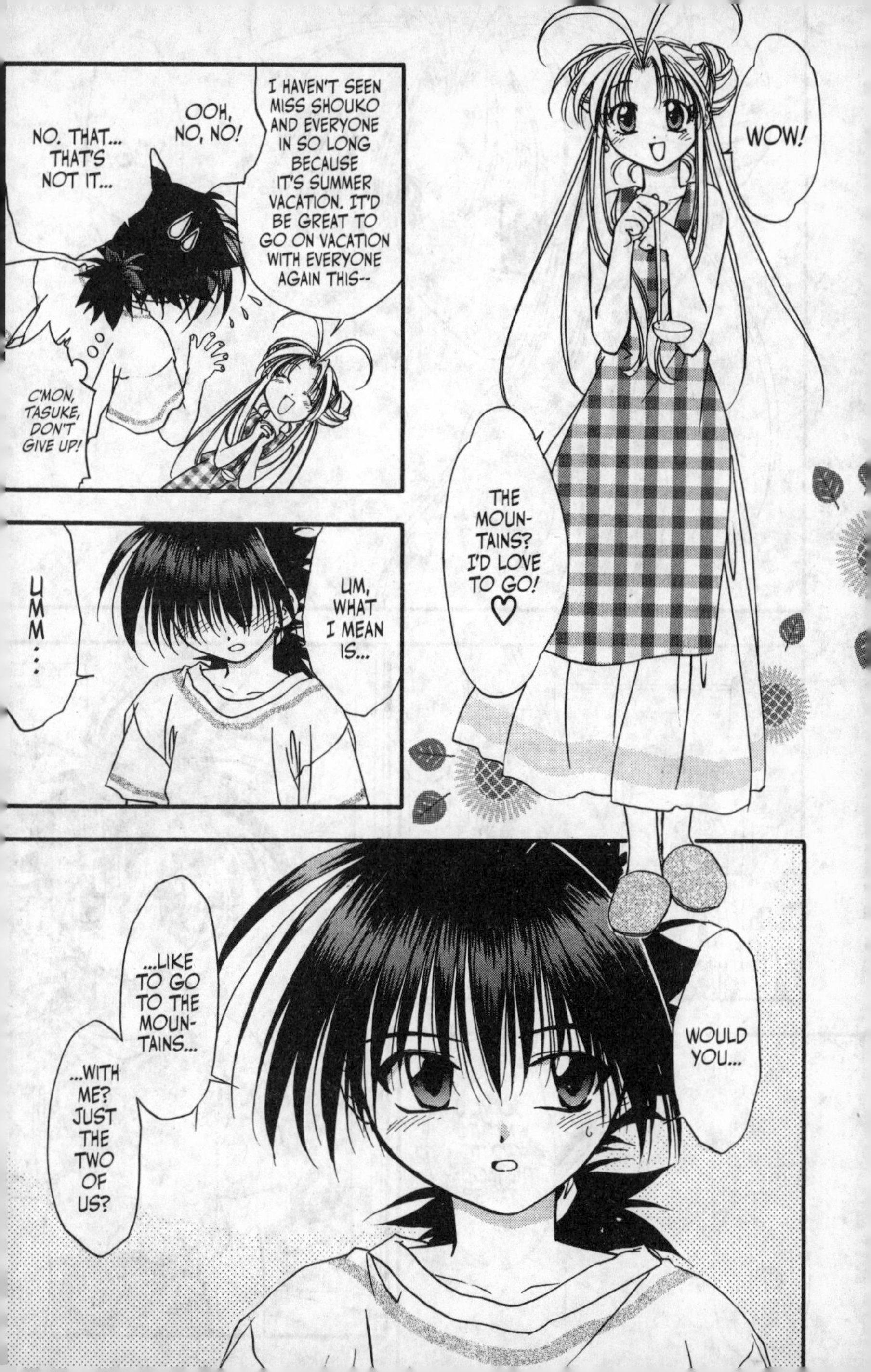
WOW!
THE MOUNTAINS? I'D LOVE TO GO! ♡
I HAVEN'T SEEN MISS SHOUKO AND EVERYONE IN SO LONG BECAUSE IT'S SUMMER VACATION. IT'D BE GREAT TO GO ON VACATION WITH EVERYONE AGAIN THIS--
OOH, NO, NO!
NO. THAT... THAT'S NOT IT...
C'MON, TASUKE, DON'T GIVE UP!
UM, WHAT I MEAN IS...
UMM...
WOULD YOU...
...LIKE TO GO TO THE MOUN-TAINS...
...WITH ME? JUST THE TWO OF US?

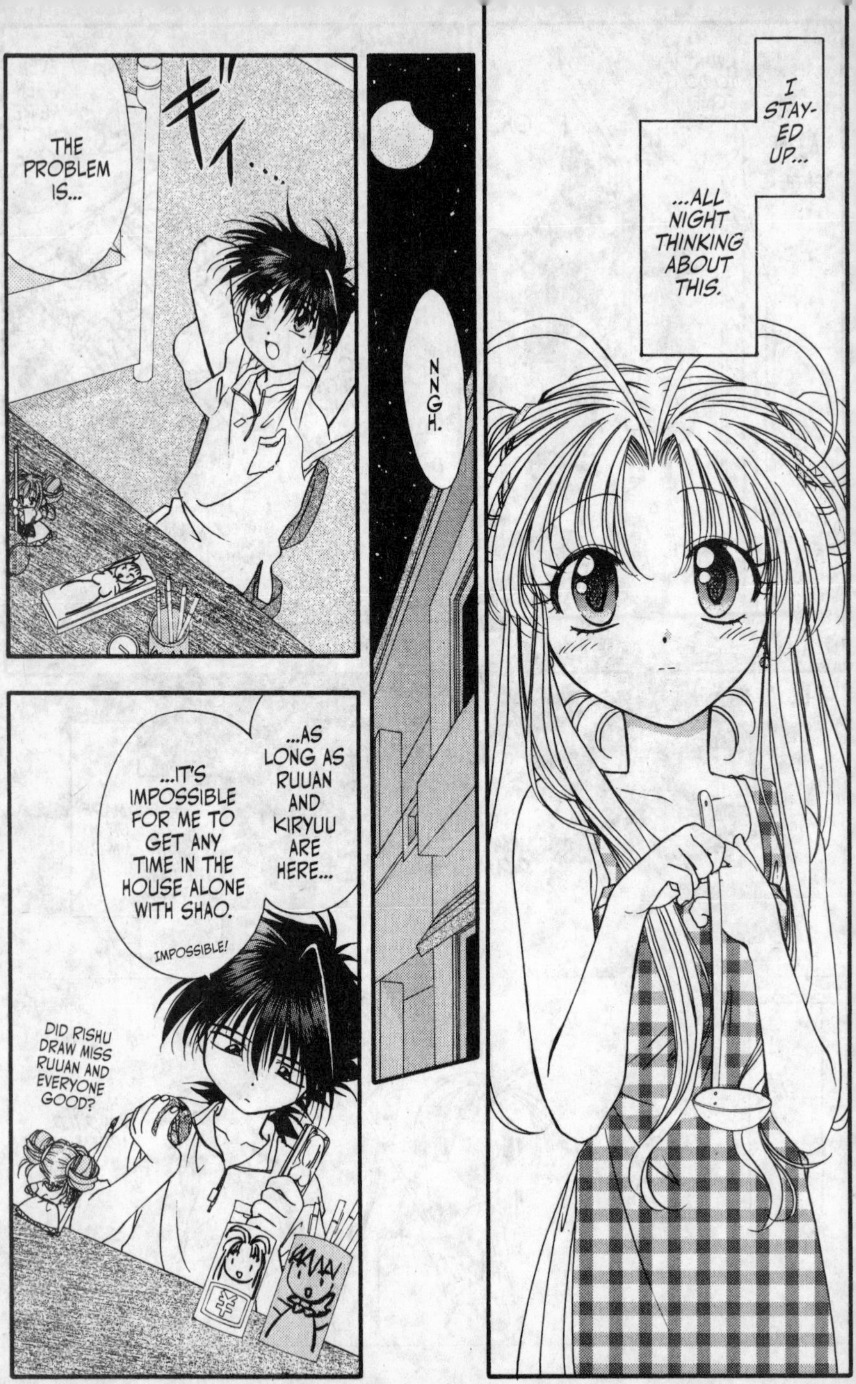
I STAYED UP...
...ALL NIGHT THINKING ABOUT THIS.
NNGH.
ギイ…
THE PROBLEM IS...
...AS LONG AS RUUAN AND KIRYUU ARE HERE...
...IT'S IMPOSSIBLE FOR ME TO GET ANY TIME IN THE HOUSE ALONE WITH SHAO.
IMPOSSIBLE!
DID RISHU DRAW MISS RUUAN AND EVERYONE GOOD?

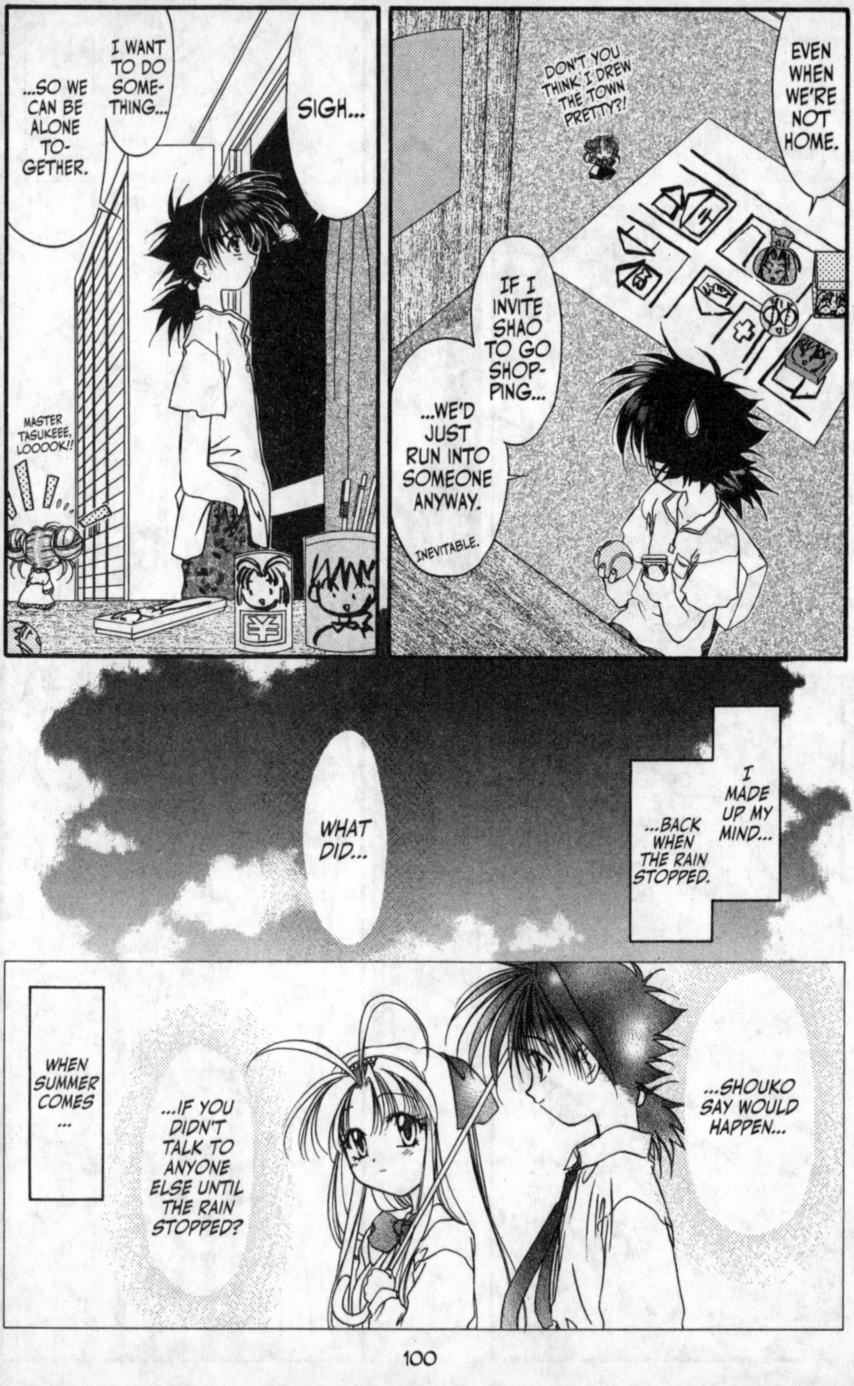
EVEN WHEN WE'RE NOT HOME.
DON'T YOU THINK I DREW THE TOWN PRETTY?!
IF I INVITE SHAO TO GO SHOP-PING...
...WE'D JUST RUN INTO SOMEONE ANYWAY.
INEVITABLE.
SIGH...
I WANT TO DO SOME-THING...
...SO WE CAN BE ALONE TO-GETHER.
MASTER TASUKEEE, LOOOOK!!
I MADE UP MY MIND...
...BACK WHEN THE RAIN STOPPED.
WHAT DID...
...SHOUKO SAY WOULD HAPPEN...
...IF YOU DIDN'T TALK TO ANYONE ELSE UNTIL THE RAIN STOPPED?
WHEN SUMMER COMES ...

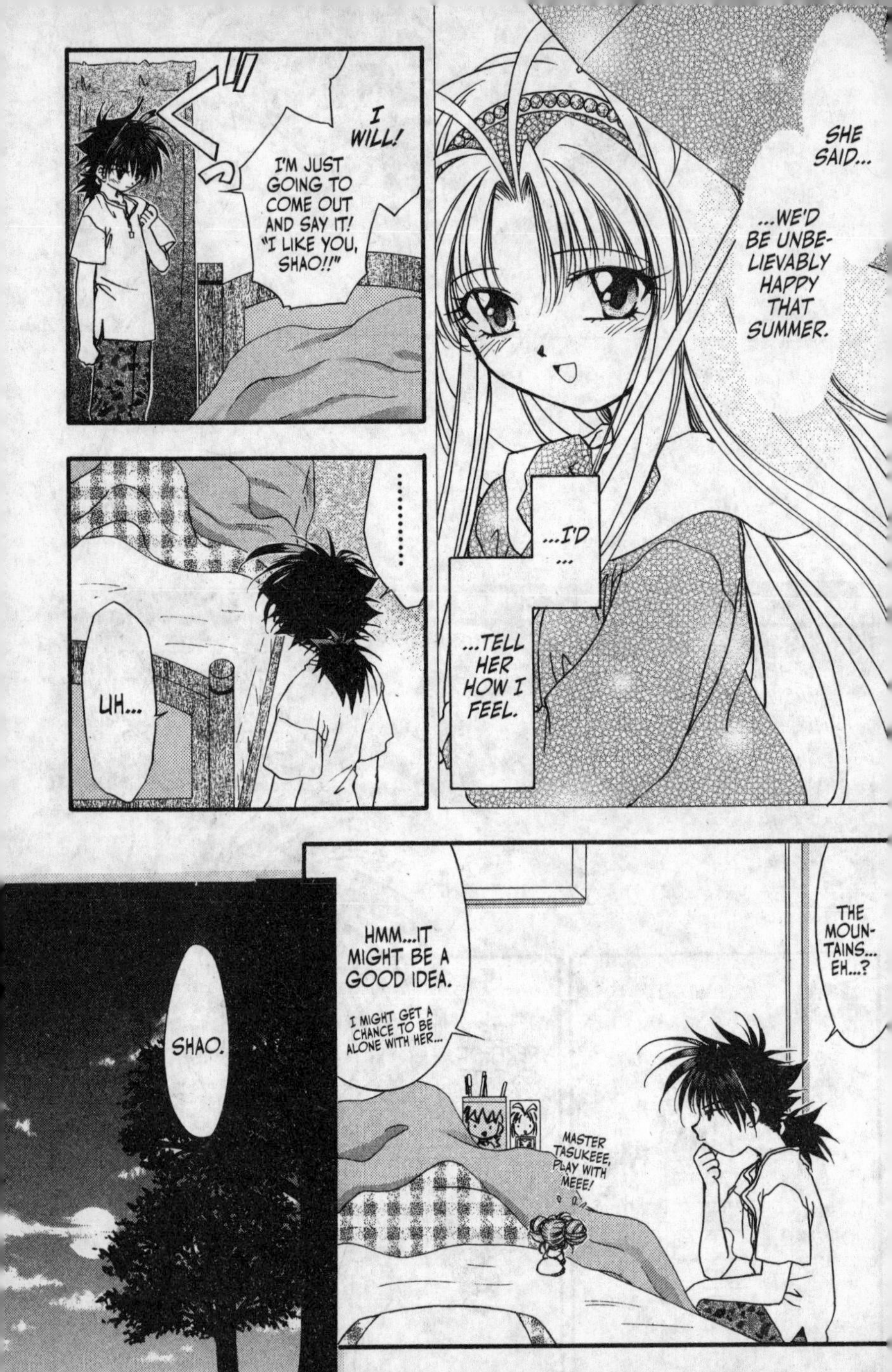
SHE SAID...
...WE'D BE UNBE-LIEVABLY HAPPY THAT SUMMER.
...I'D ...
...TELL HER HOW I FEEL.
I WILL!
I'M JUST GOING TO COME OUT AND SAY IT! "I LIKE YOU, SHAO!!"
....
UH...
THE MOUN-TAINS... EH...?
HMM...IT MIGHT BE A GOOD IDEA.
I MIGHT GET A CHANCE TO BE ALONE WITH HER...
MASTER TASUKEEE, PLAY WITH MEEE!
SHAO.

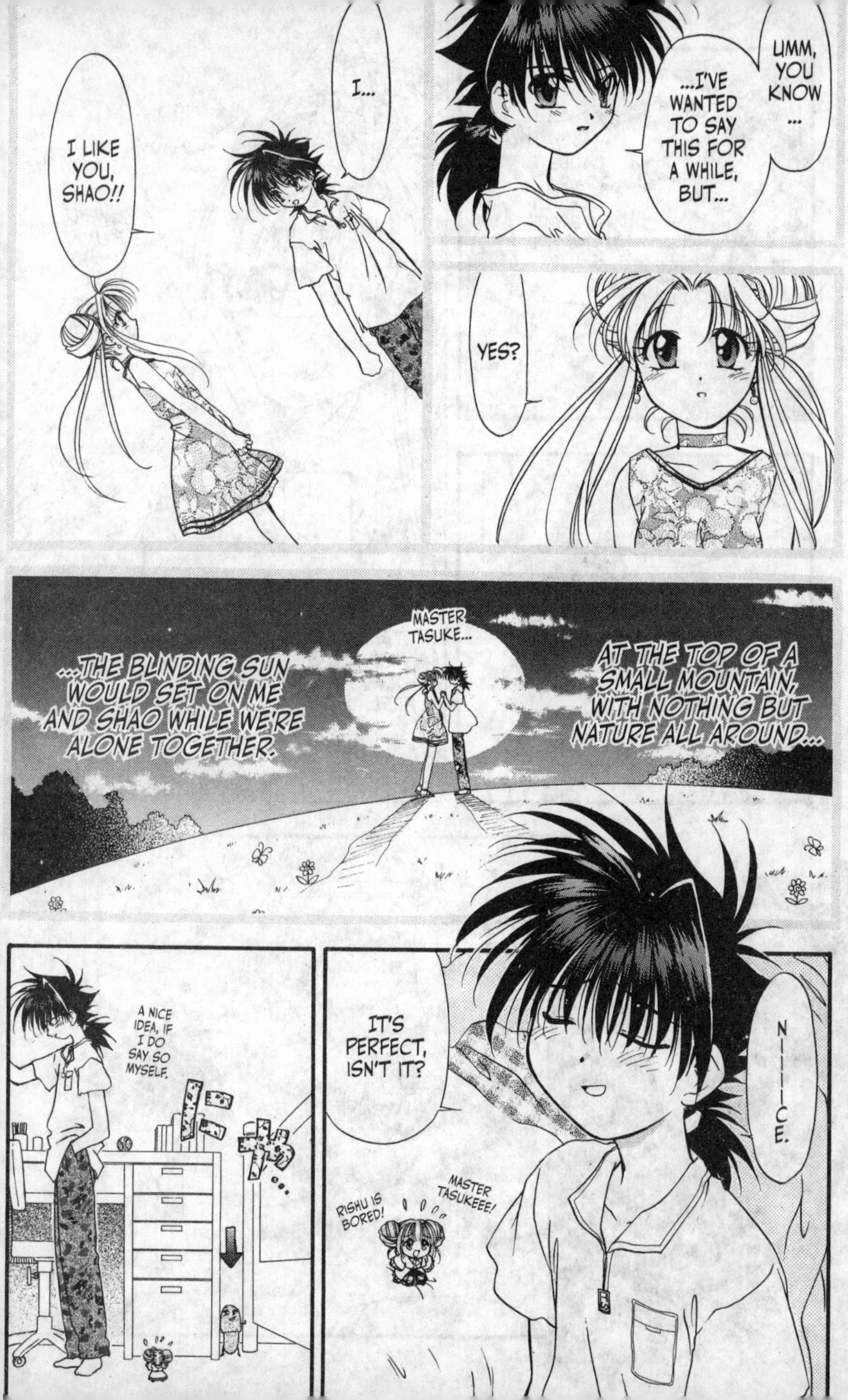
UMM, YOU KNOW ...
...I'VE WANTED TO SAY THIS FOR A WHILE, BUT...
YES?
I...
I LIKE YOU, SHAO!!
AT THE TOP OF A SMALL MOUNTAIN, WITH NOTHING BUT NATURE ALL AROUND...
MASTER TASUKE...
...THE BLINDING SUN WOULD SET ON ME AND SHAO WHILE WE'RE ALONE TOGETHER.
N-I-I-I-CE.
IT'S PERFECT, ISN'T IT?
MASTER TASUKEEE!
RISHU IS BORED!
A NICE IDEA, IF I DO SAY SO MYSELF.

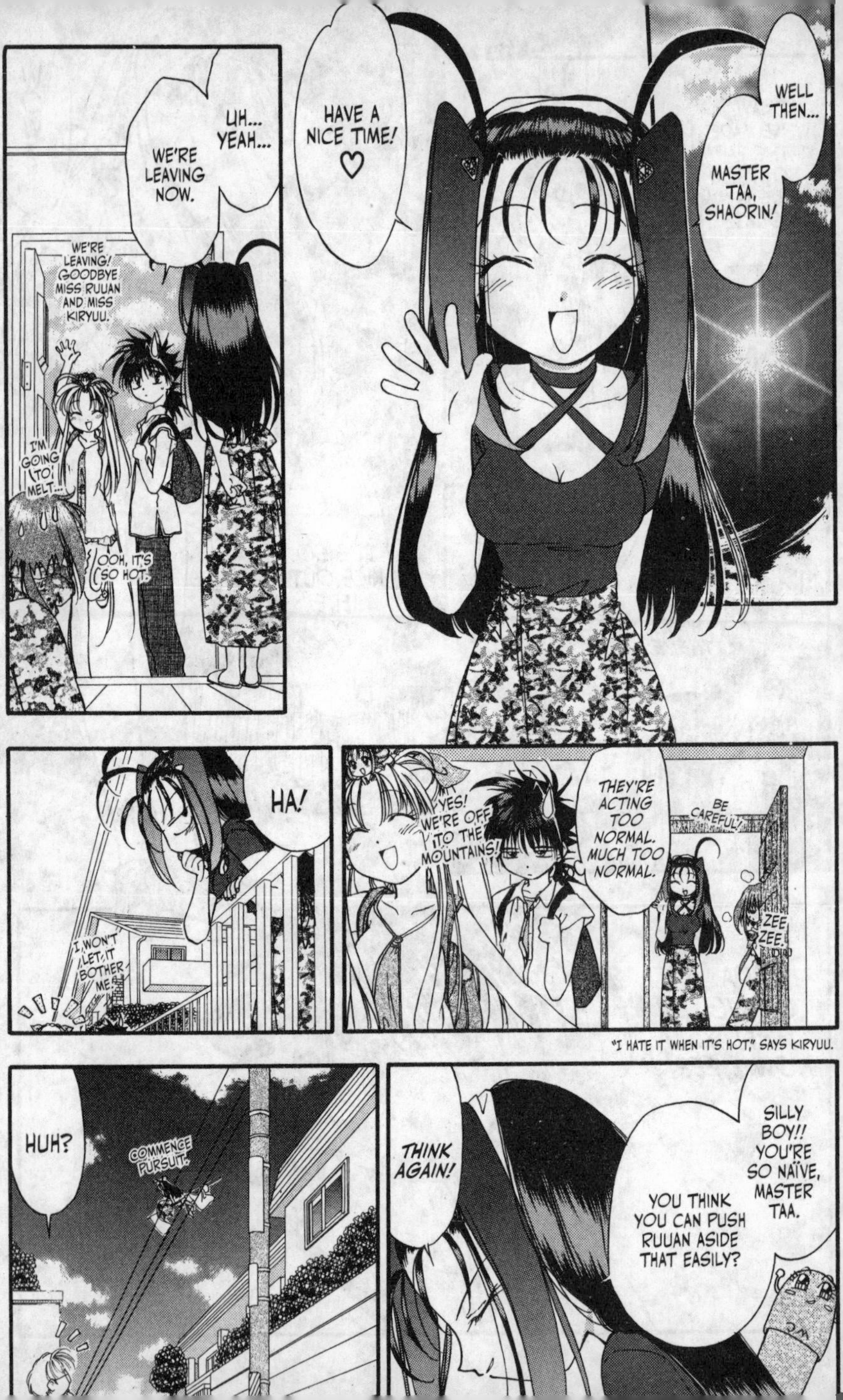
WELL THEN... MASTER TAA, SHAORIN!
HAVE A NICE TIME! ♥
UH... YEAH...
WE'RE LEAVING NOW.
WE'RE LEAVING! GOODBYE MISS RUUAN AND MISS KIRYUU.
I'M GOING TO MELT...
OOH, IT'S SO HOT.
THEY'RE ACTING TOO NORMAL. MUCH TOO NORMAL.
BE CAREFUL!
YES! WE'RE OFF TO THE MOUNTAINS!
ZEE ZEE.
HA!
I WON'T LET IT BOTHER ME.
"I HATE IT WHEN IT'S HOT," SAYS KIRYUU.
SILLY BOY!! YOU'RE SO NAÏVE, MASTER TAA.
YOU THINK YOU CAN PUSH RUUAN ASIDE THAT EASILY?
THINK AGAIN!
HUH?
COMMENCE PURSUIT.

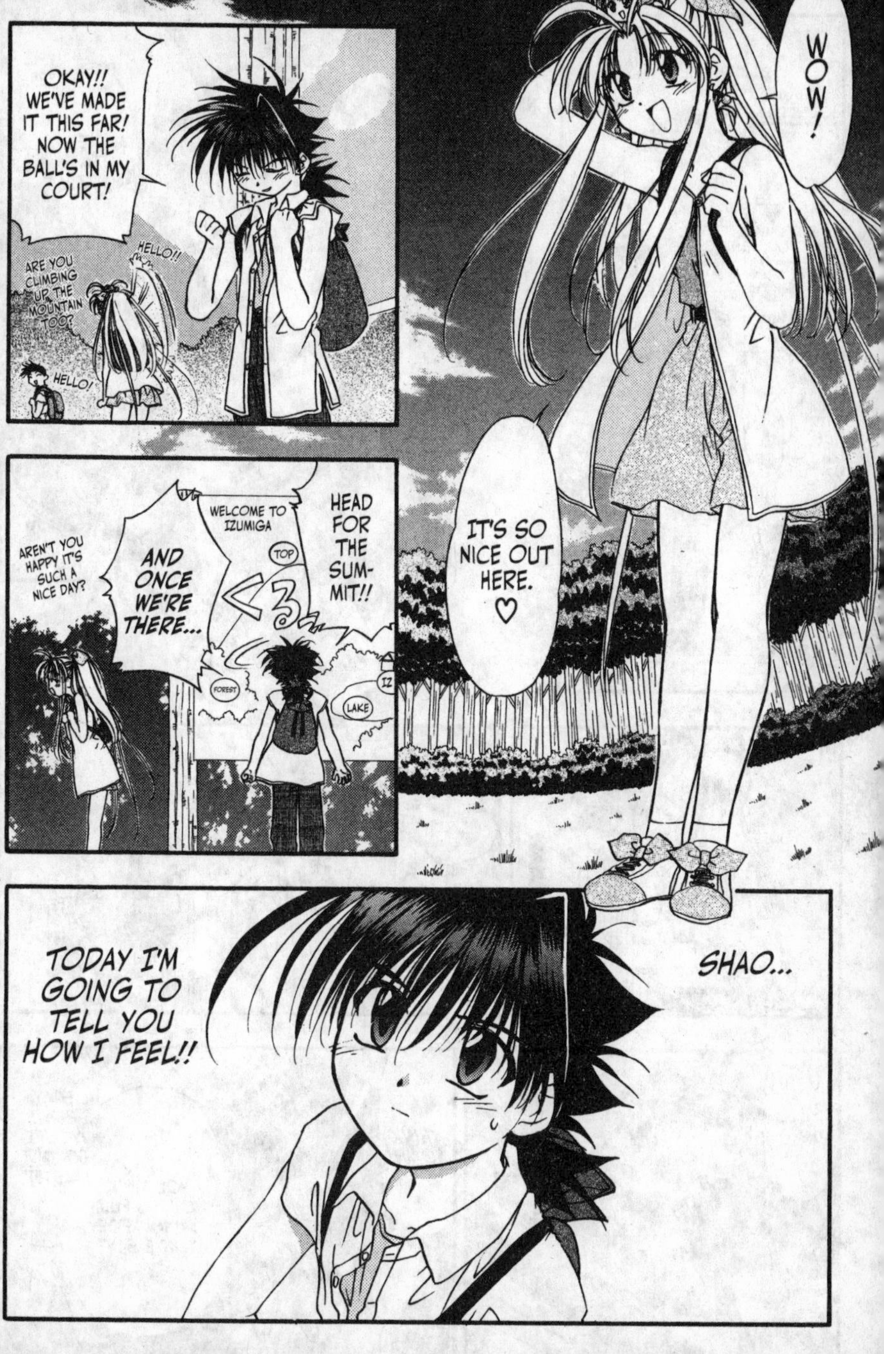
WOW!
IT'S SO NICE OUT HERE. ♥
OKAY!! WE'VE MADE IT THIS FAR! NOW THE BALL'S IN MY COURT!
HELLO!!
ARE YOU CLIMBING UP THE MOUNTAIN TOO?
HELLO!
HEAD FOR THE SUM-MIT!!
WELCOME TO IZUMIGA
TOP
AND ONCE WE'RE THERE...
くる
AREN'T YOU HAPPY IT'S SUCH A NICE DAY?
FOREST
IZ
LAKE
SHAO...
TODAY I'M GOING TO TELL YOU HOW I FEEL!!

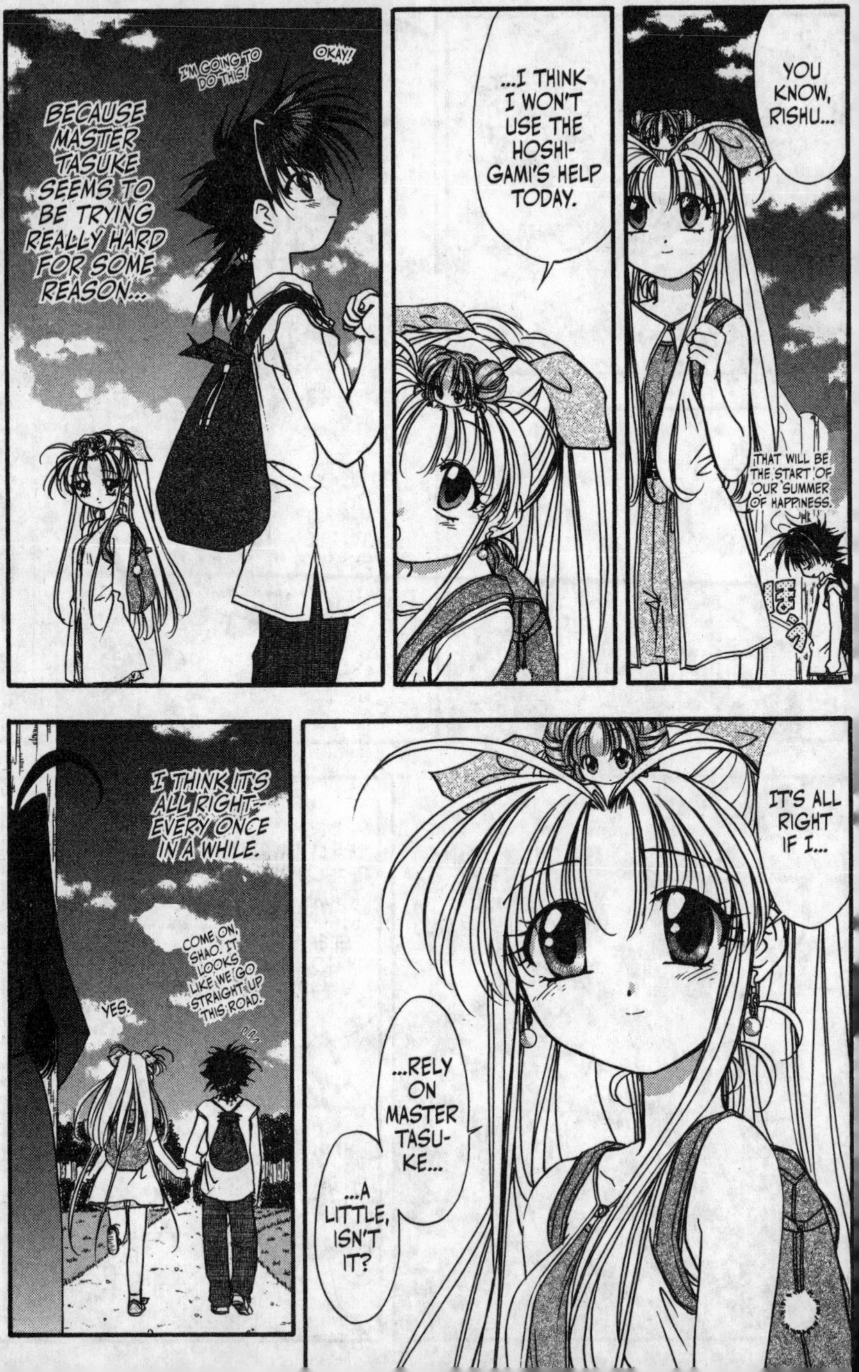
YOU KNOW, RISHU...
THAT WILL BE THE START OF OUR SUMMER OF HAPPINESS.
...I THINK I WON'T USE THE HOSHI-GAMI'S HELP TODAY.
OKAY!
I'M GOING TO DO THIS!
BECAUSE MASTER TASUKE SEEMS TO BE TRYING REALLY HARD FOR SOME REASON...
IT'S ALL RIGHT IF I...
...RELY ON MASTER TASU-KE...
...A LITTLE, ISN'T IT?
I THINK IT'S ALL RIGHT—EVERY ONCE IN A WHILE.
COME ON, SHAO. IT LOOKS LIKE WE GO STRAIGHT UP THIS ROAD.
YES.

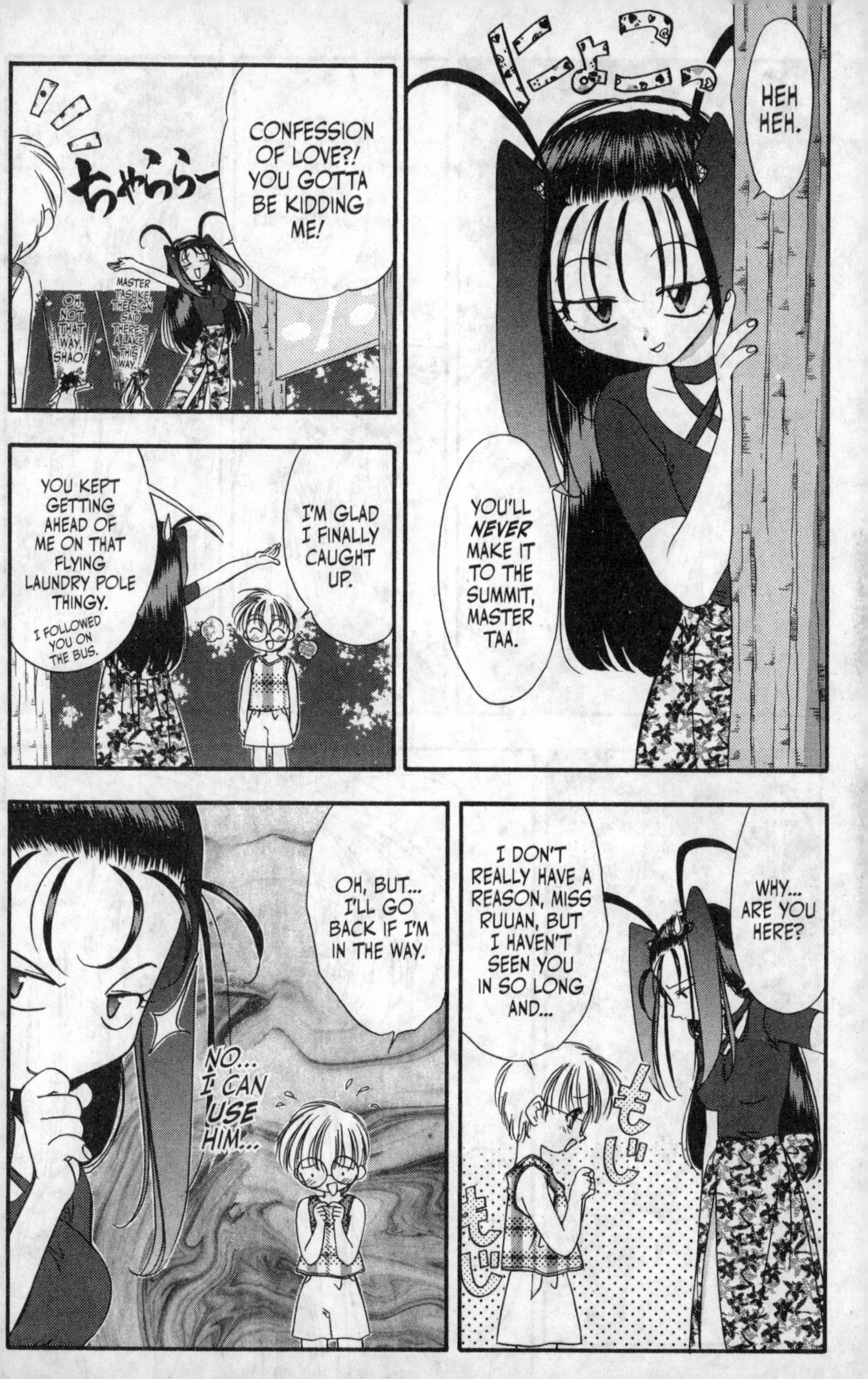
にょこっ
HEH HEH.
YOU'LL NEVER MAKE IT TO THE SUMMIT, MASTER TAA.
CONFESSION OF LOVE?! YOU GOTTA BE KIDDING ME!
ちゃららー
MASTER TASUKE, THE SIGN SAID THERE'S A LAKE THIS WAY.
OH, NOT THAT WAY, SHAO!
I'M GLAD I FINALLY CAUGHT UP.
YOU KEPT GETTING AHEAD OF ME ON THAT FLYING LAUNDRY POLE THINGY.
I FOLLOWED YOU ON THE BUS.
WHY... ARE YOU HERE?
I DON'T REALLY HAVE A REASON, MISS RUUAN, BUT I HAVEN'T SEEN YOU IN SO LONG AND...
もじもじ
OH, BUT... I'LL GO BACK IF I'M IN THE WAY.
NO... I CAN USE HIM...

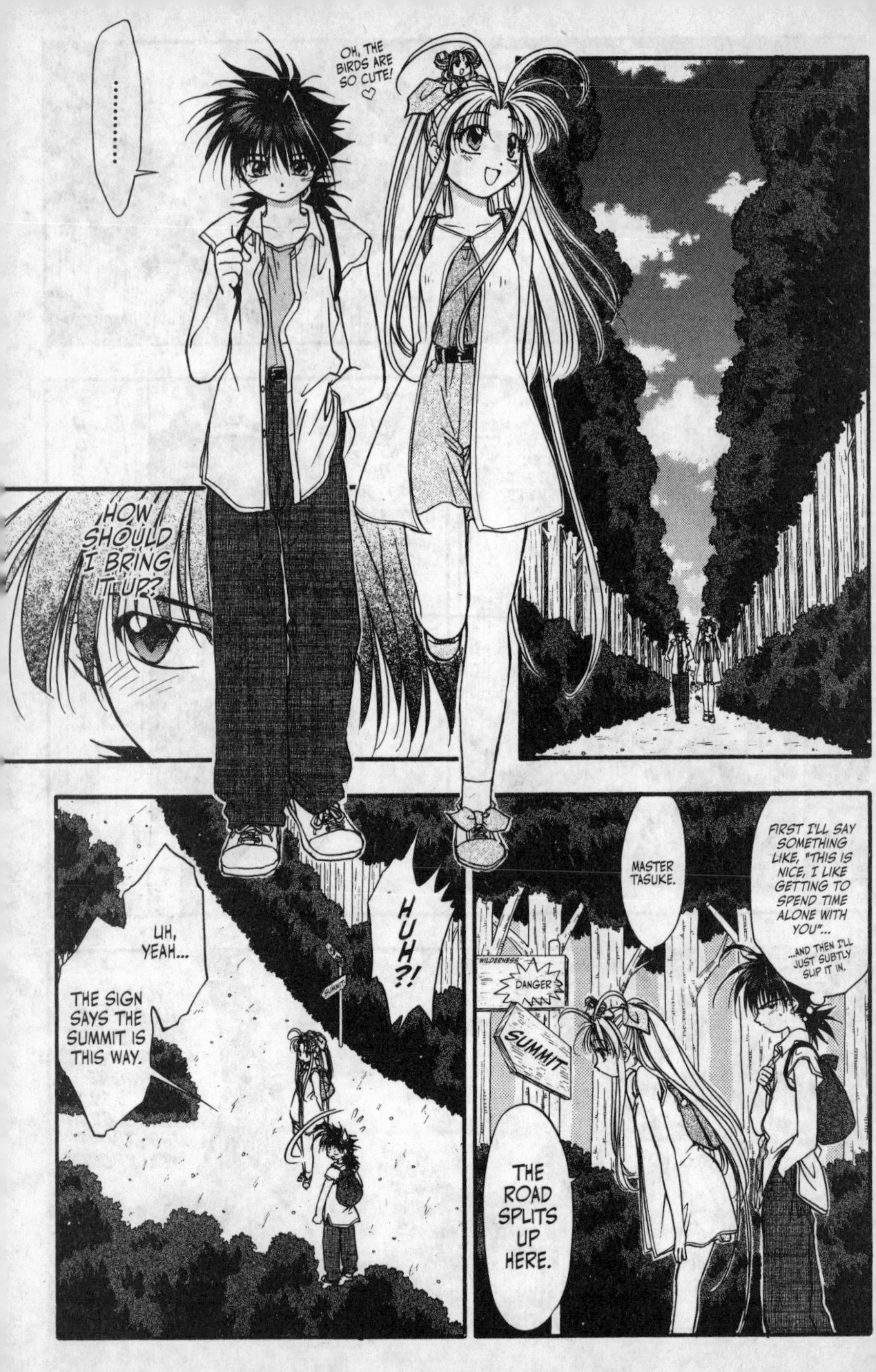
OH, THE BIRDS ARE SO CUTE! ♡
……
HOW SHOULD I BRING IT UP?
FIRST I'LL SAY SOMETHING LIKE, "THIS IS NICE, I LIKE GETTING TO SPEND TIME ALONE WITH YOU"...
...AND THEN I'LL JUST SUBTLY SLIP IT IN.
MASTER TASUKE.
WILDERNESS
DANGER
SUMMIT
THE ROAD SPLITS UP HERE.
HUH?!
UH, YEAH...
THE SIGN SAYS THE SUMMIT IS THIS WAY.
SUMMIT

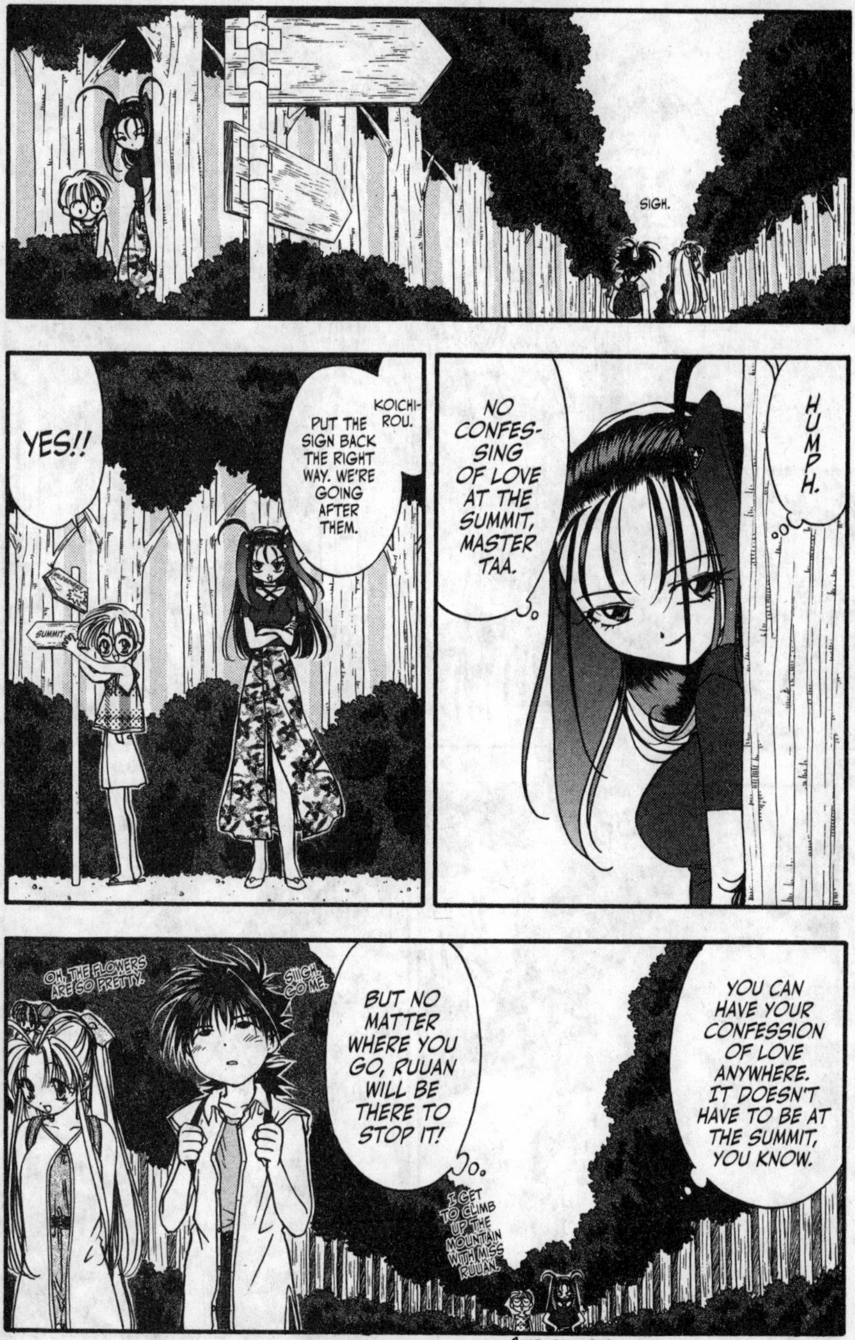
SIGH.
HUMPH.
NO CONFESSING OF LOVE AT THE SUMMIT, MASTER TAA.
KOICHIROU. PUT THE SIGN BACK THE RIGHT WAY. WE'RE GOING AFTER THEM.
YES!!
SUMMIT
YOU CAN HAVE YOUR CONFESSION OF LOVE ANYWHERE. IT DOESN'T HAVE TO BE AT THE SUMMIT, YOU KNOW.
BUT NO MATTER WHERE YOU GO, RUUAN WILL BE THERE TO STOP IT!
SIIIGH. GO ME.
OH, THE FLOWERS ARE SO PRETTY.
I GET TO CLIMB UP THE MOUNTAIN WITH MISS RUUAN.
MR. OBLIVIOUS

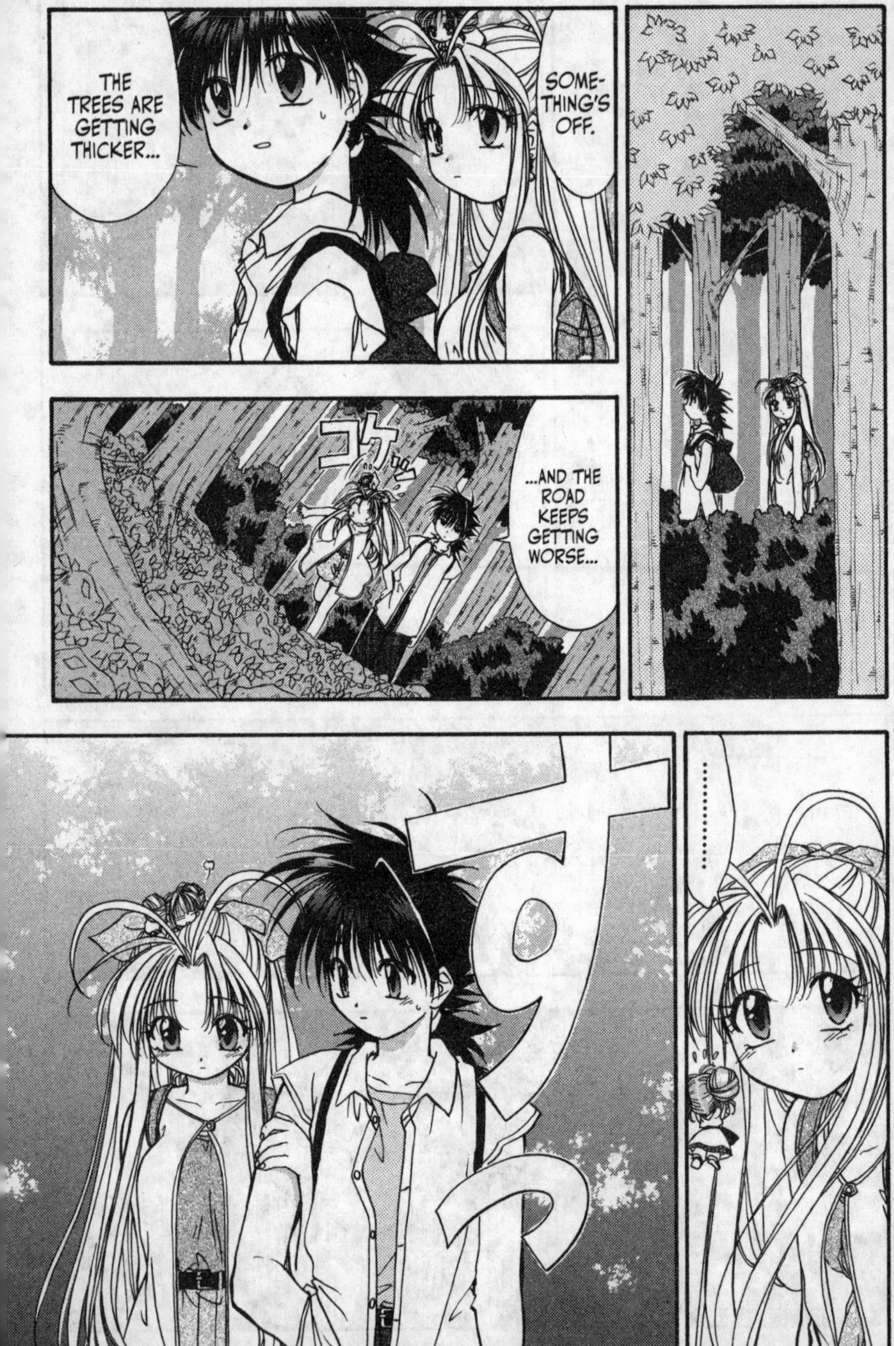
SOME-THING'S OFF.
THE TREES ARE GETTING THICKER...
...AND THE ROAD KEEPS GETTING WORSE...
コケ
....

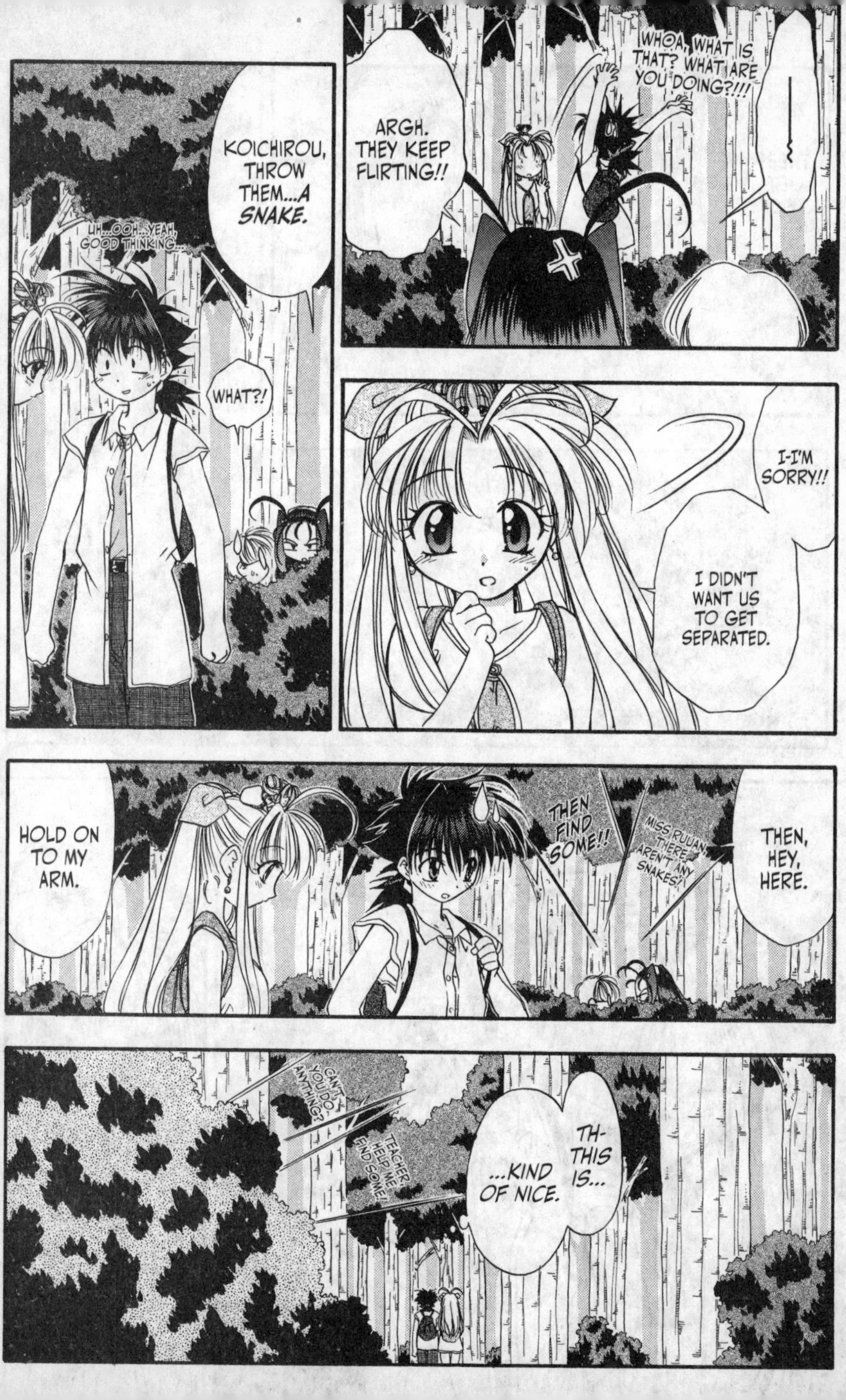
WHOA, WHAT IS THAT? WHAT ARE YOU DOING?!!!
ARGH. THEY KEEP FLIRTING!!
I-I'M SORRY!!
I DIDN'T WANT US TO GET SEPARATED.
KOICHIROU, THROW THEM...A SNAKE.
UH...OOH...YEAH, GOOD THINKING...
WHAT?!
THEN, HEY, HERE.
MISS RUUAN, THERE AREN'T ANY SNAKES!
THEN FIND SOME!!
HOLD ON TO MY ARM.
TH-THIS IS...
...KIND OF NICE.
TEACHER, HELP ME FIND SOME!
CAN'T YOU DO ANYTHING?

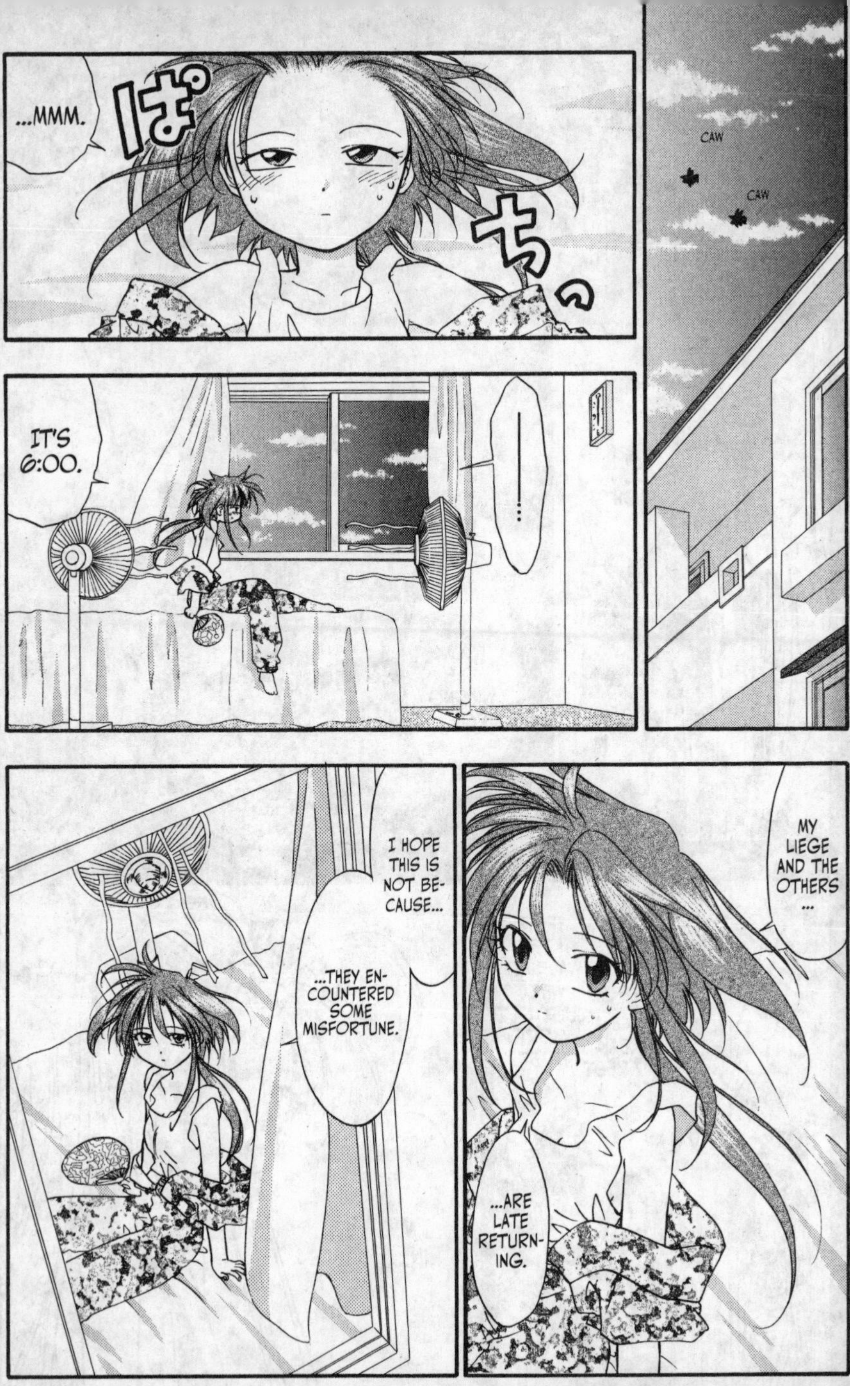
CAW
CAW
ぱちっ
...MMM.
......
IT'S 6:00.
MY LIEGE AND THE OTHERS ...
...ARE LATE RETURNING.
I HOPE THIS IS NOT BECAUSE...
...THEY ENCOUNTERED SOME MISFORTUNE.

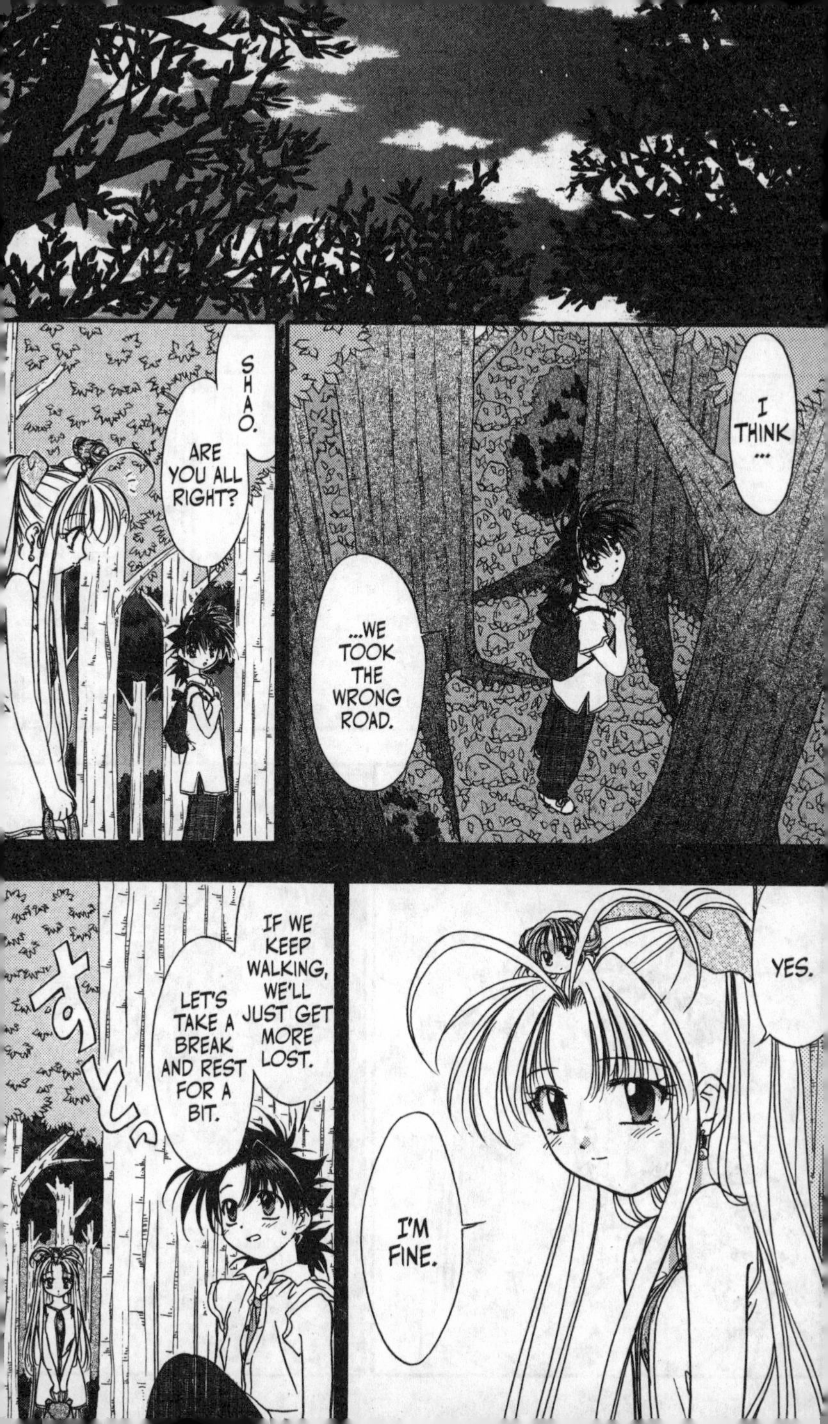
I THINK ...
...WE TOOK THE WRONG ROAD.
SHAO. ARE YOU ALL RIGHT?
YES.
I'M FINE.
IF WE KEEP WALKING, WE'LL JUST GET MORE LOST.
LET'S TAKE A BREAK AND REST FOR A BIT.

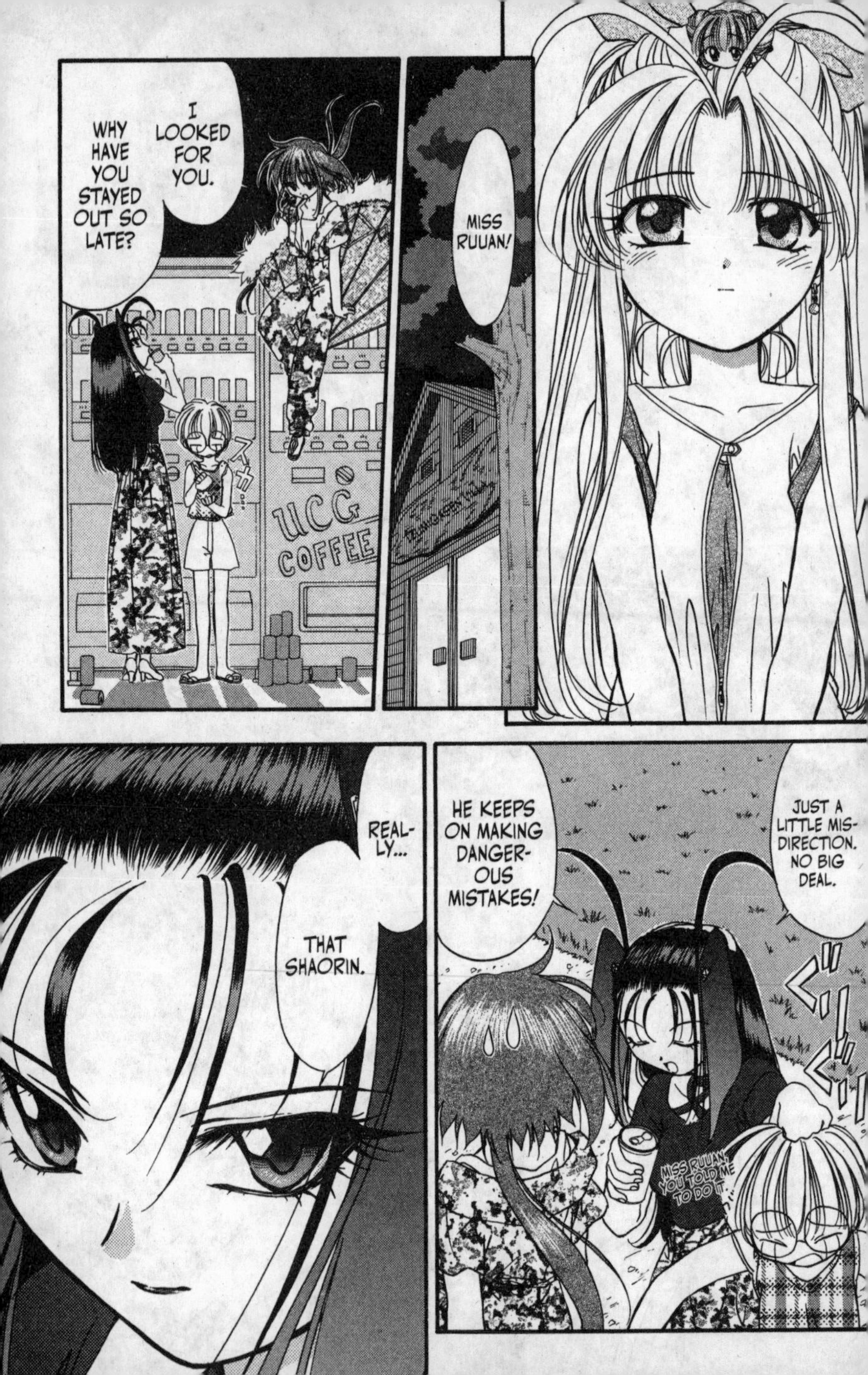
MISS RUUAN!
I LOOKED FOR YOU.
WHY HAVE YOU STAYED OUT SO LATE?
UCC COFFEE
JUST A LITTLE MIS-DIRECTION. NO BIG DEAL.
HE KEEPS ON MAKING DANGER-OUS MISTAKES!
MISS RUUAN, YOU TOLD ME TO DO IT...
REAL-LY...
THAT SHAORIN.

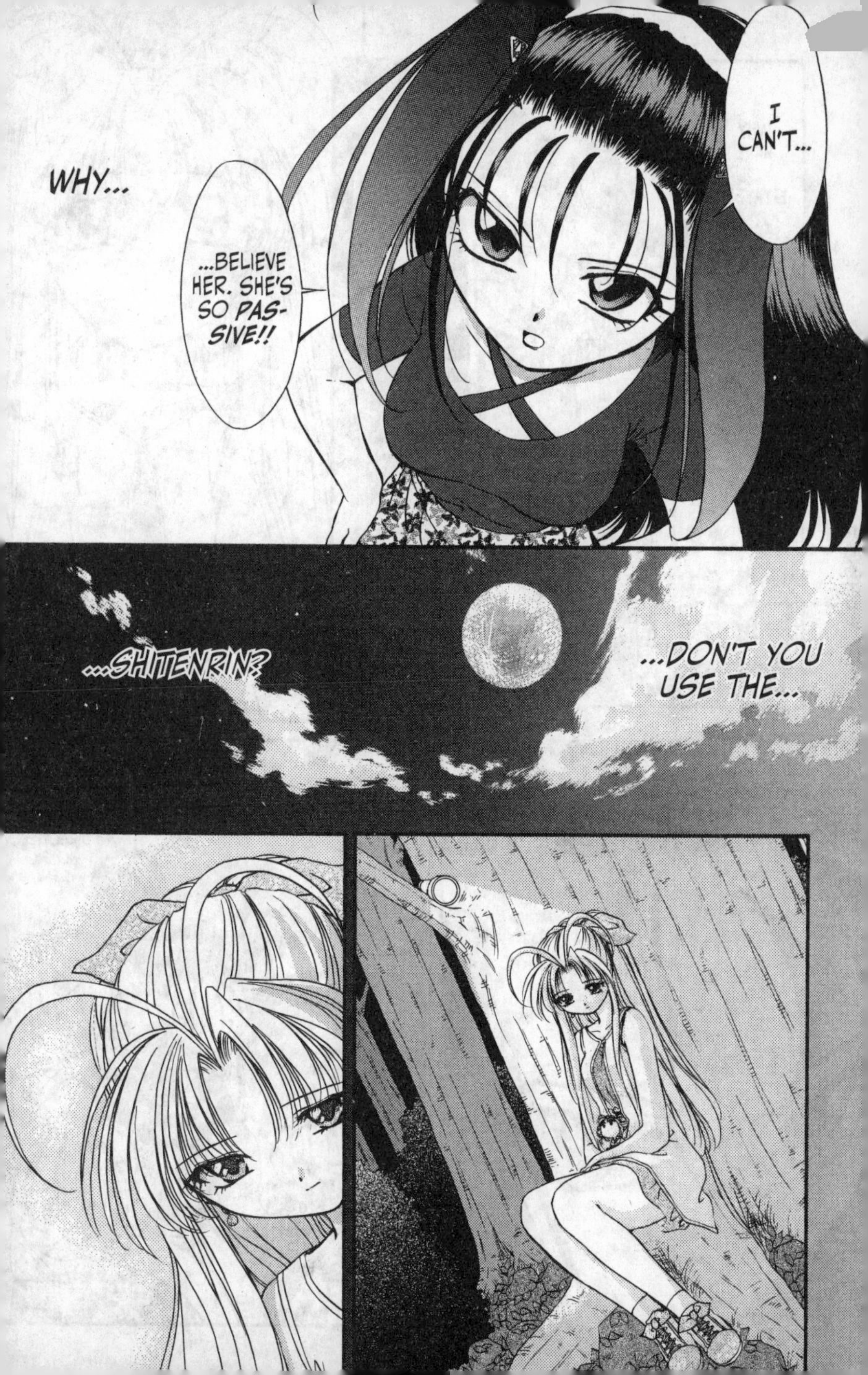
I CAN'T...
...BELIEVE HER. SHE'S SO PAS-SIVE!!
WHY...
...DON'T YOU USE THE...
...SHITENRIN?

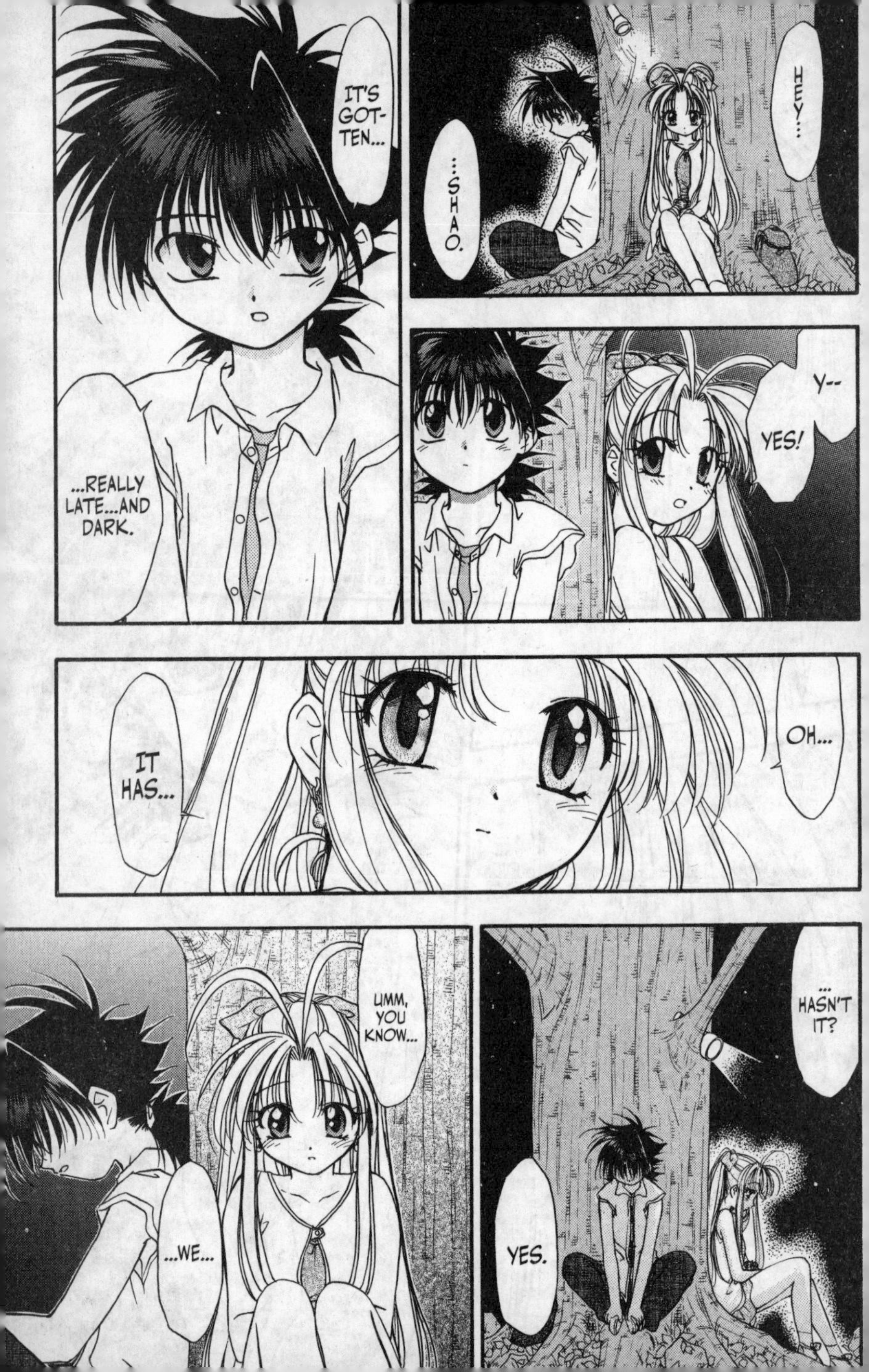
HEY...
...SHAO.
Y-- YES!
IT'S GOT-TEN...
...REALLY LATE...AND DARK.
OH...
IT HAS...
...HASN'T IT?
YES.
UMM, YOU KNOW...
...WE...

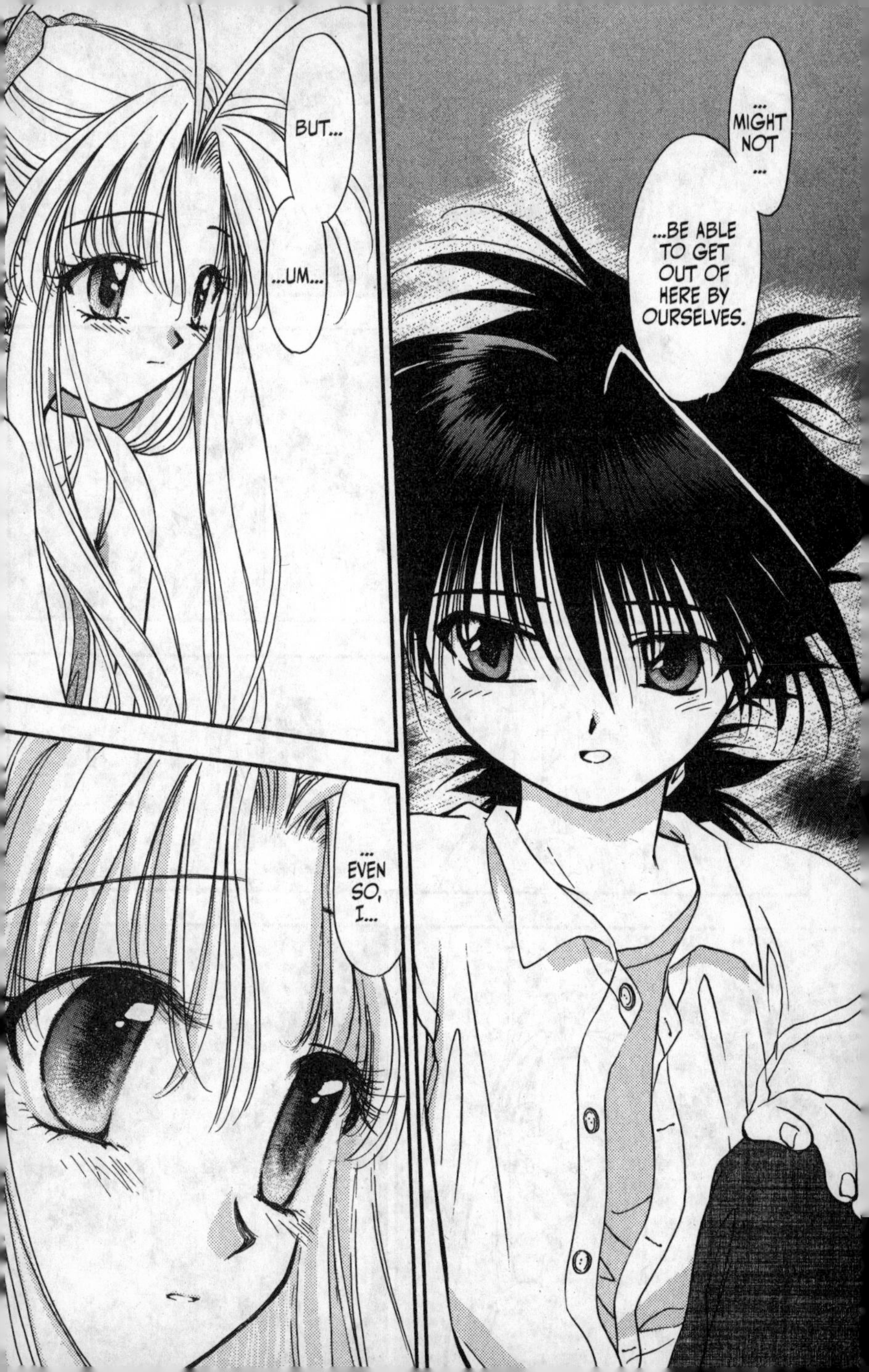
... MIGHT NOT ...
...BE ABLE TO GET OUT OF HERE BY OURSELVES.
BUT...
...UM...
... EVEN SO, I...

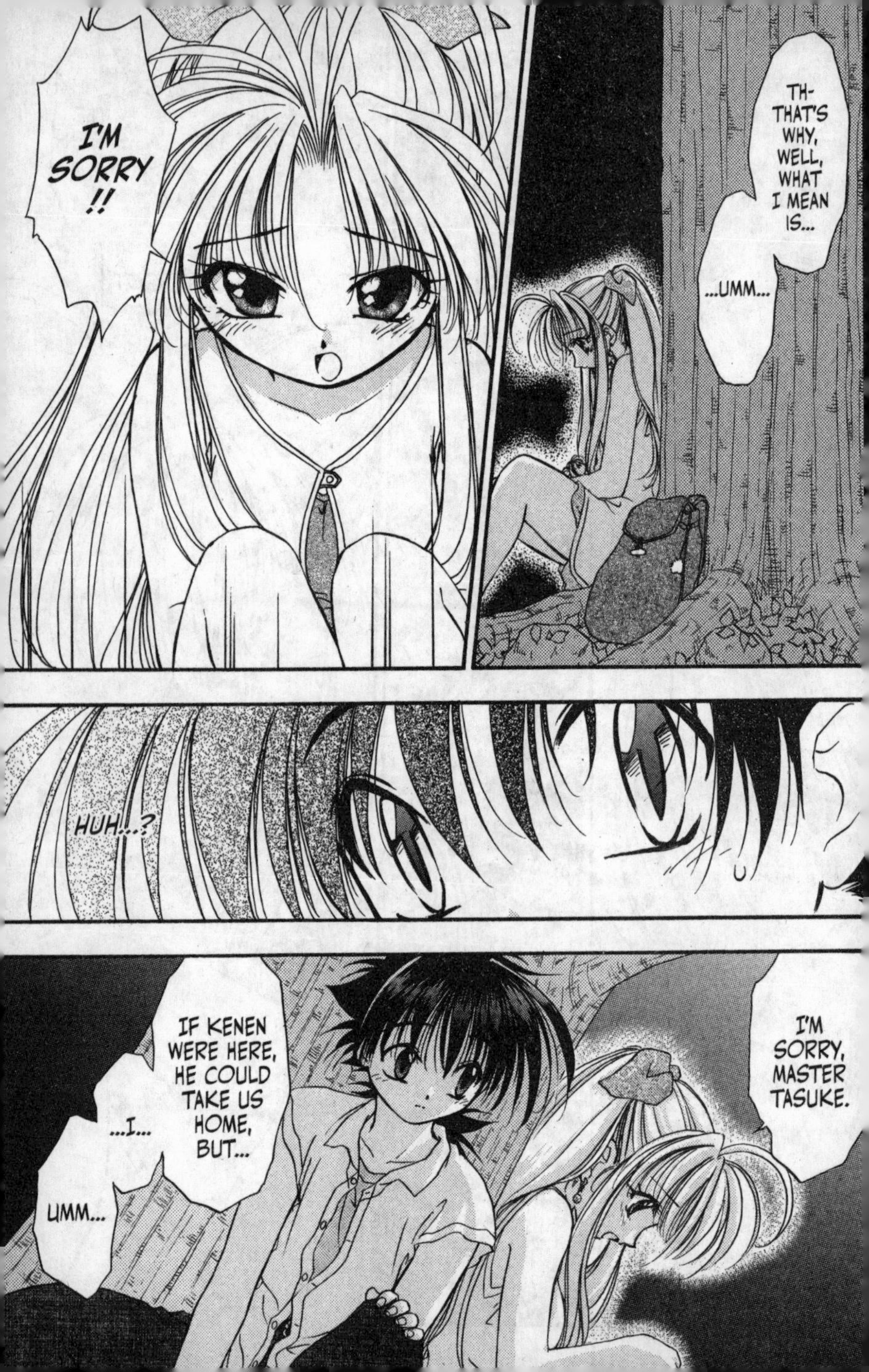
TH-THAT'S WHY, WELL, WHAT I MEAN IS...
...UMM...
I'M SORRY!!
HUH...?
I'M SORRY, MASTER TASUKE.
IF KENEN WERE HERE, HE COULD TAKE US HOME, BUT...
...I...
UMM...

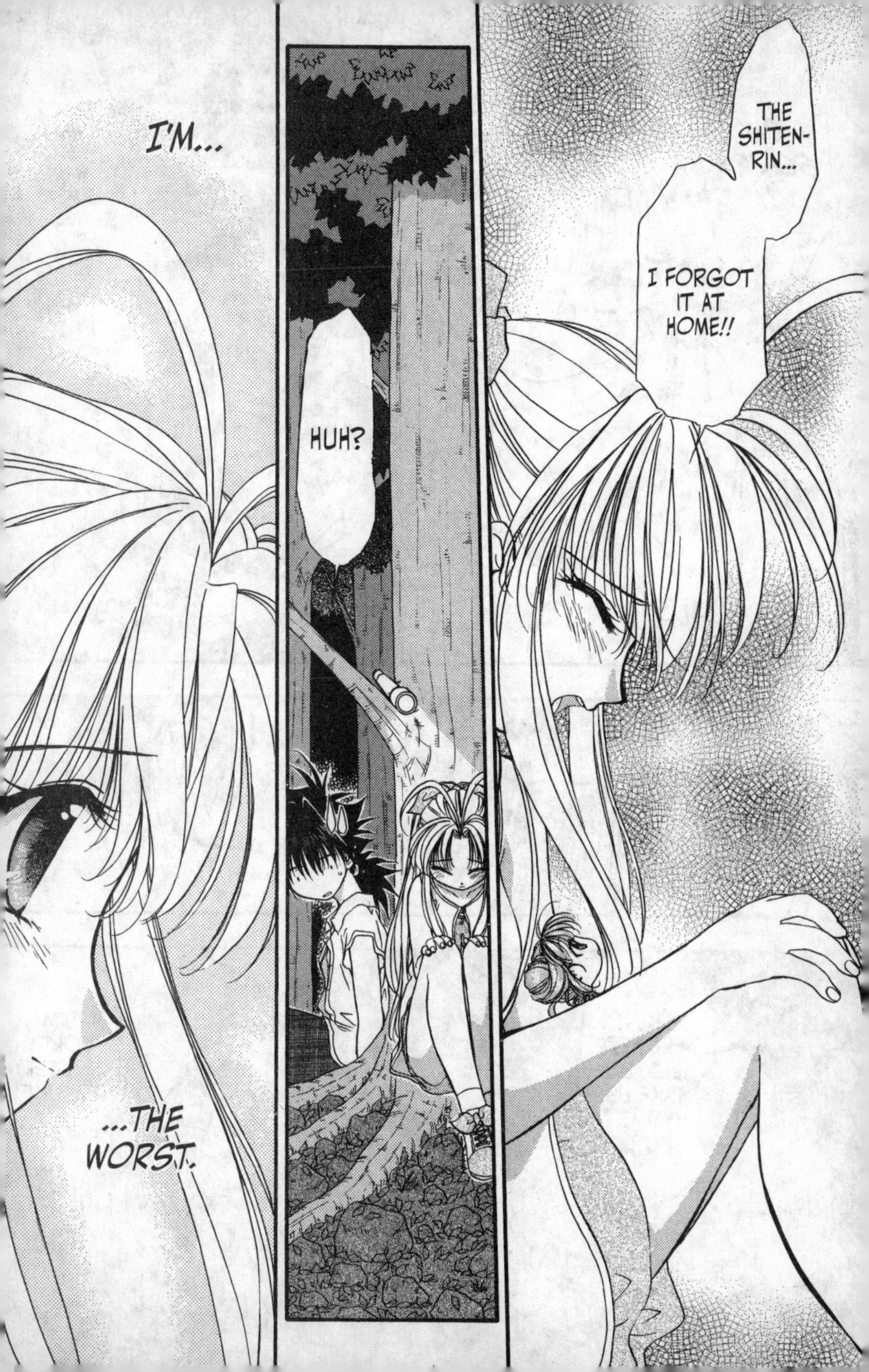
THE SHITEN-RIN...
I FORGOT IT AT HOME!!
HUH?
I'M...
...THE WORST.

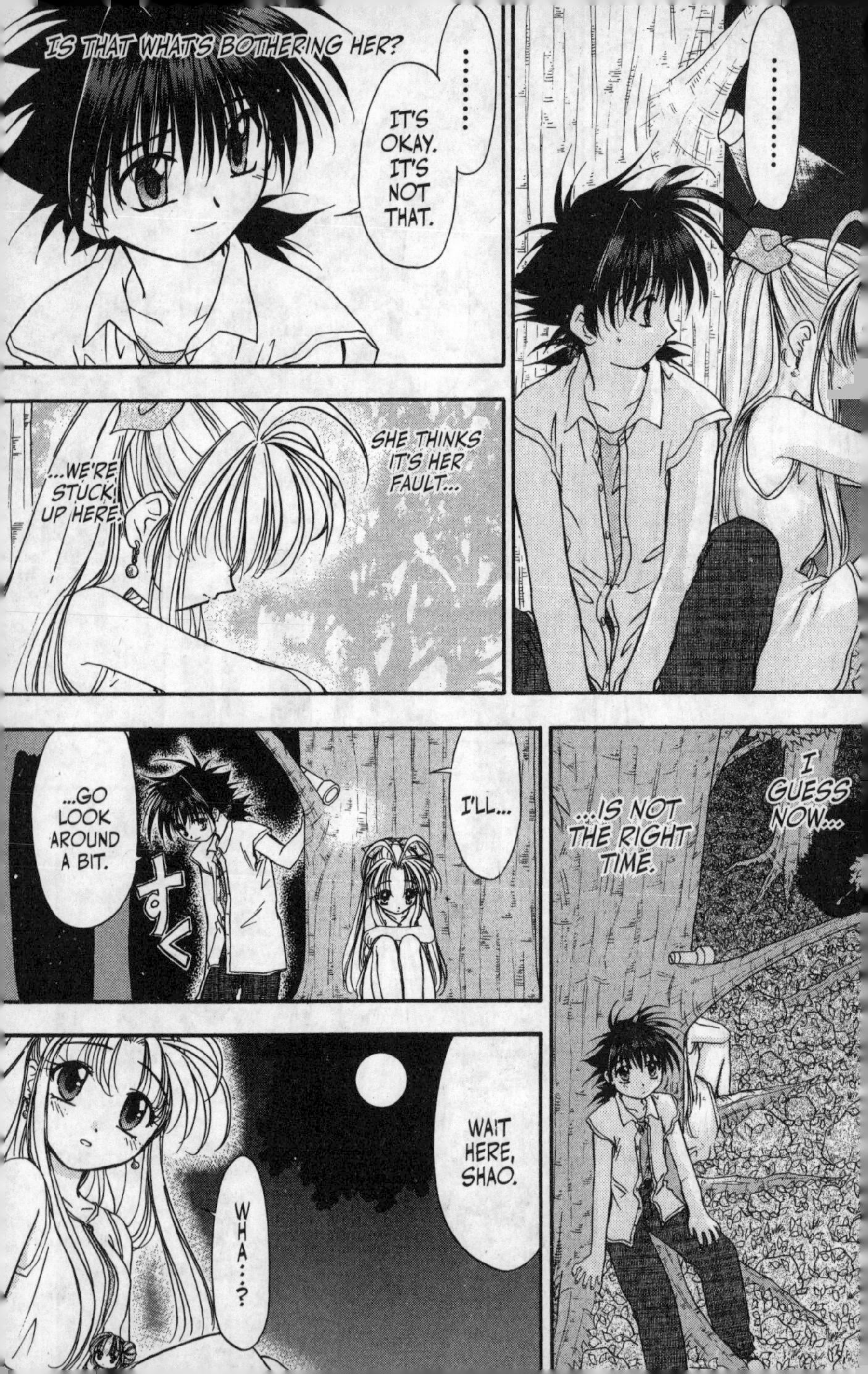
......
......
IT'S OKAY. IT'S NOT THAT.
IS THAT WHAT'S BOTHERING HER?
SHE THINKS IT'S HER FAULT...
...WE'RE STUCK UP HERE.
I GUESS NOW...
...IS NOT THE RIGHT TIME.
I'LL...
...GO LOOK AROUND A BIT.
すく
WAIT HERE, SHAO.
WHA...?

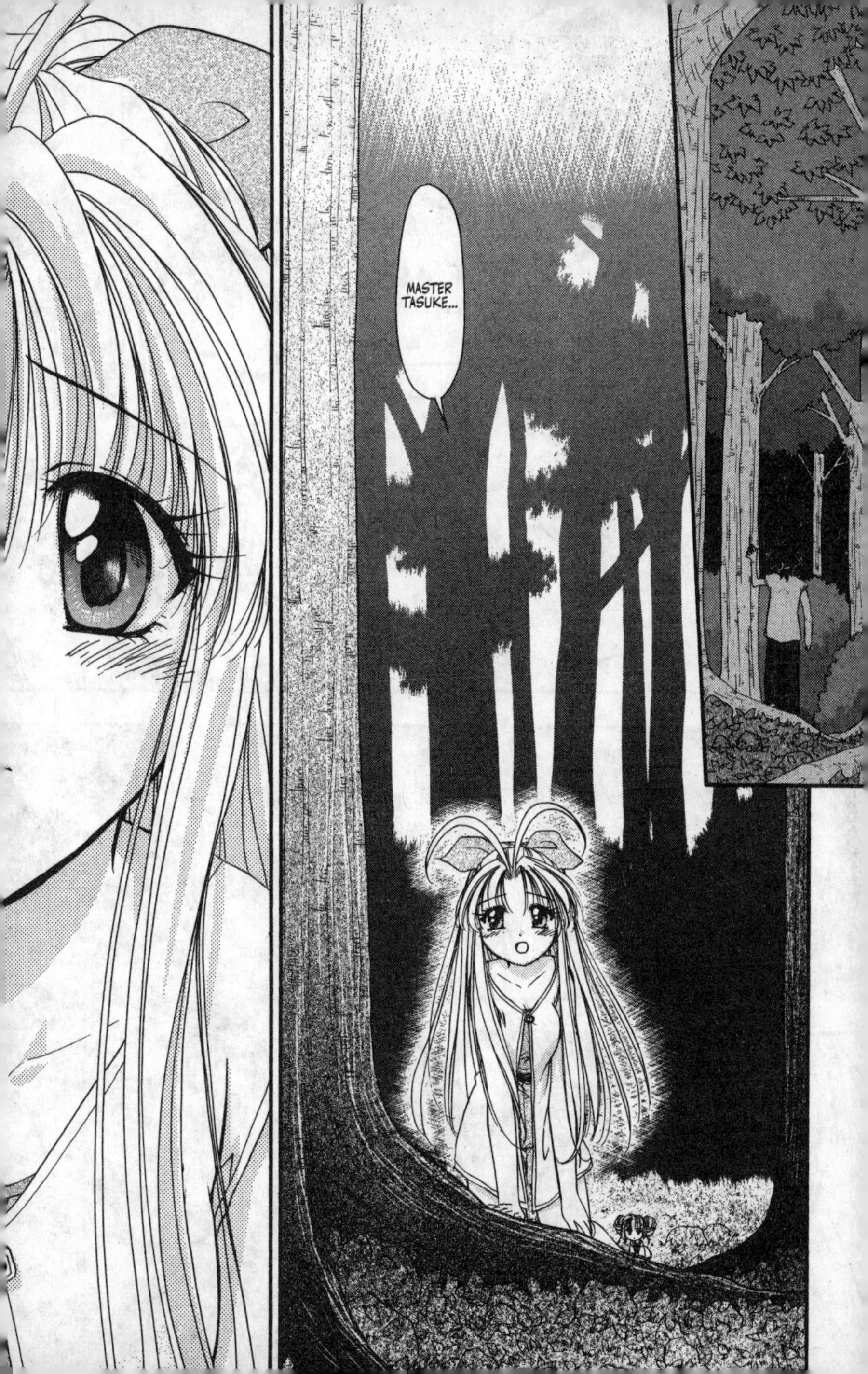
MASTER TASUKE...

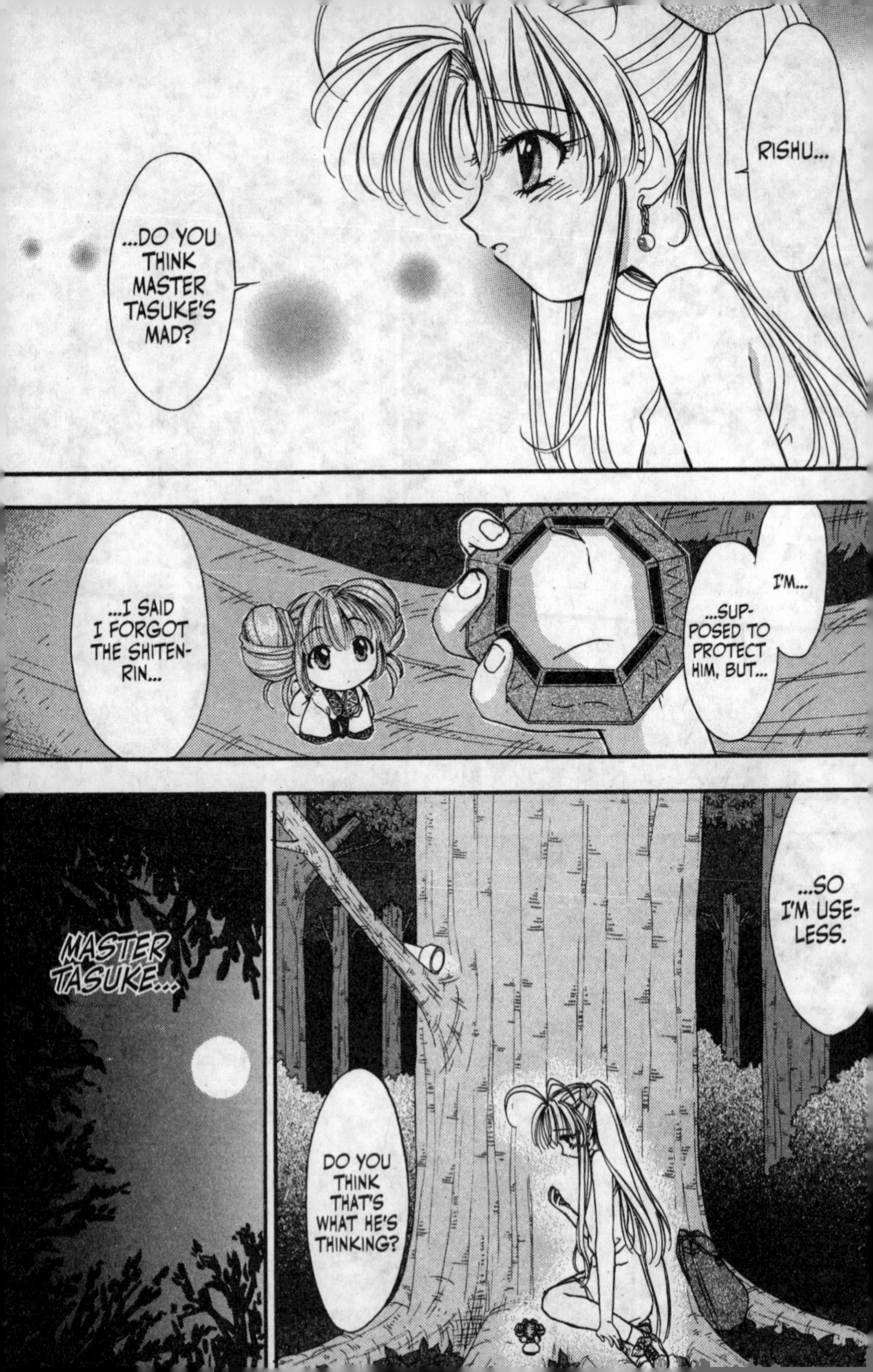
RISHU...
...DO YOU THINK MASTER TASUKE'S MAD?
I'M...
...SUP-POSED TO PROTECT HIM, BUT...
...I SAID I FORGOT THE SHITEN-RIN...
...SO I'M USE-LESS.
DO YOU THINK THAT'S WHAT HE'S THINKING?
MASTER TASUKE...

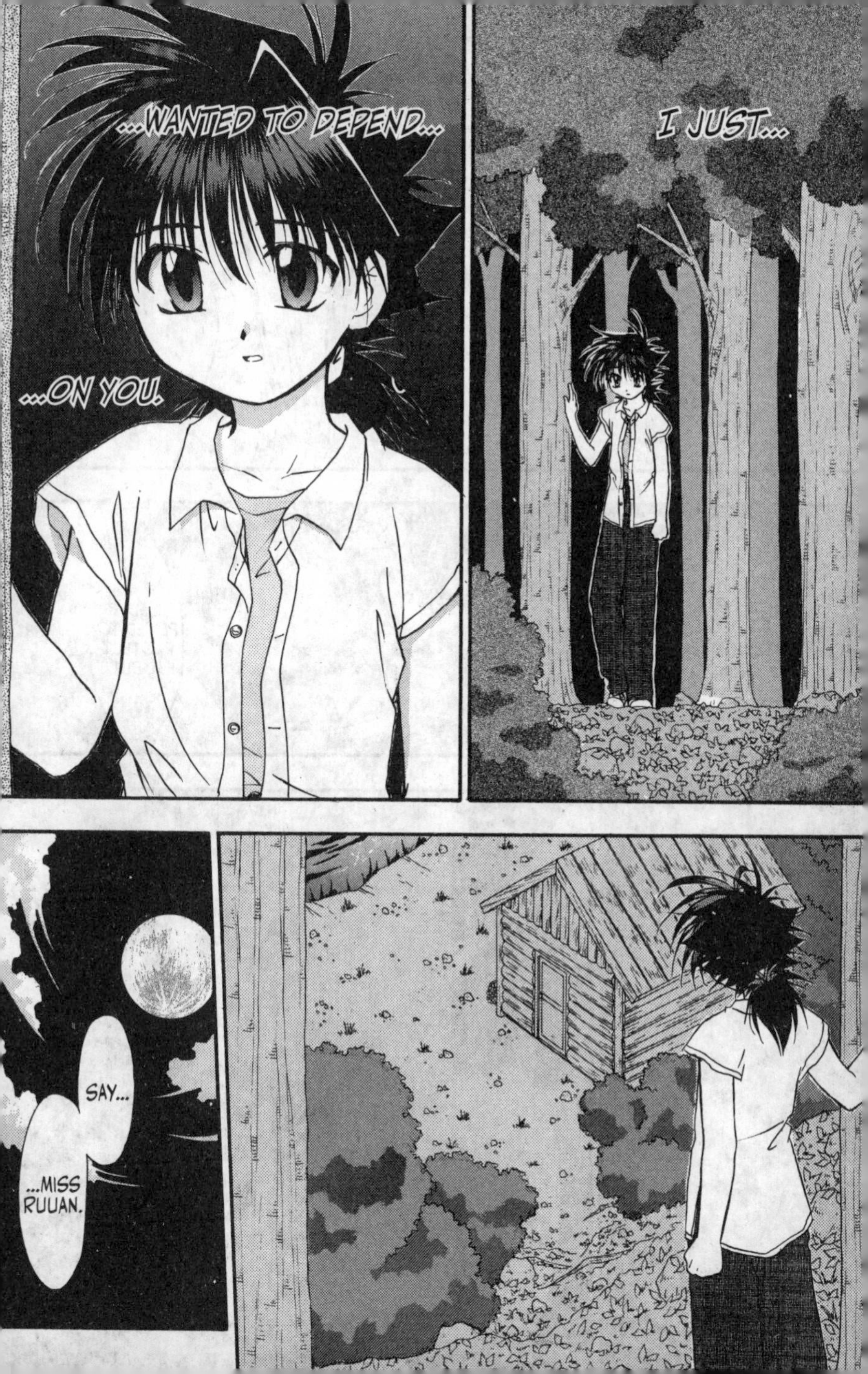
I JUST...
...WANTED TO DEPEND...
...ON YOU.
SAY...
...MISS RUUAN.

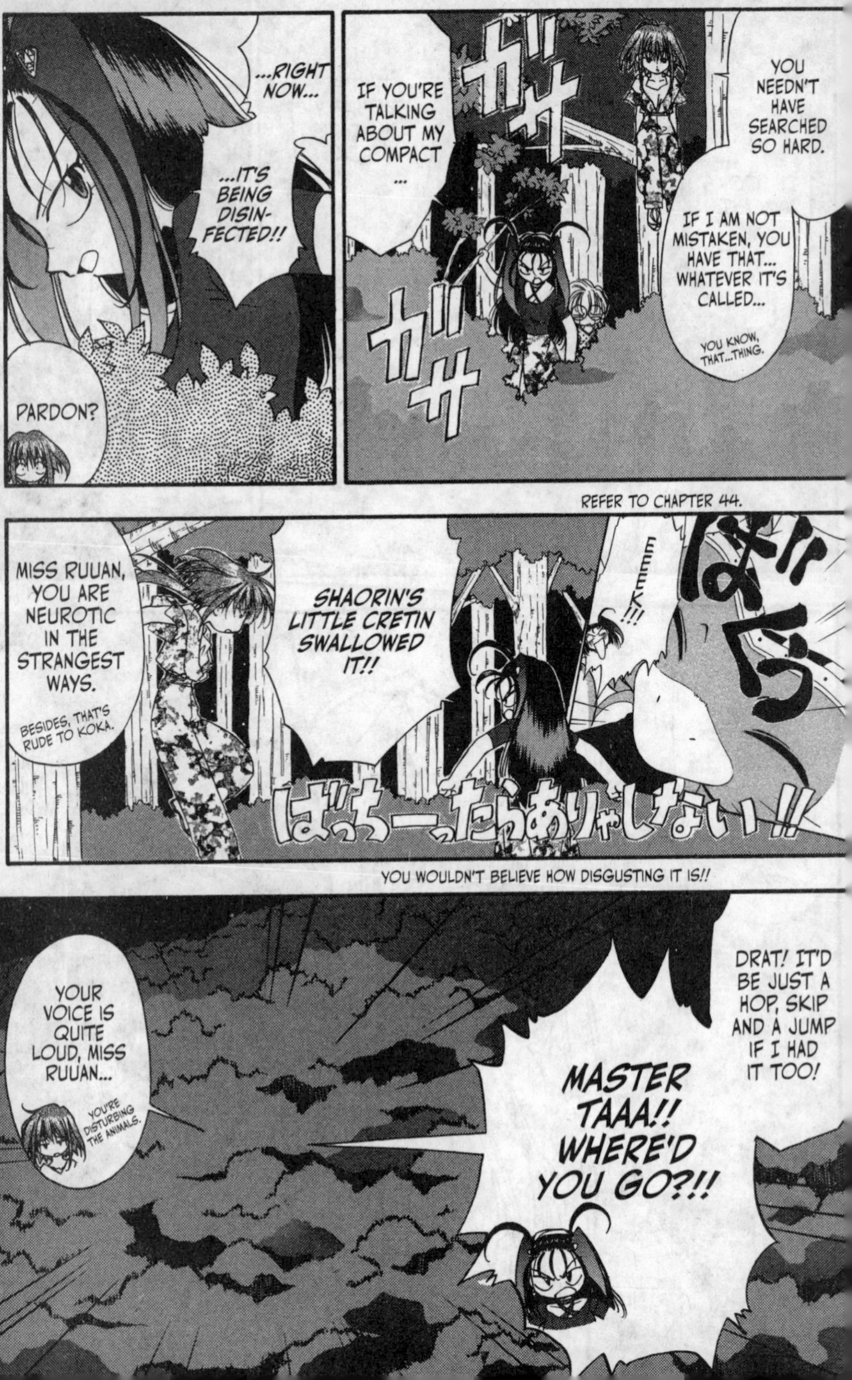
YOU NEEDN'T HAVE SEARCHED SO HARD.
IF I AM NOT MISTAKEN, YOU HAVE THAT... WHATEVER IT'S CALLED...
YOU KNOW, THAT...THING.
ガサ
ガサ
IF YOU'RE TALKING ABOUT MY COMPACT ...
...RIGHT NOW...
...IT'S BEING DISIN-FECTED!!
PARDON?
REFER TO CHAPTER 44.
EEEK!!!
SHAORIN'S LITTLE CRETIN SWALLOWED IT!!
ばっちーったらありゃしない!!
YOU WOULDN'T BELIEVE HOW DISGUSTING IT IS!!
MISS RUUAN, YOU ARE NEUROTIC IN THE STRANGEST WAYS.
BESIDES, THAT'S RUDE TO KOKA.
DRAT! IT'D BE JUST A HOP, SKIP AND A JUMP IF I HAD IT TOO!
MASTER TAAA!! WHERE'D YOU GO?!!
YOUR VOICE IS QUITE LOUD, MISS RUUAN...
YOU'RE DISTURBING THE ANIMALS.

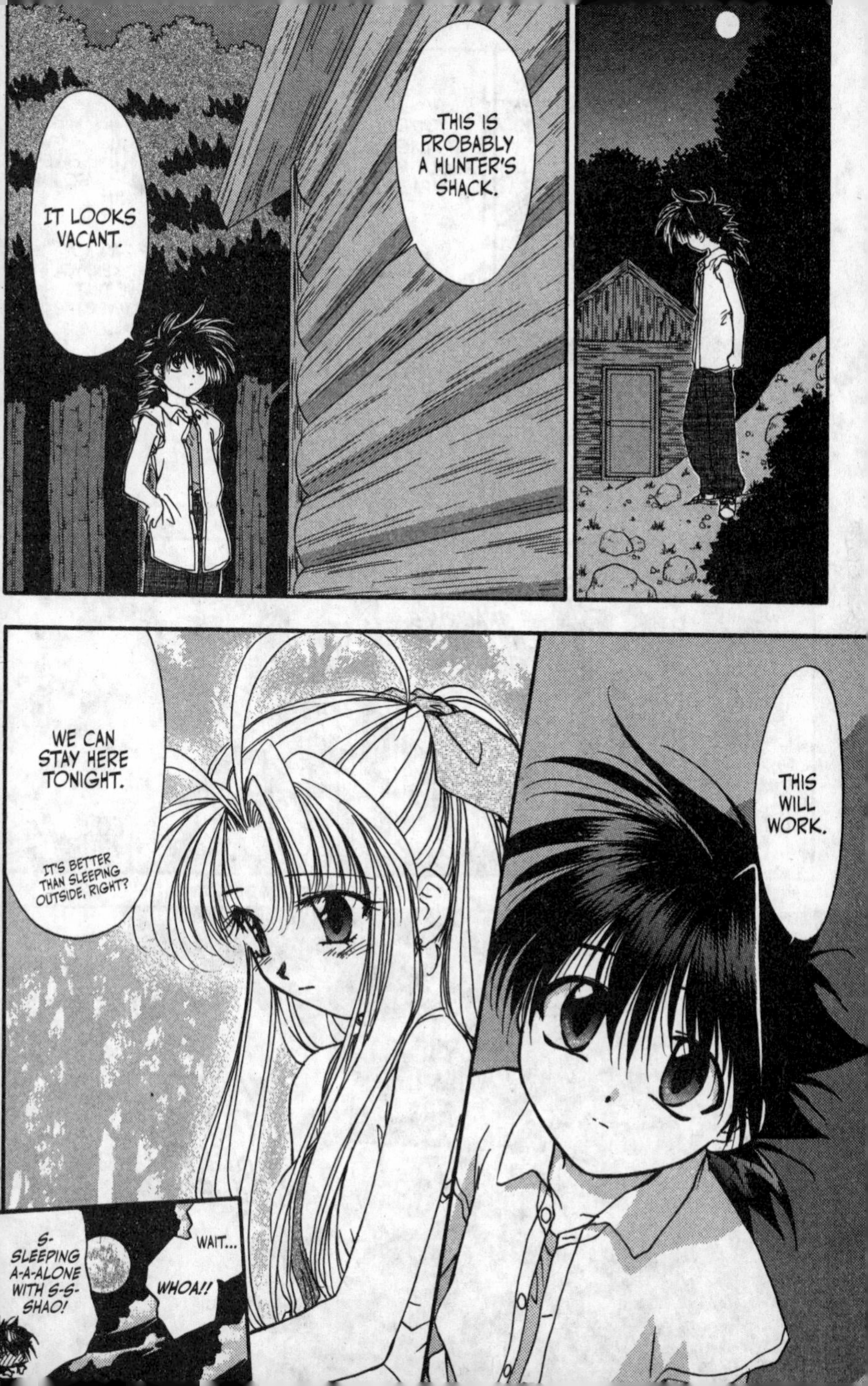
THIS IS PROBABLY A HUNTER'S SHACK.
IT LOOKS VACANT.
THIS WILL WORK.
WE CAN STAY HERE TONIGHT.
IT'S BETTER THAN SLEEPING OUTSIDE, RIGHT?
WAIT...
S-SLEEPING A-A-ALONE WITH S-S-SHAO!
WHOA!!

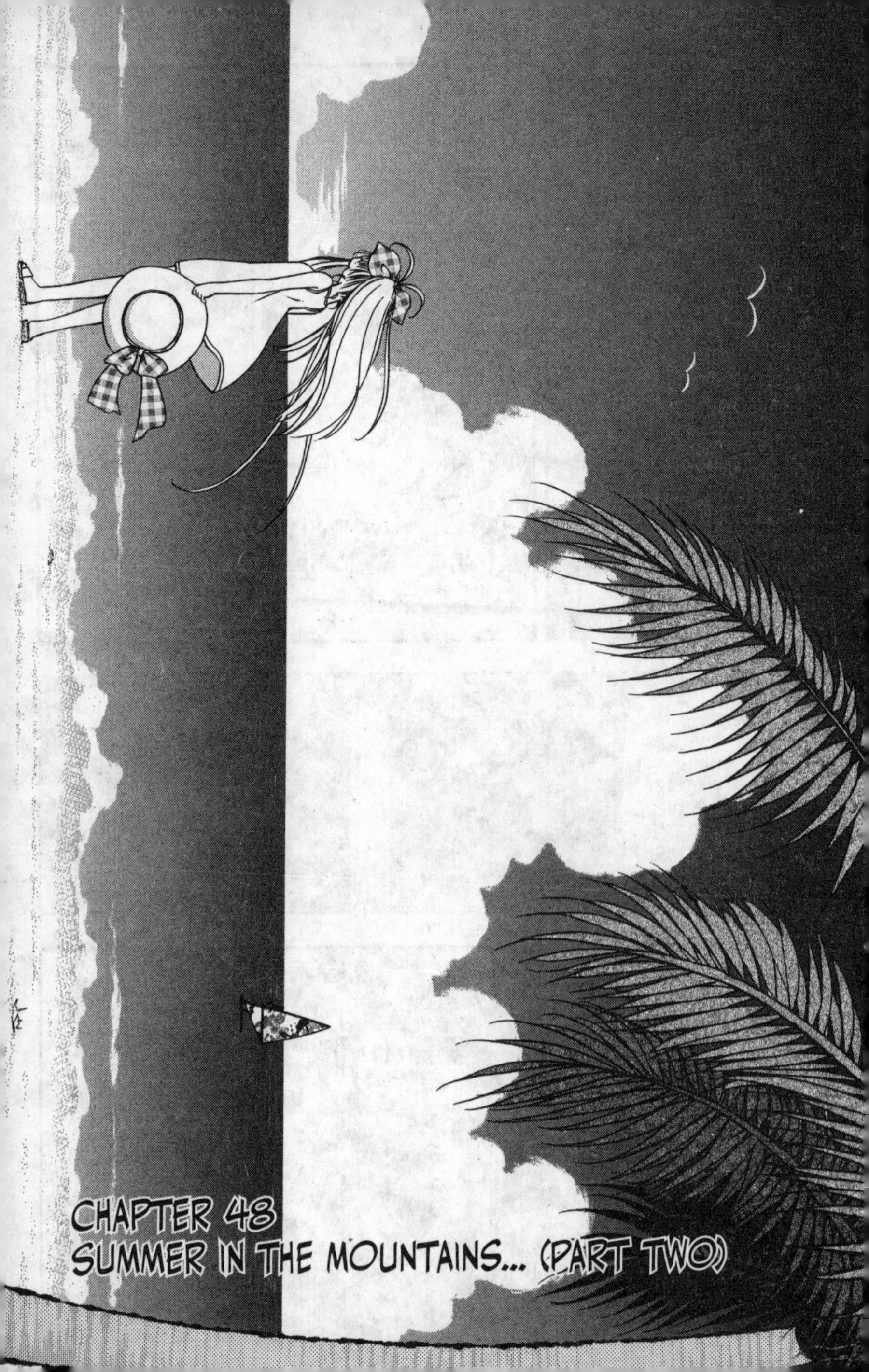
CHAPTER 48
SUMMER IN THE MOUNTAINS... (PART TWO)

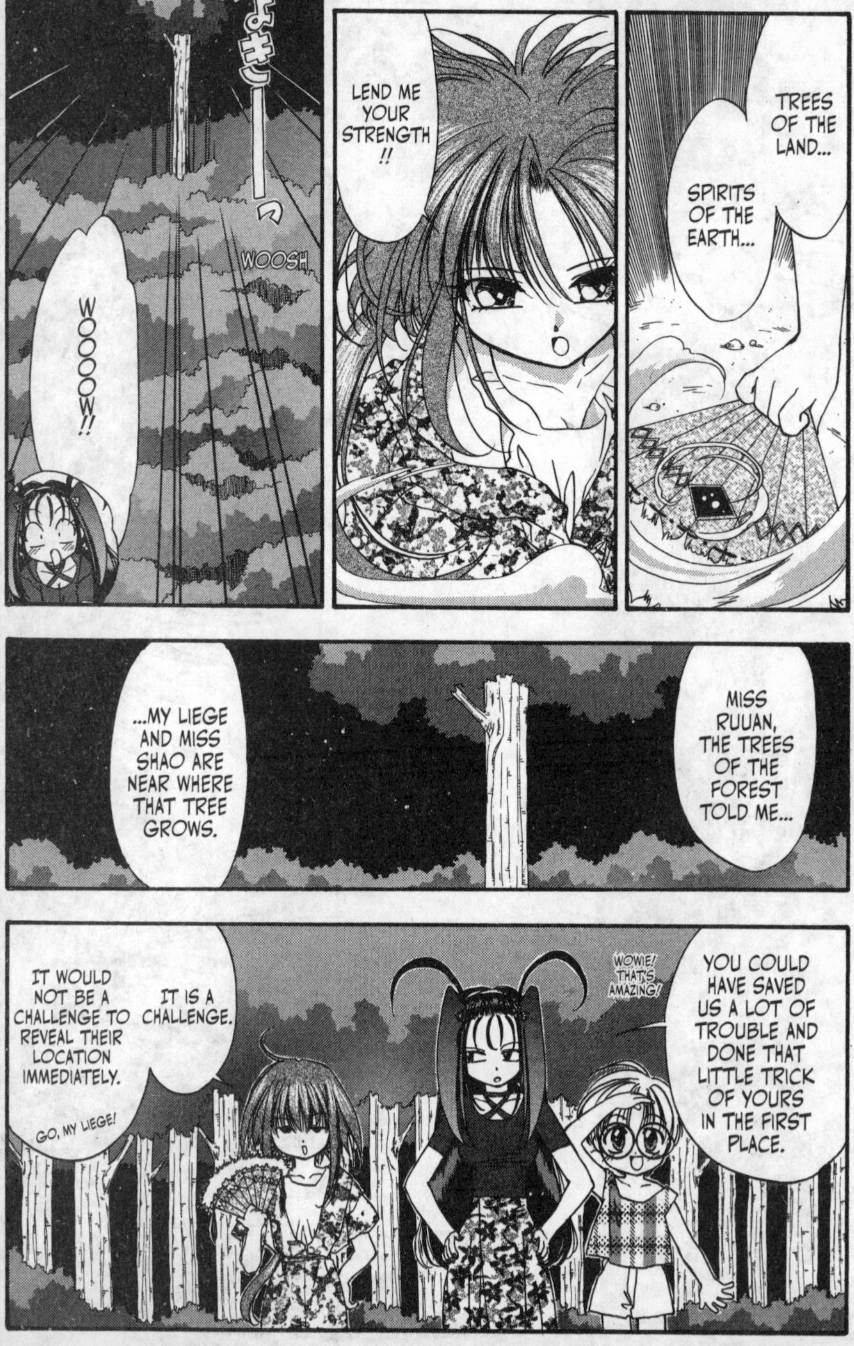
TREES OF THE LAND...
SPIRITS OF THE EARTH...
LEND ME YOUR STRENGTH!!
にょきーっ
WOOSH
WOOOOOW!!
MISS RUUAN, THE TREES OF THE FOREST TOLD ME...
...MY LIEGE AND MISS SHAO ARE NEAR WHERE THAT TREE GROWS.
YOU COULD HAVE SAVED US A LOT OF TROUBLE AND DONE THAT LITTLE TRICK OF YOURS IN THE FIRST PLACE.
WOWIE! THAT'S AMAZING!
IT IS A CHALLENGE.
IT WOULD NOT BE A CHALLENGE TO REVEAL THEIR LOCATION IMMEDIATELY.
GO, MY LIEGE!

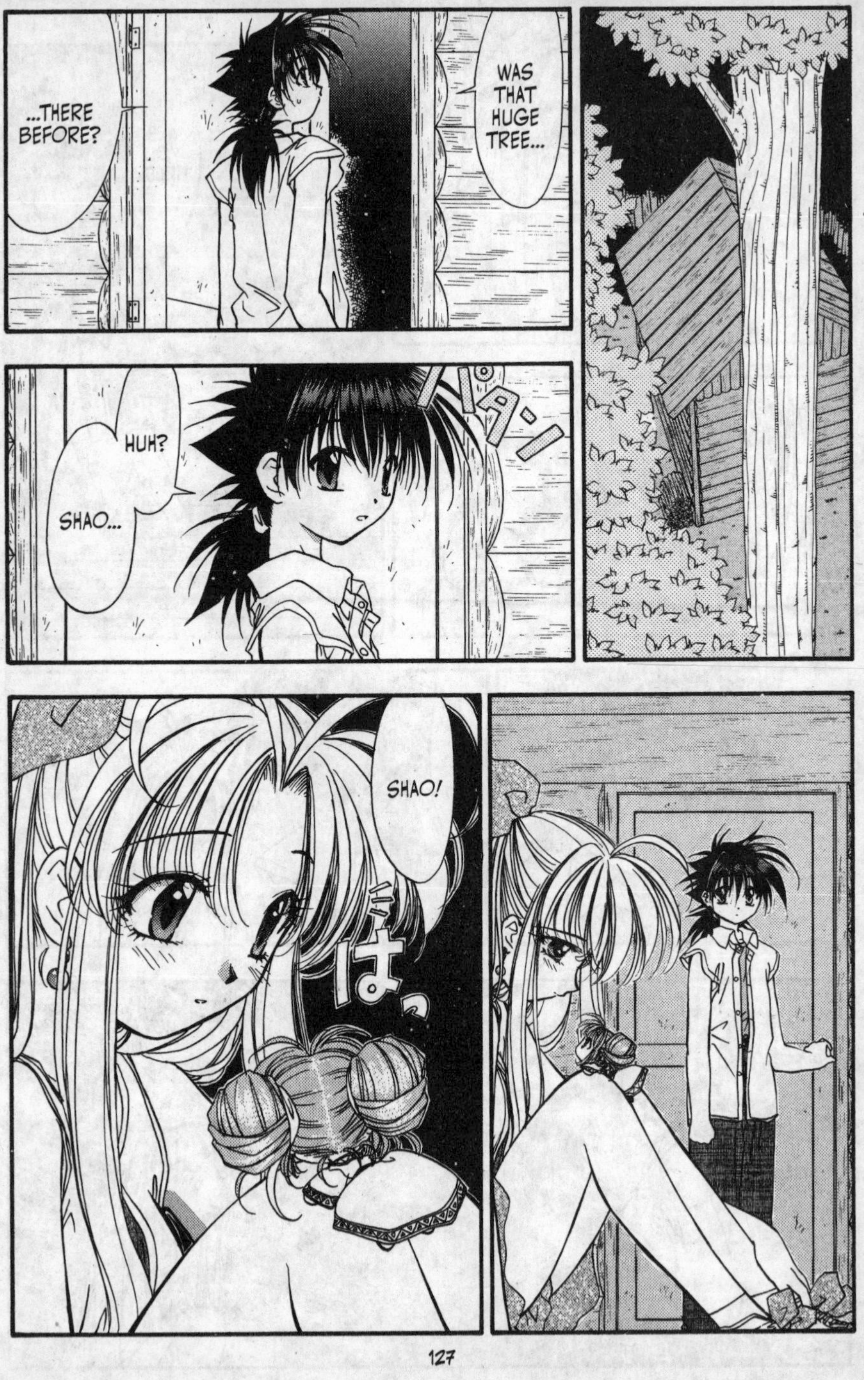
WAS THAT HUGE TREE...
...THERE BEFORE?
パタン
HUH?
SHAO...
SHAO!
はっ

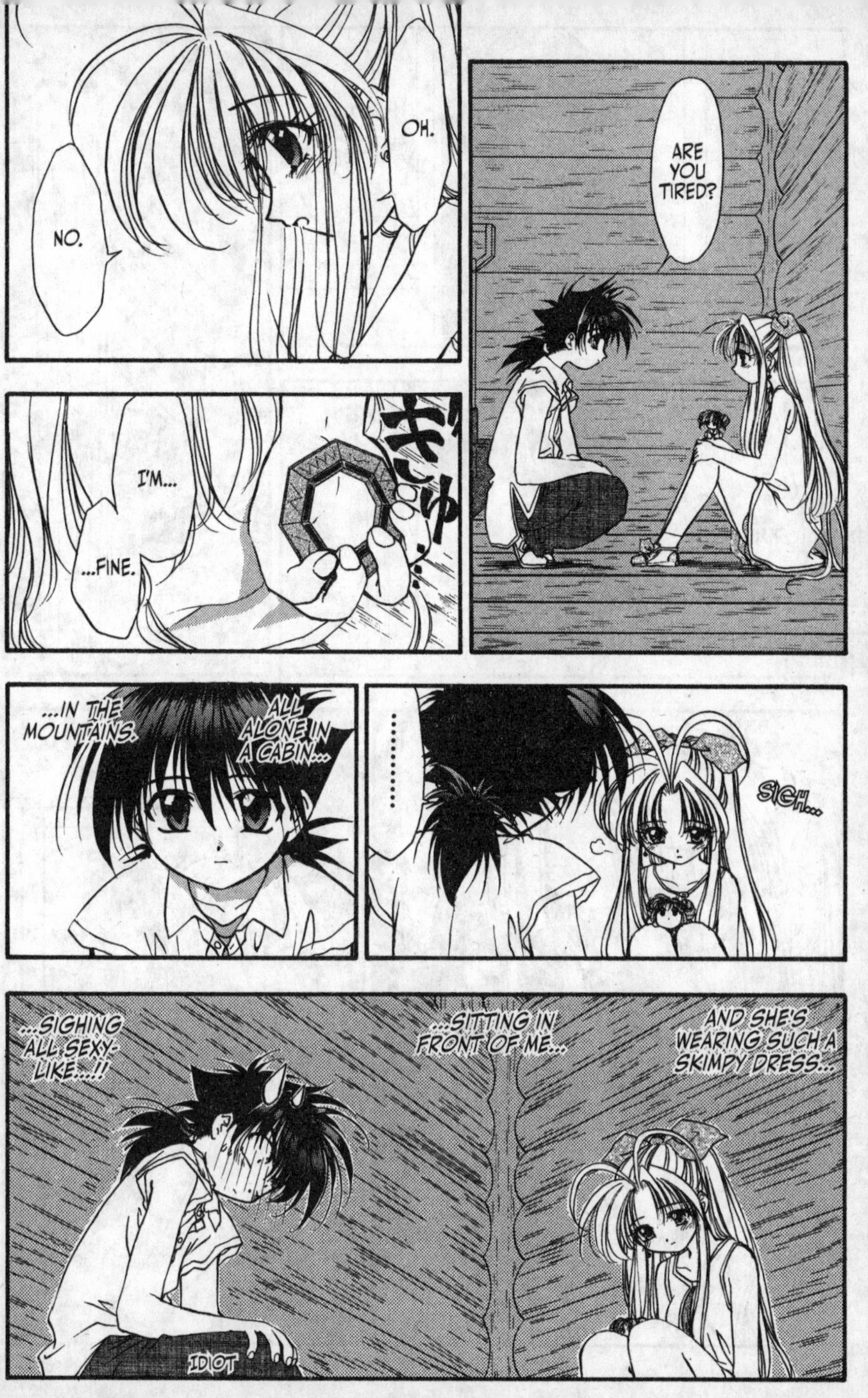
ARE YOU TIRED?
OH.
NO.
ぎゅ...
I'M...
...FINE.
SIGH...
......
ALL ALONE IN A CABIN...
...IN THE MOUNTAINS.
AND SHE'S WEARING SUCH A SKIMPY DRESS...
...SITTING IN FRONT OF ME...
...SIGHING ALL SEXY-LIKE...!!
IDIOT

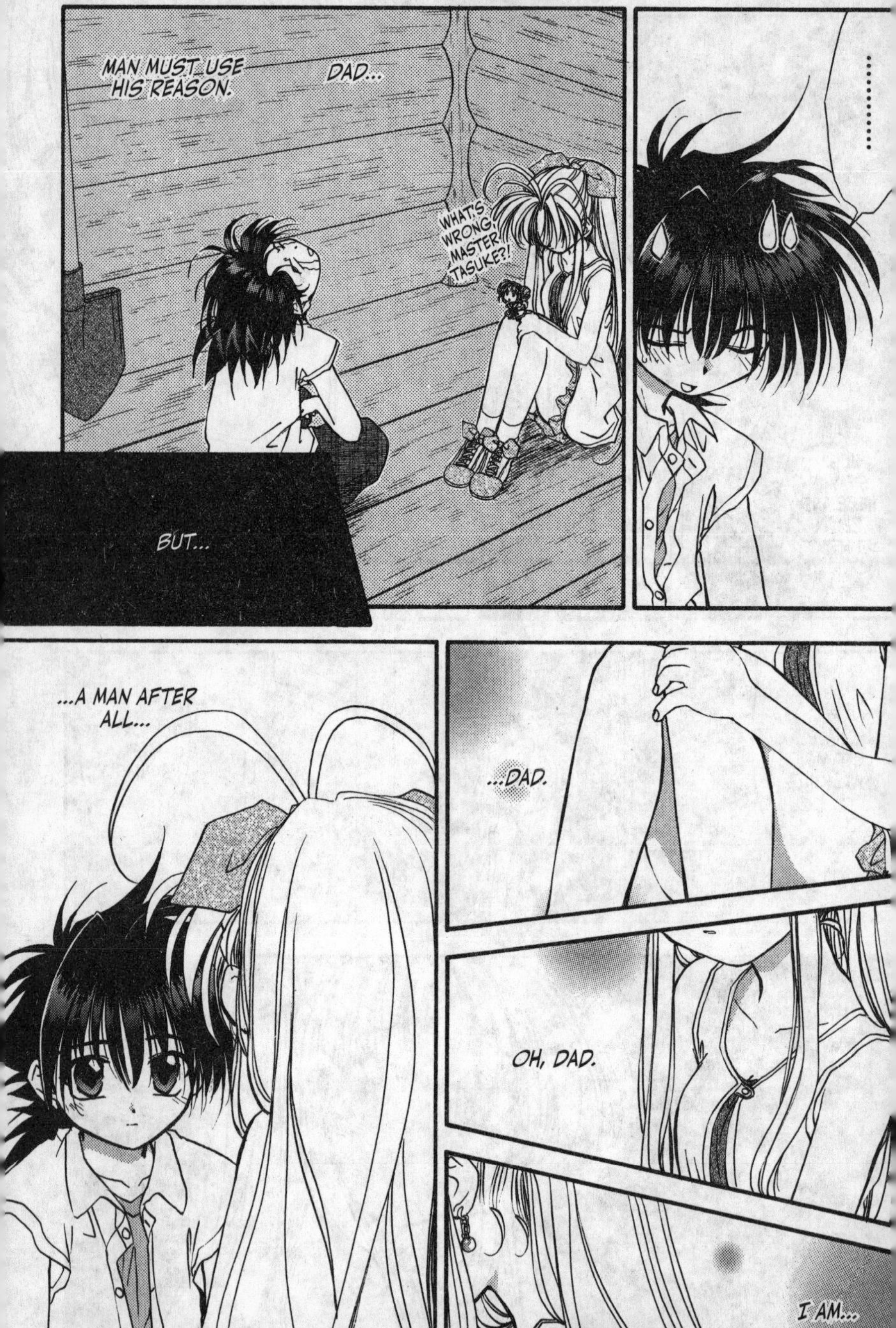
......
DAD...
MAN MUST USE HIS REASON.
WHAT'S WRONG MASTER TASUKE?!
BUT...
...DAD.
OH, DAD.
I AM...
...A MAN AFTER ALL...

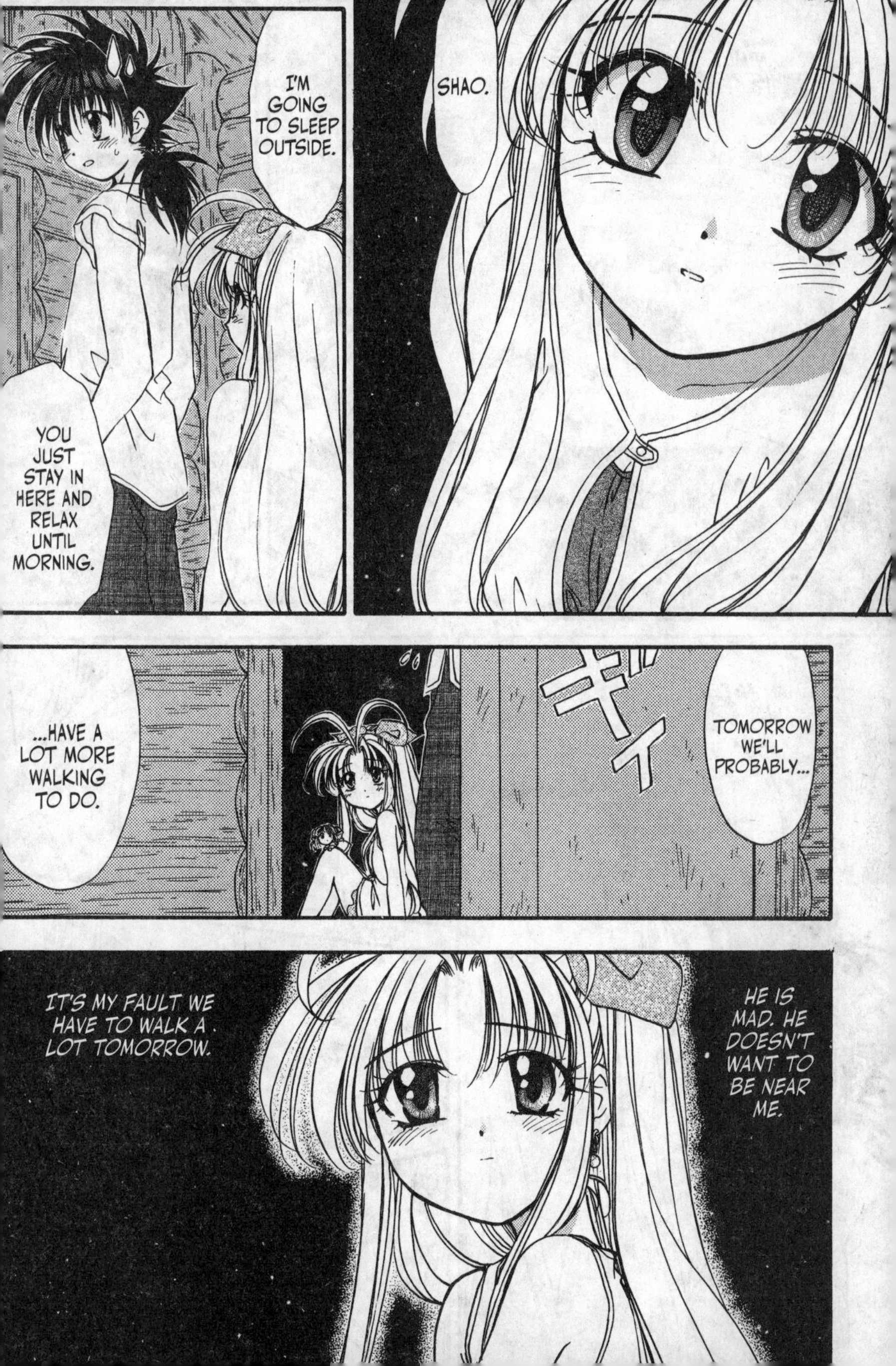
SHAO.
I'M GOING TO SLEEP OUTSIDE.
YOU JUST STAY IN HERE AND RELAX UNTIL MORNING.
TOMORROW WE'LL PROBABLY...
ギィ
...HAVE A LOT MORE WALKING TO DO.
HE IS MAD. HE DOESN'T WANT TO BE NEAR ME.
IT'S MY FAULT WE HAVE TO WALK A LOT TOMORROW.

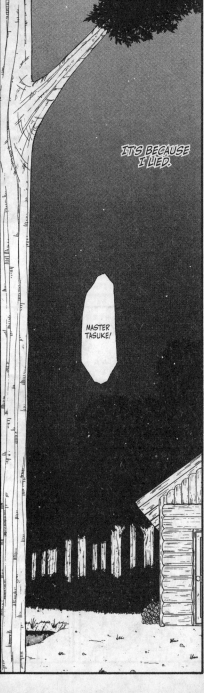

IT'S BECAUSE I LIED.

MASTER TASUKE!

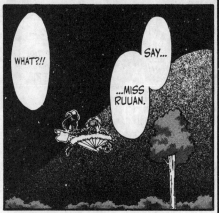

WHAT?!!

SAY...

...MISS RUUAN.

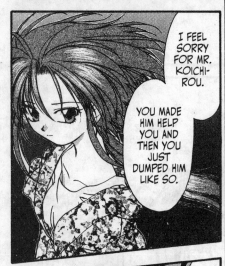

I FEEL SORRY FOR MR. KOICHIROU.

YOU MADE HIM HELP YOU AND THEN YOU JUST DUMPED HIM LIKE SO.

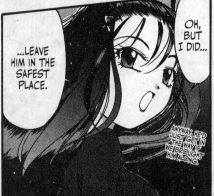

OH, BUT I DID...

...LEAVE HIM IN THE SAFEST PLACE.

ANYWAY HE'D JUST GET IN THE WAY IF WE BROUGHT HIM ALONG.

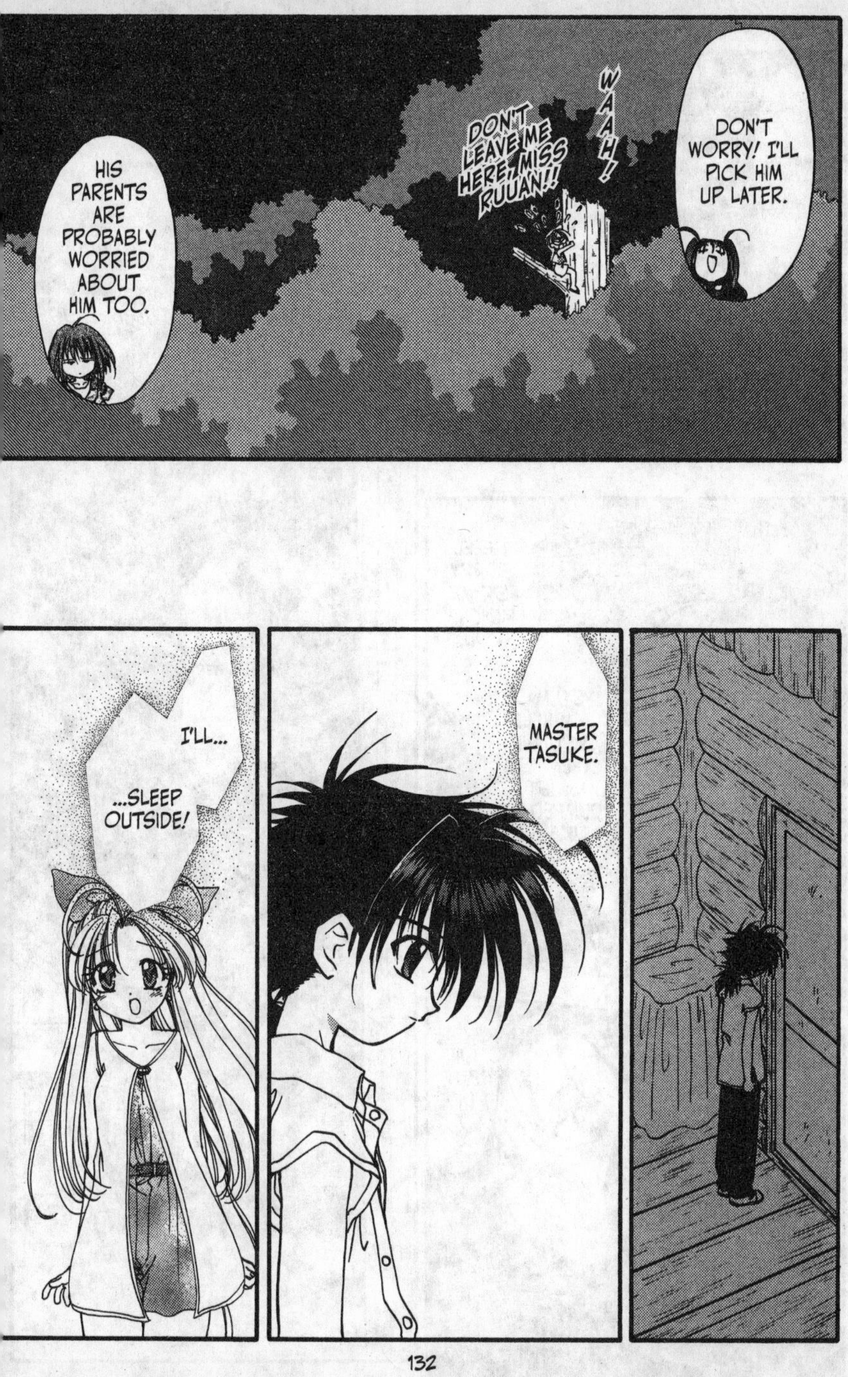
DON'T WORRY! I'LL PICK HIM UP LATER.
WAAAH!
DON'T LEAVE ME HERE, MISS RUUAN!!
HIS PARENTS ARE PROBABLY WORRIED ABOUT HIM TOO.
MASTER TASUKE.
I'LL...
...SLEEP OUTSIDE!

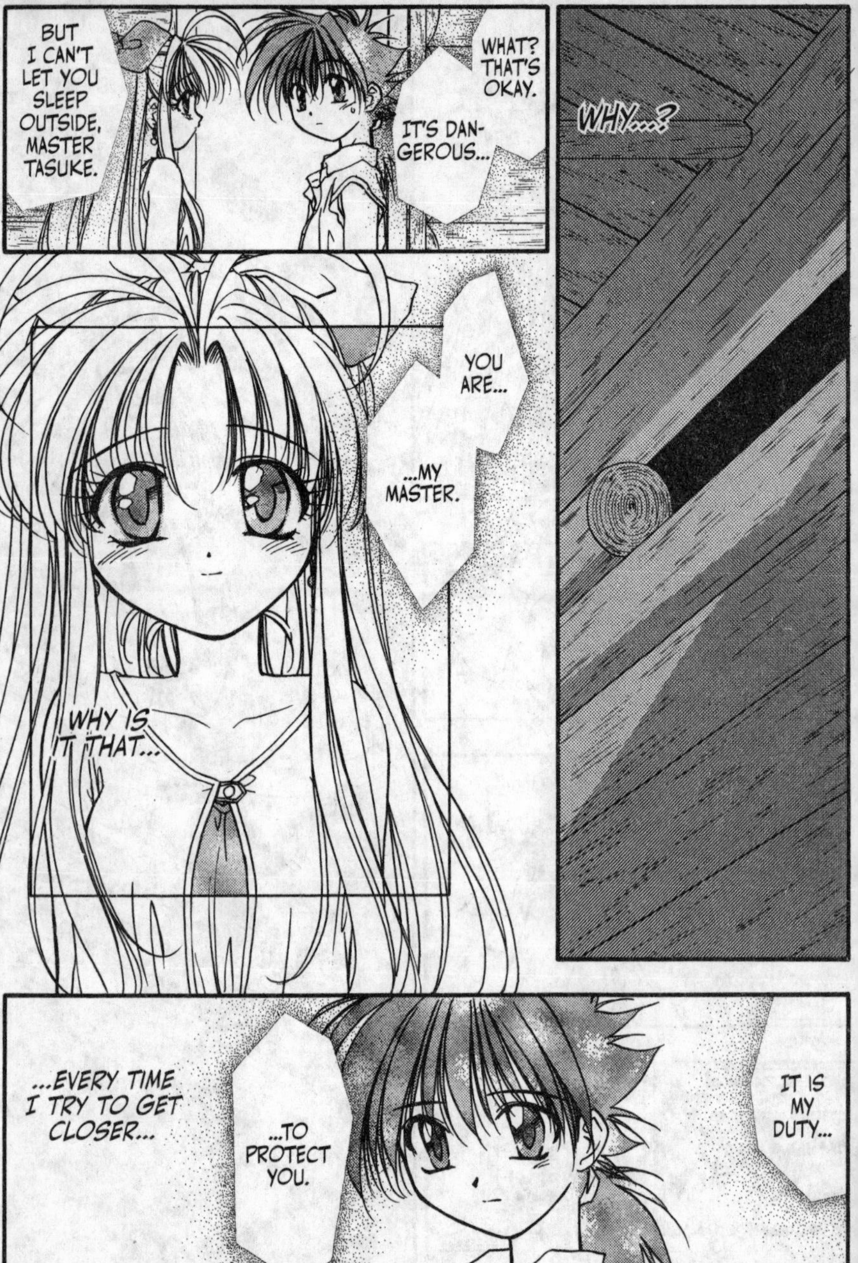
WHY...?
WHAT? THAT'S OKAY.
IT'S DAN-GEROUS...
BUT I CAN'T LET YOU SLEEP OUTSIDE, MASTER TASUKE.
YOU ARE...
...MY MASTER.
WHY IS IT THAT...
IT IS MY DUTY...
...TO PROTECT YOU.
...EVERY TIME I TRY TO GET CLOSER...

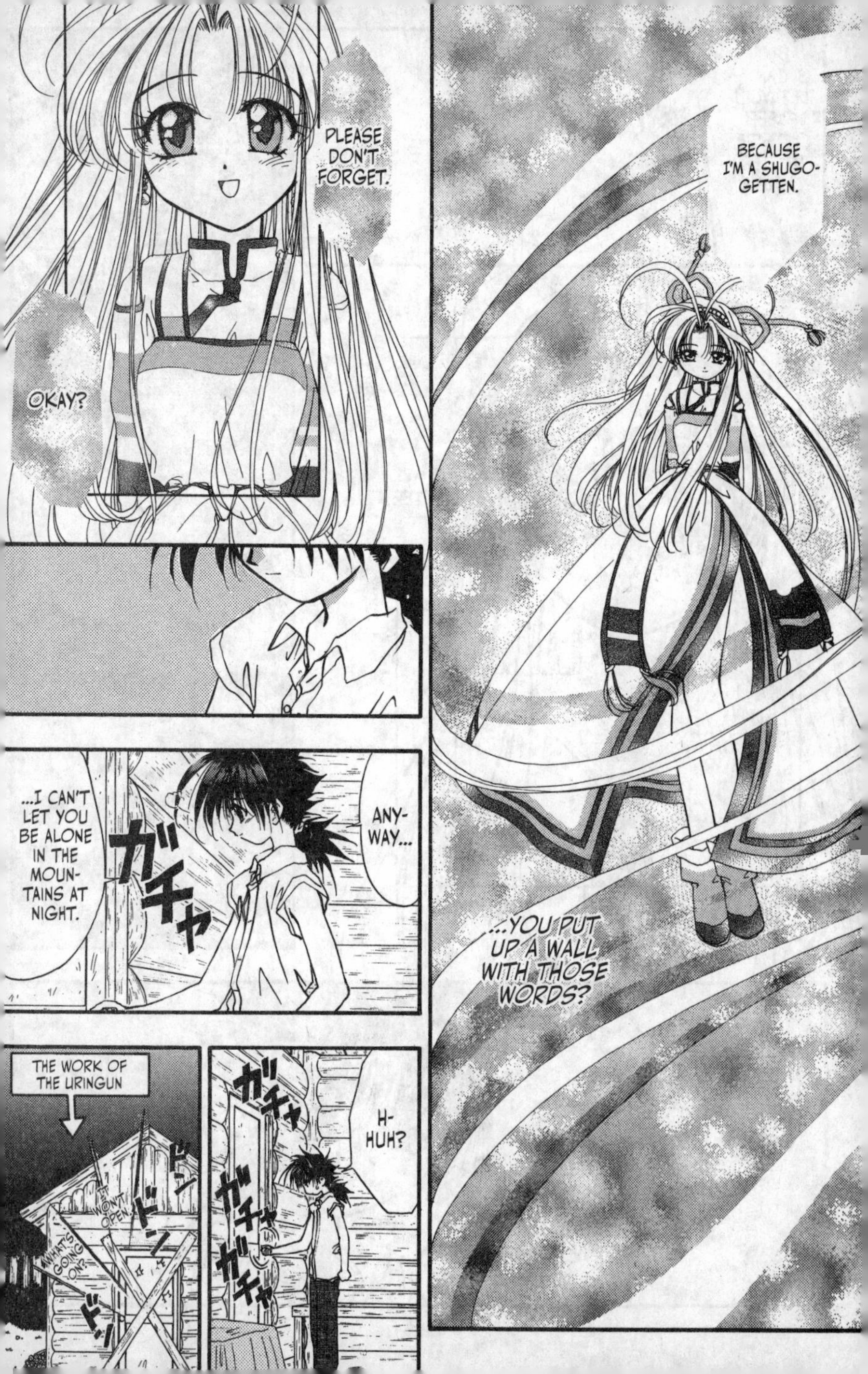
BECAUSE I'M A SHUGO-GETTEN.
...YOU PUT UP A WALL WITH THOSE WORDS?
PLEASE DON'T FORGET.
OKAY?
ANY-WAY...
...I CAN'T LET YOU BE ALONE IN THE MOUN-TAINS AT NIGHT.
ガチャ
H-HUH?
ガチャ
ガチャガチャ
THE WORK OF THE URINGUN
ドン
ドン
IT WON'T OPEN.
WHAT'S GOING ON?
ドン

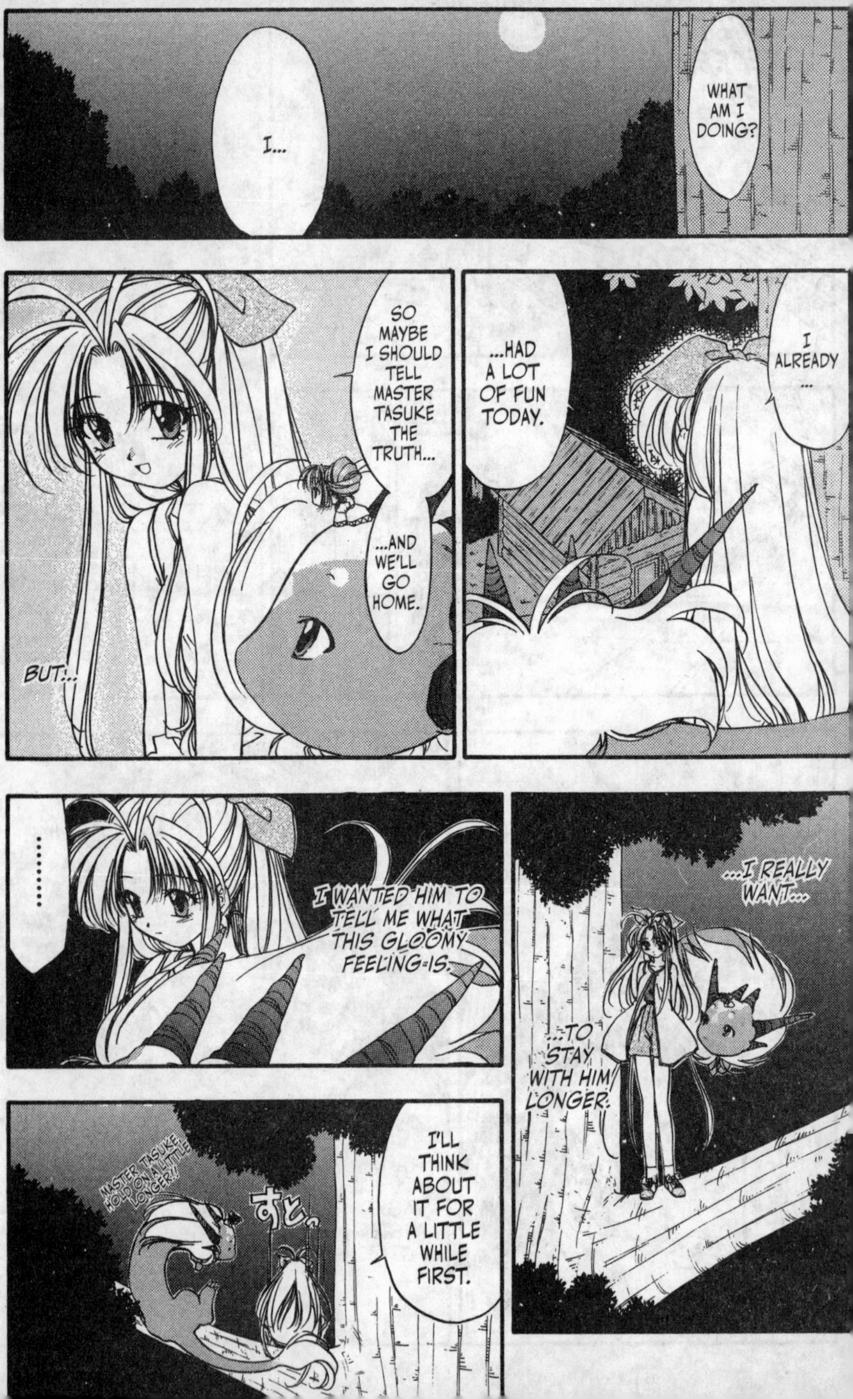
WHAT AM I DOING?
I...
I ALREADY ...
...HAD A LOT OF FUN TODAY.
SO MAYBE I SHOULD TELL MASTER TASUKE THE TRUTH...
...AND WE'LL GO HOME.
BUT...
...I REALLY WANT...
...TO STAY WITH HIM LONGER.
......
I WANTED HIM TO TELL ME WHAT THIS GLOOMY FEELING IS.
I'LL THINK ABOUT IT FOR A LITTLE WHILE FIRST.
MASTER TASUKE, HOLD ON A LITTLE LONGER!!
すとっ

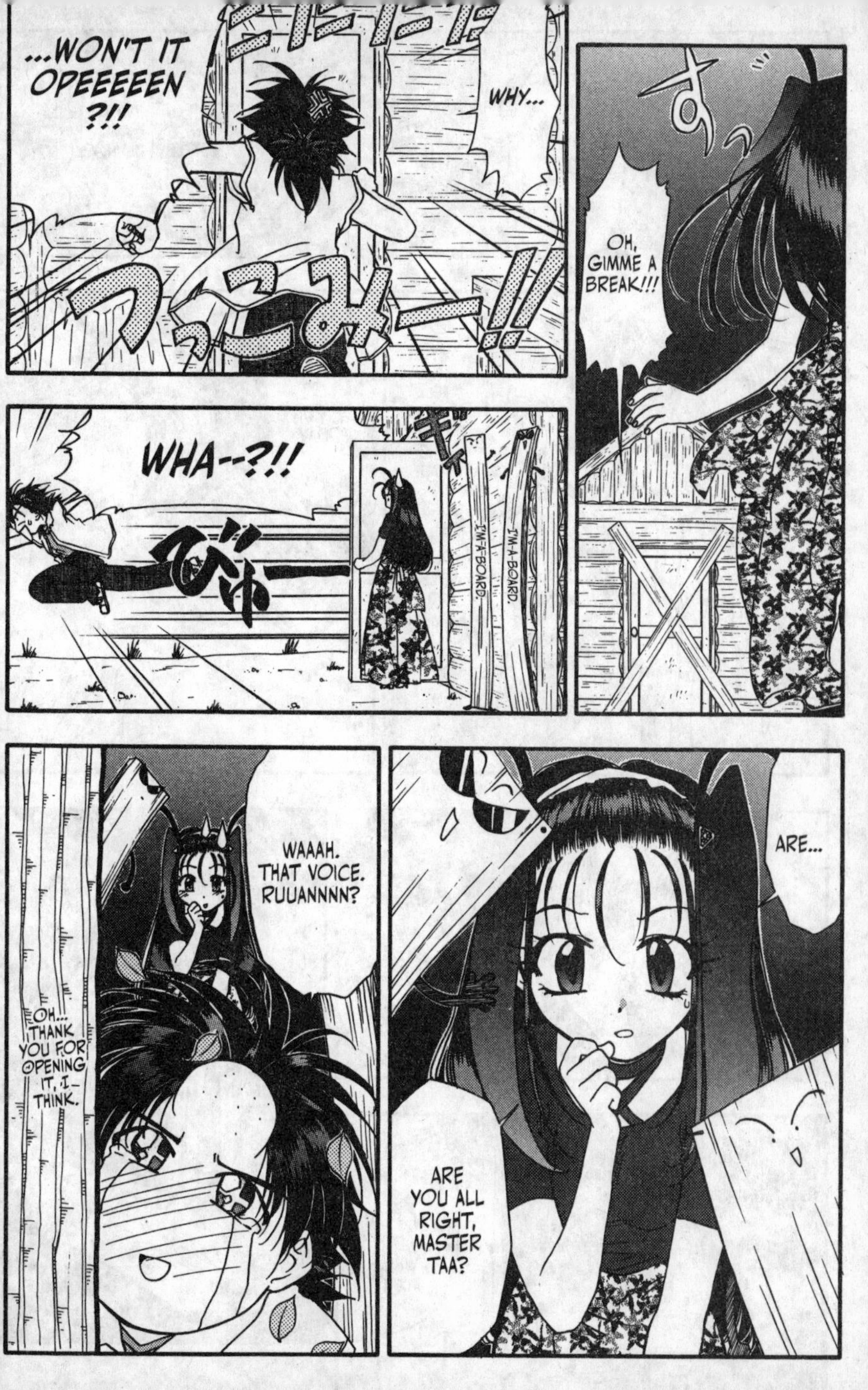
すっ
OH, GIMME A BREAK!!!
WHY...
...WON'T IT OPEEEEEN?!!
つっこみー!!
I'M-A-BOARD.
I'M-A-BOARD.
WHA--?!!
びゅー
ARE...
ARE YOU ALL RIGHT, MASTER TAA?
WAAAH. THAT VOICE. RUUANNNN?
OH... THANK YOU FOR OPENING IT, I-THINK.

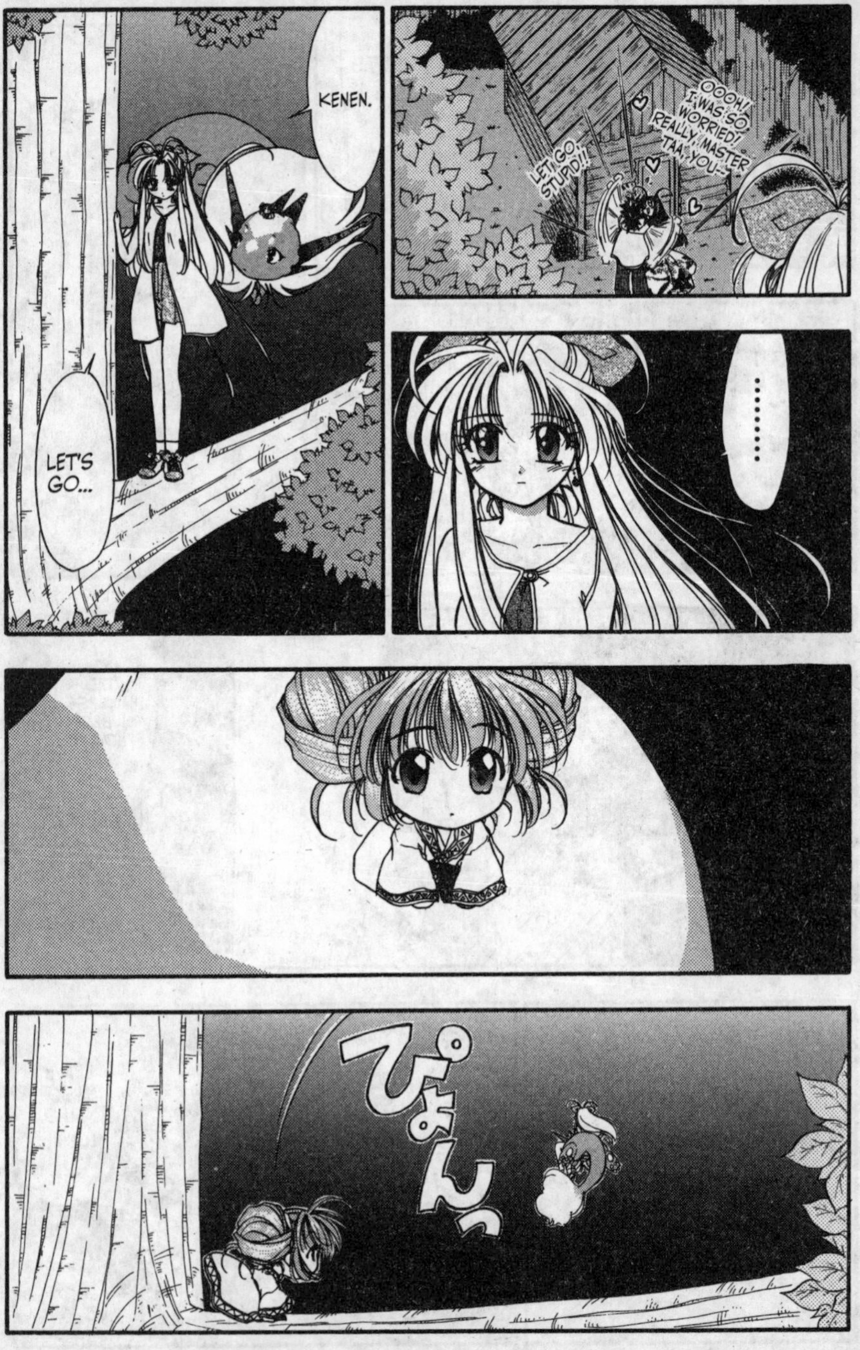
OOOH! I WAS SO WORRIED! REALLY, MASTER TAA, YOU--
LET GO, STUPID!!
......
KENEN.
LET'S GO...
ぴょんっ

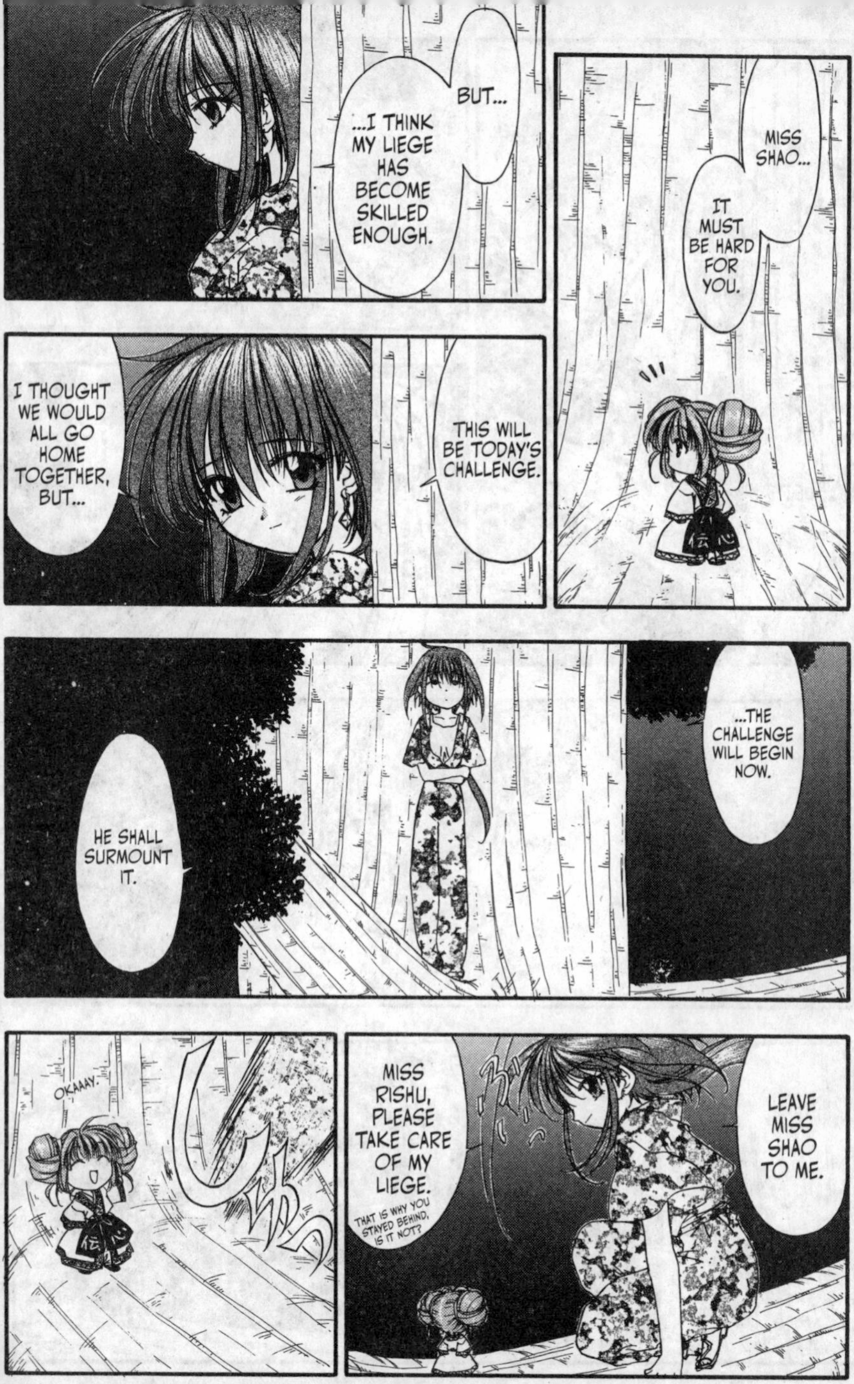
MISS SHAO...
IT MUST BE HARD FOR YOU.
BUT...
...I THINK MY LIEGE HAS BECOME SKILLED ENOUGH.
THIS WILL BE TODAY'S CHALLENGE.
I THOUGHT WE WOULD ALL GO HOME TOGETHER, BUT...
...THE CHALLENGE WILL BEGIN NOW.
HE SHALL SURMOUNT IT.
LEAVE MISS SHAO TO ME.
MISS RISHU, PLEASE TAKE CARE OF MY LIEGE.
THAT IS WHY YOU STAYED BEHIND, IS IT NOT?
OKAAAY.

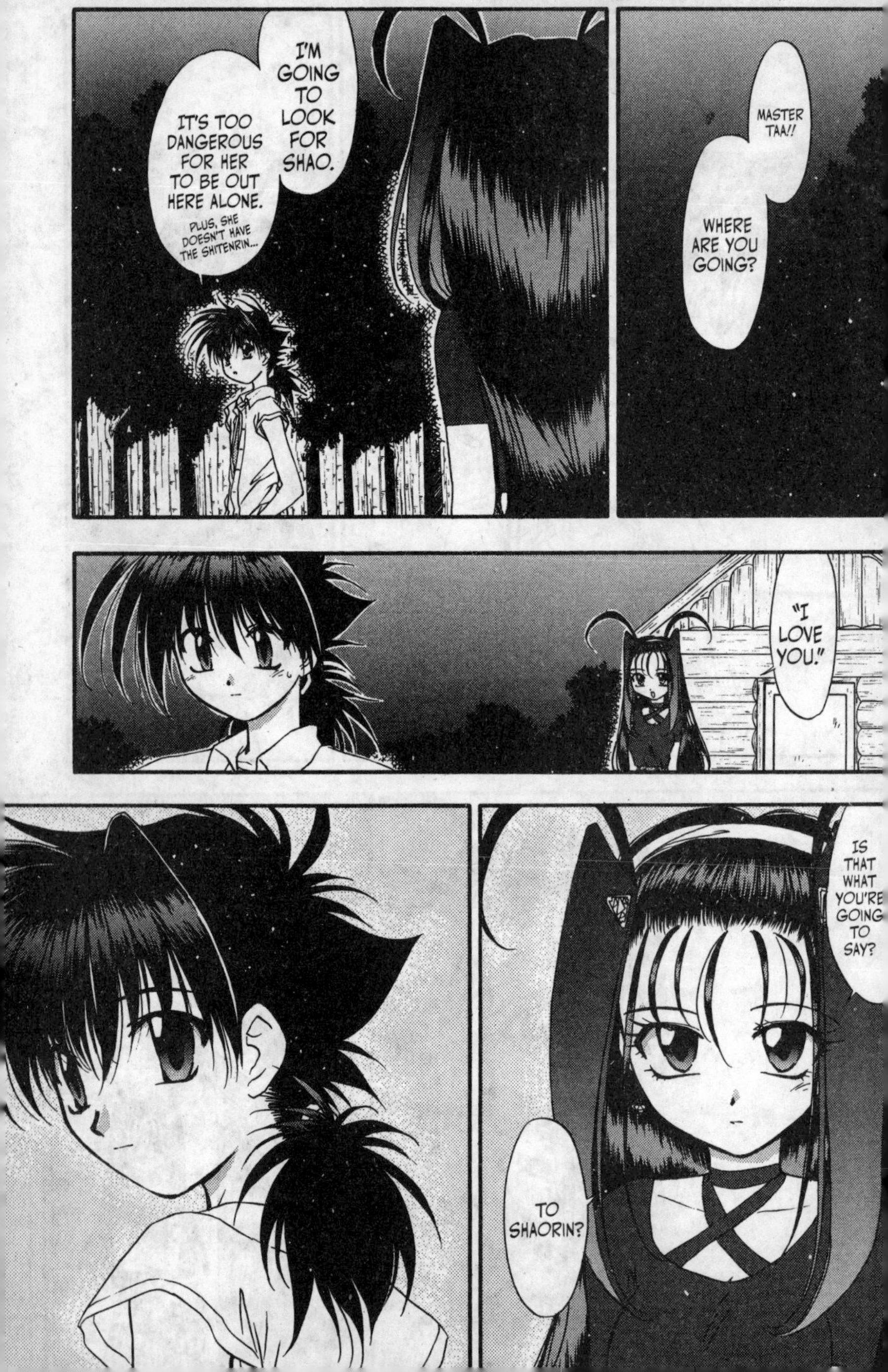
MASTER TAA!!
WHERE ARE YOU GOING?
I'M GOING TO LOOK FOR SHAO.
IT'S TOO DANGEROUS FOR HER TO BE OUT HERE ALONE.
PLUS, SHE DOESN'T HAVE THE SHITENRIN...
"I LOVE YOU."
IS THAT WHAT YOU'RE GOING TO SAY?
TO SHAORIN?

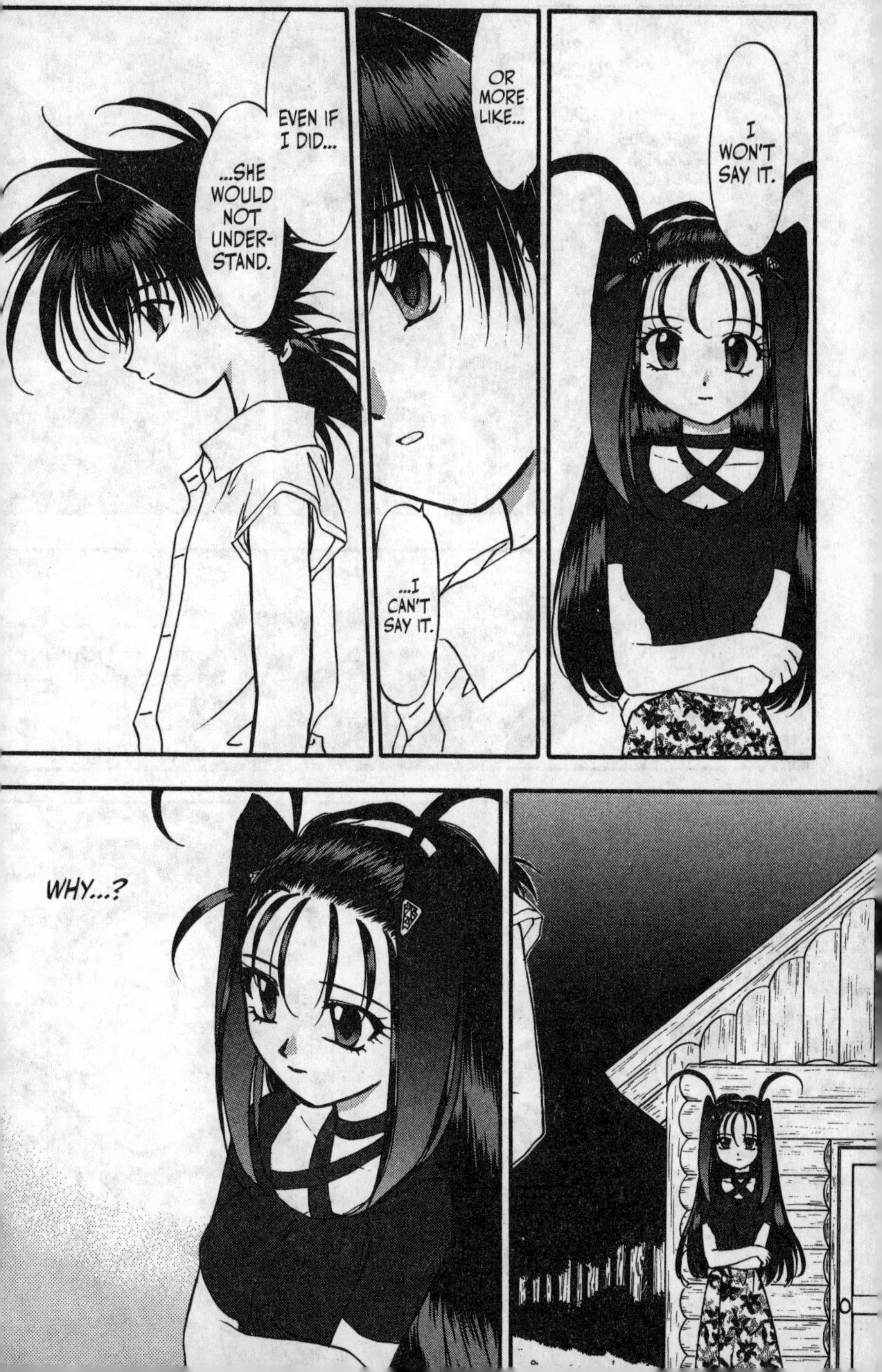
I WON'T SAY IT.
OR MORE LIKE...
...I CAN'T SAY IT.
EVEN IF I DID...
...SHE WOULD NOT UNDERSTAND.
WHY...?

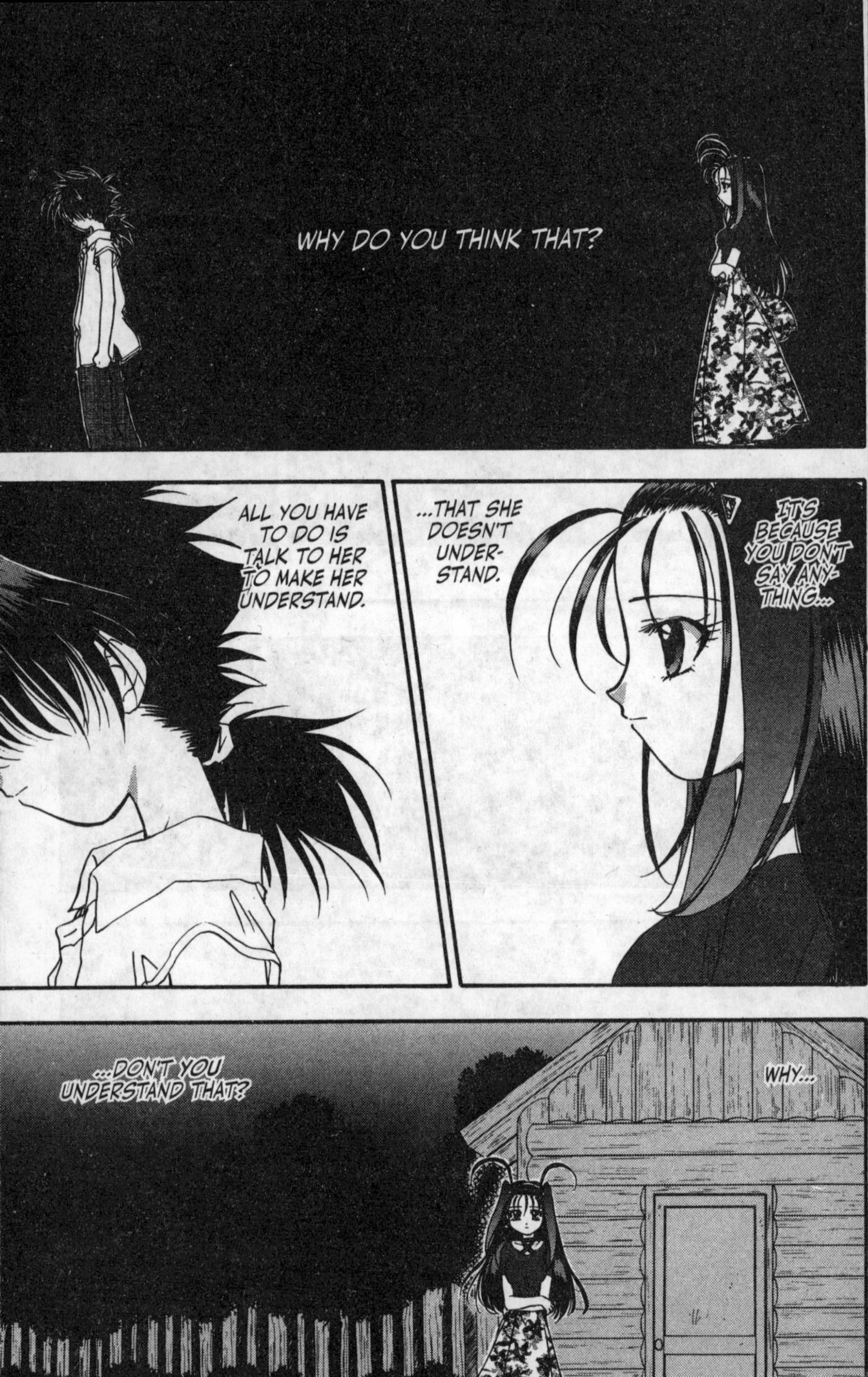
WHY DO YOU THINK THAT?
IT'S BECAUSE YOU DON'T SAY ANY-THING...
...THAT SHE DOESN'T UNDER-STAND.
ALL YOU HAVE TO DO IS TALK TO HER TO MAKE HER UNDERSTAND.
WHY...
...DON'T YOU UNDERSTAND THAT?

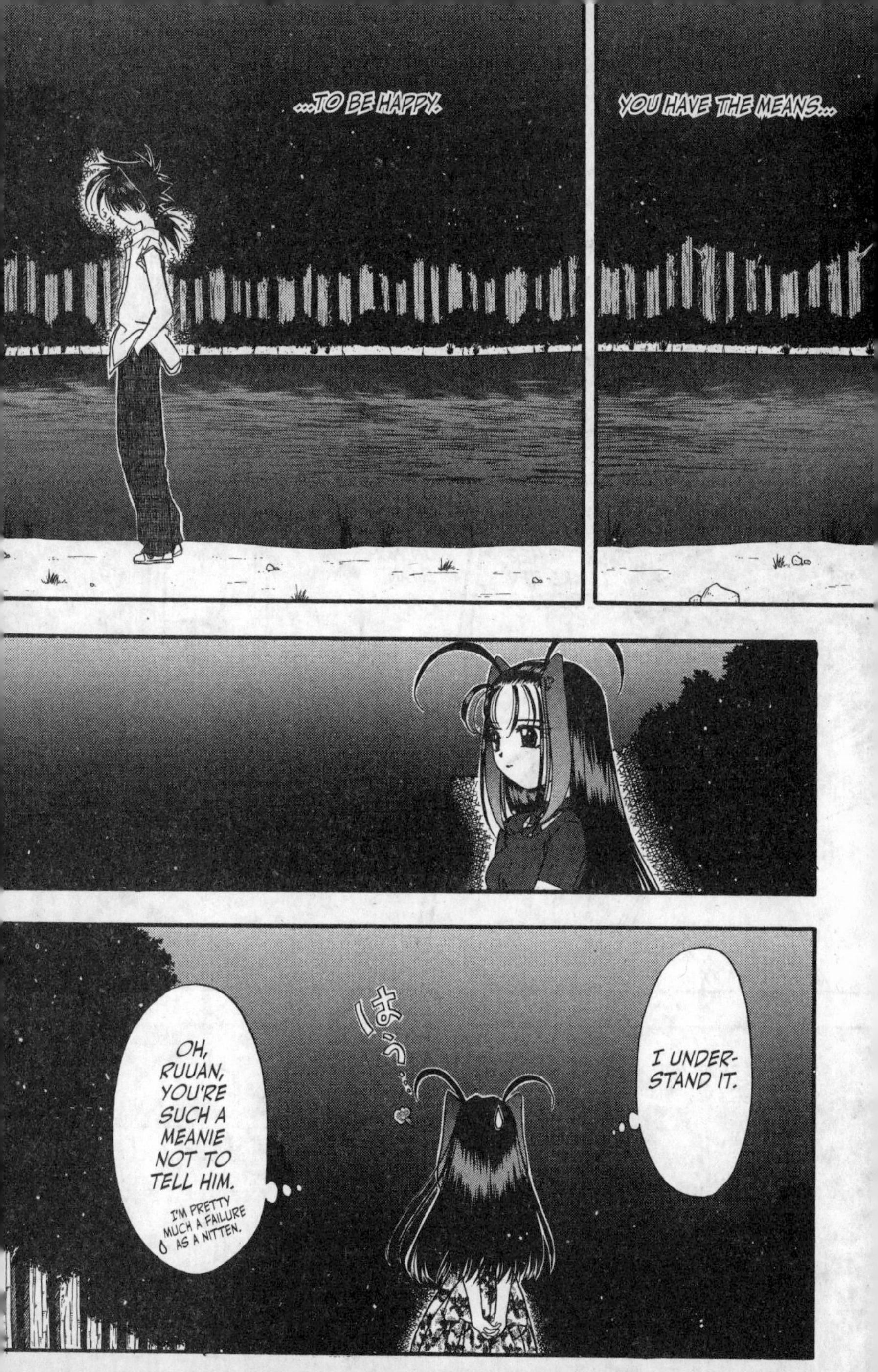
YOU HAVE THE MEANS...
...TO BE HAPPY.
I UNDER-STAND IT.
はう
OH, RUUAN, YOU'RE SUCH A MEANIE NOT TO TELL HIM.
I'M PRETTY MUCH A FAILURE AS A NITTEN.

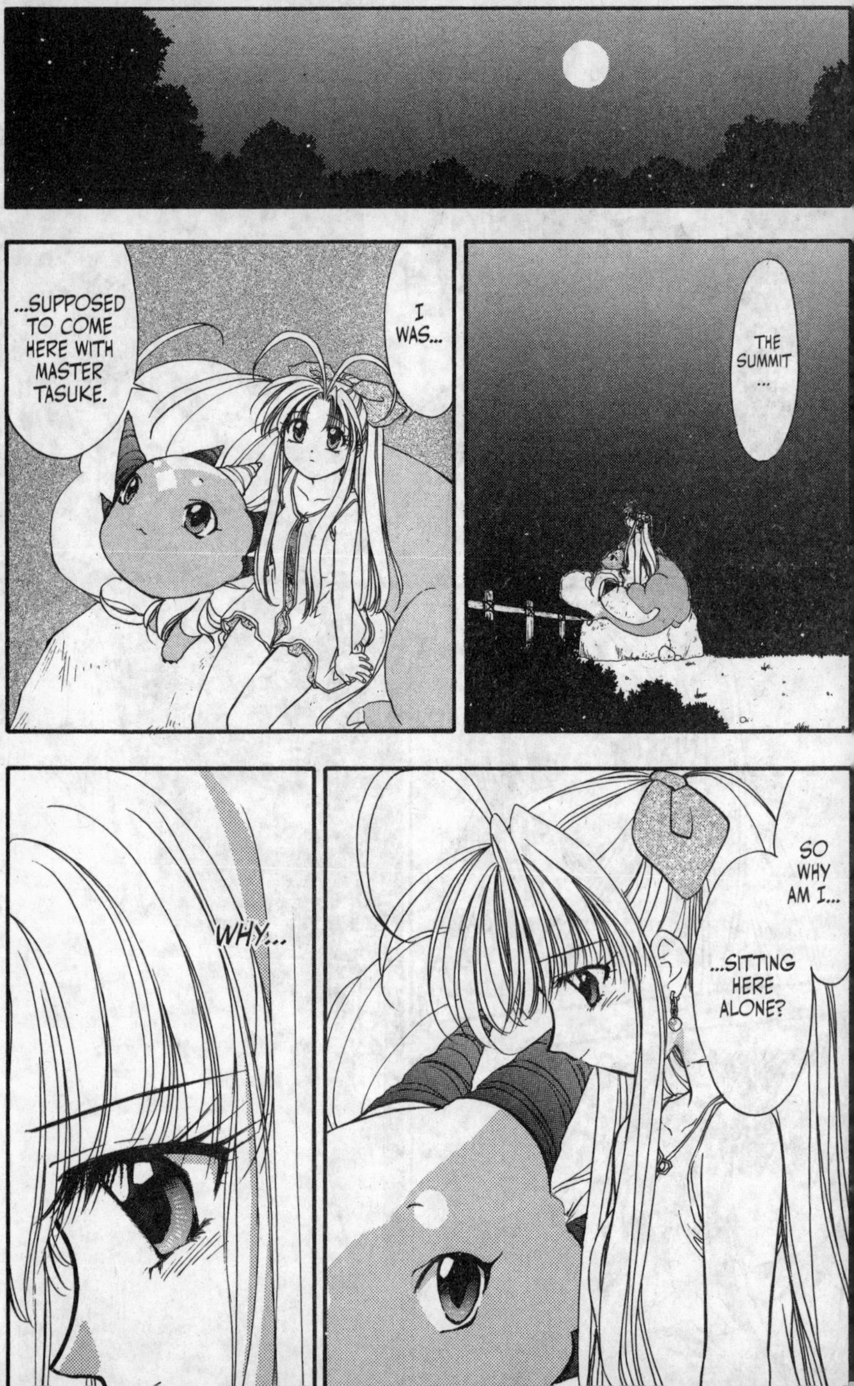
THE SUMMIT ...
I WAS...
...SUPPOSED TO COME HERE WITH MASTER TASUKE.
SO WHY AM I...
...SITTING HERE ALONE?
WHY...

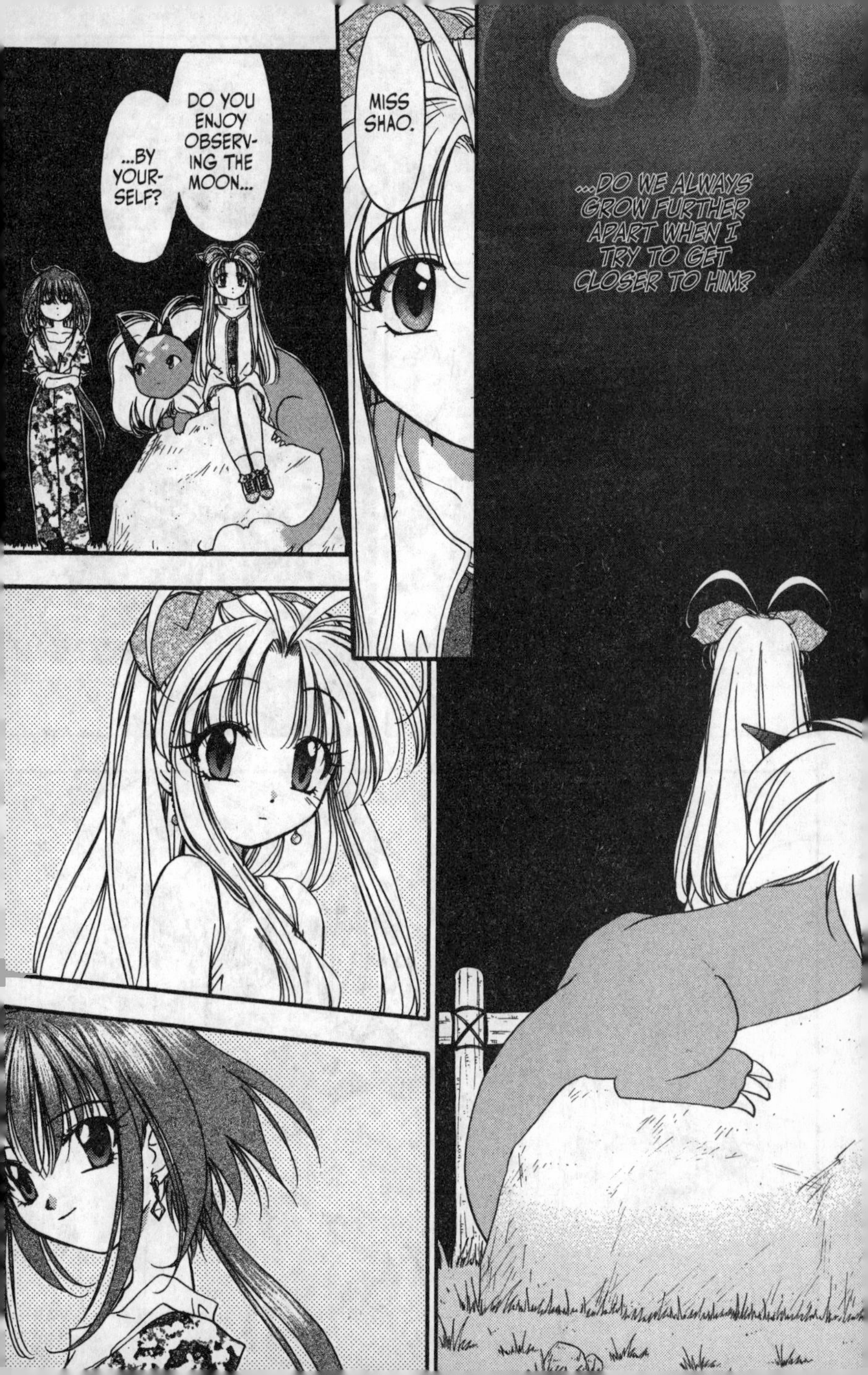
...DO WE ALWAYS GROW FURTHER APART WHEN I TRY TO GET CLOSER TO HIM?
MISS SHAO.
DO YOU ENJOY OBSERV-ING THE MOON...
...BY YOUR-SELF?

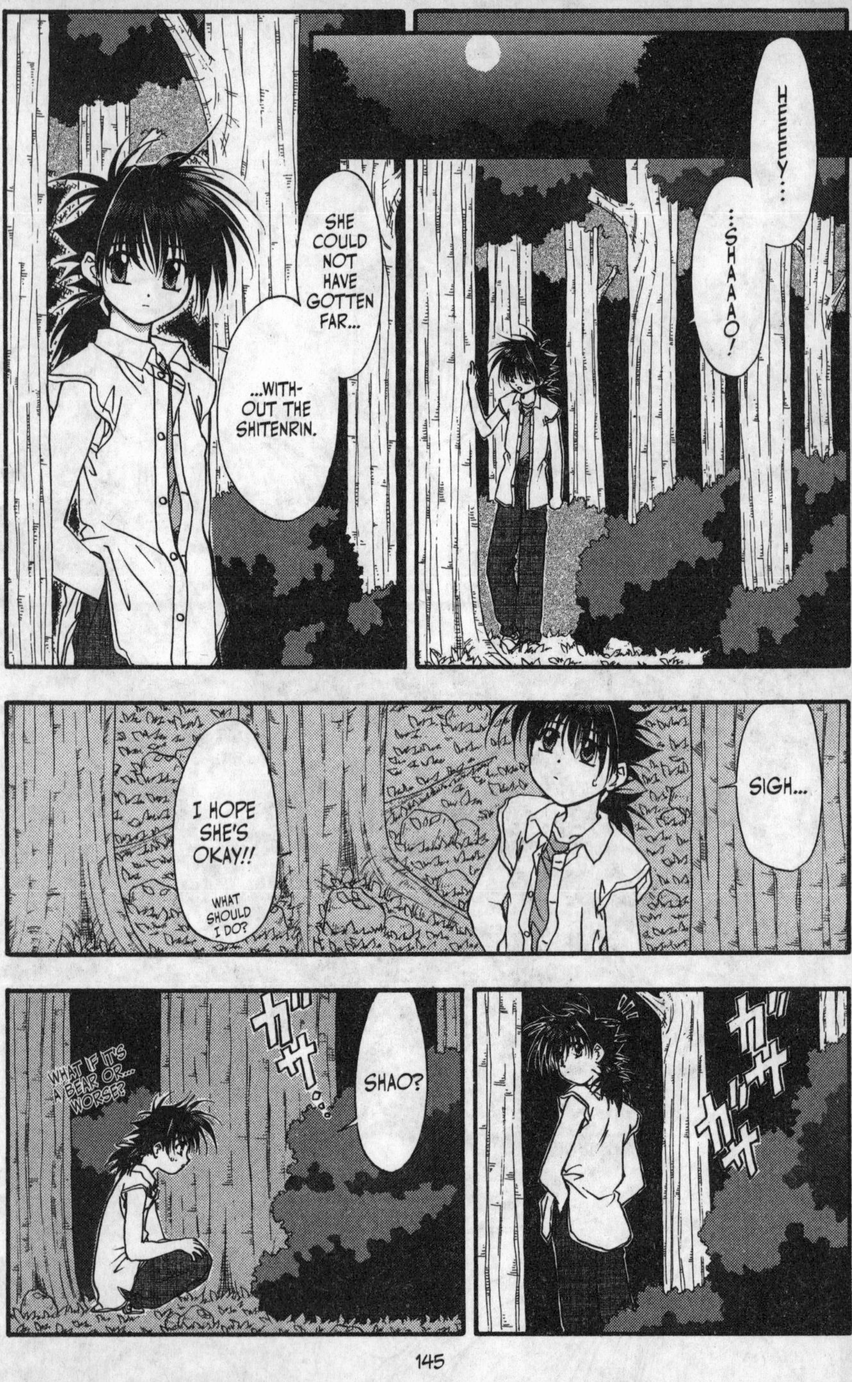
HEEEY...
...SHAAAO!
SHE COULD NOT HAVE GOTTEN FAR...
...WITH-OUT THE SHITENRIN.
SIGH...
I HOPE SHE'S OKAY!!
WHAT SHOULD I DO?
ガサ ガサ
SHAO?
ガサ
WHAT IF IT'S A BEAR OR... WORSE?

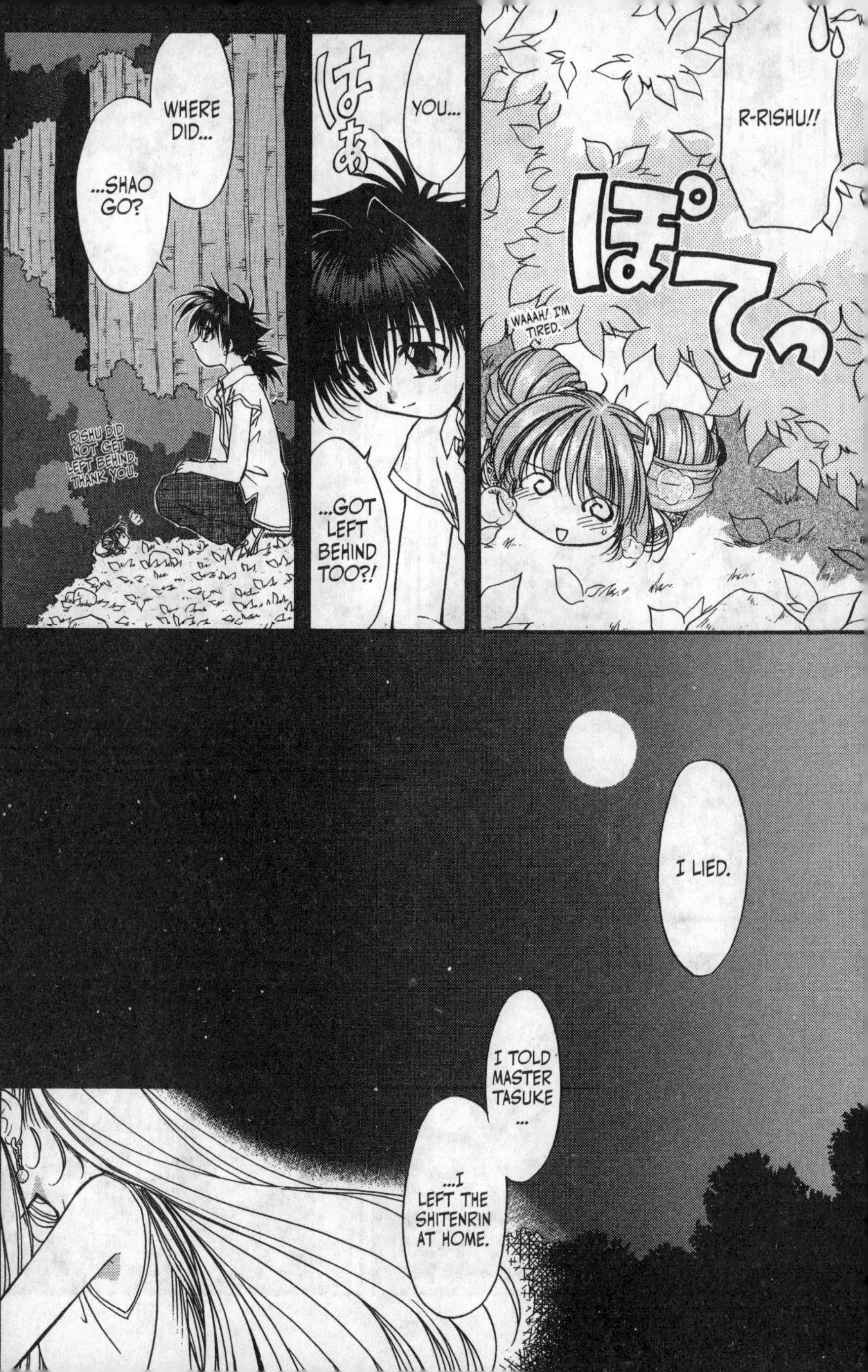
R-RISHU!!
ぽてっ
WAAAH! I'M TIRED.
はぁ
YOU...
...GOT LEFT BEHIND TOO?!
WHERE DID...
...SHAO GO?
RISHU DID NOT GET LEFT BEHIND, THANK YOU.
I LIED.
I TOLD MASTER TASUKE...
...I LEFT THE SHITENRIN AT HOME.

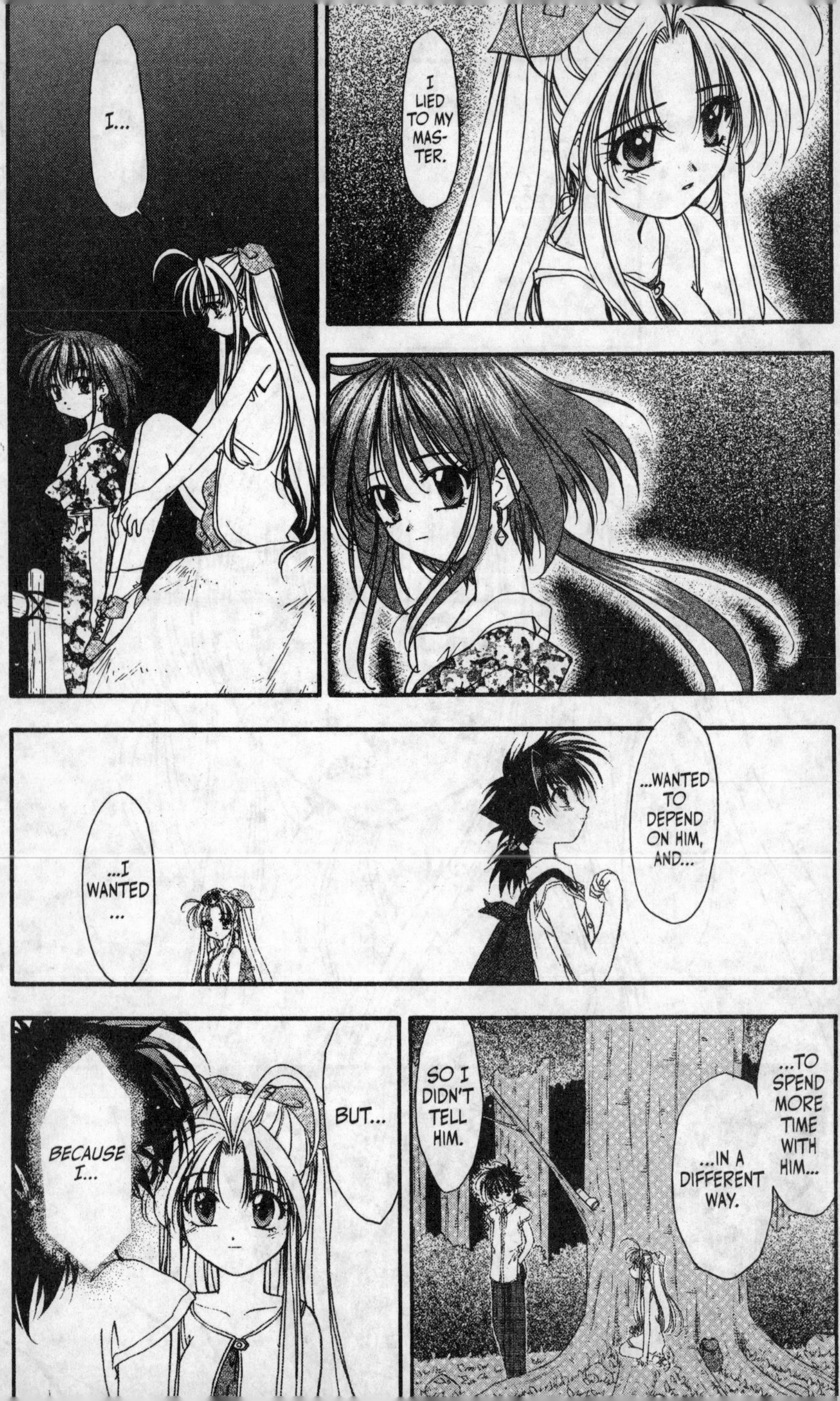
I LIED TO MY MAS-TER.
I...
...WANTED TO DEPEND ON HIM, AND...
...I WANTED ...
...TO SPEND MORE TIME WITH HIM...
...IN A DIFFERENT WAY.
SO I DIDN'T TELL HIM.
BUT...
BECAUSE I...

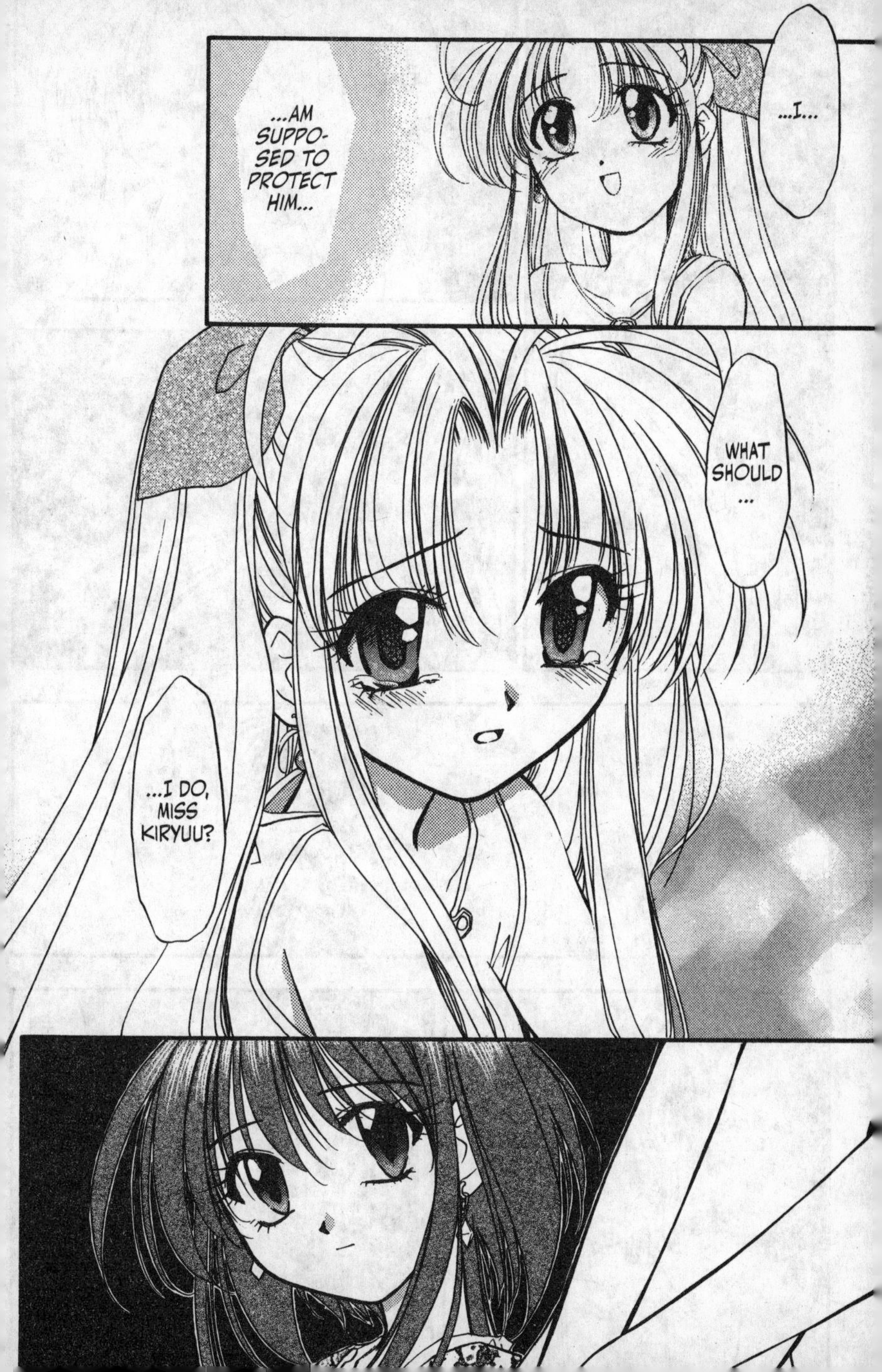
...I...
...AM SUPPOSED TO PROTECT HIM...
WHAT SHOULD ...
...I DO, MISS KIRYUU?

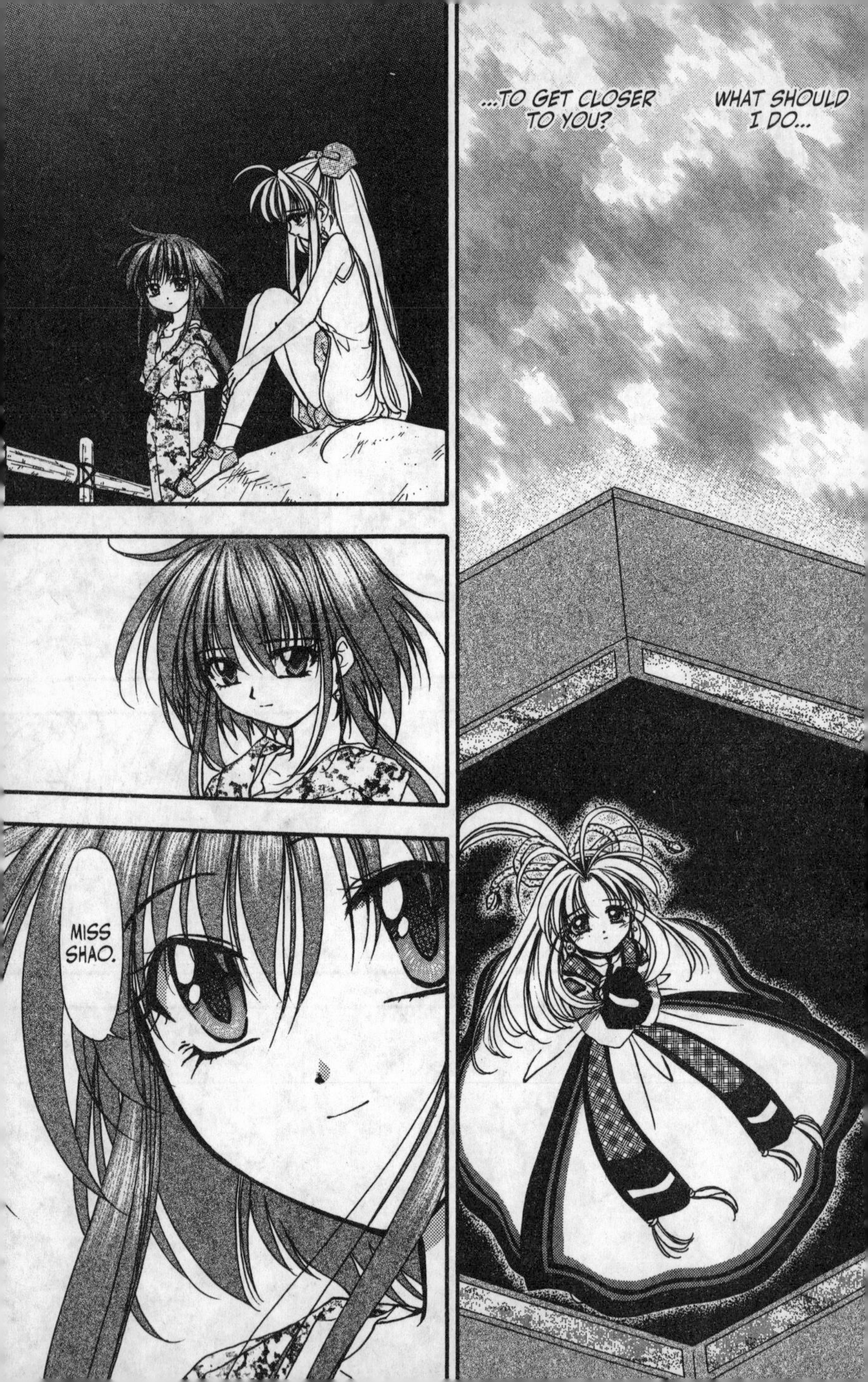
WHAT SHOULD I DO...
...TO GET CLOSER TO YOU?
MISS SHAO.

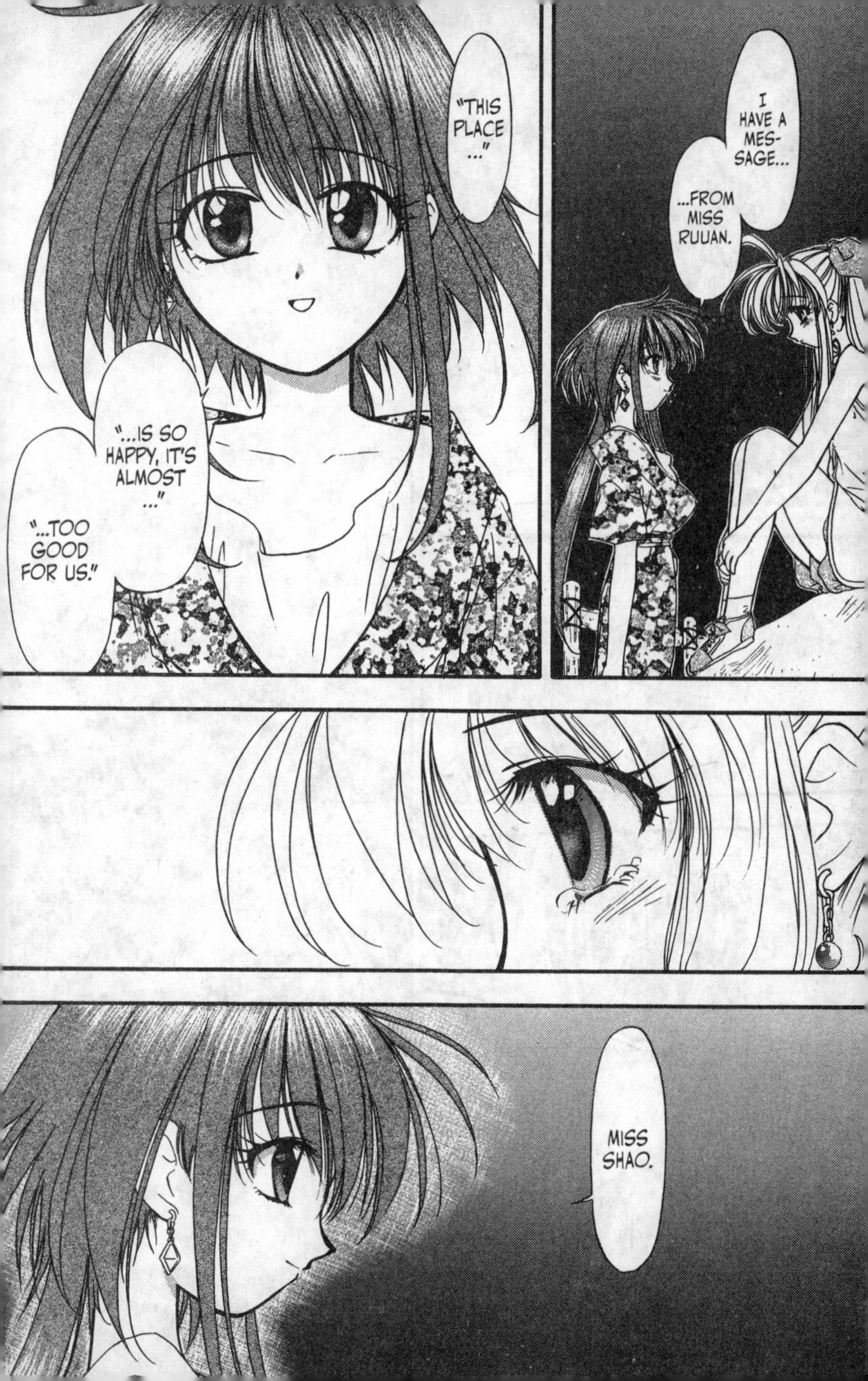
I HAVE A MES-SAGE...
...FROM MISS RUUAN.
"THIS PLACE ..."
"...IS SO HAPPY, IT'S ALMOST ..."
"...TOO GOOD FOR US."
MISS SHAO.

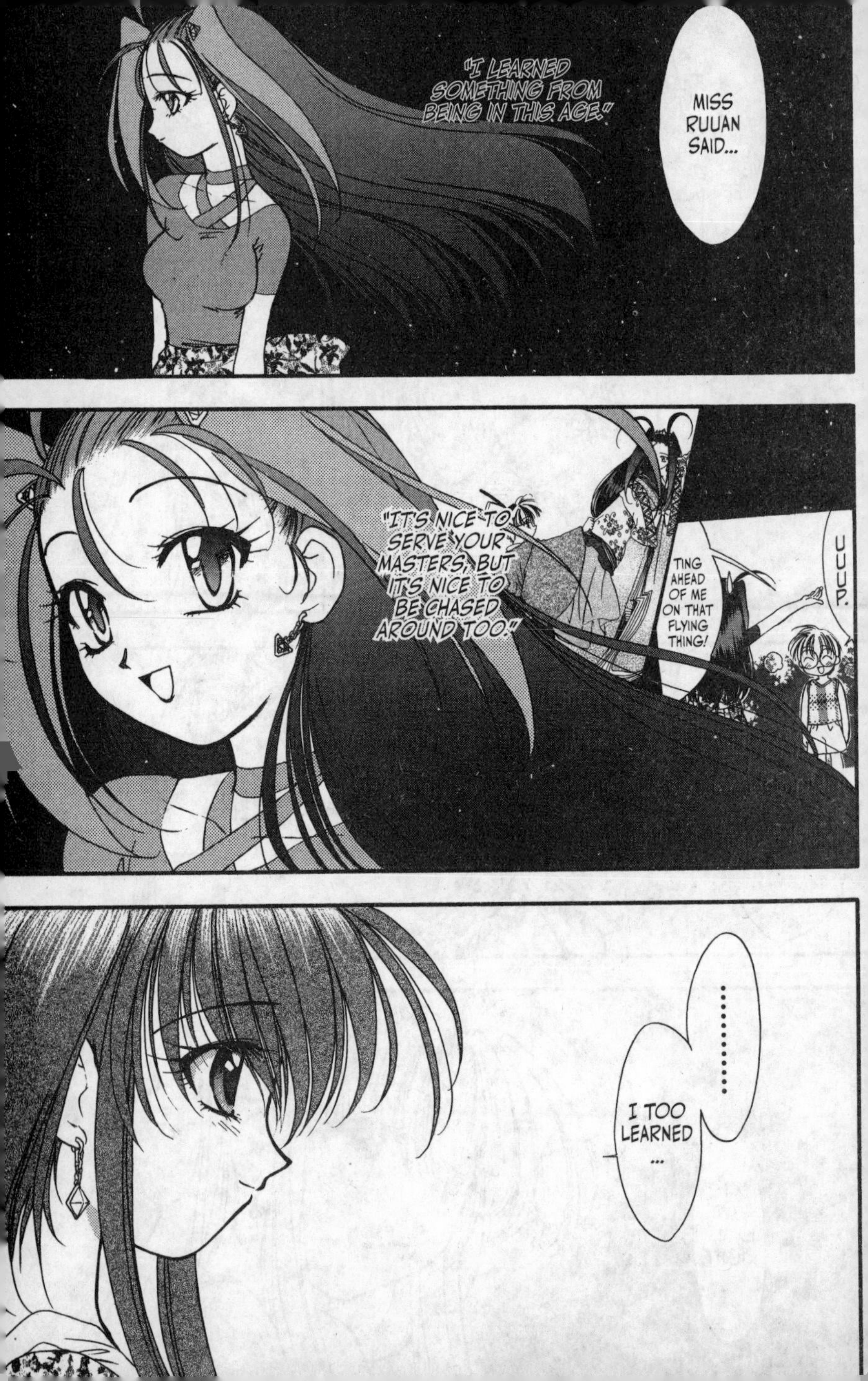
MISS RUUAN SAID...
"I LEARNED SOMETHING FROM BEING IN THIS AGE."
UUUP.
TING AHEAD OF ME ON THAT FLYING THING!
"IT'S NICE TO SERVE YOUR MASTERS, BUT IT'S NICE TO BE CHASED AROUND TOO."
....
I TOO LEARNED ...

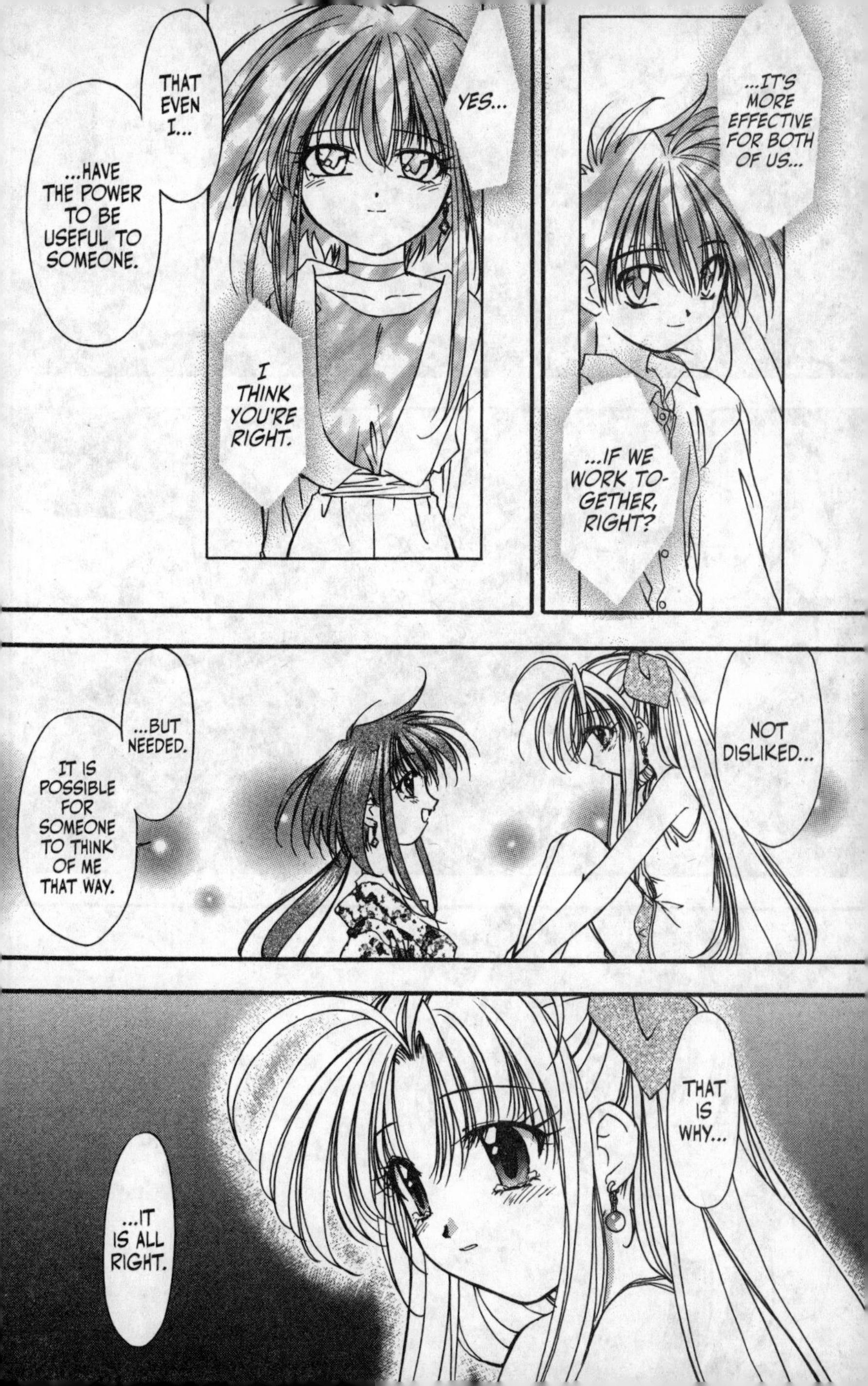
...IT'S MORE EFFECTIVE FOR BOTH OF US...
...IF WE WORK TO-GETHER, RIGHT?
YES...
I THINK YOU'RE RIGHT.
THAT EVEN I...
...HAVE THE POWER TO BE USEFUL TO SOMEONE.
NOT DISLIKED...
...BUT NEEDED.
IT IS POSSIBLE FOR SOMEONE TO THINK OF ME THAT WAY.
THAT IS WHY...
...IT IS ALL RIGHT.

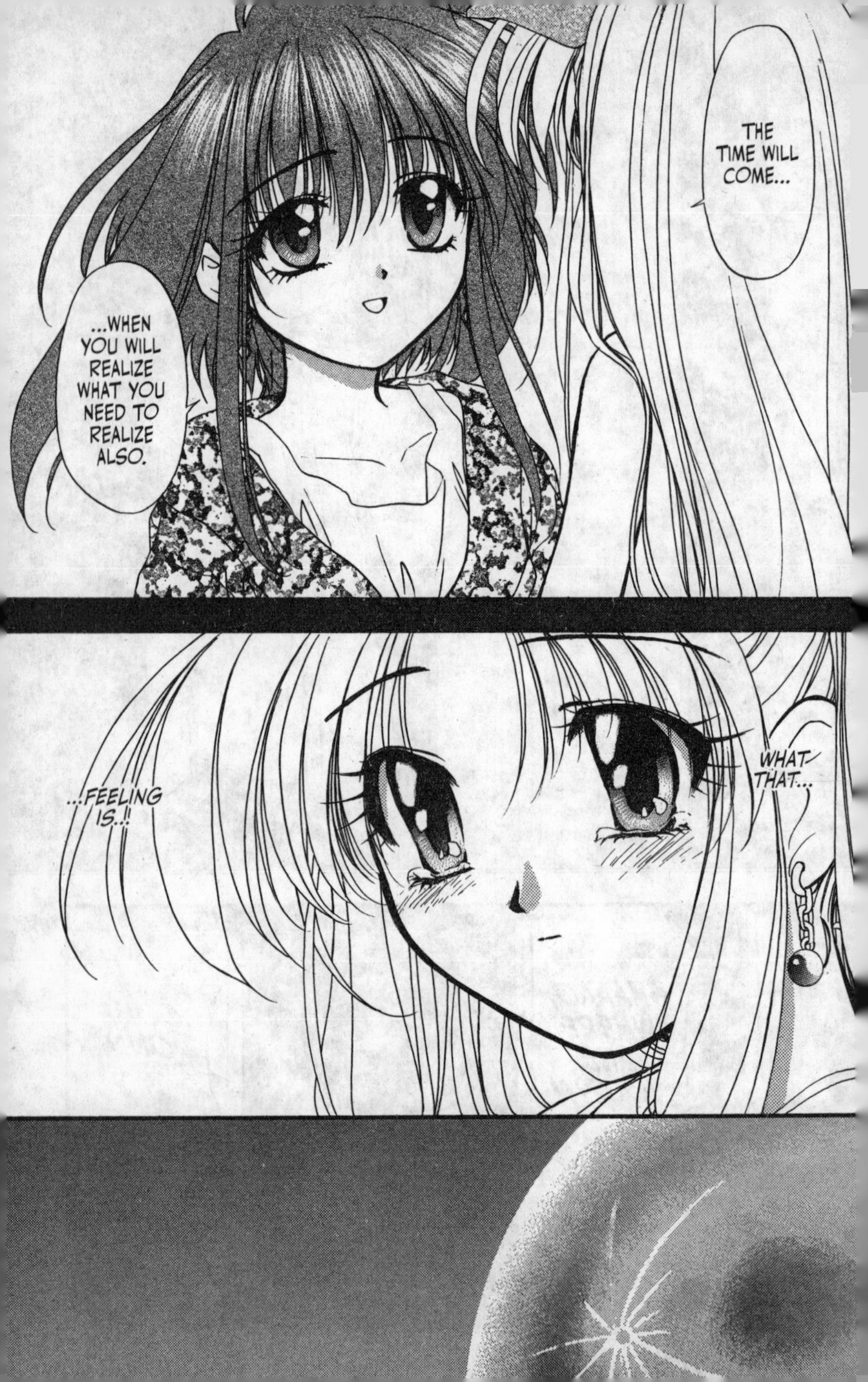
THE TIME WILL COME...
...WHEN YOU WILL REALIZE WHAT YOU NEED TO REALIZE ALSO.
WHAT THAT...
...FEELING IS..!!

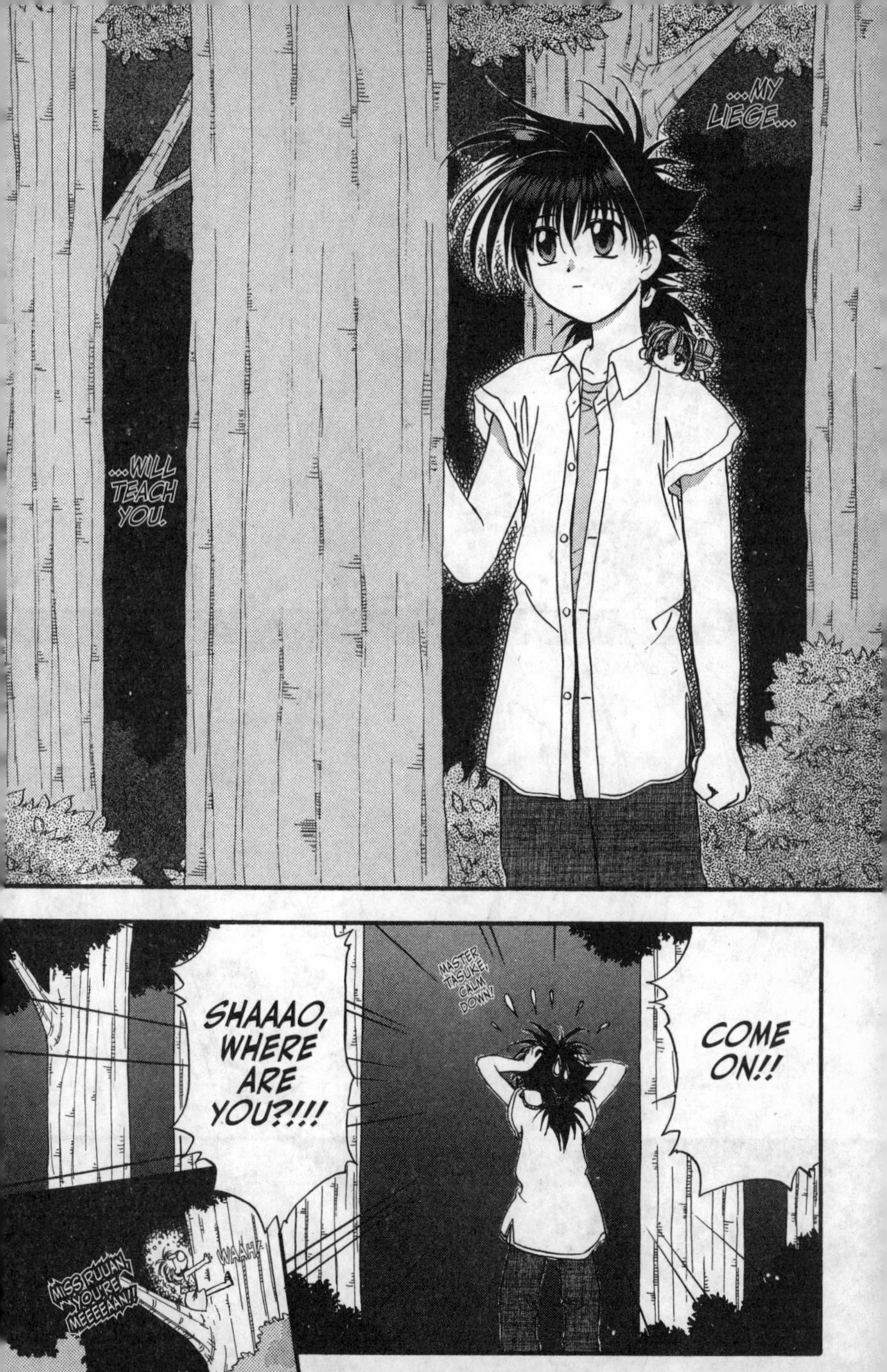
...MY LIEGE...
...WILL TEACH YOU.
COME ON!!
MASTER TASUKE, CALM DOWN!
SHAAAO, WHERE ARE YOU?!!!
WAAH!
MISS RUUAN, YOU'RE MEEEEAAN!!

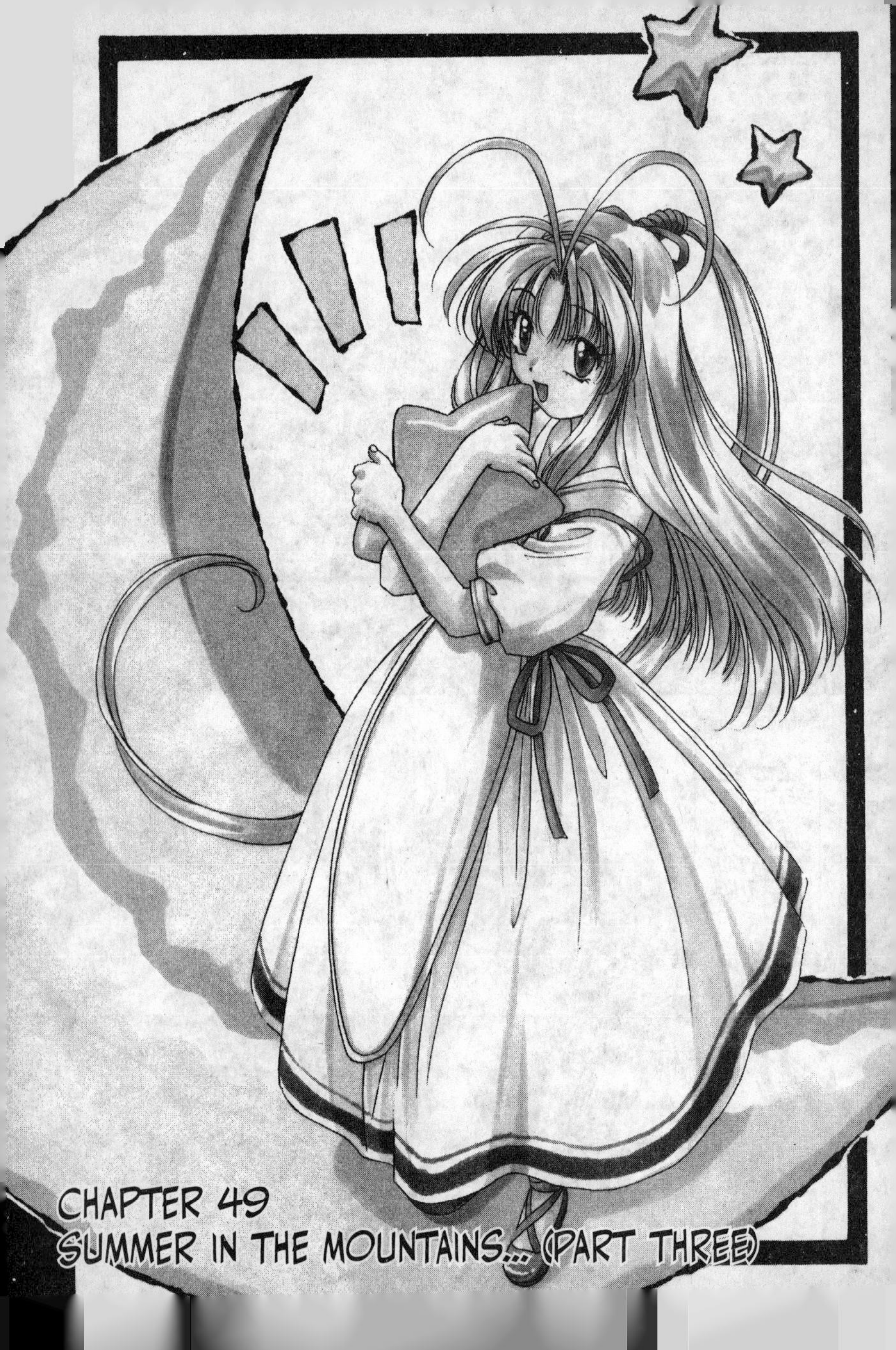
CHAPTER 49
SUMMER IN THE MOUNTAINS... (PART THREE)

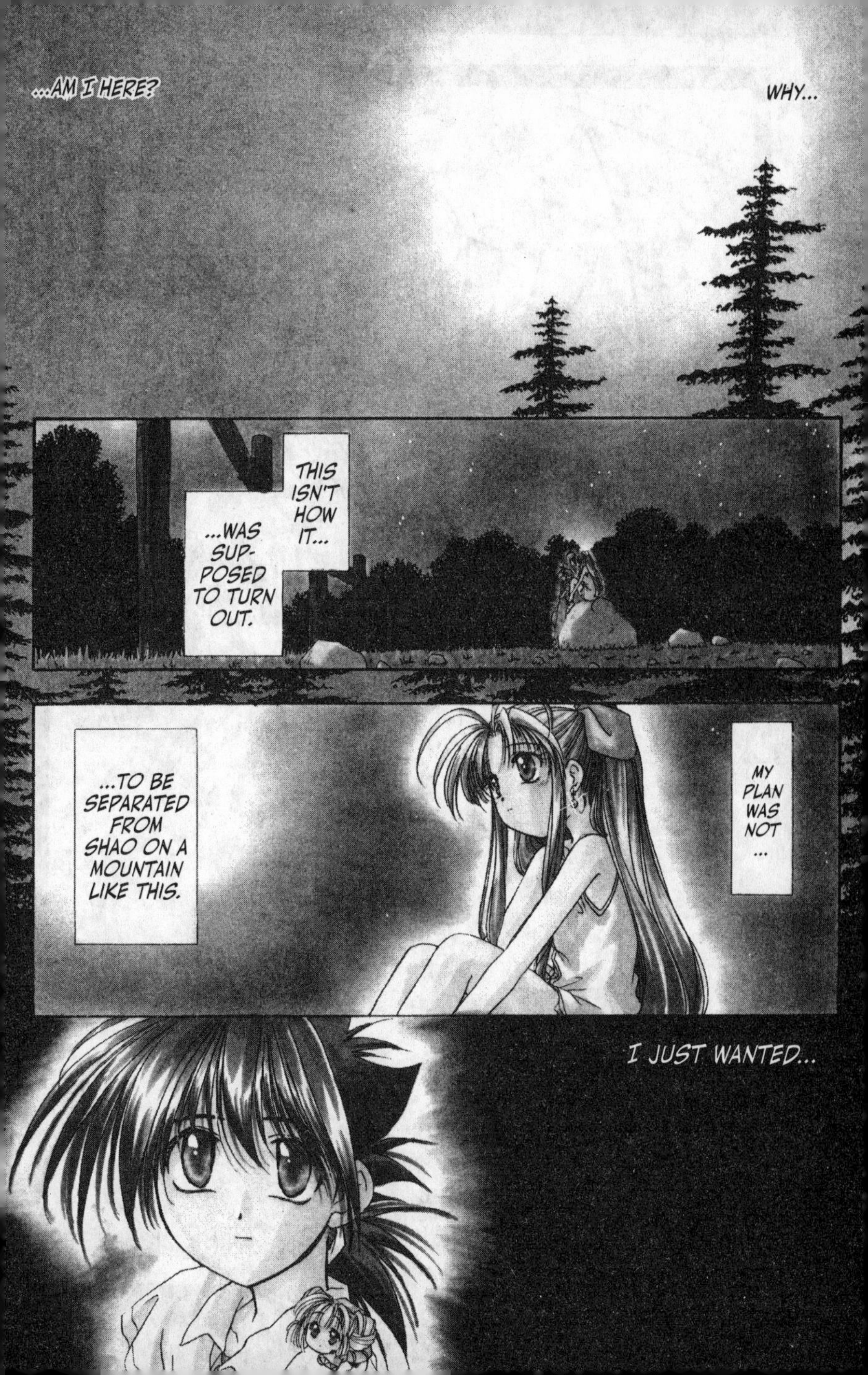
WHY...
...AM I HERE?
THIS ISN'T HOW IT...
...WAS SUP-POSED TO TURN OUT.
MY PLAN WAS NOT ...
...TO BE SEPARATED FROM SHAO ON A MOUNTAIN LIKE THIS.
I JUST WANTED...

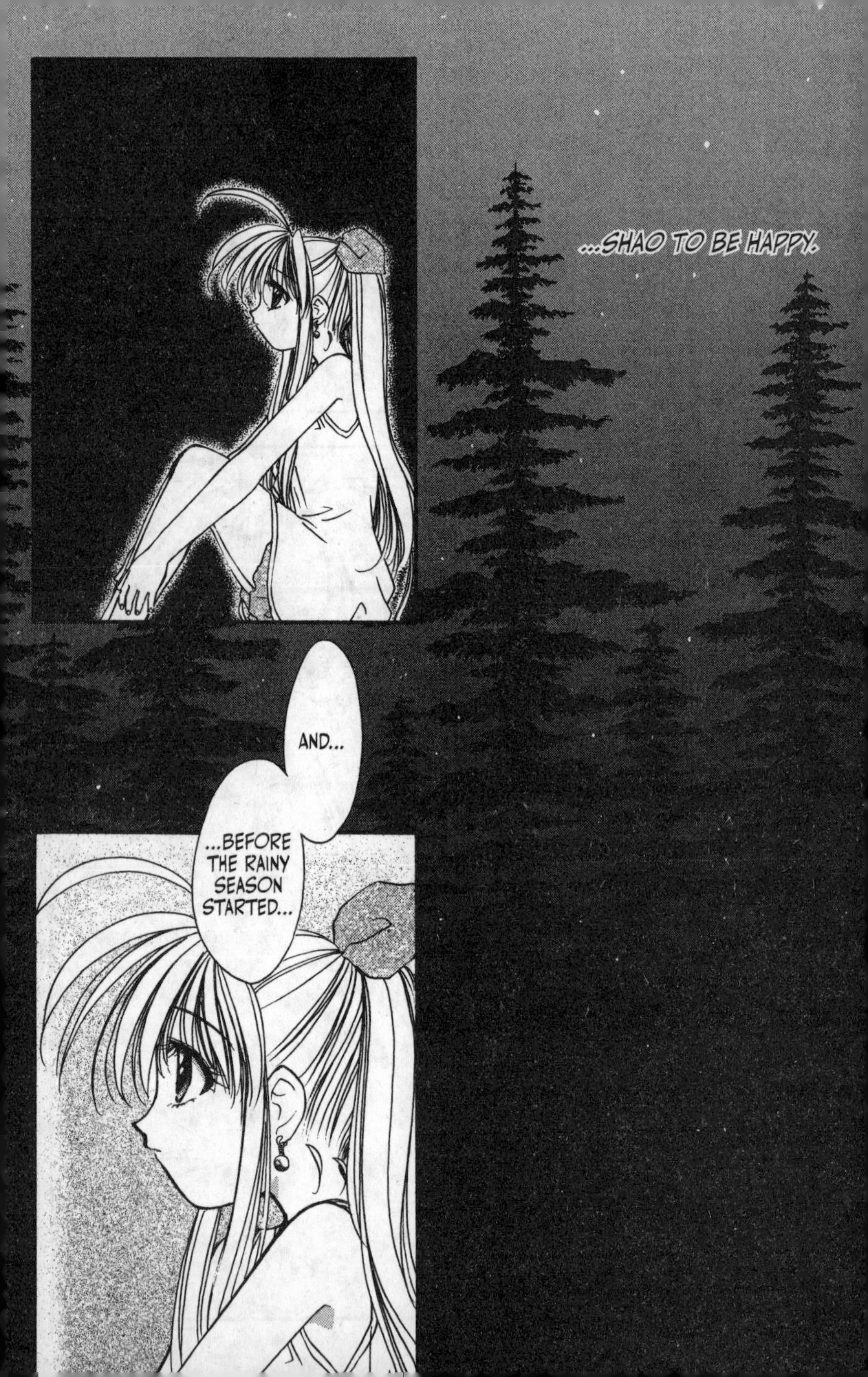
...SHAO TO BE HAPPY.
AND...
...BEFORE THE RAINY SEASON STARTED...

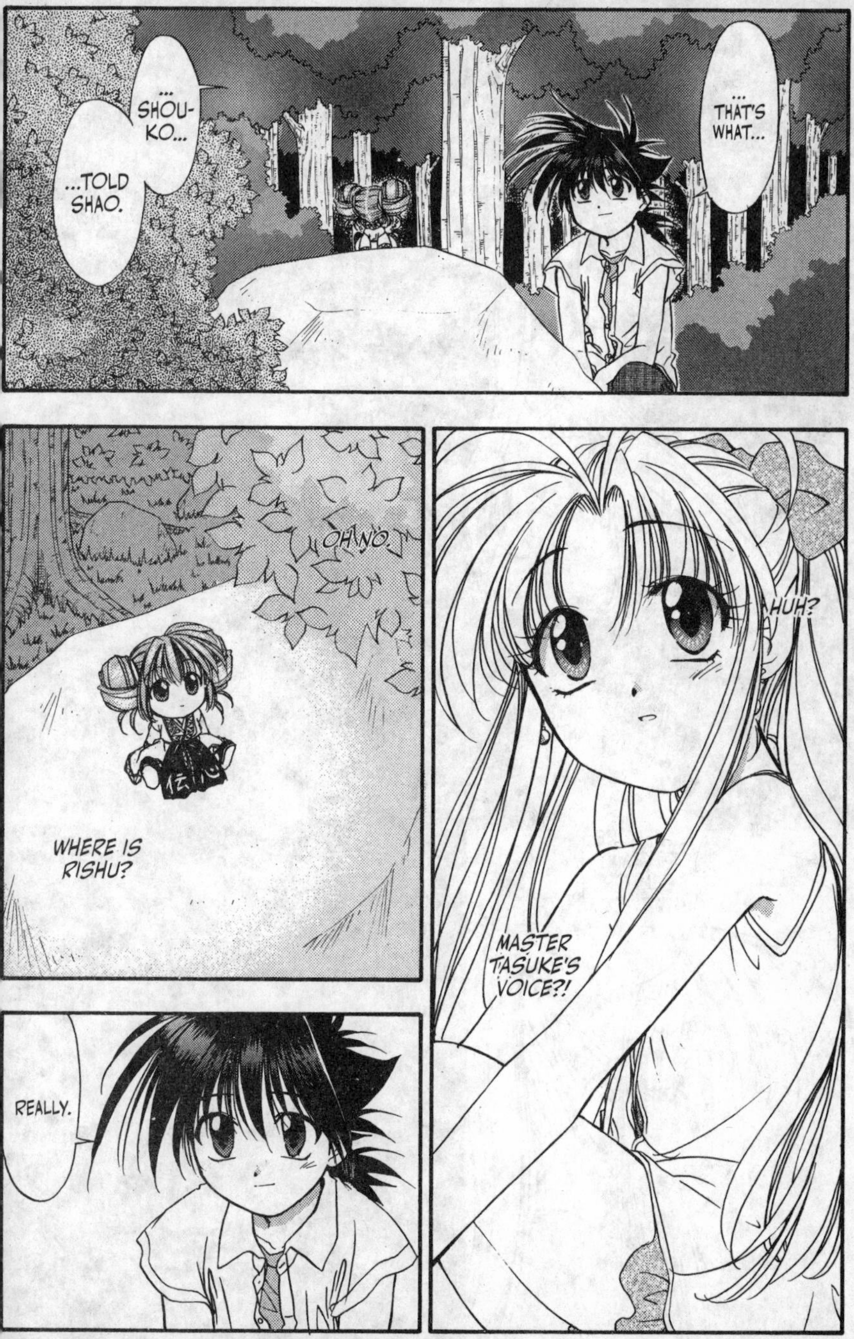
... THAT'S WHAT...
... SHOU-KO...
...TOLD SHAO.
HUH?
MASTER TASUKE'S VOICE?!
OH NO.
WHERE IS RISHU?
REALLY.

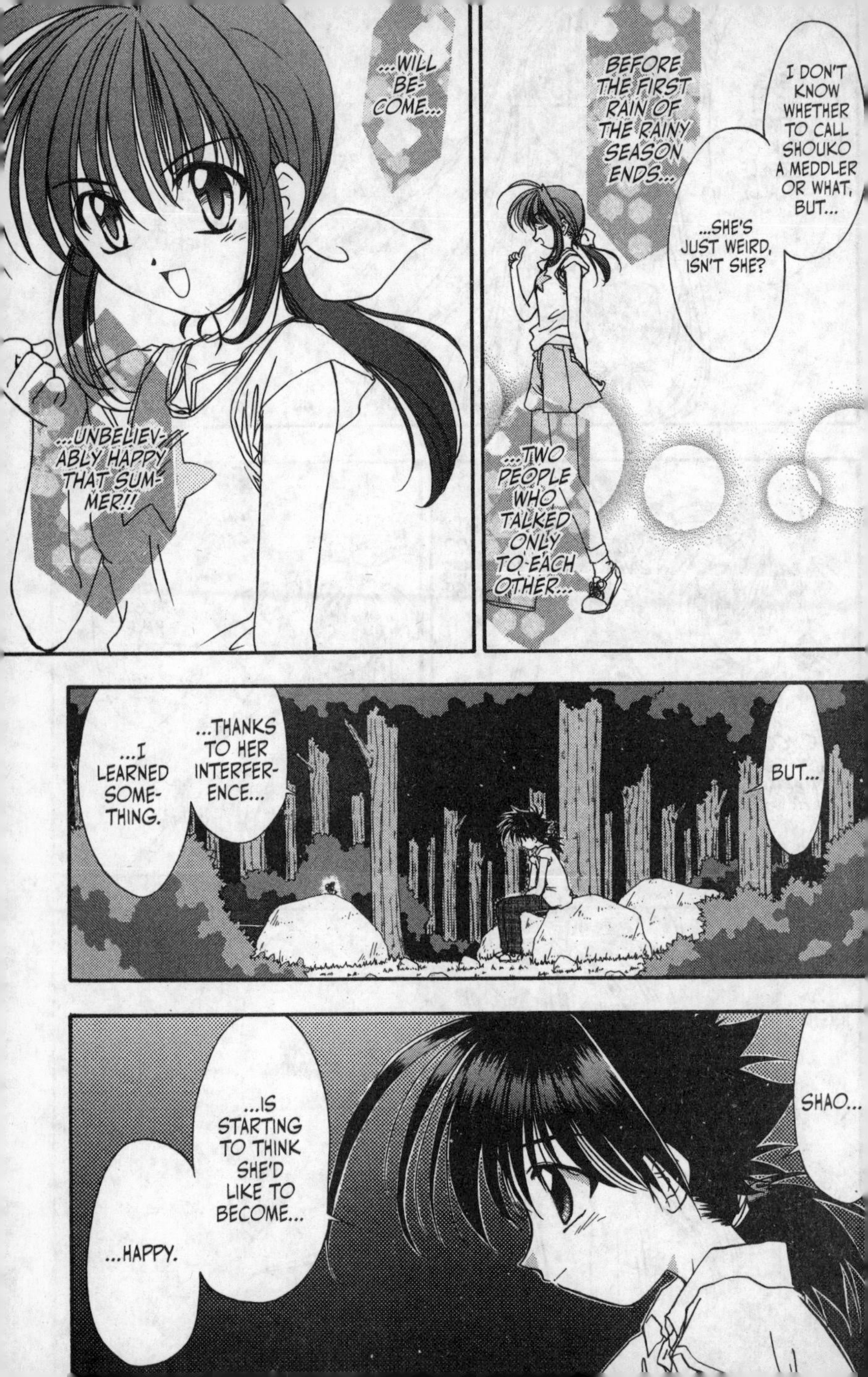
I DON'T KNOW WHETHER TO CALL SHOUKO A MEDDLER OR WHAT, BUT...
...SHE'S JUST WEIRD, ISN'T SHE?
BEFORE THE FIRST RAIN OF THE RAINY SEASON ENDS...
...TWO PEOPLE WHO TALKED ONLY TO EACH OTHER...
...WILL BE-COME...
...UNBELIEV-ABLY HAPPY THAT SUM-MER!!
BUT...
...THANKS TO HER INTERFER-ENCE...
...I LEARNED SOME-THING.
SHAO...
...IS STARTING TO THINK SHE'D LIKE TO BECOME...
...HAPPY.

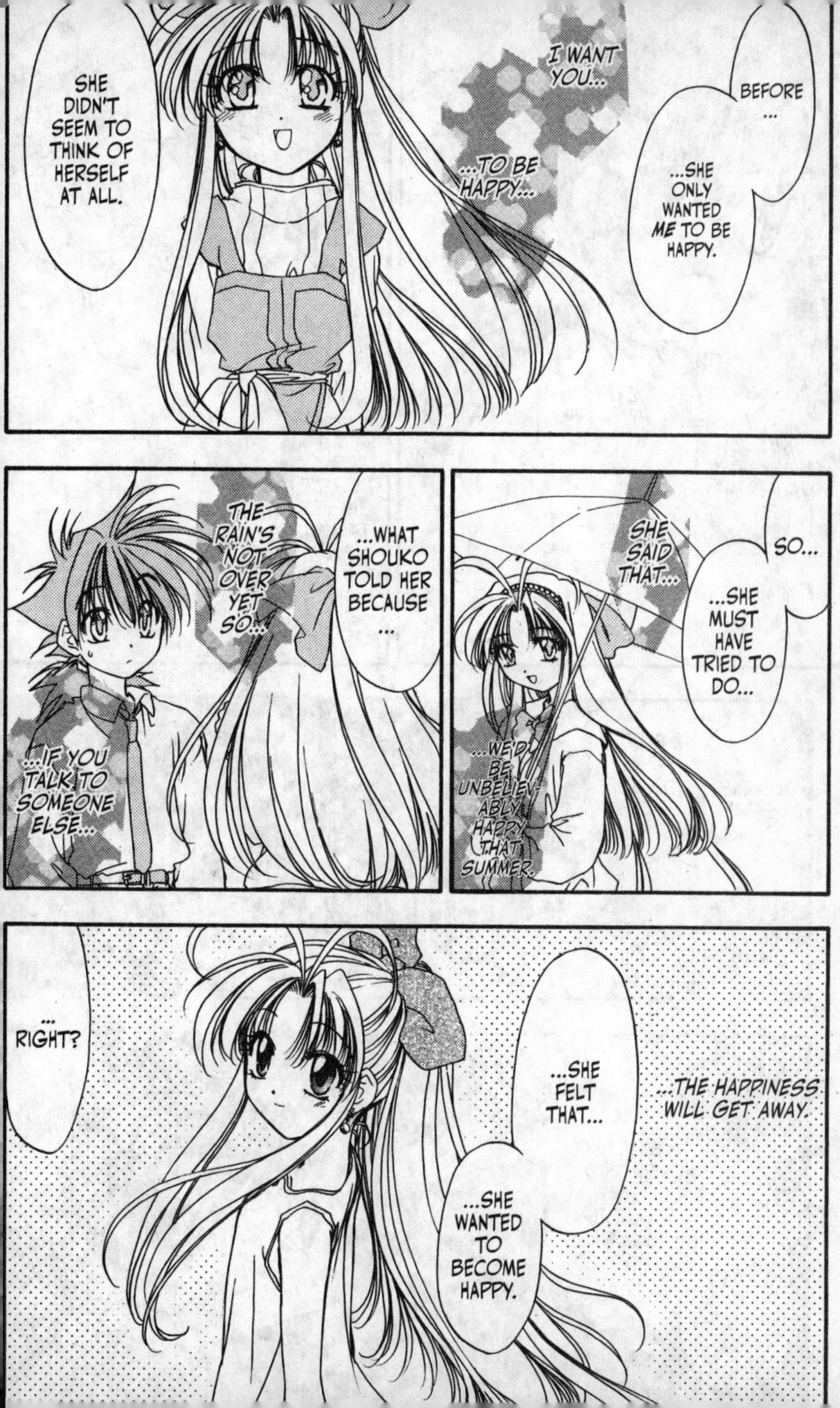
BEFORE ...
...SHE ONLY WANTED ME TO BE HAPPY.
I WANT YOU...
...TO BE HAPPY...
SHE DIDN'T SEEM TO THINK OF HERSELF AT ALL.
SO...
...SHE MUST HAVE TRIED TO DO...
SHE SAID THAT...
...WE'D BE UNBELIEV-ABLY HAPPY THAT SUMMER.
...WHAT SHOUKO TOLD HER BECAUSE ...
THE RAIN'S NOT OVER YET SO...
...IF YOU TALK TO SOMEONE ELSE...
...THE HAPPINESS WILL GET AWAY.
...SHE FELT THAT...
...SHE WANTED TO BECOME HAPPY.
... RIGHT?

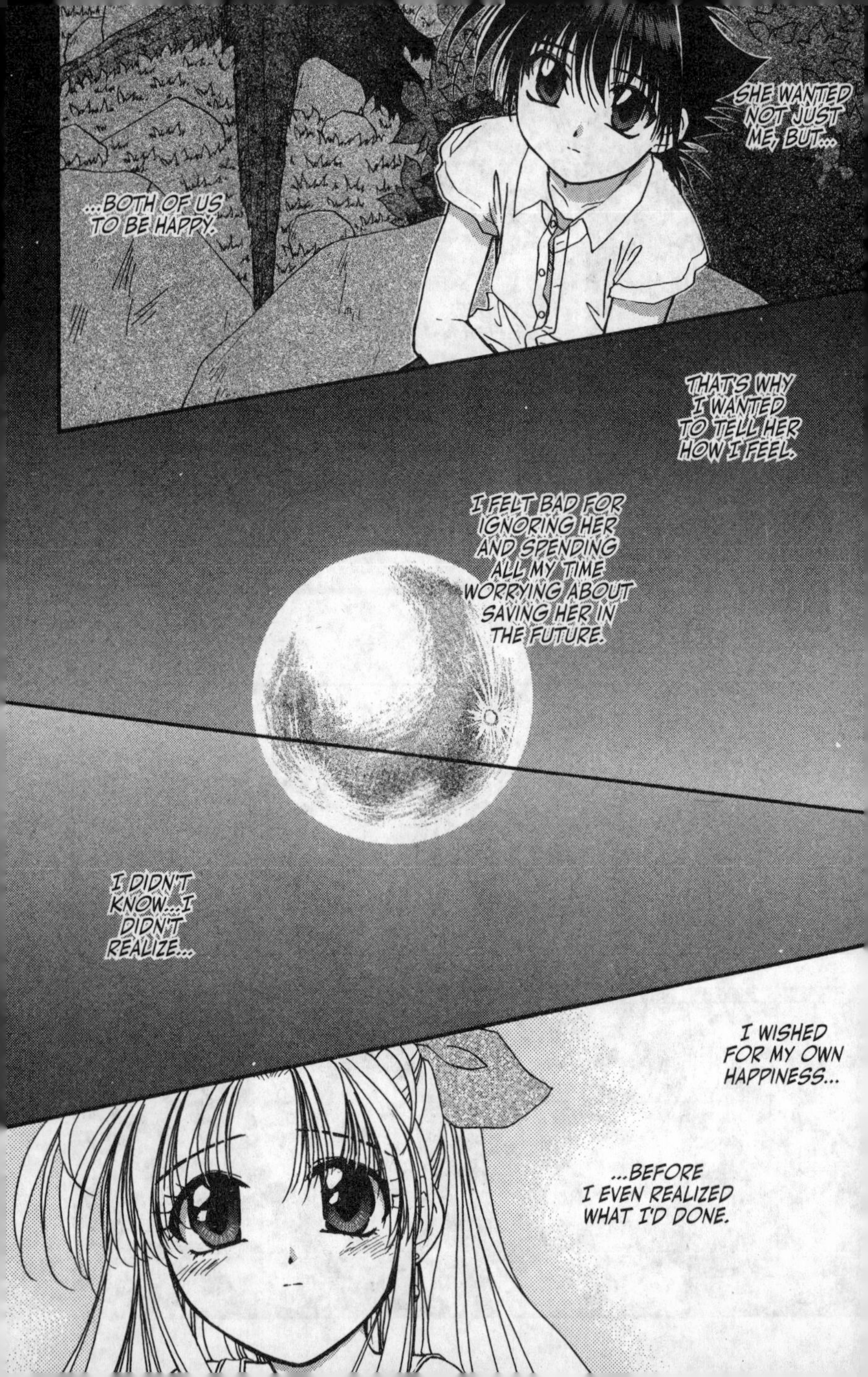
SHE WANTED NOT JUST ME, BUT...
...BOTH OF US TO BE HAPPY.
THAT'S WHY I WANTED TO TELL HER HOW I FEEL.
I FELT BAD FOR IGNORING HER AND SPENDING ALL MY TIME WORRYING ABOUT SAVING HER IN THE FUTURE.
I DIDN'T KNOW...I DIDN'T REALIZE...
I WISHED FOR MY OWN HAPPINESS...
...BEFORE I EVEN REALIZED WHAT I'D DONE.

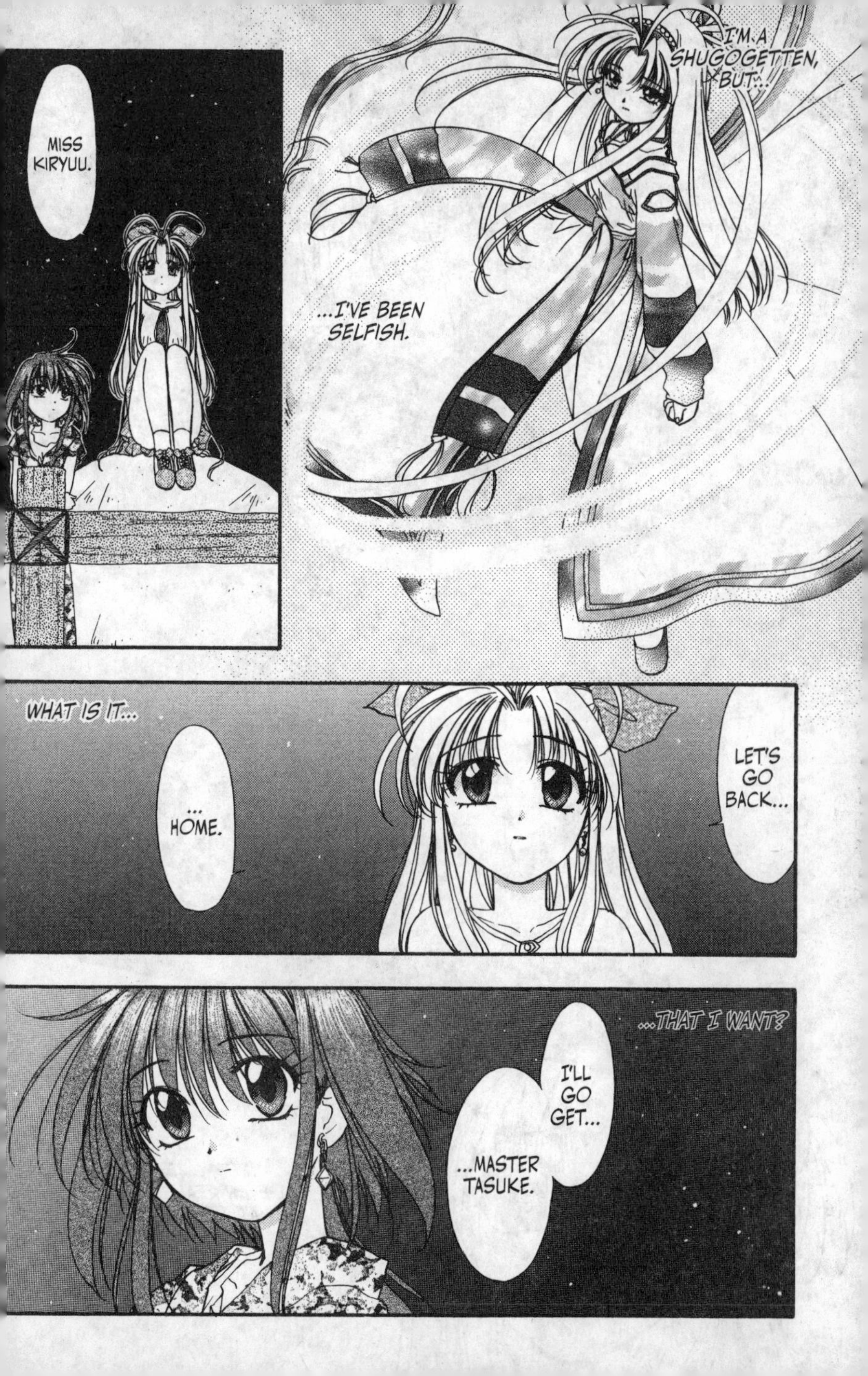
I'M A SHUGOGETTEN, BUT...
...I'VE BEEN SELFISH.
MISS KIRYUU.
LET'S GO BACK...
...HOME.
WHAT IS IT...
...THAT I WANT?
I'LL GO GET...
...MASTER TASUKE.

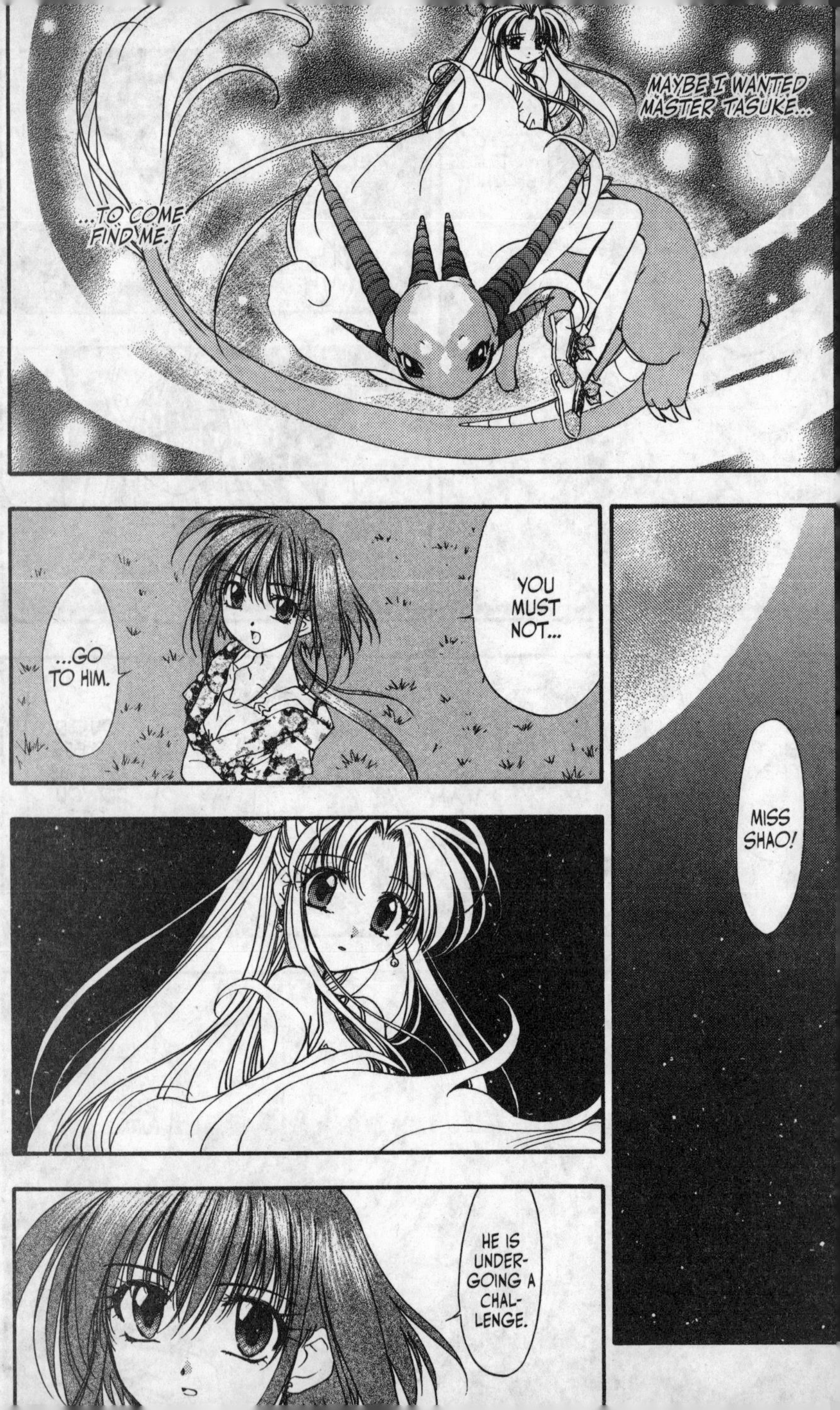
MAYBE I WANTED MASTER TASUKE...
...TO COME FIND ME.
MISS SHAO!
YOU MUST NOT...
...GO TO HIM.
HE IS UNDER-GOING A CHAL-LENGE.

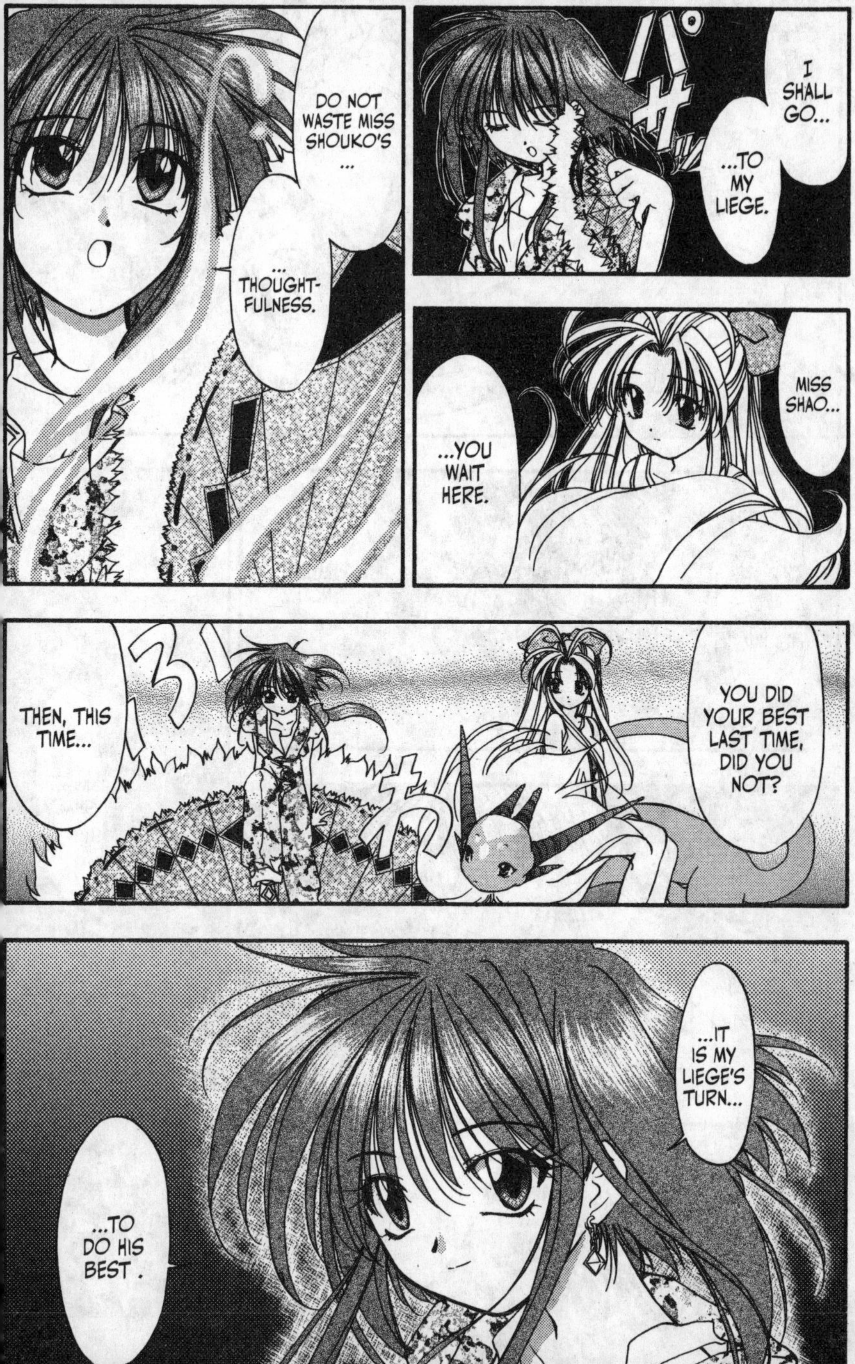
I SHALL GO...
...TO MY LIEGE.
MISS SHAO...
...YOU WAIT HERE.
DO NOT WASTE MISS SHOUKO'S ...
... THOUGHT-FULNESS.
YOU DID YOUR BEST LAST TIME, DID YOU NOT?
THEN, THIS TIME...
...IT IS MY LIEGE'S TURN...
...TO DO HIS BEST.

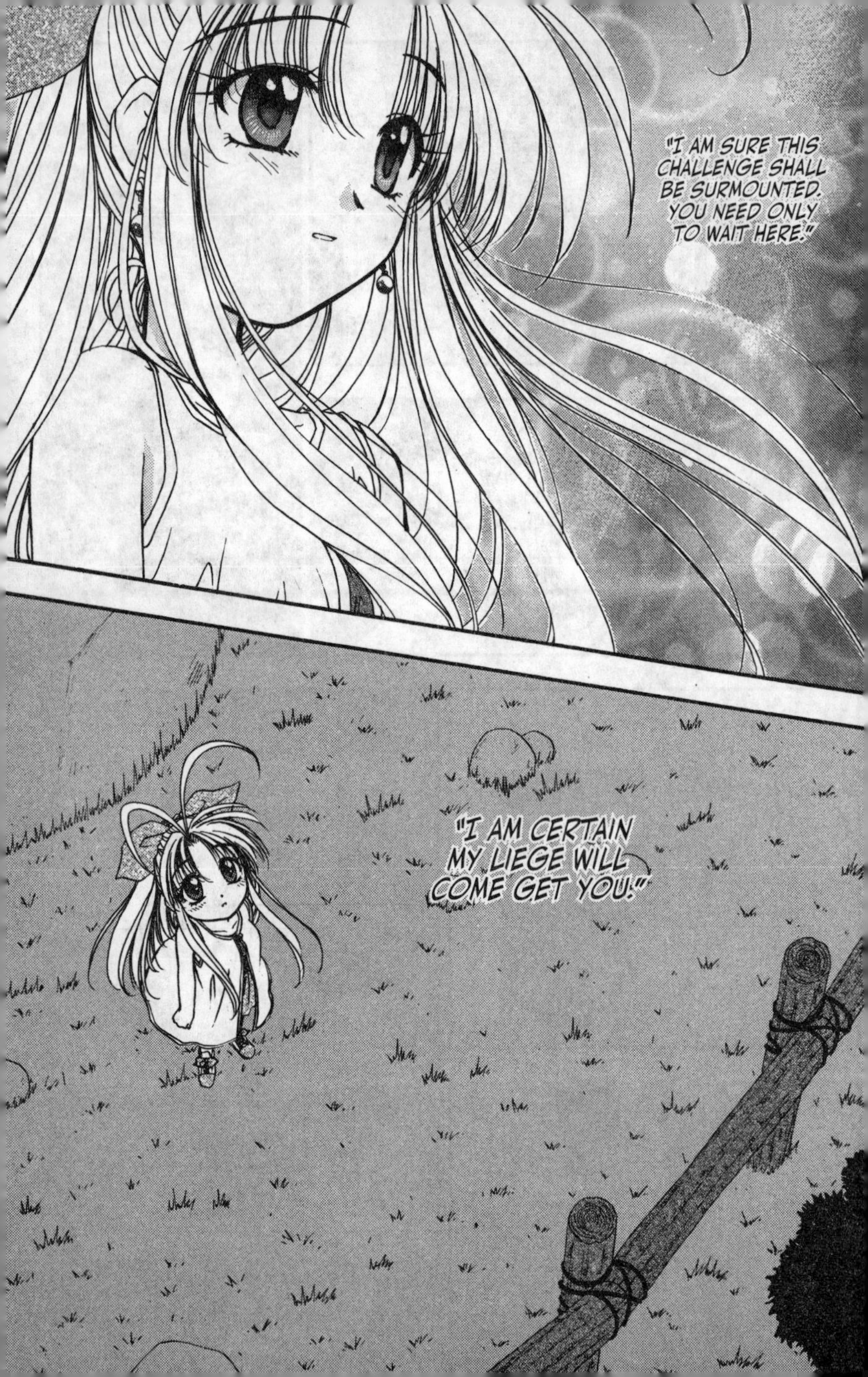
"I AM SURE THIS CHALLENGE SHALL BE SURMOUNTED. YOU NEED ONLY TO WAIT HERE."
"I AM CERTAIN MY LIEGE WILL COME GET YOU."

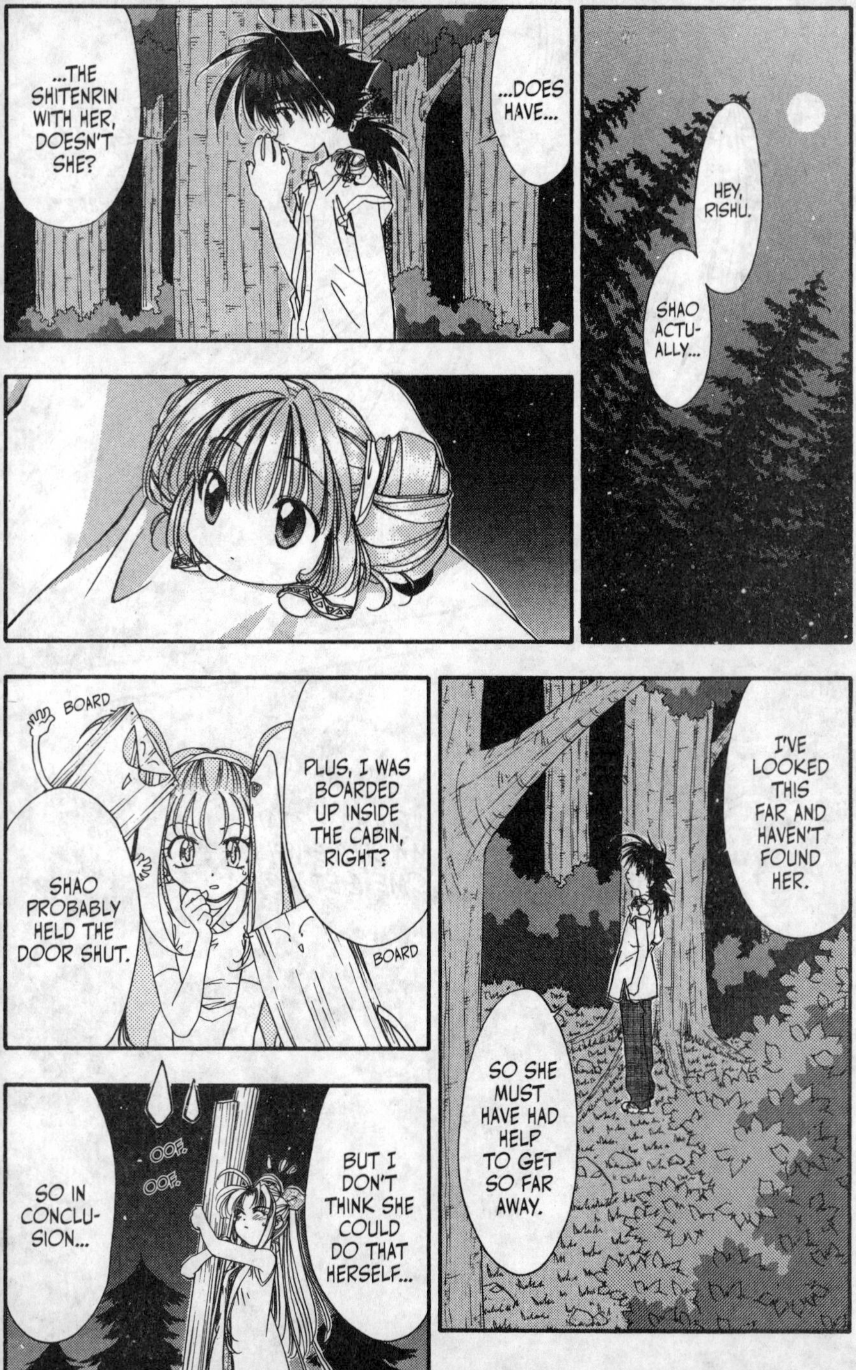
HEY, RISHU.
SHAO ACTUALLY...
...DOES HAVE...
...THE SHITENRIN WITH HER, DOESN'T SHE?
I'VE LOOKED THIS FAR AND HAVEN'T FOUND HER.
SO SHE MUST HAVE HAD HELP TO GET SO FAR AWAY.
PLUS, I WAS BOARDED UP INSIDE THE CABIN, RIGHT?
BOARD
BOARD
SHAO PROBABLY HELD THE DOOR SHUT.
BUT I DON'T THINK SHE COULD DO THAT HERSELF...
OOF.
OOF.
SO IN CONCLUSION...

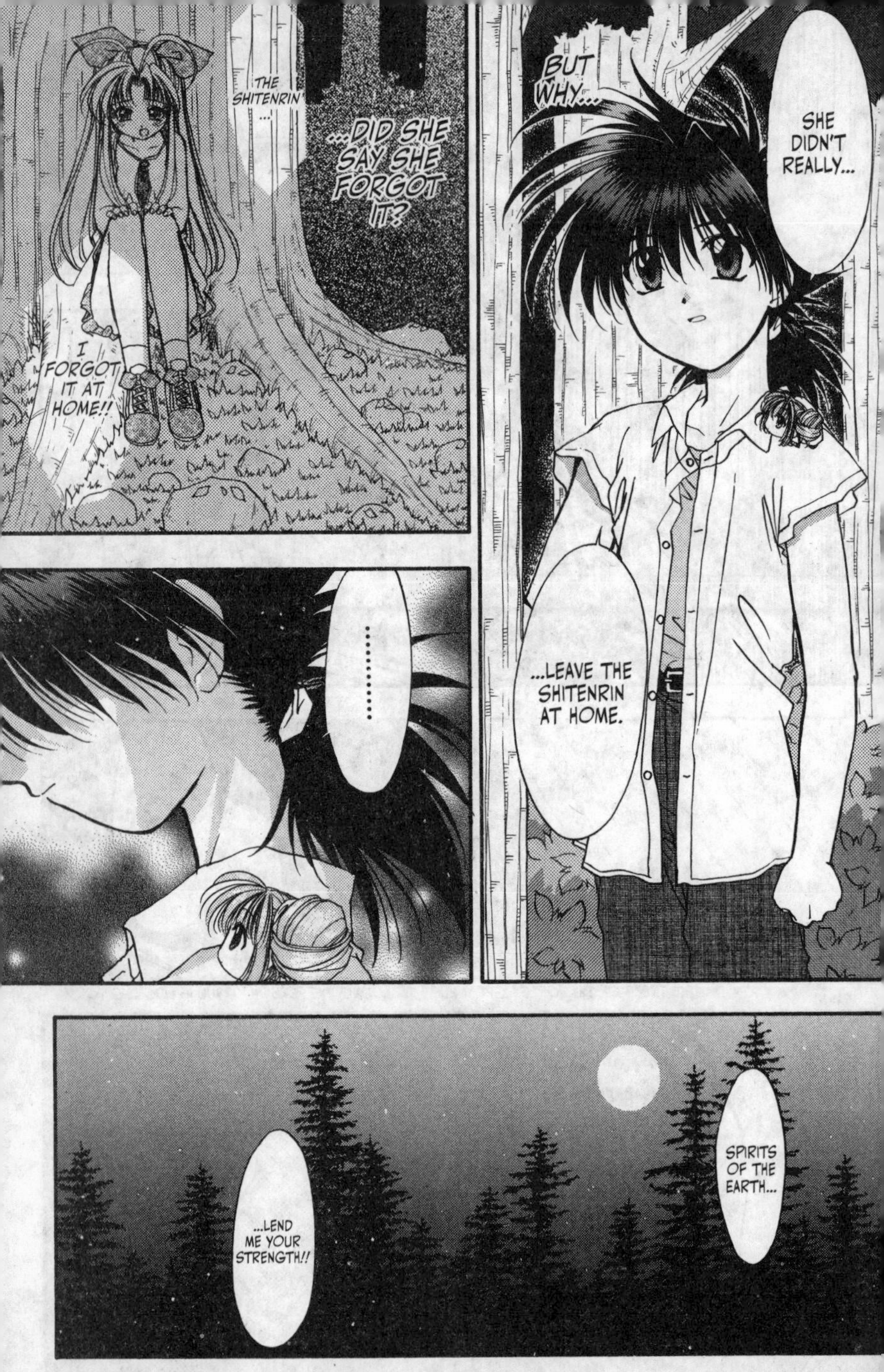
BUT WHY...
SHE DIDN'T REALLY...
...LEAVE THE SHITENRIN AT HOME.
THE SHITENRIN...
...DID SHE SAY SHE FORGOT IT?
I FORGOT IT AT HOME!!
....
SPIRITS OF THE EARTH...
...LEND ME YOUR STRENGTH!!

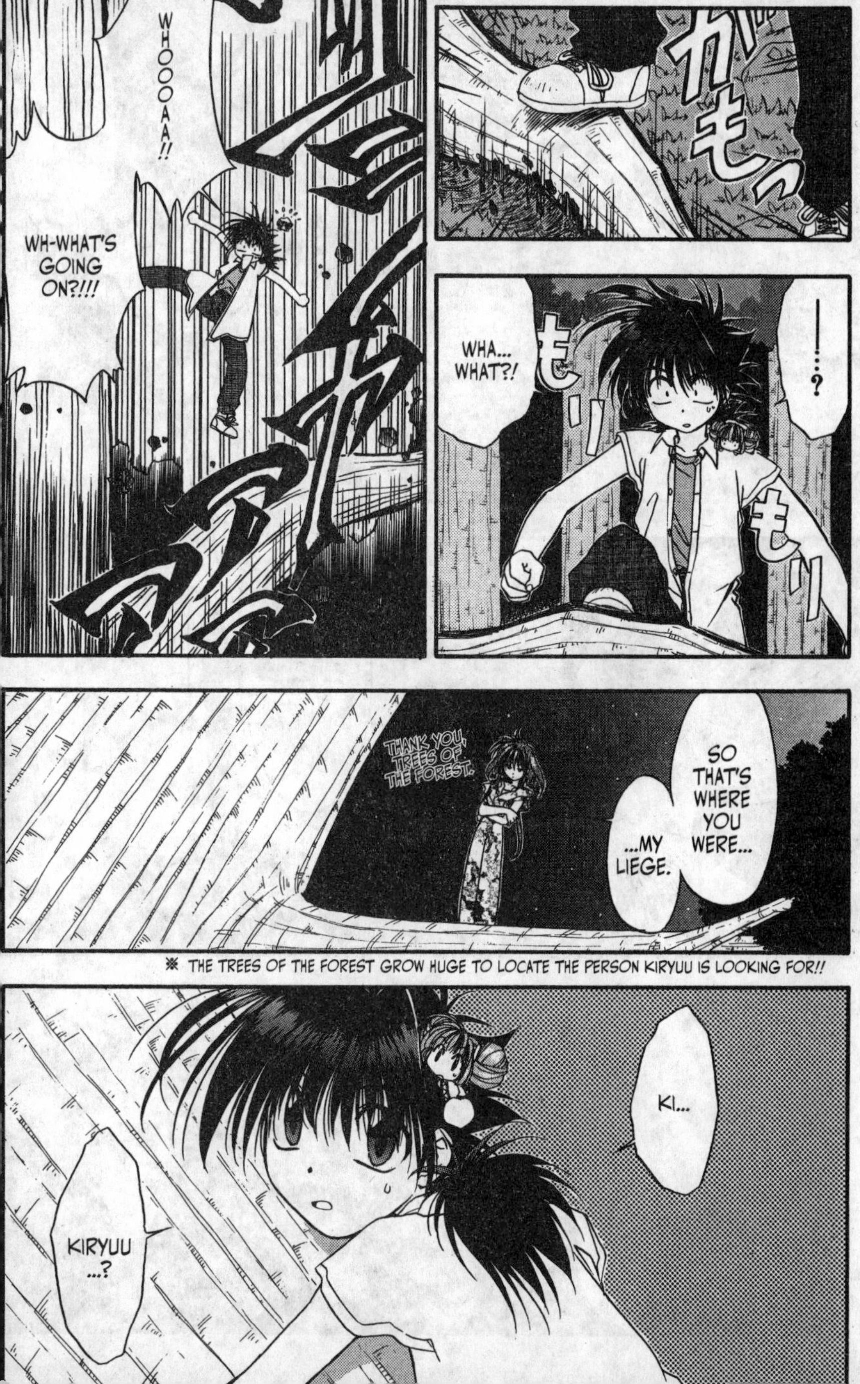
がもっ
—…?
WHA... WHAT?!
もり
もり
WHOOOAA!!
WH-WHAT'S GOING ON?!!!
SO THAT'S WHERE YOU WERE...
...MY LIEGE.
THANK YOU, TREES OF THE FOREST.
※ THE TREES OF THE FOREST GROW HUGE TO LOCATE THE PERSON KIRYUU IS LOOKING FOR!!
KI...
KIRYUU ...?

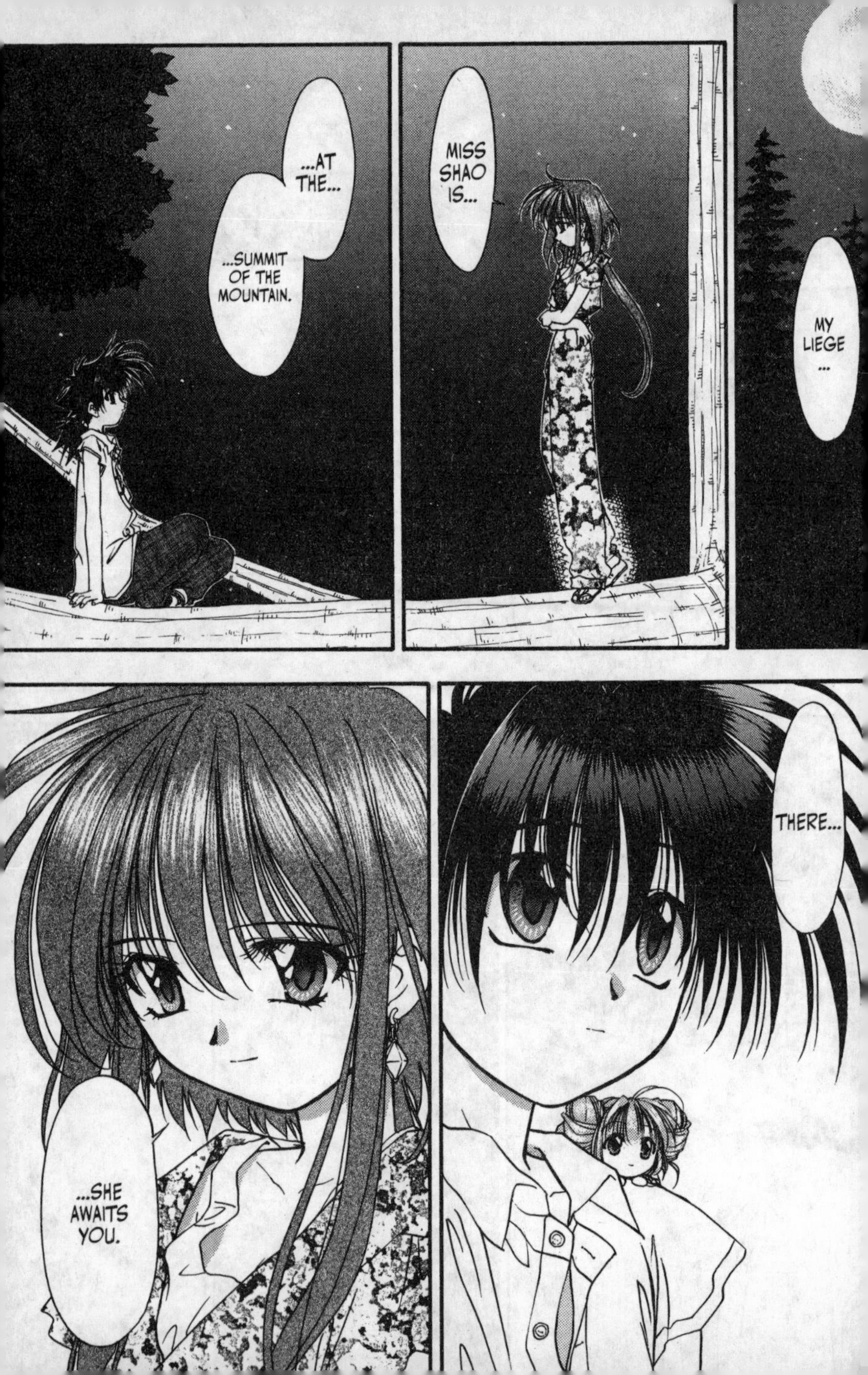
MY LIEGE ...
MISS SHAO IS...
...AT THE...
...SUMMIT OF THE MOUNTAIN.
THERE...
...SHE AWAITS YOU.

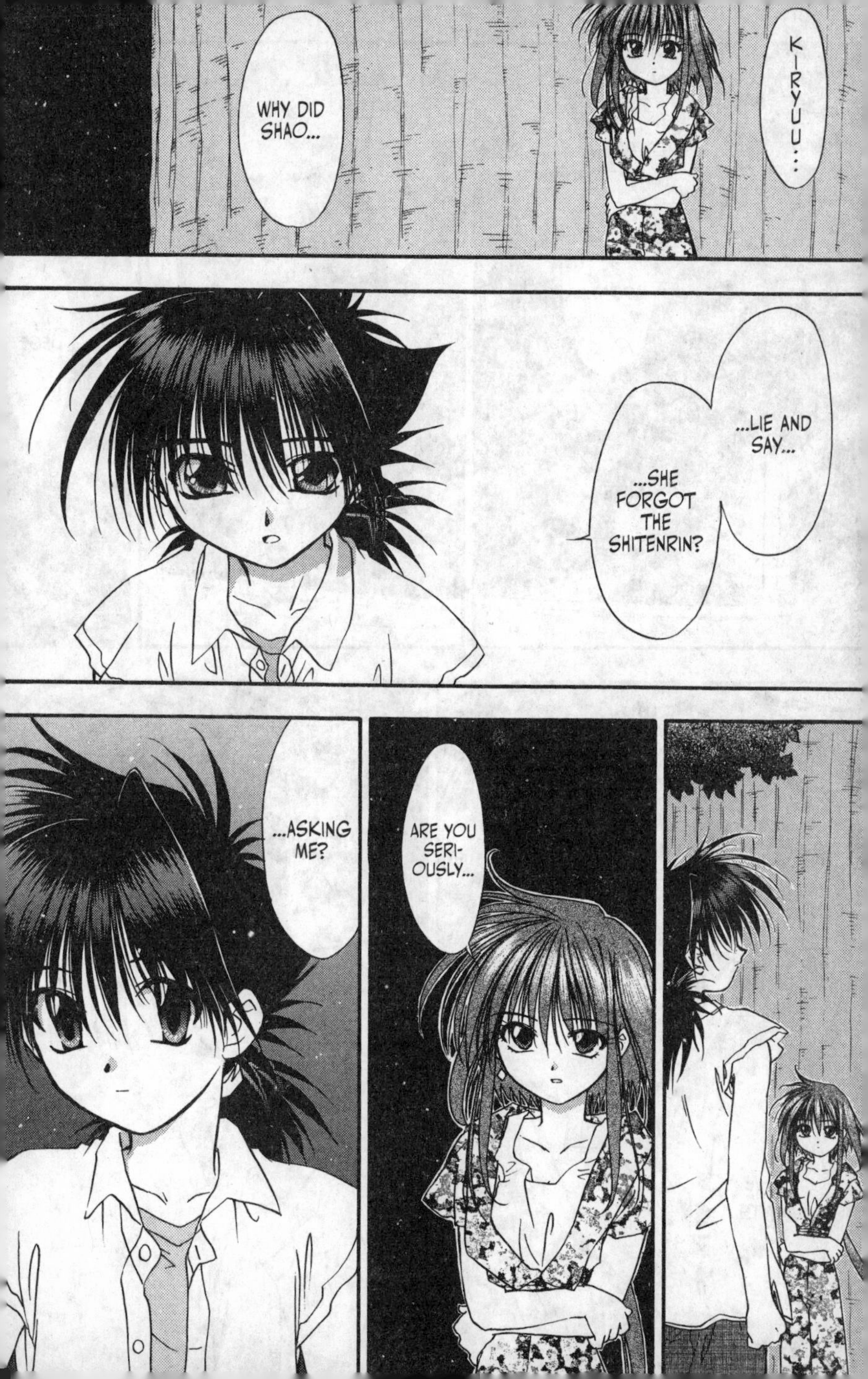
KIRYUU...
WHY DID SHAO...
...LIE AND SAY...
...SHE FORGOT THE SHITENRIN?
ARE YOU SERIOUSLY...
...ASKING ME?

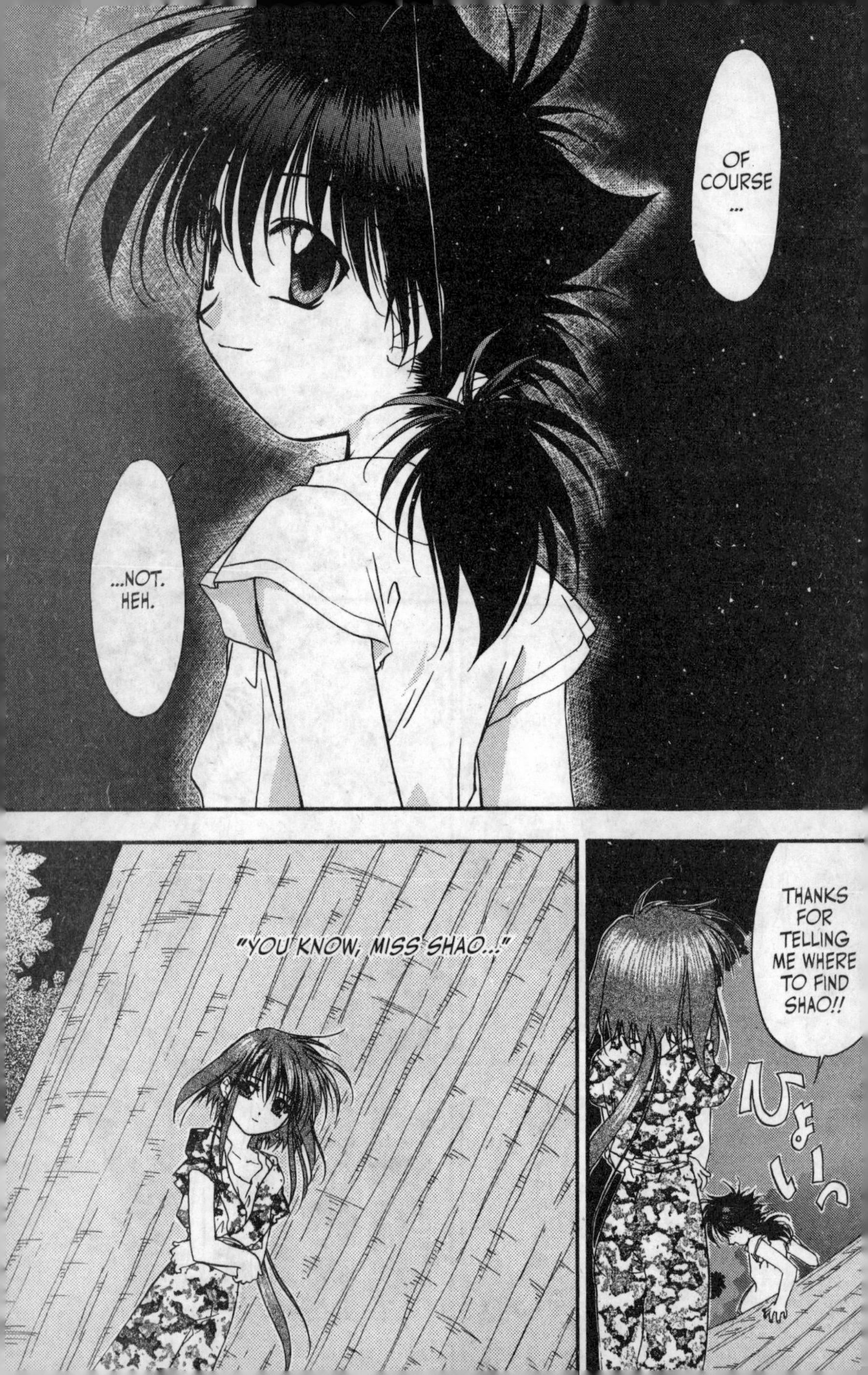
OF COURSE ...
...NOT. HEH.
THANKS FOR TELLING ME WHERE TO FIND SHAO!!
"YOU KNOW, MISS SHAO...!"

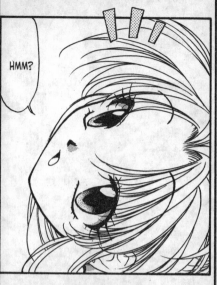

HMM?

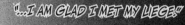

"...I AM GLAD I MET MY LIEGE."

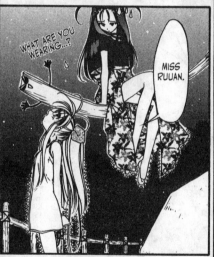

WHAT ARE YOU WEARING...?

MISS RUUAN.

I FINALLY FOUND YOU.

MASTER TAA'S WORRIED ABOUT YOU, Y'KNOW!

REALLY!

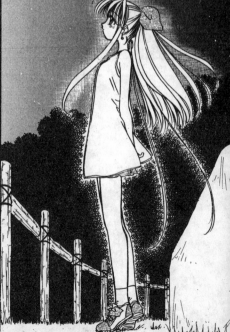

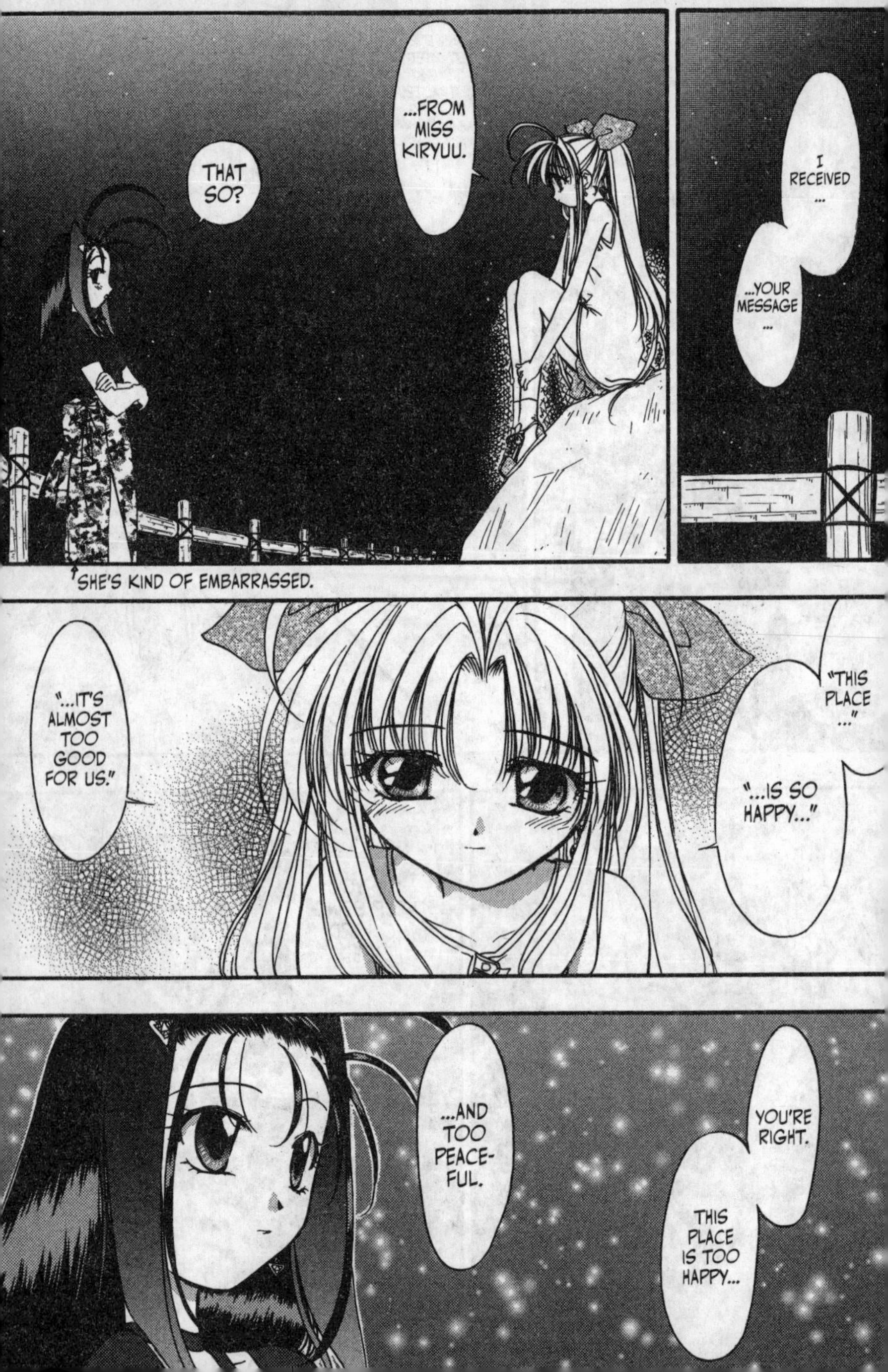
I RECEIVED...
...YOUR MESSAGE...
...FROM MISS KIRYUU.
THAT SO?
SHE'S KIND OF EMBARRASSED.
"THIS PLACE..."
"...IS SO HAPPY..."
"...IT'S ALMOST TOO GOOD FOR US."
YOU'RE RIGHT.
THIS PLACE IS TOO HAPPY...
...AND TOO PEACE-FUL.

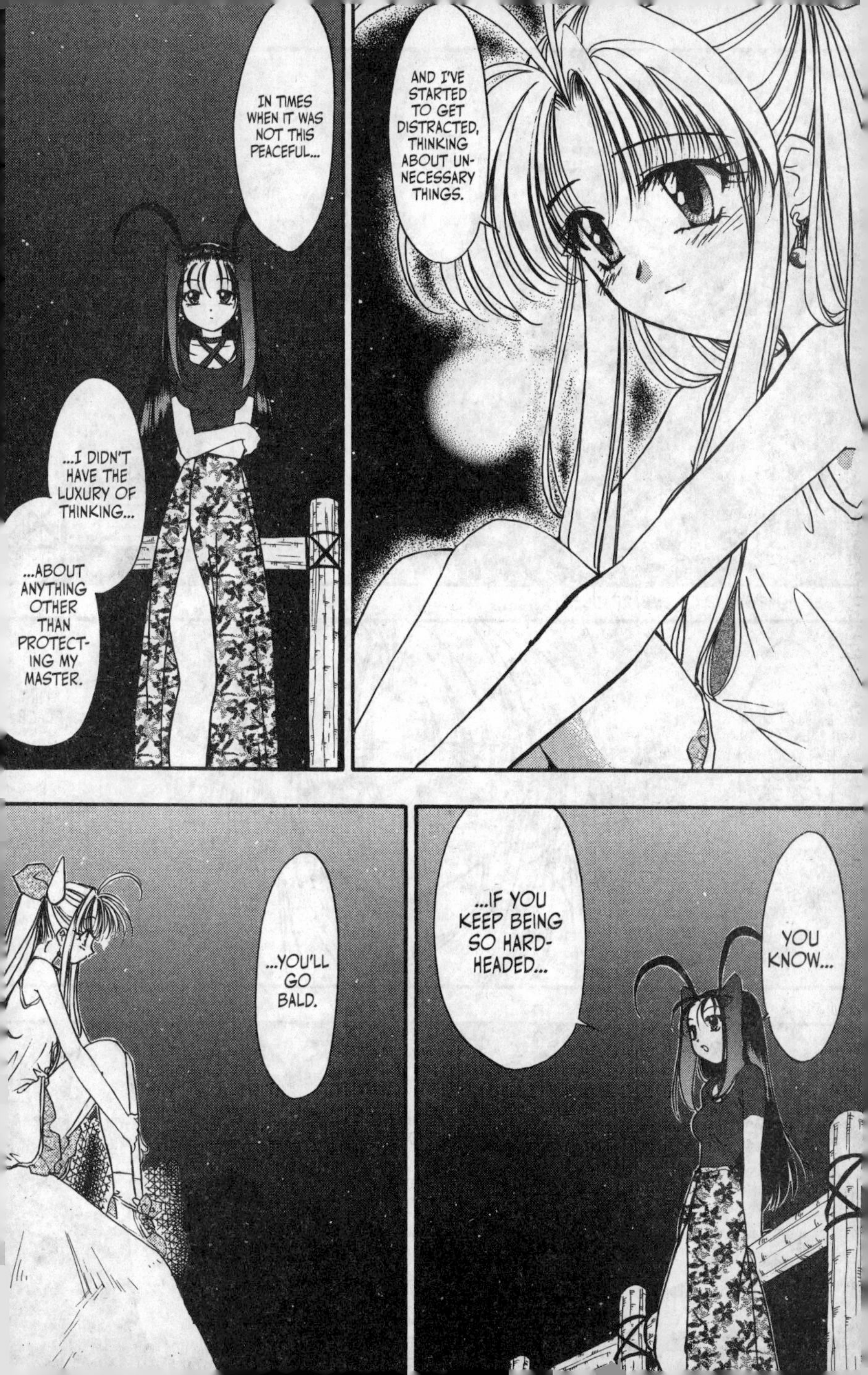
AND I'VE STARTED TO GET DISTRACTED, THINKING ABOUT UN-NECESSARY THINGS.
IN TIMES WHEN IT WAS NOT THIS PEACEFUL...
...I DIDN'T HAVE THE LUXURY OF THINKING...
...ABOUT ANYTHING OTHER THAN PROTECT-ING MY MASTER.
YOU KNOW...
...IF YOU KEEP BEING SO HARD-HEADED...
...YOU'LL GO BALD.

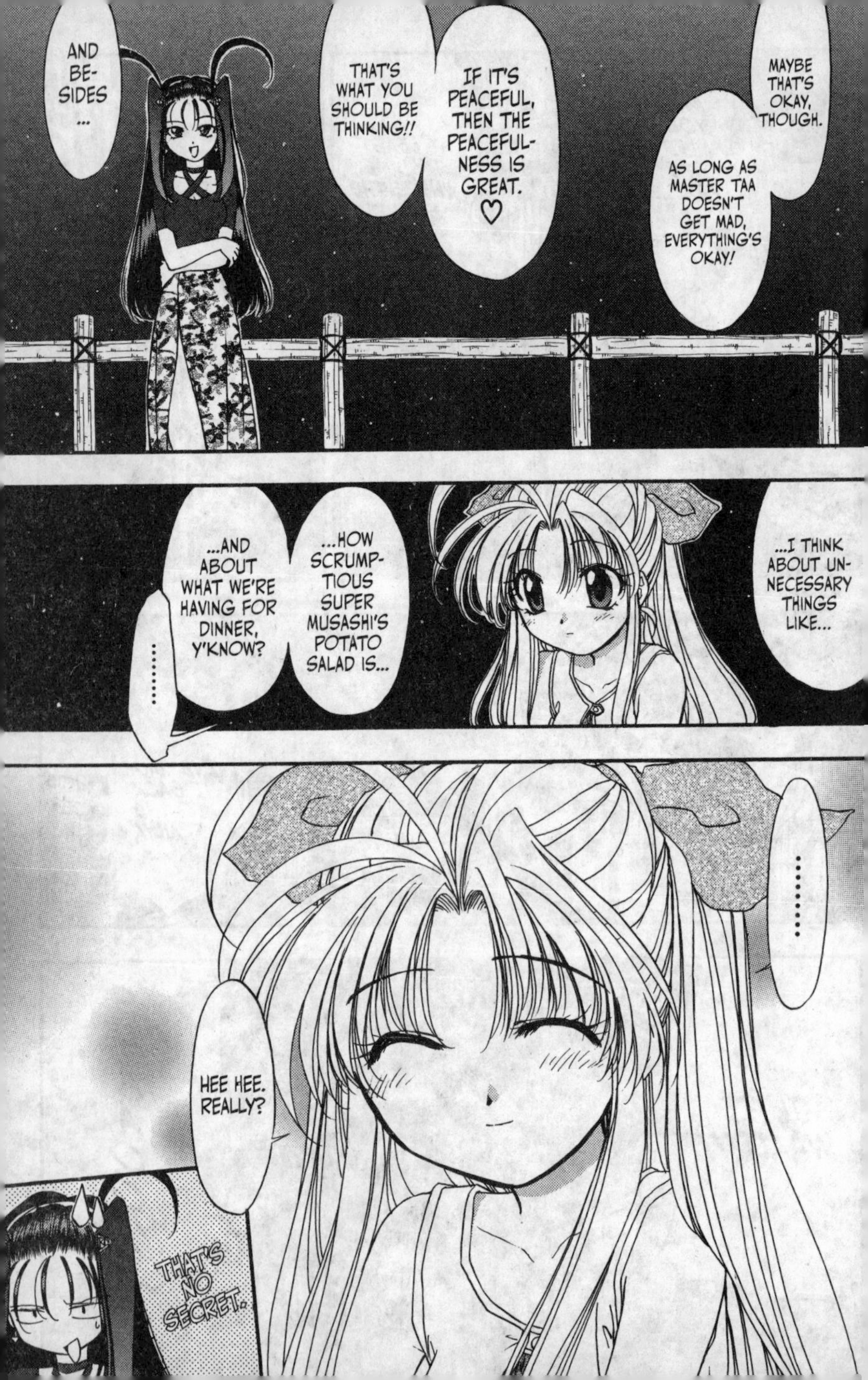

MAYBE THAT'S OKAY, THOUGH.
AS LONG AS MASTER TAA DOESN'T GET MAD, EVERYTHING'S OKAY!
IF IT'S PEACEFUL, THEN THE PEACEFULNESS IS GREAT. ♡
THAT'S WHAT YOU SHOULD BE THINKING!!
AND BESIDES ...
...I THINK ABOUT UNNECESSARY THINGS LIKE...
...HOW SCRUMPTIOUS SUPER MUSASHI'S POTATO SALAD IS...
...AND ABOUT WHAT WE'RE HAVING FOR DINNER, Y'KNOW?
....
....
HEE HEE. REALLY?
THAT'S NO SECRET.

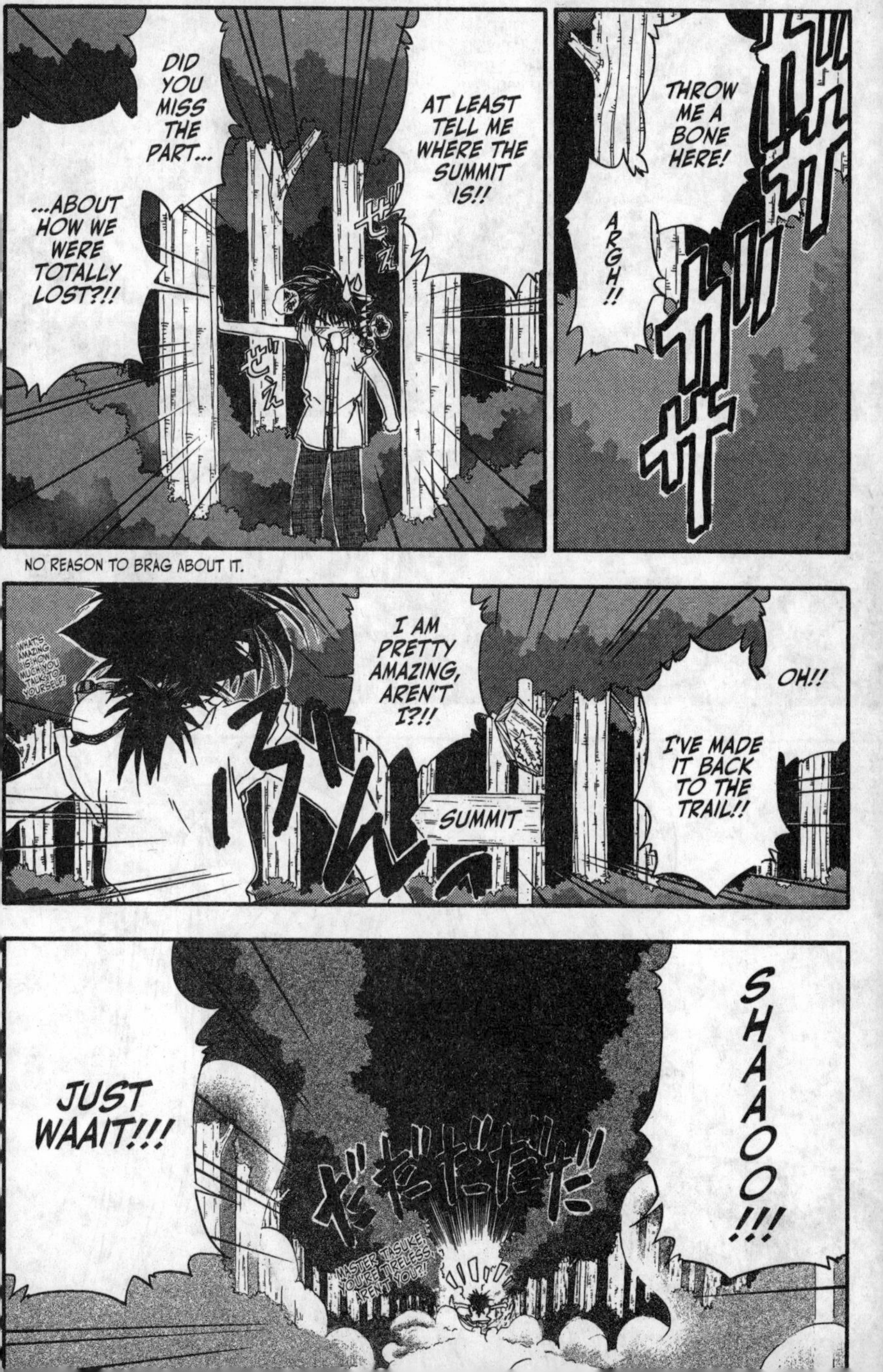
THROW ME A BONE HERE!
ARGH!!
AT LEAST TELL ME WHERE THE SUMMIT IS!!
DID YOU MISS THE PART...
...ABOUT HOW WE WERE TOTALLY LOST?!!
NO REASON TO BRAG ABOUT IT.
OH!!
I'VE MADE IT BACK TO THE TRAIL!!
I AM PRETTY AMAZING, AREN'T I?!!
SUMMIT
WHAT'S AMAZING IS HOW MUCH YOU TALK TO YOURSELF!
SHAAAOOO!!!
JUST WAAIT!!!
MASTER TASUKE, YOU'RE TIRELESS, AREN'T YOU?!

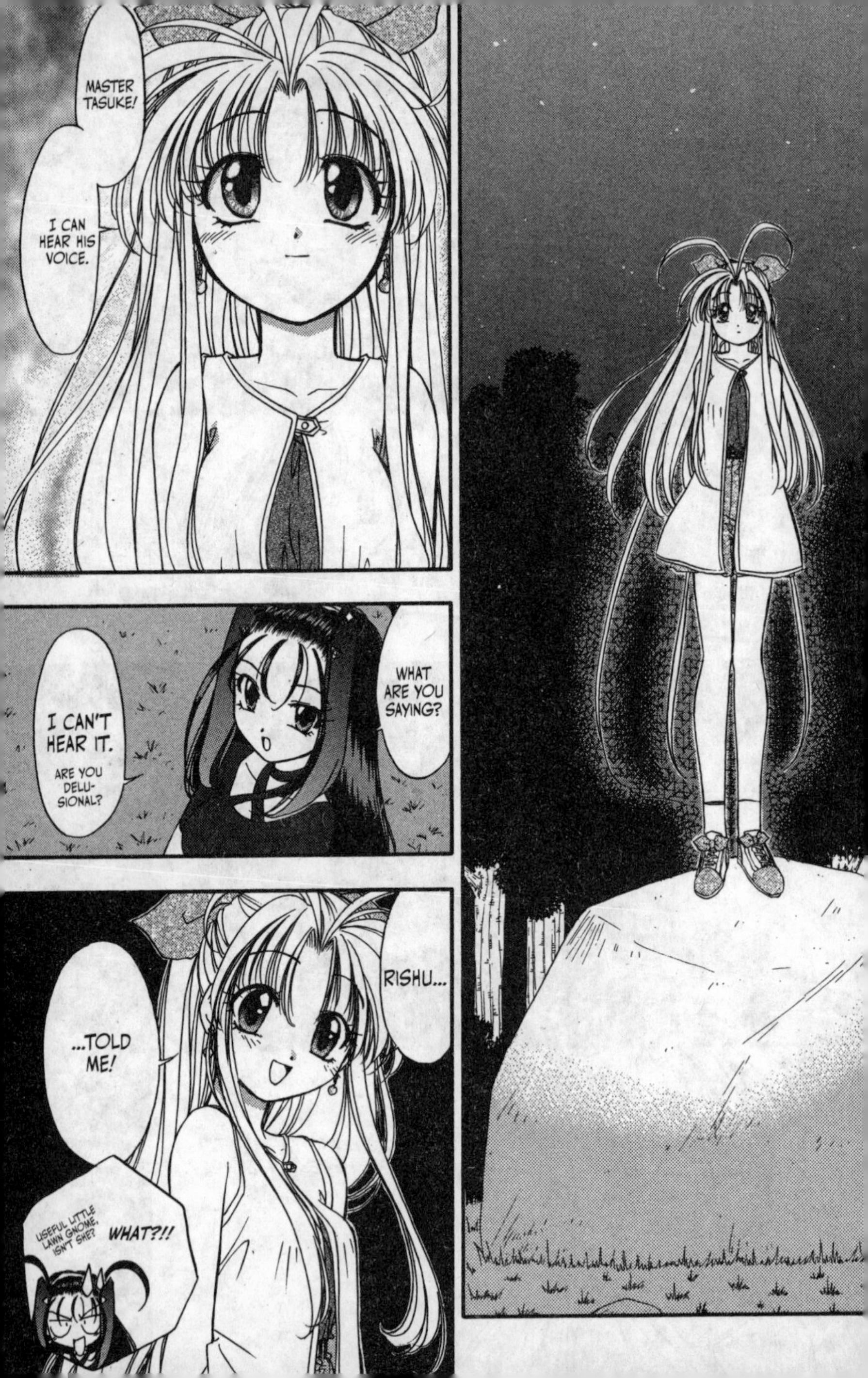
MASTER TASUKE!
I CAN HEAR HIS VOICE.
WHAT ARE YOU SAYING?
I CAN'T HEAR IT.
ARE YOU DELU-SIONAL?
RISHU...
...TOLD ME!
WHAT?!!
USEFUL LITTLE LAWN GNOME, ISN'T SHE?

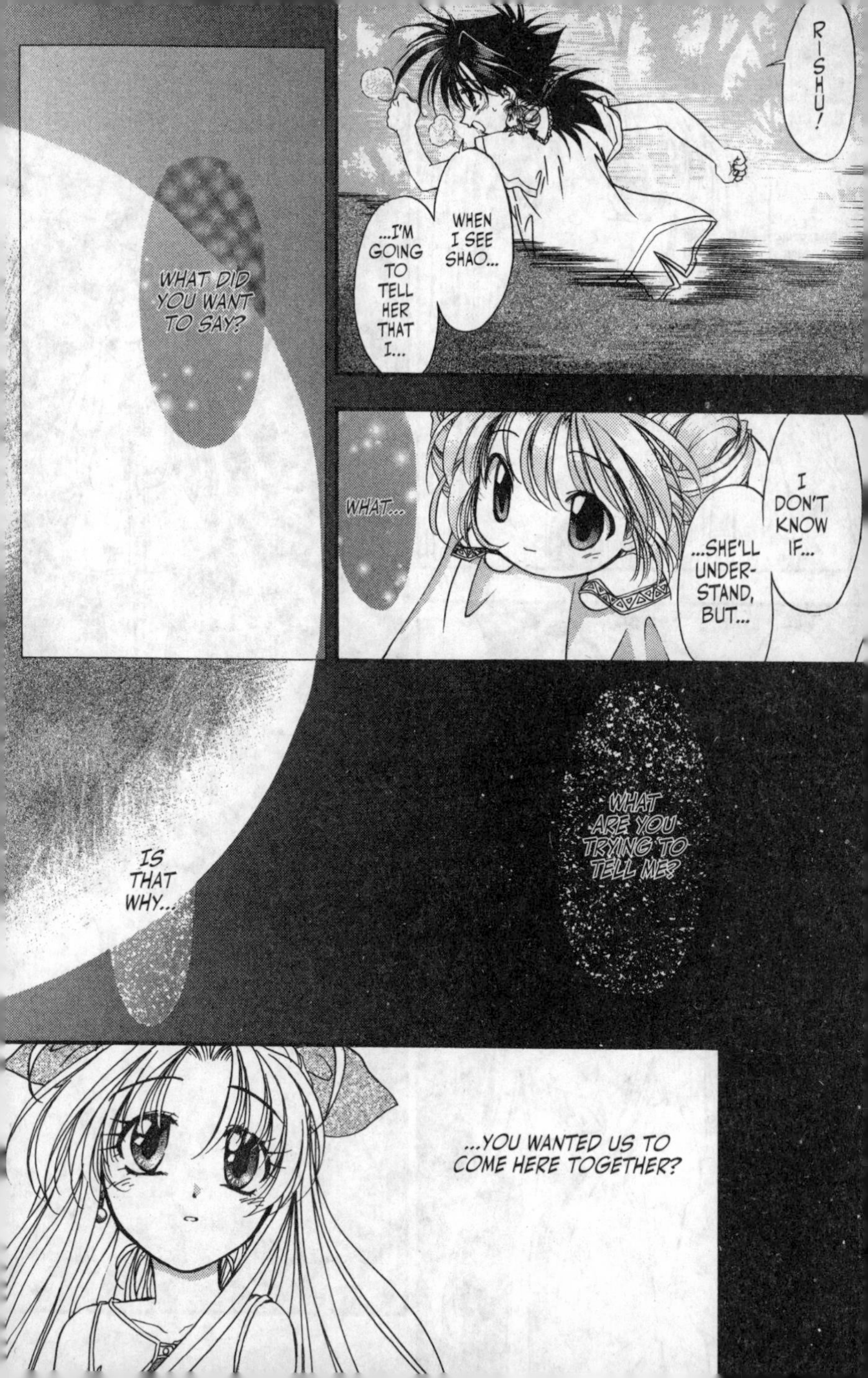
RISHU!
WHEN I SEE SHAO...
...I'M GOING TO TELL HER THAT I...
I DON'T KNOW IF...
...SHE'LL UNDER-STAND, BUT...
WHAT...
WHAT DID YOU WANT TO SAY?
WHAT ARE YOU TRYING TO TELL ME?
IS THAT WHY...
...YOU WANTED US TO COME HERE TOGETHER?

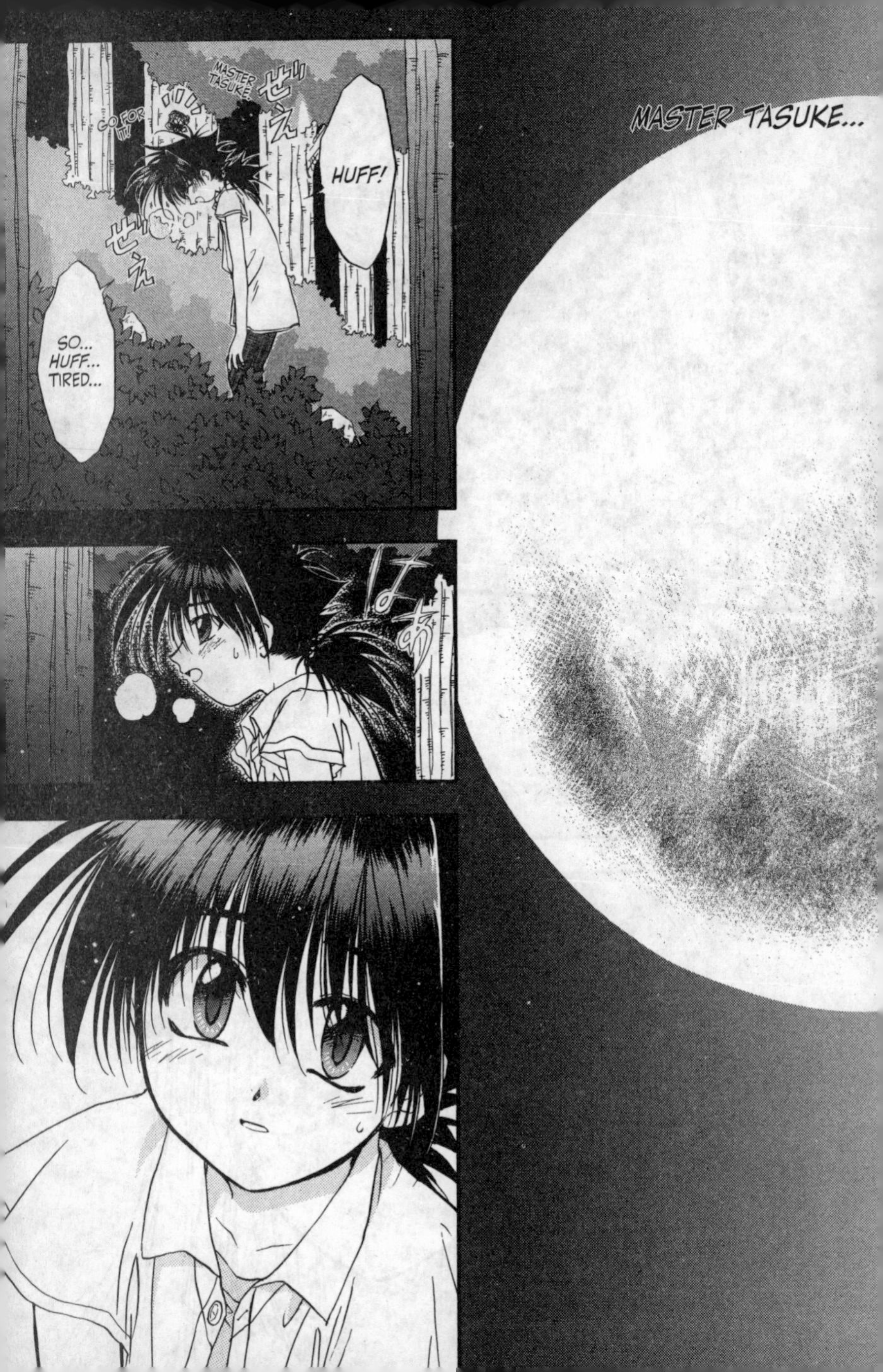
MASTER TASUKE...
HUFF!
ぜぇ
MASTER TASUKE, GO FOR IT!!
ぜぇ
SO... HUFF... TIRED...
はぁ

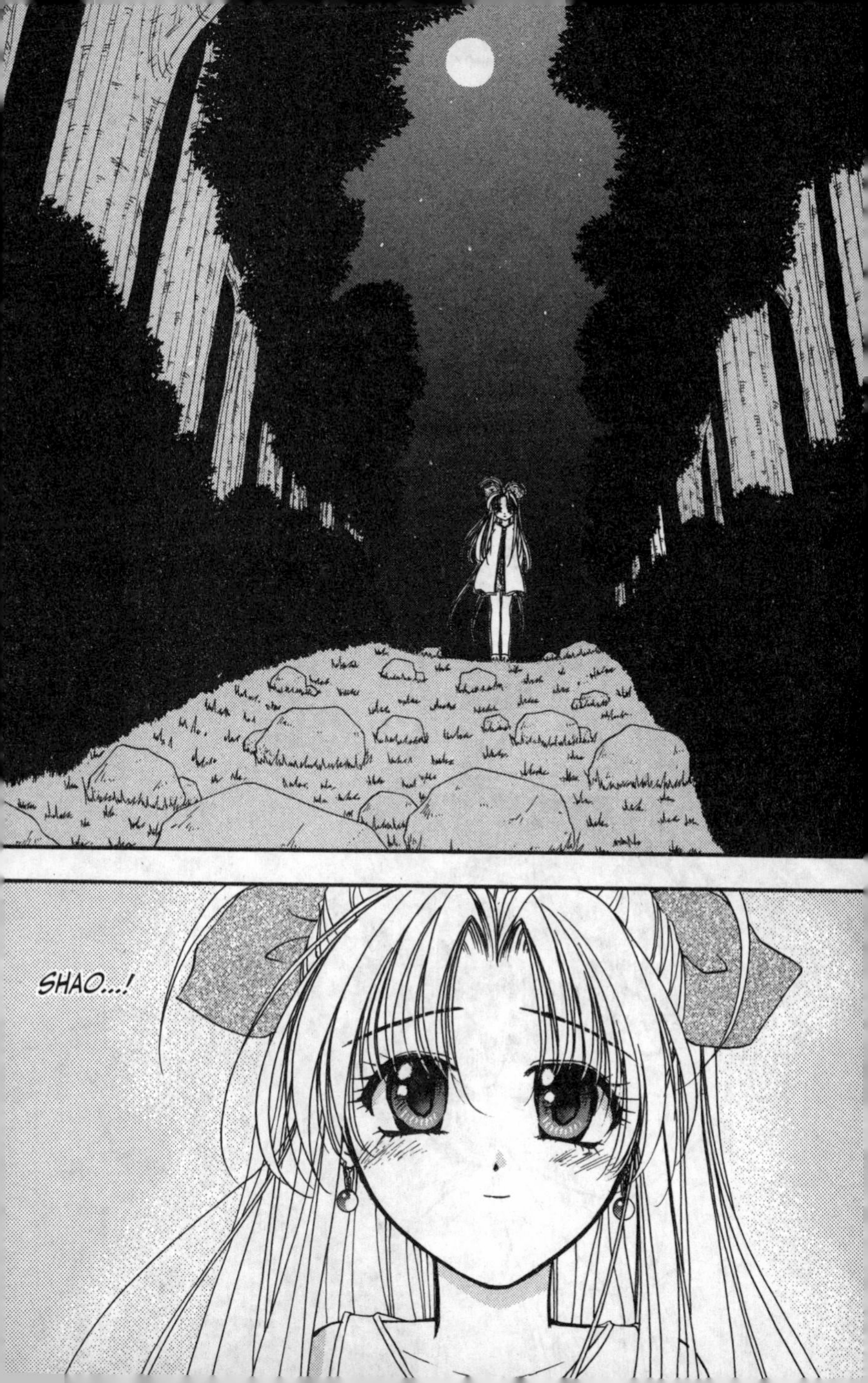
SHAO...!

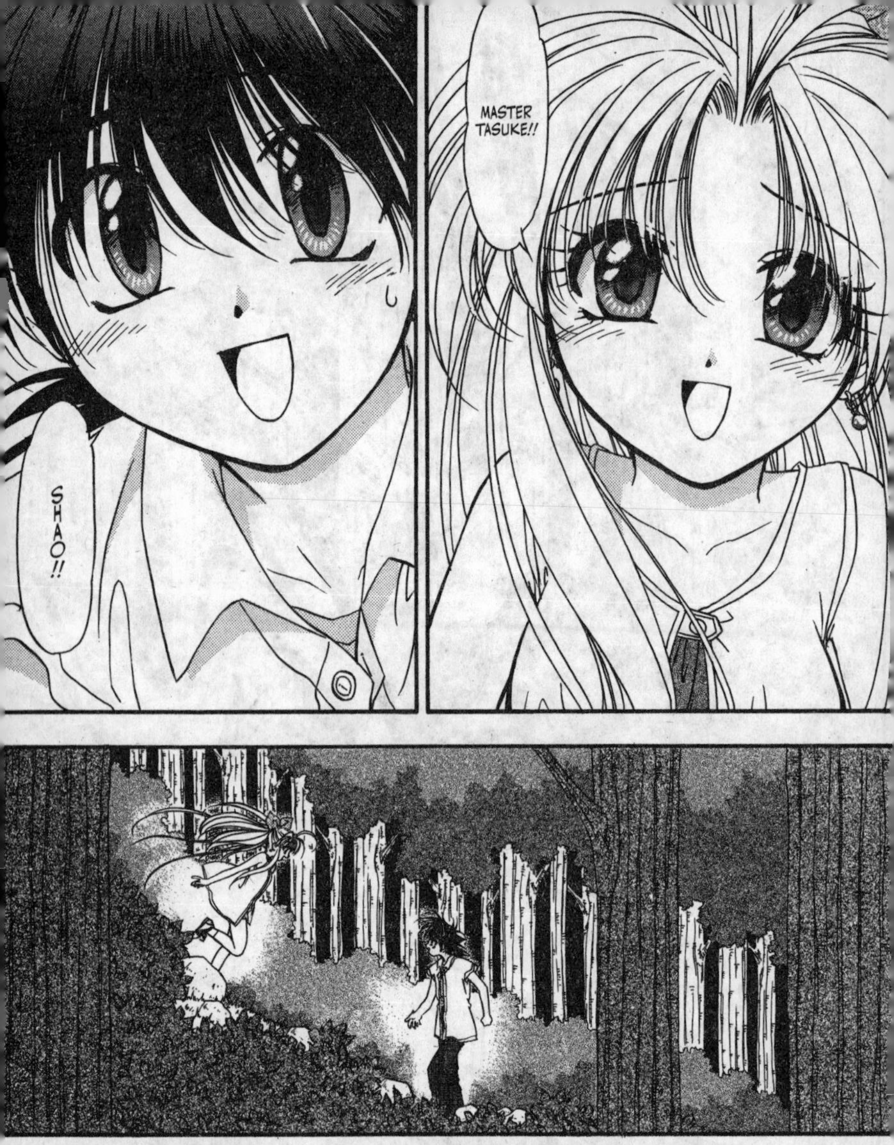
MASTER TASUKE!!
SHAO!!

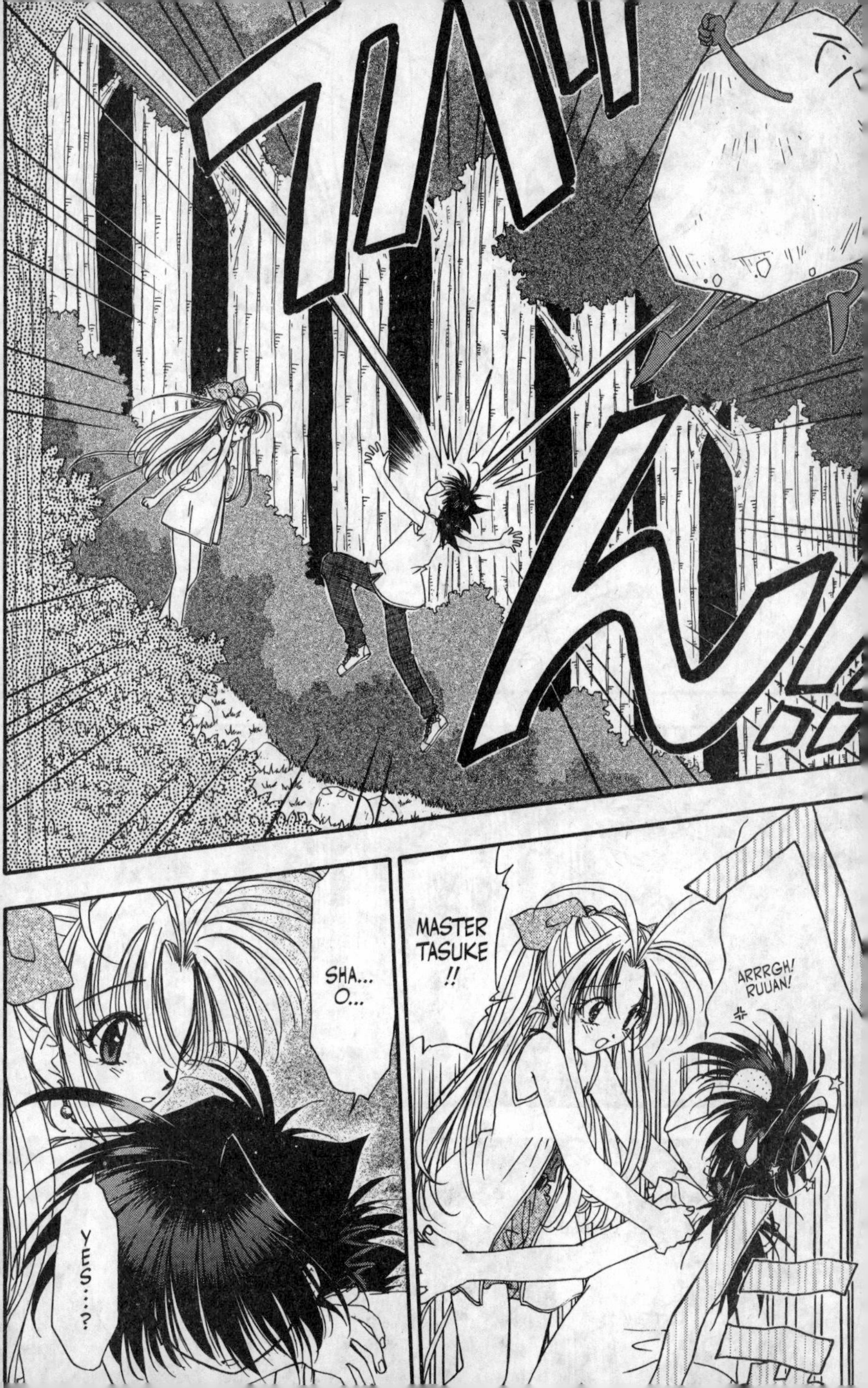
MASTER TASUKE !!
ARRRGH! RUUAN!
SHA... O...
YES...?

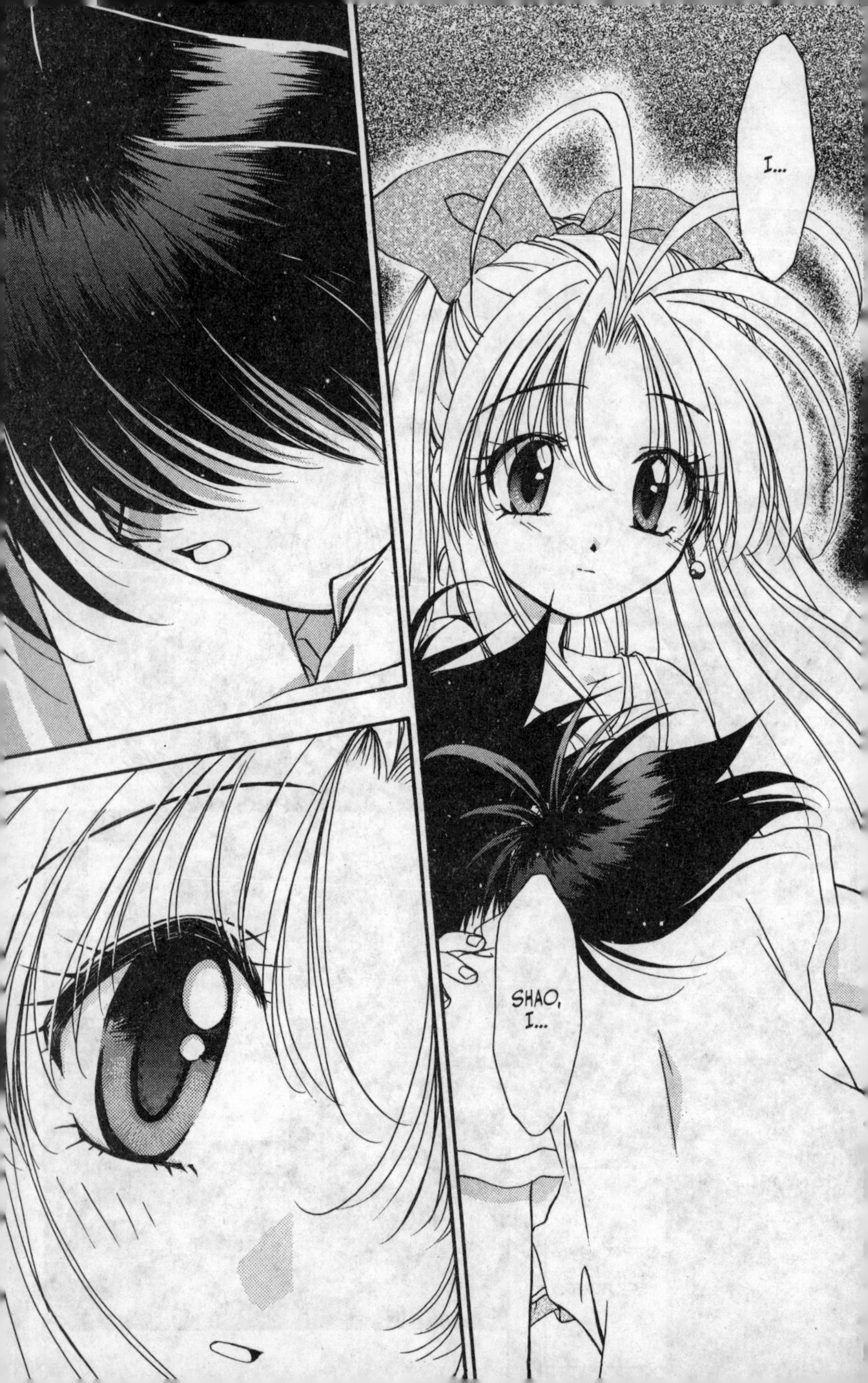
I...
SHAO, I...

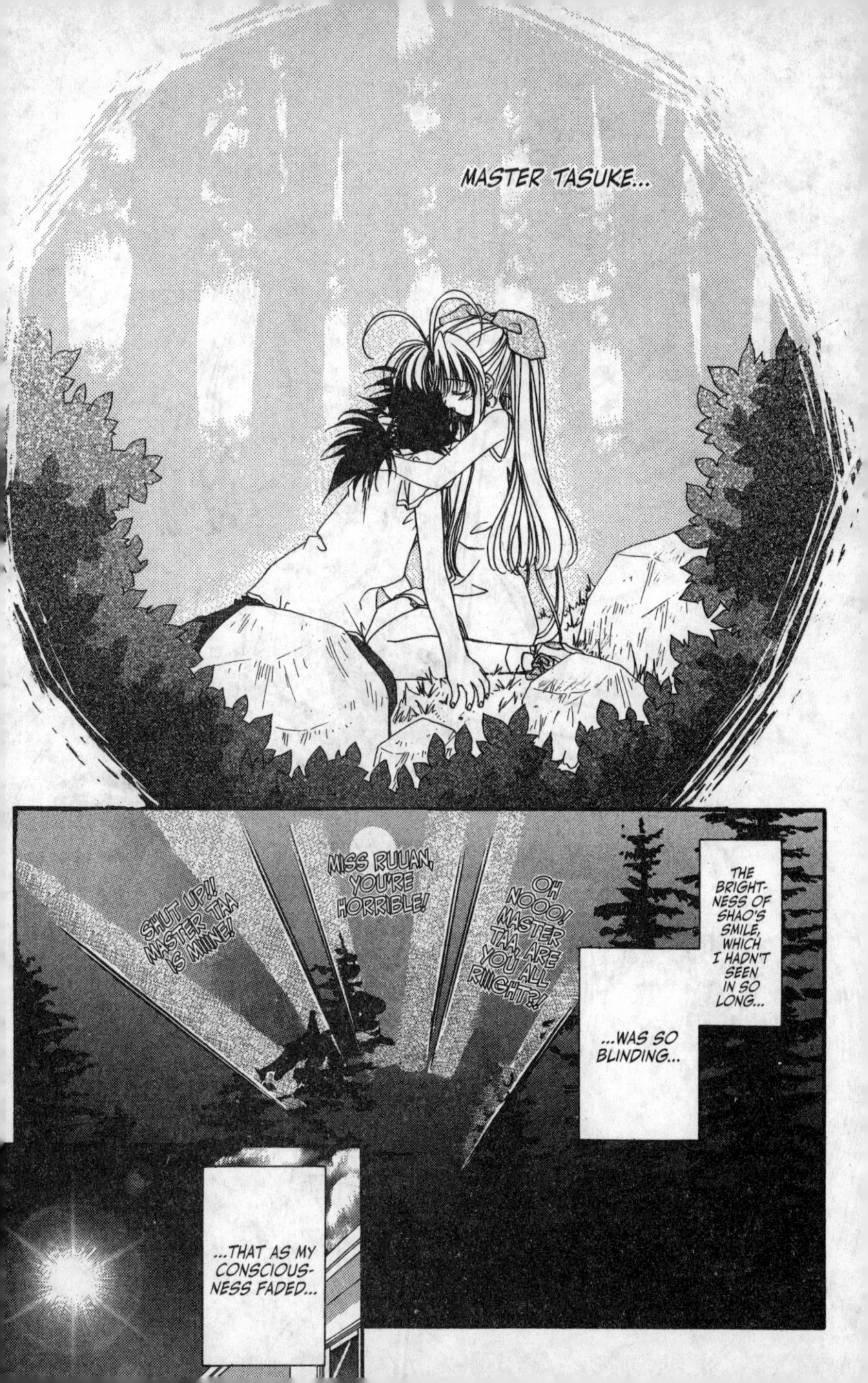
MASTER TASUKE...
THE BRIGHT-NESS OF SHAO'S SMILE, WHICH I HADN'T SEEN IN SO LONG...
...WAS SO BLINDING...
OH NOOO! MASTER TAA, ARE YOU ALL RIIIGHT?!
MISS RUUAN, YOU'RE HORRIBLE!
SHUT UP!! MASTER TAA IS MIIINE!
...THAT AS MY CONSCIOUS-NESS FADED...

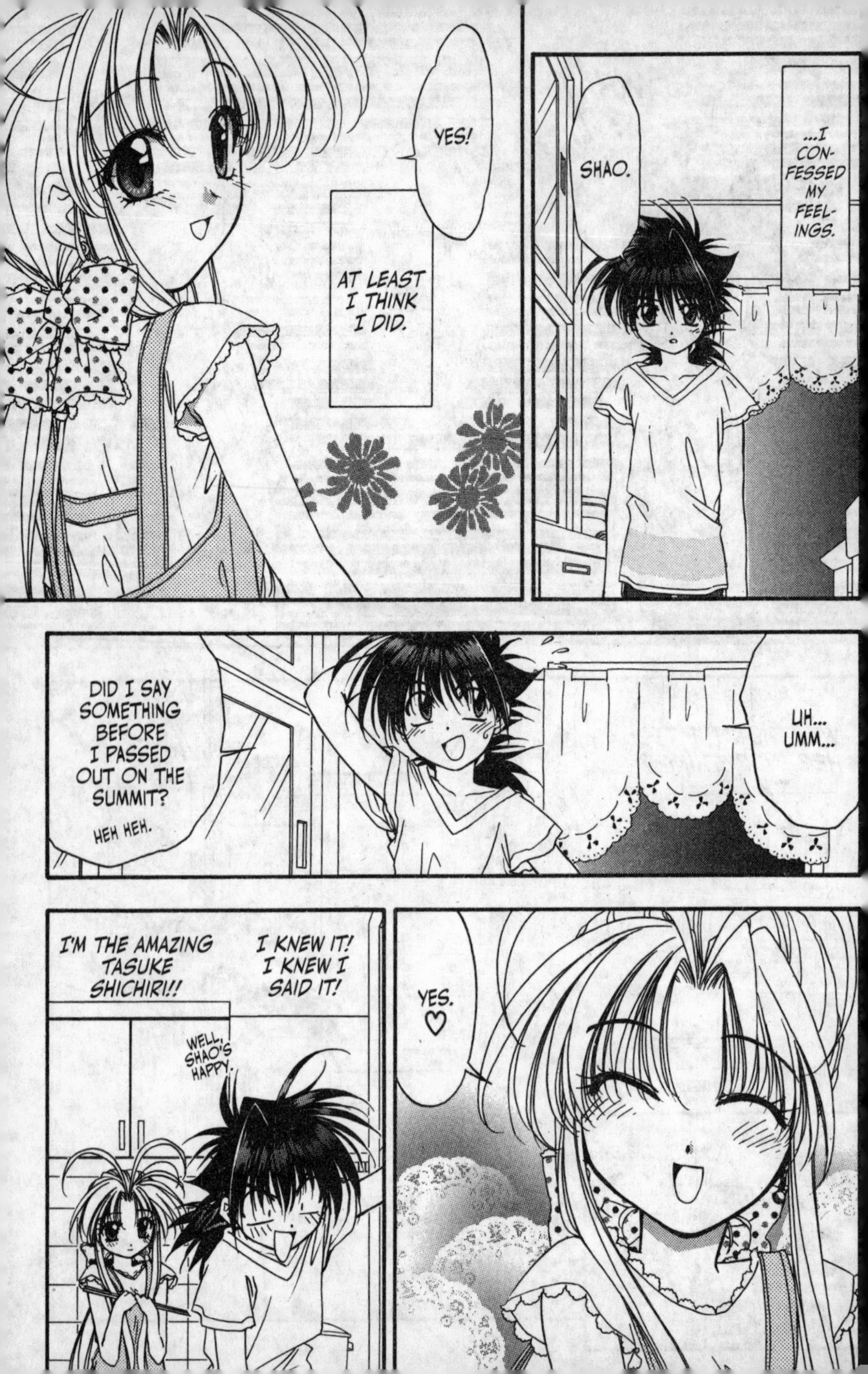
...I CONFESSED MY FEELINGS.
SHAO.
YES!
AT LEAST I THINK I DID.
UH... UMM...
DID I SAY SOMETHING BEFORE I PASSED OUT ON THE SUMMIT?
HEH HEH.
YES. ♡
I KNEW IT! I KNEW I SAID IT!
I'M THE AMAZING TASUKE SHICHIRI!!
WELL, SHAO'S HAPPY.

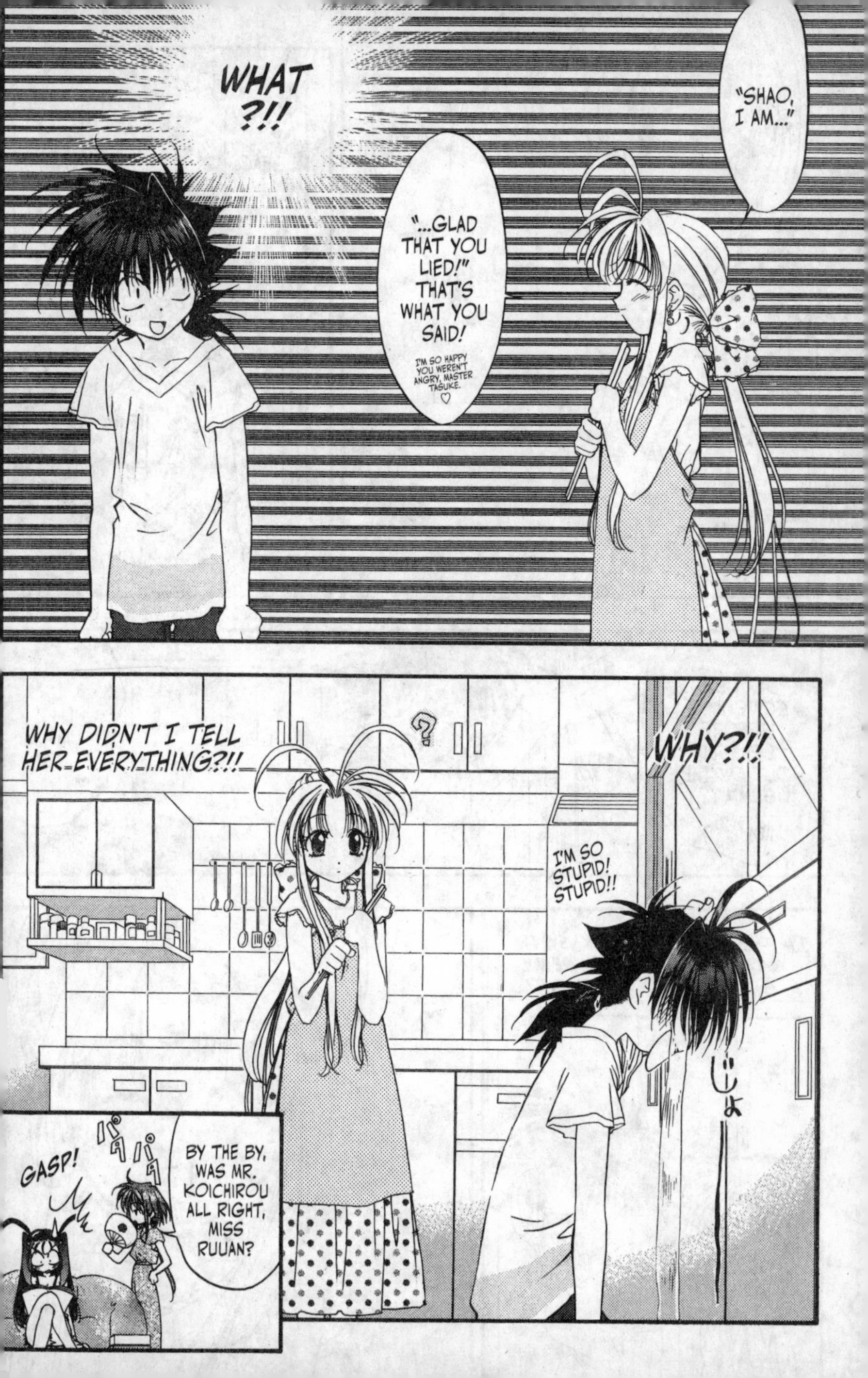
"SHAO, I AM..."
"...GLAD THAT YOU LIED!" THAT'S WHAT YOU SAID!
I'M SO HAPPY YOU WEREN'T ANGRY, MASTER TASUKE. ♡
WHAT ?!!
WHY?!!
I'M SO STUPID! STUPID!!
?
WHY DIDN'T I TELL HER EVERYTHING?!!
BY THE BY, WAS MR. KOICHIROU ALL RIGHT, MISS RUUAN?
パタパタ
GASP!

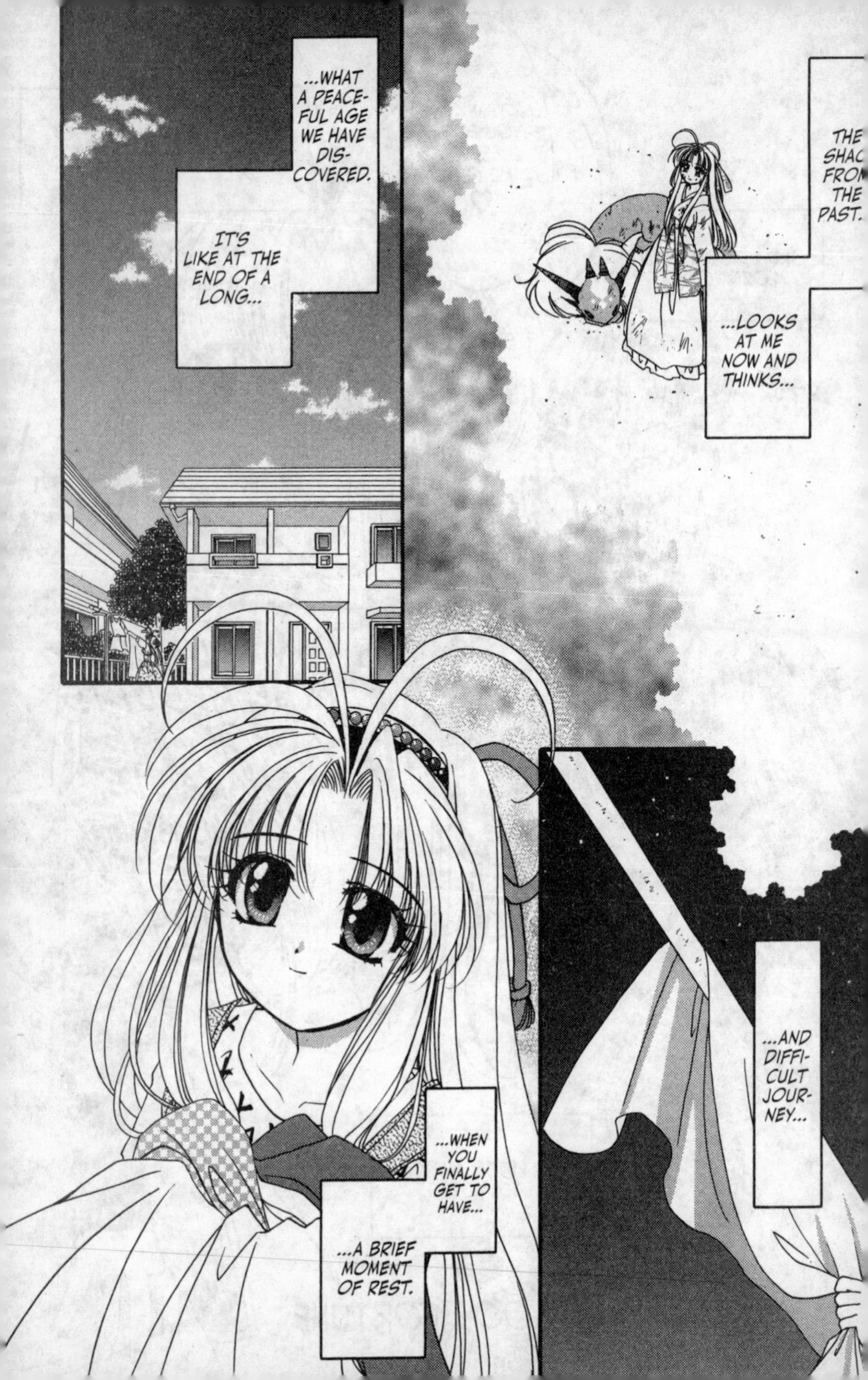

THE SHAC FROM THE PAST.
...LOOKS AT ME NOW AND THINKS...
...WHAT A PEACEFUL AGE WE HAVE DISCOVERED.
IT'S LIKE AT THE END OF A LONG...
...AND DIFFICULT JOURNEY...
...WHEN YOU FINALLY GET TO HAVE...
...A BRIEF MOMENT OF REST.

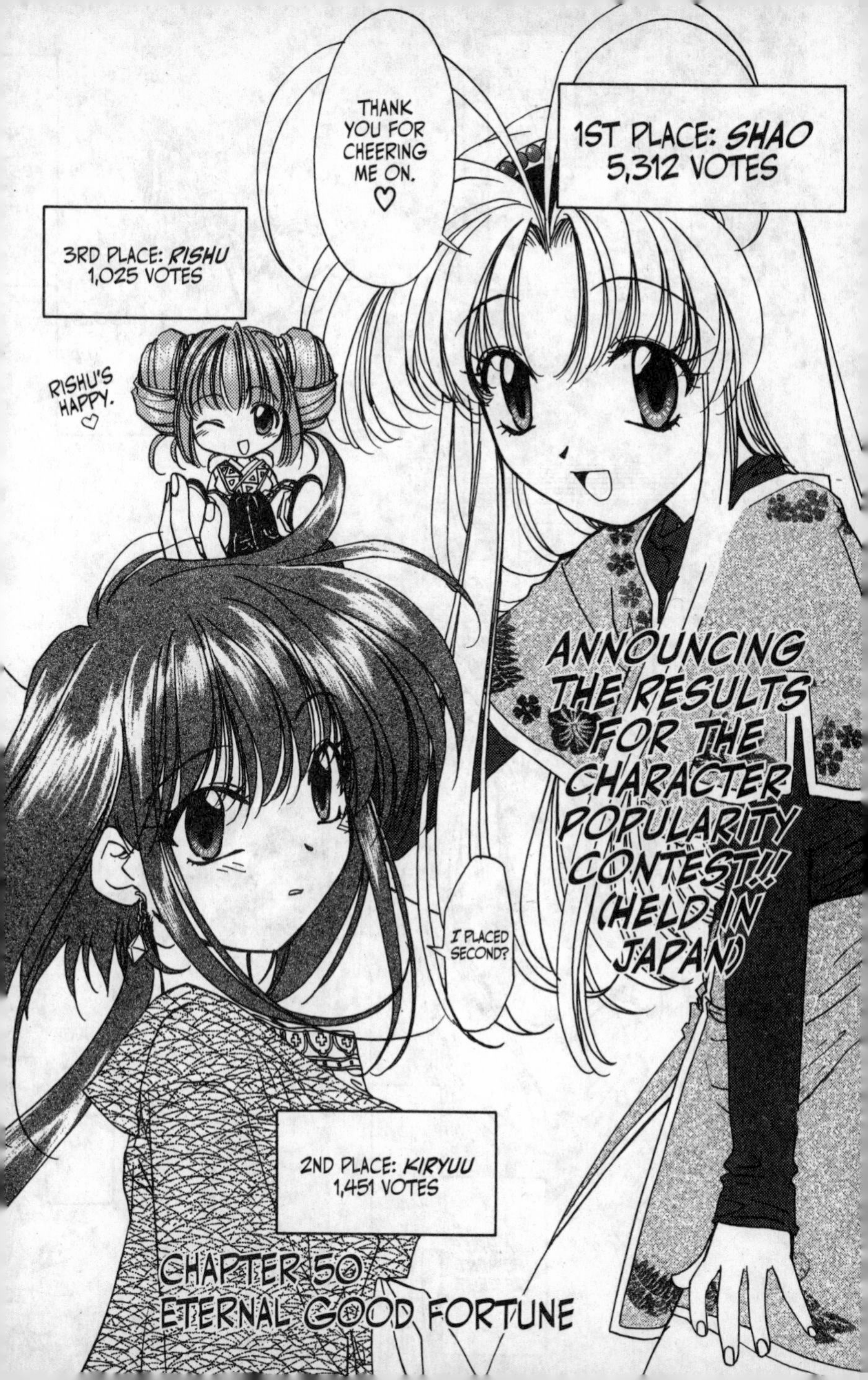
1ST PLACE: SHAO 5,312 VOTES
THANK YOU FOR CHEERING ME ON. ♡
3RD PLACE: RISHU 1,025 VOTES
RISHU'S HAPPY. ♡
ANNOUNCING THE RESULTS FOR THE CHARACTER POPULARITY CONTEST!! (HELD IN JAPAN)
I PLACED SECOND?
2ND PLACE: KIRYUU 1,451 VOTES
CHAPTER 50 ETERNAL GOOD FORTUNE

16TH	HOKUTO SHICHISEI
17TH	NANA
18TH	DEVIL RUUAN
19TH	ANGEL RUUAN
20TH	MEIHOA

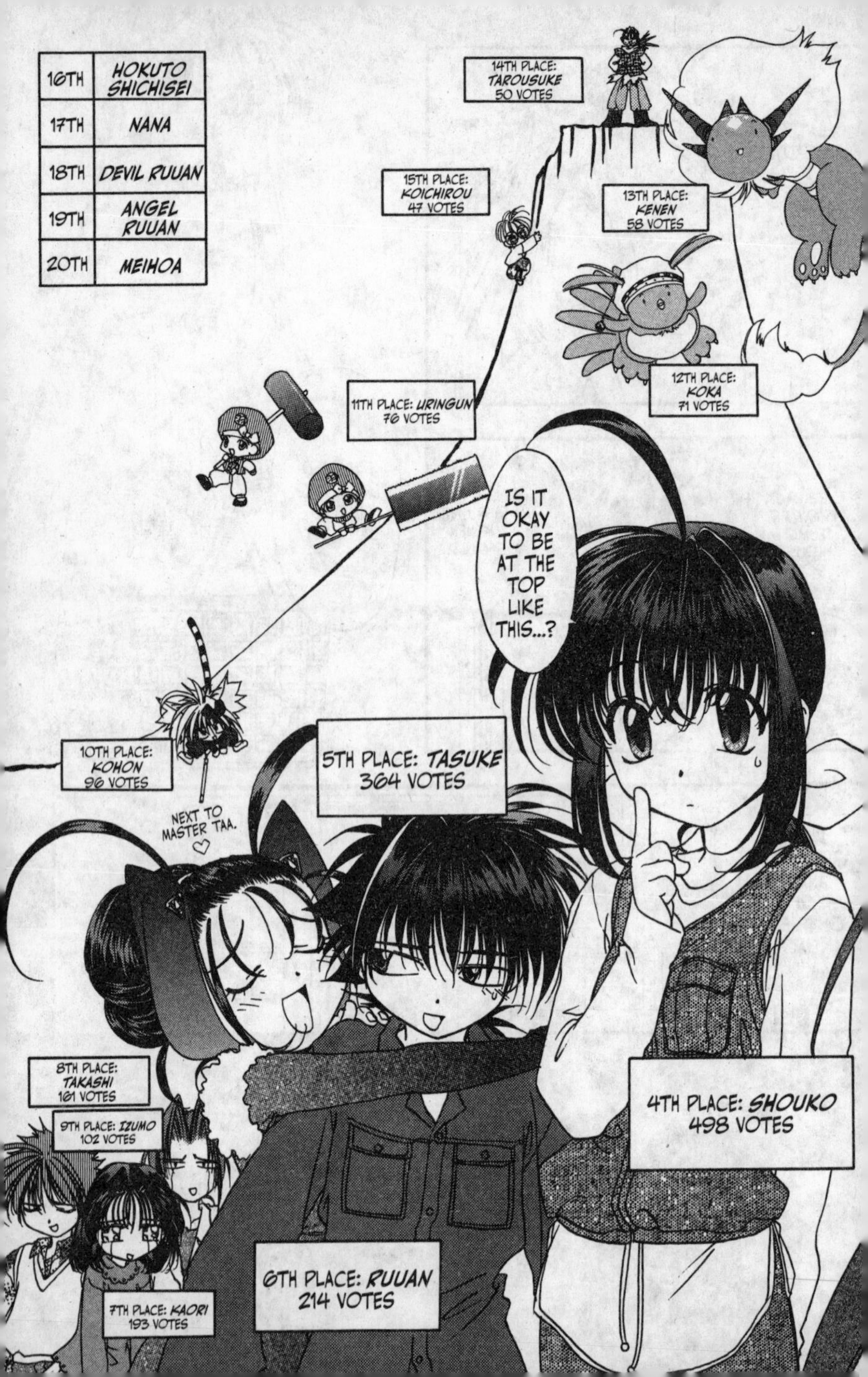
14TH PLACE: TAROUSUKE 50 VOTES
13TH PLACE: KENEN 58 VOTES
15TH PLACE: KOICHIROU 47 VOTES
12TH PLACE: KOKA 71 VOTES
11TH PLACE: URINGUN 76 VOTES
IS IT OKAY TO BE AT THE TOP LIKE THIS...?
10TH PLACE: KOHON 96 VOTES
5TH PLACE: TASUKE 364 VOTES
NEXT TO MASTER TAA. ♡
4TH PLACE: SHOUKO 498 VOTES
8TH PLACE: TAKASHI 161 VOTES
9TH PLACE: IZUMO 102 VOTES
6TH PLACE: RUUAN 214 VOTES
7TH PLACE: KAORI 193 VOTES

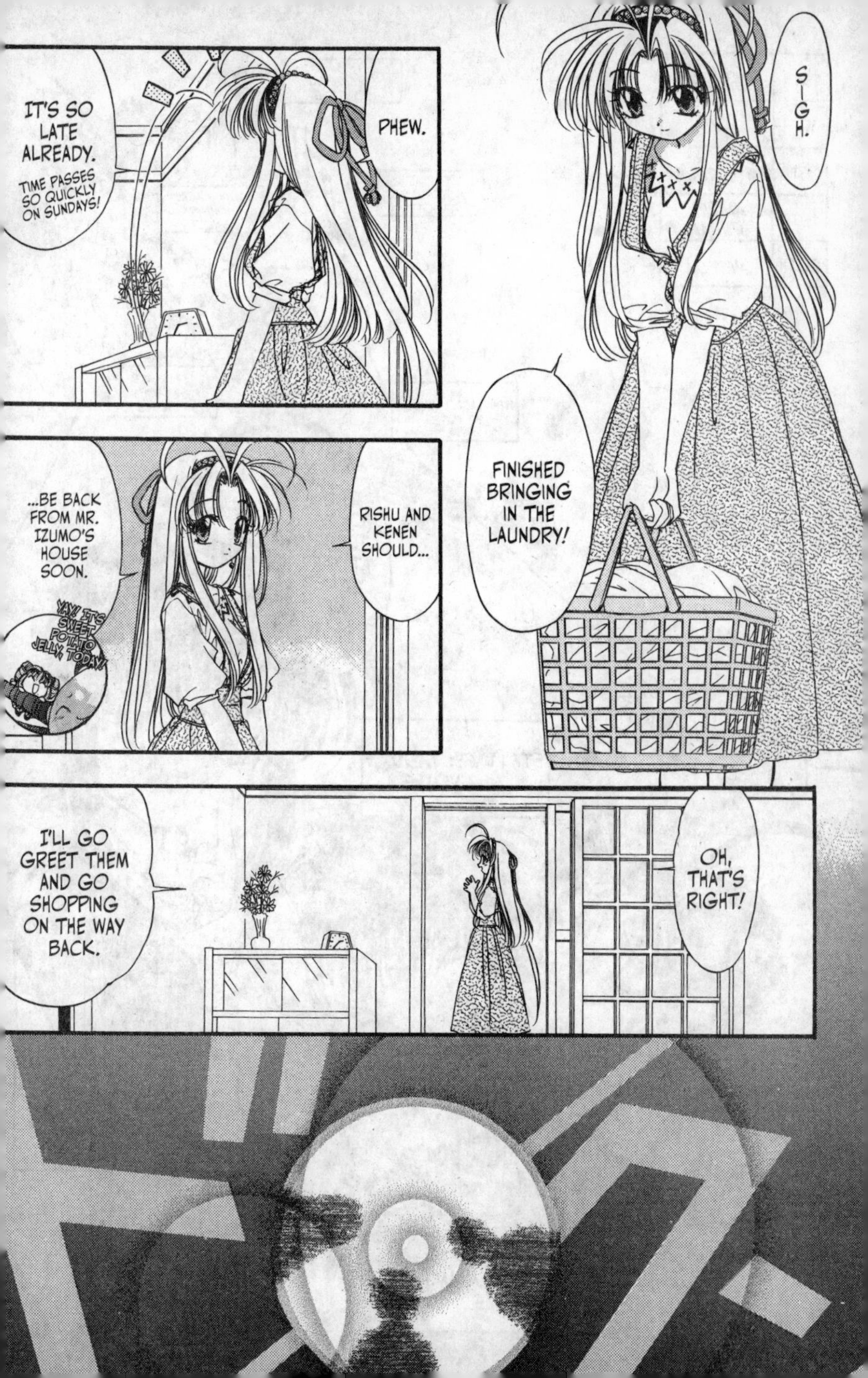
SIGH.
FINISHED BRINGING IN THE LAUNDRY!
PHEW.
IT'S SO LATE ALREADY.
TIME PASSES SO QUICKLY ON SUNDAYS!
RISHU AND KENEN SHOULD...
...BE BACK FROM MR. IZUMO'S HOUSE SOON.
YAY! IT'S SWEET POTATO JELLY, TODAY!
OH, THAT'S RIGHT!
I'LL GO GREET THEM AND GO SHOPPING ON THE WAY BACK.

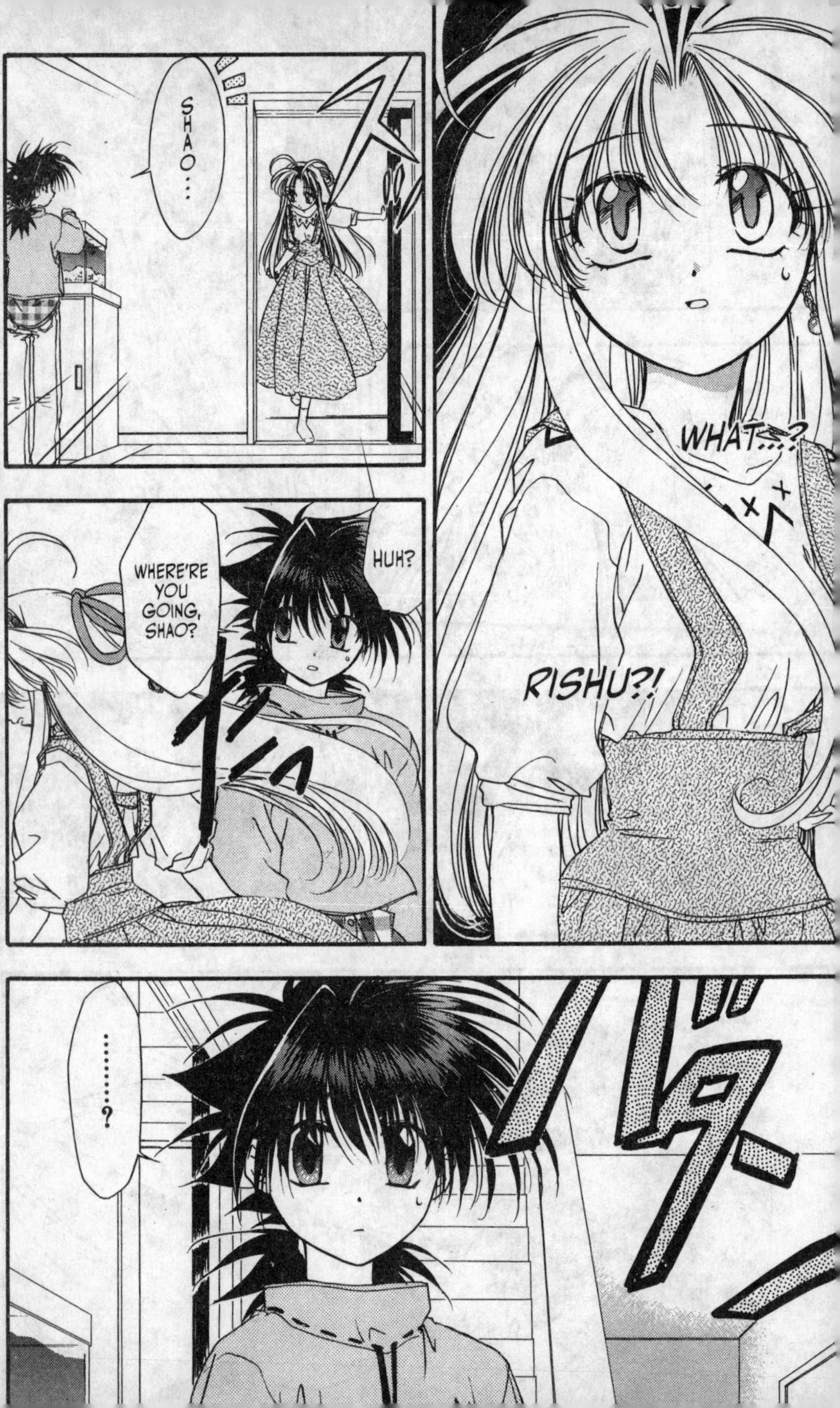
WHAT...?
RISHU?!
SHAO...
HUH?
WHERE'RE YOU GOING, SHAO?
......?

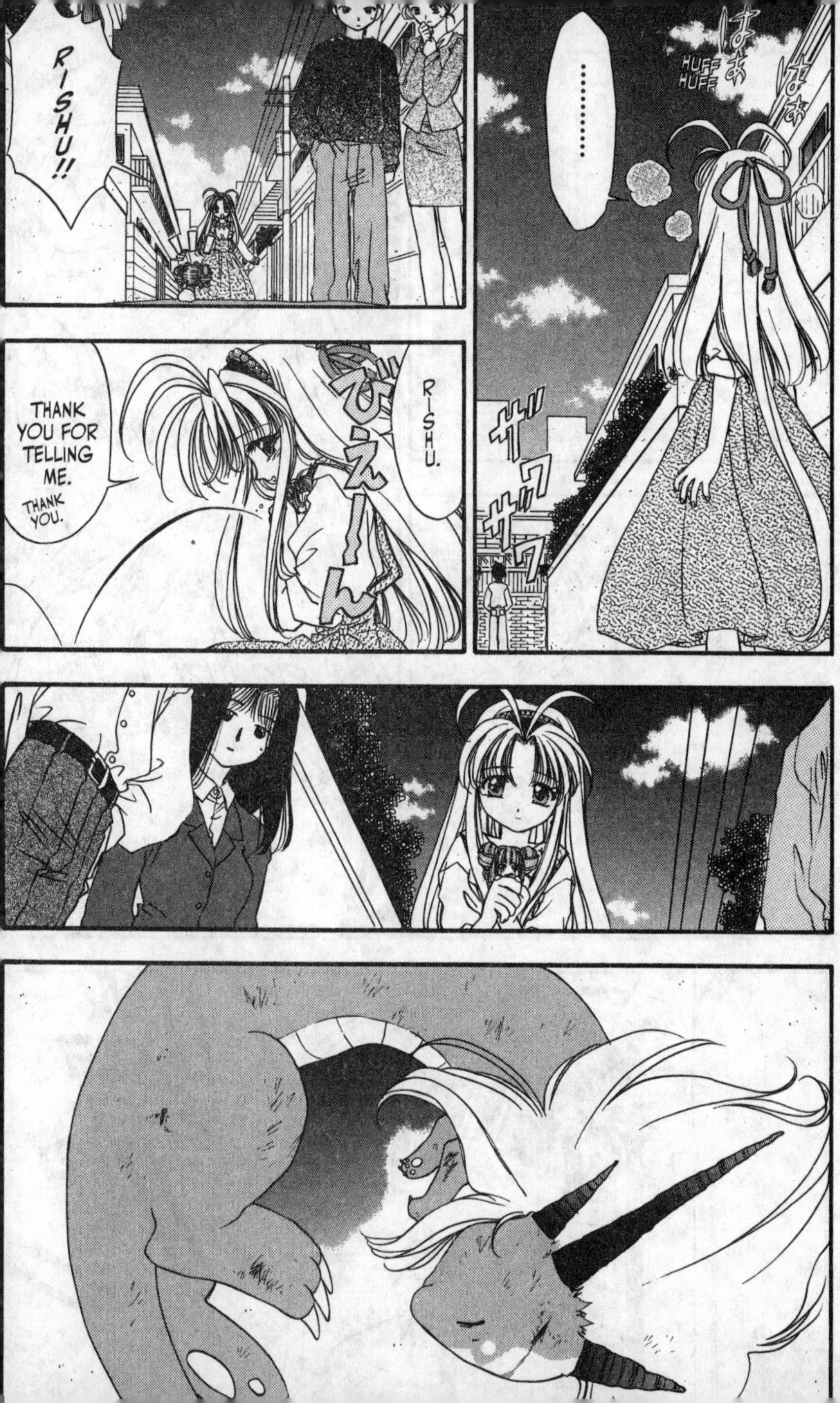
はぁ はぁ
HUFF HUFF
......
ザワ ザワ
RISHU!!
RISHU.
びえ〜ん
THANK YOU FOR TELLING ME.
THANK YOU.

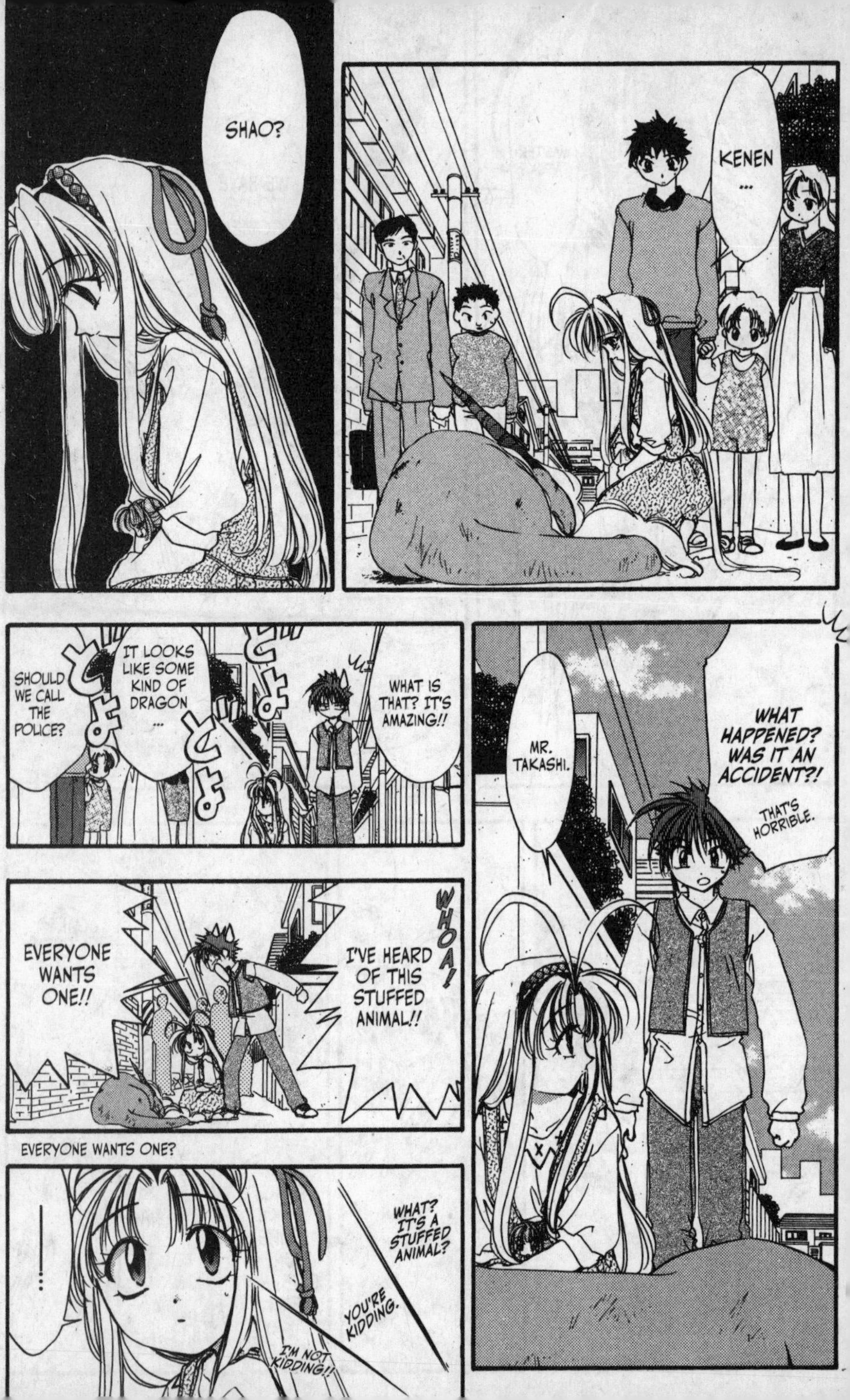
KENEN ...
SHAO?
WHAT HAPPENED? WAS IT AN ACCIDENT?!
THAT'S HORRIBLE.
MR. TAKASHI.
WHAT IS THAT? IT'S AMAZING!!
IT LOOKS LIKE SOME KIND OF DRAGON ...
SHOULD WE CALL THE POLICE?
WHOA!
I'VE HEARD OF THIS STUFFED ANIMAL!!
EVERYONE WANTS ONE!!
EVERYONE WANTS ONE?
WHAT? IT'S A STUFFED ANIMAL?
YOU'RE KIDDING.
I'M NOT KIDDING!!
......

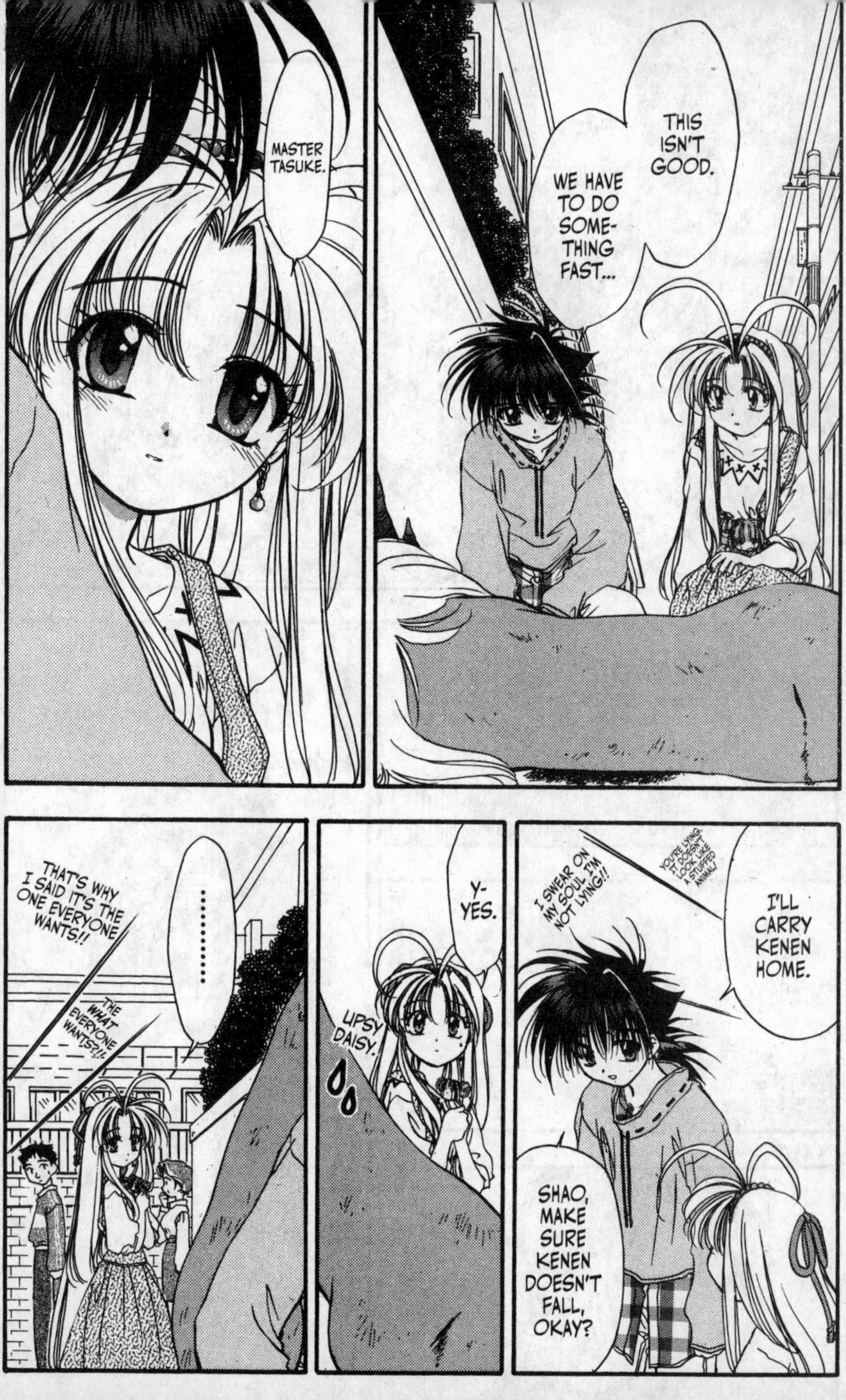
THIS ISN'T GOOD.
WE HAVE TO DO SOME-THING FAST...
MASTER TASUKE.
I'LL CARRY KENEN HOME.
YOU'RE LYING. IT DOESN'T LOOK LIKE A STUFFED ANIMAL!
I SWEAR ON MY SOUL I'M NOT LYING!!
SHAO, MAKE SURE KENEN DOESN'T FALL, OKAY?
Y-YES.
UPSY DAISY.
....
THAT'S WHY I SAID IT'S THE ONE EVERYONE WANTS!!
THE WHAT EVERYONE WANTS?!!

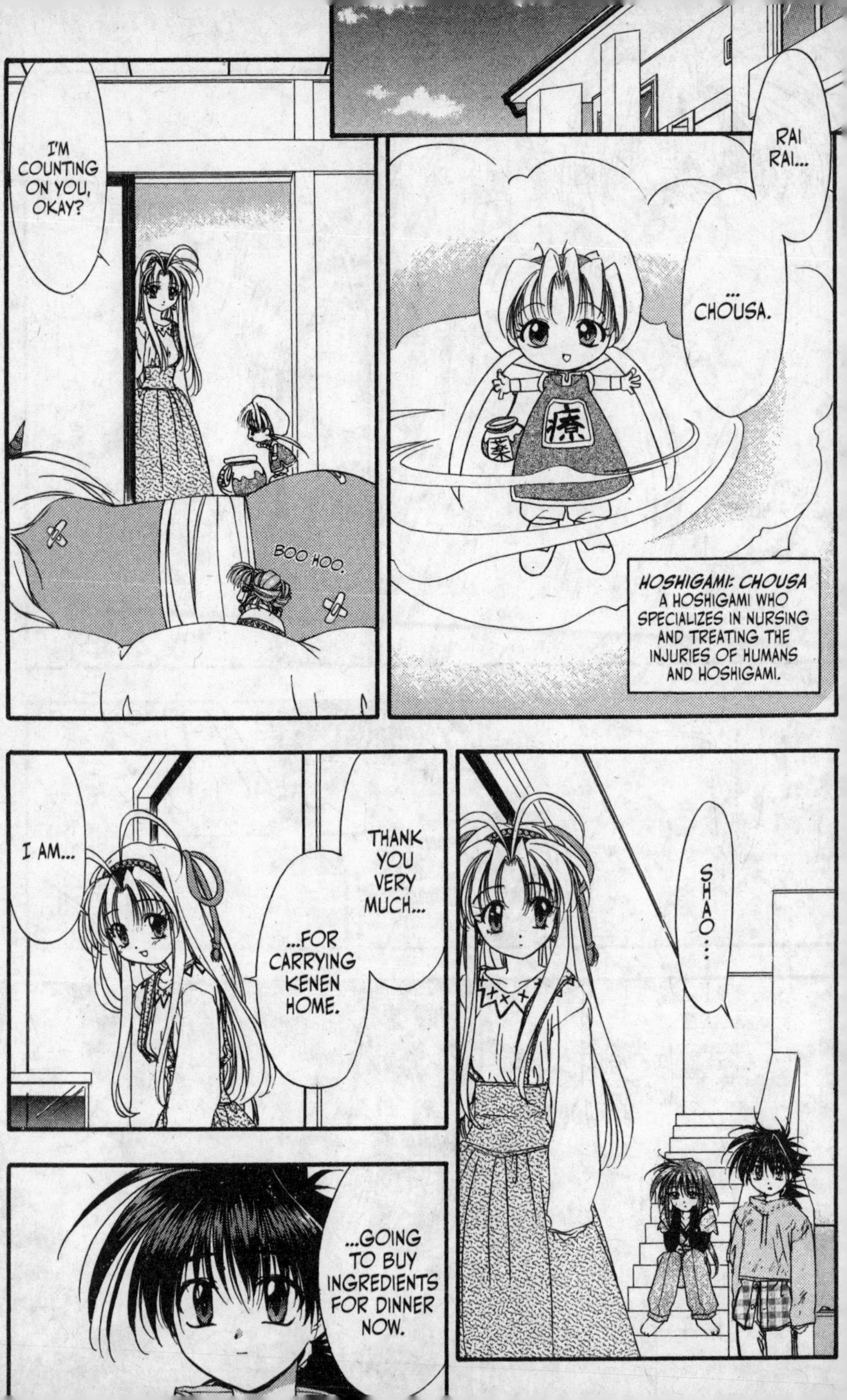
RAI RAI...
...CHOUSA.
HOSHIGAMI: CHOUSA
A HOSHIGAMI WHO SPECIALIZES IN NURSING AND TREATING THE INJURIES OF HUMANS AND HOSHIGAMI.
I'M COUNTING ON YOU, OKAY?
BOO HOO.
SHAO...
THANK YOU VERY MUCH...
...FOR CARRYING KENEN HOME.
I AM...
...GOING TO BUY INGREDIENTS FOR DINNER NOW.

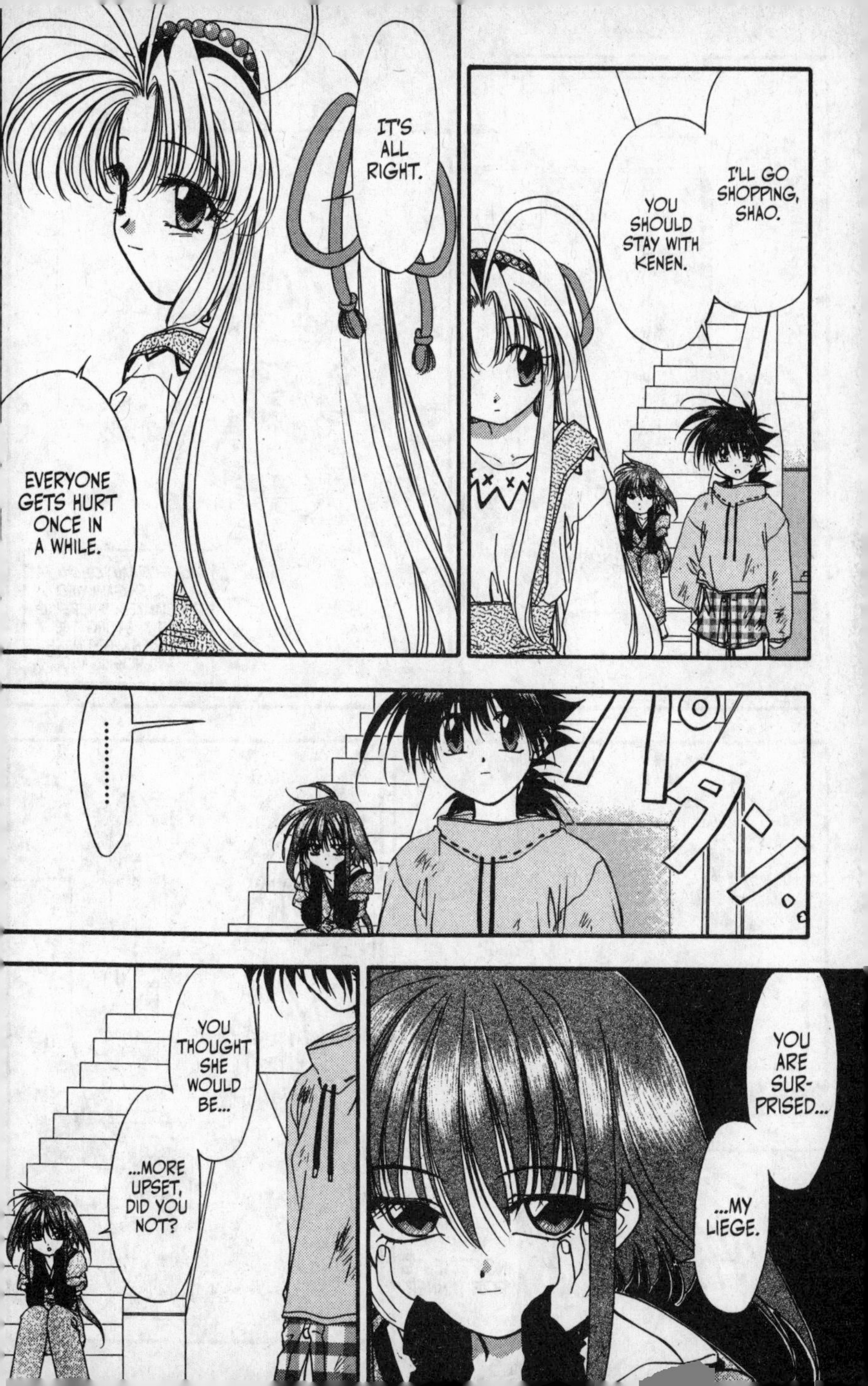
I'LL GO SHOPPING, SHAO.
YOU SHOULD STAY WITH KENEN.
IT'S ALL RIGHT.
EVERYONE GETS HURT ONCE IN A WHILE.
パタン。
……
YOU ARE SUR- PRISED...
...MY LIEGE.
YOU THOUGHT SHE WOULD BE...
...MORE UPSET, DID YOU NOT?

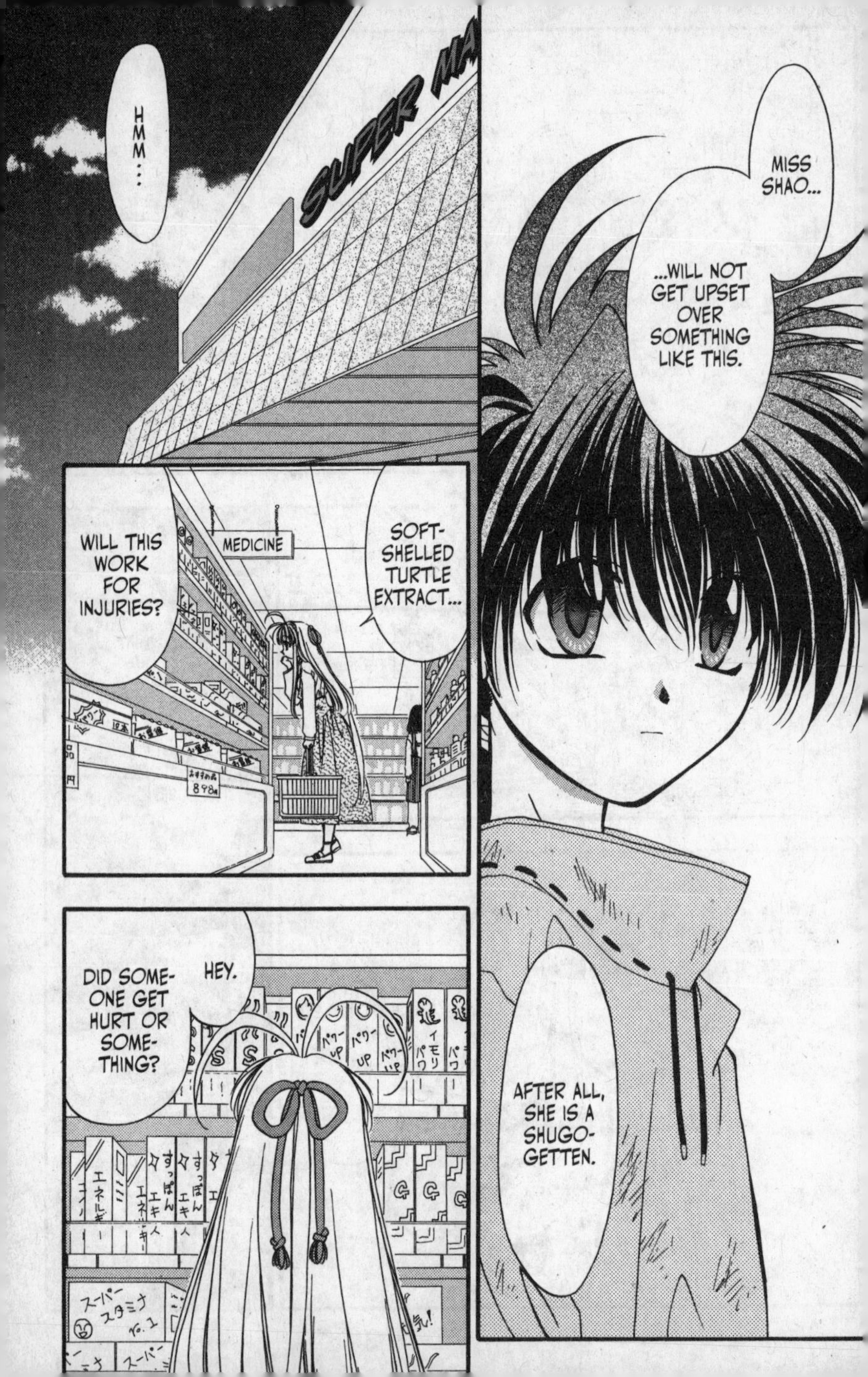
MISS SHAO...
...WILL NOT GET UPSET OVER SOMETHING LIKE THIS.
AFTER ALL, SHE IS A SHUGO-GETTEN.
SUPER MA
HMM...
MEDICINE
SOFT-SHELLED TURTLE EXTRACT...
WILL THIS WORK FOR INJURIES?
HEY.
DID SOME-ONE GET HURT OR SOME-THING?
パワーUP
パワーUP
パワーUP
イモリパワ
すっぽんエキス
すっぽんエキス
スーパースタミナ

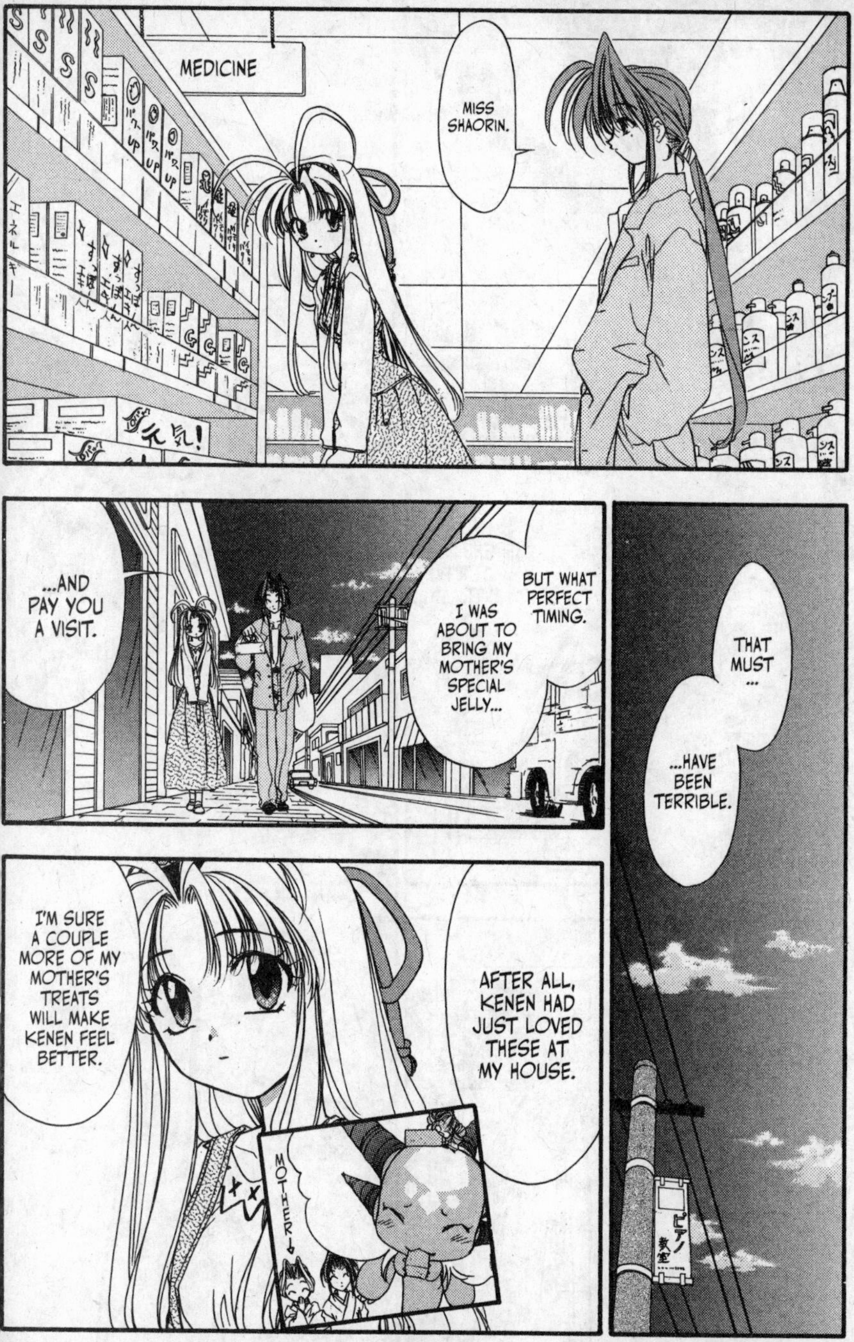
MEDICINE
MISS SHAORIN.
THAT MUST ...
...HAVE BEEN TERRIBLE.
ピアノ教室
BUT WHAT PERFECT TIMING.
I WAS ABOUT TO BRING MY MOTHER'S SPECIAL JELLY...
...AND PAY YOU A VISIT.
AFTER ALL, KENEN HAD JUST LOVED THESE AT MY HOUSE.
MOTHER
I'M SURE A COUPLE MORE OF MY MOTHER'S TREATS WILL MAKE KENEN FEEL BETTER.

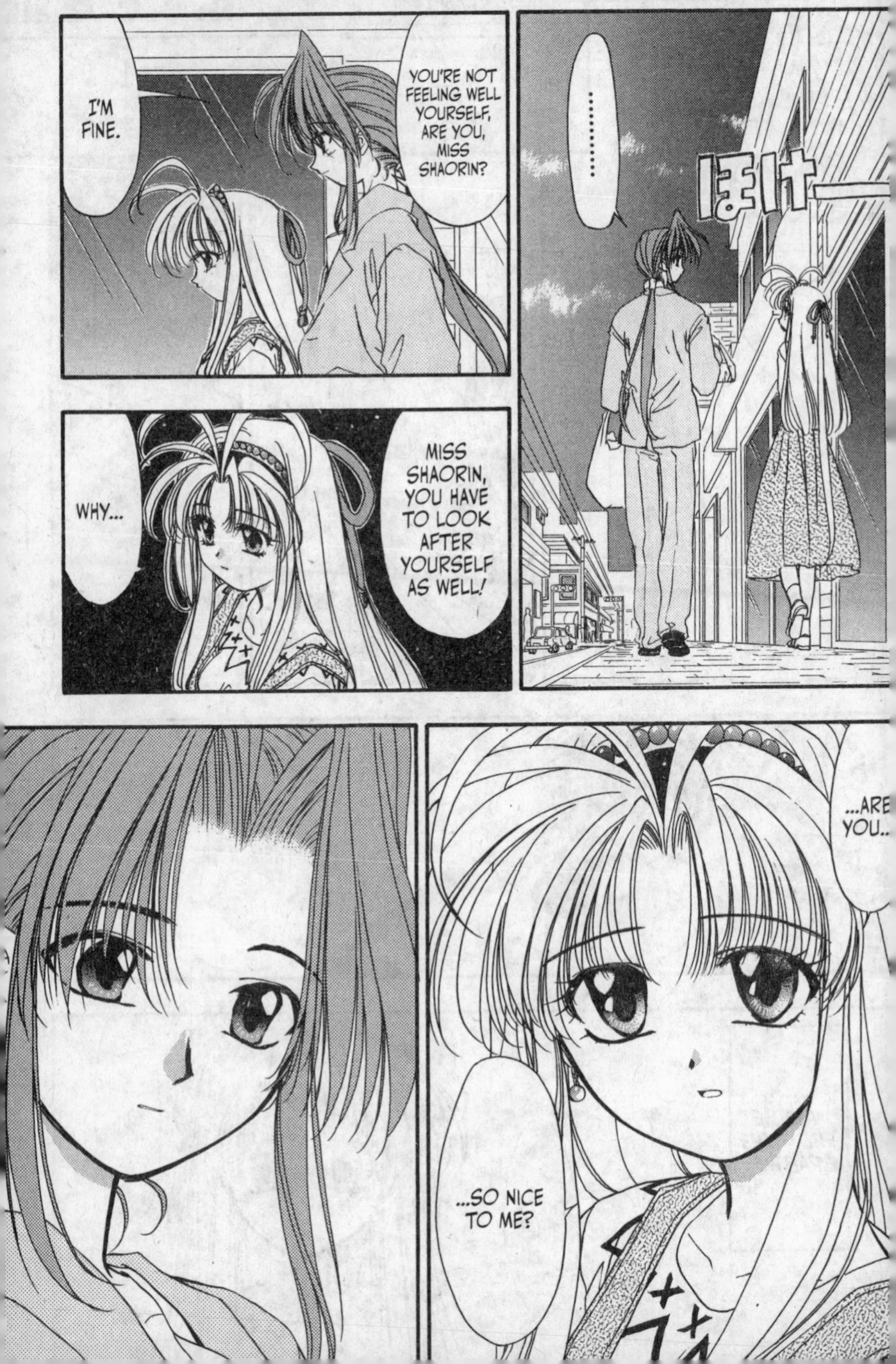
……
ほけー
YOU'RE NOT FEELING WELL YOURSELF, ARE YOU, MISS SHAORIN?
I'M FINE.
MISS SHAORIN, YOU HAVE TO LOOK AFTER YOURSELF AS WELL!
WHY...
...ARE YOU...
...SO NICE TO ME?

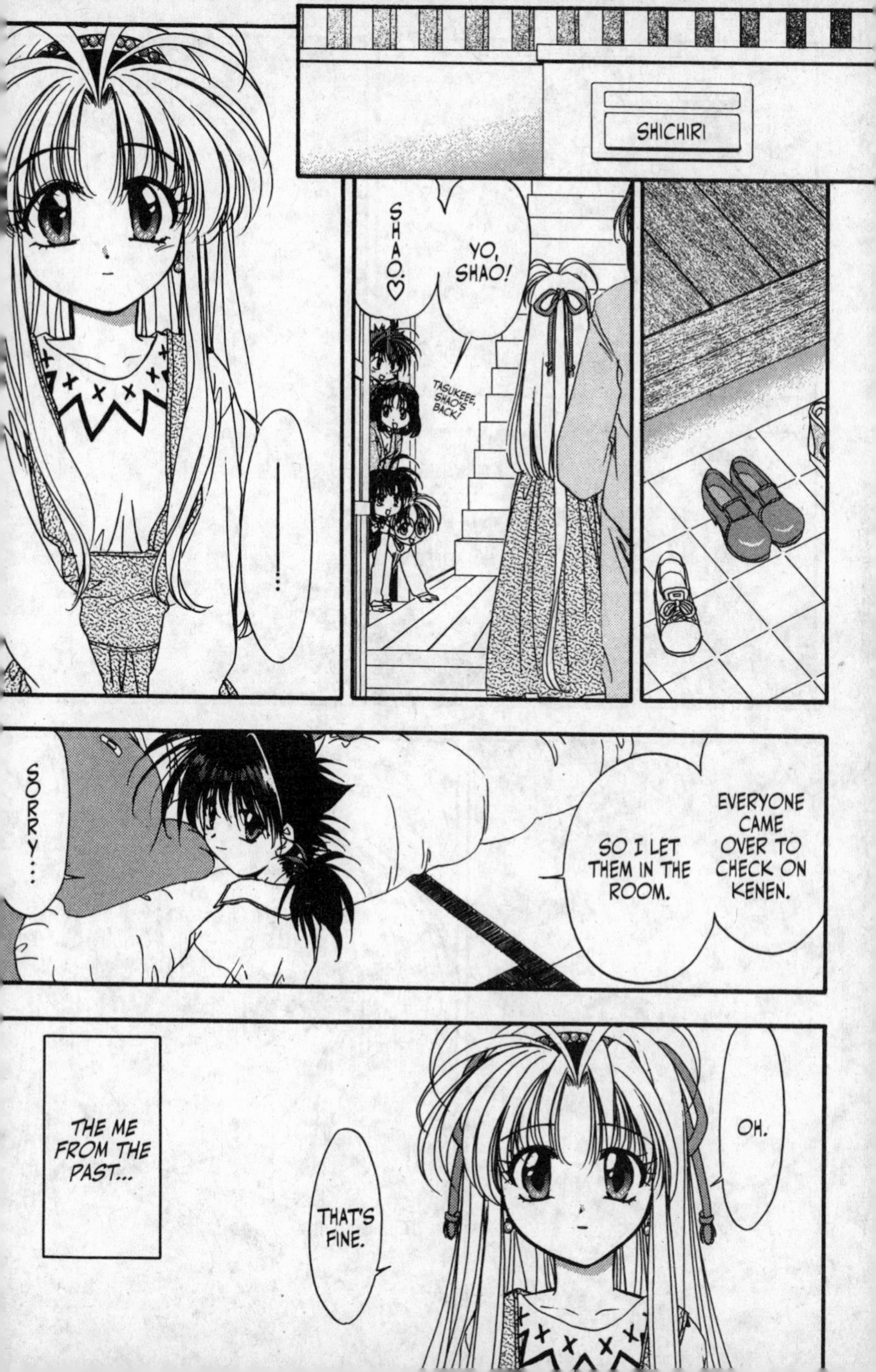

SHICHIRI
YO, SHAO!
SHAO.♡
TASUKEEE, SHAO'S BACK!
......!
EVERYONE CAME OVER TO CHECK ON KENEN.
SO I LET THEM IN THE ROOM.
SORRY...
OH.
THAT'S FINE.
THE ME FROM THE PAST...

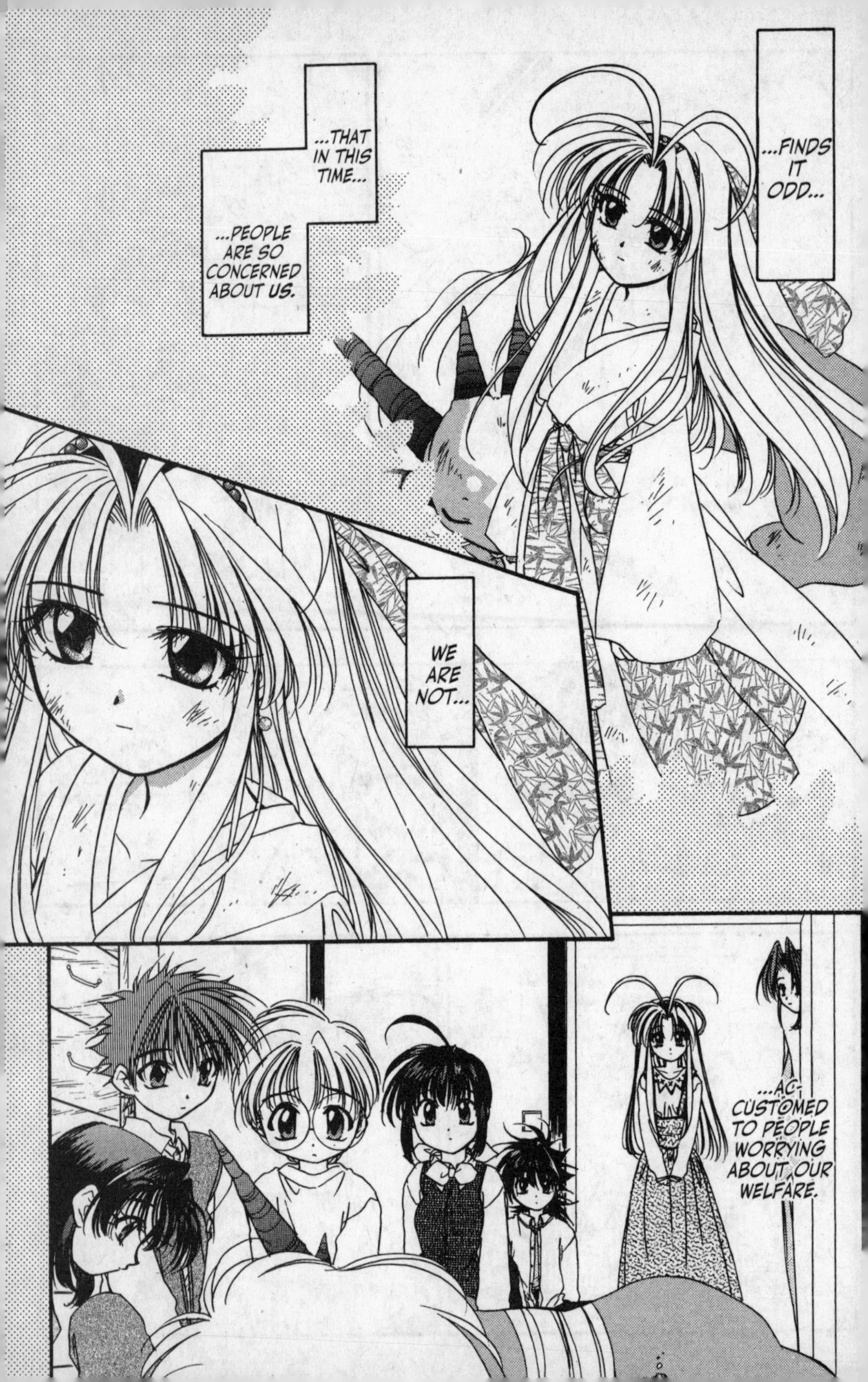
...FINDS IT ODD...
...THAT IN THIS TIME...
...PEOPLE ARE SO CONCERNED ABOUT US.
WE ARE NOT...
...AC-CUSTOMED TO PEOPLE WORRYING ABOUT OUR WELFARE.

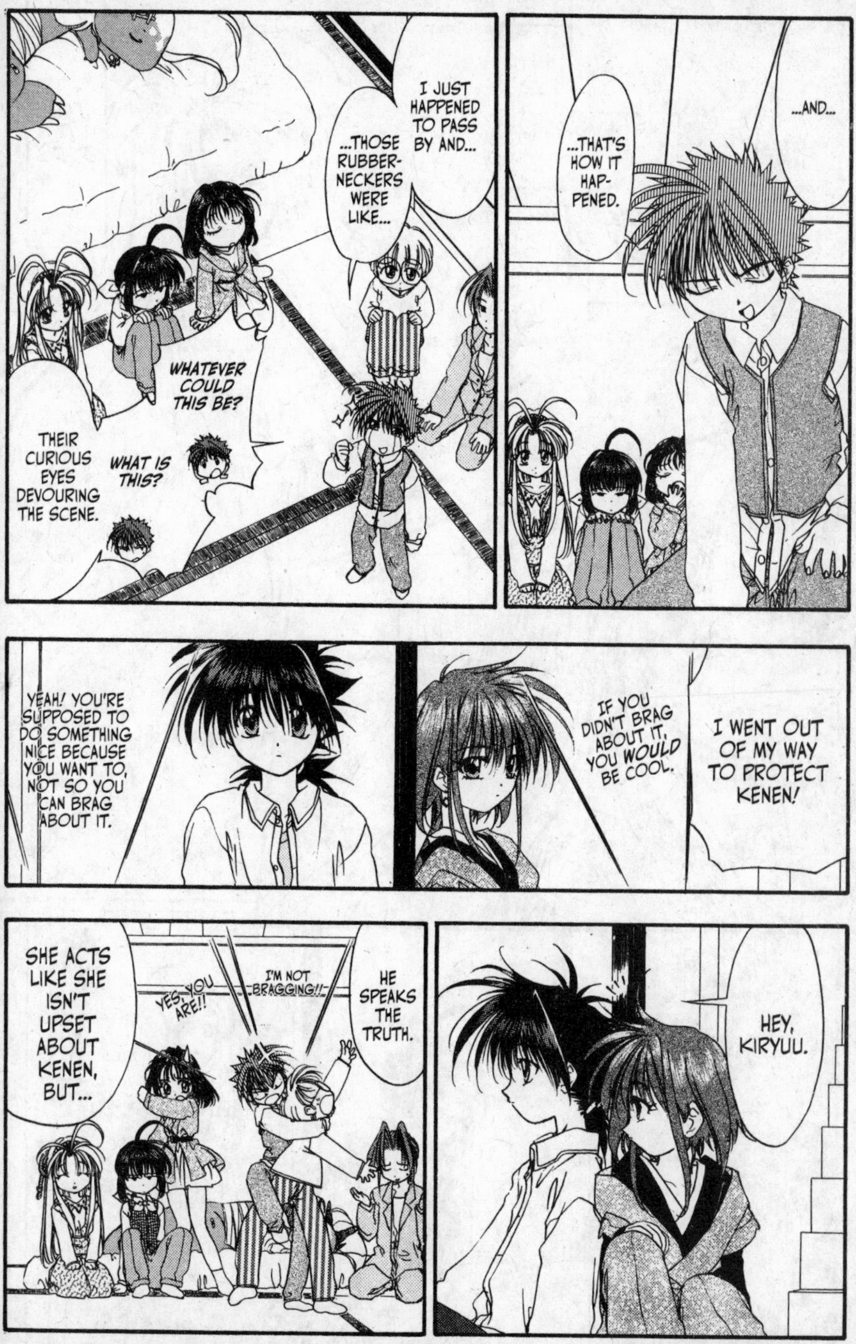
...AND...
...THAT'S HOW IT HAP-PENED.
I JUST HAPPENED TO PASS BY AND...
...THOSE RUBBER-NECKERS WERE LIKE...
WHATEVER COULD THIS BE?
WHAT IS THIS?
THEIR CURIOUS EYES DEVOURING THE SCENE.
I WENT OUT OF MY WAY TO PROTECT KENEN!
IF YOU DIDN'T BRAG ABOUT IT, YOU WOULD BE COOL.
YEAH! YOU'RE SUPPOSED TO DO SOMETHING NICE BECAUSE YOU WANT TO, NOT SO YOU CAN BRAG ABOUT IT.
HEY, KIRYUU.
HE SPEAKS THE TRUTH.
I'M NOT BRAGGING!!
YES, YOU ARE!!
SHE ACTS LIKE SHE ISN'T UPSET ABOUT KENEN, BUT...

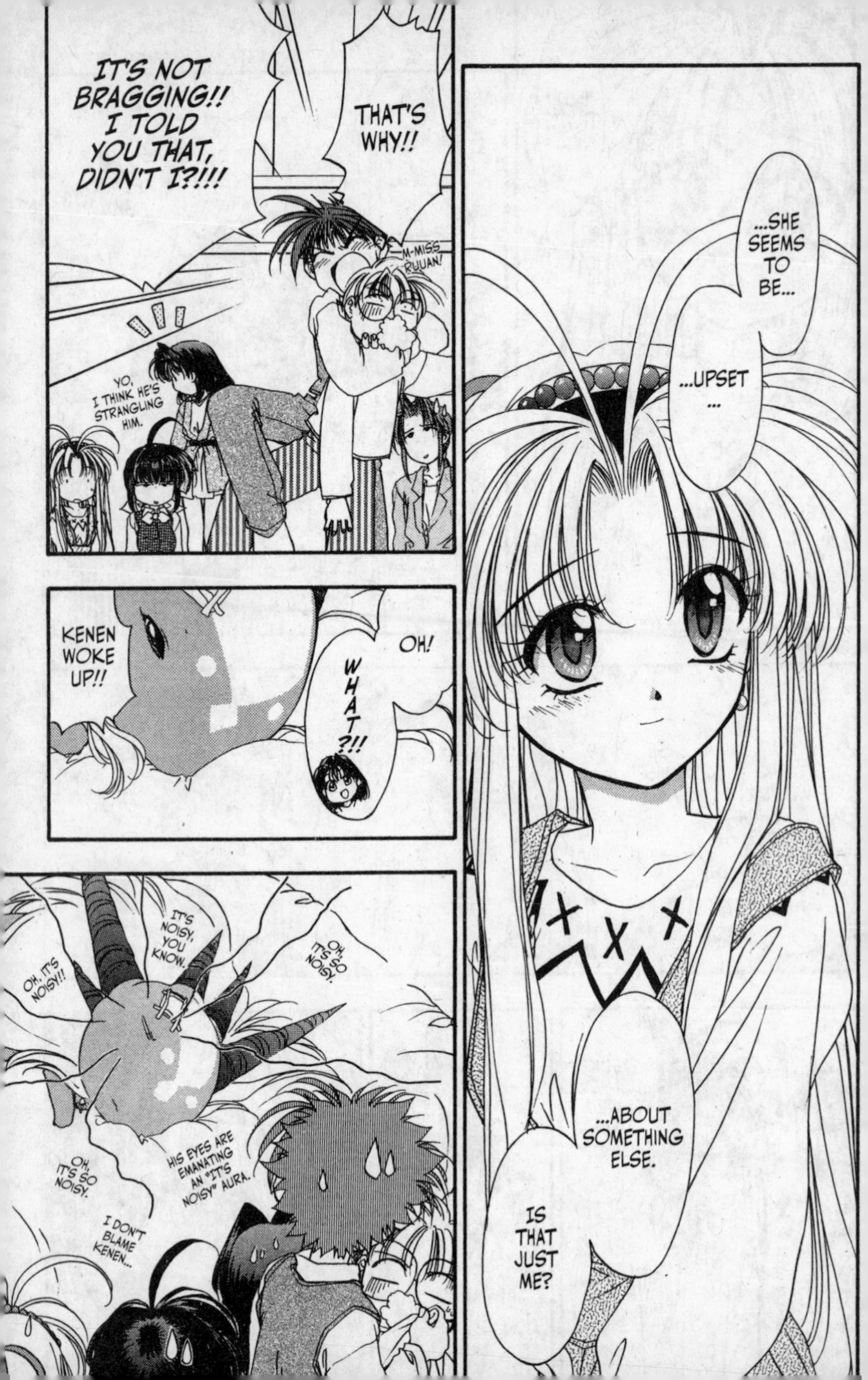
...SHE SEEMS TO BE...
...UPSET ...
...ABOUT SOMETHING ELSE.
IS THAT JUST ME?
THAT'S WHY!!
IT'S NOT BRAGGING!! I TOLD YOU THAT, DIDN'T I?!!!
M-MISS RUUAN!
YO, I THINK HE'S STRANGLING HIM.
OH!
WHAT?!!
KENEN WOKE UP!!
OH, IT'S SO NOISY.
IT'S NOISY, YOU KNOW.
OH, IT'S NOISY!!
HIS EYES ARE EMANATING AN "IT'S NOISY" AURA.
OH, IT'S SO NOISY.
I DON'T BLAME KENEN...

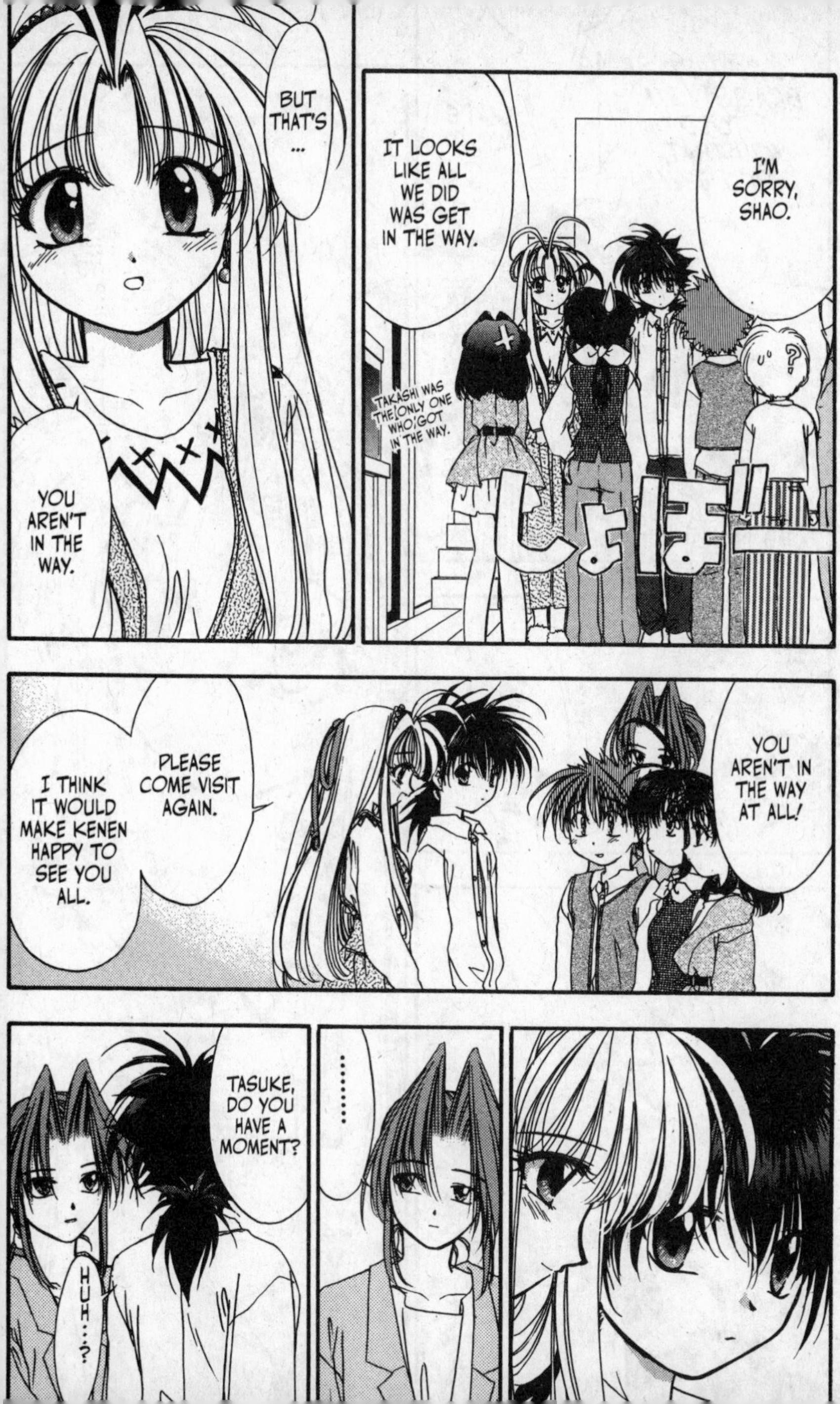
I'M SORRY, SHAO.
IT LOOKS LIKE ALL WE DID WAS GET IN THE WAY.
TAKASHI WAS THE ONLY ONE WHO GOT IN THE WAY.
しょぼー
BUT THAT'S ...
YOU AREN'T IN THE WAY.
YOU AREN'T IN THE WAY AT ALL!
PLEASE COME VISIT AGAIN.
I THINK IT WOULD MAKE KENEN HAPPY TO SEE YOU ALL.
......
TASUKE, DO YOU HAVE A MOMENT?
HUH...?

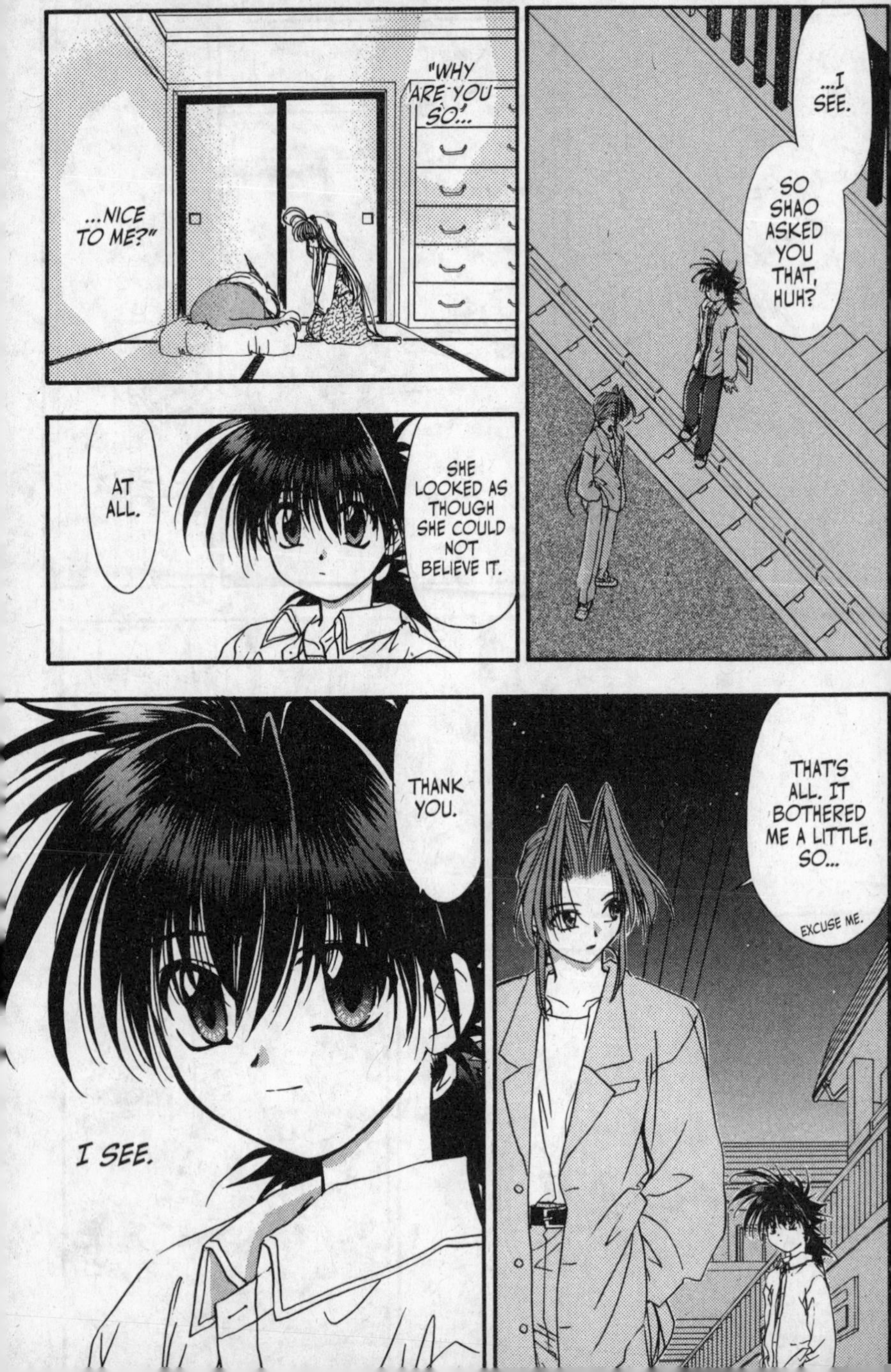
...I SEE.
SO SHAO ASKED YOU THAT, HUH?
"WHY ARE YOU SO...
...NICE TO ME?"
SHE LOOKED AS THOUGH SHE COULD NOT BELIEVE IT.
AT ALL.
THAT'S ALL. IT BOTHERED ME A LITTLE, SO...
EXCUSE ME.
THANK YOU.
I SEE.

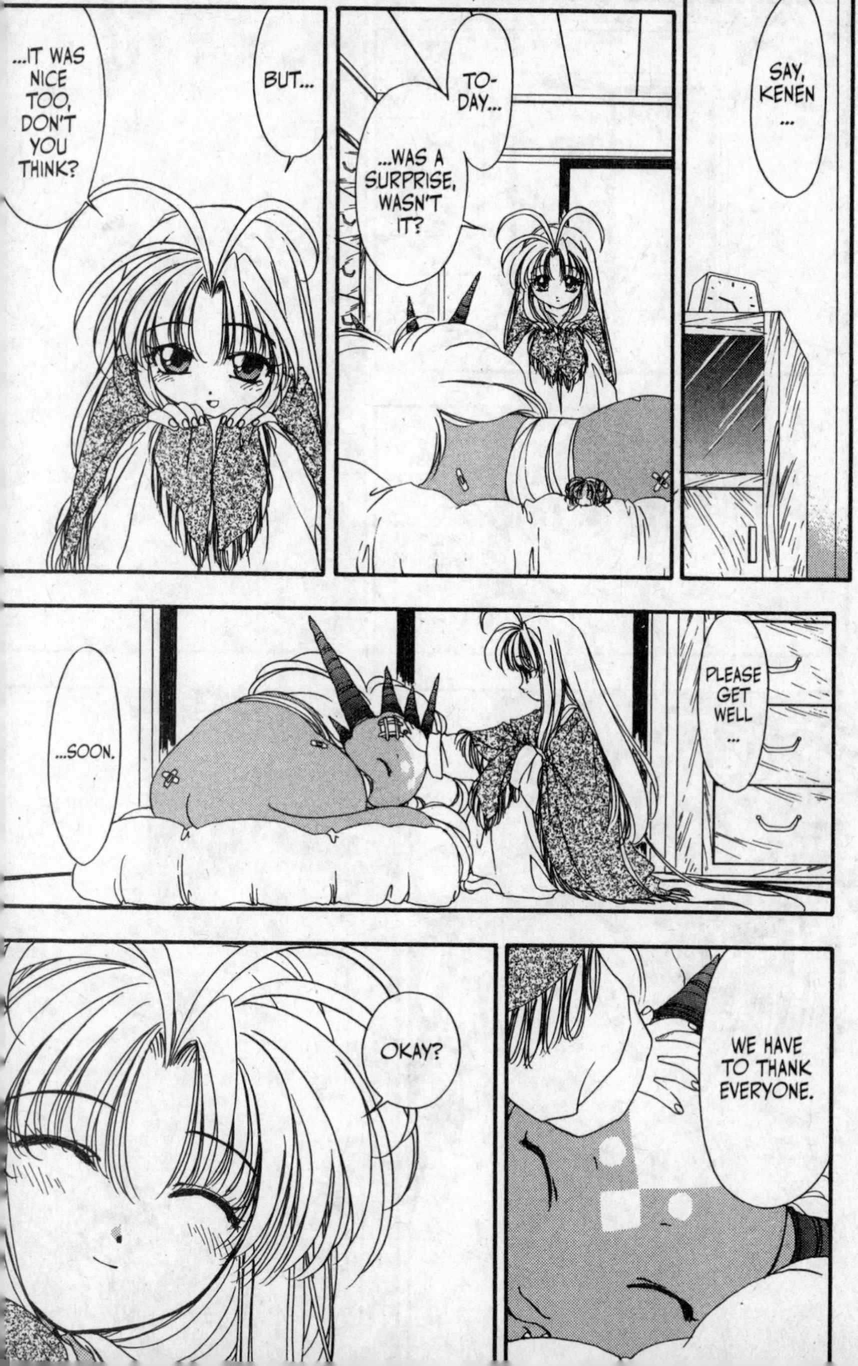
SAY, KENEN ...
TO-DAY...
...WAS A SURPRISE, WASN'T IT?
BUT...
...IT WAS NICE TOO, DON'T YOU THINK?
PLEASE GET WELL ...
...SOON.
WE HAVE TO THANK EVERYONE.
OKAY?

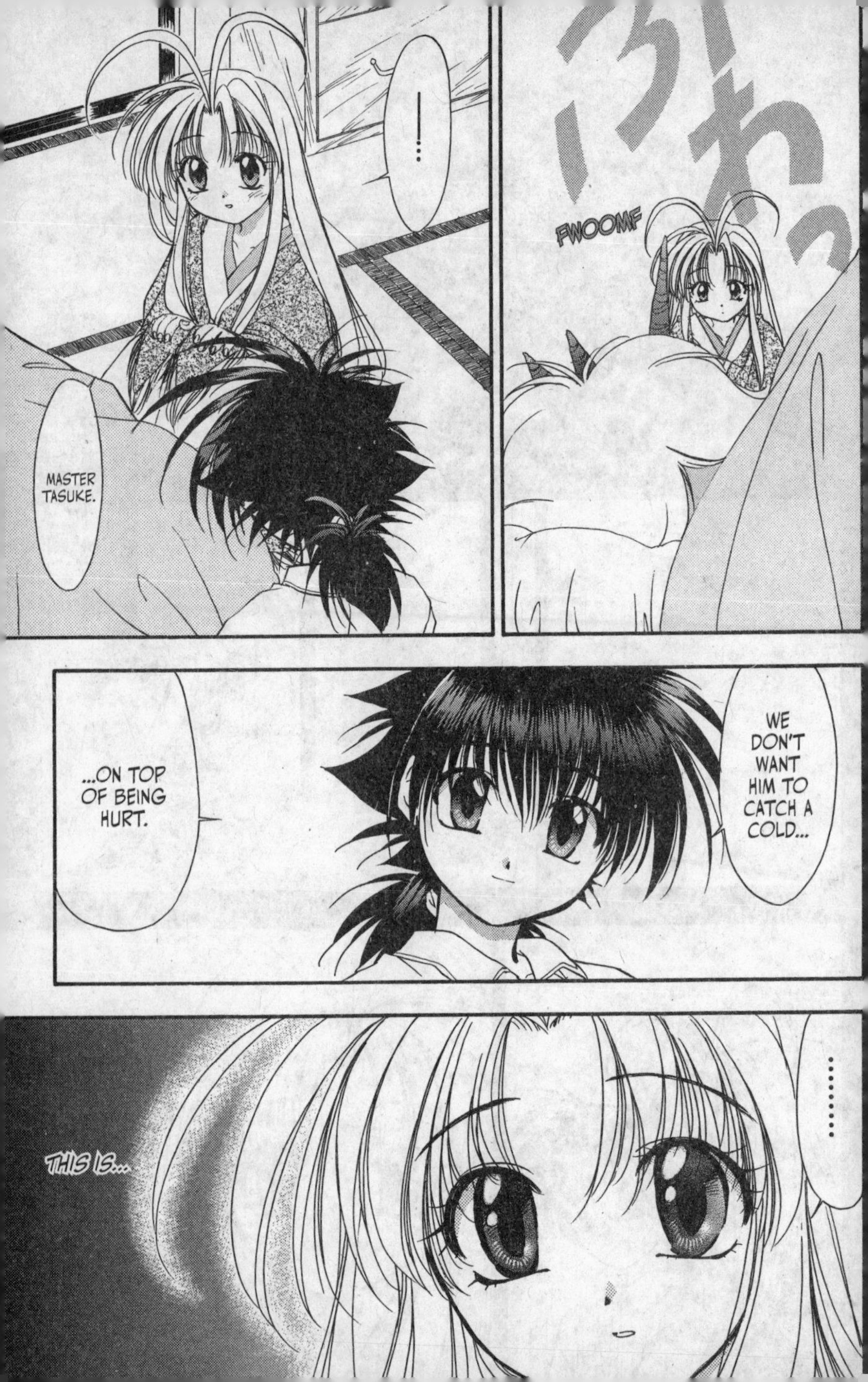
FWOOMF
......
MASTER TASUKE.
WE DON'T WANT HIM TO CATCH A COLD...
...ON TOP OF BEING HURT.
......
THIS IS...

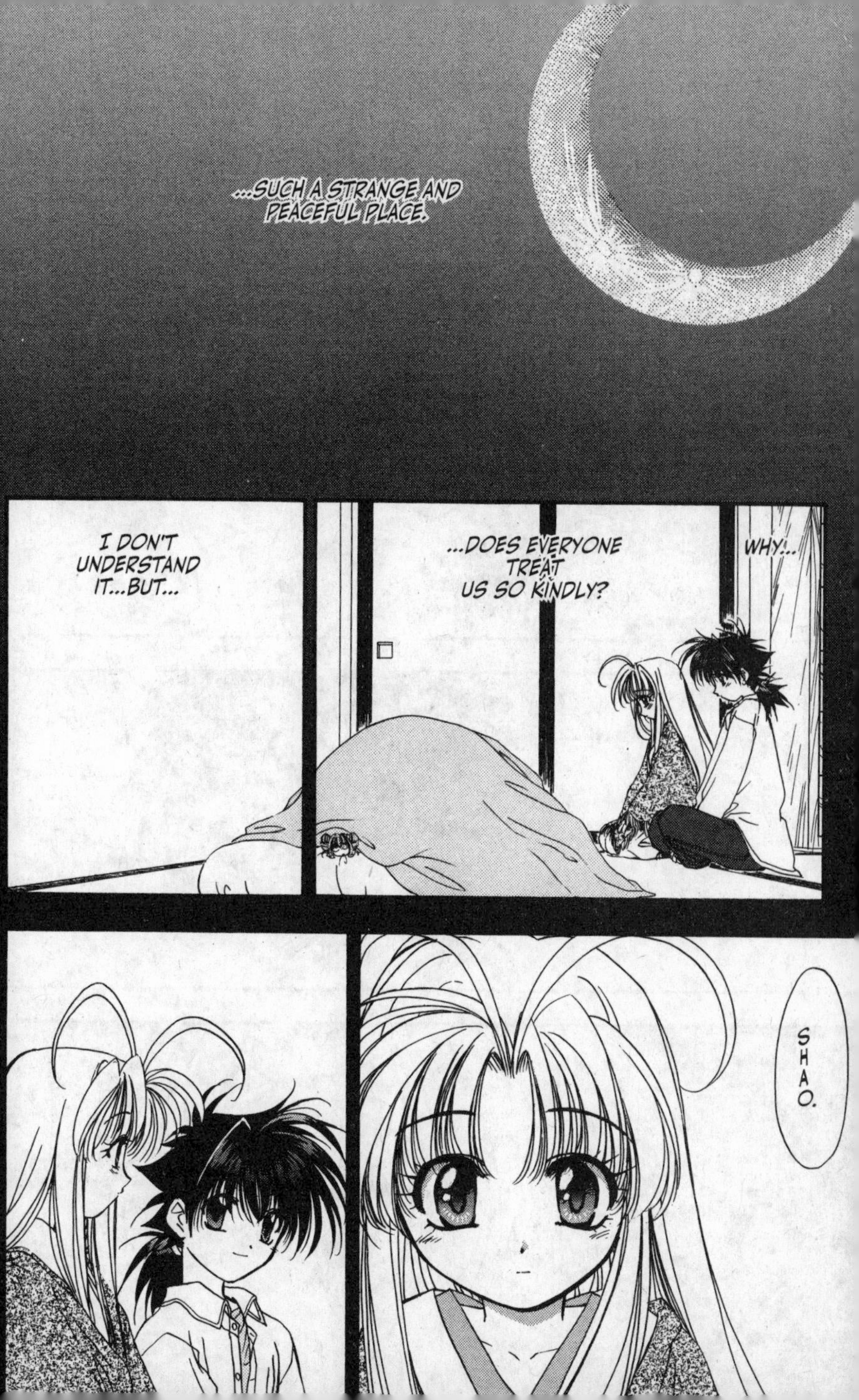
...SUCH A STRANGE AND PEACEFUL PLACE.
WHY...
...DOES EVERYONE TREAT US SO KINDLY?
I DON'T UNDERSTAND IT...BUT...
SHAO.

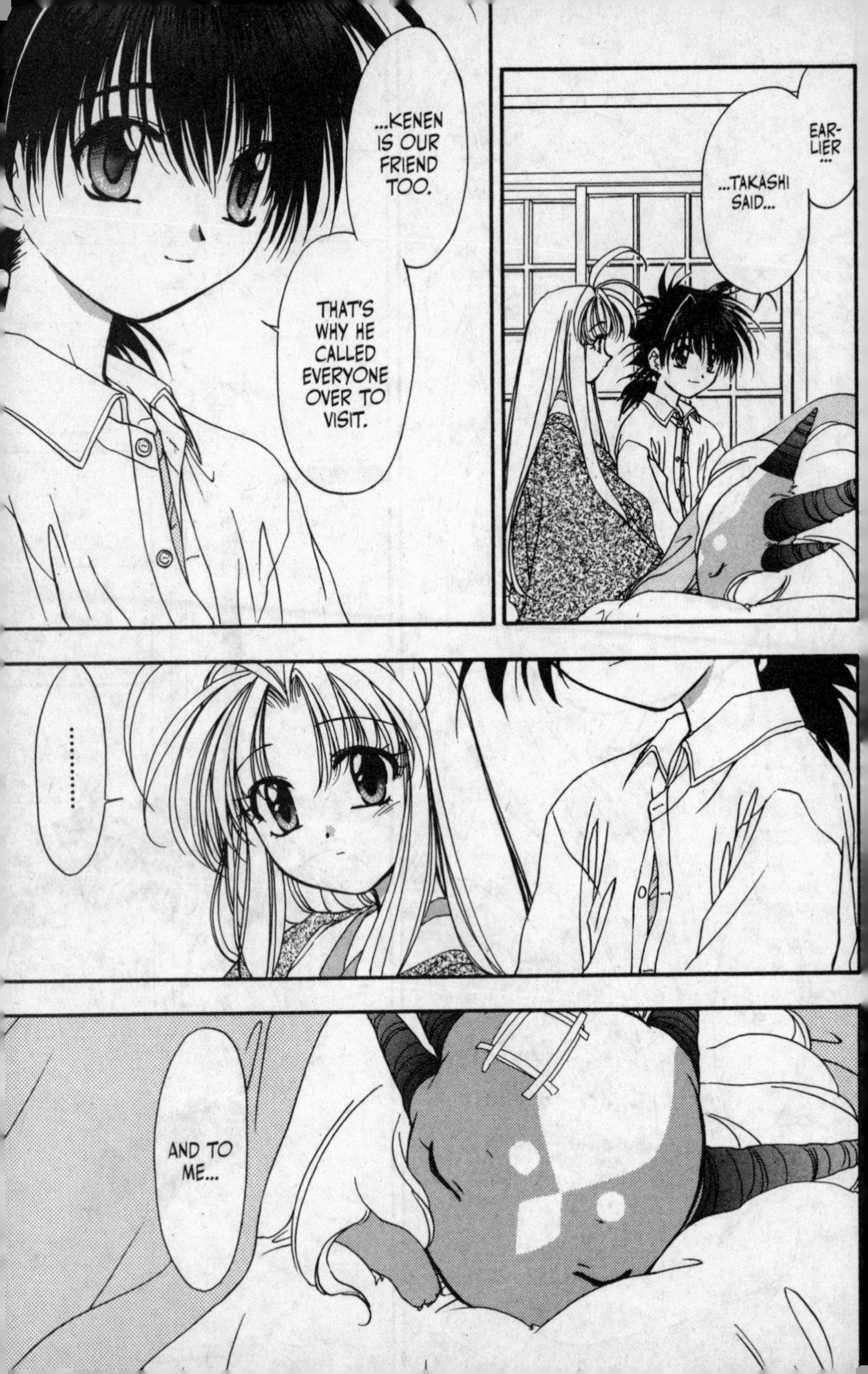
EAR-LIER...
...TAKASHI SAID...
...KENEN IS OUR FRIEND TOO.
THAT'S WHY HE CALLED EVERYONE OVER TO VISIT.
....
AND TO ME...

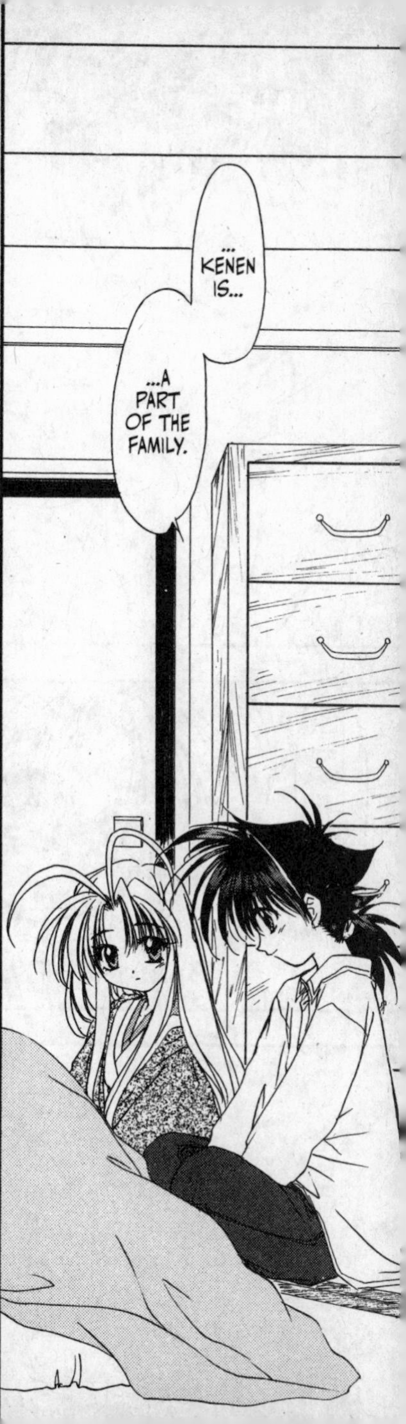
...KENEN IS...
...A PART OF THE FAMILY.

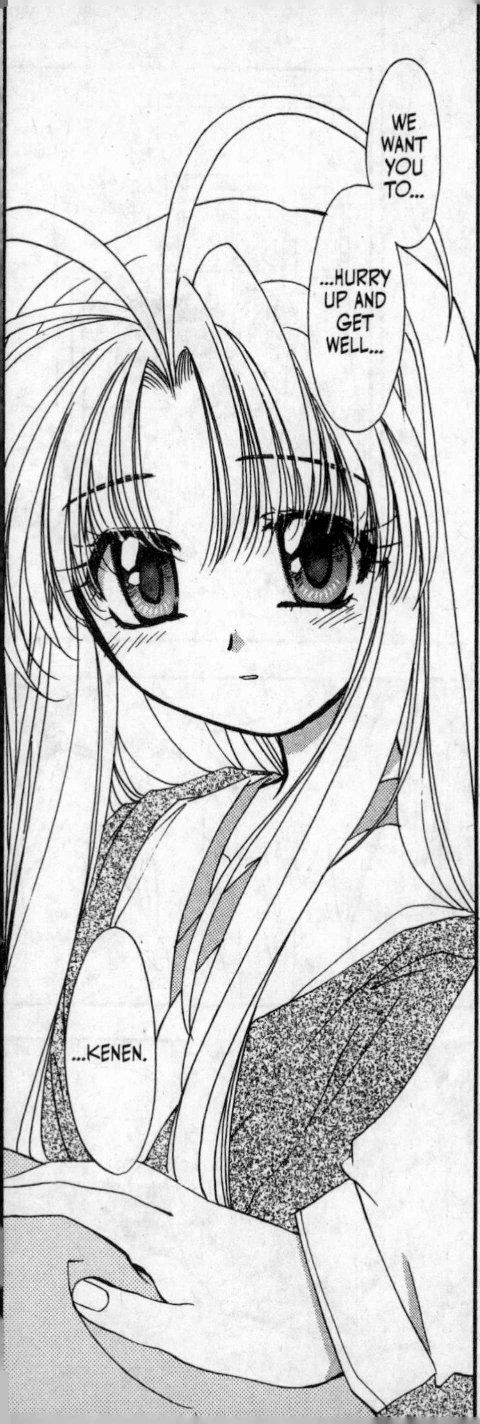
WE WANT YOU TO...
...HURRY UP AND GET WELL...
...KENEN.

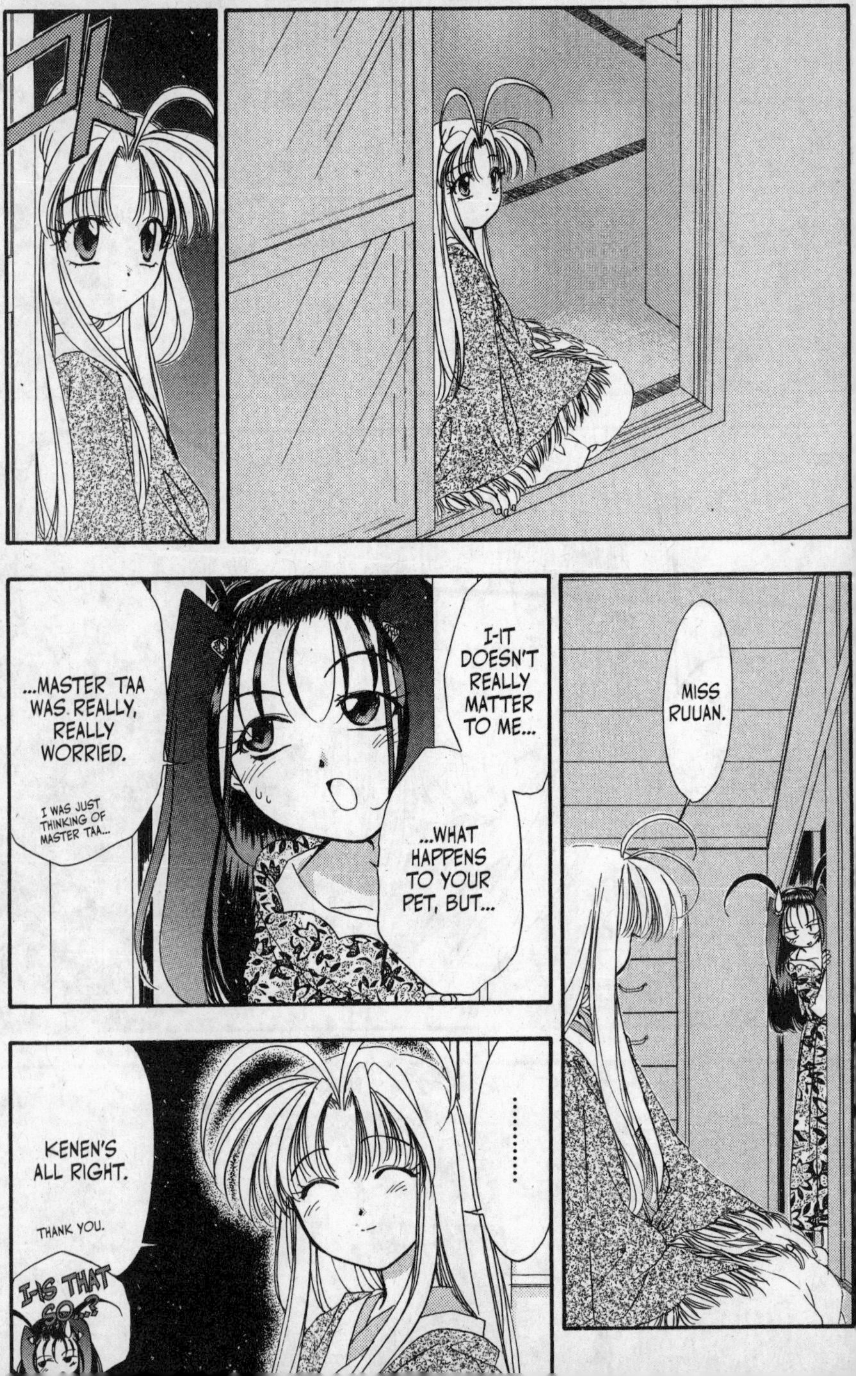
MISS RUUAN.
I-IT DOESN'T REALLY MATTER TO ME...
...WHAT HAPPENS TO YOUR PET, BUT...
...MASTER TAA WAS REALLY, REALLY WORRIED.
I WAS JUST THINKING OF MASTER TAA...
......
KENEN'S ALL RIGHT.
THANK YOU.
I-IS THAT SO...?

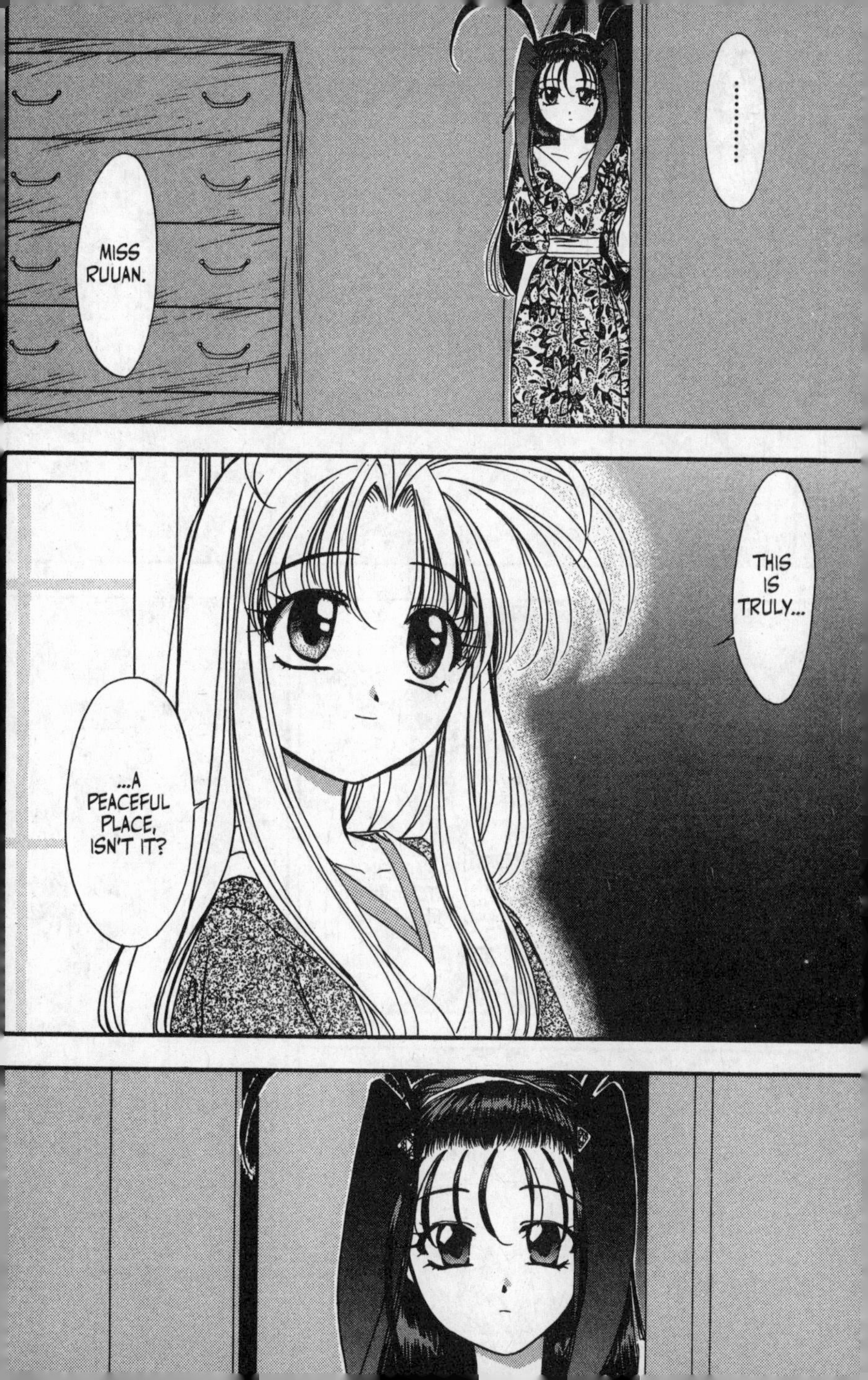
......
MISS RUUAN.
THIS IS TRULY...
...A PEACEFUL PLACE, ISN'T IT?

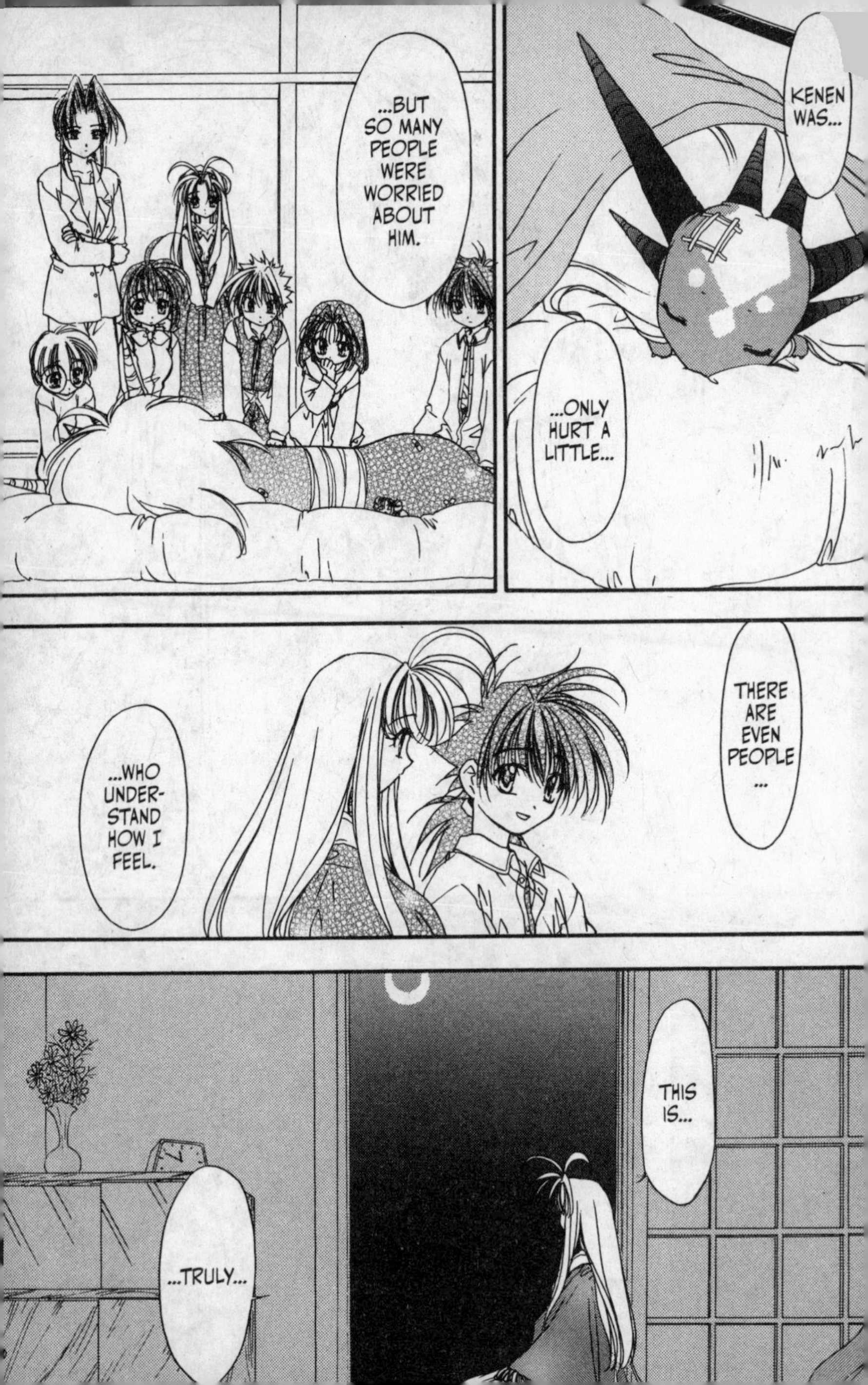
KENEN WAS...
...ONLY HURT A LITTLE...
...BUT SO MANY PEOPLE WERE WORRIED ABOUT HIM.
THERE ARE EVEN PEOPLE...
...WHO UNDER-STAND HOW I FEEL.
THIS IS...
...TRULY...

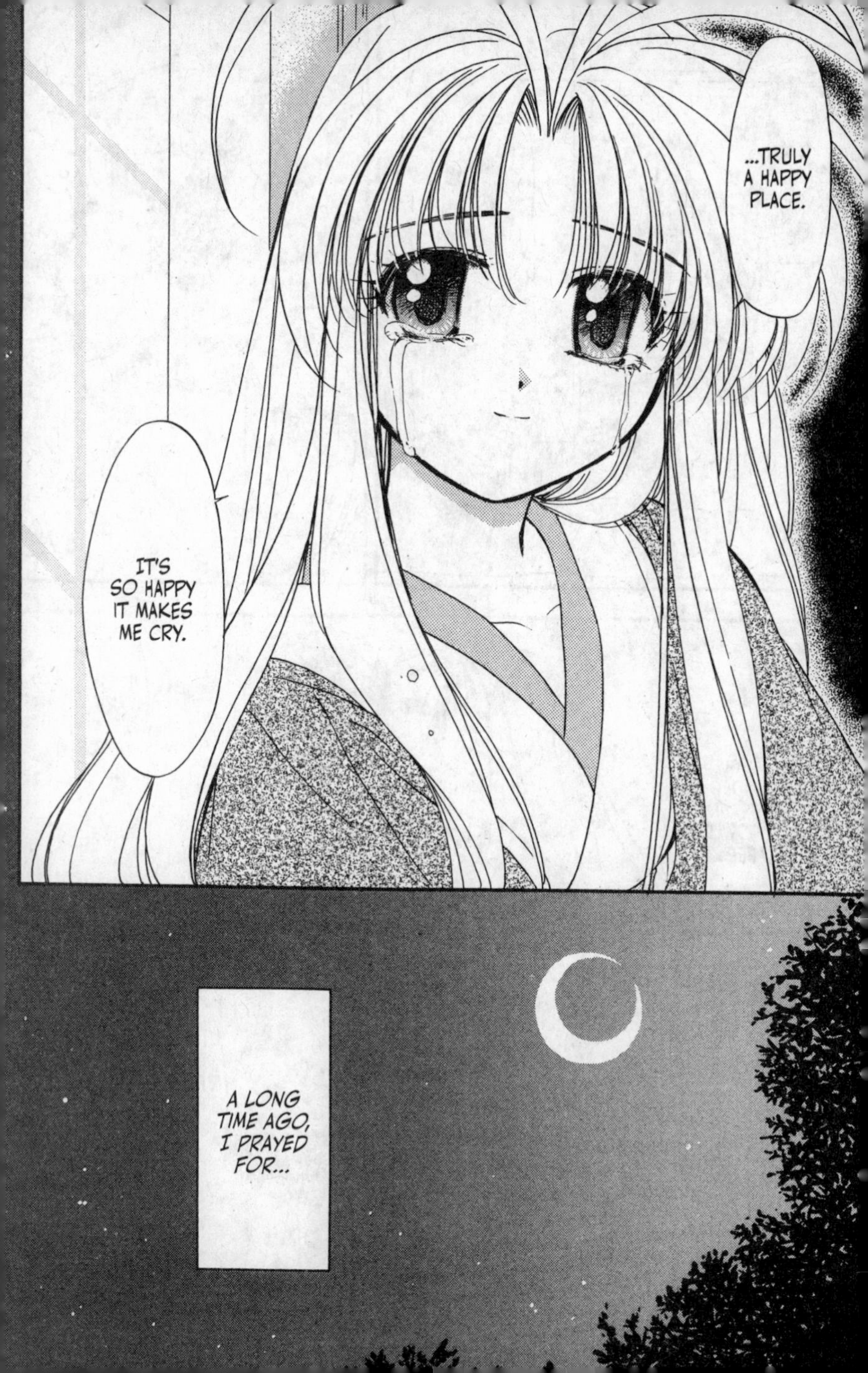
...TRULY A HAPPY PLACE.
IT'S SO HAPPY IT MAKES ME CRY.
A LONG TIME AGO, I PRAYED FOR...

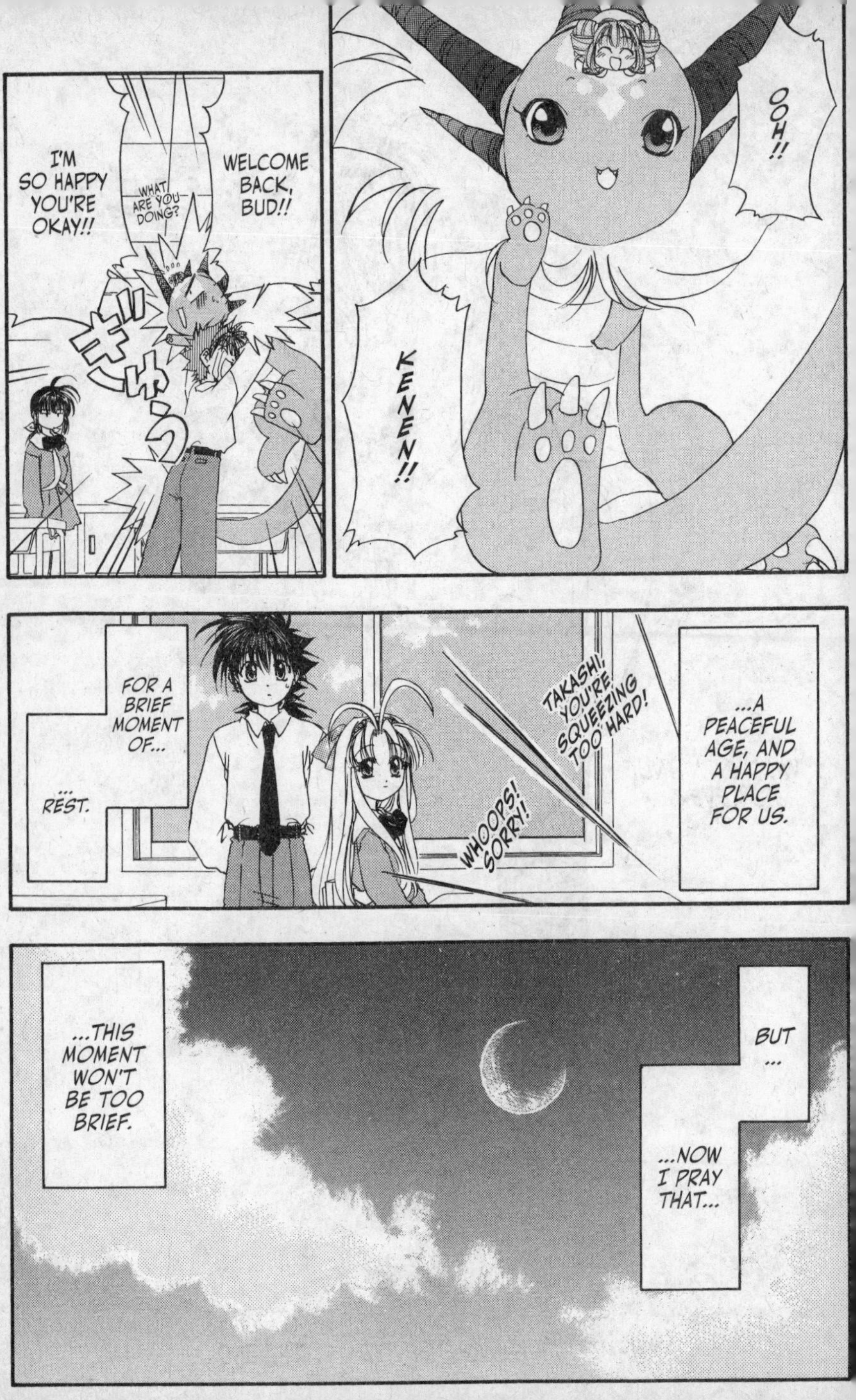
OOH!!
KENEN!!
WELCOME BACK, BUD!!
WHAT ARE YOU DOING?
I'M SO HAPPY YOU'RE OKAY!!
ぎゅう
...A PEACEFUL AGE, AND A HAPPY PLACE FOR US.
TAKASHI, YOU'RE SQUEEZING TOO HARD!
WHOOPS! SORRY!!
FOR A BRIEF MOMENT OF...
...REST.
BUT...
...NOW I PRAY THAT...
...THIS MOMENT WON'T BE TOO BRIEF.

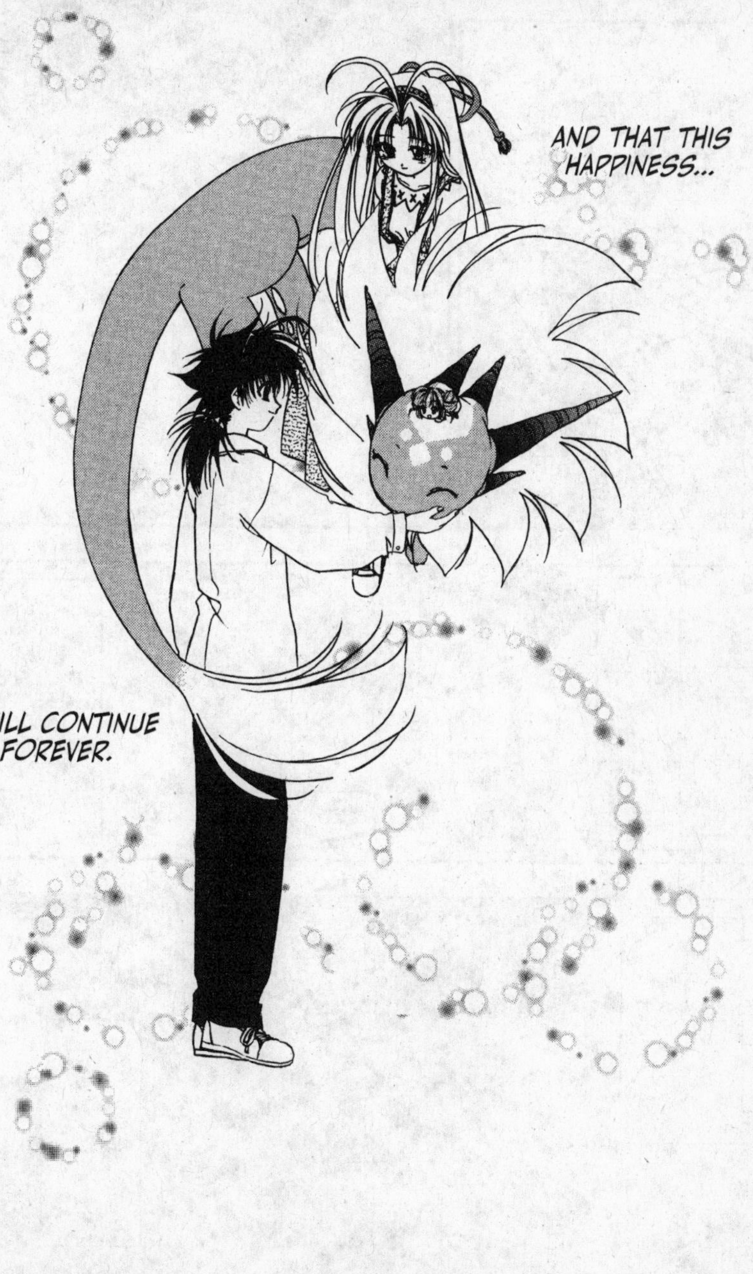
AND THAT THIS HAPPINESS...
...WILL CONTINUE FOREVER.

MAMOTTE SHUGOGETTEN 7: THE END

mamotte
shugogetten

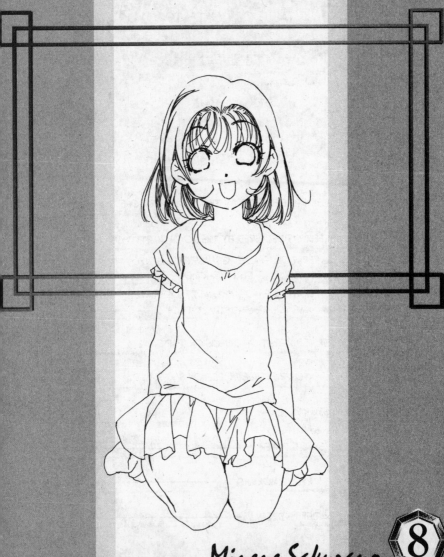

8

Minene Sakurano.

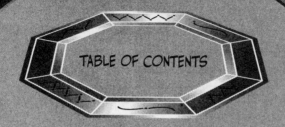

TABLE OF CONTENTS

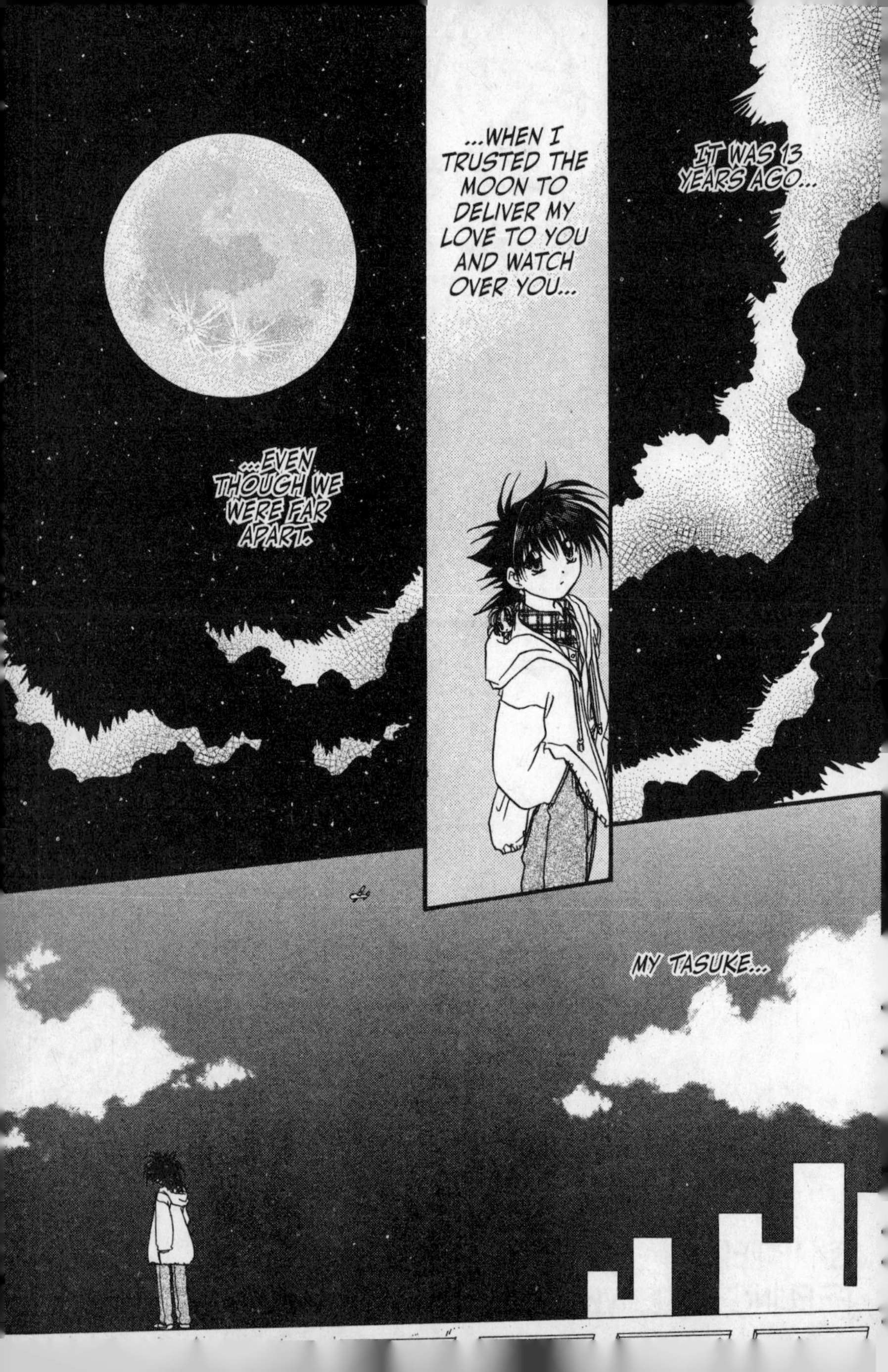
IT WAS 13 YEARS AGO...
...WHEN I TRUSTED THE MOON TO DELIVER MY LOVE TO YOU AND WATCH OVER YOU...
...EVEN THOUGH WE WERE FAR APART.
MY TASUKE...

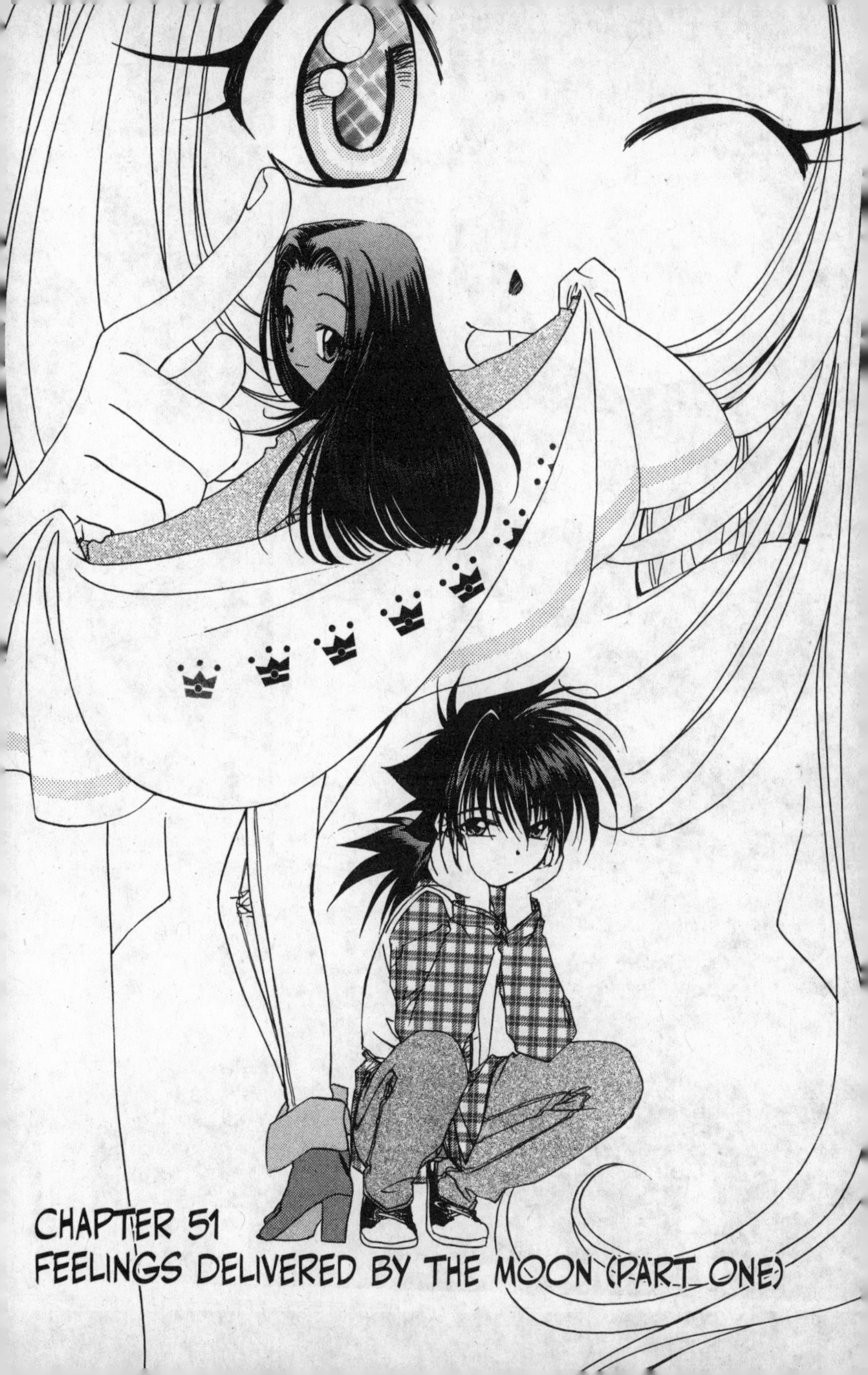
CHAPTER 51
FEELINGS DELIVERED BY THE MOON (PART ONE)

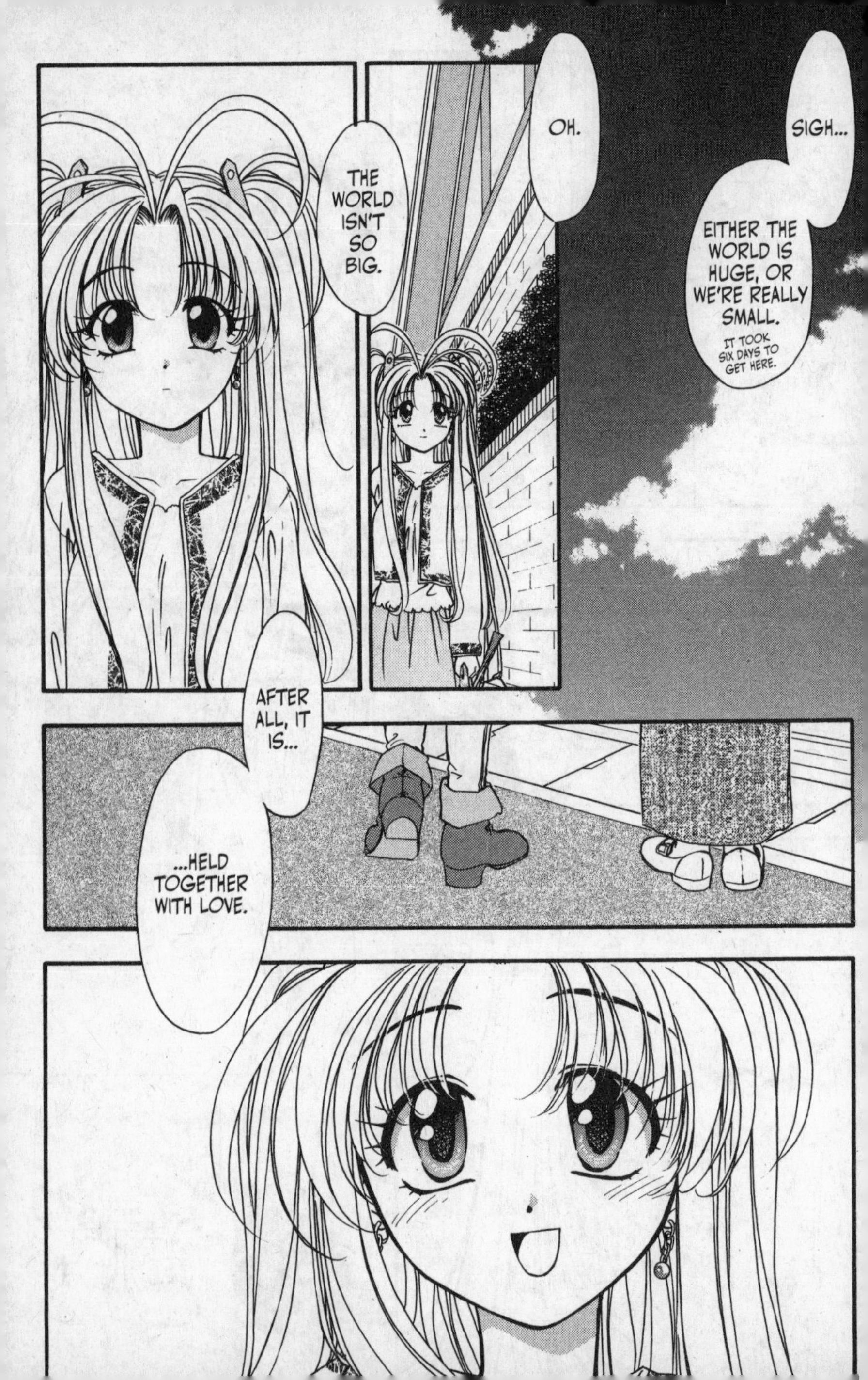

SIGH...
EITHER THE WORLD IS HUGE, OR WE'RE REALLY SMALL.
IT TOOK SIX DAYS TO GET HERE.
OH.
THE WORLD ISN'T SO BIG.
AFTER ALL, IT IS...
...HELD TOGETHER WITH LOVE.

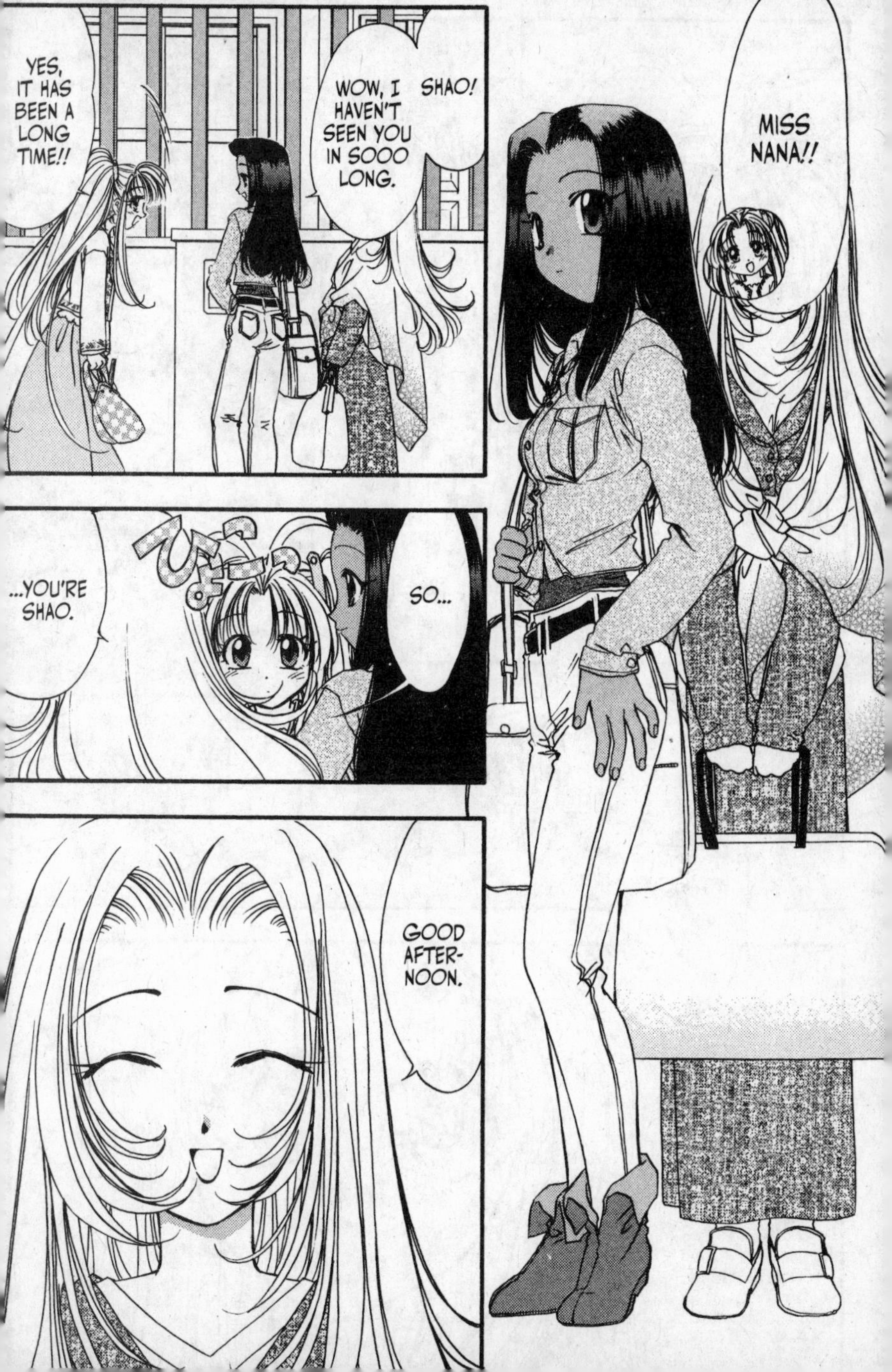
MISS NANA!!
SHAO!
WOW, I HAVEN'T SEEN YOU IN SOOO LONG.
YES, IT HAS BEEN A LONG TIME!!
SO...
...YOU'RE SHAO.
GOOD AFTERNOON.

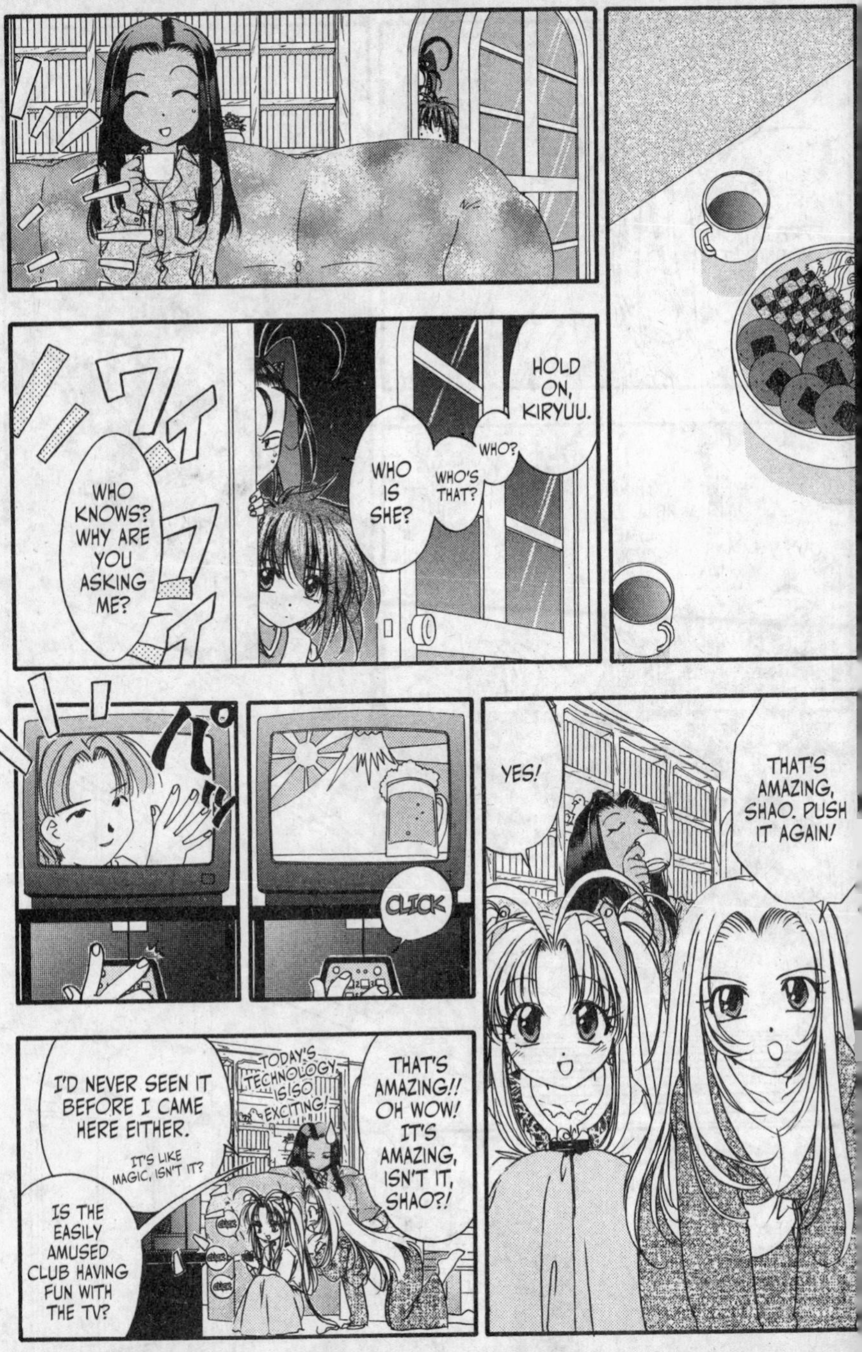
HOLD ON, KIRYUU.
WHO?
WHO'S THAT?
WHO IS SHE?
WHO KNOWS? WHY ARE YOU ASKING ME?
THAT'S AMAZING, SHAO. PUSH IT AGAIN!
YES!
CLICK
THAT'S AMAZING!! OH WOW! IT'S AMAZING, ISN'T IT, SHAO?!
TODAY'S TECHNOLOGY IS SO EXCITING!
I'D NEVER SEEN IT BEFORE I CAME HERE EITHER.
IT'S LIKE MAGIC, ISN'T IT?
IS THE EASILY AMUSED CLUB HAVING FUN WITH THE TV?

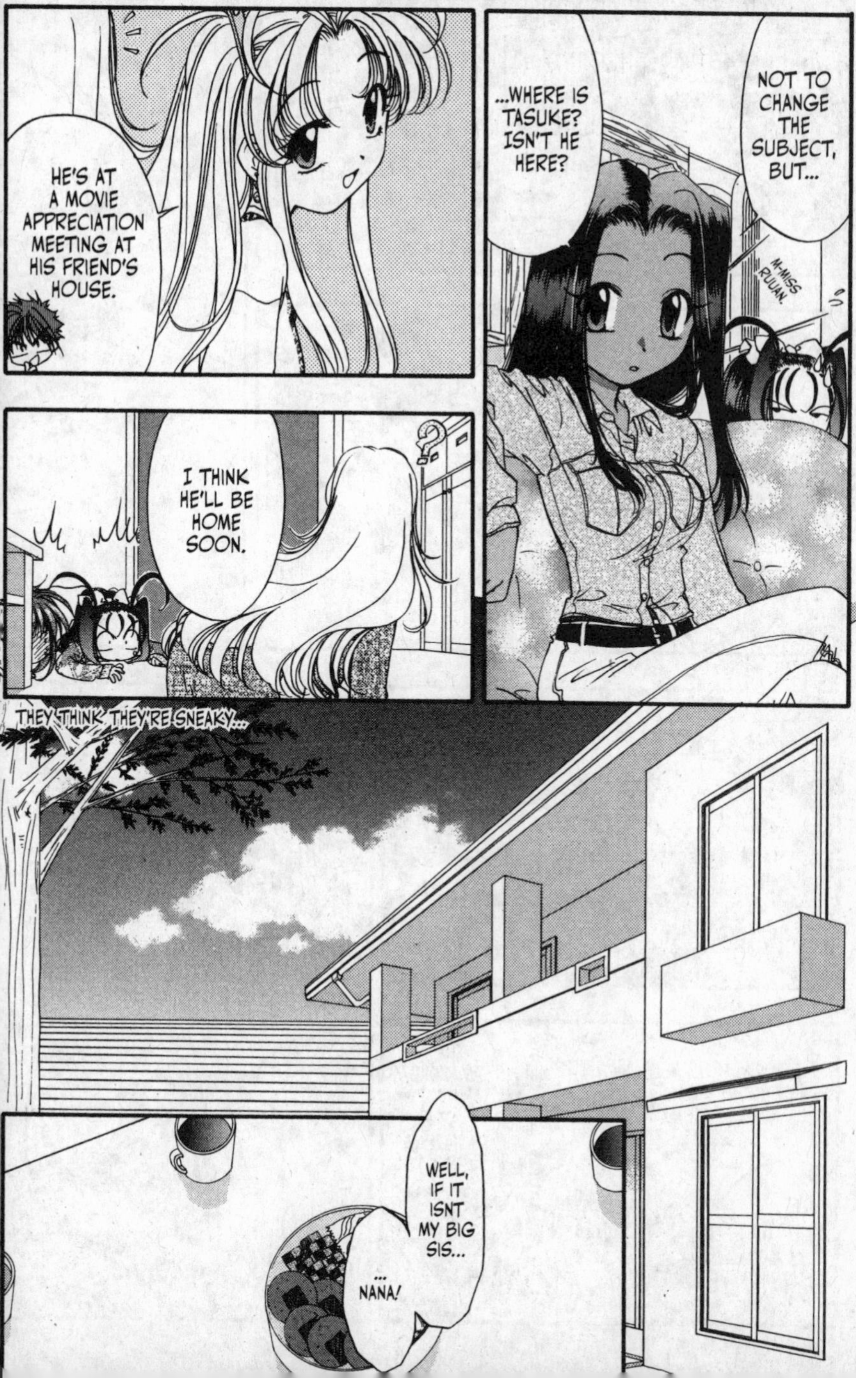
NOT TO CHANGE THE SUBJECT, BUT...
...WHERE IS TASUKE? ISN'T HE HERE?
M-MISS RUUAN.
HE'S AT A MOVIE APPRECIATION MEETING AT HIS FRIEND'S HOUSE.
I THINK HE'LL BE HOME SOON.
THEY THINK THEY'RE SNEAKY...
WELL, IF IT ISNT MY BIG SIS...
...NANA!

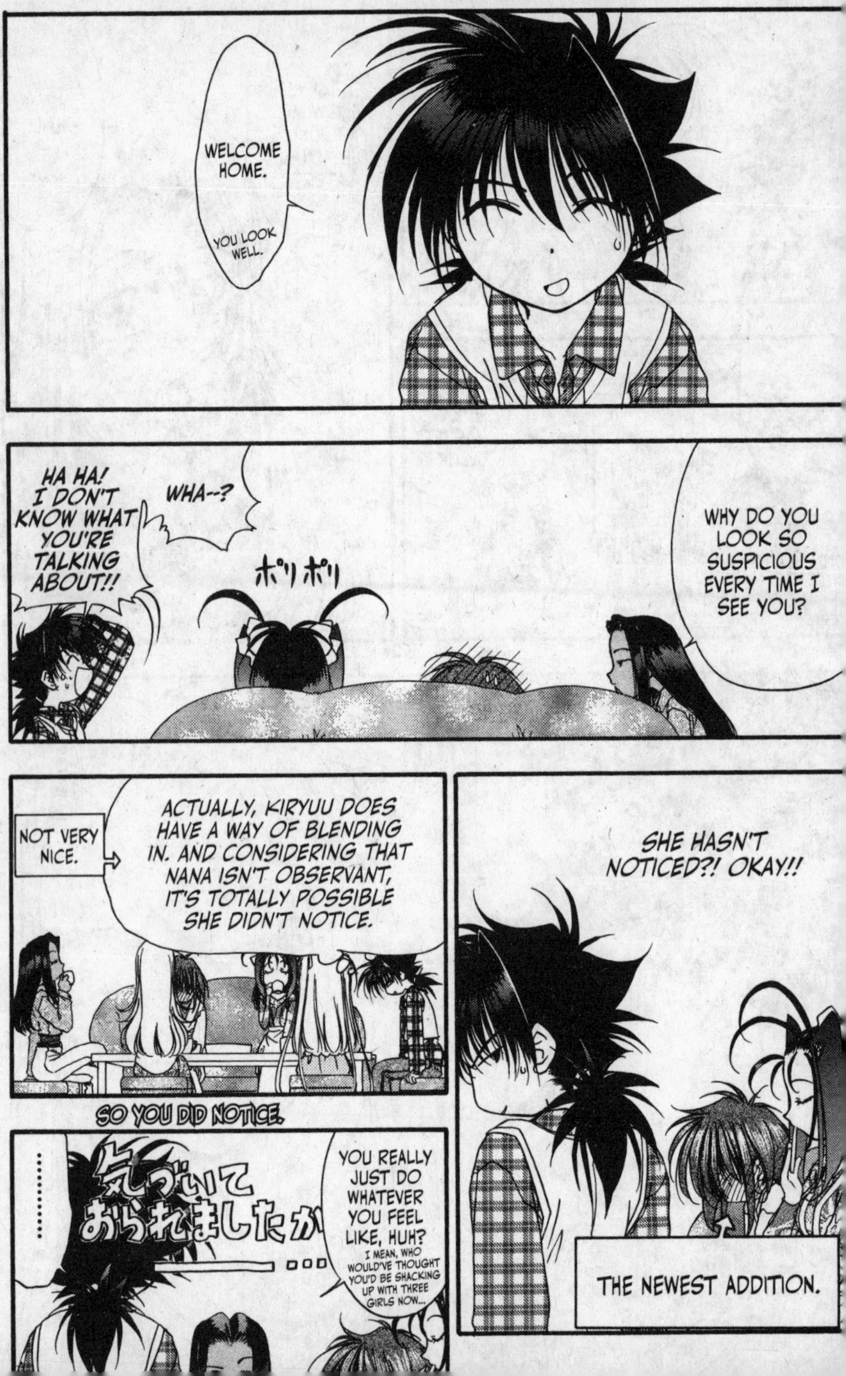
WELCOME HOME.
YOU LOOK WELL.
WHY DO YOU LOOK SO SUSPICIOUS EVERY TIME I SEE YOU?
WHA--?
HA HA! I DON'T KNOW WHAT YOU'RE TALKING ABOUT!!
ポリポリ
SHE HASN'T NOTICED?! OKAY!!
THE NEWEST ADDITION.
ACTUALLY, KIRYUU DOES HAVE A WAY OF BLENDING IN. AND CONSIDERING THAT NANA ISN'T OBSERVANT, IT'S TOTALLY POSSIBLE SHE DIDN'T NOTICE.
NOT VERY NICE.
SO YOU DID NOTICE.
YOU REALLY JUST DO WHATEVER YOU FEEL LIKE, HUH?
I MEAN, WHO WOULD'VE THOUGHT YOU'D BE SHACKING UP WITH THREE GIRLS NOW...
気づいておられましたか
……
...

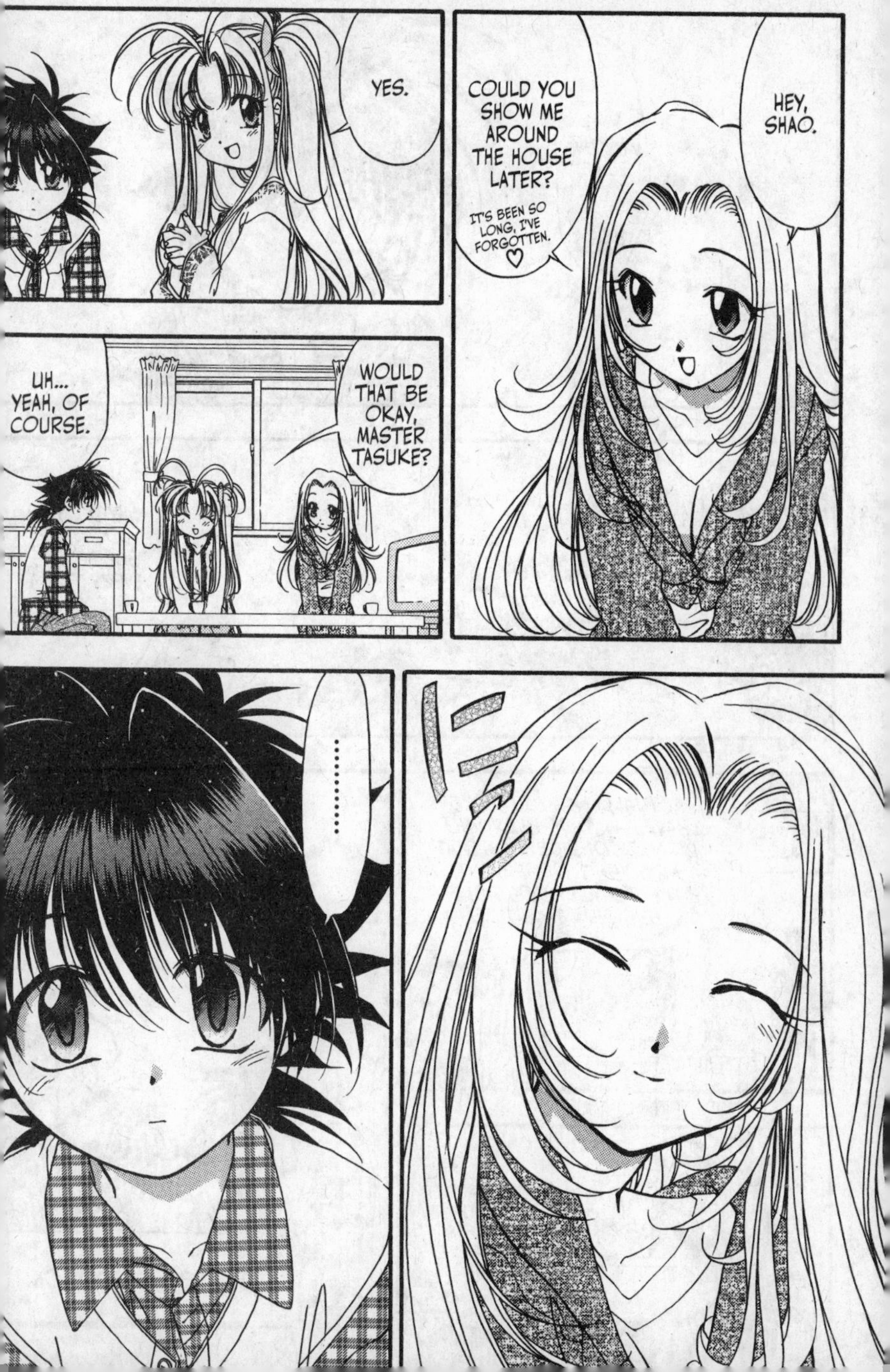
HEY, SHAO.
COULD YOU SHOW ME AROUND THE HOUSE LATER?
IT'S BEEN SO LONG, I'VE FORGOTTEN. ♡
YES.
WOULD THAT BE OKAY, MASTER TASUKE?
UH... YEAH, OF COURSE.
....

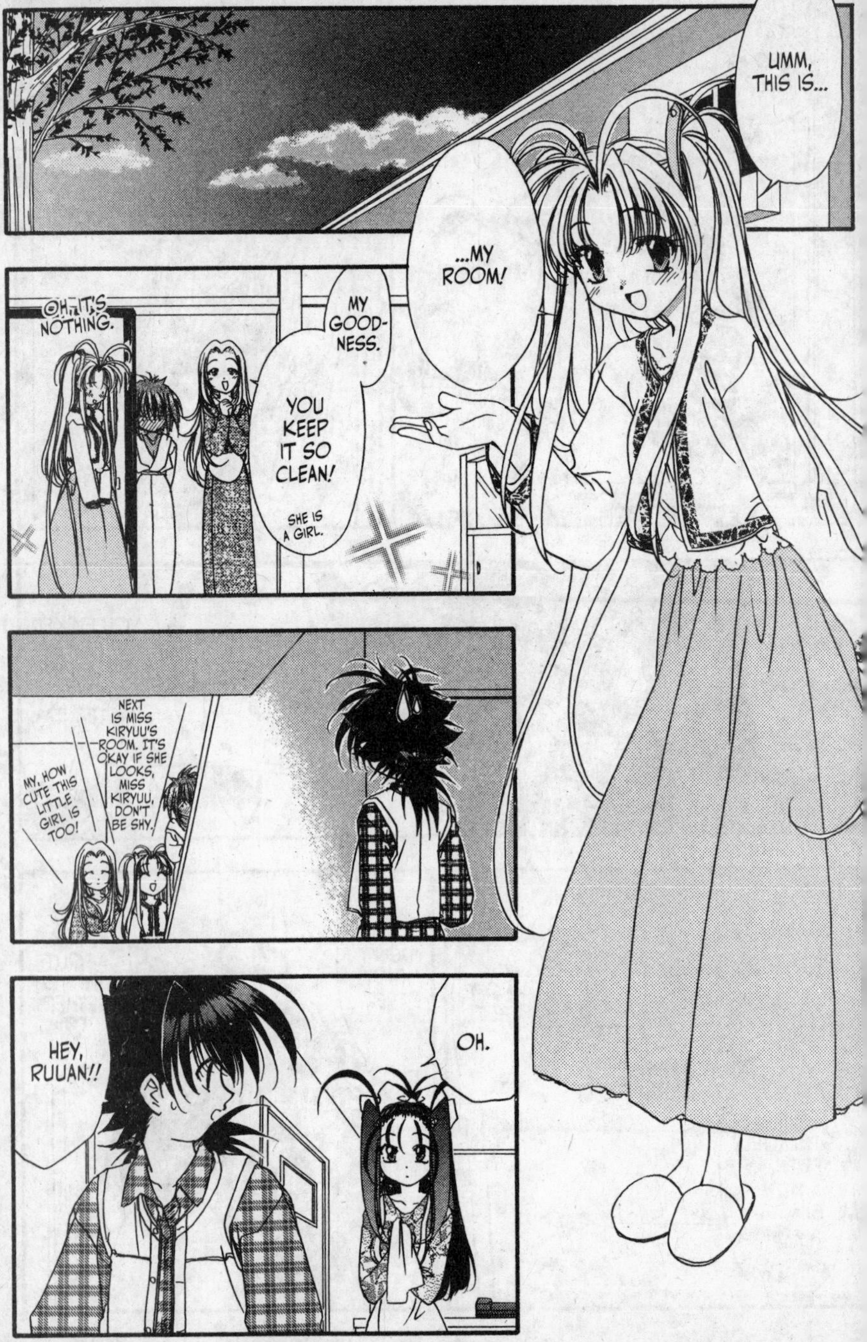
UMM, THIS IS...
...MY ROOM!
MY GOODNESS.
YOU KEEP IT SO CLEAN!
SHE IS A GIRL.
OH, IT'S NOTHING.
NEXT IS MISS KIRYUU'S ROOM. IT'S OKAY IF SHE LOOKS, MISS KIRYUU, DON'T BE SHY.
MY, HOW CUTE THIS LITTLE GIRL IS TOO!
OH.
HEY, RUUAN!!

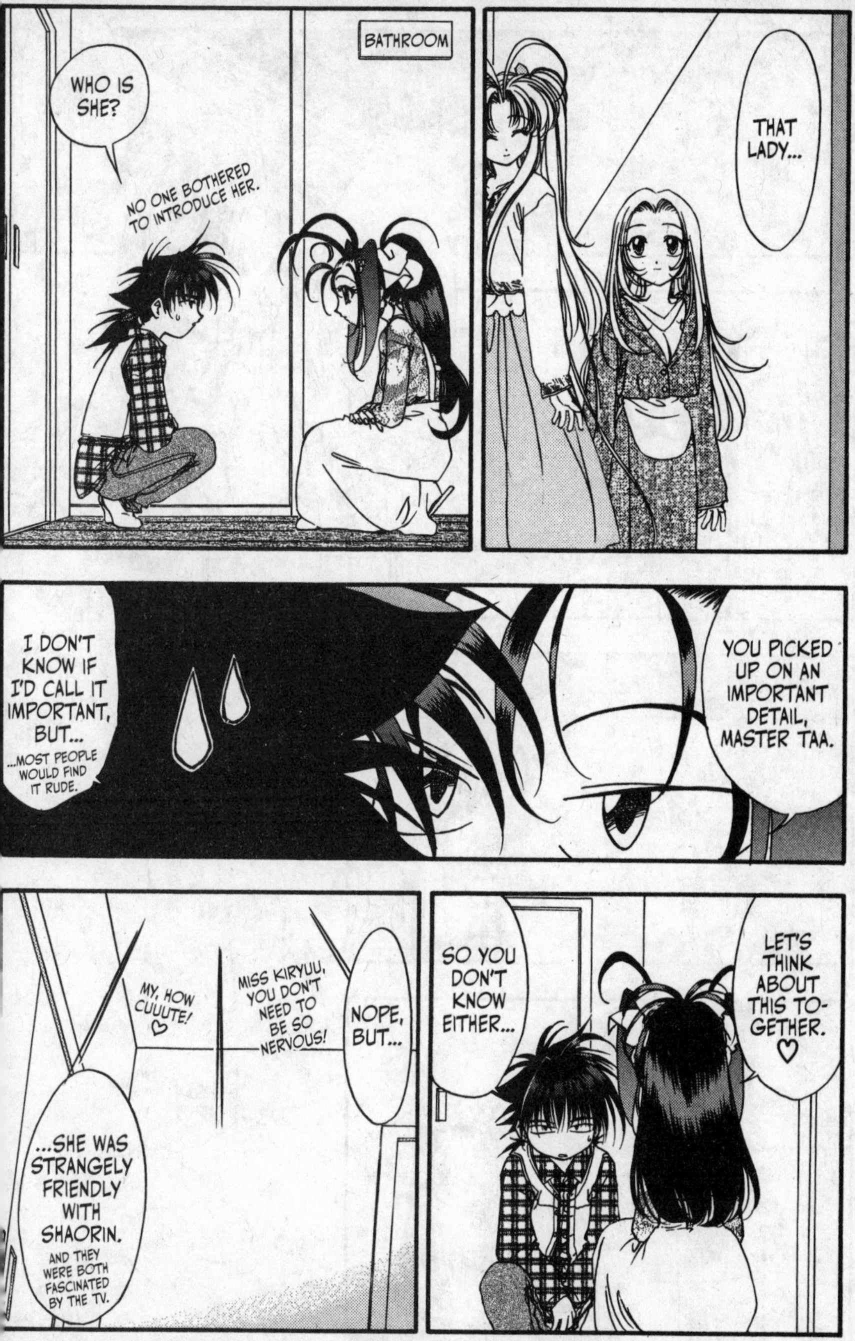
BATHROOM
THAT LADY...
WHO IS SHE?
NO ONE BOTHERED TO INTRODUCE HER.
YOU PICKED UP ON AN IMPORTANT DETAIL, MASTER TAA.
I DON'T KNOW IF I'D CALL IT IMPORTANT, BUT...
...MOST PEOPLE WOULD FIND IT RUDE.
LET'S THINK ABOUT THIS TO-GETHER. ♡
SO YOU DON'T KNOW EITHER...
NOPE, BUT...
MISS KIRYUU, YOU DON'T NEED TO BE SO NERVOUS!
MY, HOW CUUUTE! ♡
...SHE WAS STRANGELY FRIENDLY WITH SHAORIN.
AND THEY WERE BOTH FASCINATED BY THE TV.

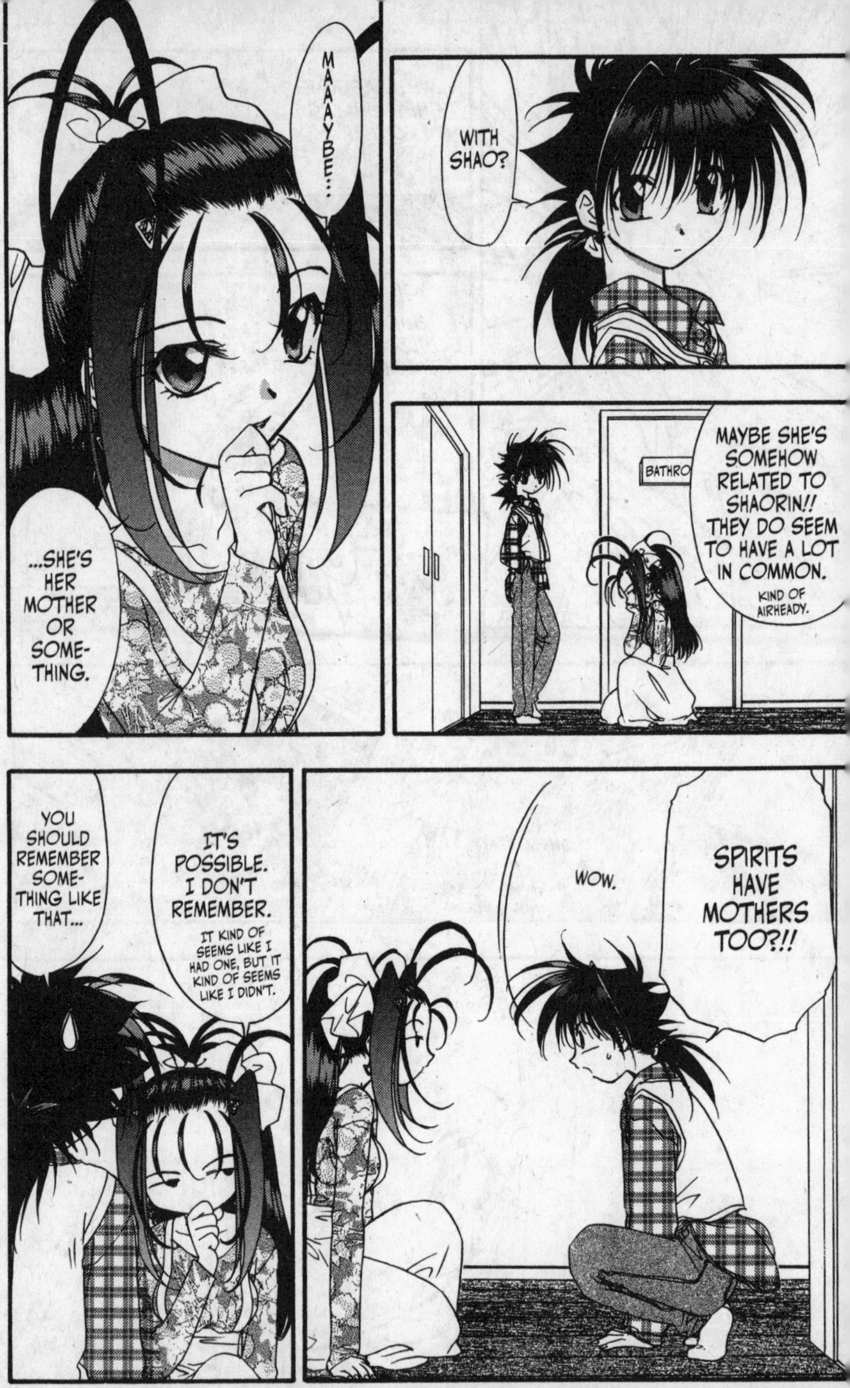
WITH SHAO?
MAYBE SHE'S SOMEHOW RELATED TO SHAORIN!! THEY DO SEEM TO HAVE A LOT IN COMMON.
KIND OF AIRHEADY.
BATHRO
MAAAYBE...
...SHE'S HER MOTHER OR SOME-THING.
SPIRITS HAVE MOTHERS TOO?!!
WOW.
IT'S POSSIBLE. I DON'T REMEMBER.
IT KIND OF SEEMS LIKE I HAD ONE, BUT IT KIND OF SEEMS LIKE I DIDN'T.
YOU SHOULD REMEMBER SOME-THING LIKE THAT...

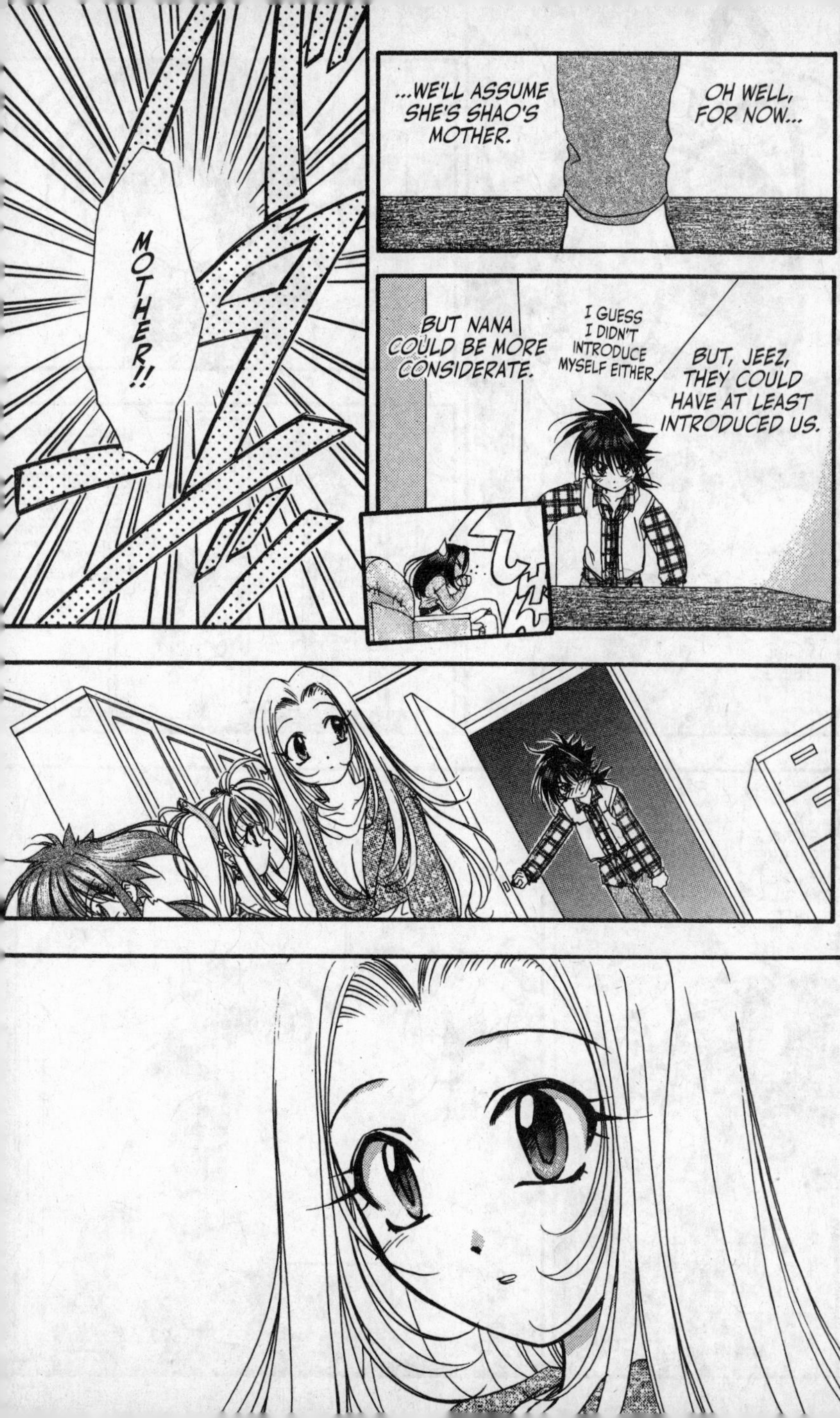
OH WELL, FOR NOW...
...WE'LL ASSUME SHE'S SHAO'S MOTHER.
BUT, JEEZ, THEY COULD HAVE AT LEAST INTRODUCED US.
I GUESS I DIDN'T INTRODUCE MYSELF EITHER.
BUT NANA COULD BE MORE CONSIDERATE.
MOTHER!!

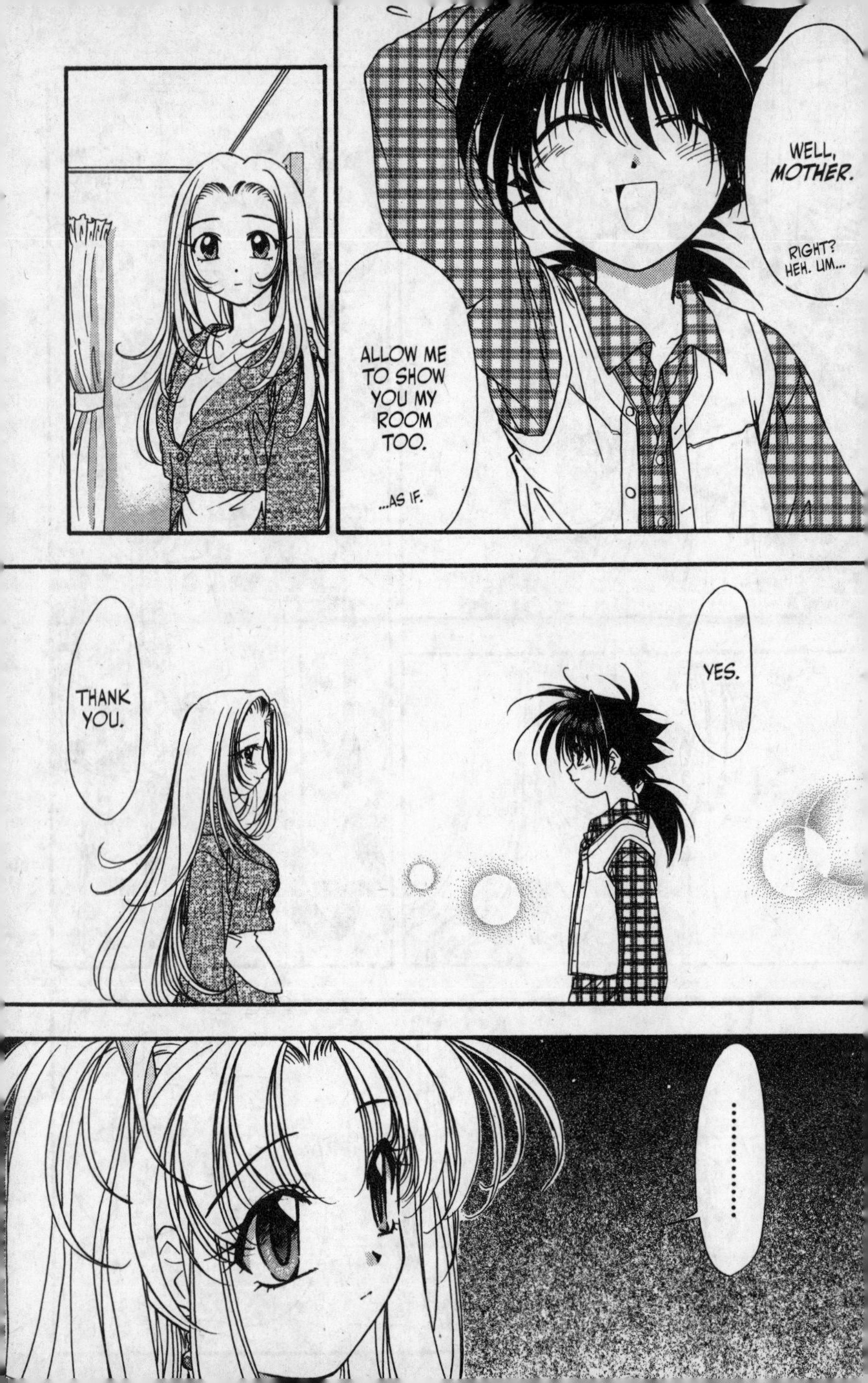
WELL, MOTHER.
RIGHT? HEH. UM...
ALLOW ME TO SHOW YOU MY ROOM TOO.
...AS IF.
YES.
THANK YOU.
....

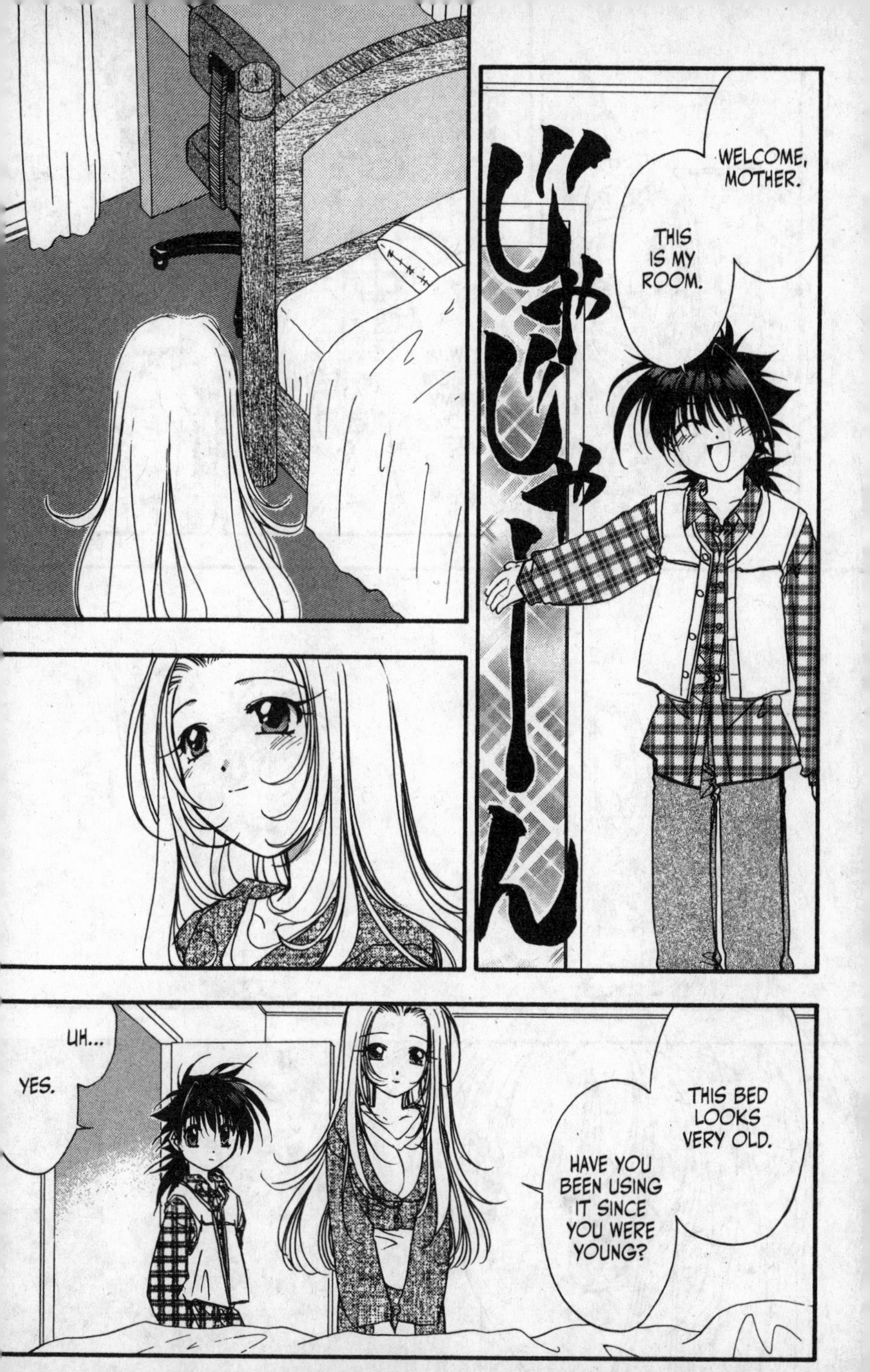
WELCOME, MOTHER.
THIS IS MY ROOM.
じゃじゃーん
THIS BED LOOKS VERY OLD.
HAVE YOU BEEN USING IT SINCE YOU WERE YOUNG?
UH...
YES.

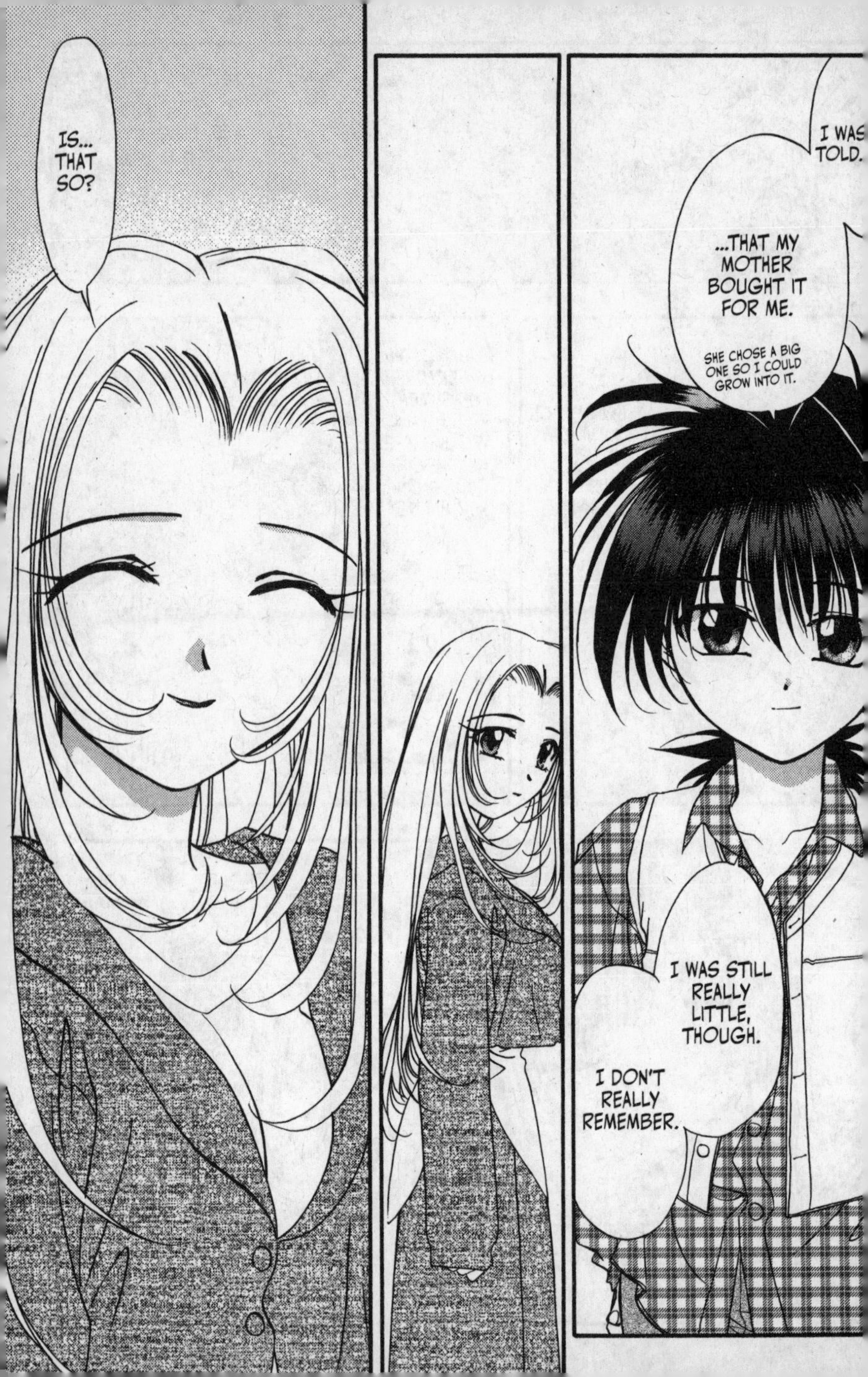
I WAS TOLD.
...THAT MY MOTHER BOUGHT IT FOR ME.
SHE CHOSE A BIG ONE SO I COULD GROW INTO IT.
I WAS STILL REALLY LITTLE, THOUGH.
I DON'T REALLY REMEMBER.
IS... THAT SO?

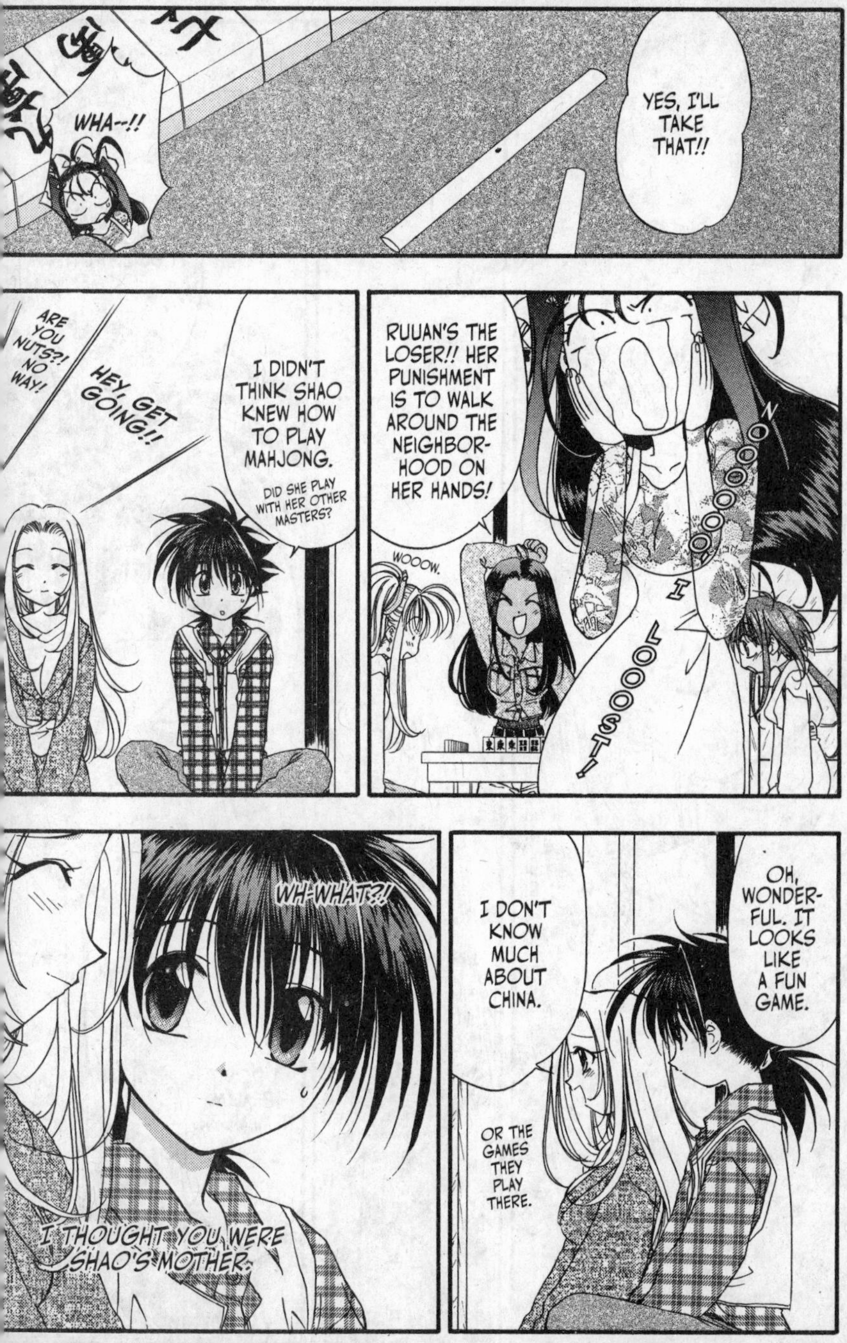
YES, I'LL TAKE THAT!!
WHA--!!
RUUAN'S THE LOSER!! HER PUNISHMENT IS TO WALK AROUND THE NEIGHBOR-HOOD ON HER HANDS!
NOOOOOO, I LOOOOST!
WOOOW.
I DIDN'T THINK SHAO KNEW HOW TO PLAY MAHJONG.
DID SHE PLAY WITH HER OTHER MASTERS?
HEY, GET GOING!!
ARE YOU NUTS?!! NO WAY!
OH, WONDER-FUL. IT LOOKS LIKE A FUN GAME.
I DON'T KNOW MUCH ABOUT CHINA.
OR THE GAMES THEY PLAY THERE.
WH-WHAT?!
I THOUGHT YOU WERE SHAO'S MOTHER.

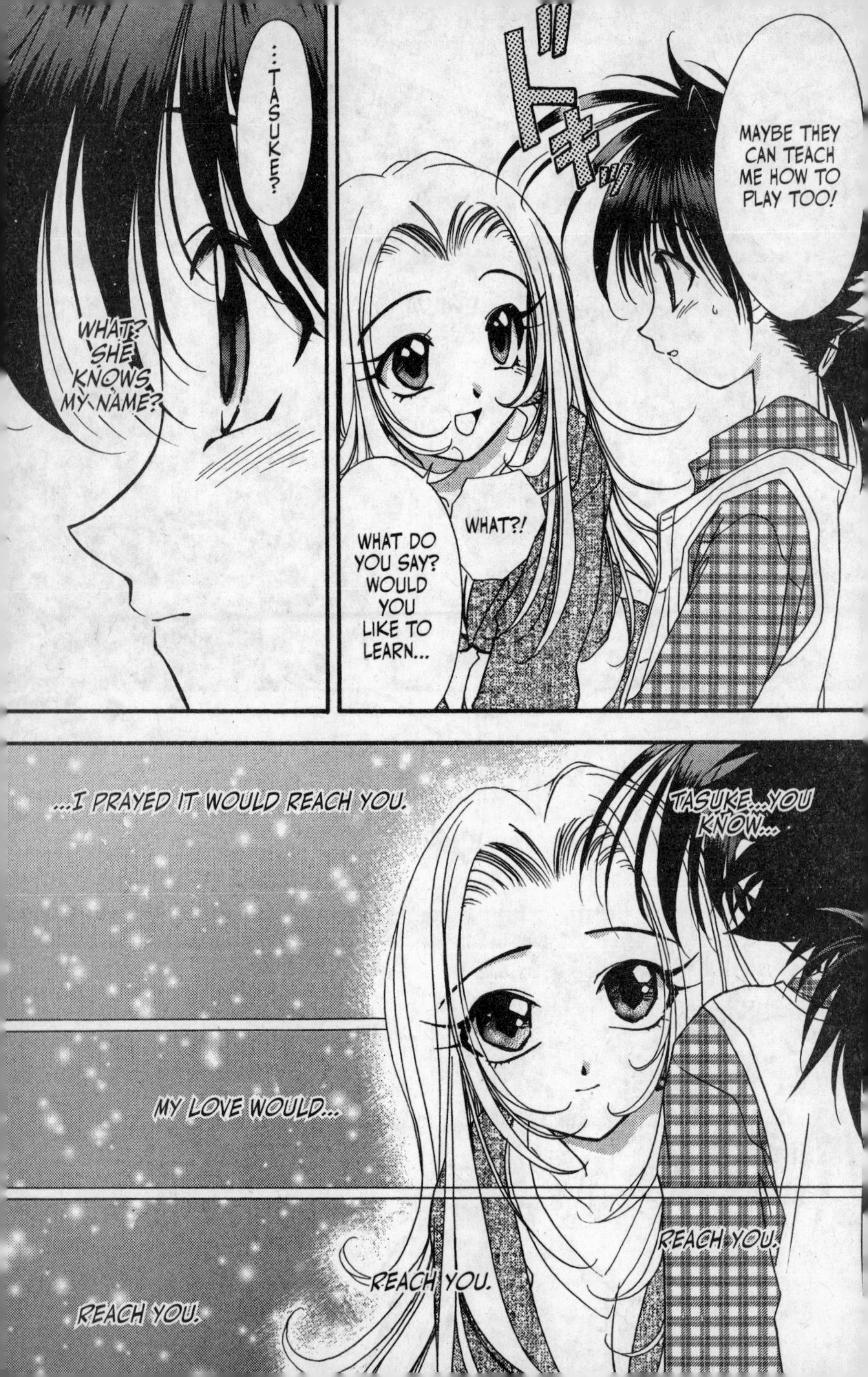

ドキッ
MAYBE THEY CAN TEACH ME HOW TO PLAY TOO!
WHAT?!
WHAT DO YOU SAY? WOULD YOU LIKE TO LEARN...
...TASUKE?
WHAT? SHE KNOWS MY NAME?
TASUKE...YOU KNOW...
...I PRAYED IT WOULD REACH YOU.
MY LOVE WOULD...
REACH YOU.
REACH YOU.
REACH YOU.

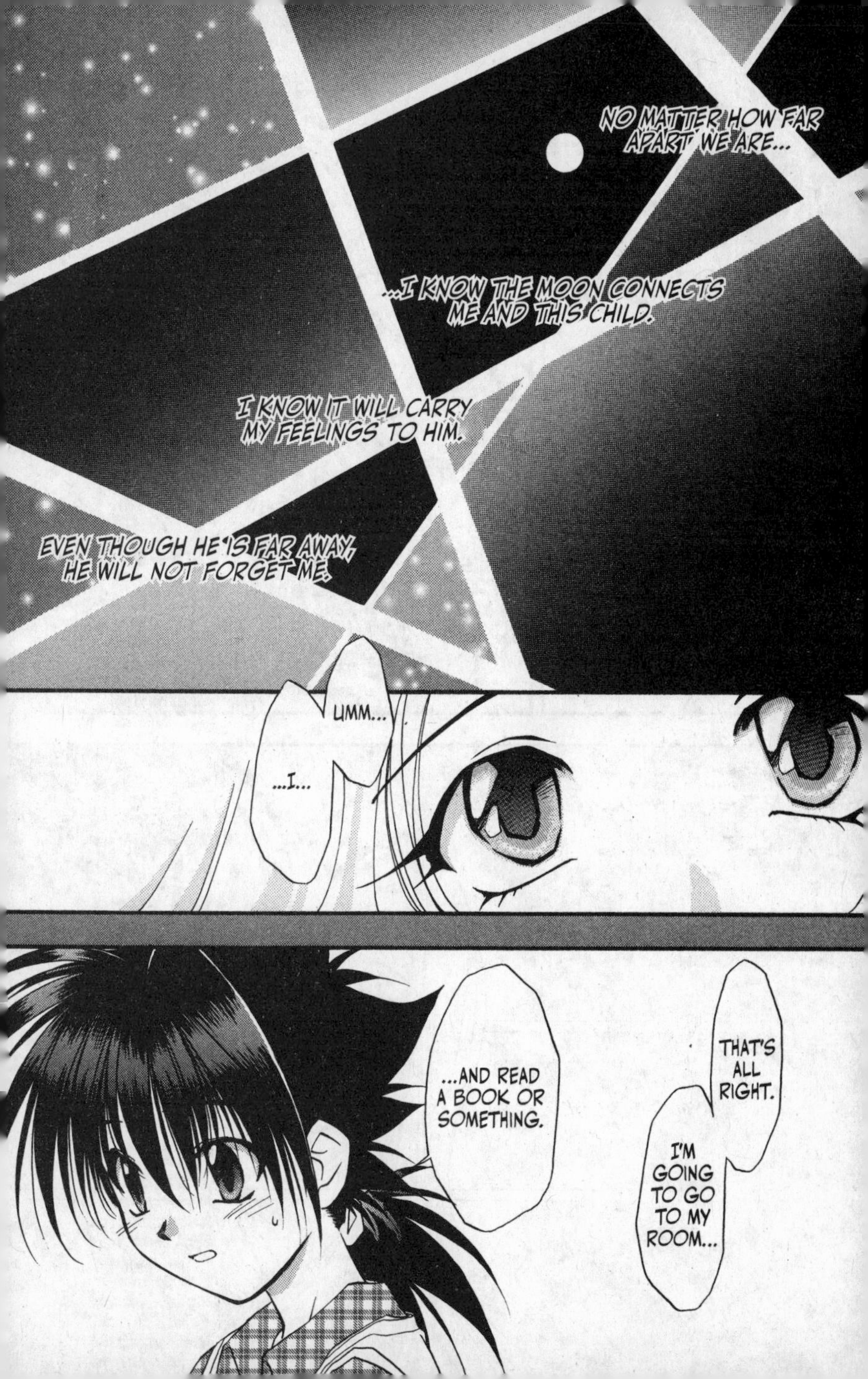
NO MATTER HOW FAR APART WE ARE...
...I KNOW THE MOON CONNECTS ME AND THIS CHILD.
I KNOW IT WILL CARRY MY FEELINGS TO HIM.
EVEN THOUGH HE IS FAR AWAY, HE WILL NOT FORGET ME.
UMM...
...I...
THAT'S ALL RIGHT.
I'M GOING TO GO TO MY ROOM...
...AND READ A BOOK OR SOMETHING.

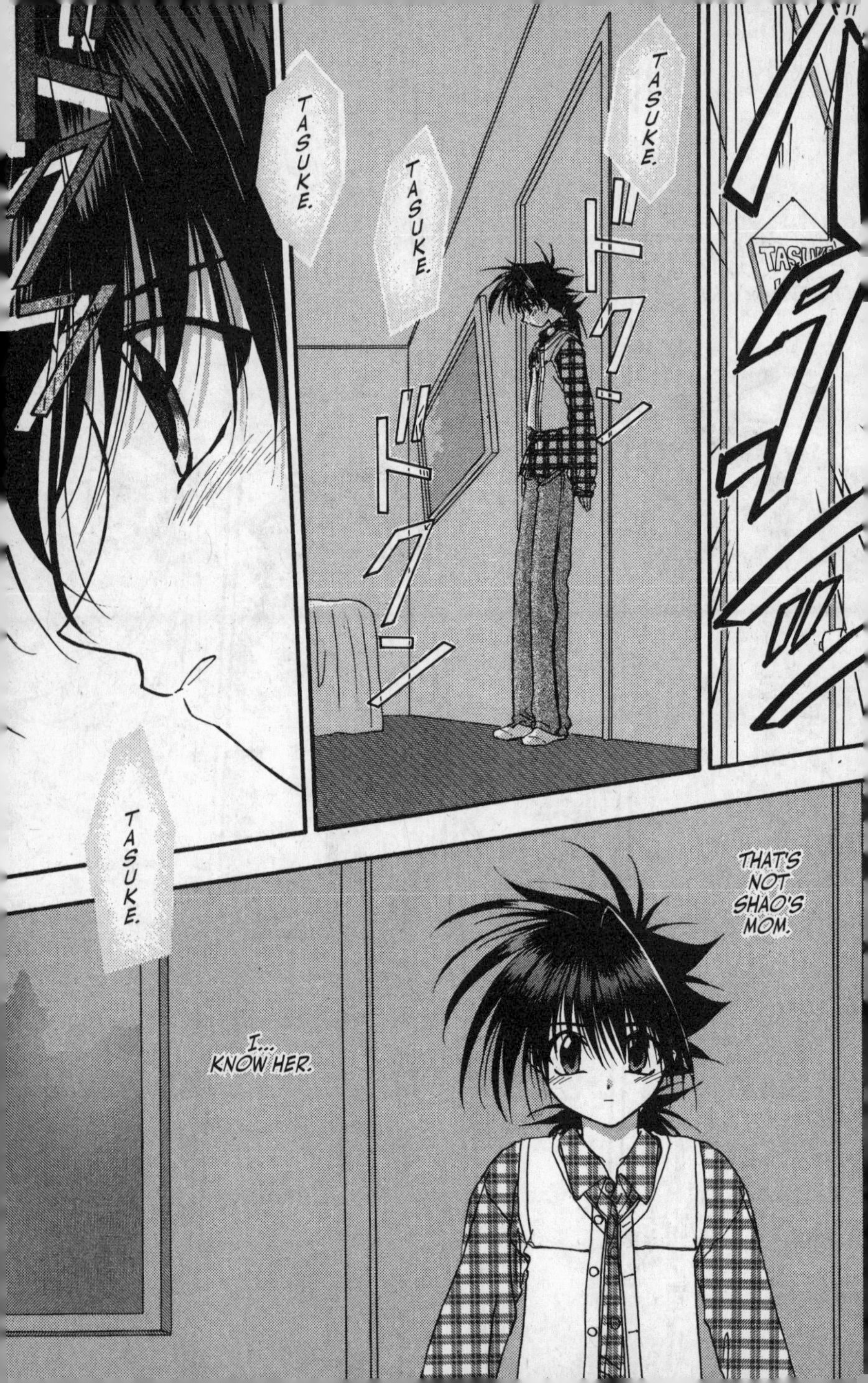
TASUKE.
TASUKE.
TASUKE.
TASUKE.
THAT'S NOT SHAO'S MOM.
I... KNOW HER.

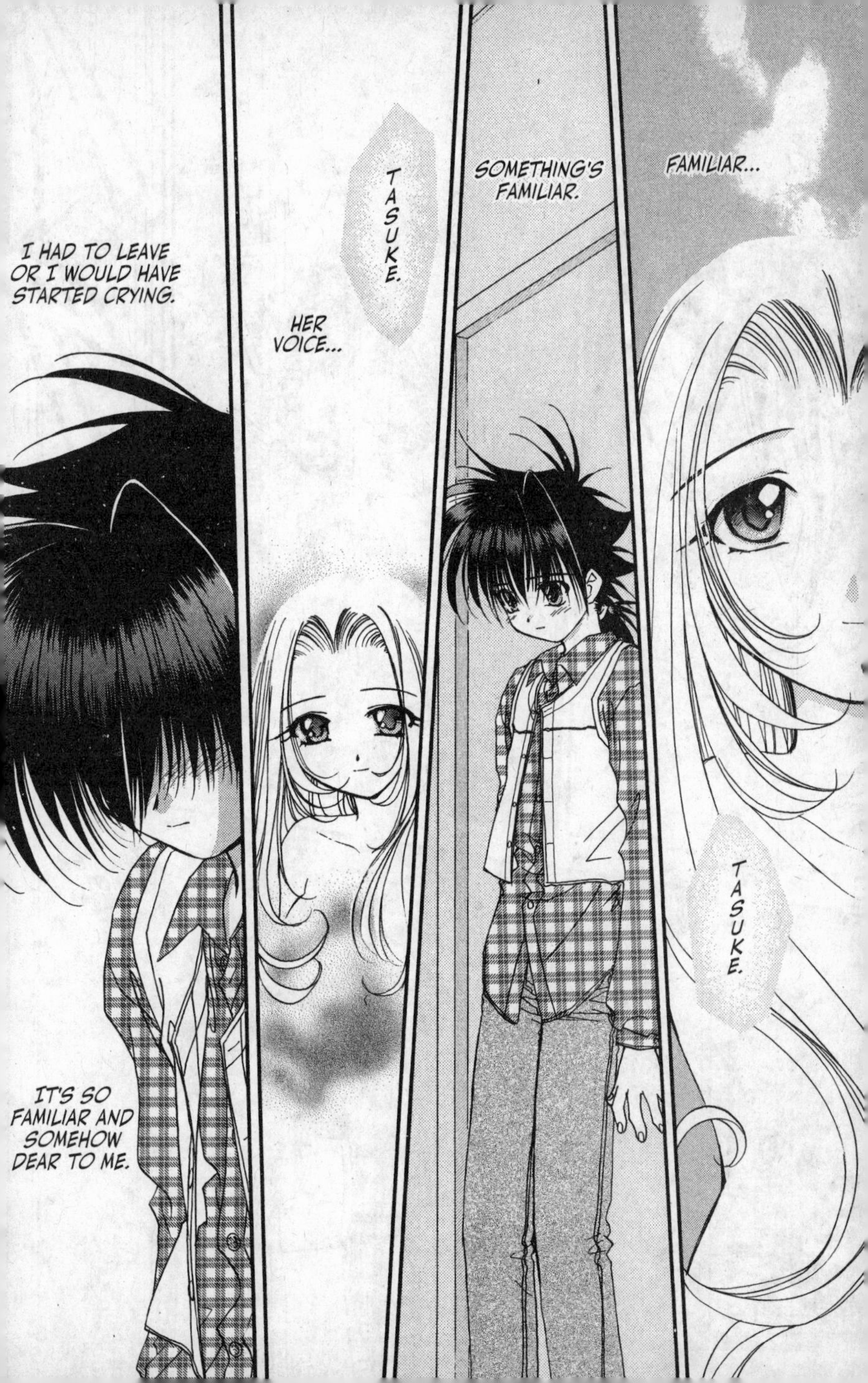
FAMILIAR...
TASUKE.
SOMETHING'S FAMILIAR.
TASUKE.
HER VOICE...
I HAD TO LEAVE OR I WOULD HAVE STARTED CRYING.
IT'S SO FAMILIAR AND SOMEHOW DEAR TO ME.

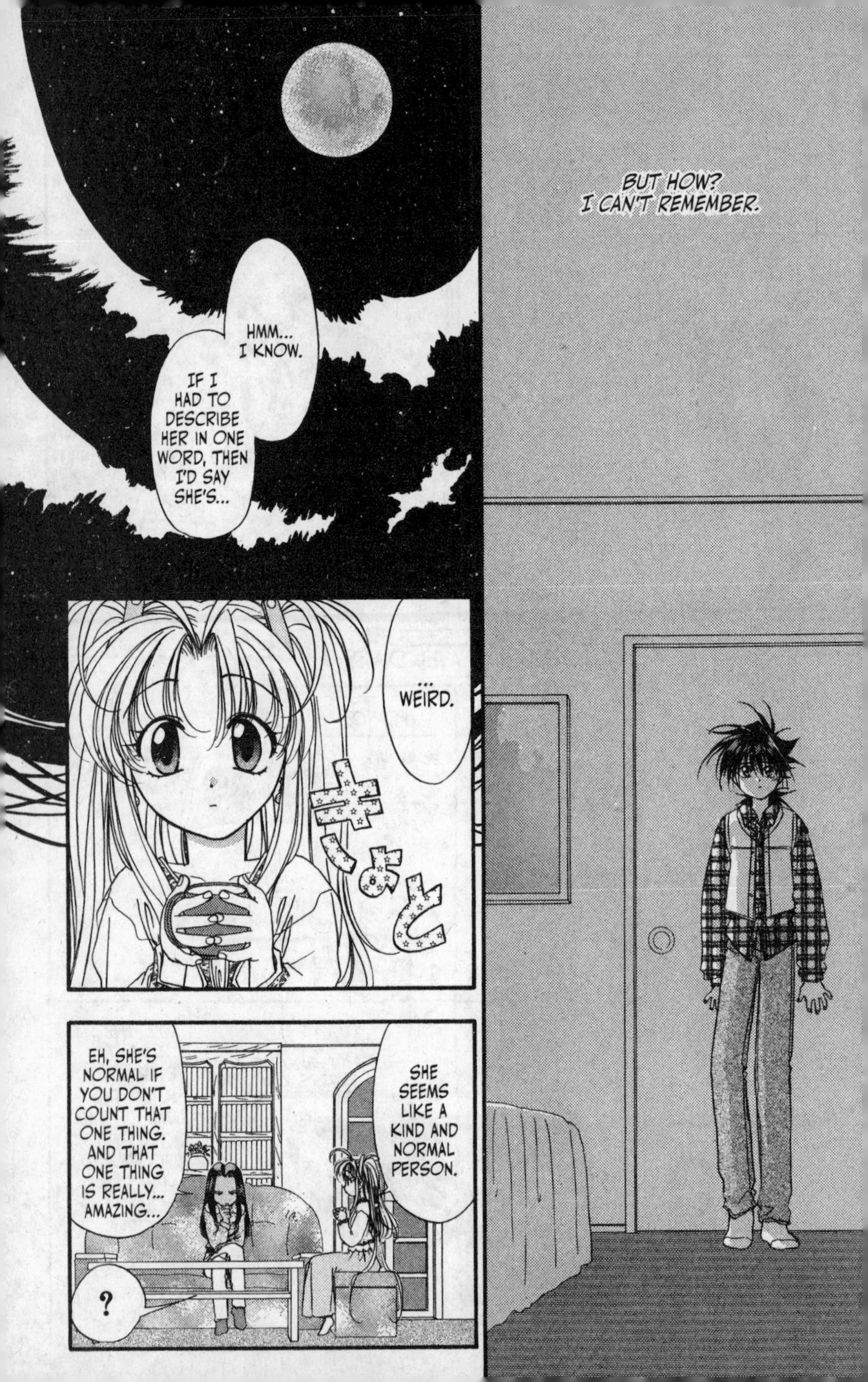
BUT HOW? I CAN'T REMEMBER.
HMM... I KNOW.
IF I HAD TO DESCRIBE HER IN ONE WORD, THEN I'D SAY SHE'S...
...WEIRD.
SHE SEEMS LIKE A KIND AND NORMAL PERSON.
EH, SHE'S NORMAL IF YOU DON'T COUNT THAT ONE THING. AND THAT ONE THING IS REALLY... AMAZING...
?

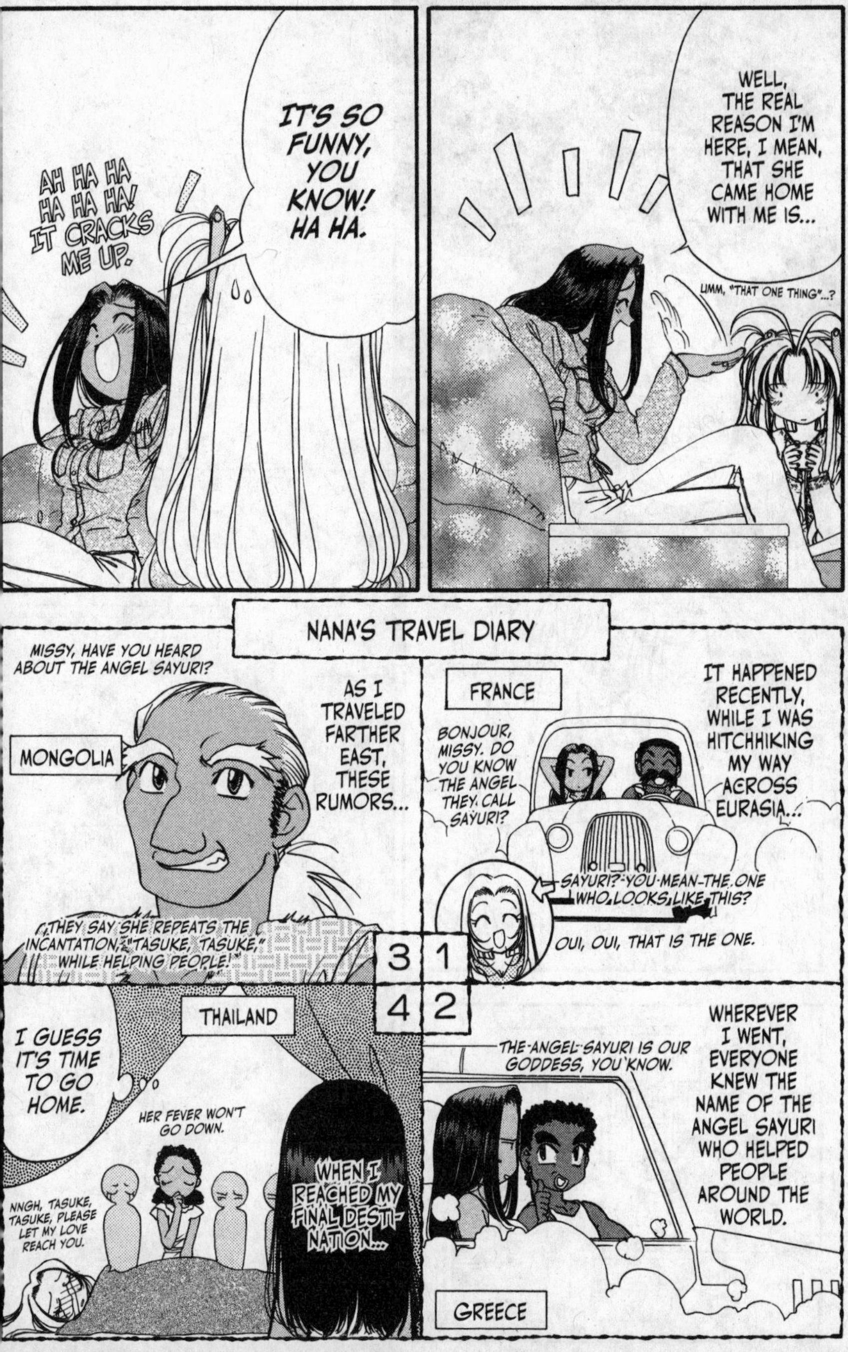
WELL, THE REAL REASON I'M HERE, I MEAN, THAT SHE CAME HOME WITH ME IS...
UMM, "THAT ONE THING"...?
IT'S SO FUNNY, YOU KNOW! HA HA.
AH HA HA HA HA HA! IT CRACKS ME UP.
NANA'S TRAVEL DIARY
IT HAPPENED RECENTLY, WHILE I WAS HITCHHIKING MY WAY ACROSS EURASIA...
FRANCE
BONJOUR, MISSY. DO YOU KNOW THE ANGEL THEY CALL SAYURI?
SAYURI? YOU MEAN THE ONE WHO LOOKS LIKE THIS?
OUI, OUI, THAT IS THE ONE.
1
2
WHEREVER I WENT, EVERYONE KNEW THE NAME OF THE ANGEL SAYURI WHO HELPED PEOPLE AROUND THE WORLD.
THE ANGEL SAYURI IS OUR GODDESS, YOU KNOW.
GREECE
3
AS I TRAVELED FARTHER EAST, THESE RUMORS...
MISSY, HAVE YOU HEARD ABOUT THE ANGEL SAYURI?
MONGOLIA
THEY SAY SHE REPEATS THE INCANTATION, "TASUKE, TASUKE," WHILE HELPING PEOPLE!
4
THAILAND
WHEN I REACHED MY FINAL DESTINATION...
HER FEVER WON'T GO DOWN.
I GUESS IT'S TIME TO GO HOME.
NNGH, TASUKE, TASUKE, PLEASE LET MY LOVE REACH YOU.

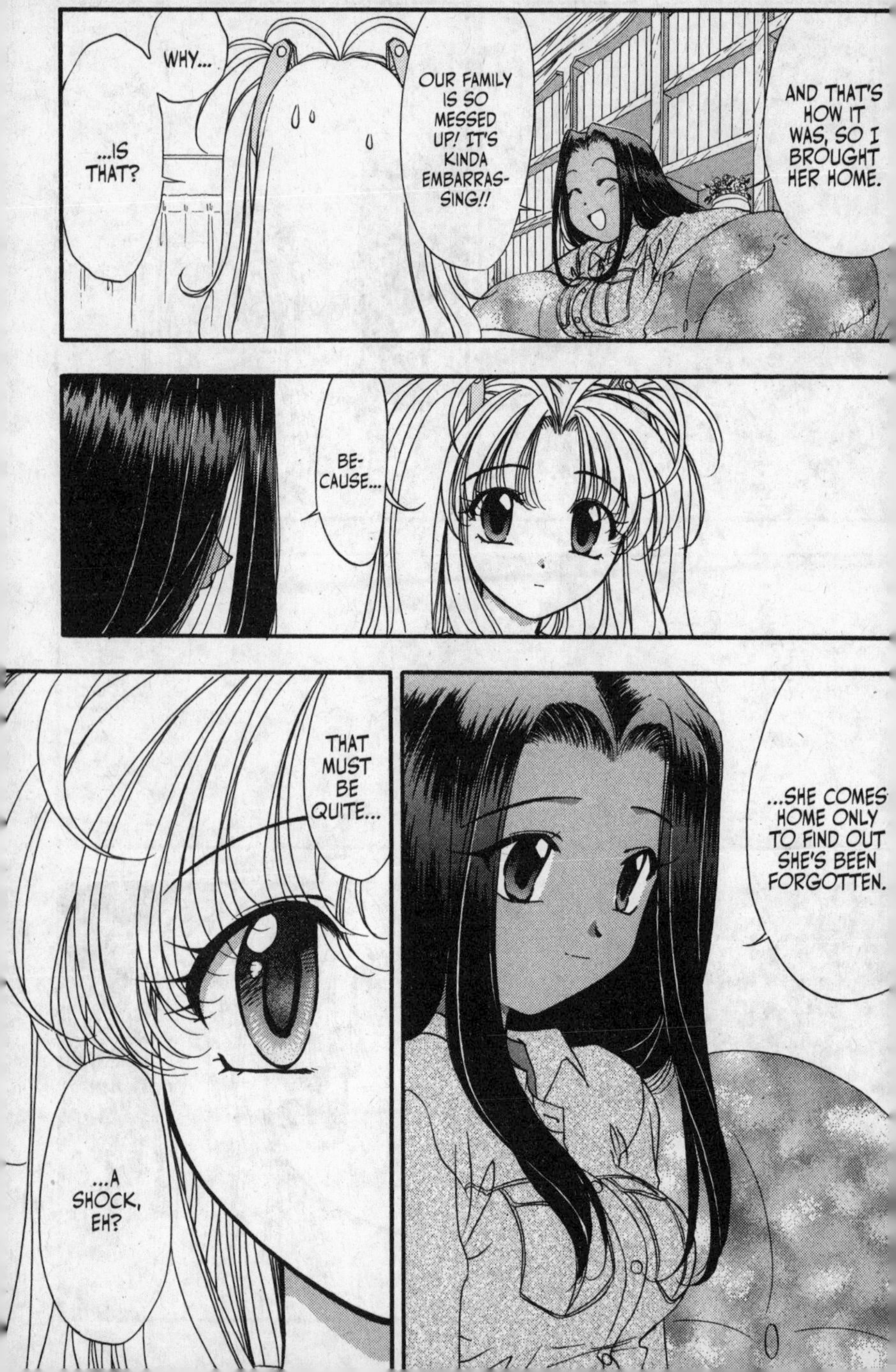
AND THAT'S HOW IT WAS, SO I BROUGHT HER HOME.
OUR FAMILY IS SO MESSED UP! IT'S KINDA EMBARRAS-SING!!
WHY...
...IS THAT?
BE-CAUSE...
...SHE COMES HOME ONLY TO FIND OUT SHE'S BEEN FORGOTTEN.
THAT MUST BE QUITE...
...A SHOCK, EH?

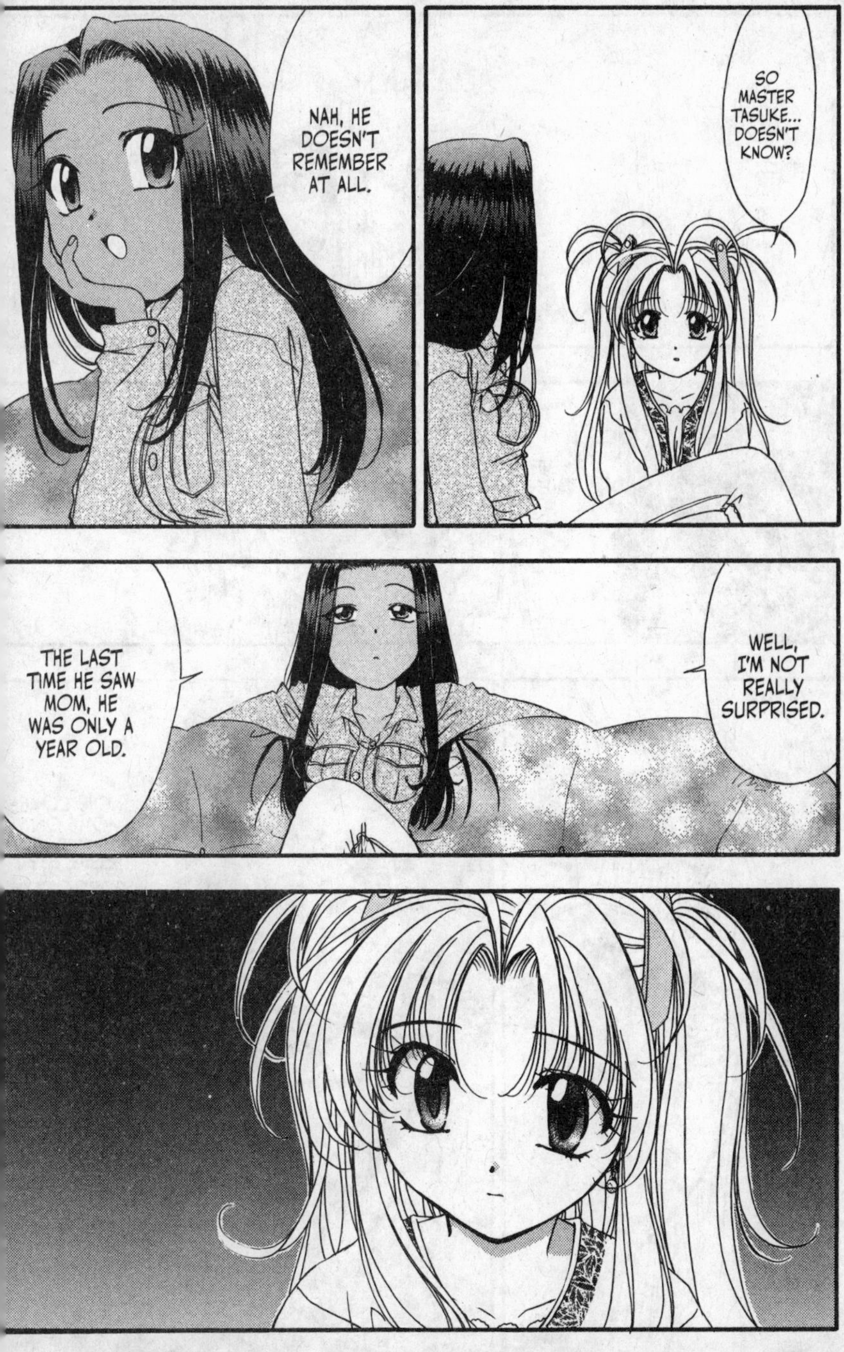
SO MASTER TASUKE... DOESN'T KNOW?
NAH, HE DOESN'T REMEMBER AT ALL.
WELL, I'M NOT REALLY SURPRISED.
THE LAST TIME HE SAW MOM, HE WAS ONLY A YEAR OLD.

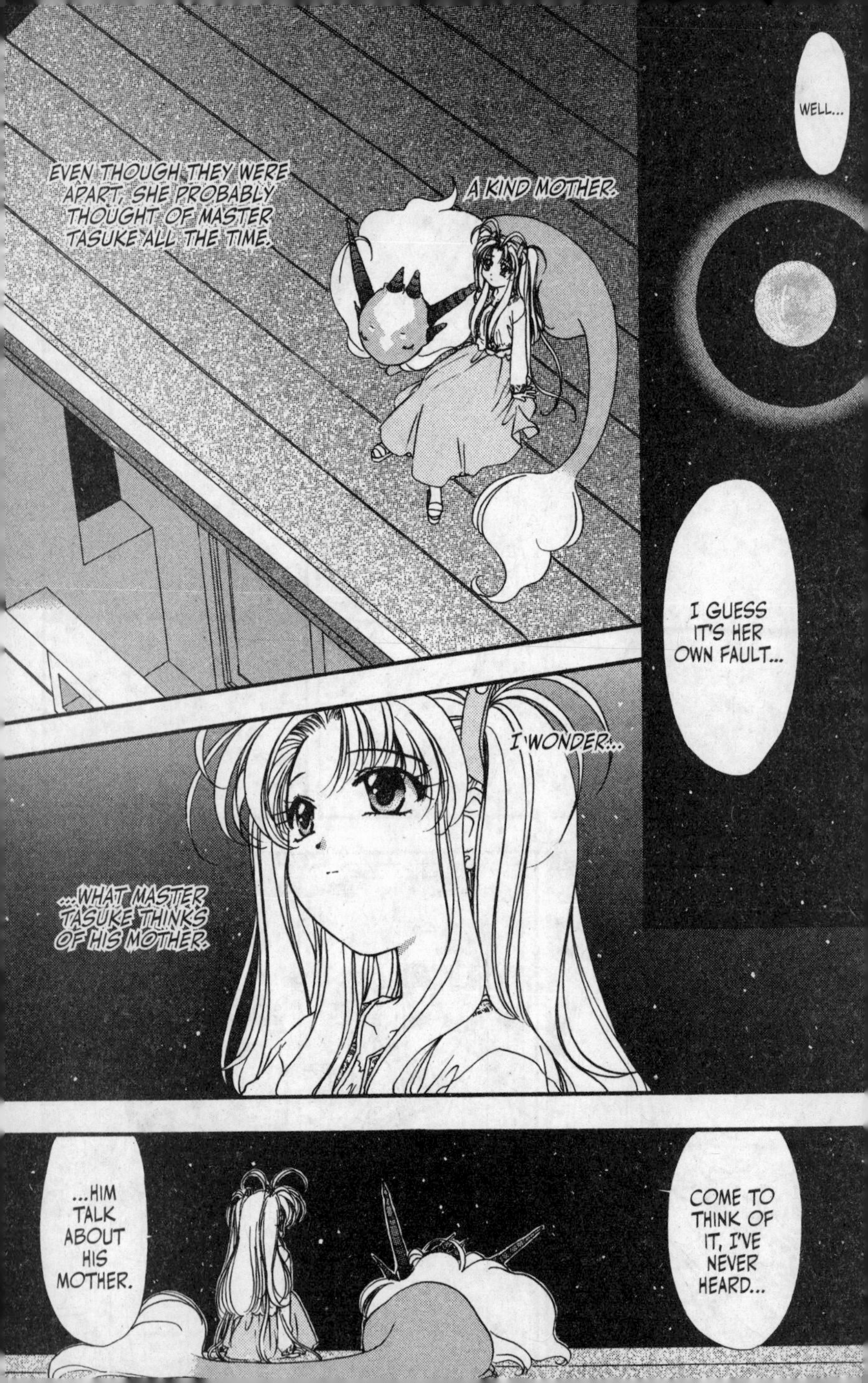
WELL...
I GUESS IT'S HER OWN FAULT...
A KIND MOTHER.
EVEN THOUGH THEY WERE APART, SHE PROBABLY THOUGHT OF MASTER TASUKE ALL THE TIME.
I WONDER...
...WHAT MASTER TASUKE THINKS OF HIS MOTHER.
COME TO THINK OF IT, I'VE NEVER HEARD...
...HIM TALK ABOUT HIS MOTHER.

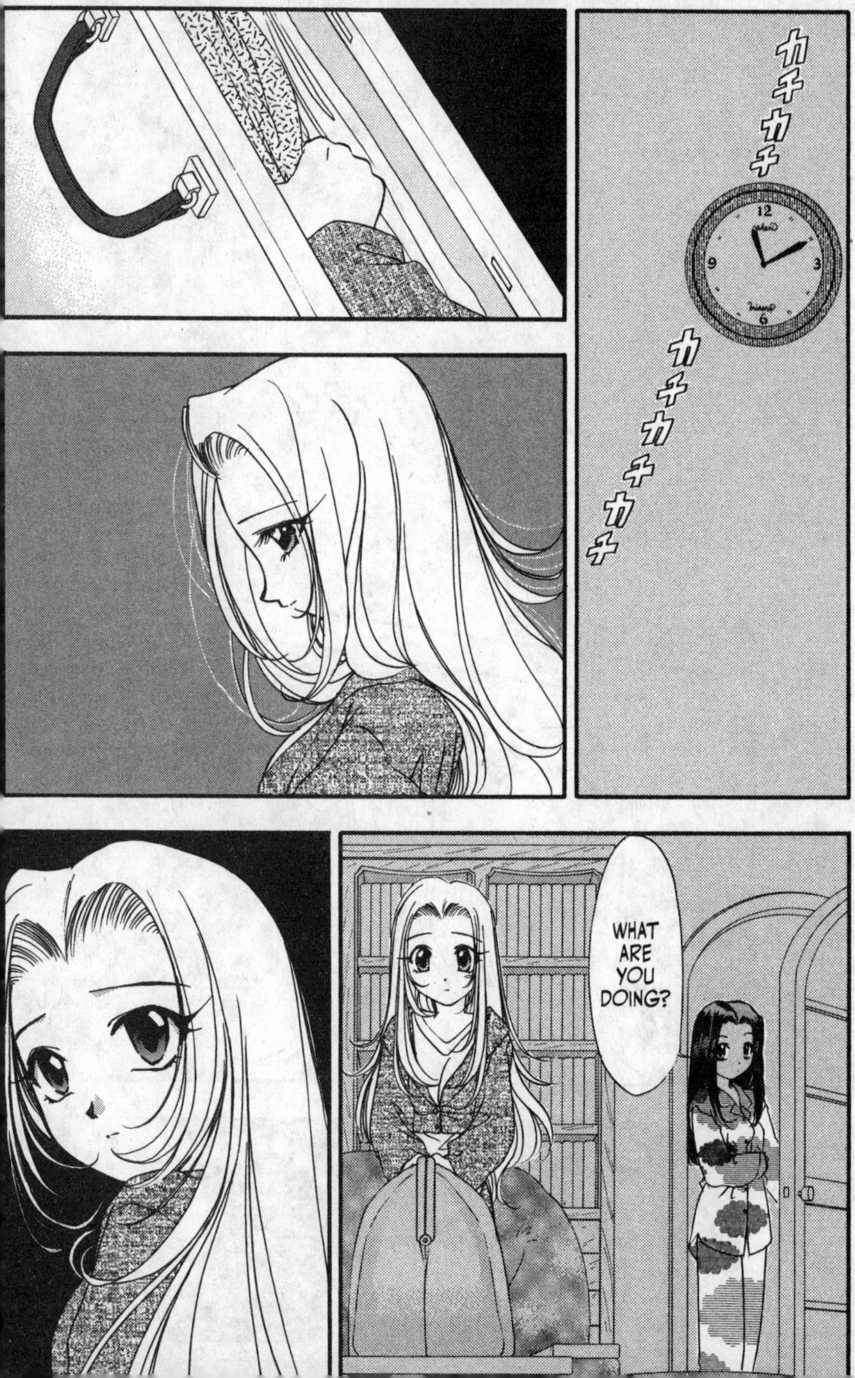
カチカチ
カチカチカチカチ
WHAT ARE YOU DOING?

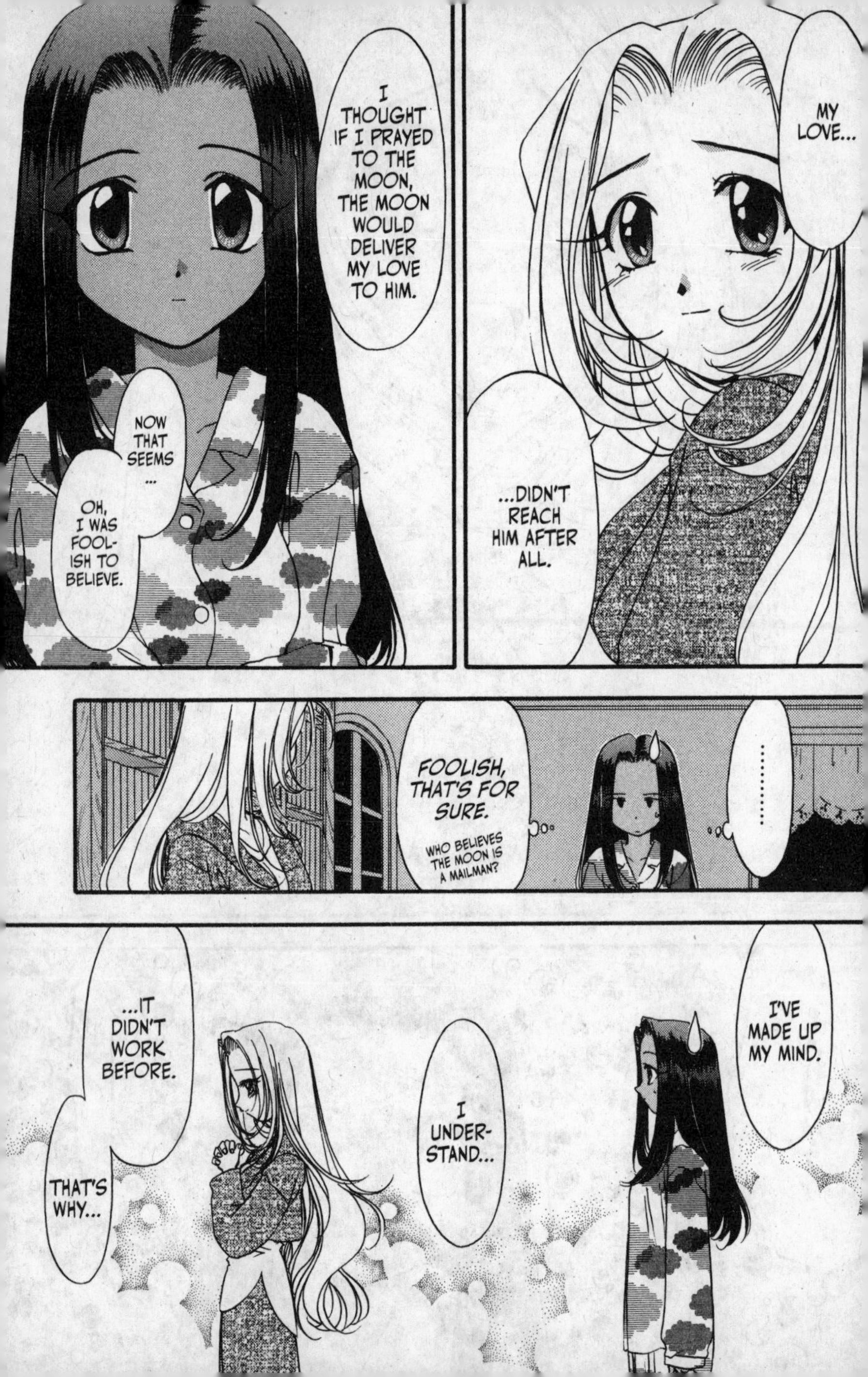
MY LOVE...
...DIDN'T REACH HIM AFTER ALL.
I THOUGHT IF I PRAYED TO THE MOON, THE MOON WOULD DELIVER MY LOVE TO HIM.
NOW THAT SEEMS ...
OH, I WAS FOOL-ISH TO BELIEVE.
......
FOOLISH, THAT'S FOR SURE.
WHO BELIEVES THE MOON IS A MAILMAN?
I'VE MADE UP MY MIND.
I UNDER-STAND...
...IT DIDN'T WORK BEFORE.
THAT'S WHY...

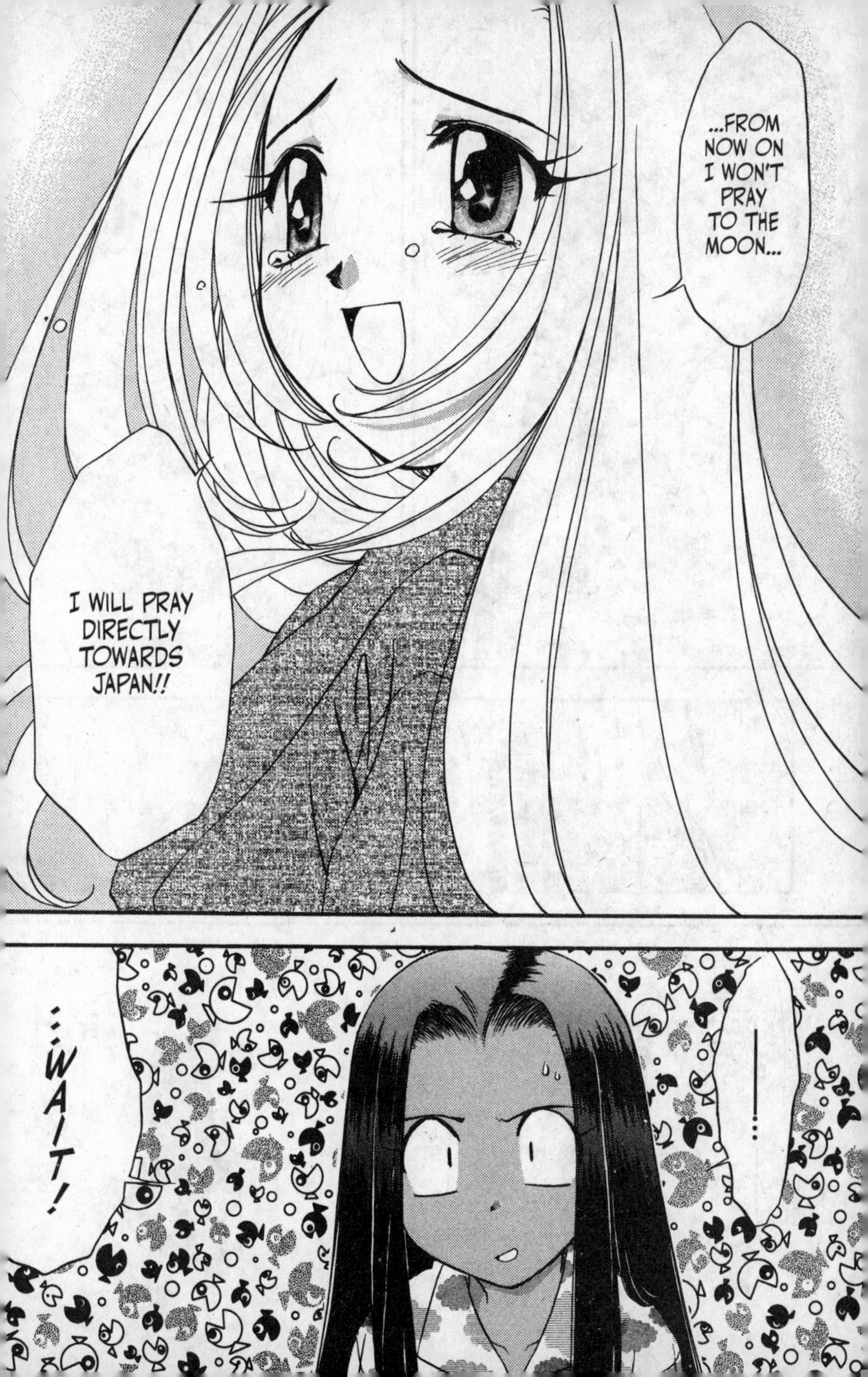
...FROM NOW ON I WON'T PRAY TO THE MOON...
I WILL PRAY DIRECTLY TOWARDS JAPAN!!
...!
...WAIT!

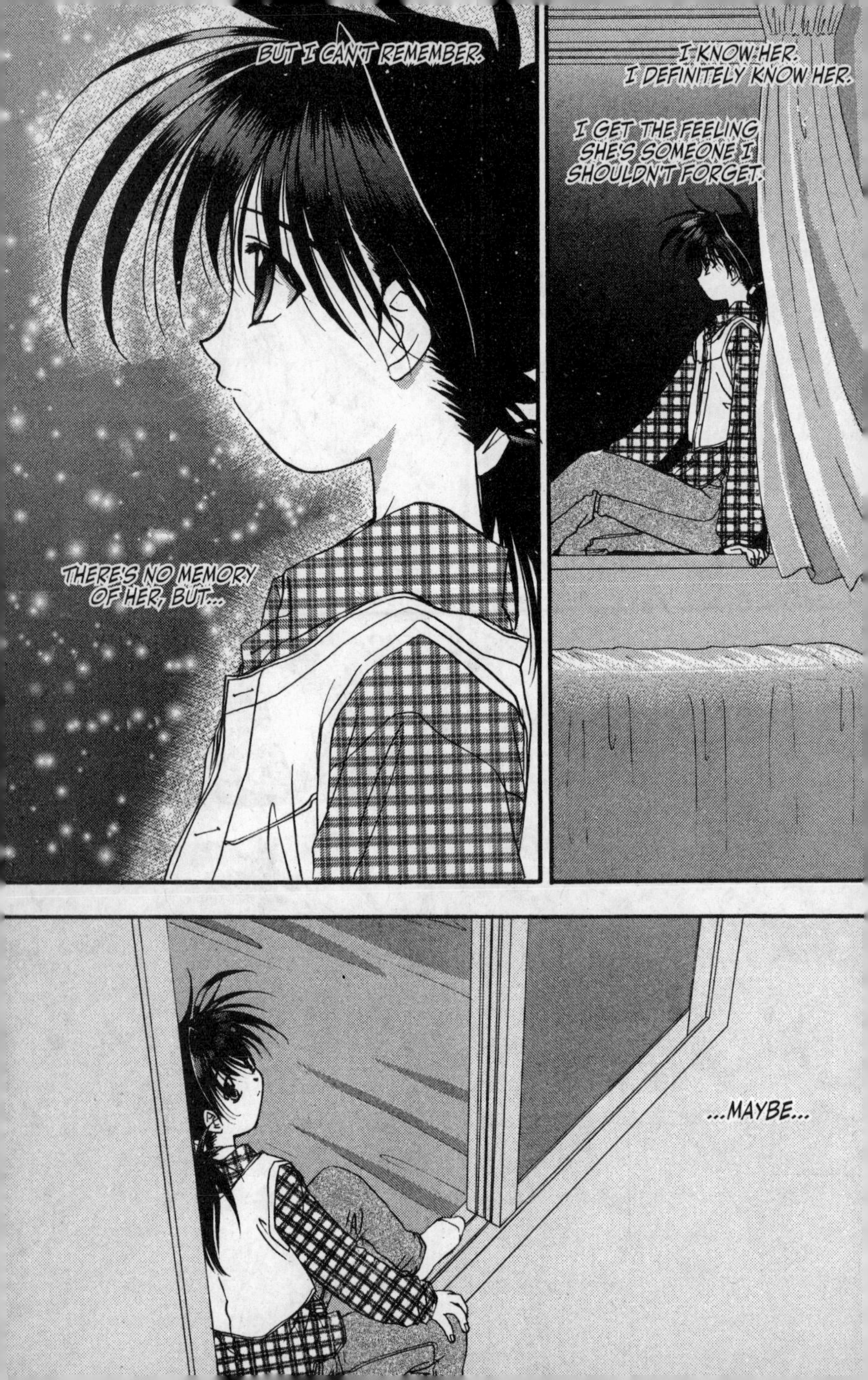
I KNOW HER. I DEFINITELY KNOW HER.
I GET THE FEELING SHE'S SOMEONE I SHOULDN'T FORGET.
BUT I CAN'T REMEMBER.
THERE'S NO MEMORY OF HER, BUT...
...MAYBE...

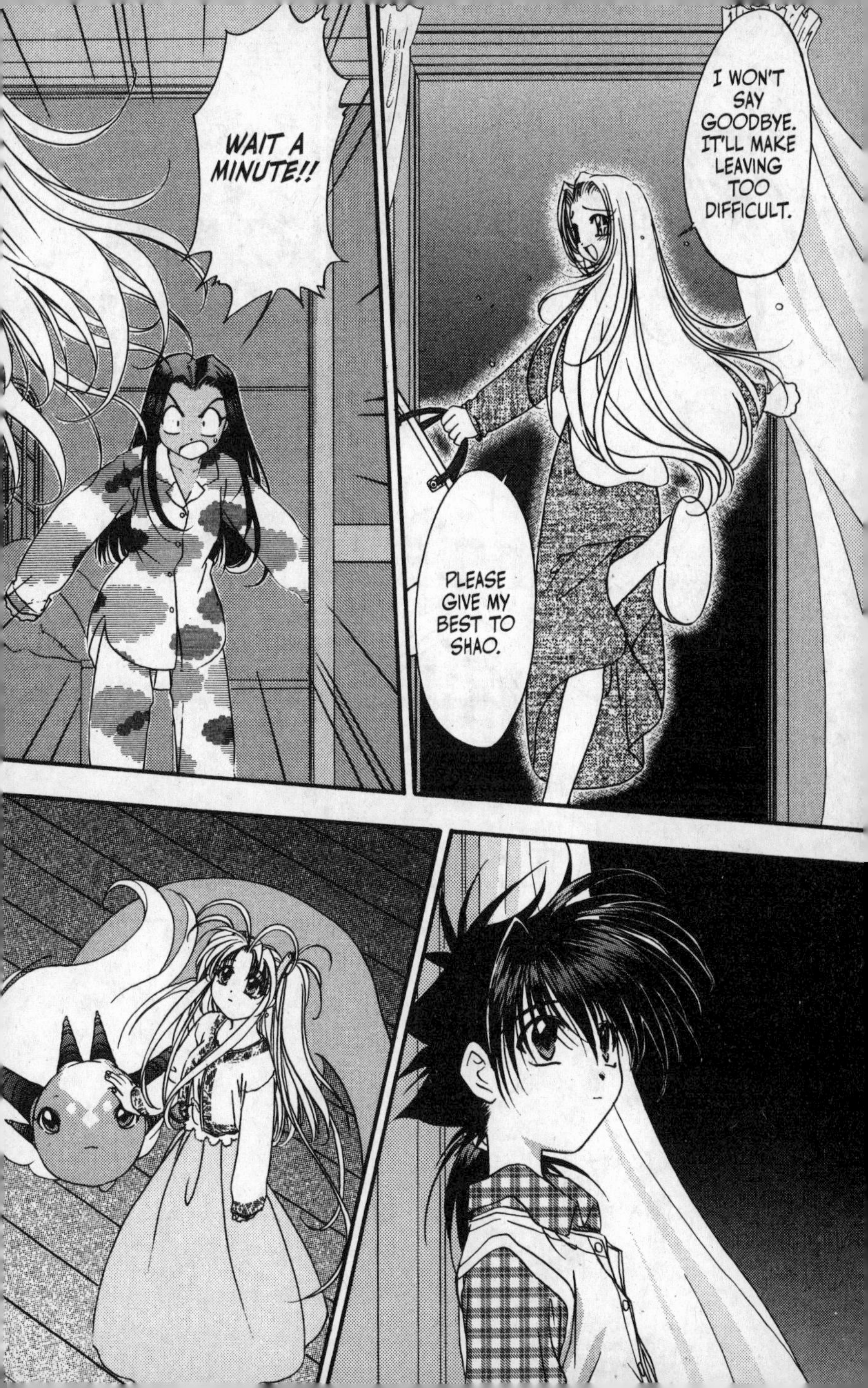
I WON'T SAY GOODBYE. IT'LL MAKE LEAVING TOO DIFFICULT.
PLEASE GIVE MY BEST TO SHAO.
WAIT A MINUTE!!

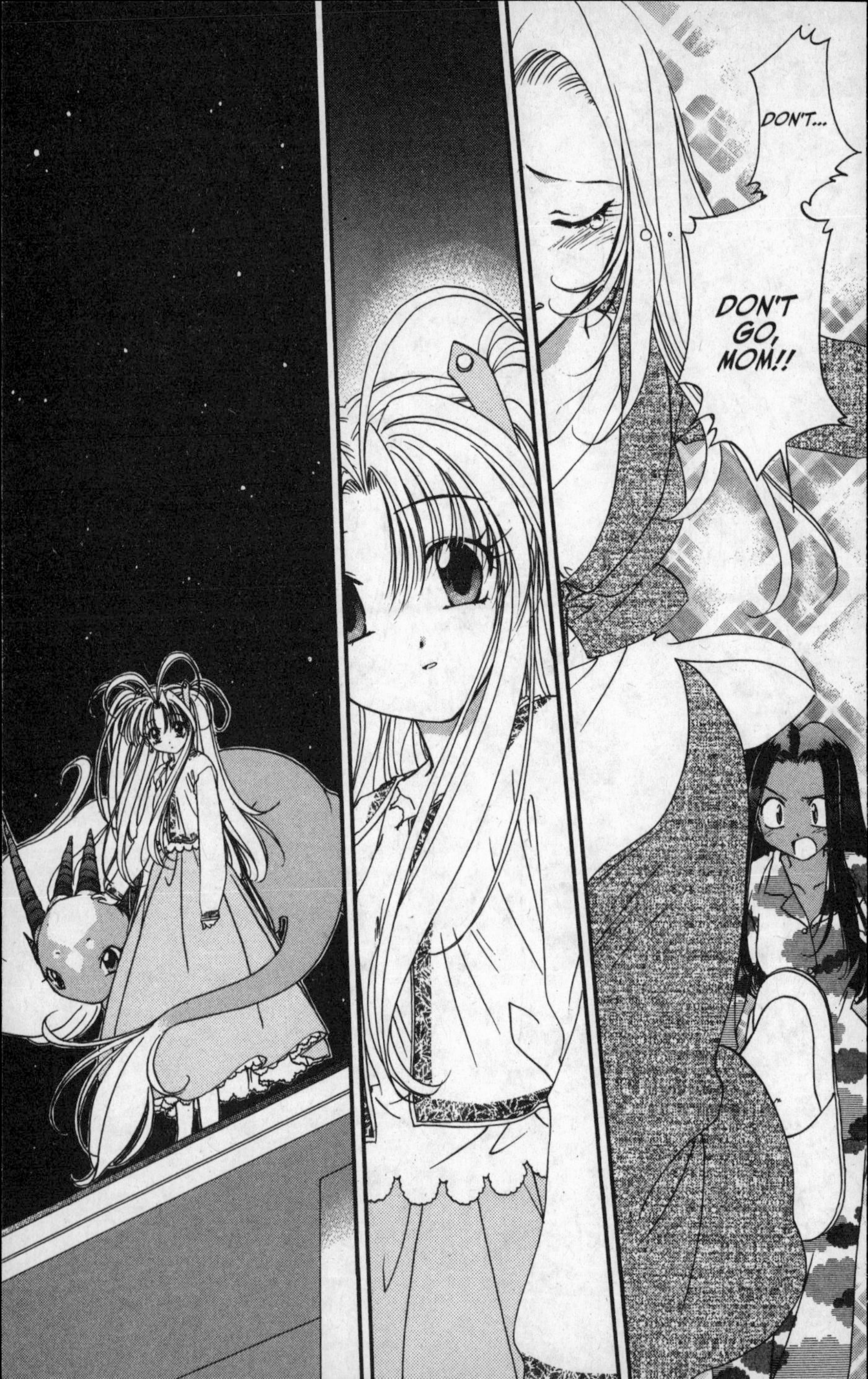
DON'T...
DON'T GO, MOM!!

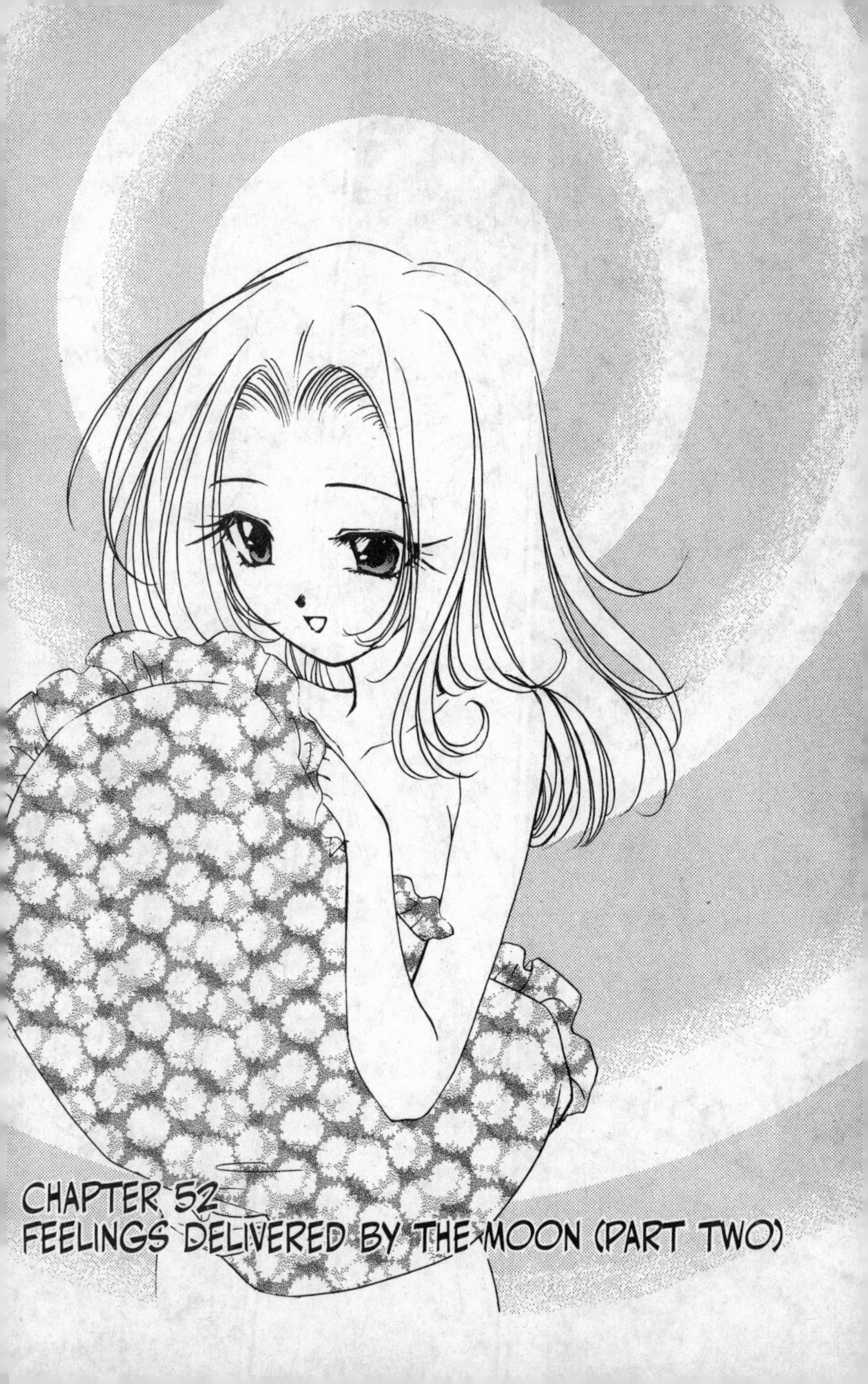

CHAPTER 52
FEELINGS DELIVERED BY THE MOON (PART TWO)

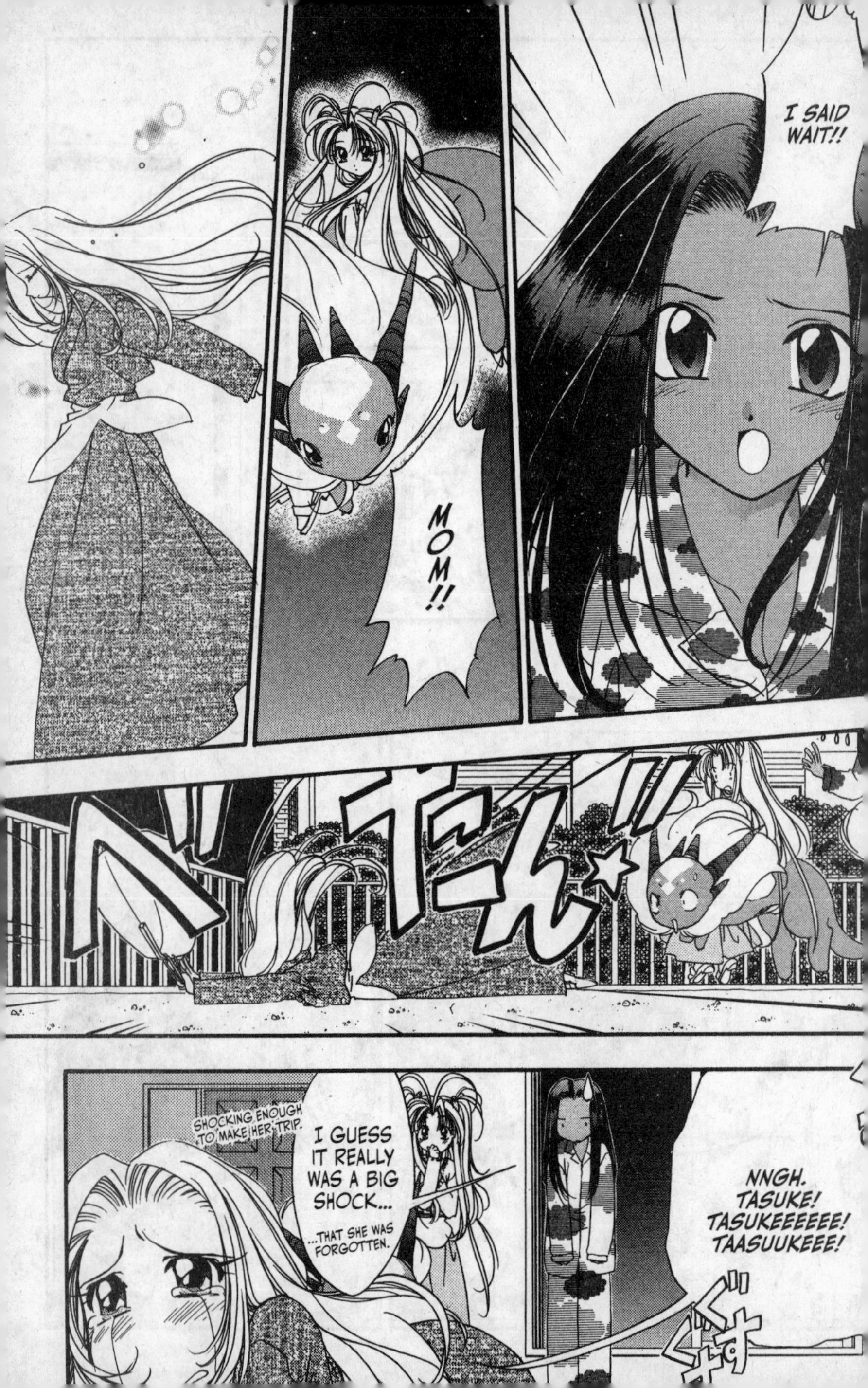
I SAID WAIT!!
MOM!!
べたん!!
NNGH. TASUKE! TASUKEEEEEE! TAASUUKEEE!
ぐす
ぐす
I GUESS IT REALLY WAS A BIG SHOCK...
...THAT SHE WAS FORGOTTEN.
SHOCKING ENOUGH TO MAKE HER TRIP.

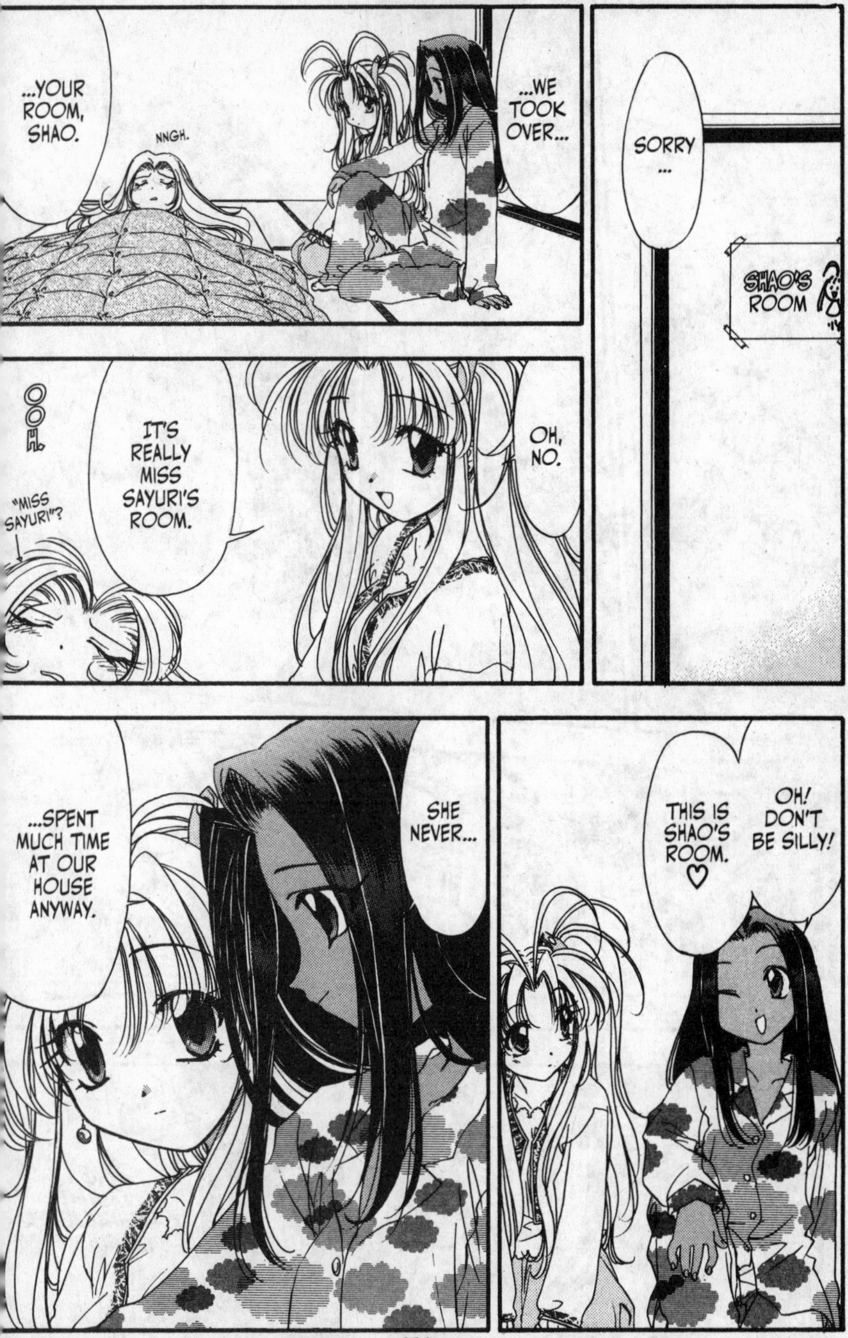
SORRY...
SHAO'S ROOM
...WE TOOK OVER...
...YOUR ROOM, SHAO.
NNGH.
OH, NO.
IT'S REALLY MISS SAYURI'S ROOM.
"MISS SAYURI"?
OOH
OH! DON'T BE SILLY!
THIS IS SHAO'S ROOM. ♡
SHE NEVER...
...SPENT MUCH TIME AT OUR HOUSE ANYWAY.

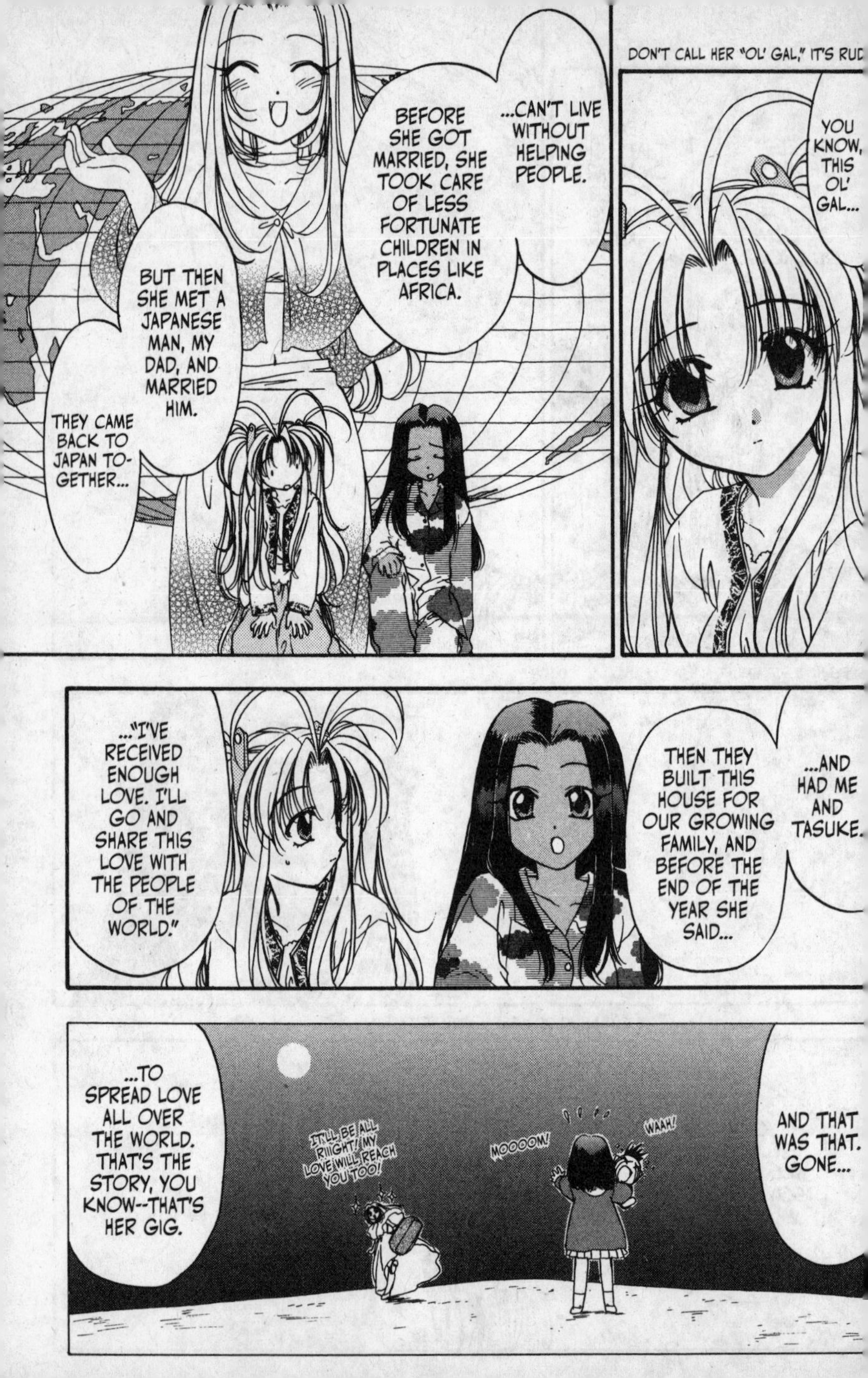

DON'T CALL HER "OL' GAL," IT'S RUD
YOU KNOW, THIS OL' GAL...
...CAN'T LIVE WITHOUT HELPING PEOPLE.
BEFORE SHE GOT MARRIED, SHE TOOK CARE OF LESS FORTUNATE CHILDREN IN PLACES LIKE AFRICA.
BUT THEN SHE MET A JAPANESE MAN, MY DAD, AND MARRIED HIM.
THEY CAME BACK TO JAPAN TO-GETHER...
...AND HAD ME AND TASUKE.
THEN THEY BUILT THIS HOUSE FOR OUR GROWING FAMILY, AND BEFORE THE END OF THE YEAR SHE SAID...
..."I'VE RECEIVED ENOUGH LOVE. I'LL GO AND SHARE THIS LOVE WITH THE PEOPLE OF THE WORLD."
AND THAT WAS THAT. GONE...
WAAH!
MOOOOM!
IT'LL BE ALL RIIIGHT! MY LOVE WILL REACH YOU TOO!
...TO SPREAD LOVE ALL OVER THE WORLD. THAT'S THE STORY, YOU KNOW--THAT'S HER GIG.

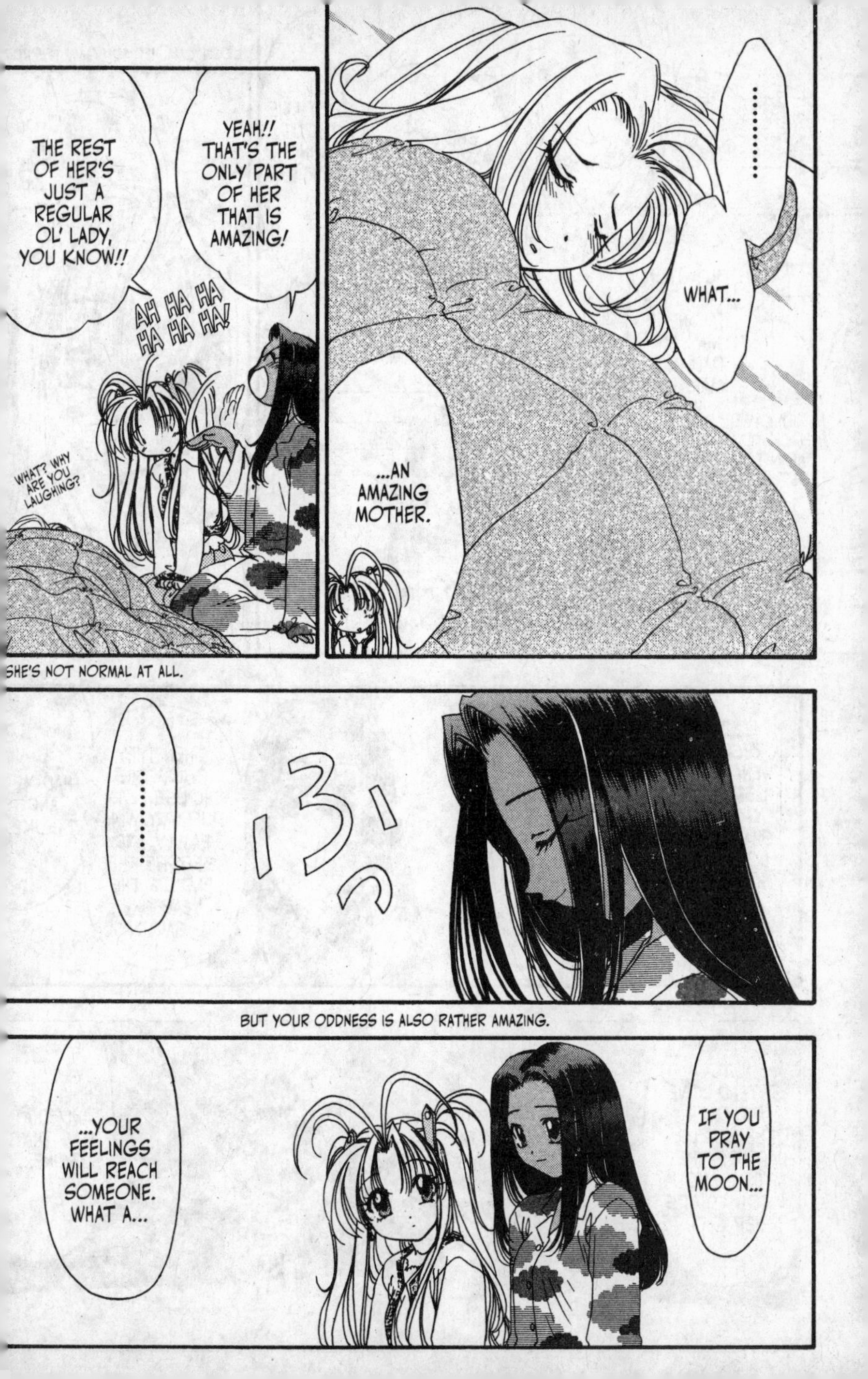
......
WHAT...
...AN AMAZING MOTHER.
YEAH!! THAT'S THE ONLY PART OF HER THAT IS AMAZING!
THE REST OF HER'S JUST A REGULAR OL' LADY, YOU KNOW!!
AH HA HA HA HA HA!
WHAT? WHY ARE YOU LAUGHING?
SHE'S NOT NORMAL AT ALL.
ふっ
......
BUT YOUR ODDNESS IS ALSO RATHER AMAZING.
IF YOU PRAY TO THE MOON...
...YOUR FEELINGS WILL REACH SOMEONE. WHAT A...

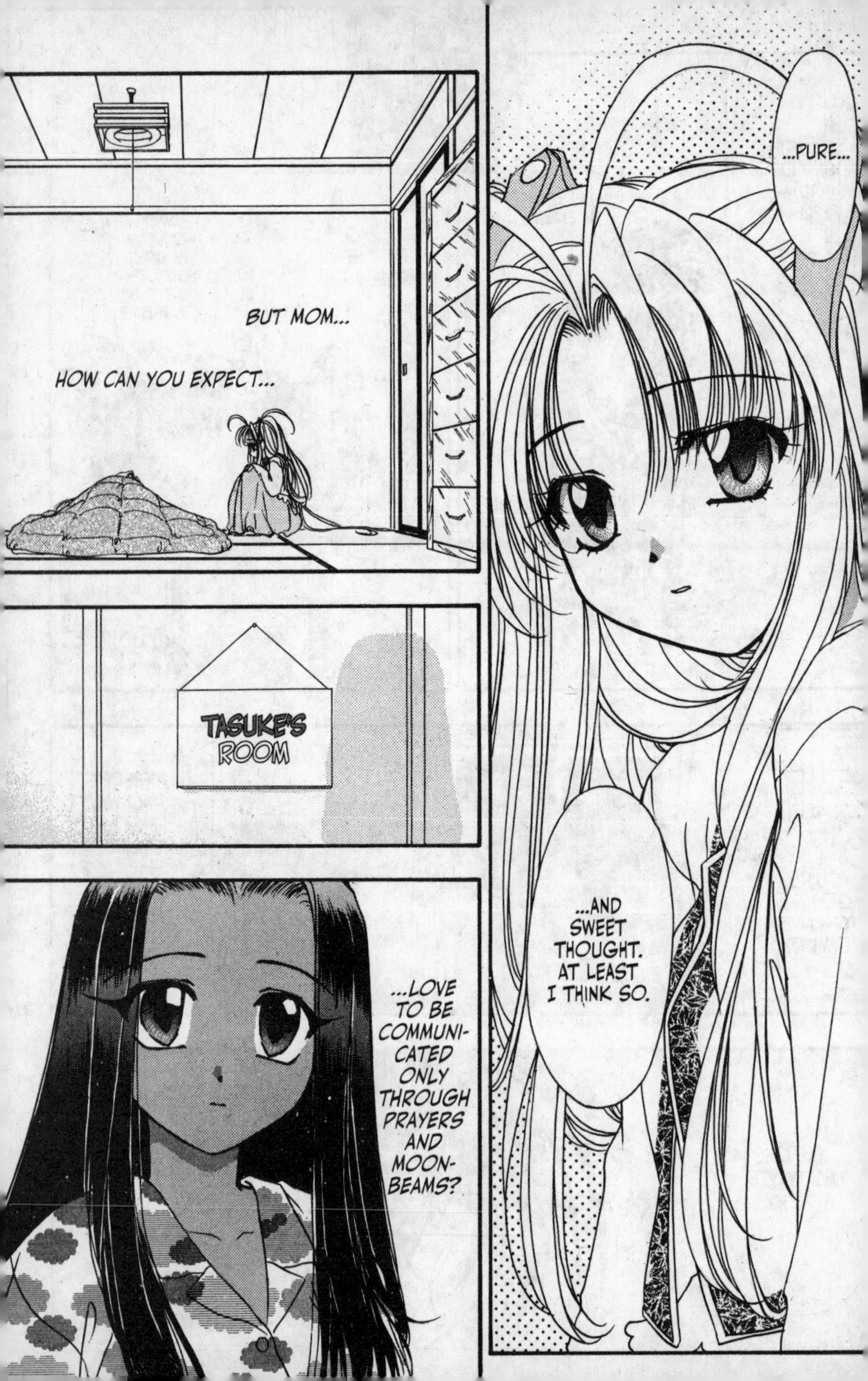
...PURE...
...AND SWEET THOUGHT. AT LEAST I THINK SO.
BUT MOM...
HOW CAN YOU EXPECT...
TASUKE'S ROOM
...LOVE TO BE COMMUNICATED ONLY THROUGH PRAYERS AND MOON-BEAMS?

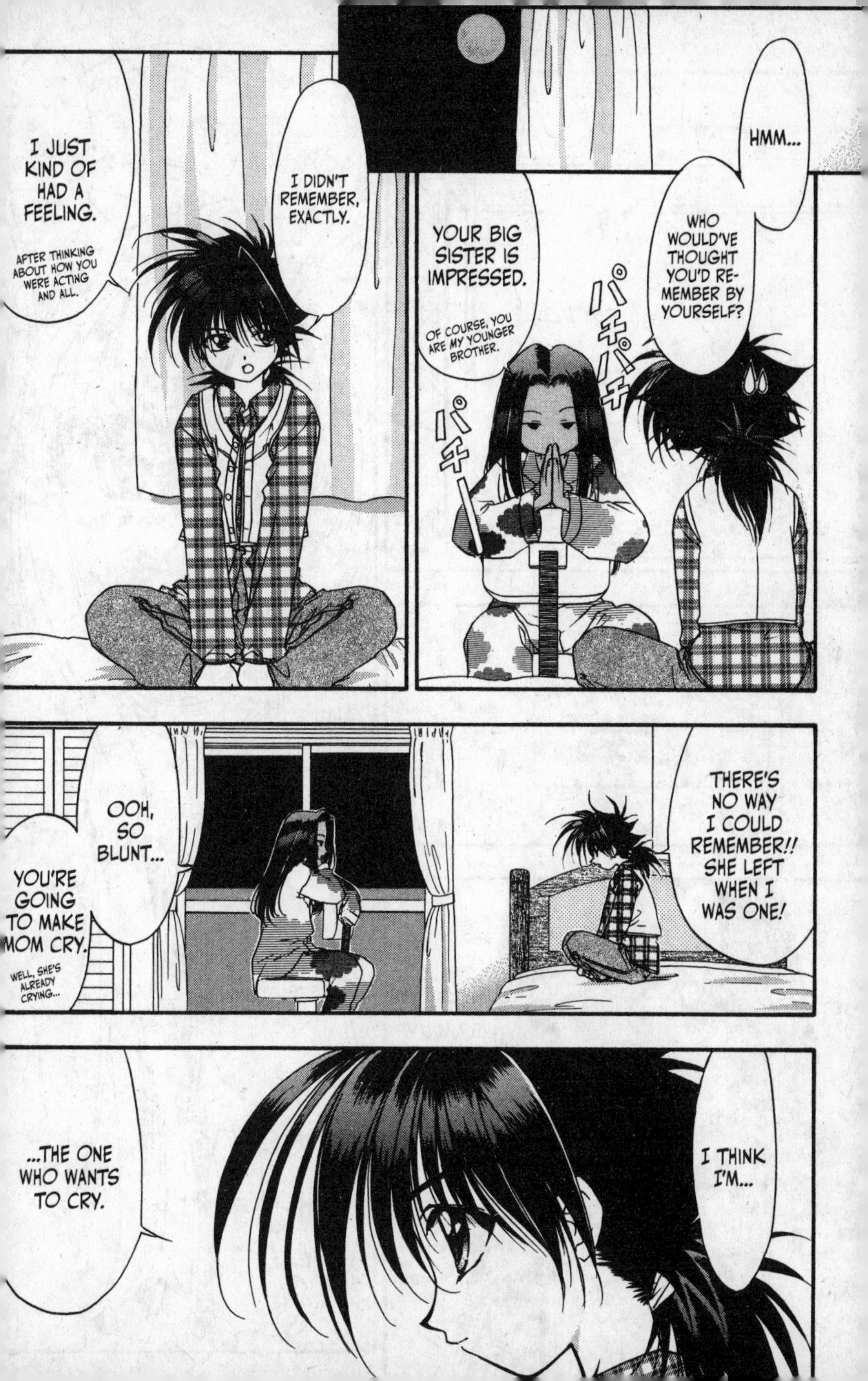
HMM...
WHO WOULD'VE THOUGHT YOU'D RE-MEMBER BY YOURSELF?
パチパチ
パチ
YOUR BIG SISTER IS IMPRESSED.
OF COURSE, YOU ARE MY YOUNGER BROTHER.
I DIDN'T REMEMBER, EXACTLY.
I JUST KIND OF HAD A FEELING.
AFTER THINKING ABOUT HOW YOU WERE ACTING AND ALL.
THERE'S NO WAY I COULD REMEMBER!! SHE LEFT WHEN I WAS ONE!
OOH, SO BLUNT...
YOU'RE GOING TO MAKE MOM CRY.
WELL, SHE'S ALREADY CRYING...
I THINK I'M...
...THE ONE WHO WANTS TO CRY.

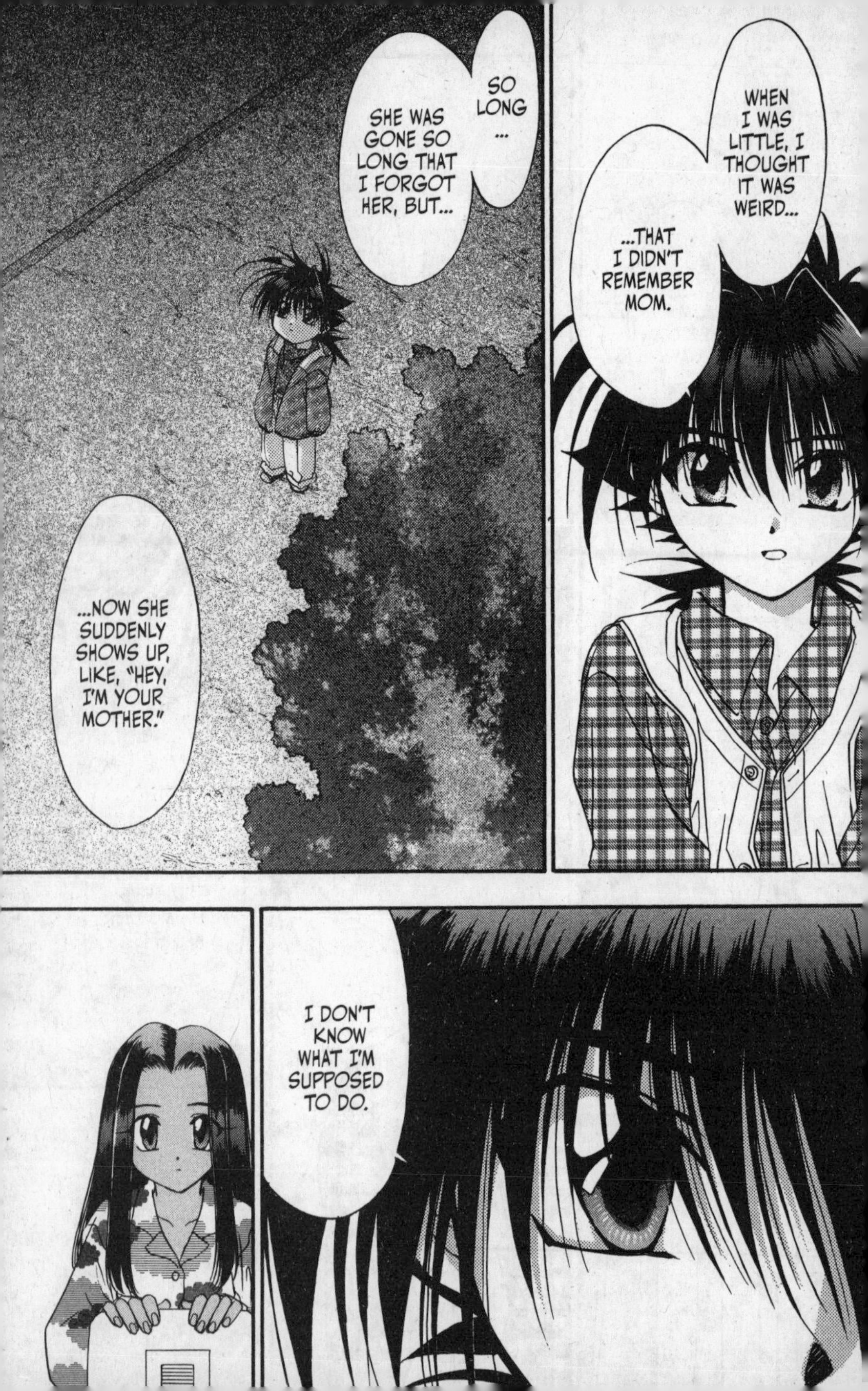
WHEN I WAS LITTLE, I THOUGHT IT WAS WEIRD...
...THAT I DIDN'T REMEMBER MOM.
SO LONG ...
SHE WAS GONE SO LONG THAT I FORGOT HER, BUT...
...NOW SHE SUDDENLY SHOWS UP, LIKE, "HEY, I'M YOUR MOTHER."
I DON'T KNOW WHAT I'M SUPPOSED TO DO.

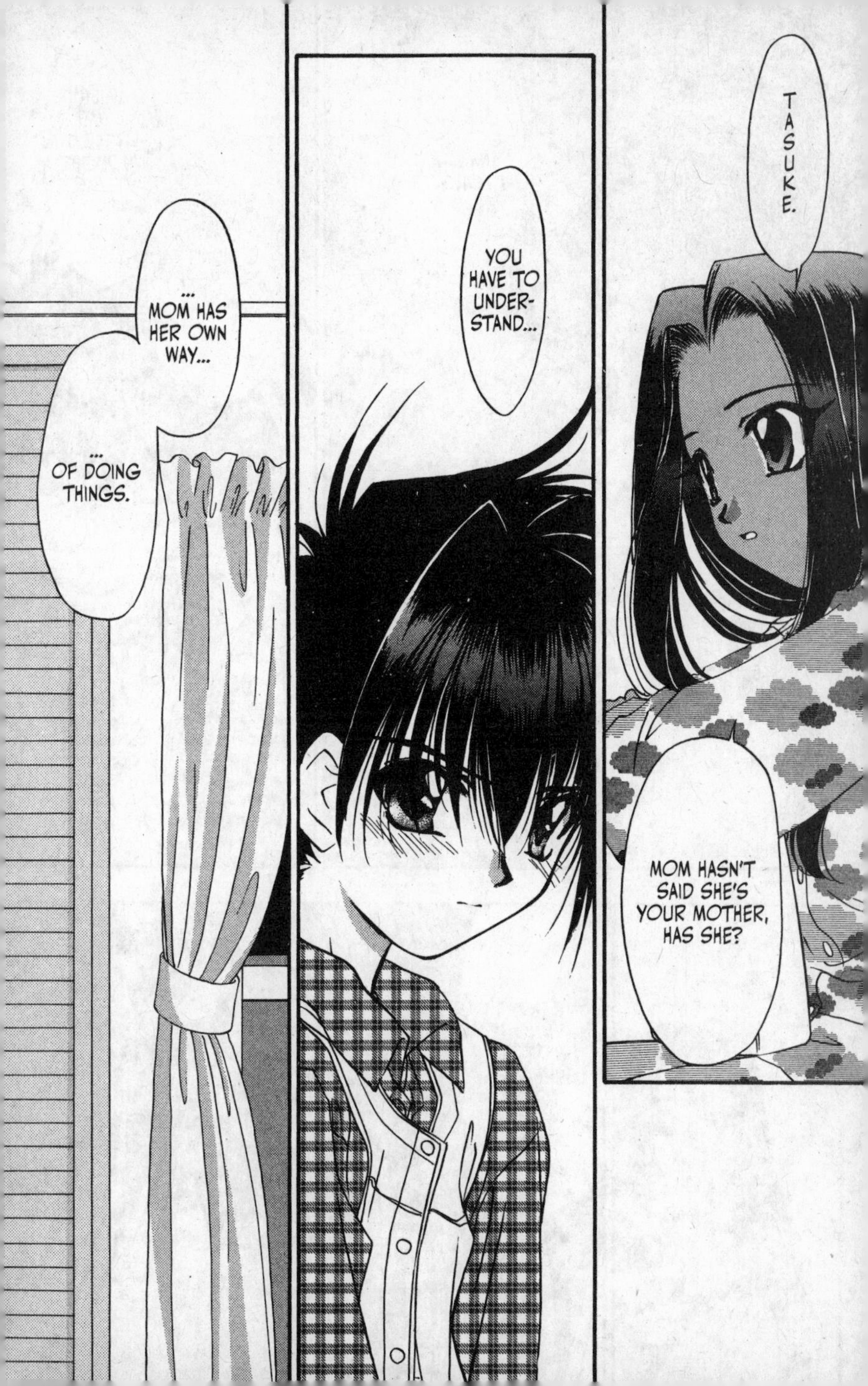
TASUKE.
MOM HASN'T SAID SHE'S YOUR MOTHER, HAS SHE?
YOU HAVE TO UNDER-STAND...
... MOM HAS HER OWN WAY...
... OF DOING THINGS.

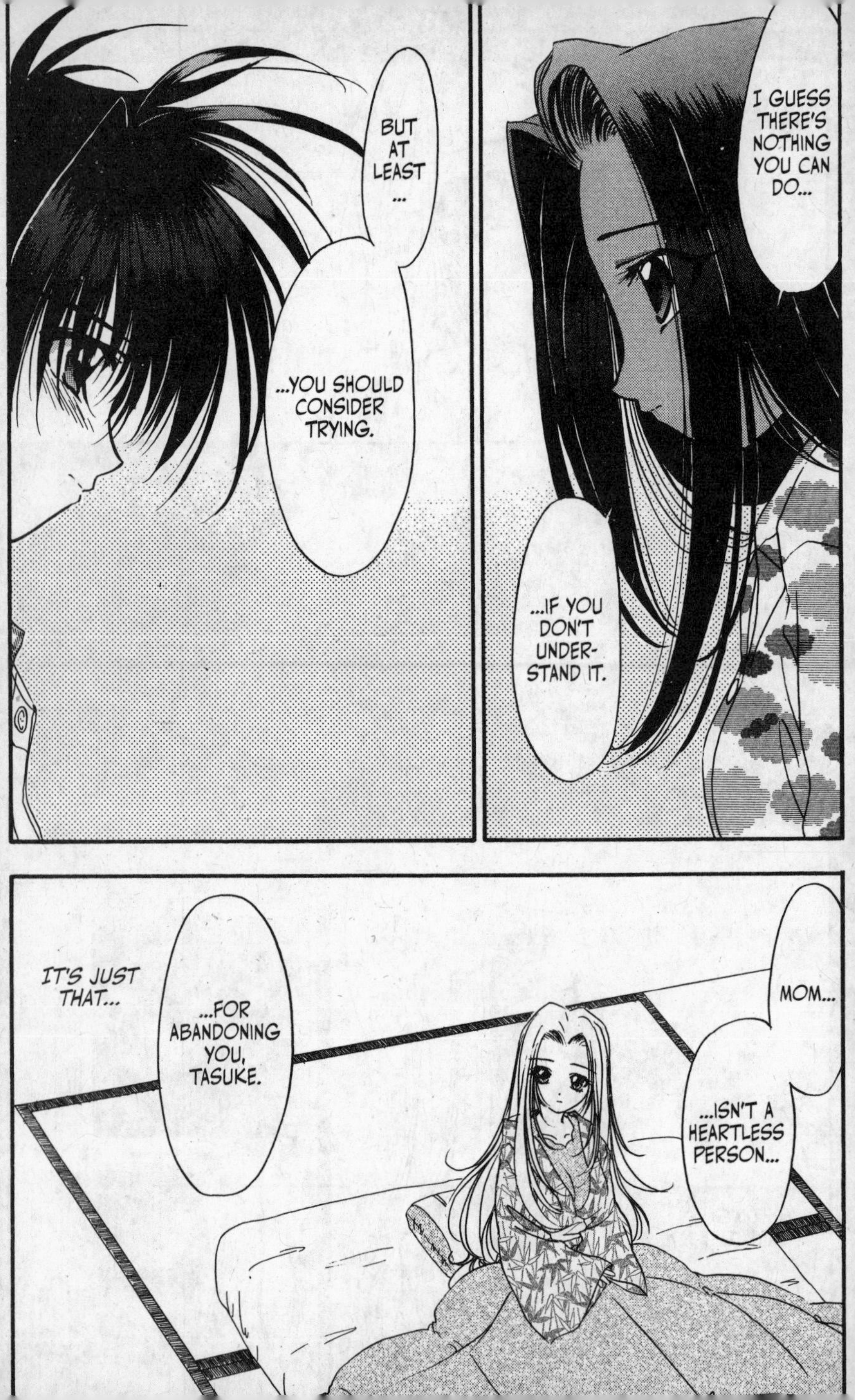
I GUESS THERE'S NOTHING YOU CAN DO...
...IF YOU DON'T UNDER-STAND IT.
BUT AT LEAST ...
...YOU SHOULD CONSIDER TRYING.
MOM...
...ISN'T A HEARTLESS PERSON...
...FOR ABANDONING YOU, TASUKE.
IT'S JUST THAT...

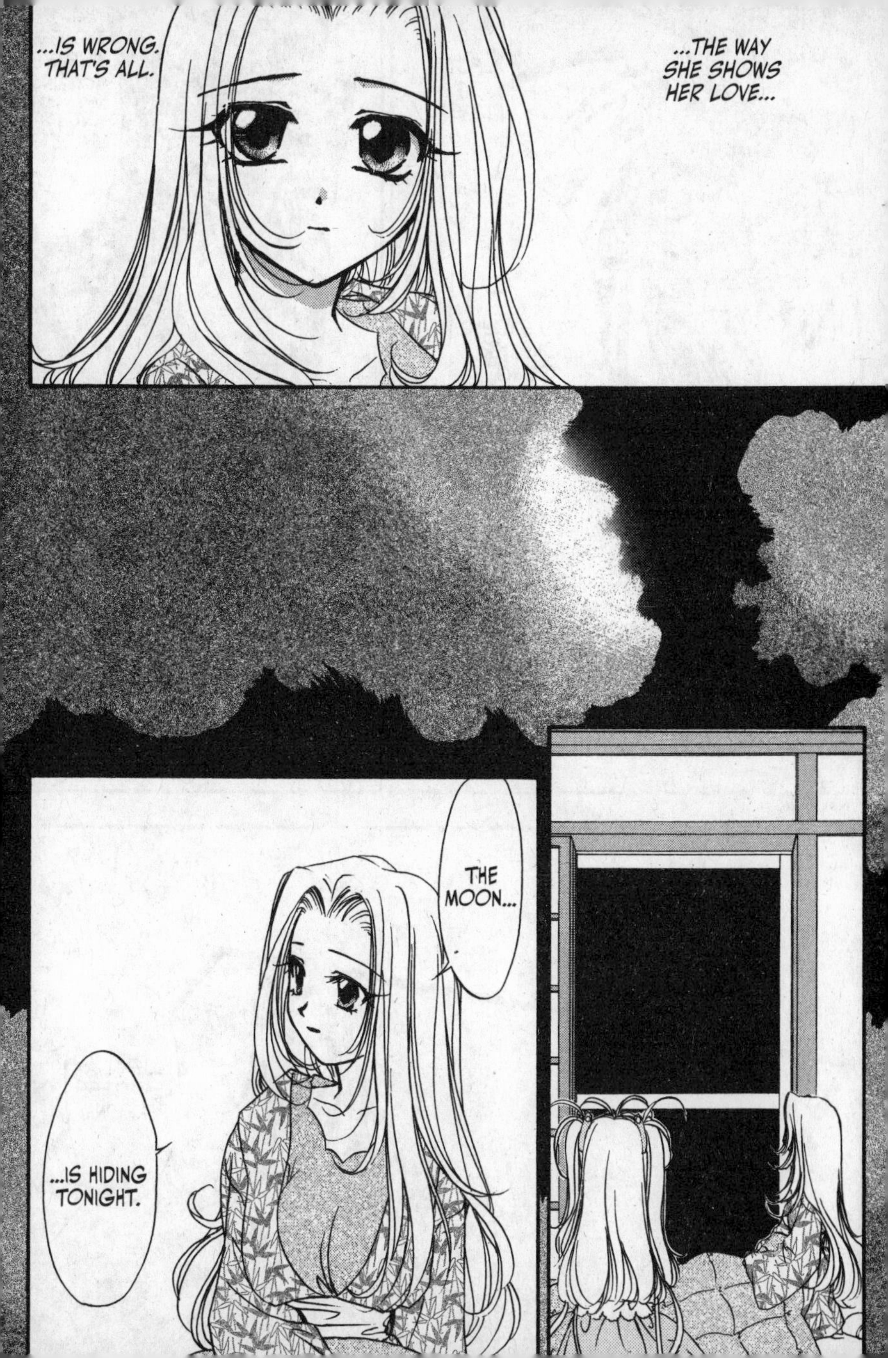
...THE WAY SHE SHOWS HER LOVE...
...IS WRONG. THAT'S ALL.
THE MOON...
...IS HIDING TONIGHT.

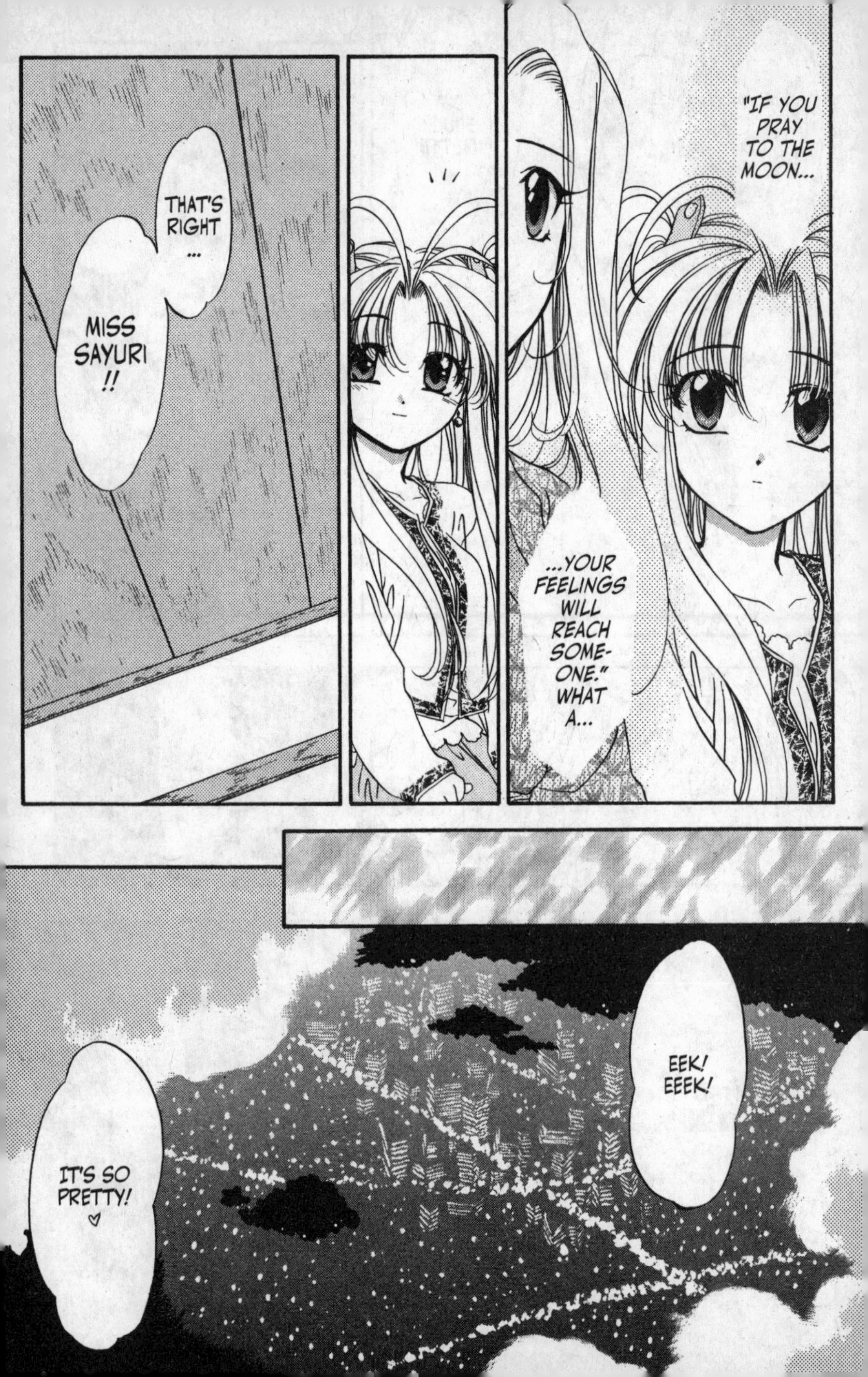
"IF YOU PRAY TO THE MOON...
...YOUR FEELINGS WILL REACH SOME-ONE." WHAT A...
THAT'S RIGHT ...
MISS SAYURI !!
EEK! EEEK!
IT'S SO PRETTY! ♥

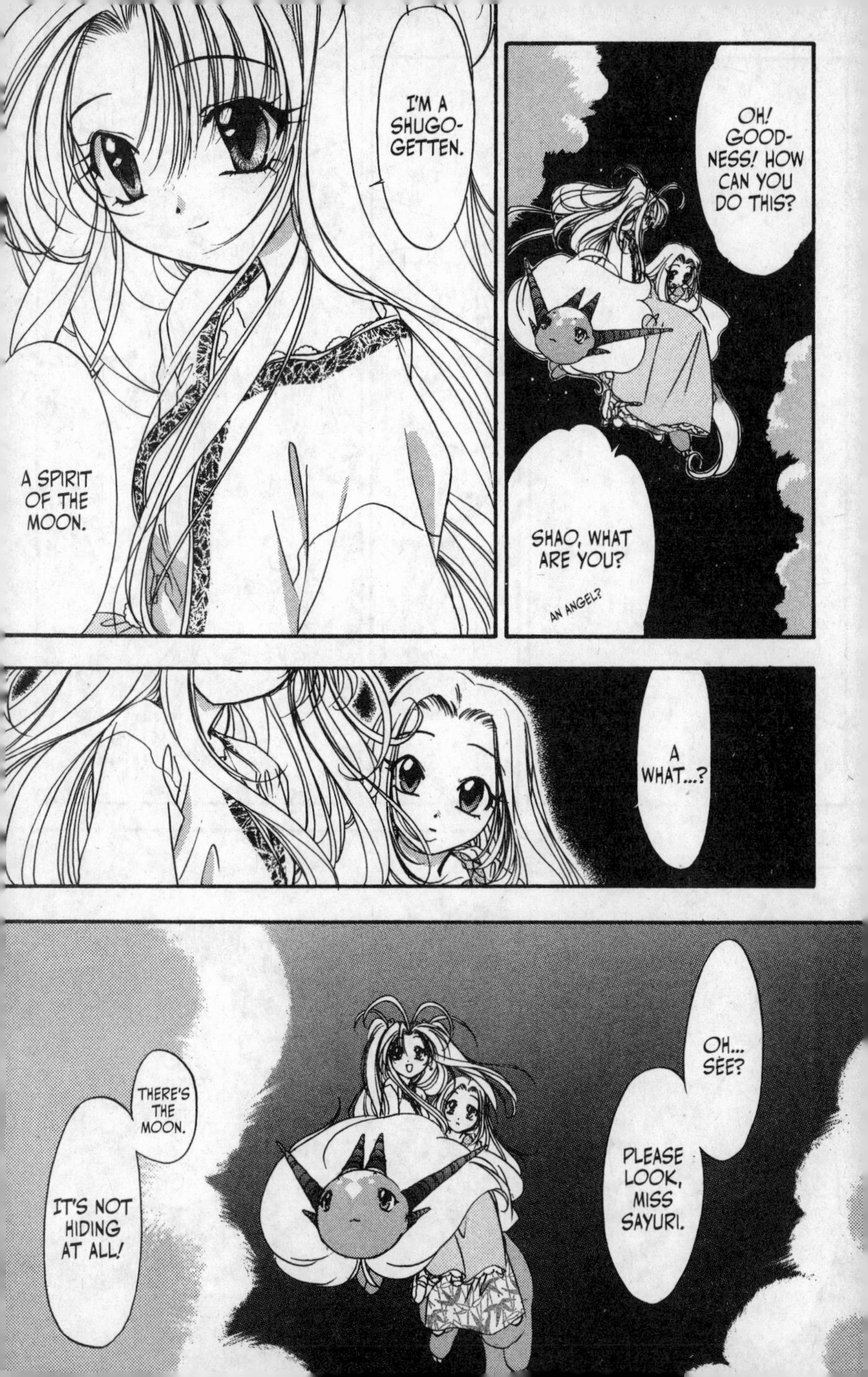
OH! GOODNESS! HOW CAN YOU DO THIS?
SHAO, WHAT ARE YOU?
AN ANGEL?
I'M A SHUGO-GETTEN.
A SPIRIT OF THE MOON.
A WHAT...?
OH... SEE?
PLEASE LOOK, MISS SAYURI.
THERE'S THE MOON.
IT'S NOT HIDING AT ALL!

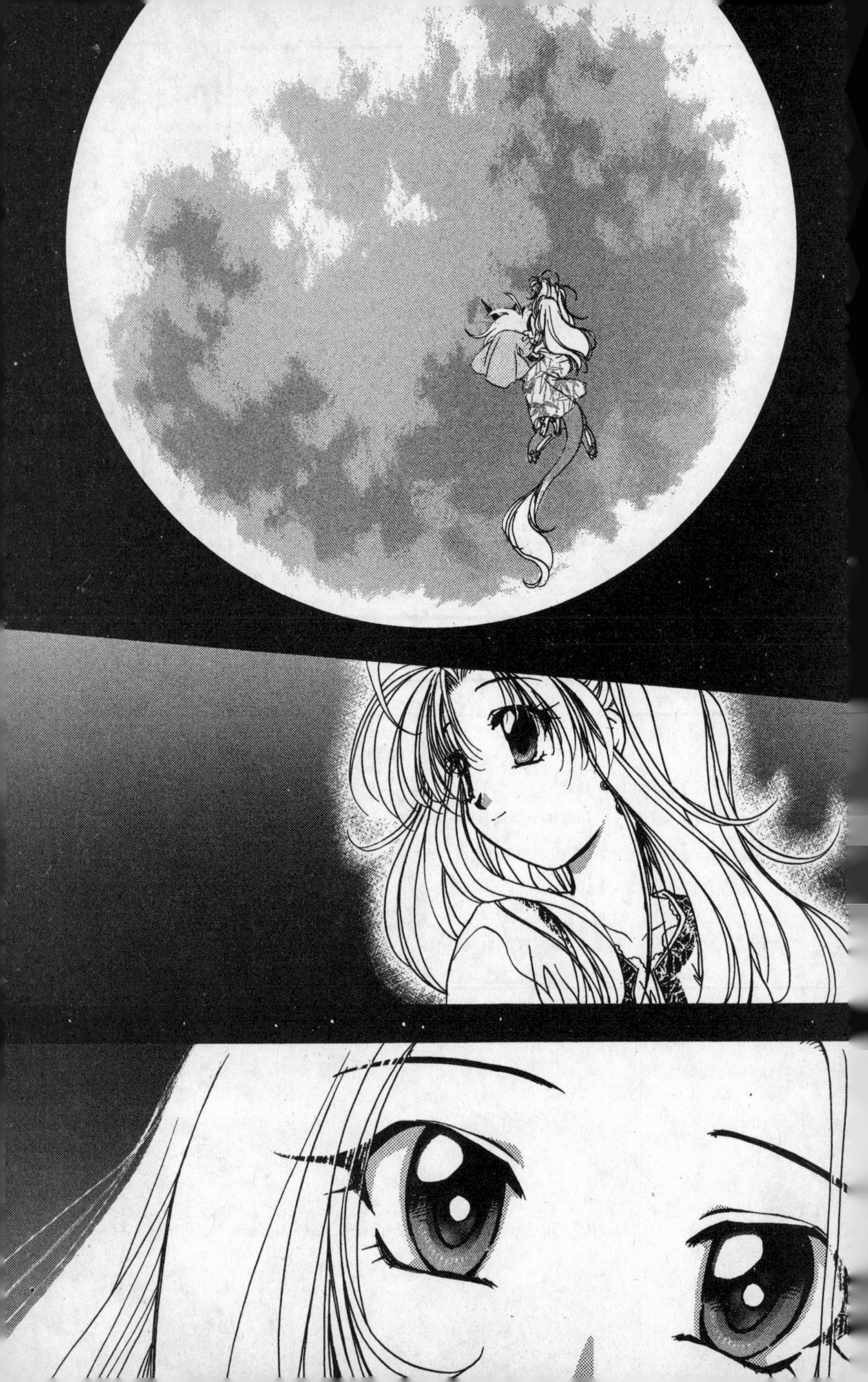

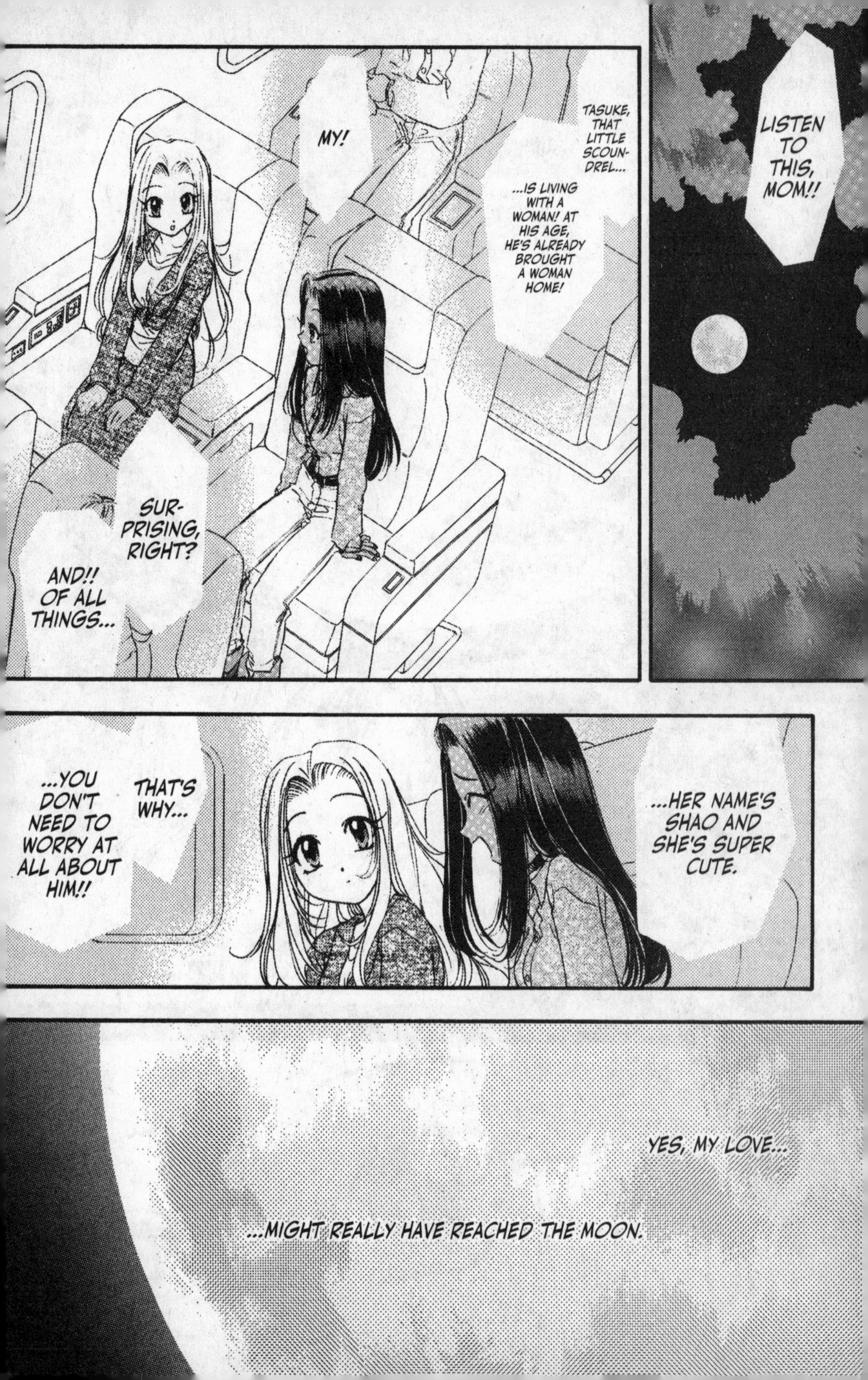
LISTEN TO THIS, MOM!!
TASUKE, THAT LITTLE SCOUNDREL...
...IS LIVING WITH A WOMAN! AT HIS AGE, HE'S ALREADY BROUGHT A WOMAN HOME!
MY!
SURPRISING, RIGHT?
AND!! OF ALL THINGS...
...HER NAME'S SHAO AND SHE'S SUPER CUTE.
THAT'S WHY...
...YOU DON'T NEED TO WORRY AT ALL ABOUT HIM!!
YES, MY LOVE...
...MIGHT REALLY HAVE REACHED THE MOON.

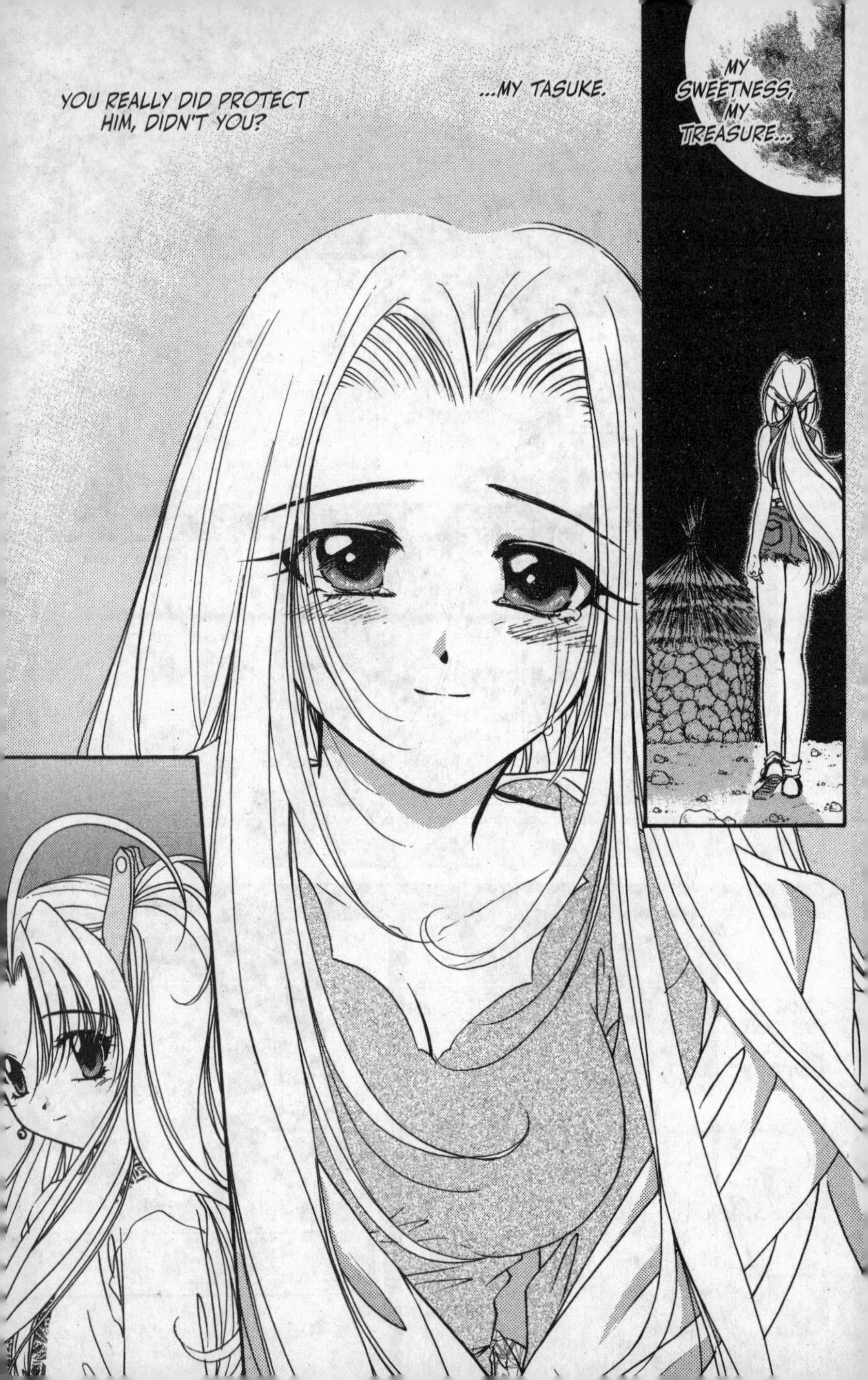
MY SWEETNESS, MY TREASURE...
...MY TASUKE.
YOU REALLY DID PROTECT HIM, DIDN'T YOU?

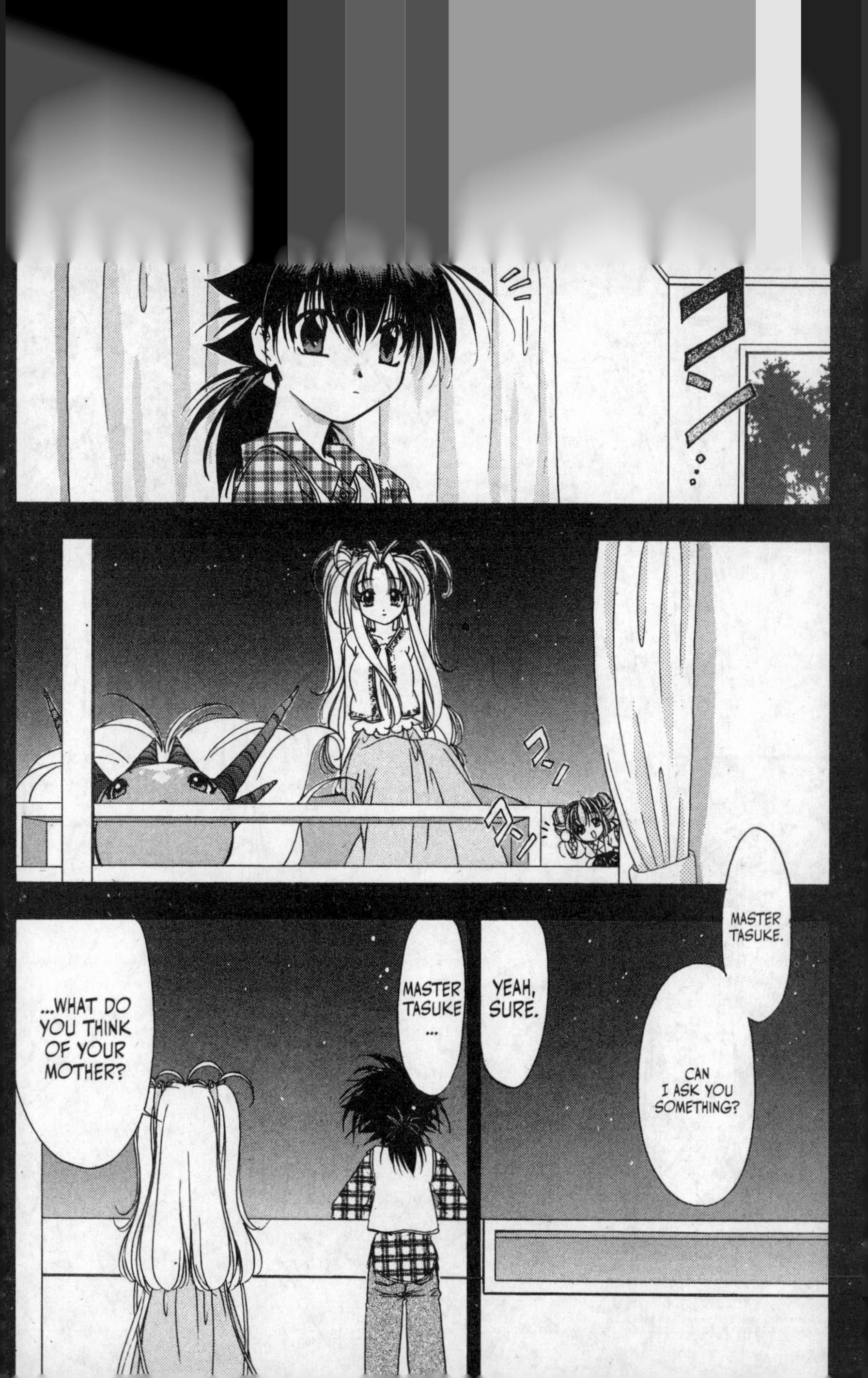
MASTER TASUKE.
CAN I ASK YOU SOMETHING?
YEAH, SURE.
MASTER TASUKE ...
...WHAT DO YOU THINK OF YOUR MOTHER?

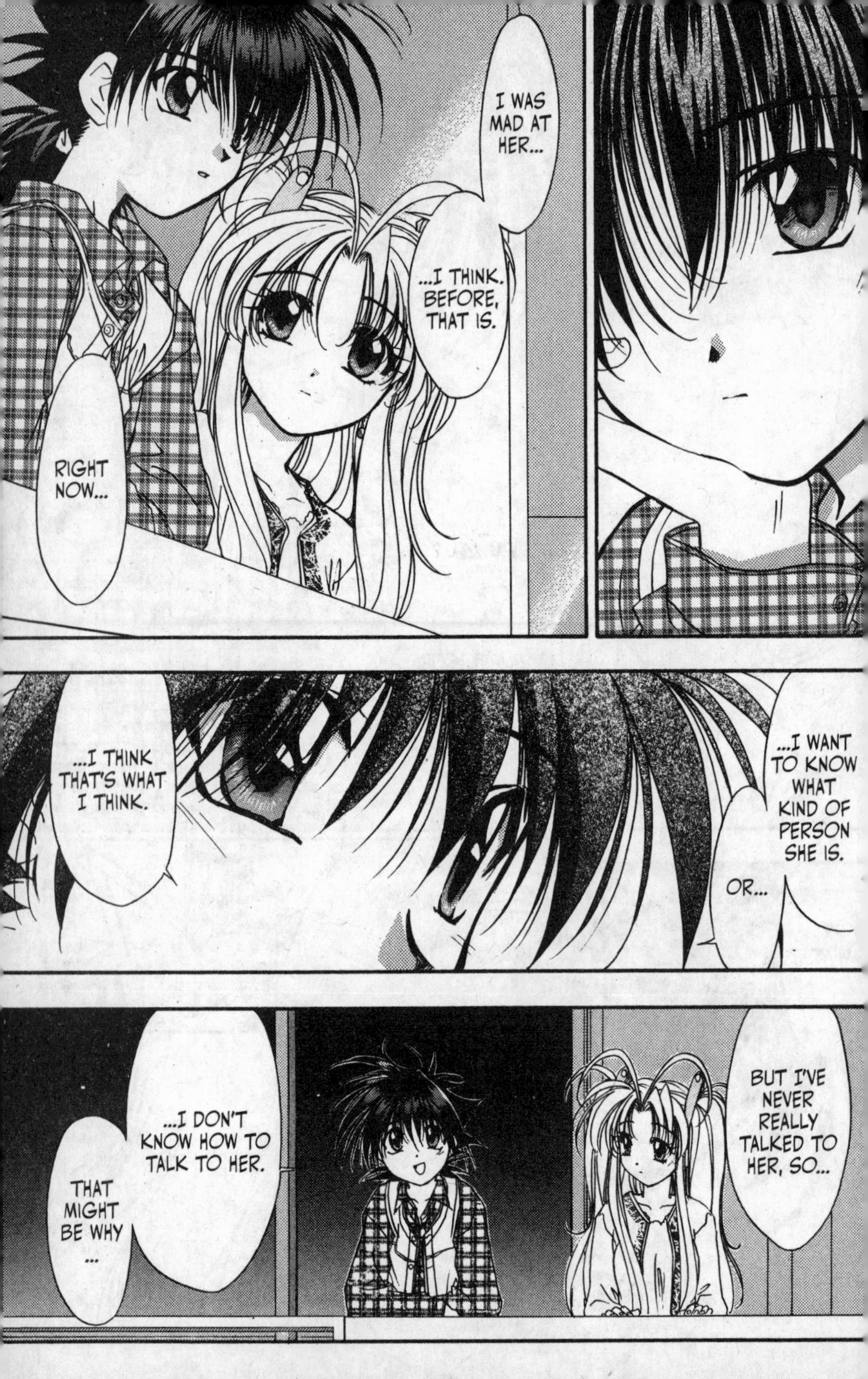
I WAS MAD AT HER...
...I THINK. BEFORE, THAT IS.
RIGHT NOW...
...I WANT TO KNOW WHAT KIND OF PERSON SHE IS.
OR...
...I THINK THAT'S WHAT I THINK.
BUT I'VE NEVER REALLY TALKED TO HER, SO...
...I DON'T KNOW HOW TO TALK TO HER.
THAT MIGHT BE WHY ...

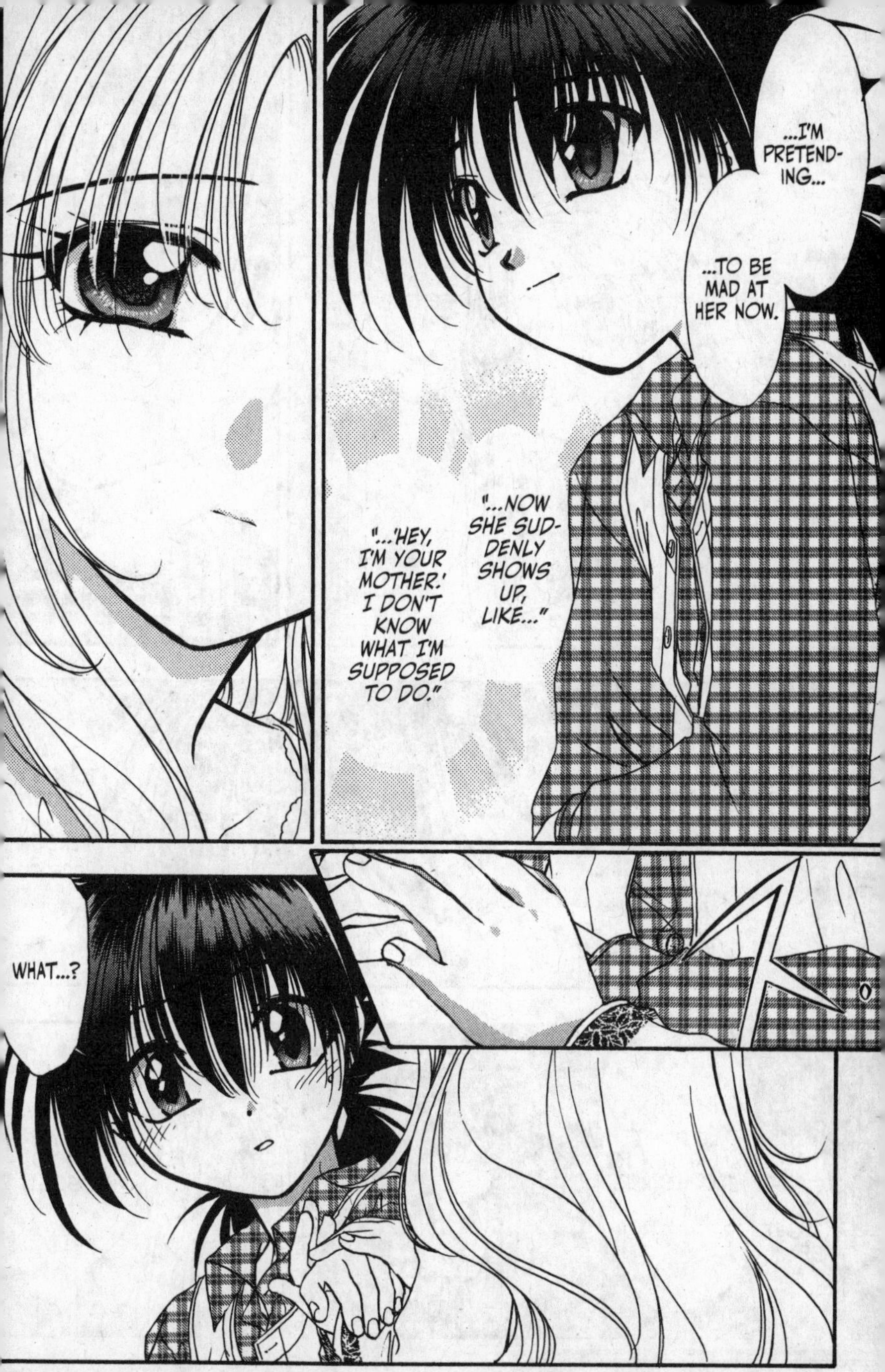
...I'M PRETENDING...
...TO BE MAD AT HER NOW.
"...NOW SHE SUDDENLY SHOWS UP, LIKE..."
"...'HEY, I'M YOUR MOTHER.' I DON'T KNOW WHAT I'M SUPPOSED TO DO."
WHAT...?

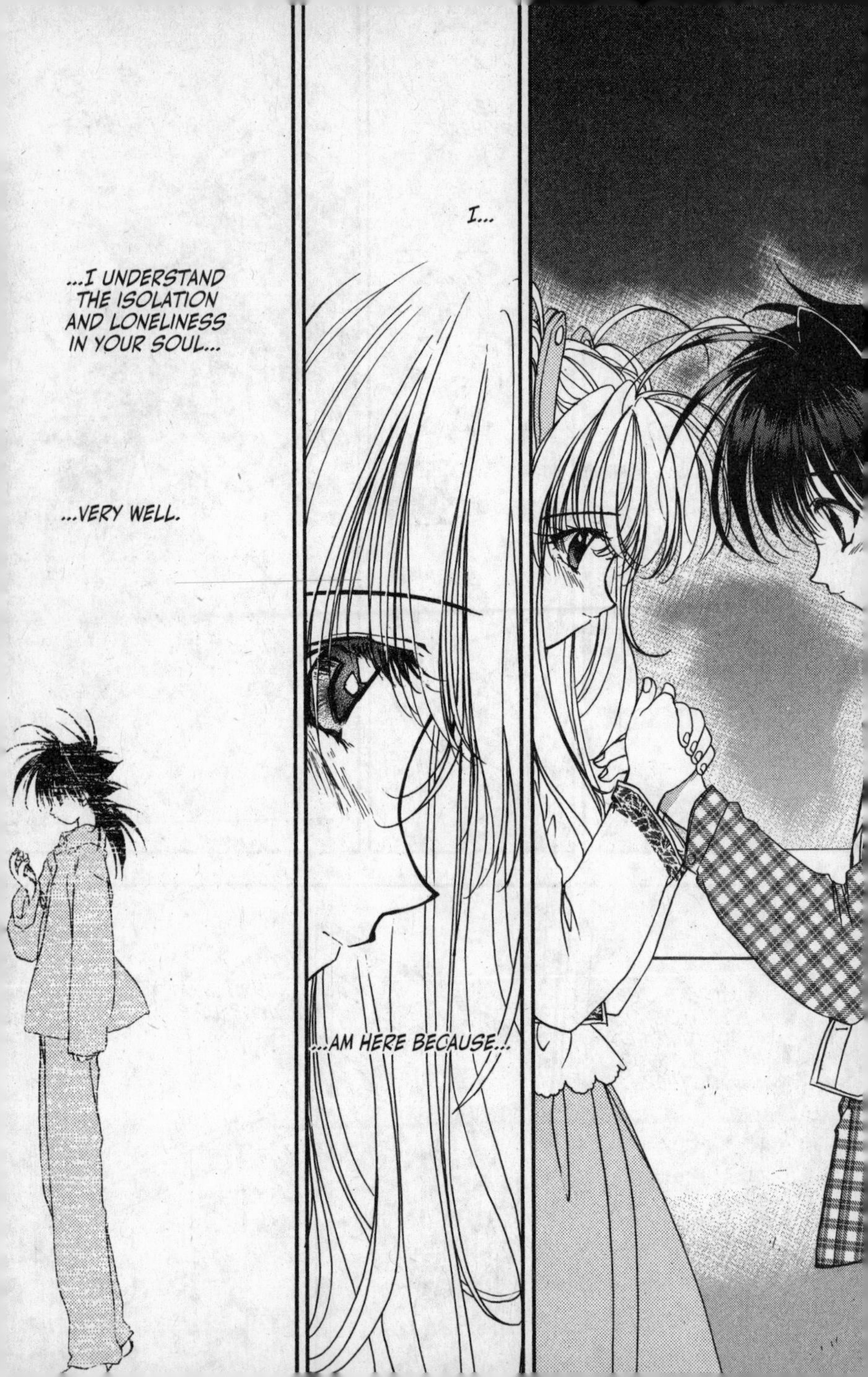
I...
...AM HERE BECAUSE...
...I UNDERSTAND THE ISOLATION AND LONELINESS IN YOUR SOUL...
...VERY WELL.

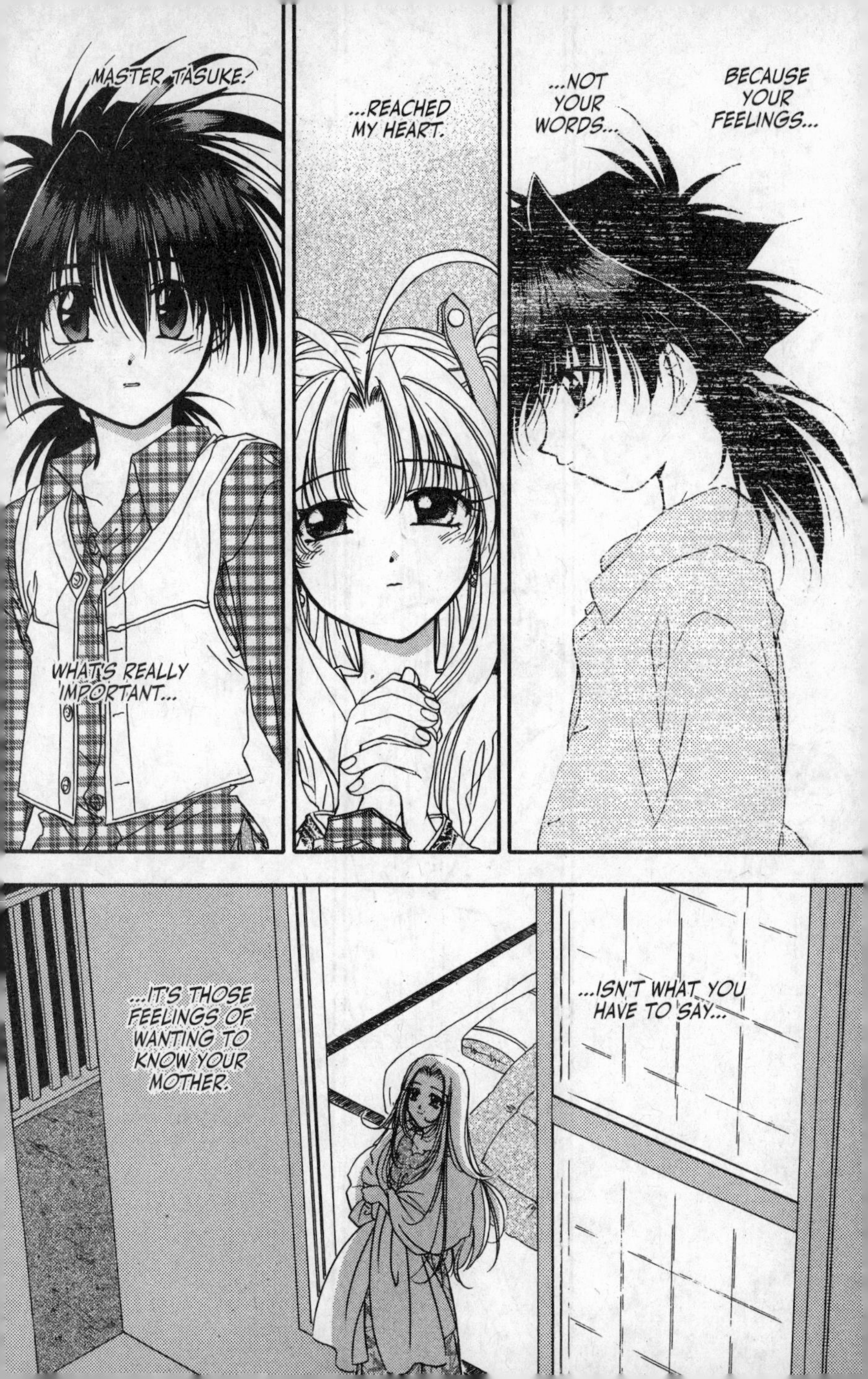
BECAUSE YOUR FEELINGS...
...NOT YOUR WORDS...
...REACHED MY HEART.
MASTER TASUKE.
WHAT'S REALLY IMPORTANT...
...ISN'T WHAT YOU HAVE TO SAY...
...IT'S THOSE FEELINGS OF WANTING TO KNOW YOUR MOTHER.

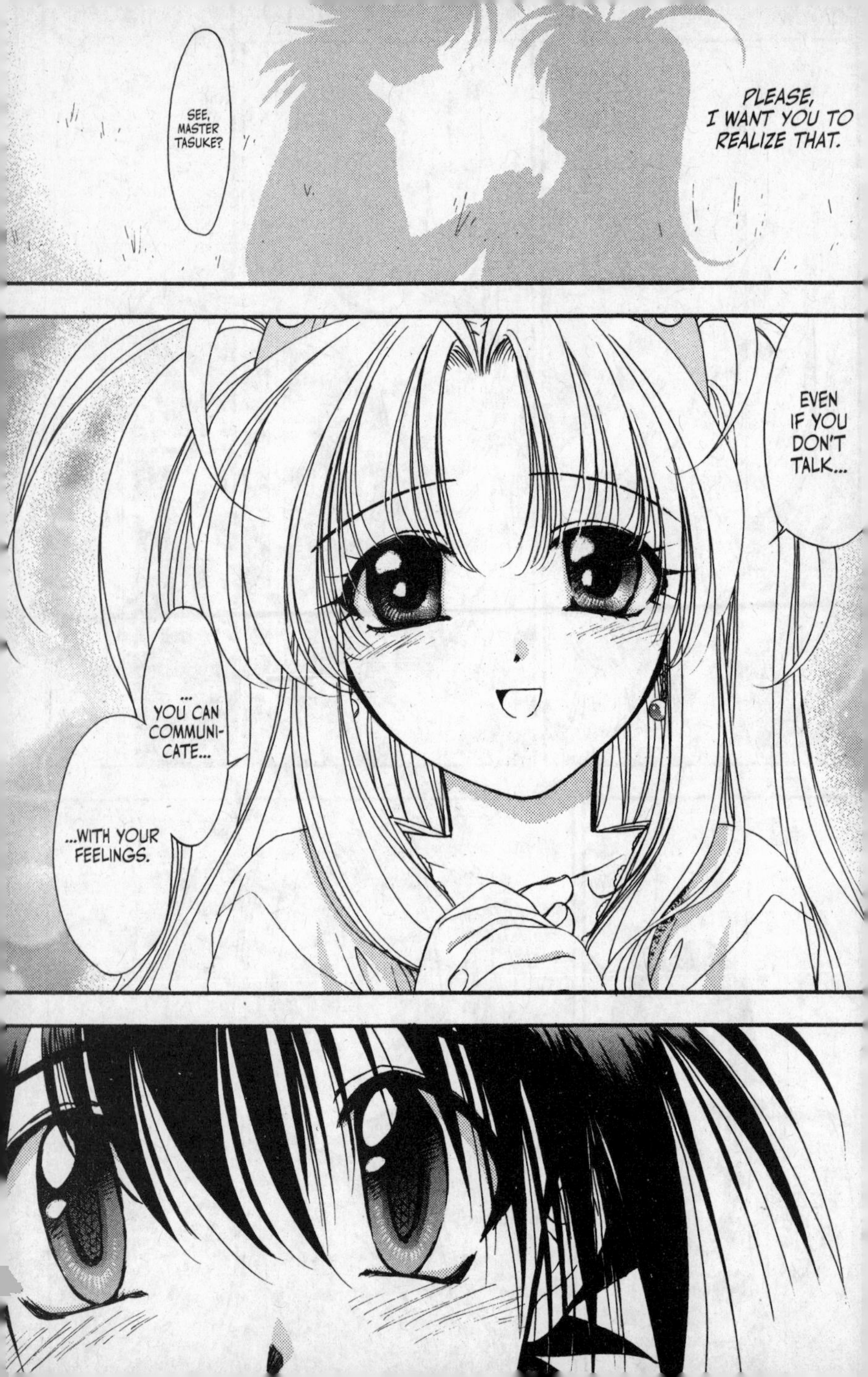
PLEASE, I WANT YOU TO REALIZE THAT.
SEE, MASTER TASUKE?
EVEN IF YOU DON'T TALK...
...YOU CAN COMMUNICATE...
...WITH YOUR FEELINGS.

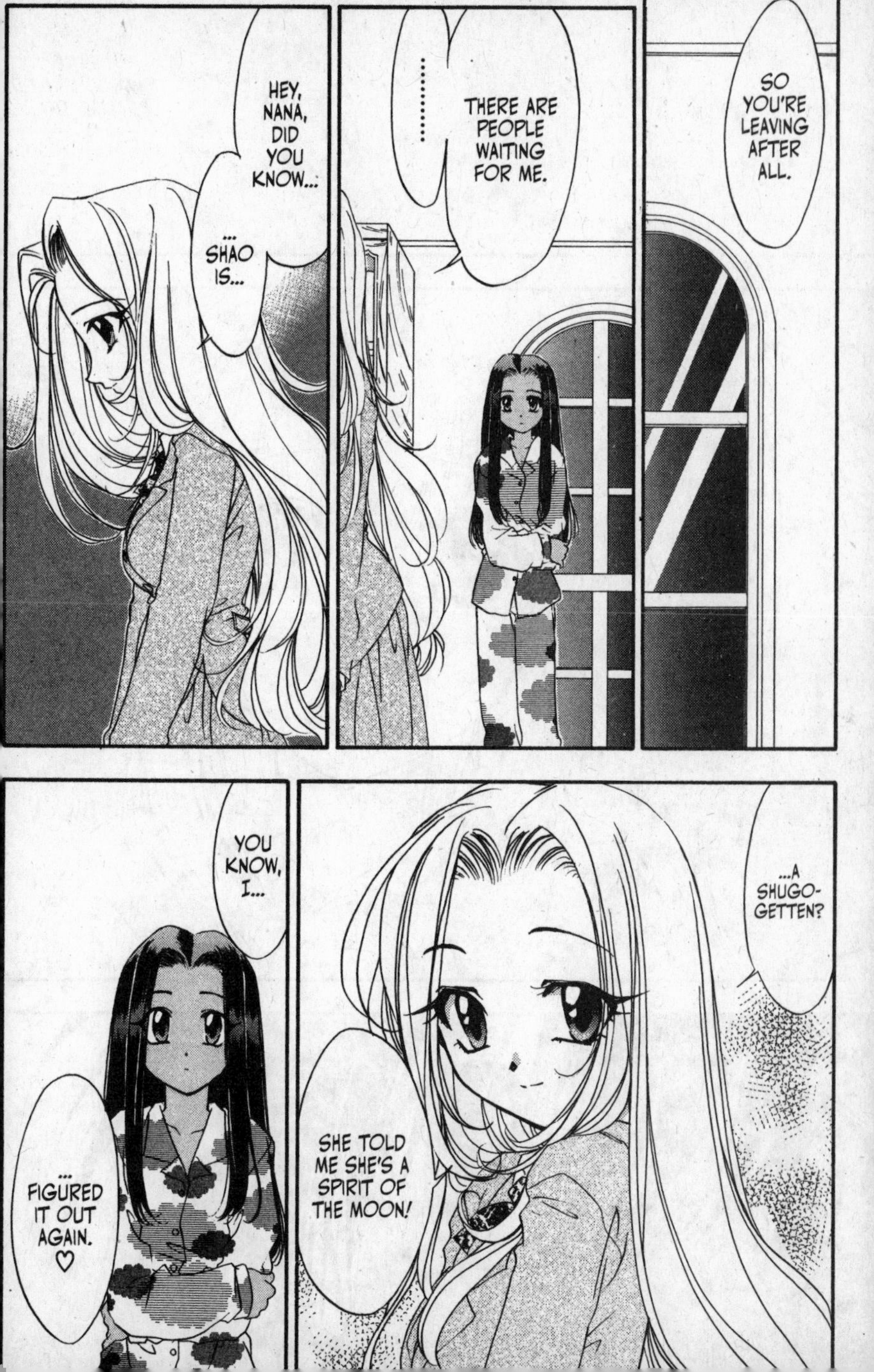
SO YOU'RE LEAVING AFTER ALL.
THERE ARE PEOPLE WAITING FOR ME.
....
HEY, NANA, DID YOU KNOW...
...SHAO IS...
...A SHUGO-GETTEN?
SHE TOLD ME SHE'S A SPIRIT OF THE MOON!
YOU KNOW, I...
...FIGURED IT OUT AGAIN. ♡

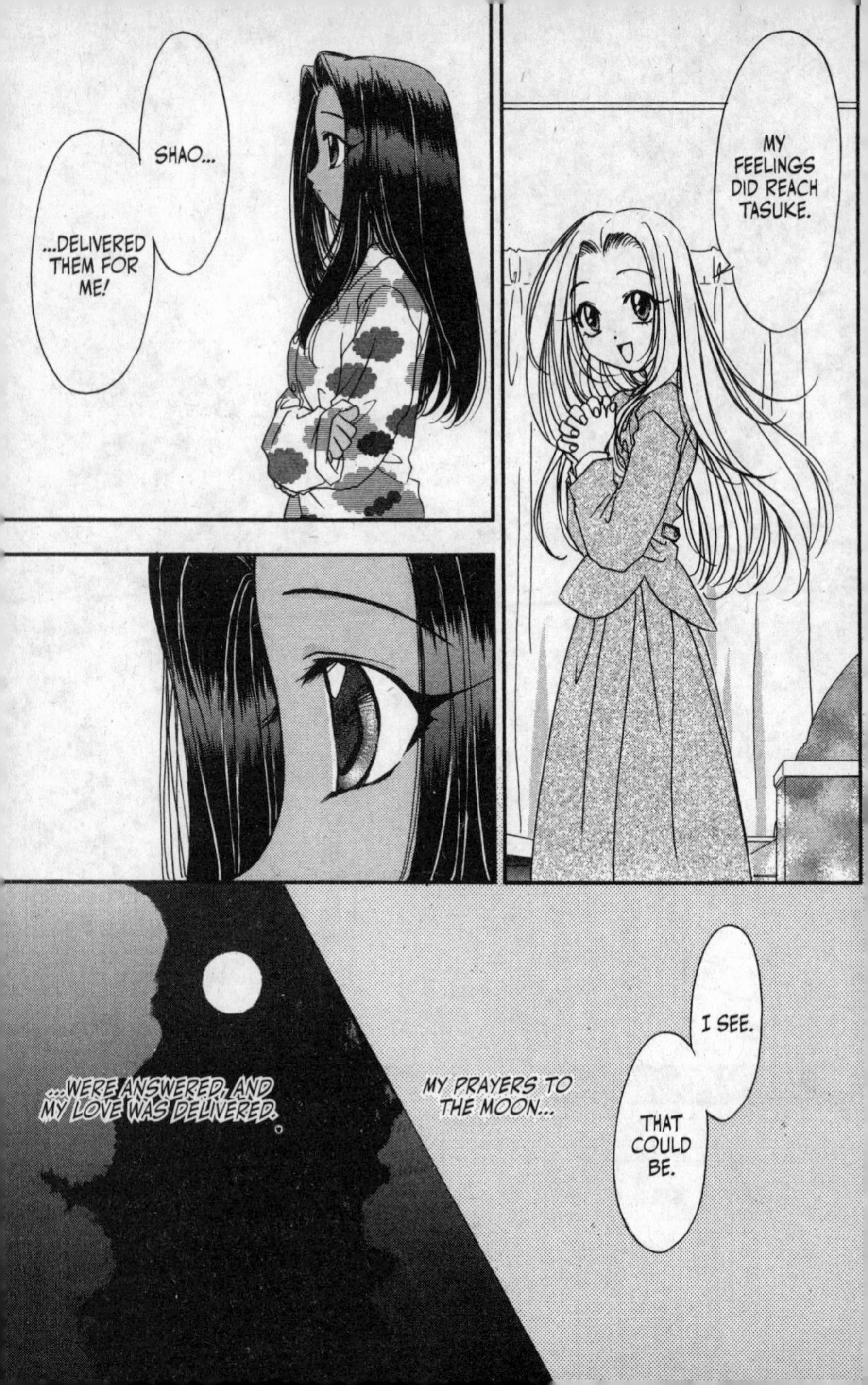
MY FEELINGS DID REACH TASUKE.
SHAO...
...DELIVERED THEM FOR ME!
I SEE.
THAT COULD BE.
MY PRAYERS TO THE MOON...
...WERE ANSWERED, AND MY LOVE WAS DELIVERED.

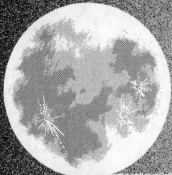

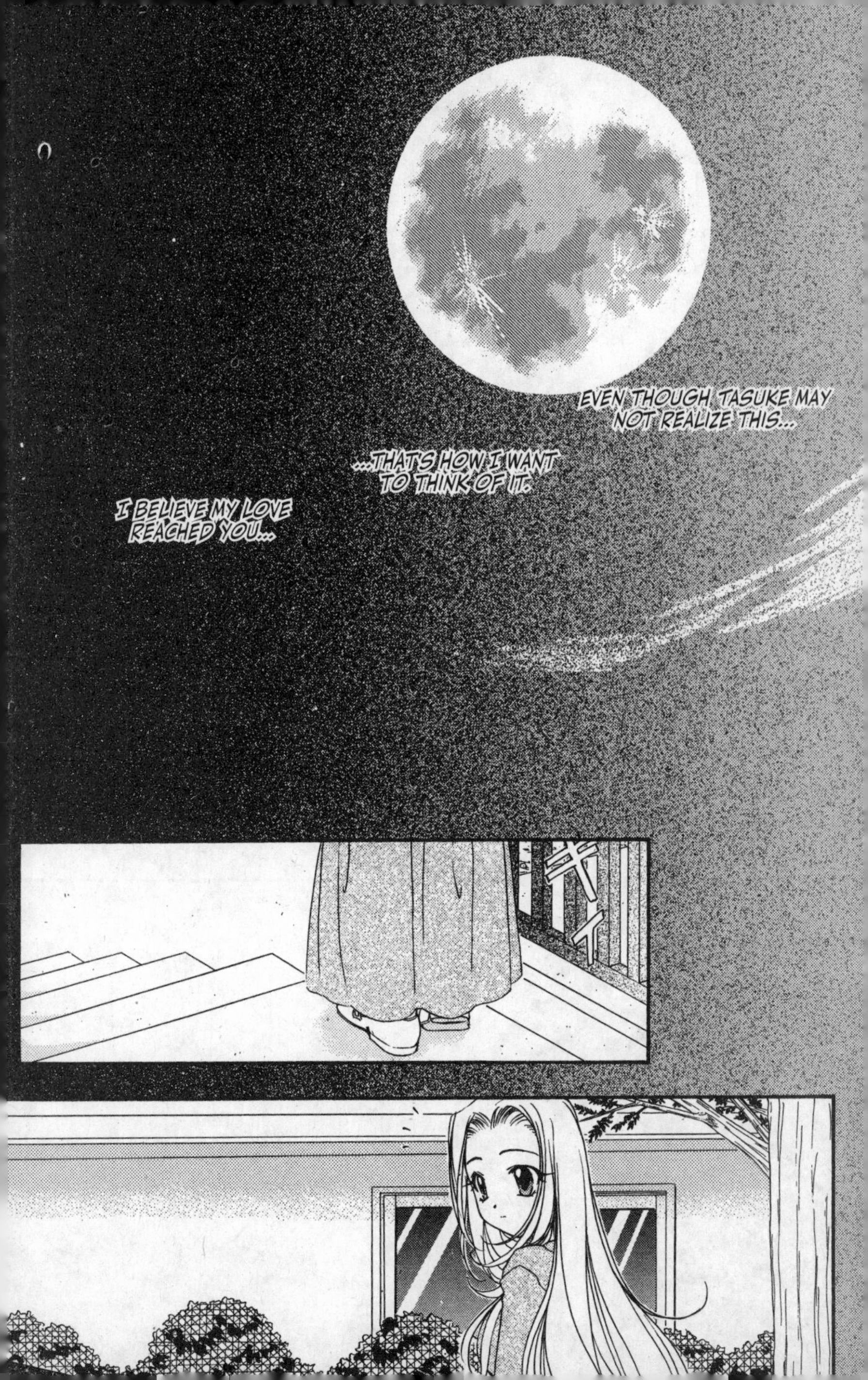

EVEN THOUGH TASUKE MAY
NOT REALIZE THIS...

...THAT'S HOW I WANT
TO THINK OF IT.

I BELIEVE MY LOVE
REACHED YOU...

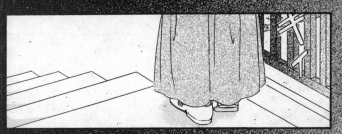

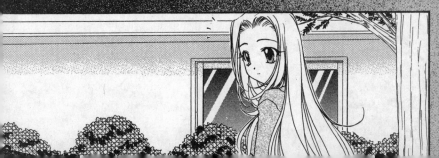

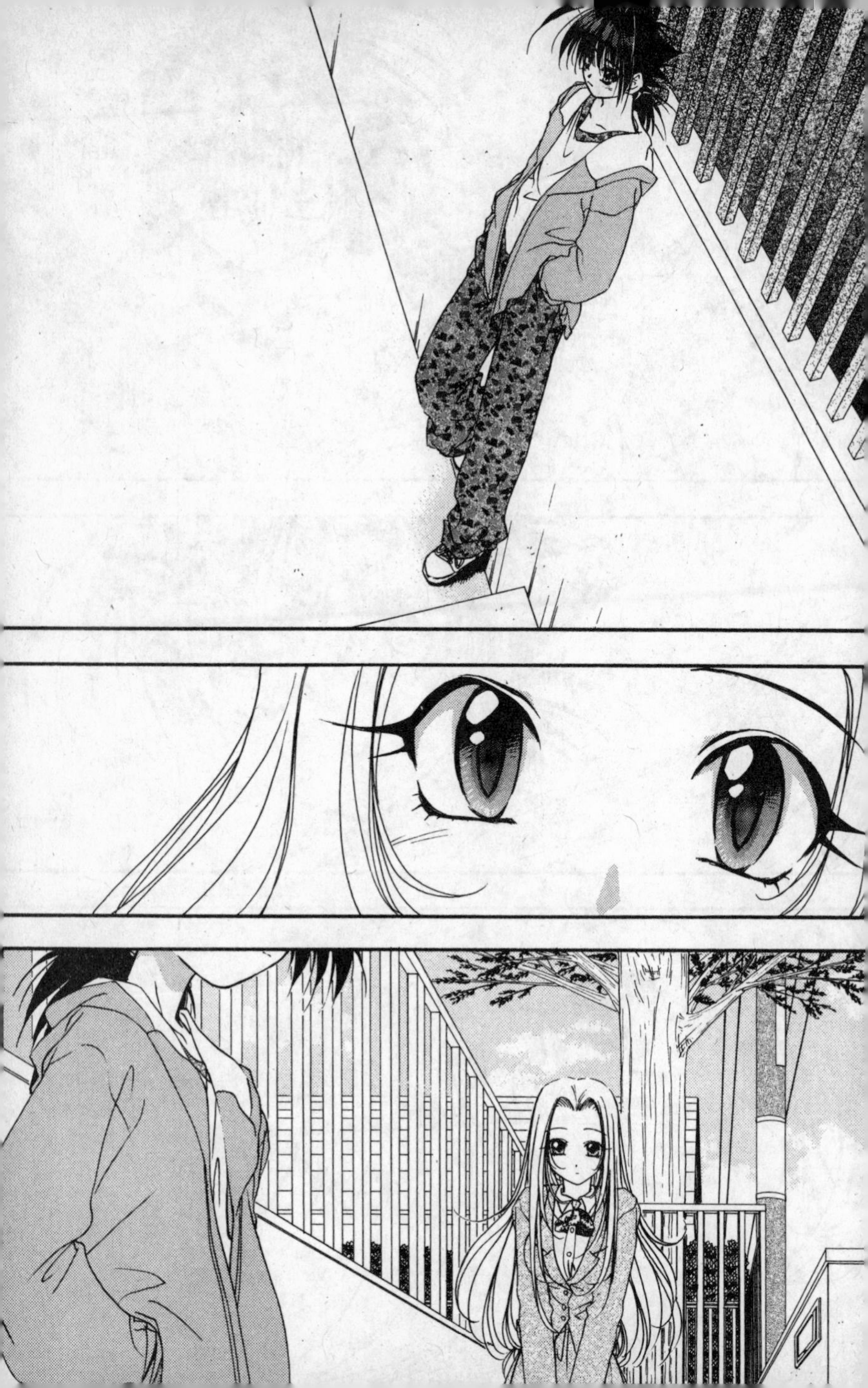

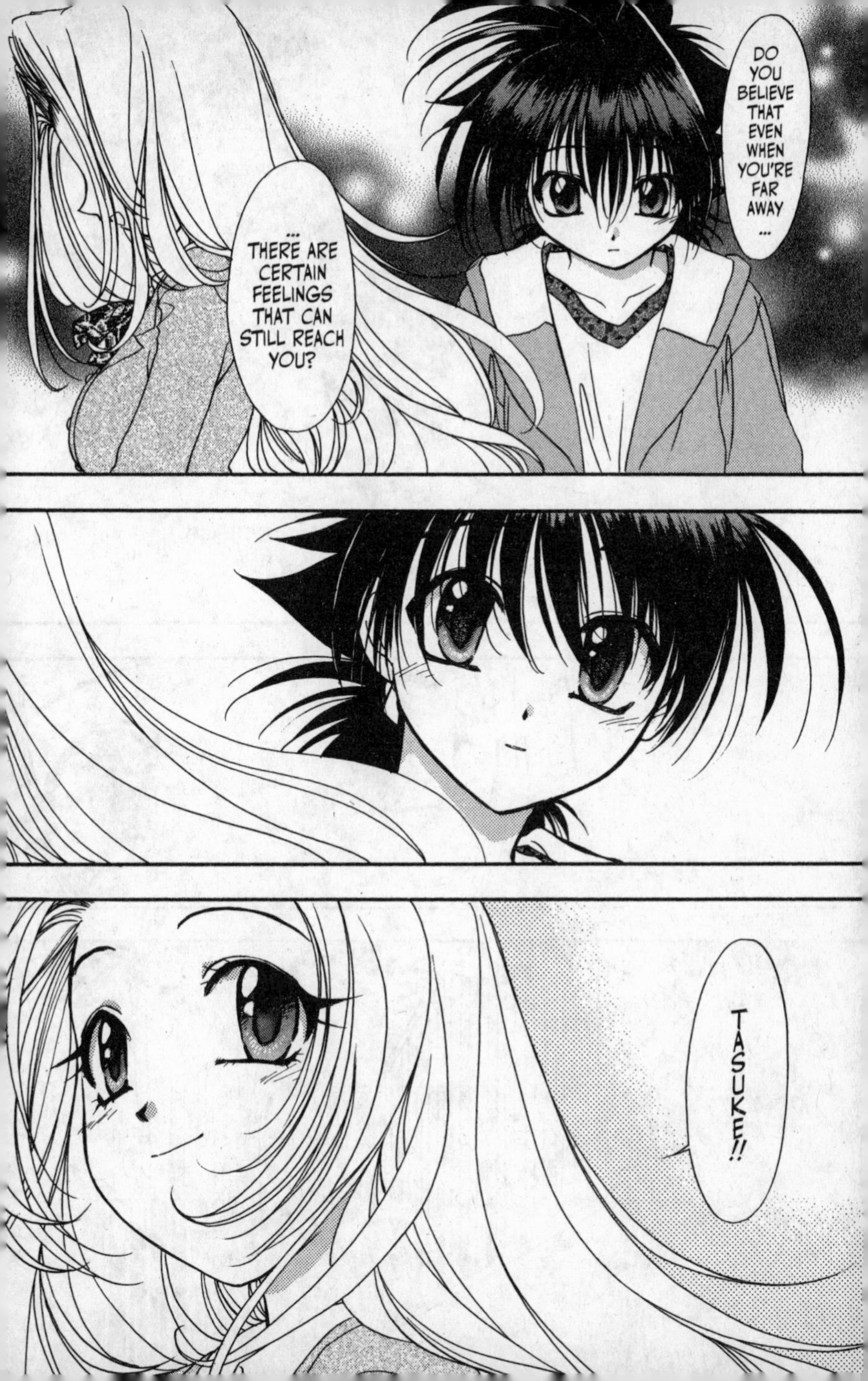
DO YOU BELIEVE THAT EVEN WHEN YOU'RE FAR AWAY ...
... THERE ARE CERTAIN FEELINGS THAT CAN STILL REACH YOU?
TASUKE!!

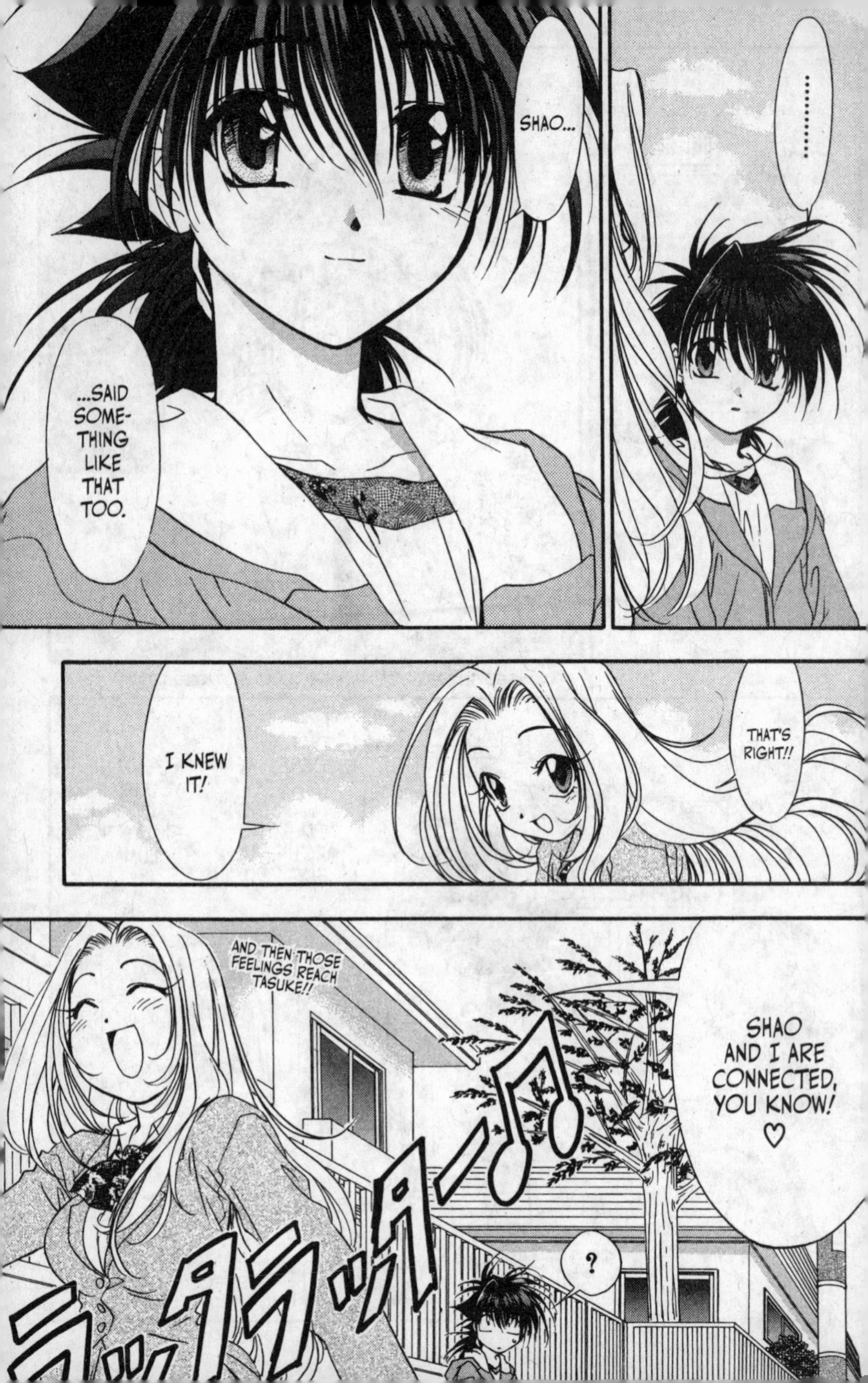
......
SHAO...
...SAID SOMETHING-THING LIKE THAT TOO.
THAT'S RIGHT!!
I KNEW IT!
SHAO AND I ARE CONNECTED, YOU KNOW! ♡
AND THEN THOSE FEELINGS REACH TASUKE!!
ラッタラッター♪
?

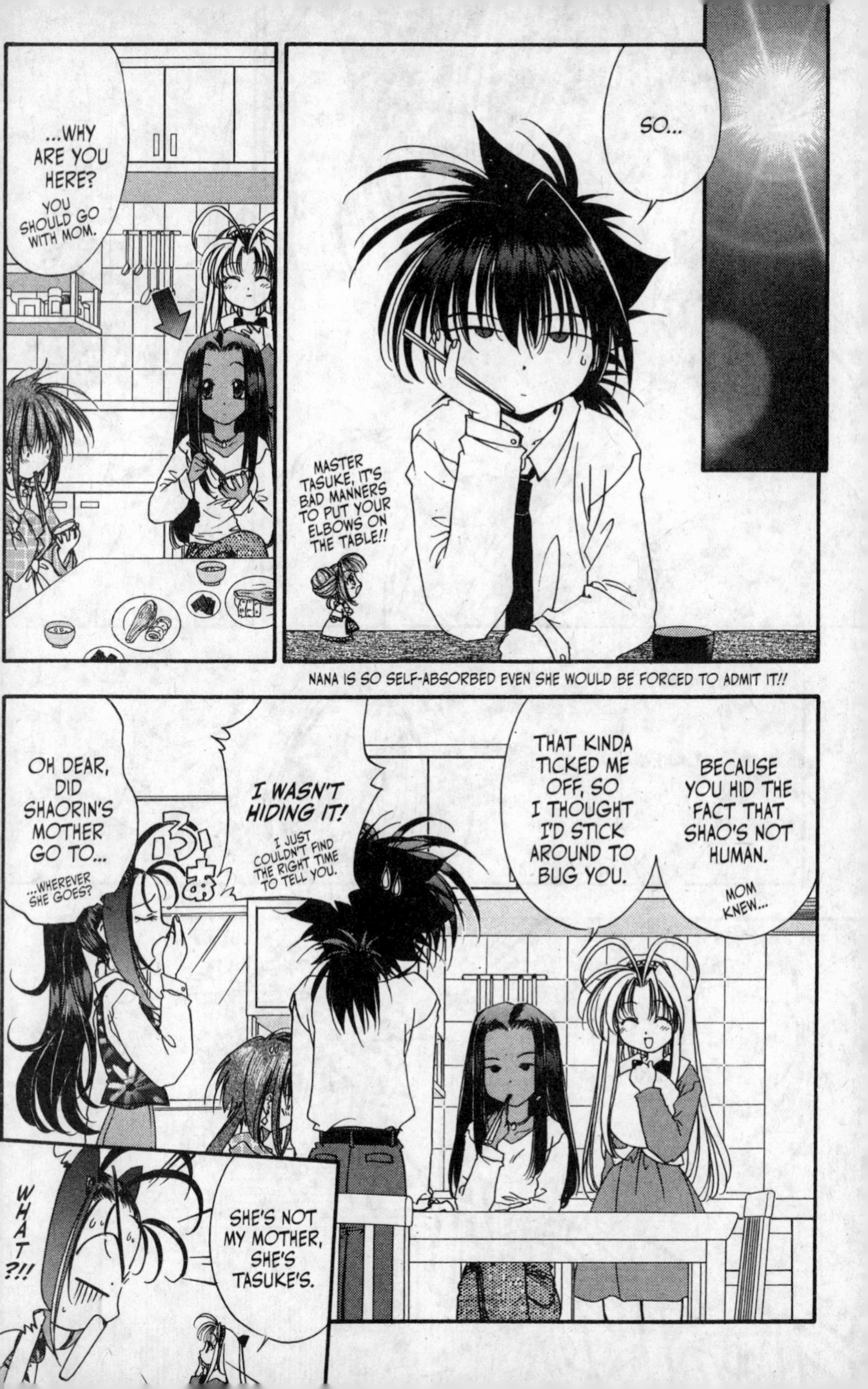
SO...
MASTER TASUKE, IT'S BAD MANNERS TO PUT YOUR ELBOWS ON THE TABLE!!
...WHY ARE YOU HERE?
YOU SHOULD GO WITH MOM.
NANA IS SO SELF-ABSORBED EVEN SHE WOULD BE FORCED TO ADMIT IT!!
BECAUSE YOU HID THE FACT THAT SHAO'S NOT HUMAN.
MOM KNEW...
THAT KINDA TICKED ME OFF, SO I THOUGHT I'D STICK AROUND TO BUG YOU.
I WASN'T HIDING IT!
I JUST COULDN'T FIND THE RIGHT TIME TO TELL YOU.
OH DEAR, DID SHAORIN'S MOTHER GO TO...
...WHEREVER SHE GOES?
SHE'S NOT MY MOTHER, SHE'S TASUKE'S.
WHAT?!!

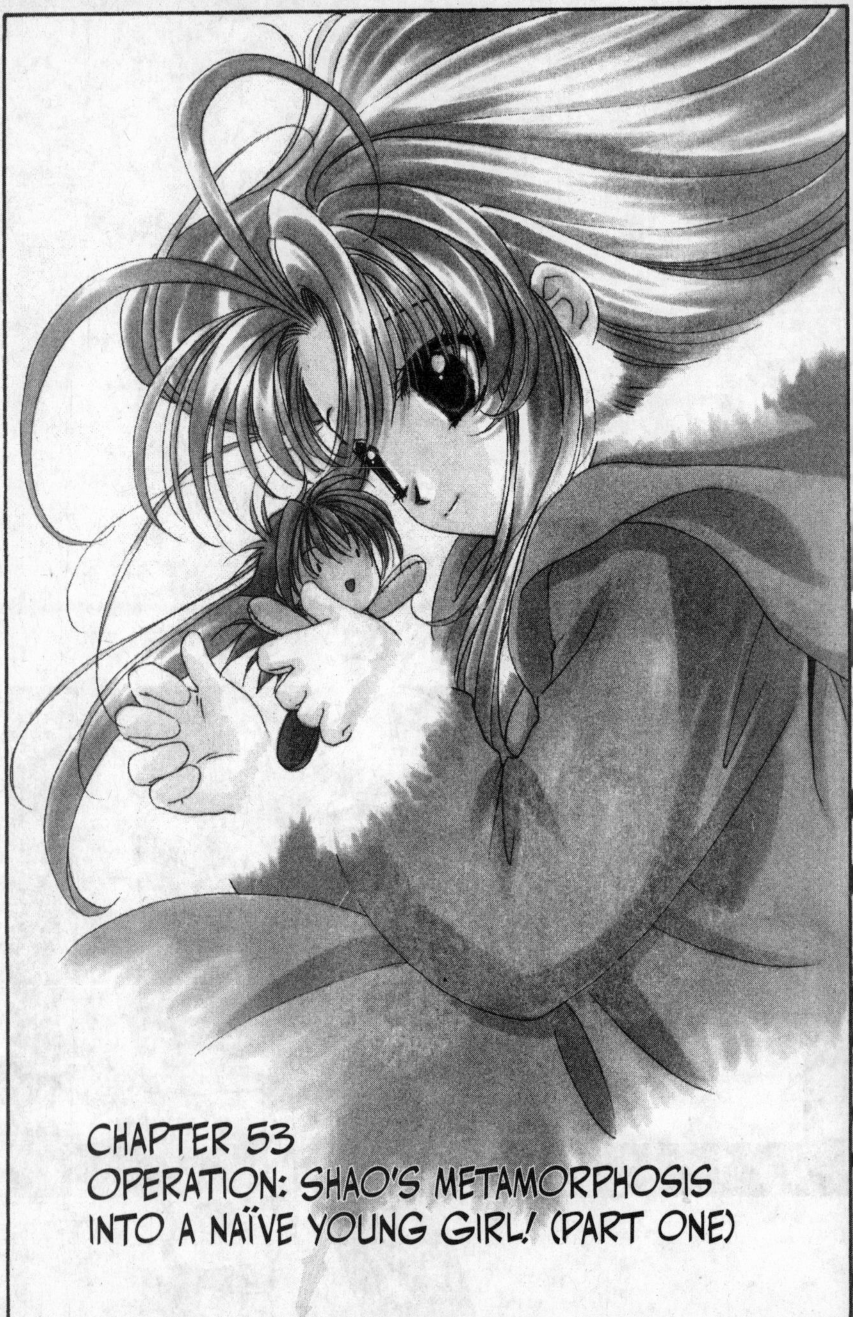

CHAPTER 53
OPERATION: SHAO'S METAMORPHOSIS INTO A NAÏVE YOUNG GIRL! (PART ONE)

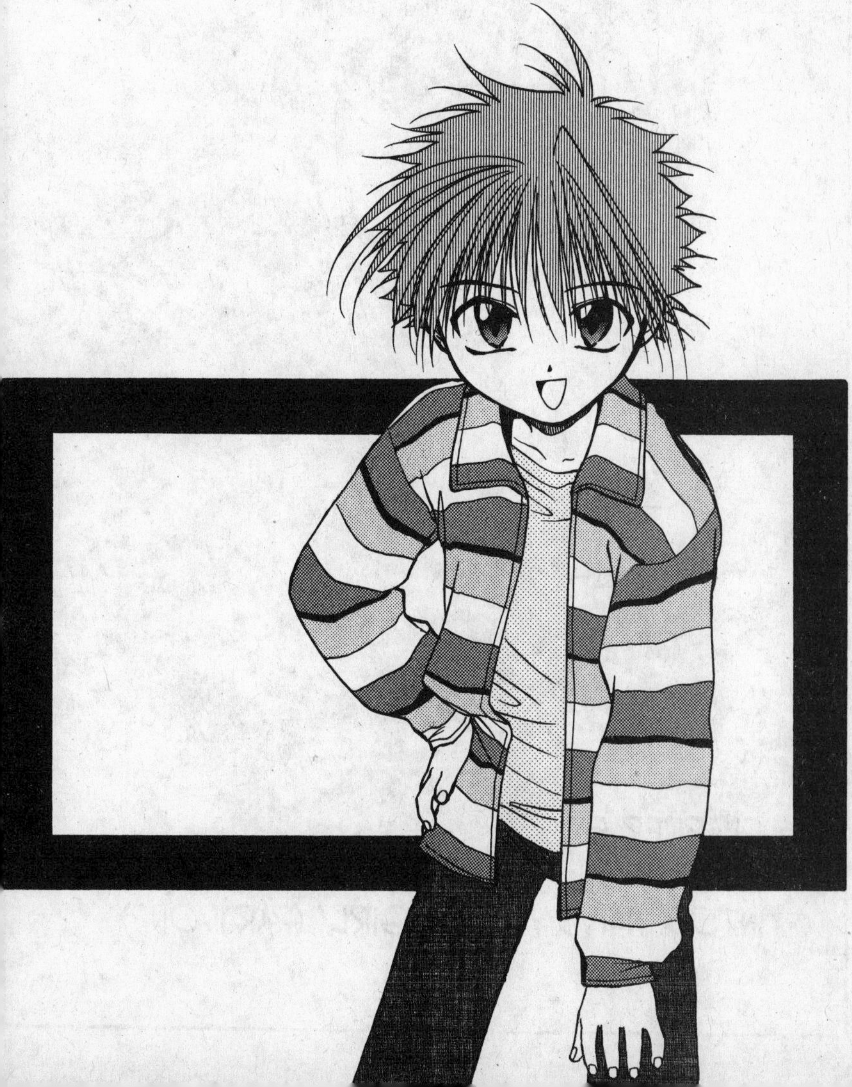

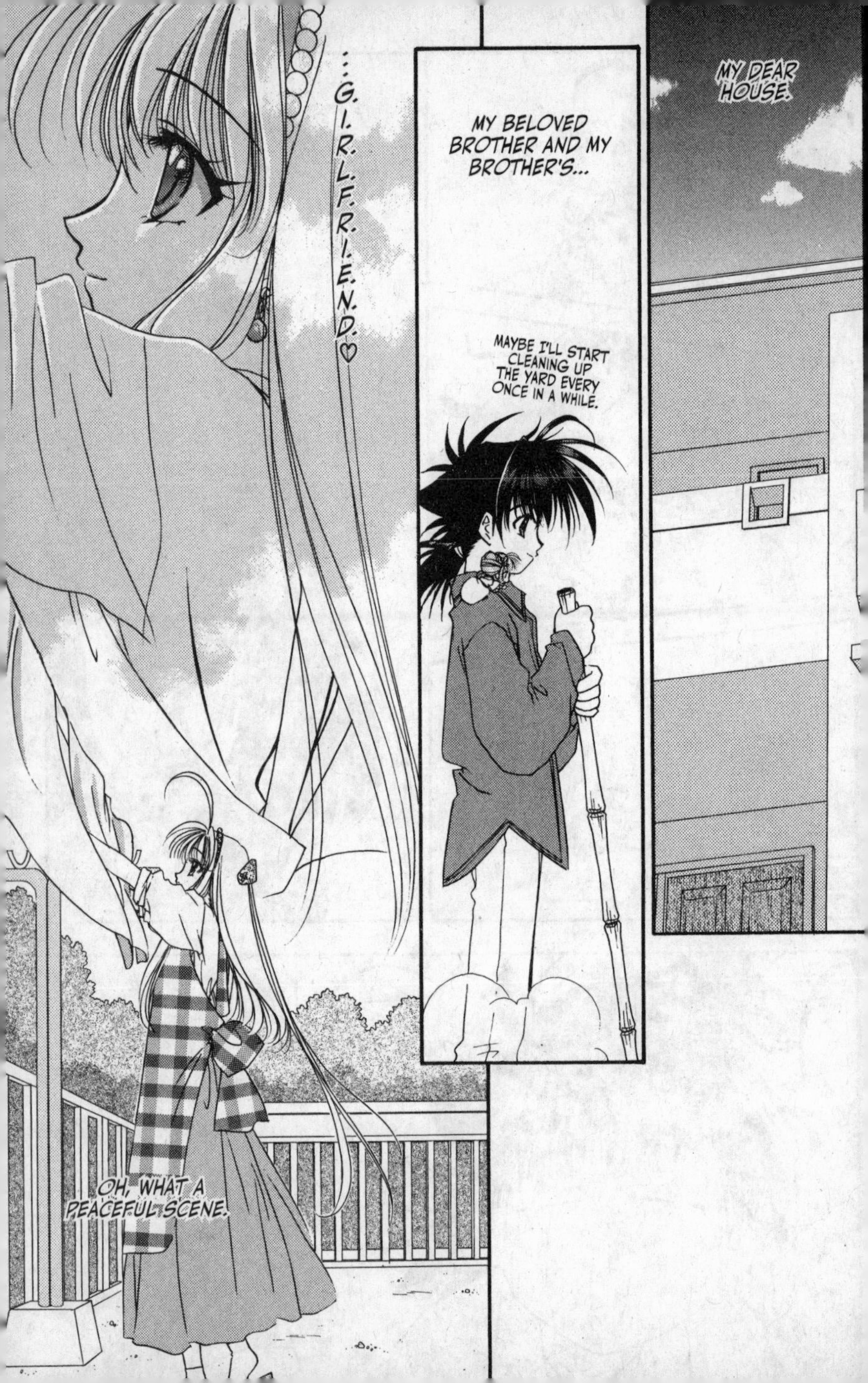
MY DEAR HOUSE.
MY BELOVED BROTHER AND MY BROTHER'S...
MAYBE I'LL START CLEANING UP THE YARD EVERY ONCE IN A WHILE.
...G.I.R.L.F.R.I.E.N.D.♡
OH, WHAT A PEACEFUL SCENE.

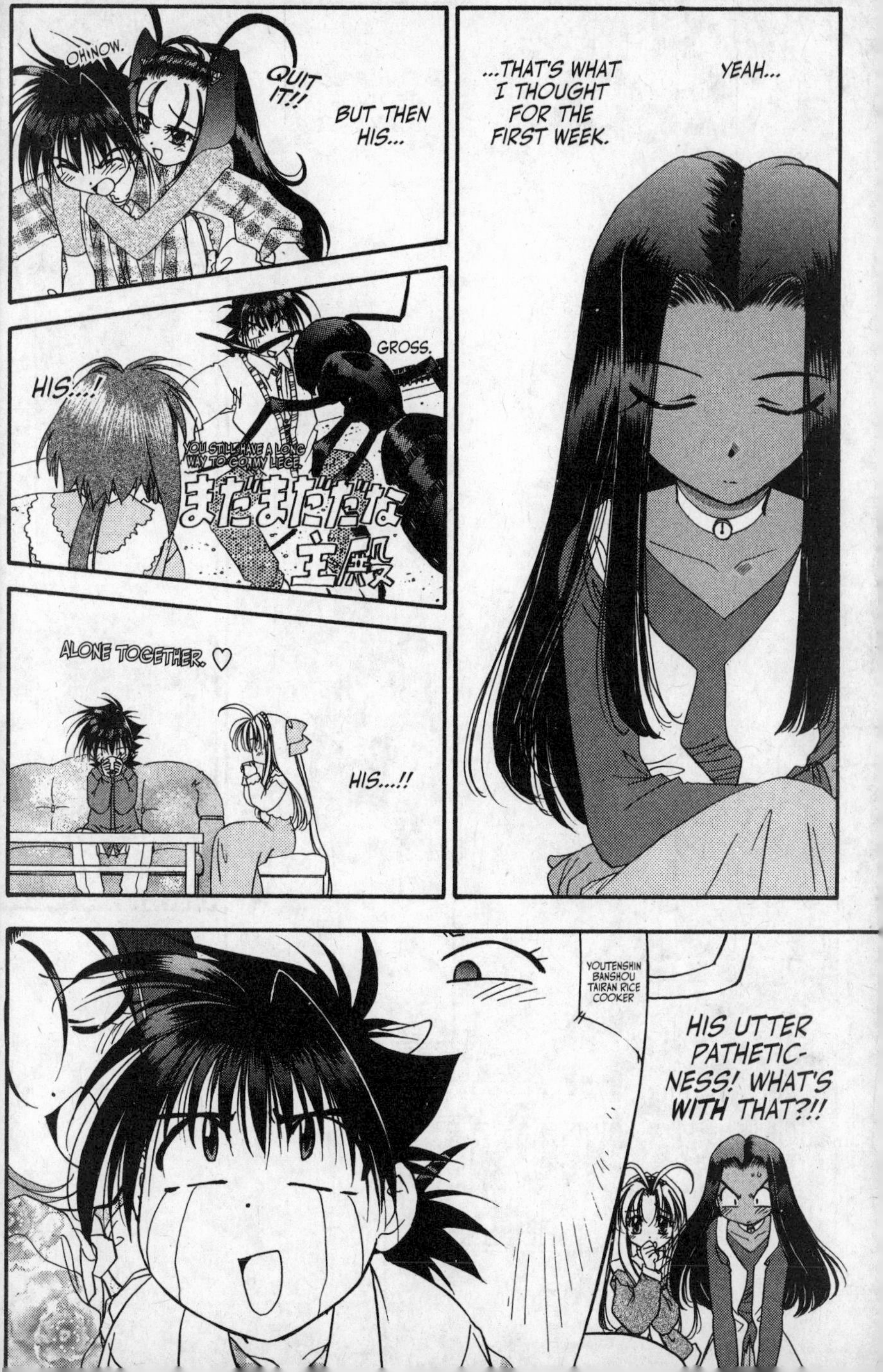
YEAH...
...THAT'S WHAT I THOUGHT FOR THE FIRST WEEK.
BUT THEN HIS...
QUIT IT!!
OH...NOW.
GROSS.
HIS...!
YOU STILL HAVE A LONG WAY TO GO, MY LIEGE.
まだまだだな主殿
HIS...!!
ALONE TOGETHER. ♡
HIS UTTER PATHETIC-NESS! WHAT'S WITH THAT?!!
YOUTENSHIN BANSHOU TAIRAN RICE COOKER

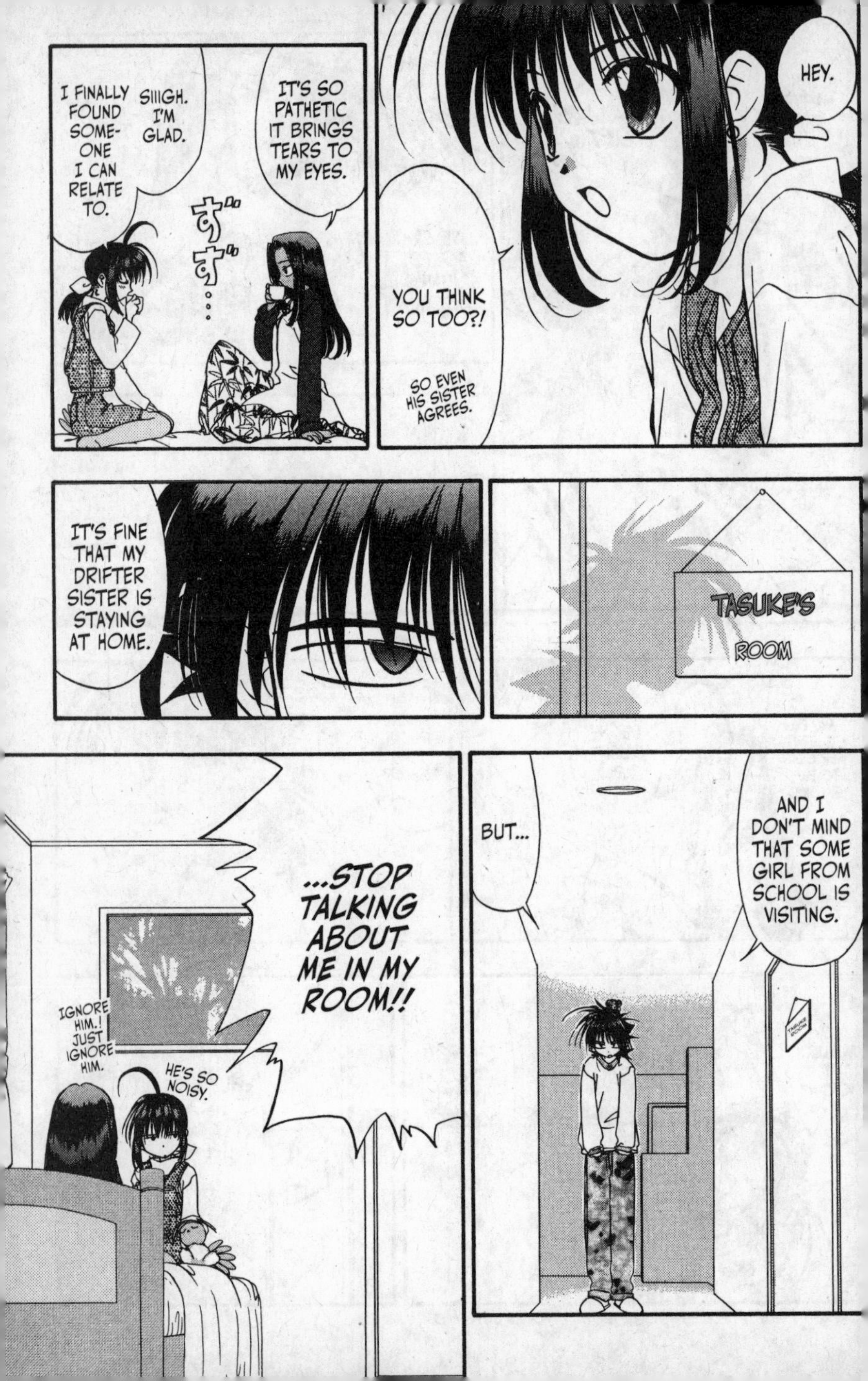
HEY.
YOU THINK SO TOO?!
SO EVEN HIS SISTER AGREES.
IT'S SO PATHETIC IT BRINGS TEARS TO MY EYES.
SIIIGH. I'M GLAD.
I FINALLY FOUND SOME-ONE I CAN RELATE TO.
ずず…
TASUKE'S ROOM
IT'S FINE THAT MY DRIFTER SISTER IS STAYING AT HOME.
AND I DON'T MIND THAT SOME GIRL FROM SCHOOL IS VISITING.
BUT...
...STOP TALKING ABOUT ME IN MY ROOM!!
HE'S SO NOISY.
IGNORE HIM.! JUST IGNORE HIM.

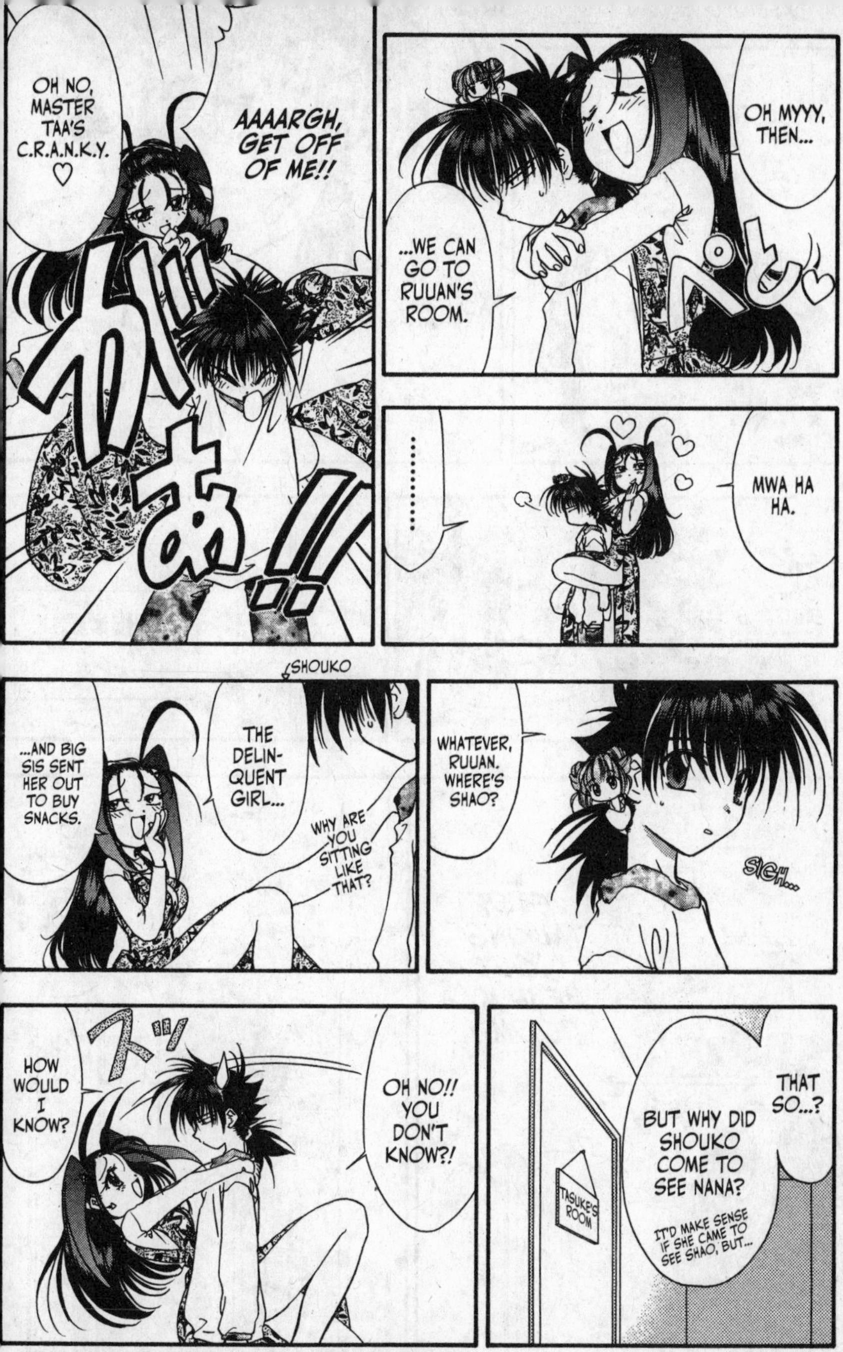
OH MYYY, THEN...
...WE CAN GO TO RUUAN'S ROOM.
MWA HA HA.
....
AAAARGH, GET OFF OF ME!!
OH NO, MASTER TAA'S C.R.A.N.K.Y. ♡
WHATEVER, RUUAN. WHERE'S SHAO?
SIGH...
SHOUKO
THE DELIN-QUENT GIRL...
...AND BIG SIS SENT HER OUT TO BUY SNACKS.
WHY ARE YOU SITTING LIKE THAT?
THAT SO...?
BUT WHY DID SHOUKO COME TO SEE NANA?
IT'D MAKE SENSE IF SHE CAME TO SEE SHAO, BUT...
TASUKE'S ROOM
OH NO!! YOU DON'T KNOW?!
HOW WOULD I KNOW?

HERE'S A GUY WHO DOESN'T CARE ABOUT ANYTHING BUT SHAO.

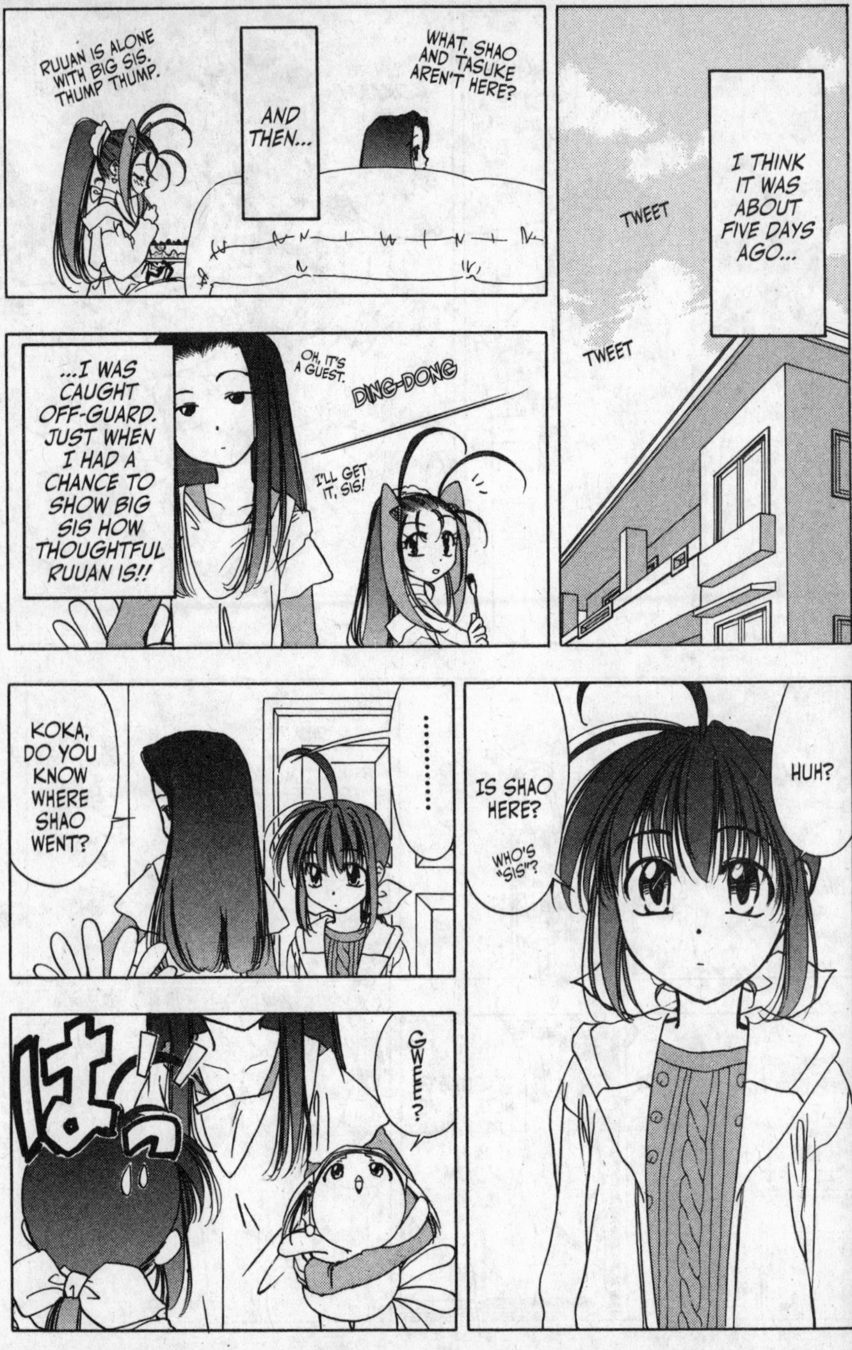
I THINK IT WAS ABOUT FIVE DAYS AGO...
TWEET
TWEET
WHAT, SHAO AND TASUKE AREN'T HERE?
AND THEN...
RUUAN IS ALONE WITH BIG SIS. THUMP THUMP.
OH, IT'S A GUEST.
DING-DONG
...I WAS CAUGHT OFF-GUARD. JUST WHEN I HAD A CHANCE TO SHOW BIG SIS HOW THOUGHTFUL RUUAN IS!!
I'LL GET IT, SIS!
HUH?
IS SHAO HERE?
WHO'S "SIS"?
....
KOKA, DO YOU KNOW WHERE SHAO WENT?
GWEE?
はっ

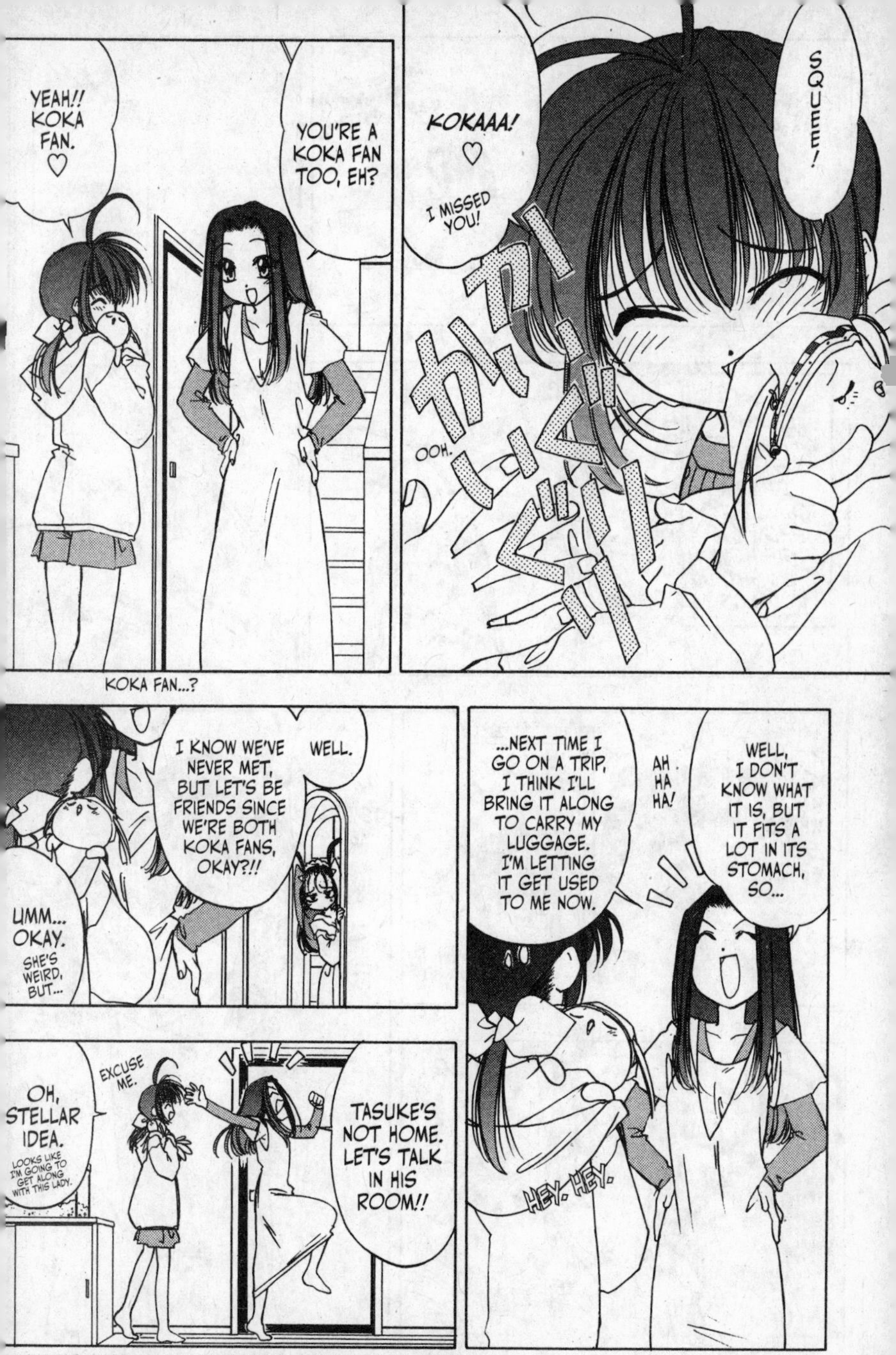
SQUEE!
KOKAAA! ♡
I MISSED YOU!
OOH.
YOU'RE A KOKA FAN TOO, EH?
YEAH!! KOKA FAN. ♡
KOKA FAN...?
WELL, I DON'T KNOW WHAT IT IS, BUT IT FITS A LOT IN ITS STOMACH, SO...
AH HA HA!
...NEXT TIME I GO ON A TRIP, I THINK I'LL BRING IT ALONG TO CARRY MY LUGGAGE. I'M LETTING IT GET USED TO ME NOW.
HEY. HEY.
WELL.
I KNOW WE'VE NEVER MET, BUT LET'S BE FRIENDS SINCE WE'RE BOTH KOKA FANS, OKAY?!!
UMM... OKAY.
SHE'S WEIRD, BUT...
TASUKE'S NOT HOME. LET'S TALK IN HIS ROOM!!
EXCUSE ME.
OH, STELLAR IDEA.
LOOKS LIKE I'M GOING TO GET ALONG WITH THIS LADY.

※ AND THIS IS HOW LITTLE BROTHER'S ROOM BECAME BIG SIS'S ROOM.

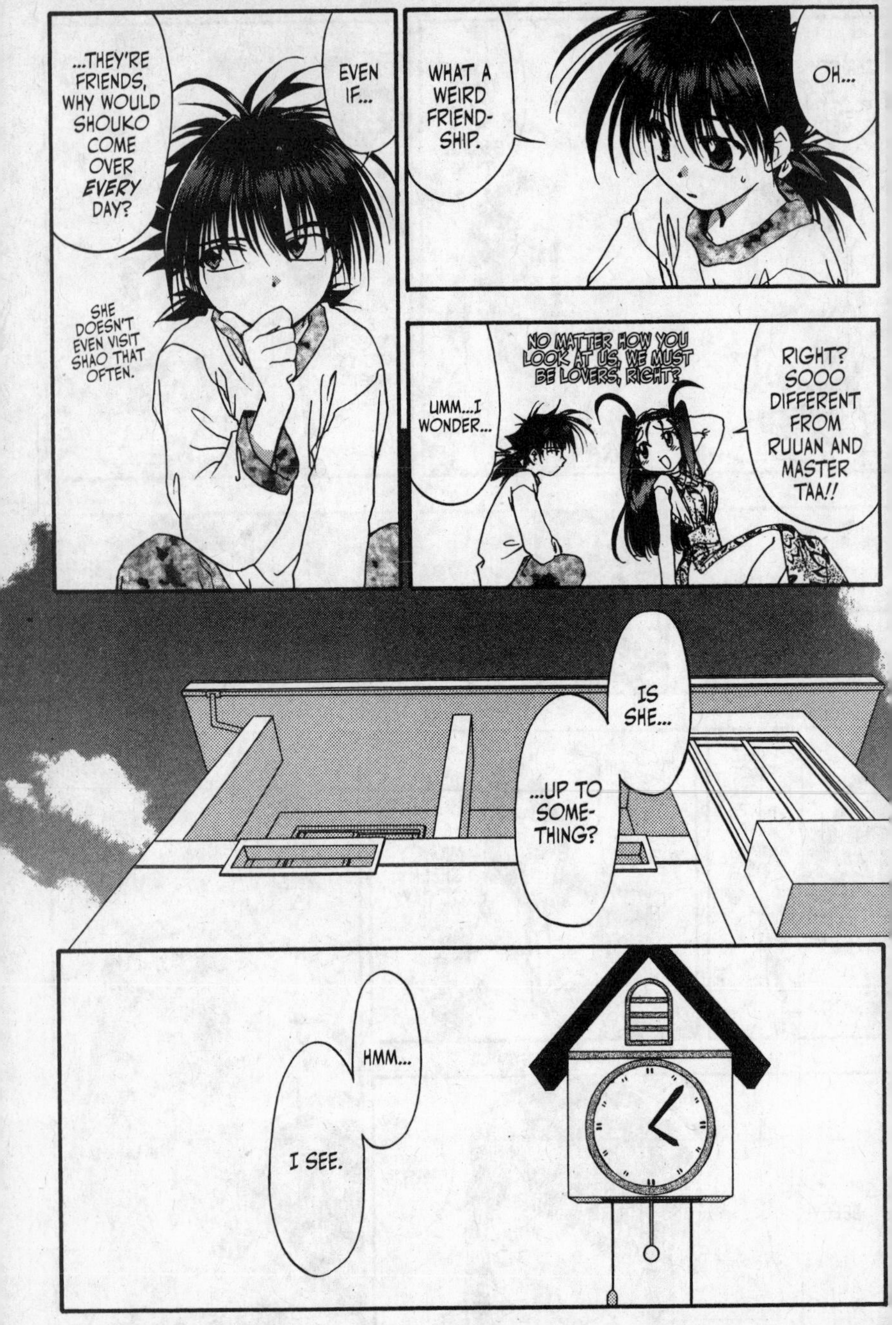
OH...
WHAT A WEIRD FRIENDSHIP.
RIGHT? SOOO DIFFERENT FROM RUUAN AND MASTER TAA!!
NO MATTER HOW YOU LOOK AT US, WE MUST BE LOVERS, RIGHT?
UMM...I WONDER...
EVEN IF...
...THEY'RE FRIENDS, WHY WOULD SHOUKO COME OVER *EVERY* DAY?
SHE DOESN'T EVEN VISIT SHAO THAT OFTEN.
IS SHE...
...UP TO SOMETHING?
HMM...
I SEE.

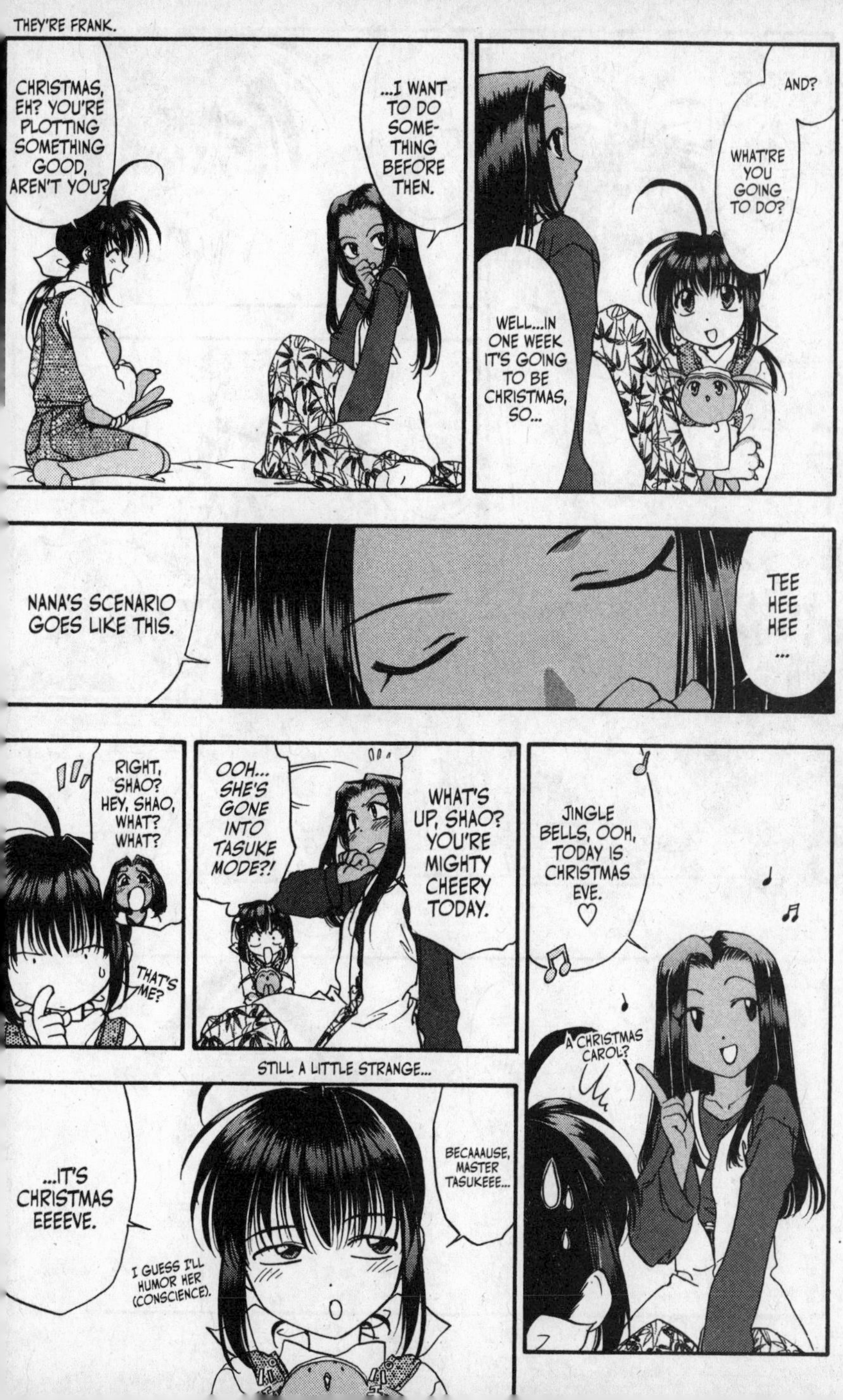
THEY'RE FRANK.
AND?
WHAT'RE YOU GOING TO DO?
WELL...IN ONE WEEK IT'S GOING TO BE CHRISTMAS, SO...
...I WANT TO DO SOMETHING BEFORE THEN.
CHRISTMAS, EH? YOU'RE PLOTTING SOMETHING GOOD, AREN'T YOU?
TEE HEE HEE ...
NANA'S SCENARIO GOES LIKE THIS.
JINGLE BELLS, OOH, TODAY IS CHRISTMAS EVE. ♡
A CHRISTMAS CAROL?
WHAT'S UP, SHAO? YOU'RE MIGHTY CHEERY TODAY.
OOH... SHE'S GONE INTO TASUKE MODE?!
RIGHT, SHAO? HEY, SHAO, WHAT? WHAT?
THAT'S ME?
STILL A LITTLE STRANGE...
BECAAAUSE, MASTER TASUKEEE...
...IT'S CHRISTMAS EEEEVE.
I GUESS I'LL HUMOR HER (CONSCIENCE).

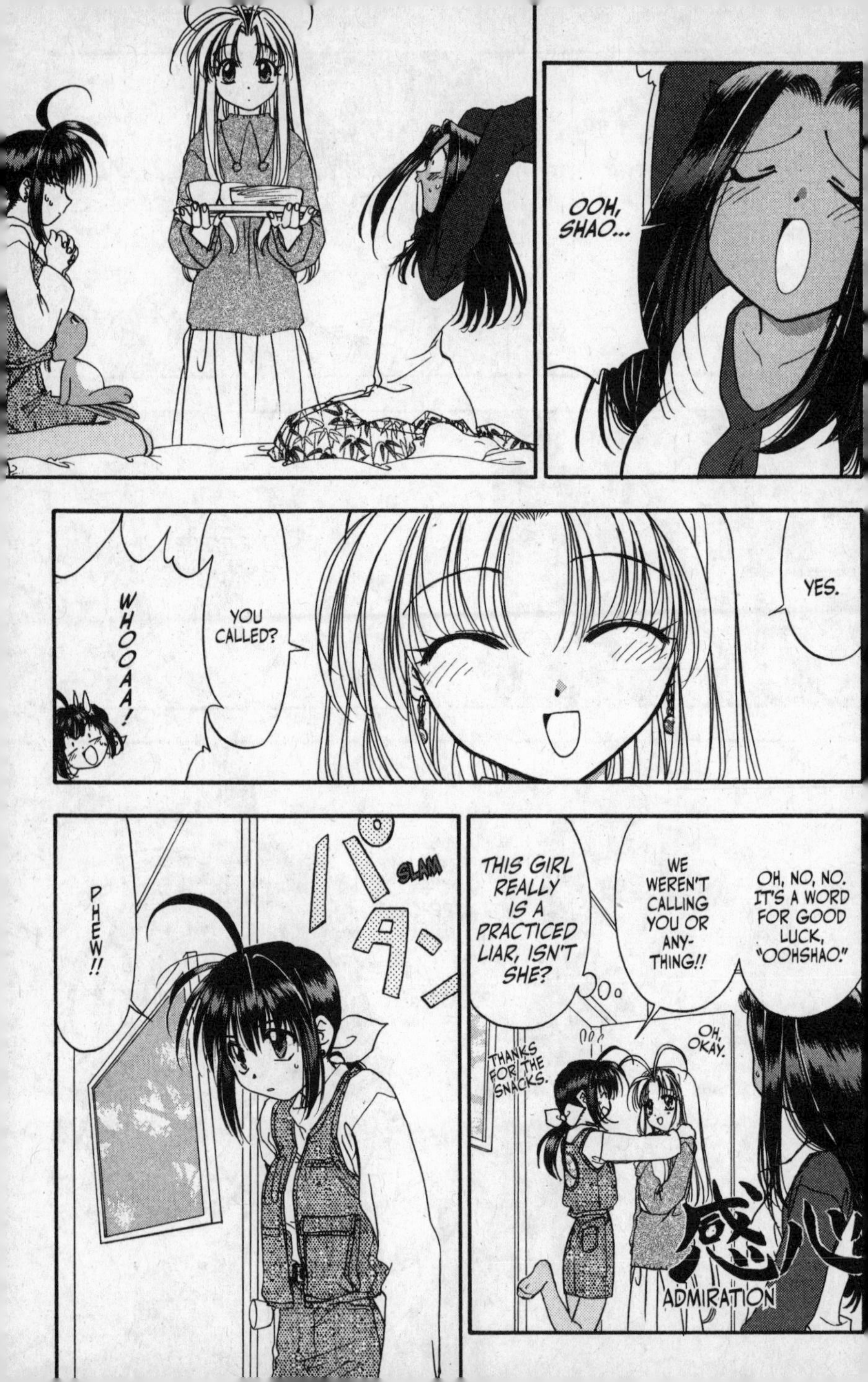
OOH, SHAO...
YES.
YOU CALLED?
WHOOOAA!
OH, NO, NO. IT'S A WORD FOR GOOD LUCK, "OOHSHAO."
WE WEREN'T CALLING YOU OR ANY-THING!!
THIS GIRL REALLY IS A PRACTICED LIAR, ISN'T SHE?
OH, OKAY.
THANKS FOR THE SNACKS.
感心
ADMIRATION
パタン
SLAM
PHEW!!

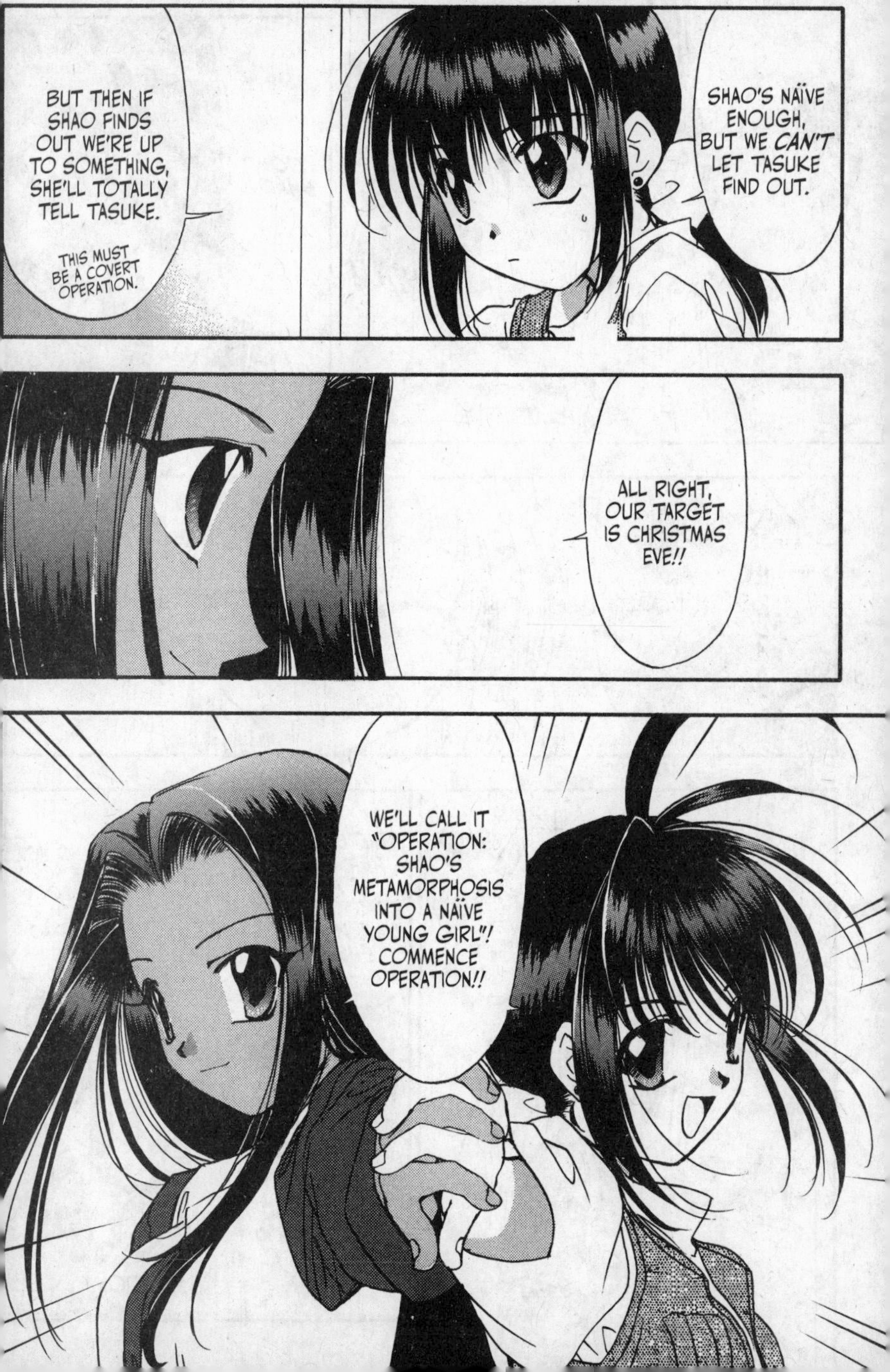
SHAO'S NAÏVE ENOUGH, BUT WE *CAN'T* LET TASUKE FIND OUT.
BUT THEN IF SHAO FINDS OUT WE'RE UP TO SOMETHING, SHE'LL TOTALLY TELL TASUKE.
THIS MUST BE A COVERT OPERATION.
ALL RIGHT, OUR TARGET IS CHRISTMAS EVE!!
WE'LL CALL IT "OPERATION: SHAO'S METAMORPHOSIS INTO A NAÏVE YOUNG GIRL"! COMMENCE OPERATION!!

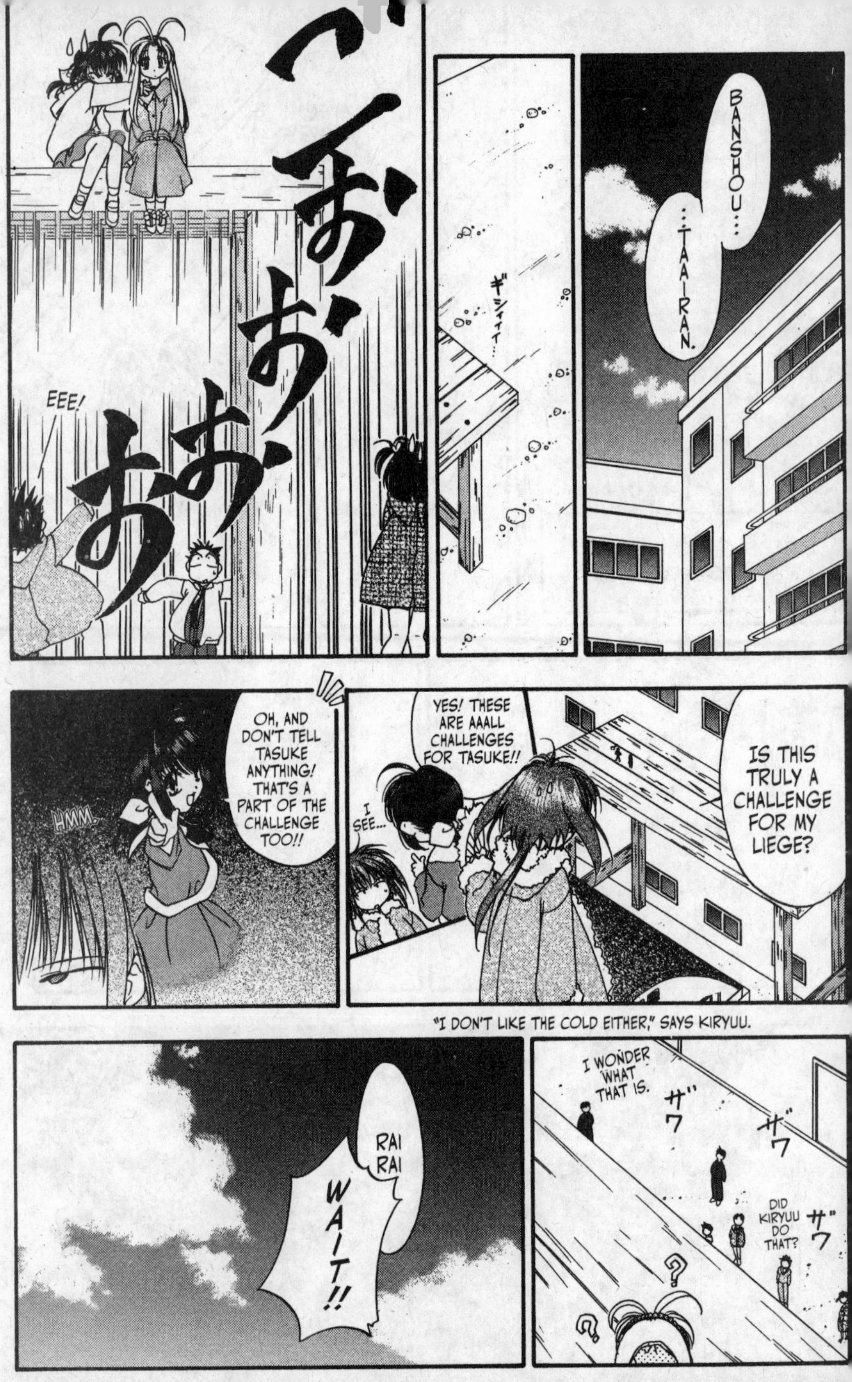
BANSHOU...
...TAAIRAN.
ギシィィィ...
EEE!
IS THIS TRULY A CHALLENGE FOR MY LIEGE?
YES! THESE ARE AAALL CHALLENGES FOR TASUKE!!
I SEE...
OH, AND DON'T TELL TASUKE ANYTHING! THAT'S A PART OF THE CHALLENGE TOO!!
HMM.
"I DON'T LIKE THE COLD EITHER," SAYS KIRYUU.
I WONDER WHAT THAT IS.
ザワ
ザワ
DID KIRYUU DO THAT?
ザワ
RAI RAI
WAIT!!

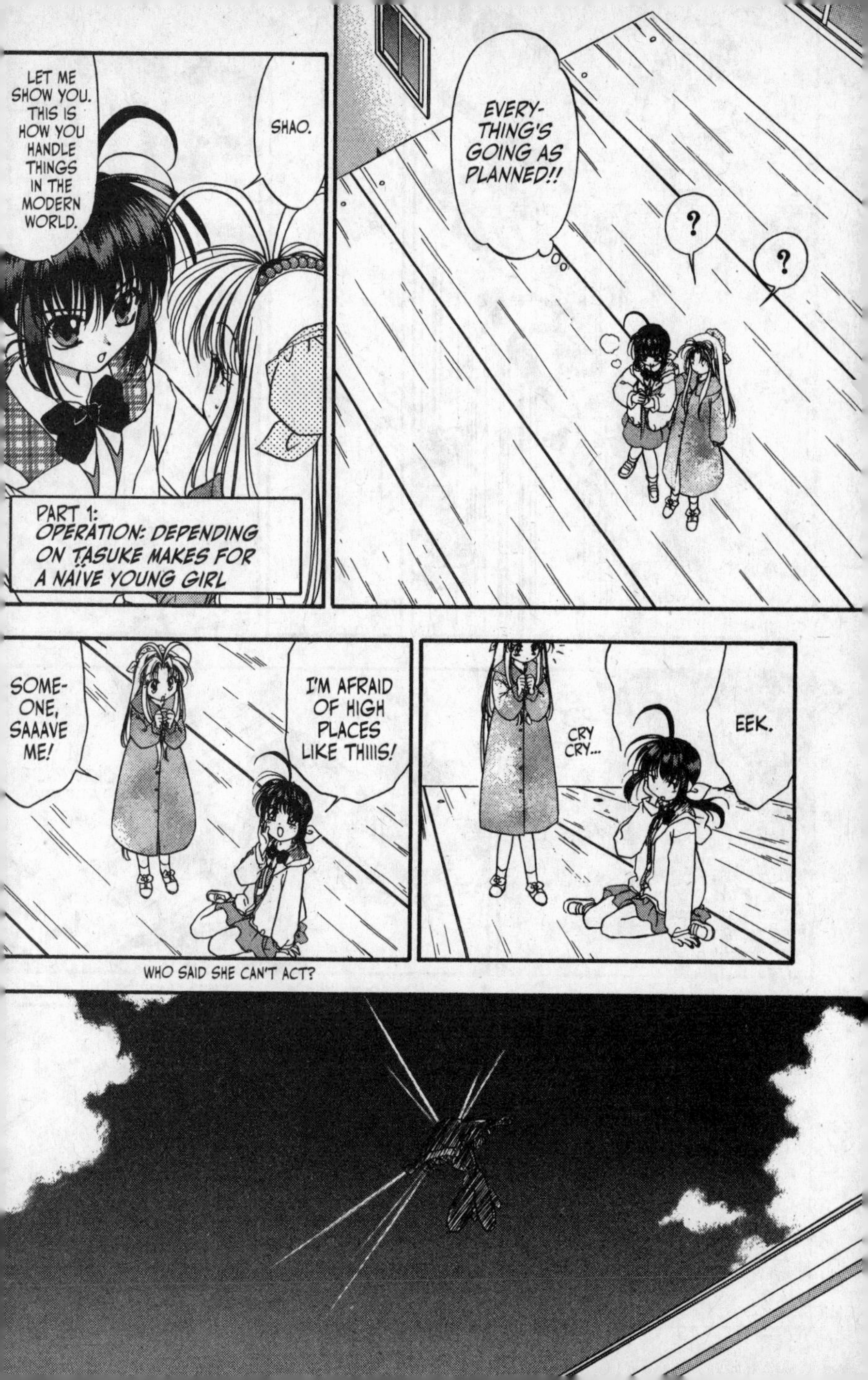
EVERY-THING'S GOING AS PLANNED!!
?
?
SHAO.
LET ME SHOW YOU. THIS IS HOW YOU HANDLE THINGS IN THE MODERN WORLD.
PART 1: OPERATION: DEPENDING ON TASUKE MAKES FOR A NAÏVE YOUNG GIRL
EEK.
CRY CRY...
I'M AFRAID OF HIGH PLACES LIKE THIIIS!
SOME-ONE, SAAAVE ME!
WHO SAID SHE CAN'T ACT?

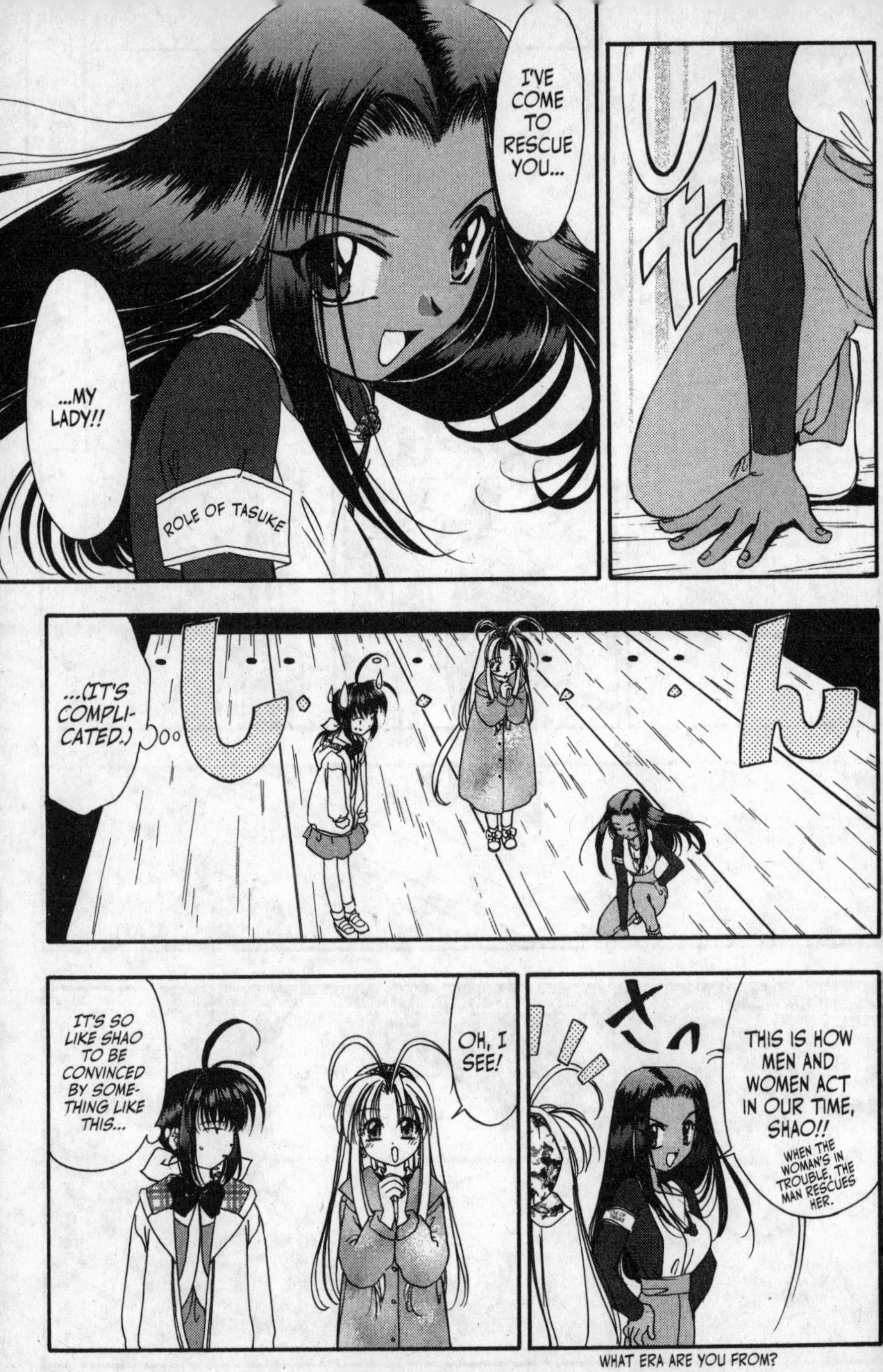
I'VE COME TO RESCUE YOU...
...MY LADY!!
ROLE OF TASUKE
...(IT'S COMPLICATED.)
THIS IS HOW MEN AND WOMEN ACT IN OUR TIME, SHAO!!
WHEN THE WOMAN'S IN TROUBLE, THE MAN RESCUES HER.
OH, I SEE!
IT'S SO LIKE SHAO TO BE CONVINCED BY SOMETHING LIKE THIS...
WHAT ERA ARE YOU FROM?

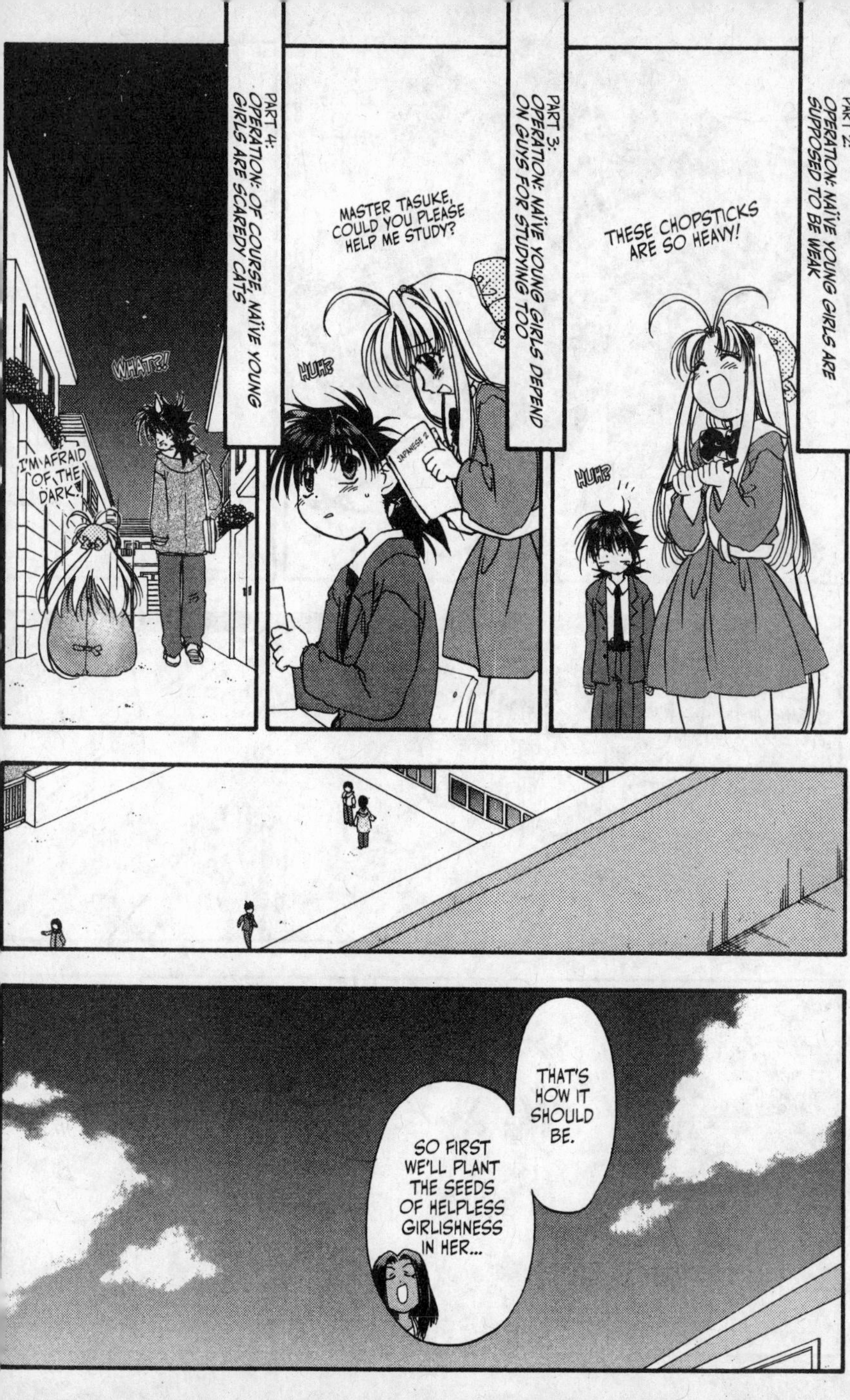
PART 2:
OPERATION: NAÏVE YOUNG GIRLS ARE SUPPOSED TO BE WEAK
THESE CHOPSTICKS ARE SO HEAVY!
HUH?
PART 3:
OPERATION: NAÏVE YOUNG GIRLS DEPEND ON GUYS FOR STUDYING TOO
MASTER TASUKE, COULD YOU PLEASE HELP ME STUDY?
JAPANESE 2
HUH?
PART 4:
OPERATION: OF COURSE, NAÏVE YOUNG GIRLS ARE SCAREDY CATS
WHAT?!
I'M AFRAID OF THE DARK!
THAT'S HOW IT SHOULD BE.
SO FIRST WE'LL PLANT THE SEEDS OF HELPLESS GIRLISHNESS IN HER...

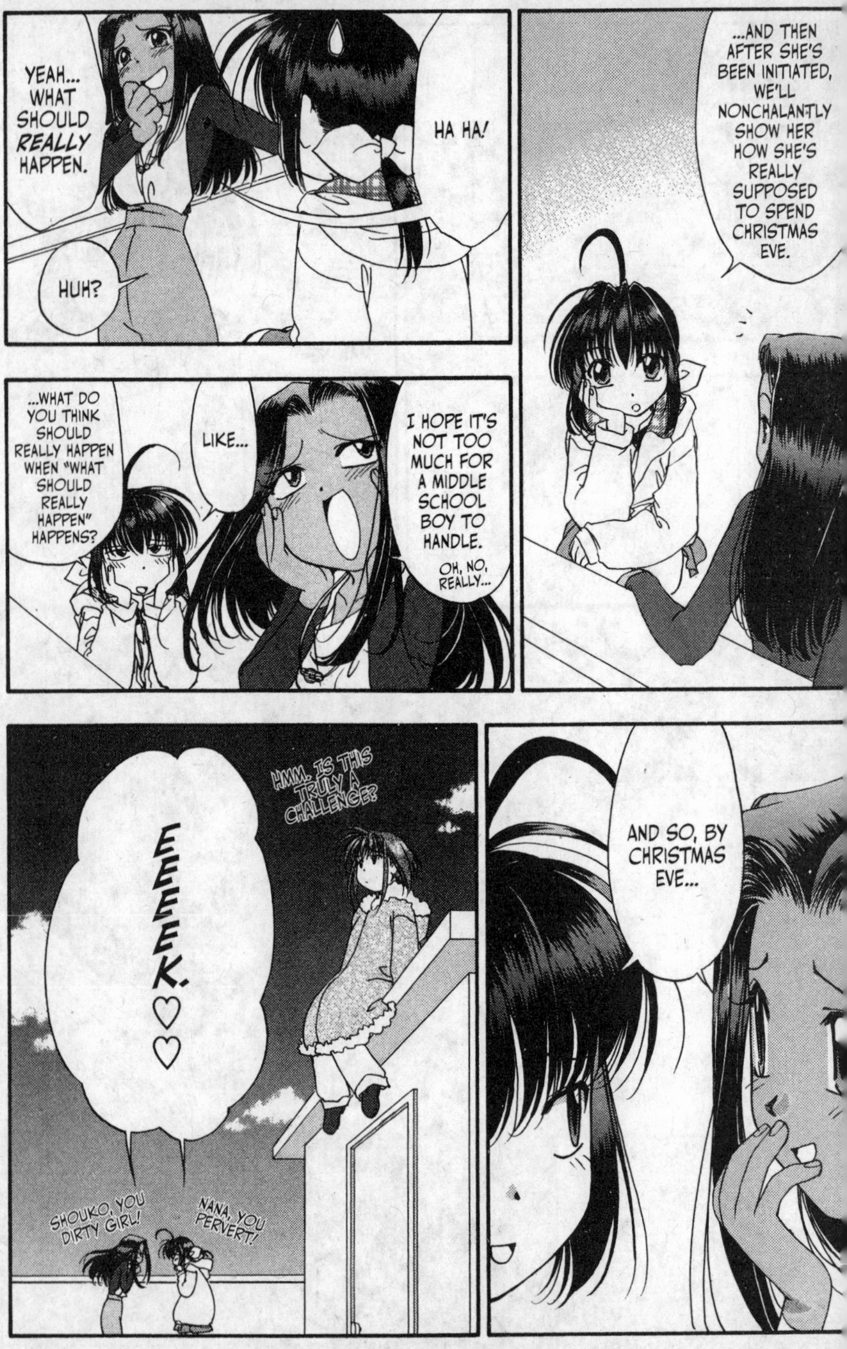
...AND THEN AFTER SHE'S BEEN INITIATED, WE'LL NONCHALANTLY SHOW HER HOW SHE'S REALLY SUPPOSED TO SPEND CHRISTMAS EVE.
YEAH... WHAT SHOULD *REALLY* HAPPEN.
HA HA!
HUH?
I HOPE IT'S NOT TOO MUCH FOR A MIDDLE SCHOOL BOY TO HANDLE.
OH, NO, REALLY...
LIKE...
...WHAT DO YOU THINK SHOULD REALLY HAPPEN WHEN "WHAT SHOULD REALLY HAPPEN" HAPPENS?
AND SO, BY CHRISTMAS EVE...
HMM. IS THIS TRULY A CHALLENGE?
EEEEK. ♡ ♡
NANA, YOU PERVERT!
SHOUKO, YOU DIRTY GIRL!

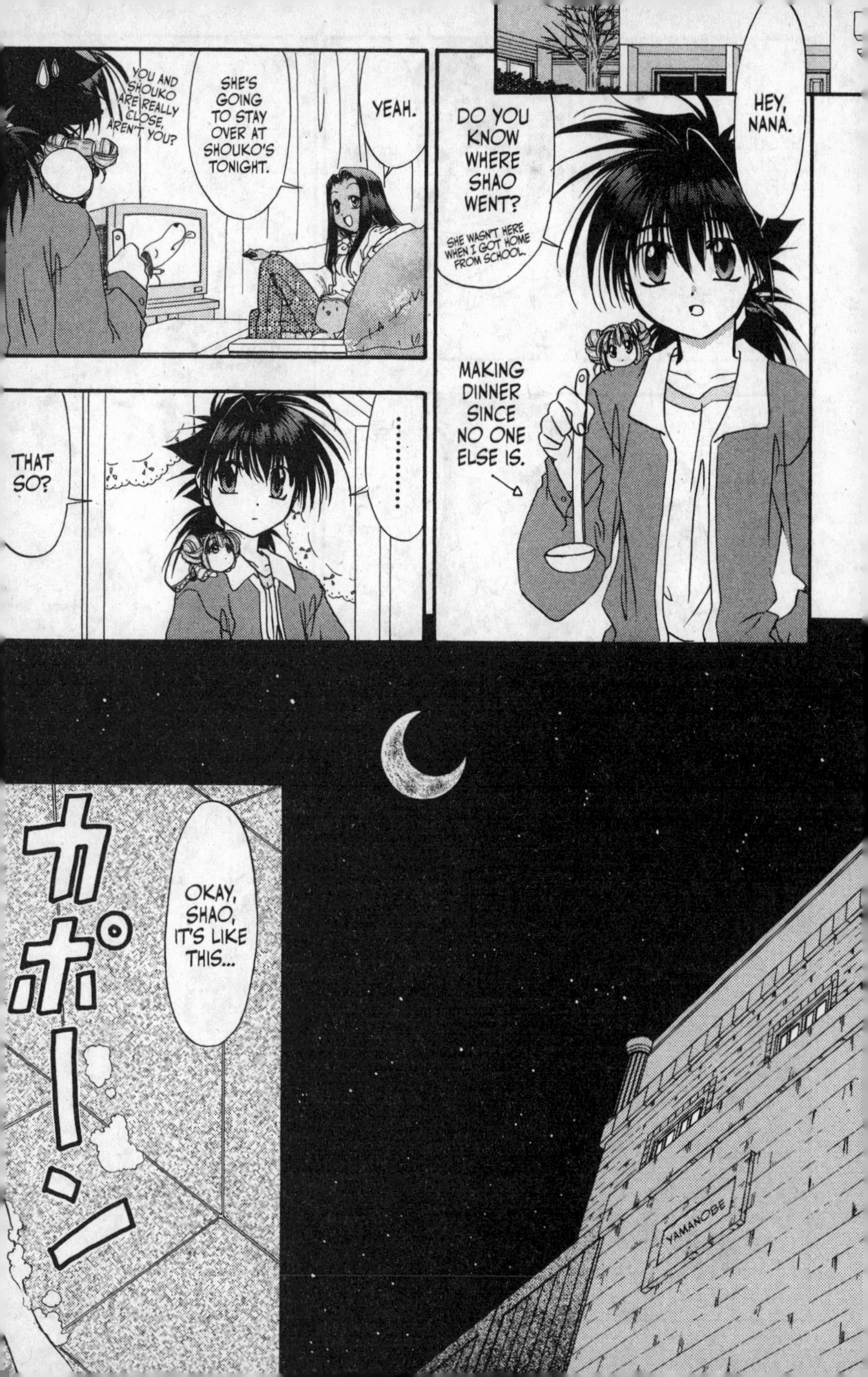
HEY, NANA.
DO YOU KNOW WHERE SHAO WENT?
SHE WASN'T HERE WHEN I GOT HOME FROM SCHOOL.
MAKING DINNER SINCE NO ONE ELSE IS.
YEAH.
SHE'S GOING TO STAY OVER AT SHOUKO'S TONIGHT.
YOU AND SHOUKO ARE REALLY CLOSE, AREN'T YOU?
......
THAT SO?
YAMANOBE
OKAY, SHAO, IT'S LIKE THIS...
カポーン

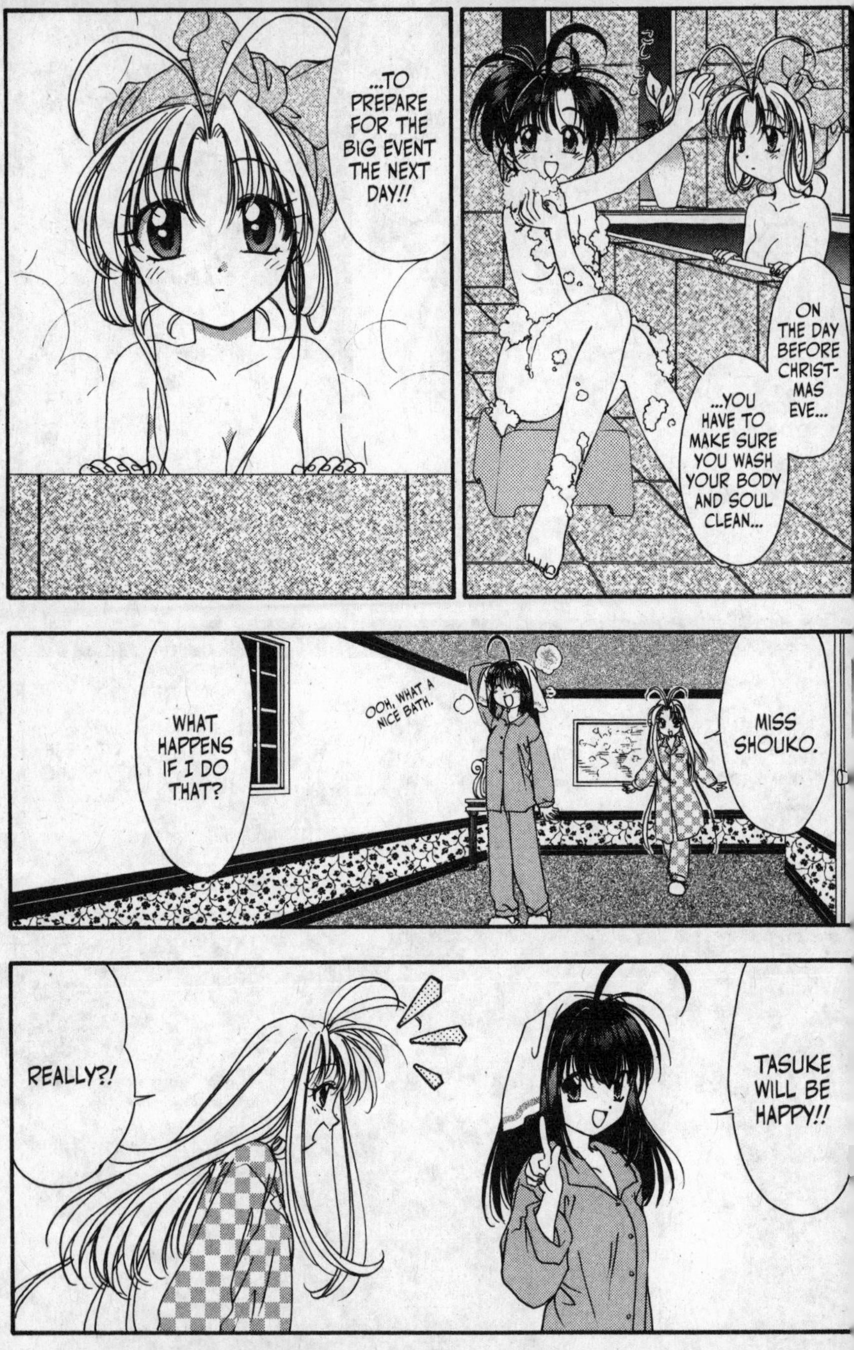
ON THE DAY BEFORE CHRISTMAS EVE...
...YOU HAVE TO MAKE SURE YOU WASH YOUR BODY AND SOUL CLEAN...
...TO PREPARE FOR THE BIG EVENT THE NEXT DAY!!
MISS SHOUKO.
OOH, WHAT A NICE BATH.
WHAT HAPPENS IF I DO THAT?
TASUKE WILL BE HAPPY!!
REALLY?!

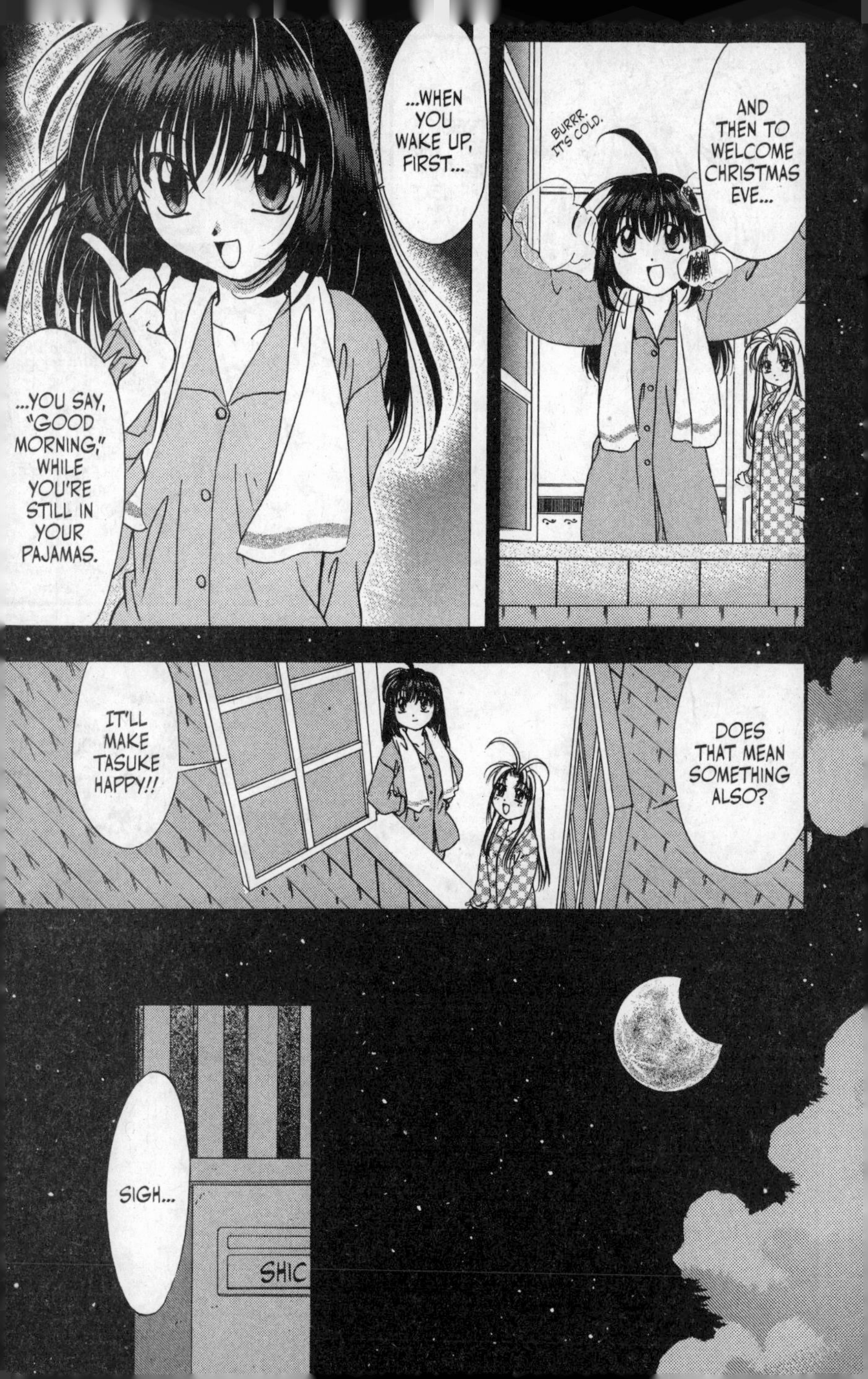
AND THEN TO WELCOME CHRISTMAS EVE...
BURRR. IT'S COLD.
...WHEN YOU WAKE UP, FIRST...
...YOU SAY, "GOOD MORNING," WHILE YOU'RE STILL IN YOUR PAJAMAS.
DOES THAT MEAN SOMETHING ALSO?
IT'LL MAKE TASUKE HAPPY!!
SIGH...
SHIC

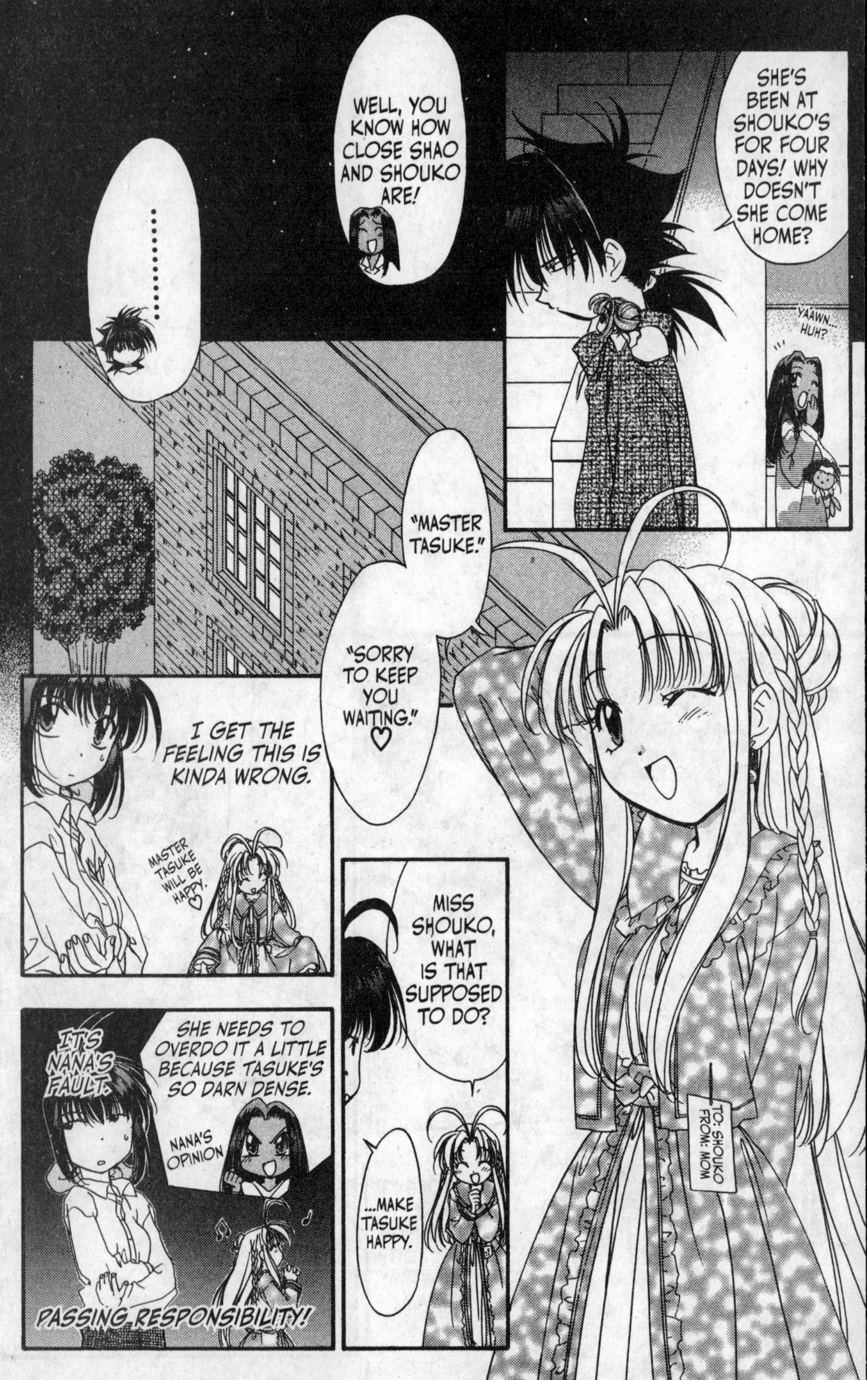
SHE'S BEEN AT SHOUKO'S FOR FOUR DAYS! WHY DOESN'T SHE COME HOME?
YAAWN... HUH?
WELL, YOU KNOW HOW CLOSE SHAO AND SHOUKO ARE!
......
"MASTER TASUKE."
"SORRY TO KEEP YOU WAITING." ♡
TO: SHOUKO FROM: MOM
I GET THE FEELING THIS IS KINDA WRONG.
MASTER TASUKE WILL BE HAPPY. ♡
MISS SHOUKO, WHAT IS THAT SUPPOSED TO DO?
...MAKE TASUKE HAPPY.
SHE NEEDS TO OVERDO IT A LITTLE BECAUSE TASUKE'S SO DARN DENSE.
NANA'S OPINION
IT'S NANA'S FAULT.
PASSING RESPONSIBILITY!

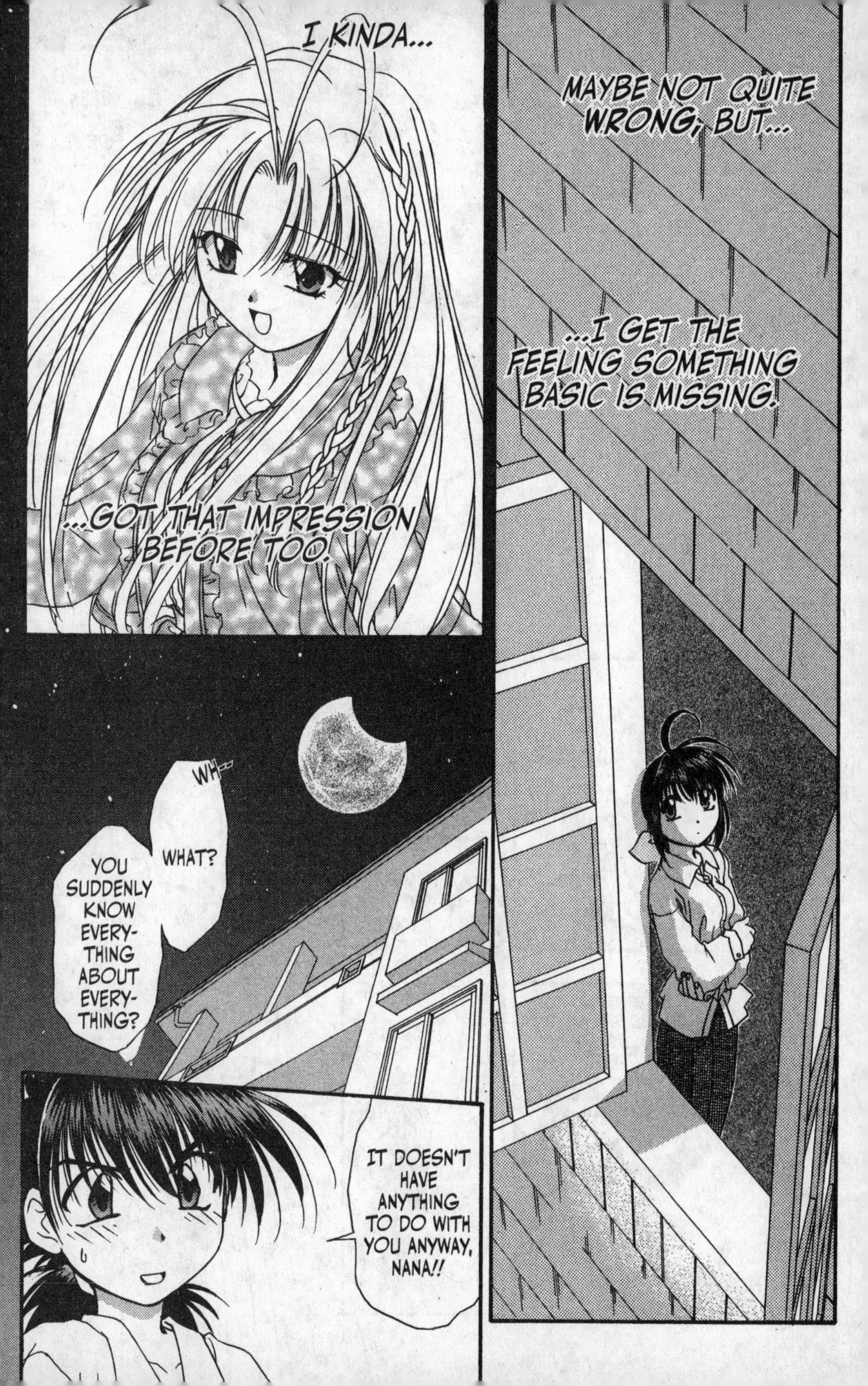
MAYBE NOT QUITE WRONG, BUT...
...I GET THE FEELING SOMETHING BASIC IS MISSING.
I KINDA...
...GOT THAT IMPRESSION BEFORE TOO.
WH--
WHAT?
YOU SUDDENLY KNOW EVERY-THING ABOUT EVERY-THING?
IT DOESN'T HAVE ANYTHING TO DO WITH YOU ANYWAY, NANA!!

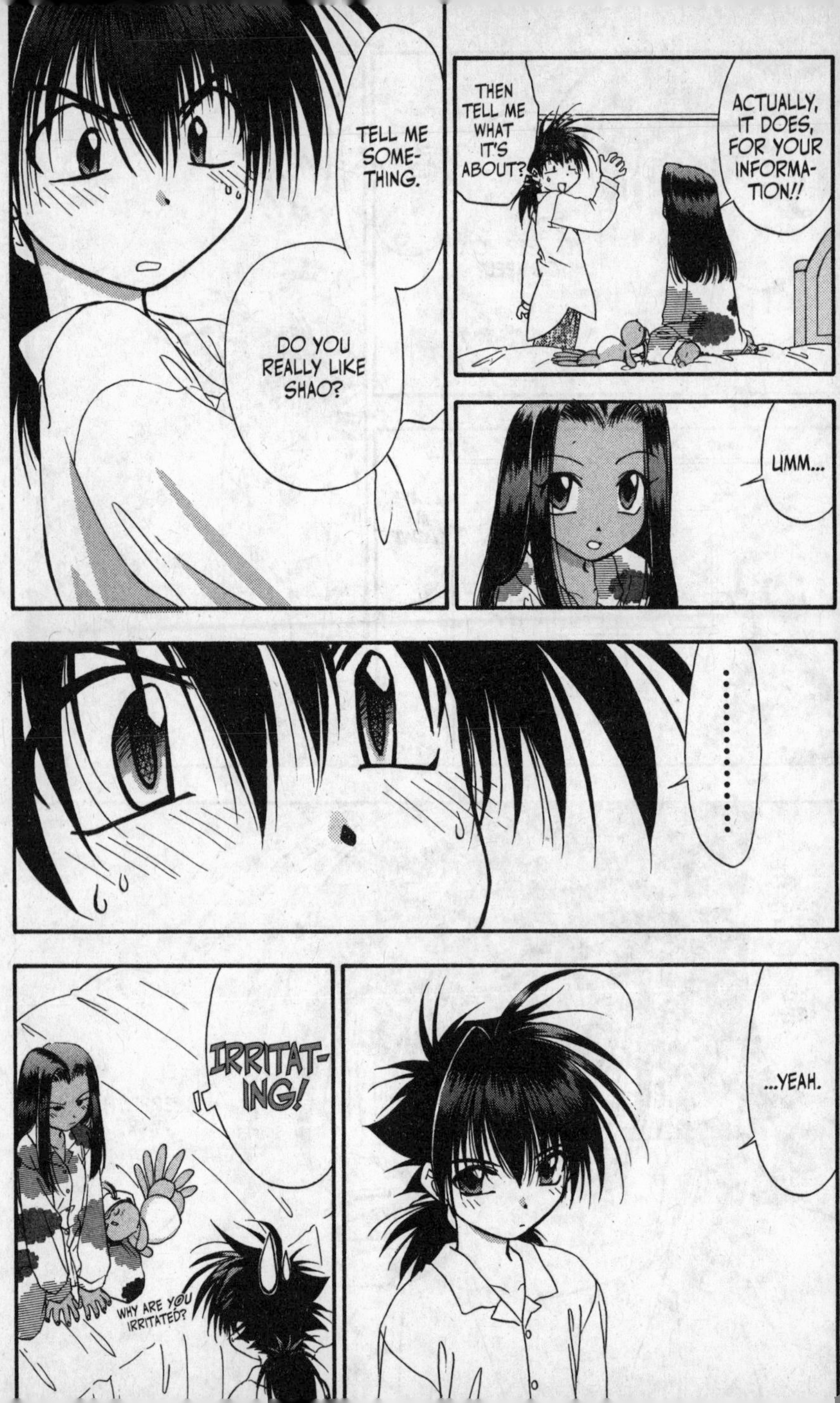
ACTUALLY, IT DOES, FOR YOUR INFORMATION!!
THEN TELL ME WHAT IT'S ABOUT?
UMM...
TELL ME SOMETHING.
DO YOU REALLY LIKE SHAO?
......
...YEAH.
IRRITATING!
WHY ARE YOU IRRITATED?

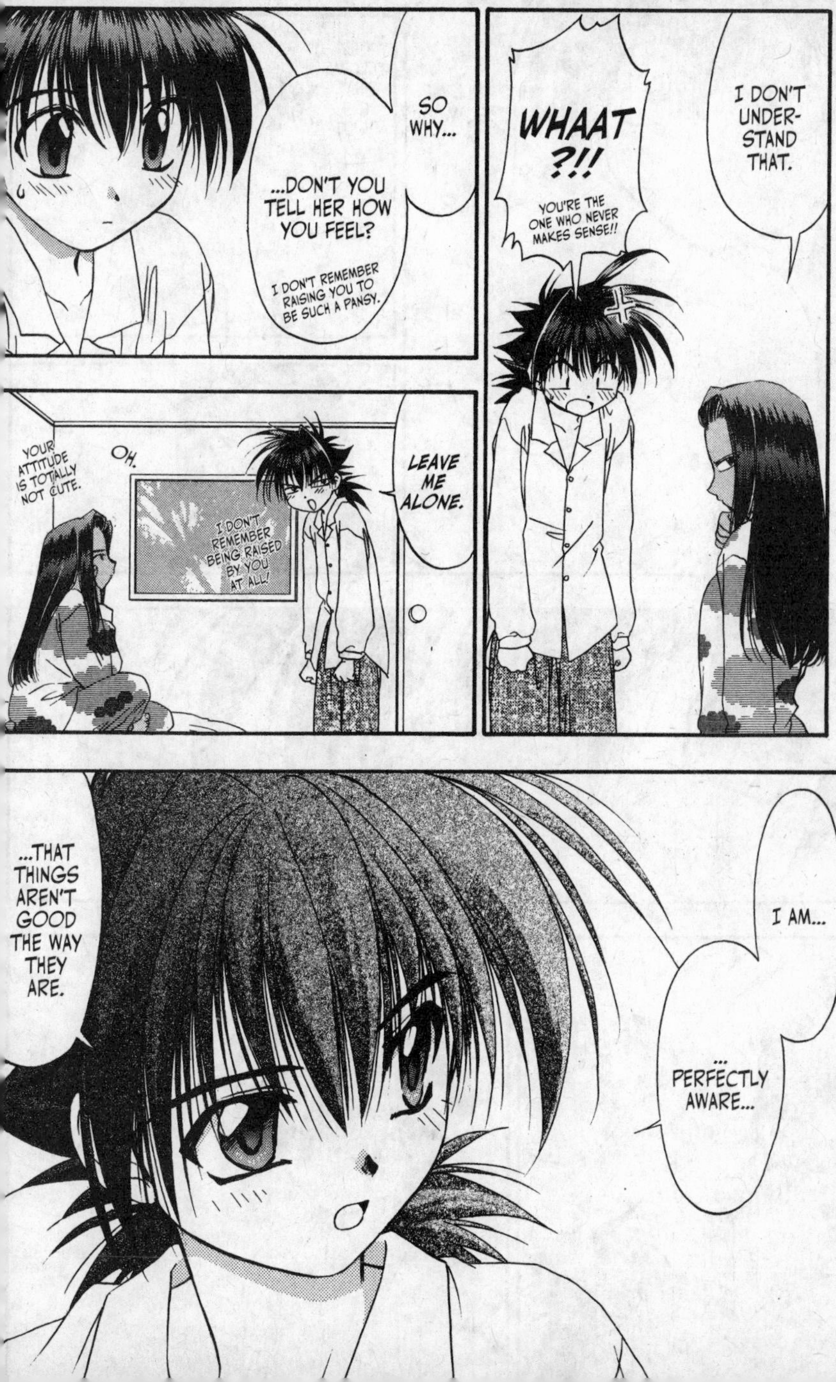
I DON'T UNDER-STAND THAT.
WHAAT ?!!
YOU'RE THE ONE WHO NEVER MAKES SENSE!!
SO WHY...
...DON'T YOU TELL HER HOW YOU FEEL?
I DON'T REMEMBER RAISING YOU TO BE SUCH A PANSY.
LEAVE ME ALONE.
I DON'T REMEMBER BEING RAISED BY YOU AT ALL!
OH.
YOUR ATTITUDE IS TOTALLY NOT CUTE.
I AM...
... PERFECTLY AWARE...
...THAT THINGS AREN'T GOOD THE WAY THEY ARE.

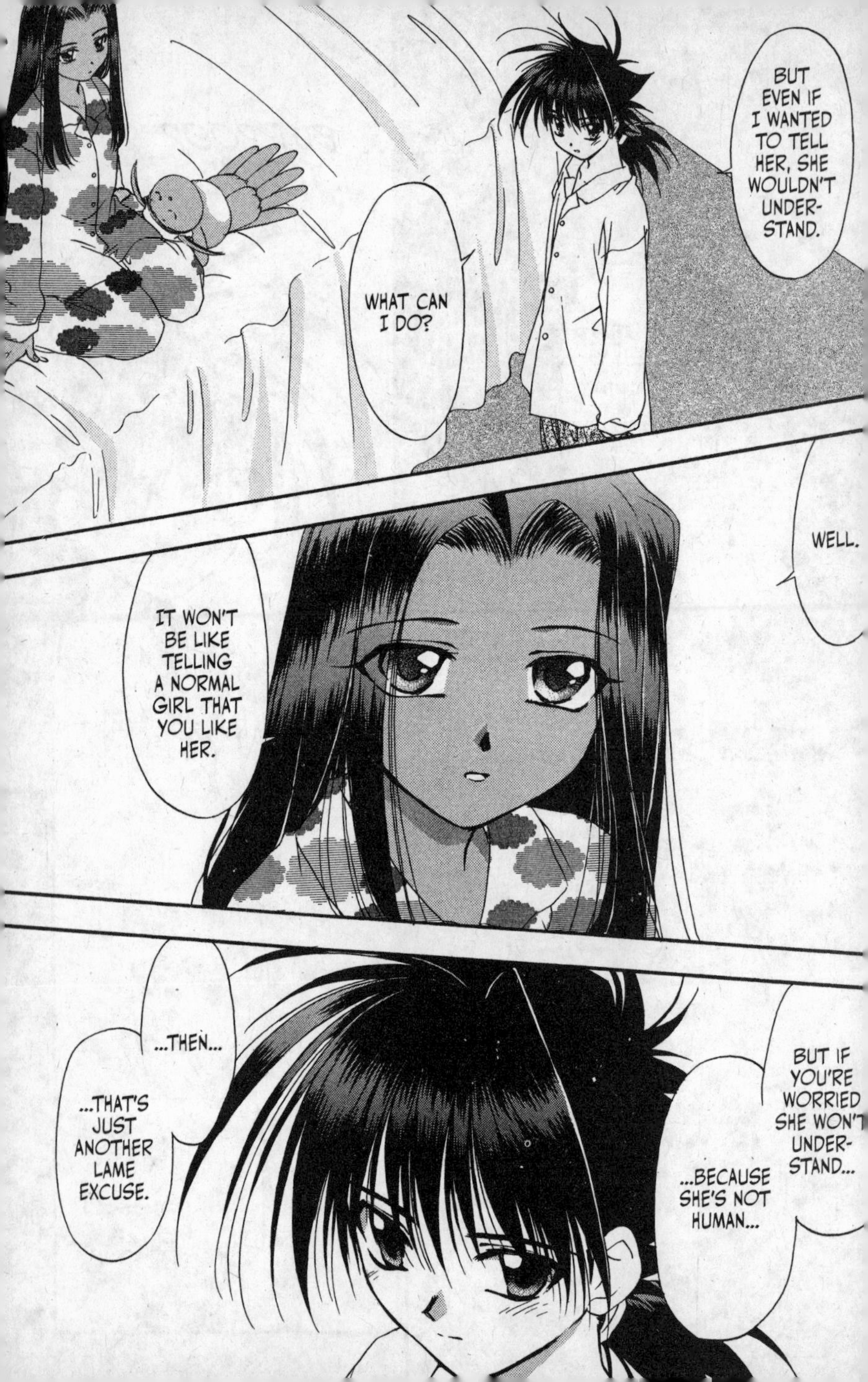
BUT EVEN IF I WANTED TO TELL HER, SHE WOULDN'T UNDER-STAND.
WHAT CAN I DO?
WELL.
IT WON'T BE LIKE TELLING A NORMAL GIRL THAT YOU LIKE HER.
BUT IF YOU'RE WORRIED SHE WON'T UNDER-STAND...
...BECAUSE SHE'S NOT HUMAN...
...THEN...
...THAT'S JUST ANOTHER LAME EXCUSE.

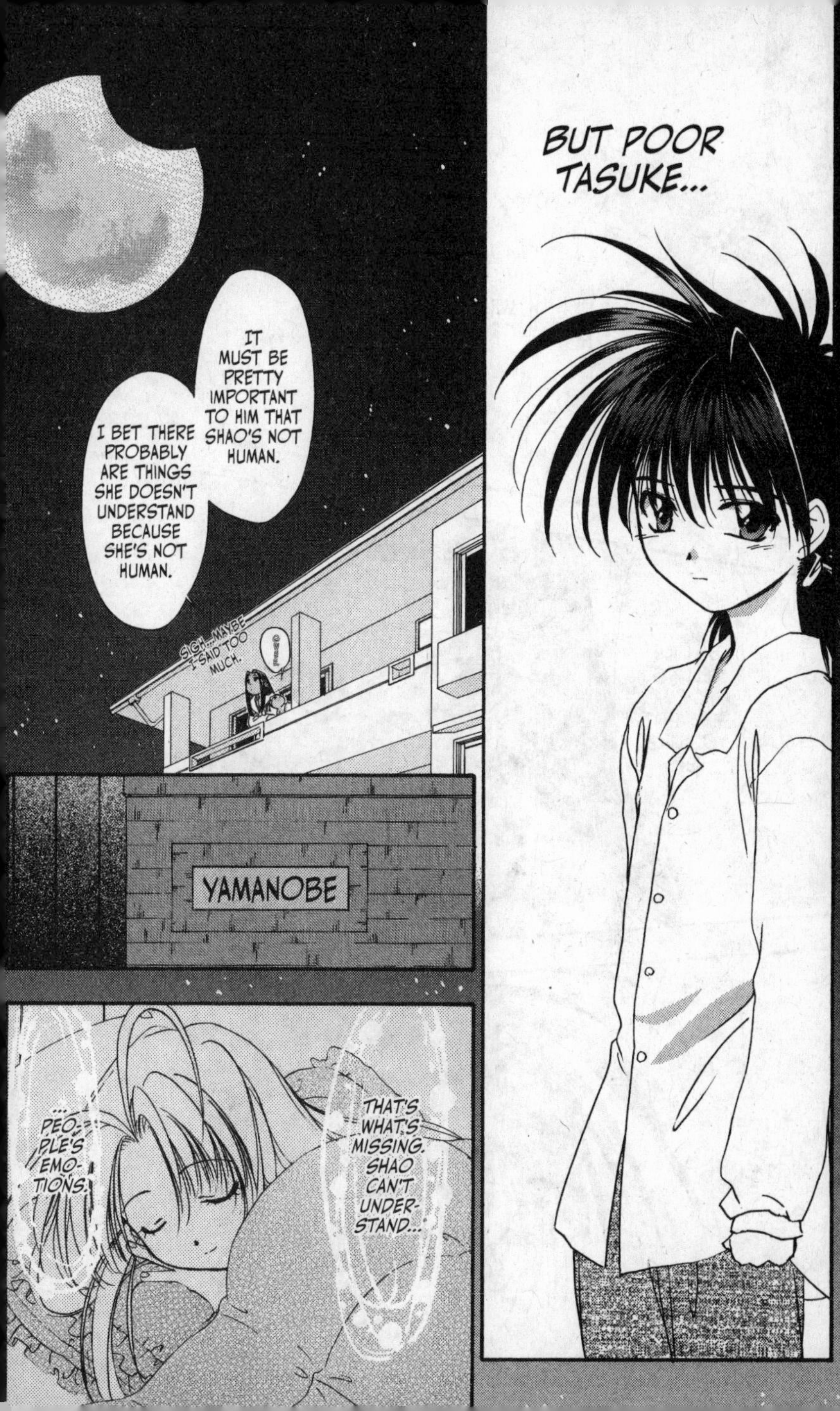
BUT POOR TASUKE...
IT MUST BE PRETTY IMPORTANT TO HIM THAT SHAO'S NOT HUMAN.
I BET THERE PROBABLY ARE THINGS SHE DOESN'T UNDERSTAND BECAUSE SHE'S NOT HUMAN.
SIGH... MAYBE I SAID TOO MUCH.
YAMANOBE
THAT'S WHAT'S MISSING. SHAO CAN'T UNDERSTAND...
...PEOPLE'S EMOTIONS.

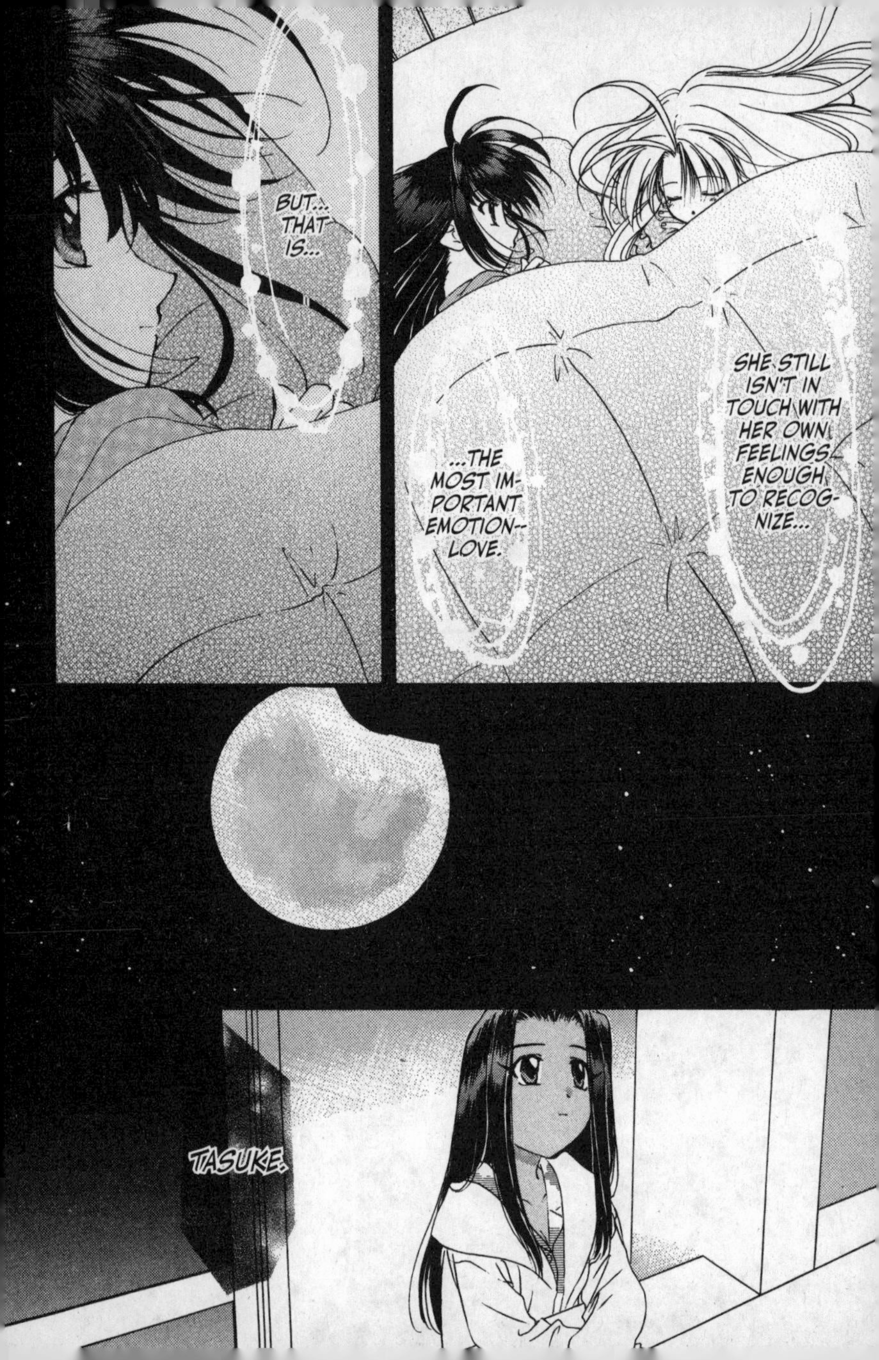
SHE STILL ISN'T IN TOUCH WITH HER OWN FEELINGS ENOUGH TO RECOG-NIZE...
...THE MOST IM-PORTANT EMOTION--LOVE.
BUT... THAT IS...
TASUKE.

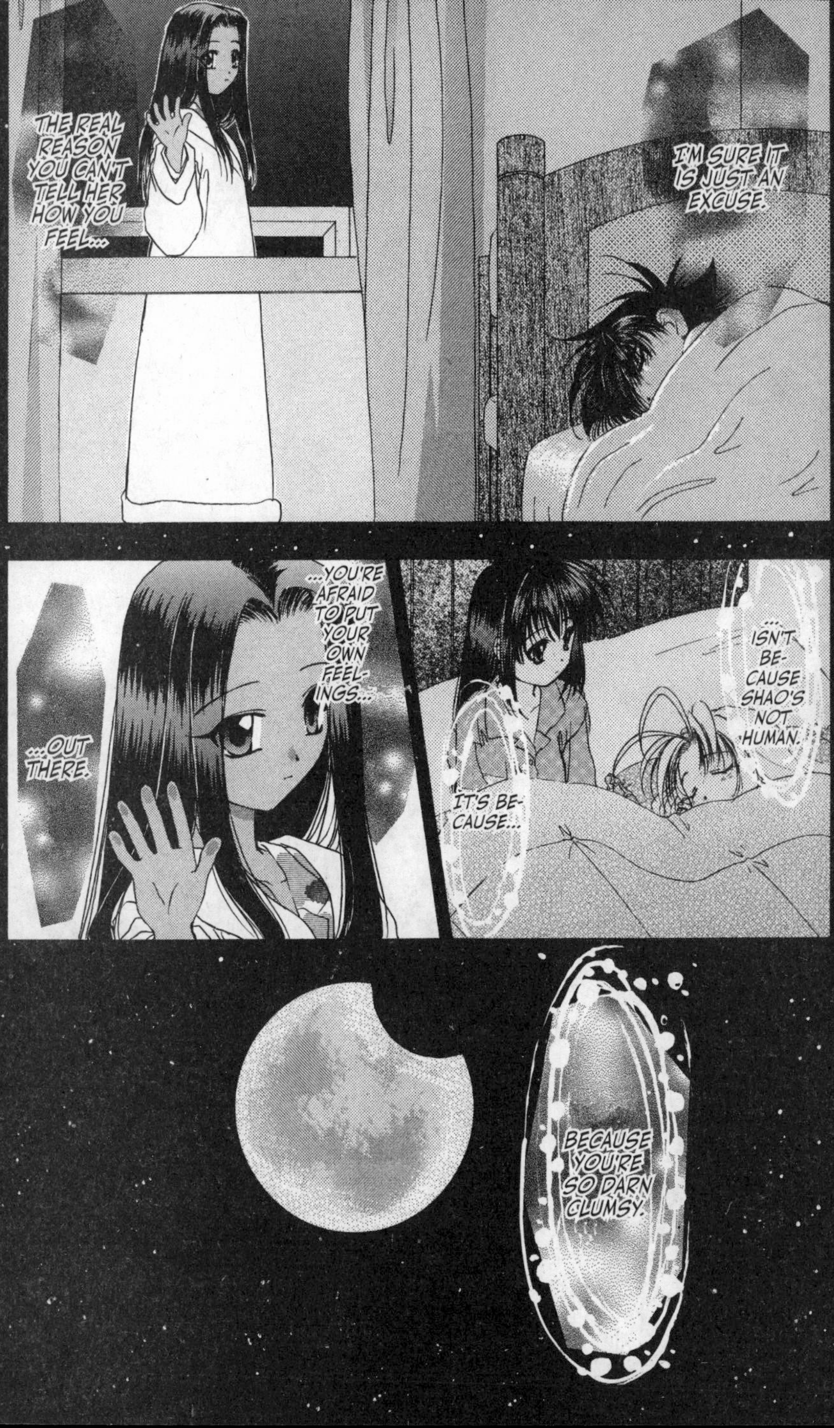
I'M SURE IT IS JUST AN EXCUSE.
THE REAL REASON YOU CAN'T TELL HER HOW YOU FEEL...
...ISN'T BECAUSE SHAO'S NOT HUMAN.
IT'S BECAUSE...
...YOU'RE AFRAID TO PUT YOUR OWN FEELINGS...
...OUT THERE.
BECAUSE YOU'RE SO DARN CLUMSY.

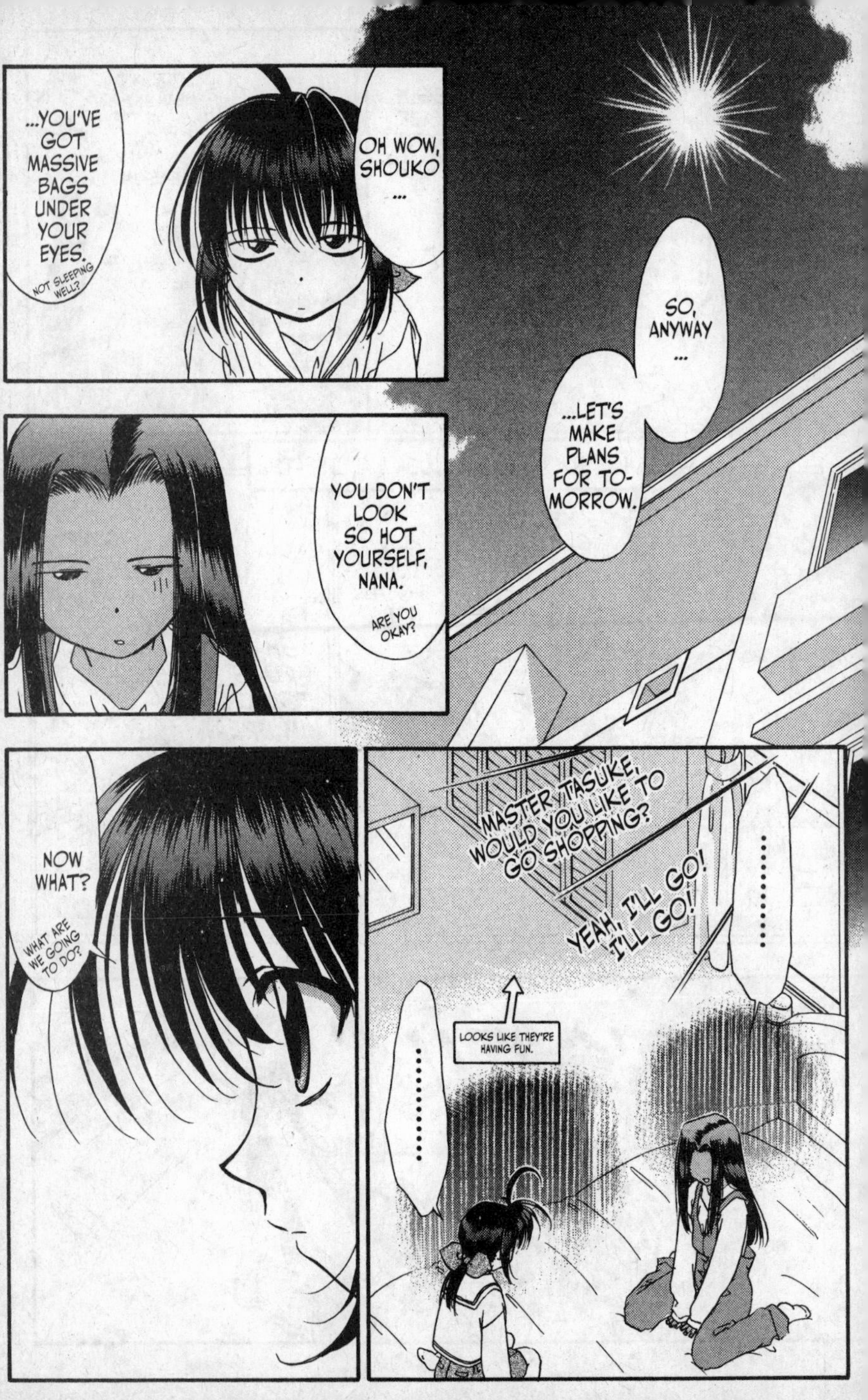
OH WOW, SHOUKO ...
...YOU'VE GOT MASSIVE BAGS UNDER YOUR EYES.
NOT SLEEPING WELL?
YOU DON'T LOOK SO HOT YOURSELF, NANA.
ARE YOU OKAY?
SO, ANYWAY ...
...LET'S MAKE PLANS FOR TO-MORROW.
MASTER TASUKE, WOULD YOU LIKE TO GO SHOPPING?
YEAH, I'LL GO! I'LL GO!
......
......
LOOKS LIKE THEY'RE HAVING FUN.
NOW WHAT?
WHAT ARE WE GOING TO DO?

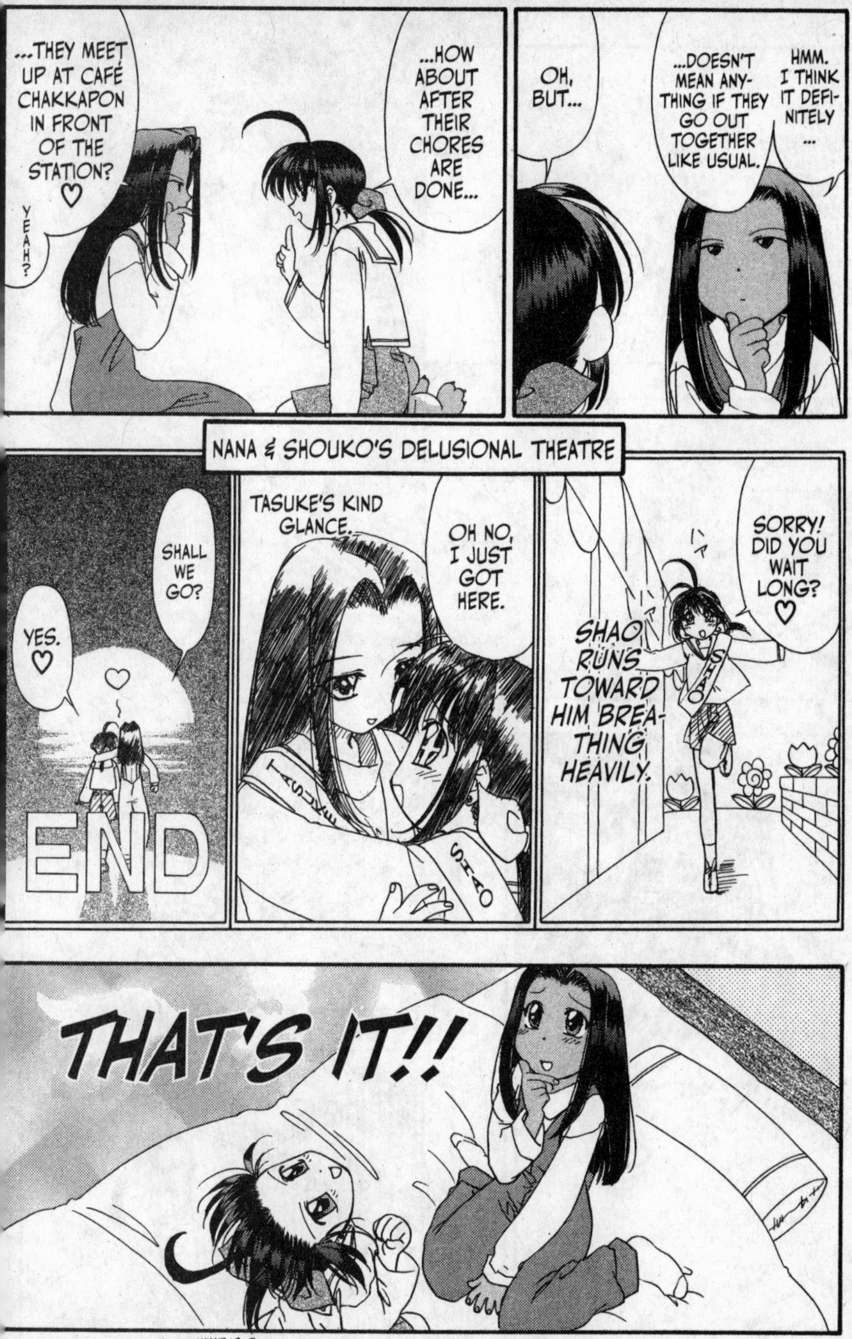
HMM. I THINK IT DEFINITELY...
...DOESN'T MEAN ANYTHING IF THEY GO OUT TOGETHER LIKE USUAL.
OH, BUT...
...HOW ABOUT AFTER THEIR CHORES ARE DONE...
...THEY MEET UP AT CAFÉ CHAKKAPON IN FRONT OF THE STATION? ♡
YEAH?
NANA & SHOUKO'S DELUSIONAL THEATRE
SORRY! DID YOU WAIT LONG? ♡
SHAO RUNS TOWARD HIM BREATHING HEAVILY.
SHAO
TASUKE'S KIND GLANCE.
OH NO, I JUST GOT HERE.
TASUKE
SHAO
SHALL WE GO?
YES. ♡
END
THAT'S IT!!

WHAT IS...?

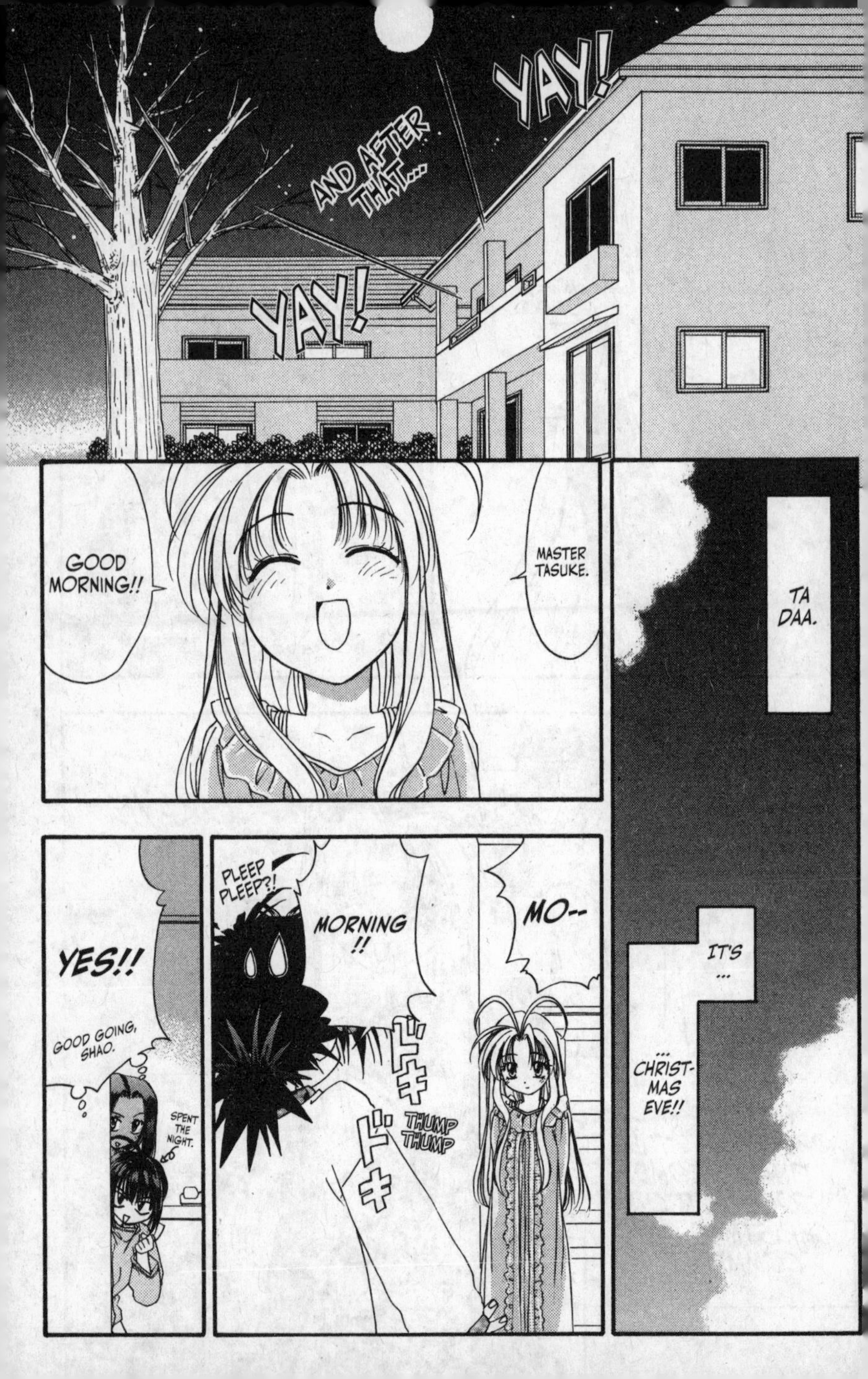

YAY!
AND AFTER THAT...
YAY!
TA DAA.
IT'S ...
... CHRIST-MAS EVE!!
MASTER TASUKE.
GOOD MORNING!!
MO--
MORNING !!
PLEEP PLEEP?!
ドキドキ
THUMP THUMP
YES!!
GOOD GOING, SHAO.
SPENT THE NIGHT.

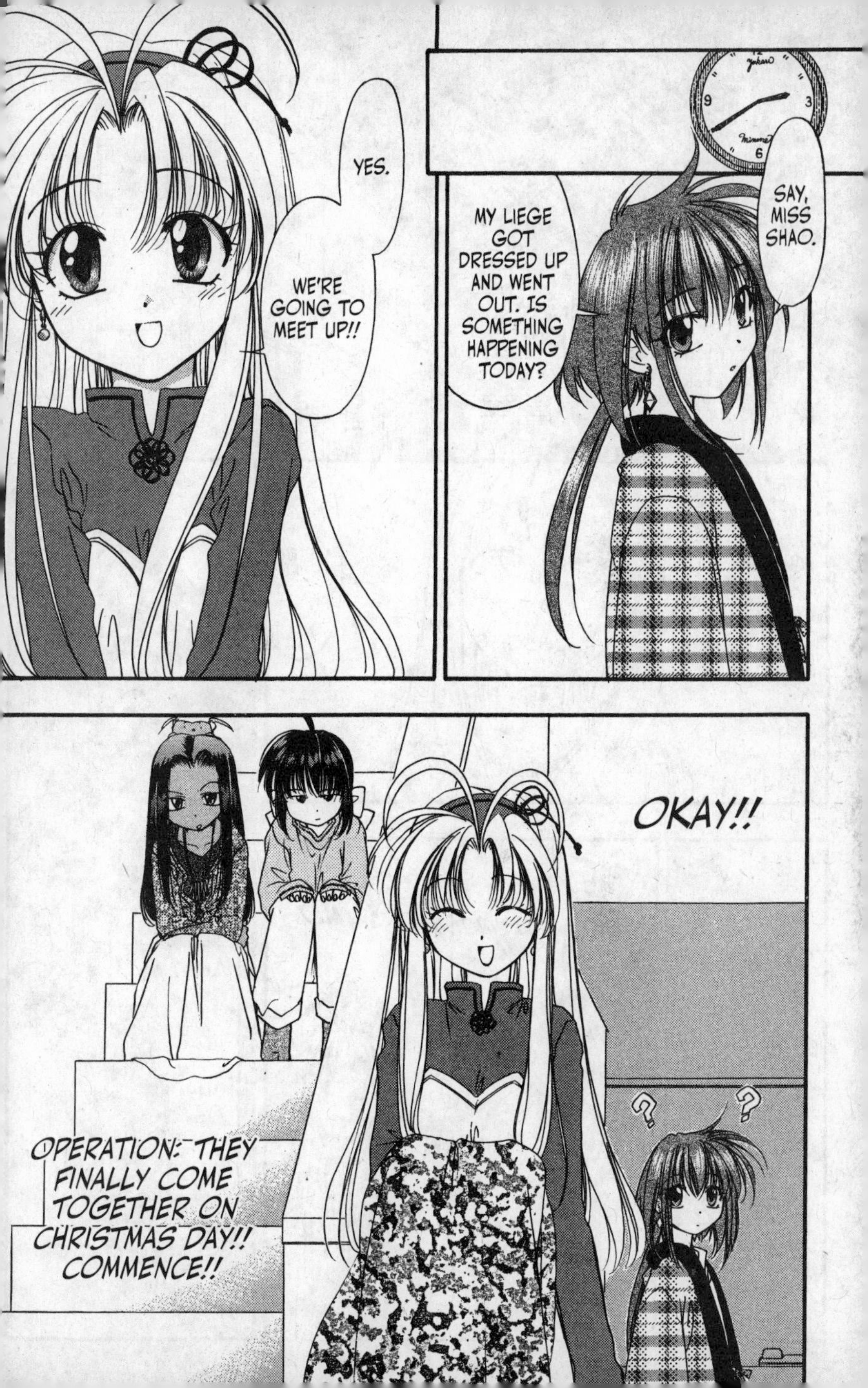
SAY, MISS SHAO.
MY LIEGE GOT DRESSED UP AND WENT OUT. IS SOMETHING HAPPENING TODAY?
YES.
WE'RE GOING TO MEET UP!!
OKAY!!
OPERATION: THEY FINALLY COME TOGETHER ON CHRISTMAS DAY!! COMMENCE!!

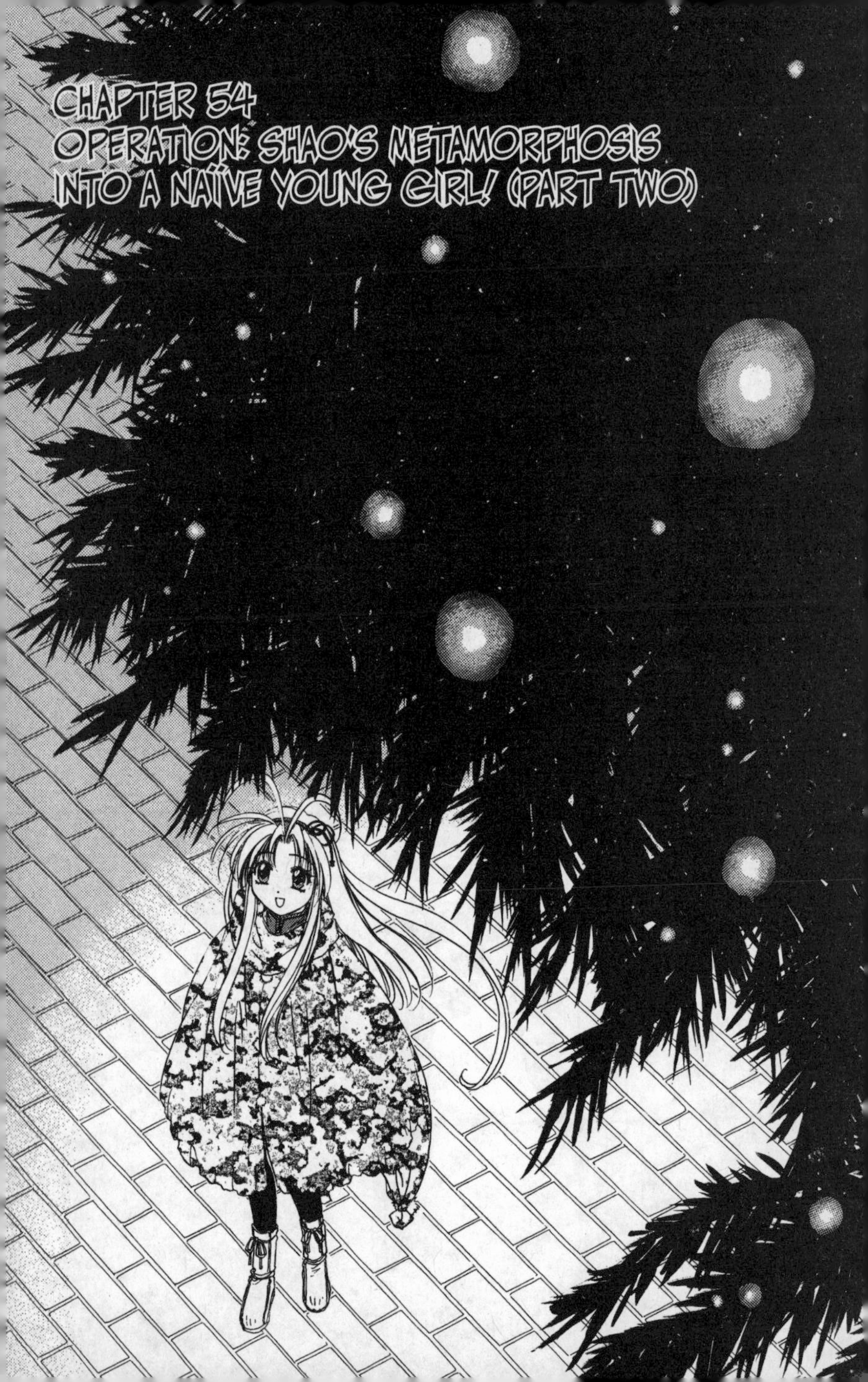
CHAPTER 54
OPERATION: SHAO'S METAMORPHOSIS INTO A NAÏVE YOUNG GIRL! (PART TWO)

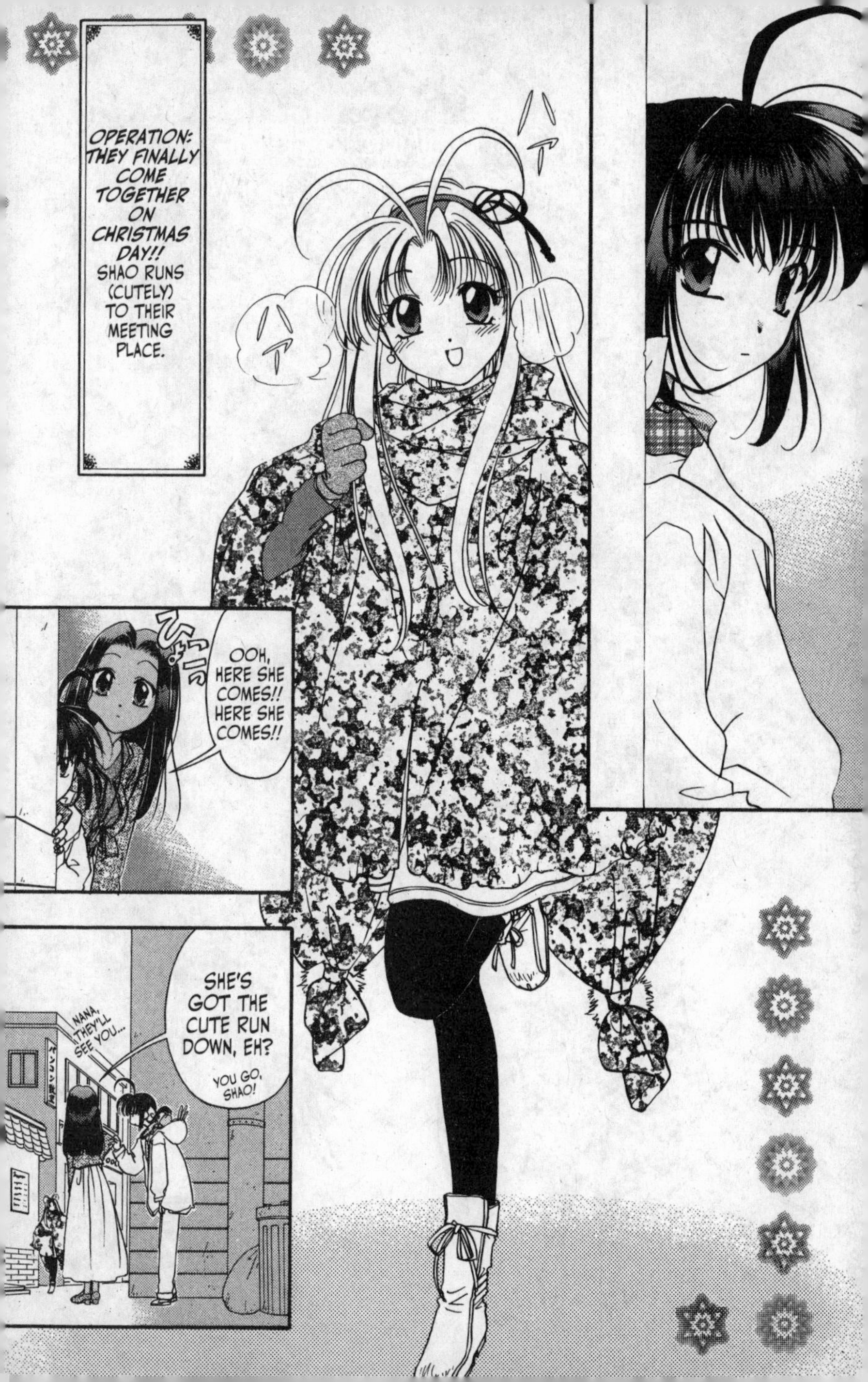
OPERATION: THEY FINALLY COME TOGETHER ON CHRISTMAS DAY!! SHAO RUNS (CUTELY) TO THEIR MEETING PLACE.
OOH, HERE SHE COMES!! HERE SHE COMES!!
SHE'S GOT THE CUTE RUN DOWN, EH?
YOU GO, SHAO!
NANA, THEY'LL SEE YOU...

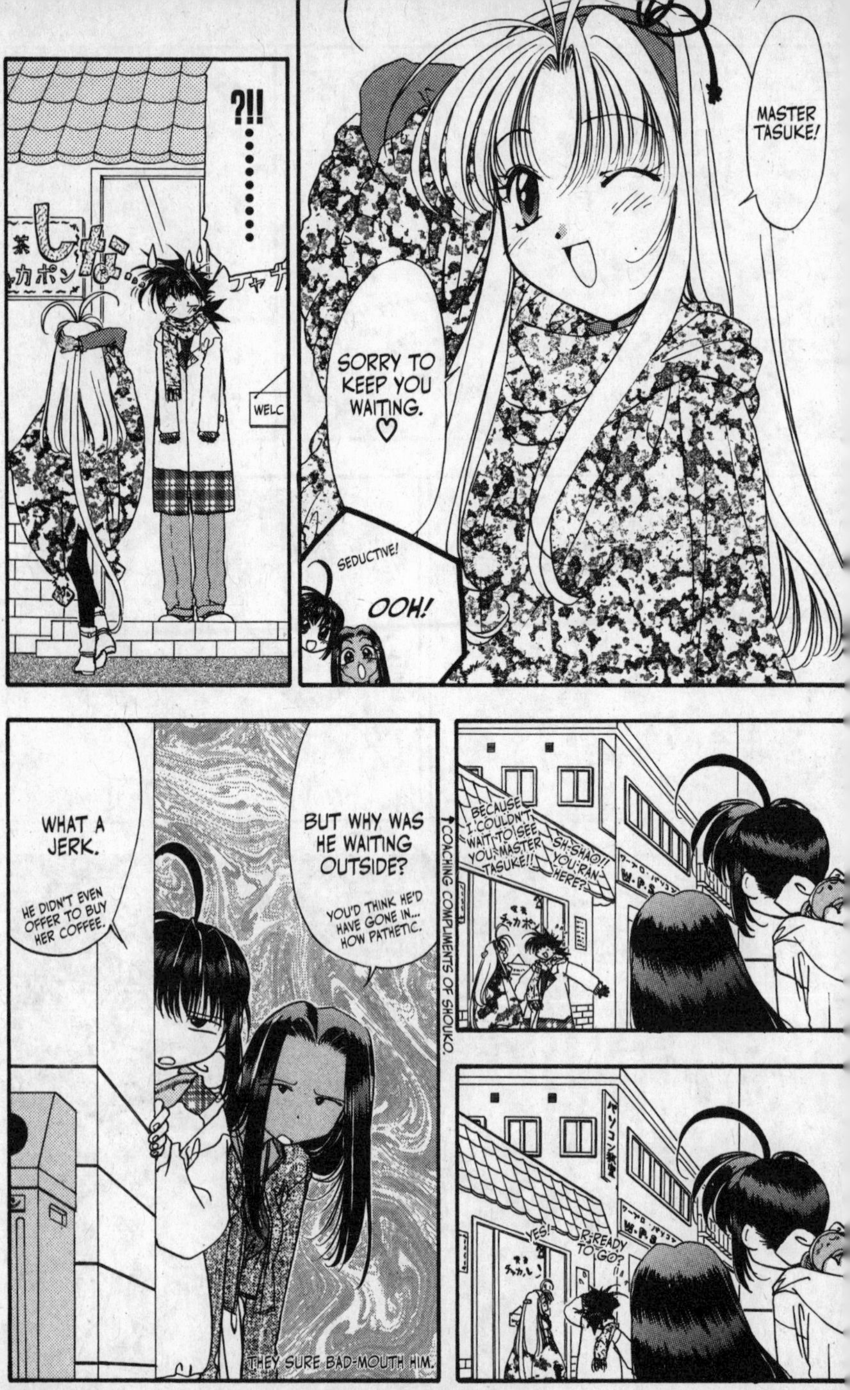
MASTER TASUKE!
SORRY TO KEEP YOU WAITING. ♡
SEDUCTIVE!
OOH!
?!!
......
WELC
SH-SHAO!! YOU RAN HERE?
BECAUSE I COULDN'T WAIT TO SEE YOU, MASTER TASUKE!!
R-READY TO GO?
YES!
↑COACHING COMPLIMENTS OF SHOUKO.
BUT WHY WAS HE WAITING OUTSIDE?
YOU'D THINK HE'D HAVE GONE IN... HOW PATHETIC.
WHAT A JERK.
HE DIDN'T EVEN OFFER TO BUY HER COFFEE.
THEY SURE BAD-MOUTH HIM.

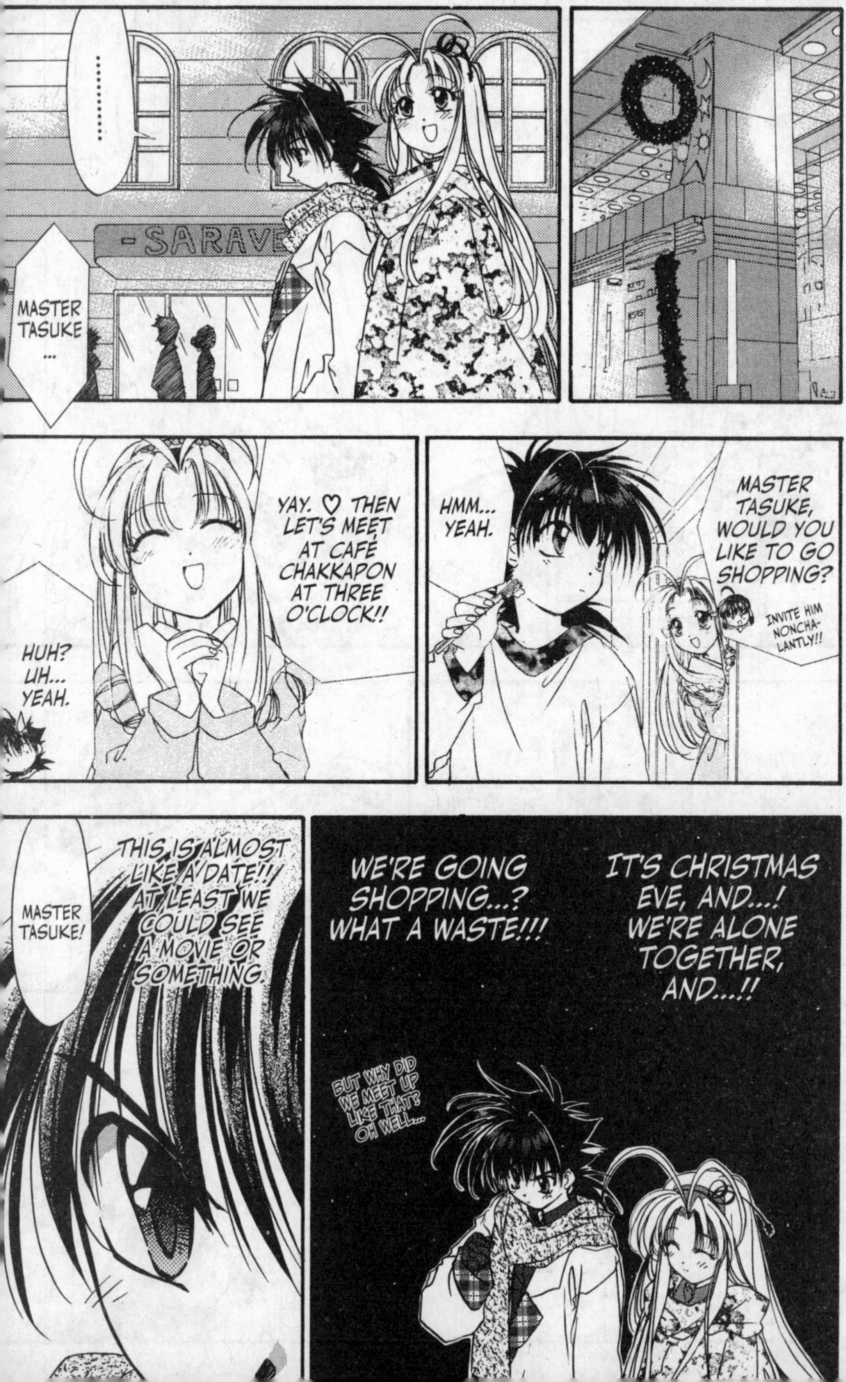
......
MASTER TASUKE ...
MASTER TASUKE, WOULD YOU LIKE TO GO SHOPPING?
INVITE HIM NONCHALANTLY!!
HMM... YEAH.
YAY. ♡ THEN LET'S MEET AT CAFÉ CHAKKAPON AT THREE O'CLOCK!!
HUH? UH... YEAH.
IT'S CHRISTMAS EVE, AND...! WE'RE ALONE TOGETHER, AND...!!
WE'RE GOING SHOPPING...? WHAT A WASTE!!!
BUT WHY DID WE MEET UP LIKE THAT? OH WELL...
THIS IS ALMOST LIKE A DATE!! AT LEAST WE COULD SEE A MOVIE OR SOMETHING.
MASTER TASUKE!

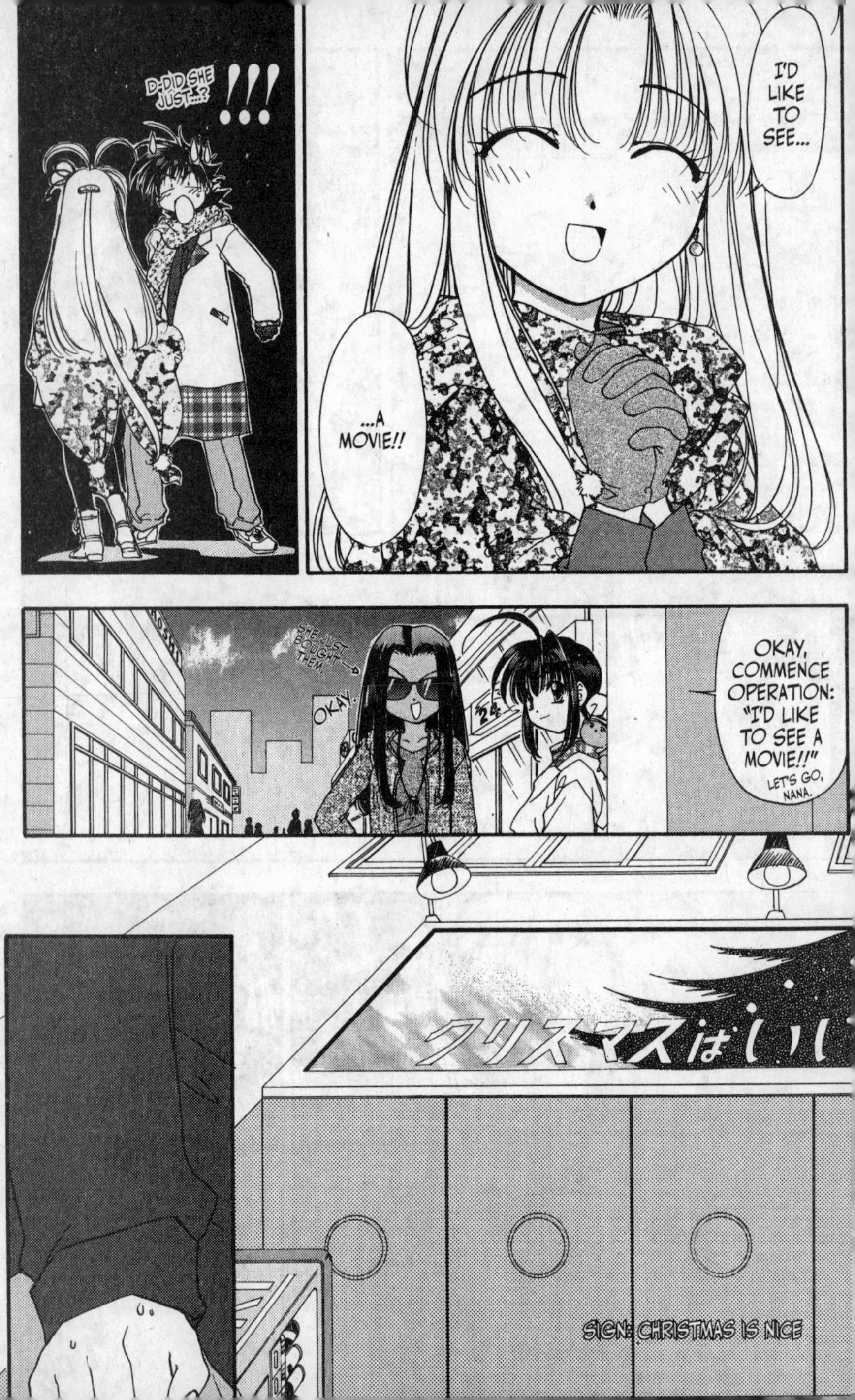
I'D LIKE TO SEE...
...A MOVIE!!
D-DID SHE JUST...?
!!!
OKAY, COMMENCE OPERATION: "I'D LIKE TO SEE A MOVIE!!"
LET'S GO, NANA.
SHE JUST BOUGHT THEM.
OKAY.
クリスマスはいい
SIGN: CHRISTMAS IS NICE

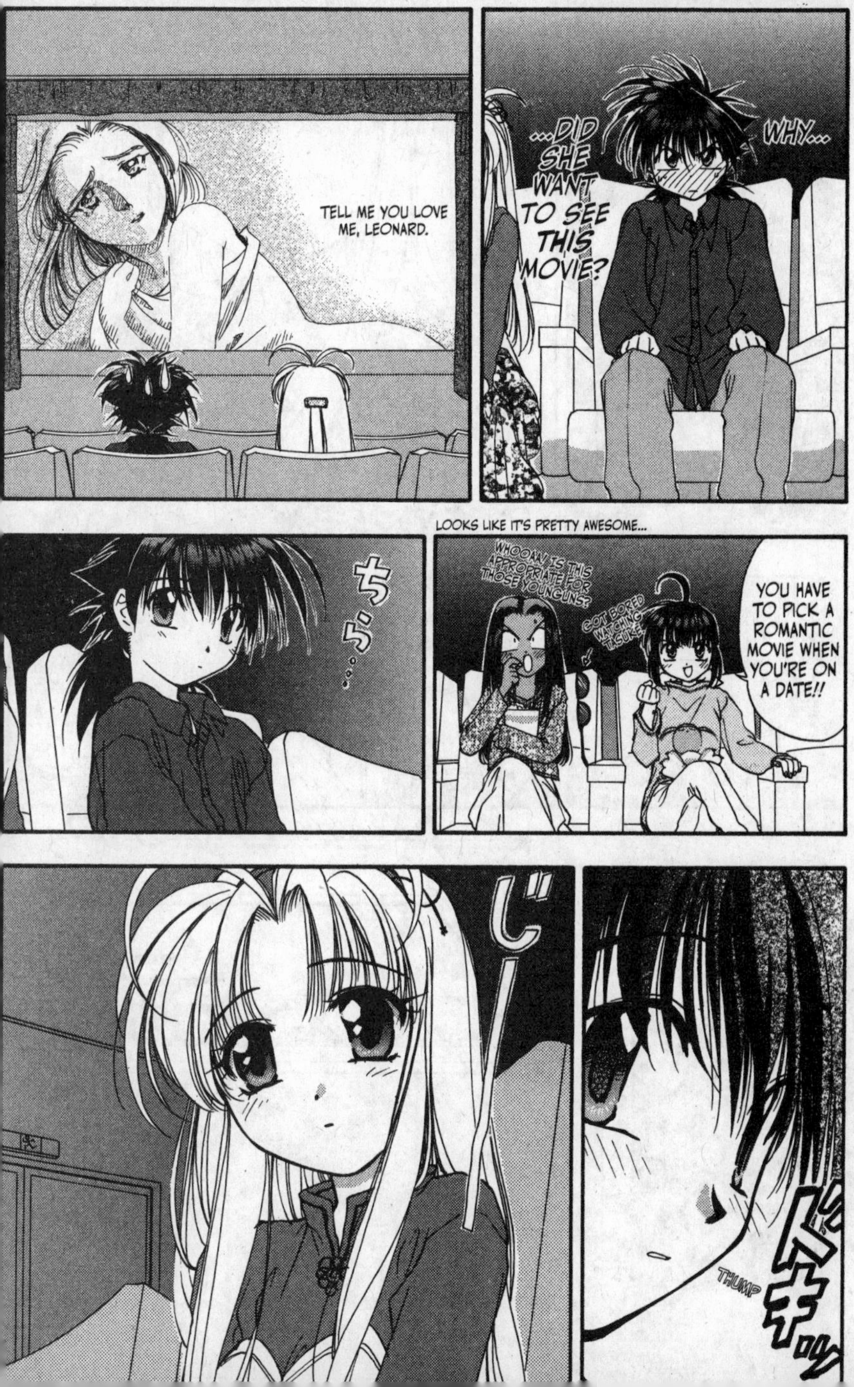
WHY...
...DID SHE WANT TO SEE THIS MOVIE?
TELL ME YOU LOVE ME, LEONARD.
LOOKS LIKE IT'S PRETTY AWESOME...
YOU HAVE TO PICK A ROMANTIC MOVIE WHEN YOU'RE ON A DATE!!
GOT BORED WATCHING TASUKE
WHOOAA! IS THIS APPROPRIATE FOR THOSE YOUNGUNS?
ちら…
ドキッ
THUMP
じ

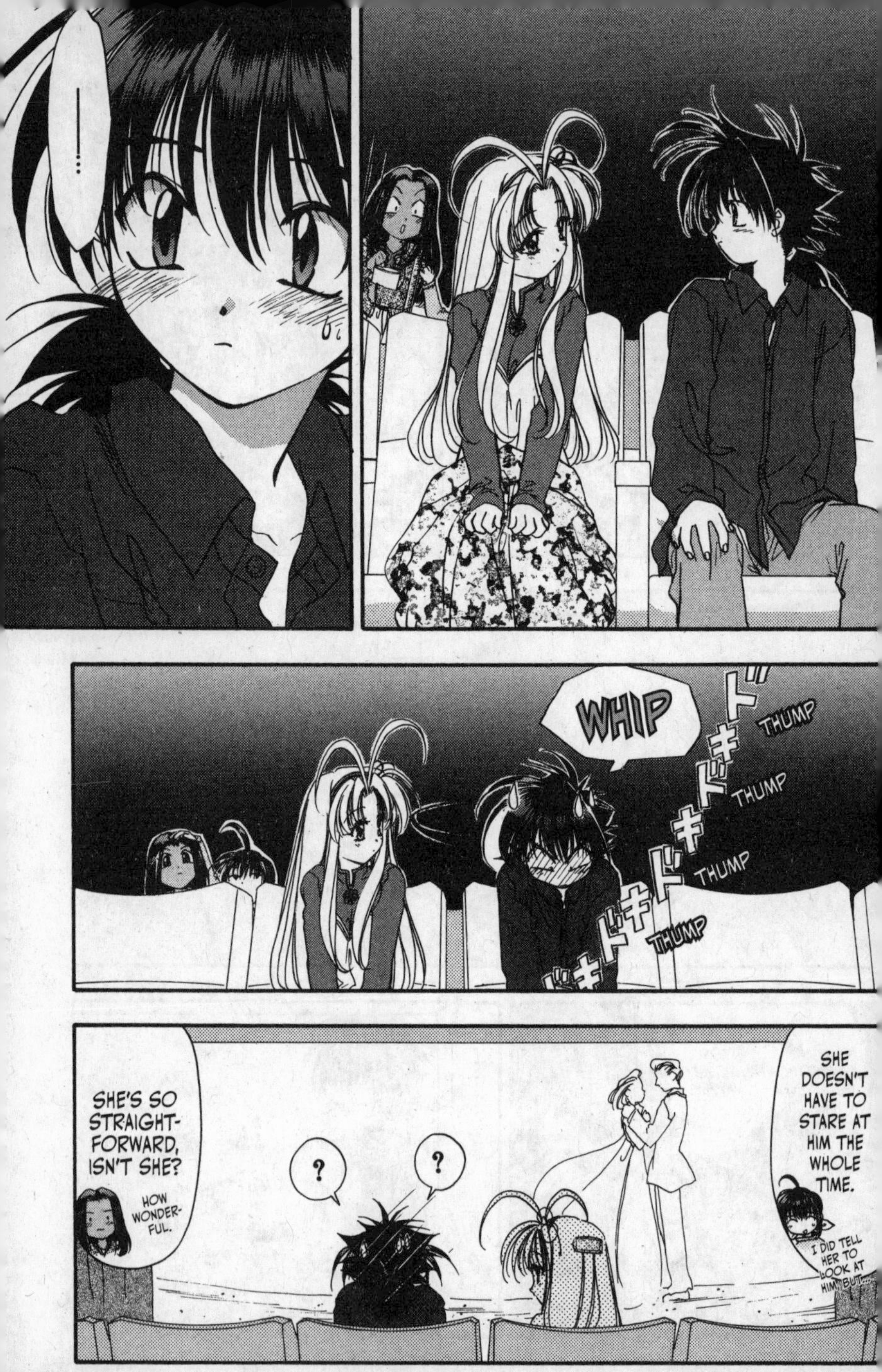
......!
WHIP
ドキ
THUMP
ドキ
THUMP
ドキ
THUMP
ドキ
THUMP
SHE DOESN'T HAVE TO STARE AT HIM THE WHOLE TIME.
I DID TELL HER TO LOOK AT HIM, BUT...
?
?
SHE'S SO STRAIGHT-FORWARD, ISN'T SHE?
HOW WONDER-FUL.

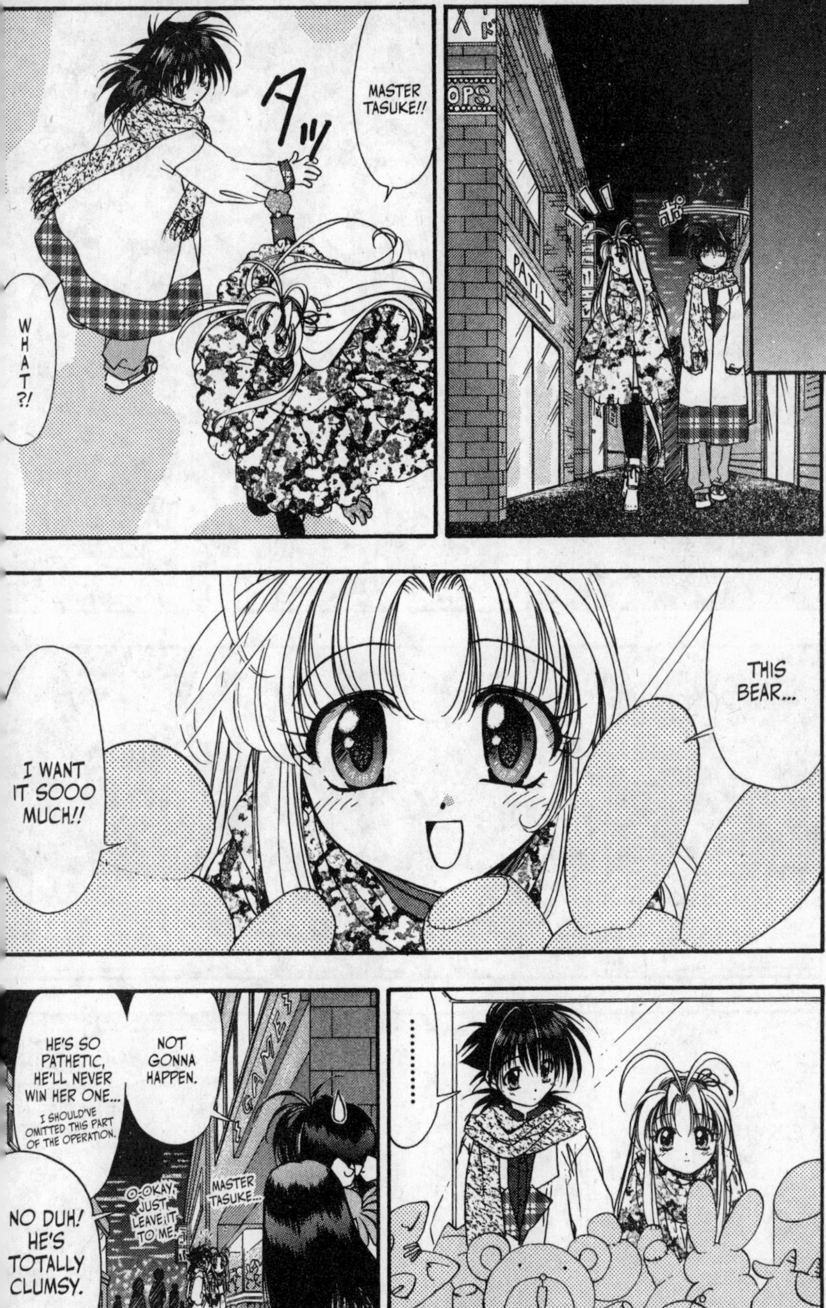
ポ
MASTER TASUKE!!
アッ
WHAT?!
THIS BEAR...
I WANT IT SOOO MUCH!!
......
NOT GONNA HAPPEN.
HE'S SO PATHETIC, HE'LL NEVER WIN HER ONE...
I SHOULD'VE OMITTED THIS PART OF THE OPERATION.
MASTER TASUKE...
O-OKAY, JUST LEAVE IT TO ME.
NO DUH! HE'S TOTALLY CLUMSY.

BAD-MOUTHING, TAKE 2.

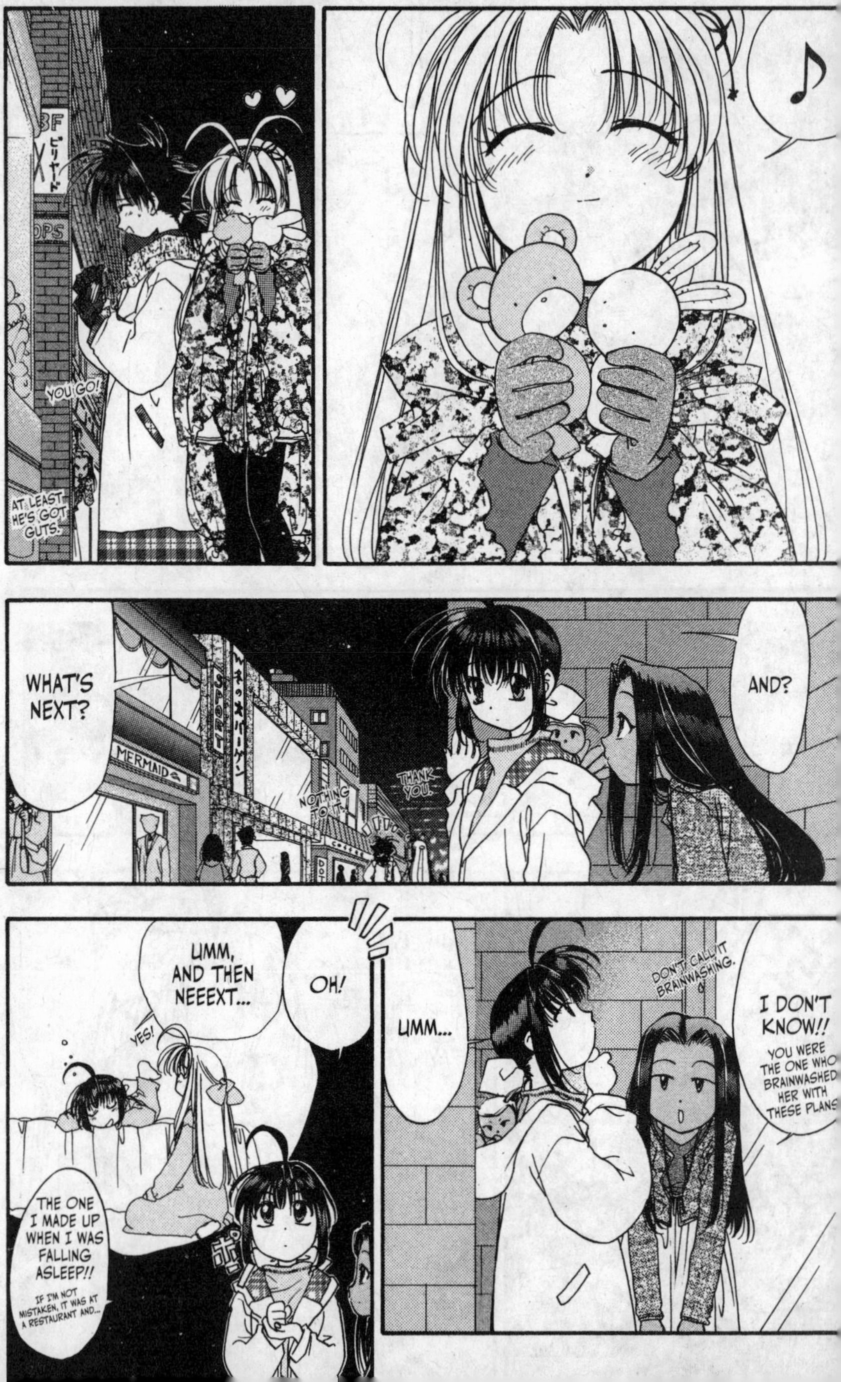
♪
3F ビリヤード
YOU GO!
AT LEAST HE'S GOT GUTS.
AND?
THANK YOU.
NOTHING TO T—
WHAT'S NEXT?
MERMAID
SPORT
I DON'T KNOW!!
YOU WERE THE ONE WHO BRAINWASHED HER WITH THESE PLANS
DON'T CALL IT BRAINWASHING.
UMM...
OH!
UMM, AND THEN NEEEXT...
YES!
THE ONE I MADE UP WHEN I WAS FALLING ASLEEP!!
IF I'M NOT MISTAKEN, IT WAS AT A RESTAURANT AND...

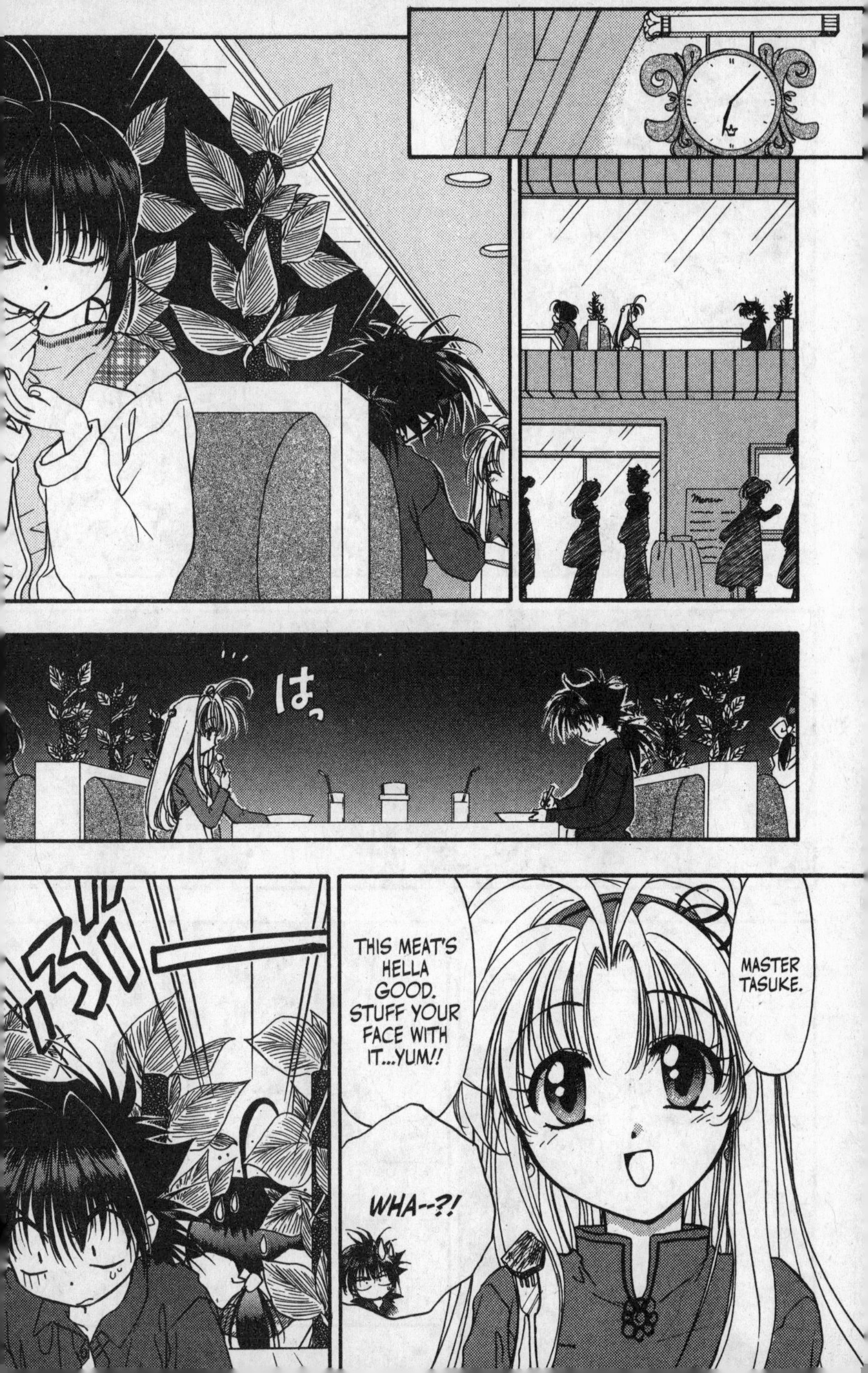
はっ
MASTER TASUKE.
THIS MEAT'S HELLA GOOD. STUFF YOUR FACE WITH IT...YUM!!
WHA--?!

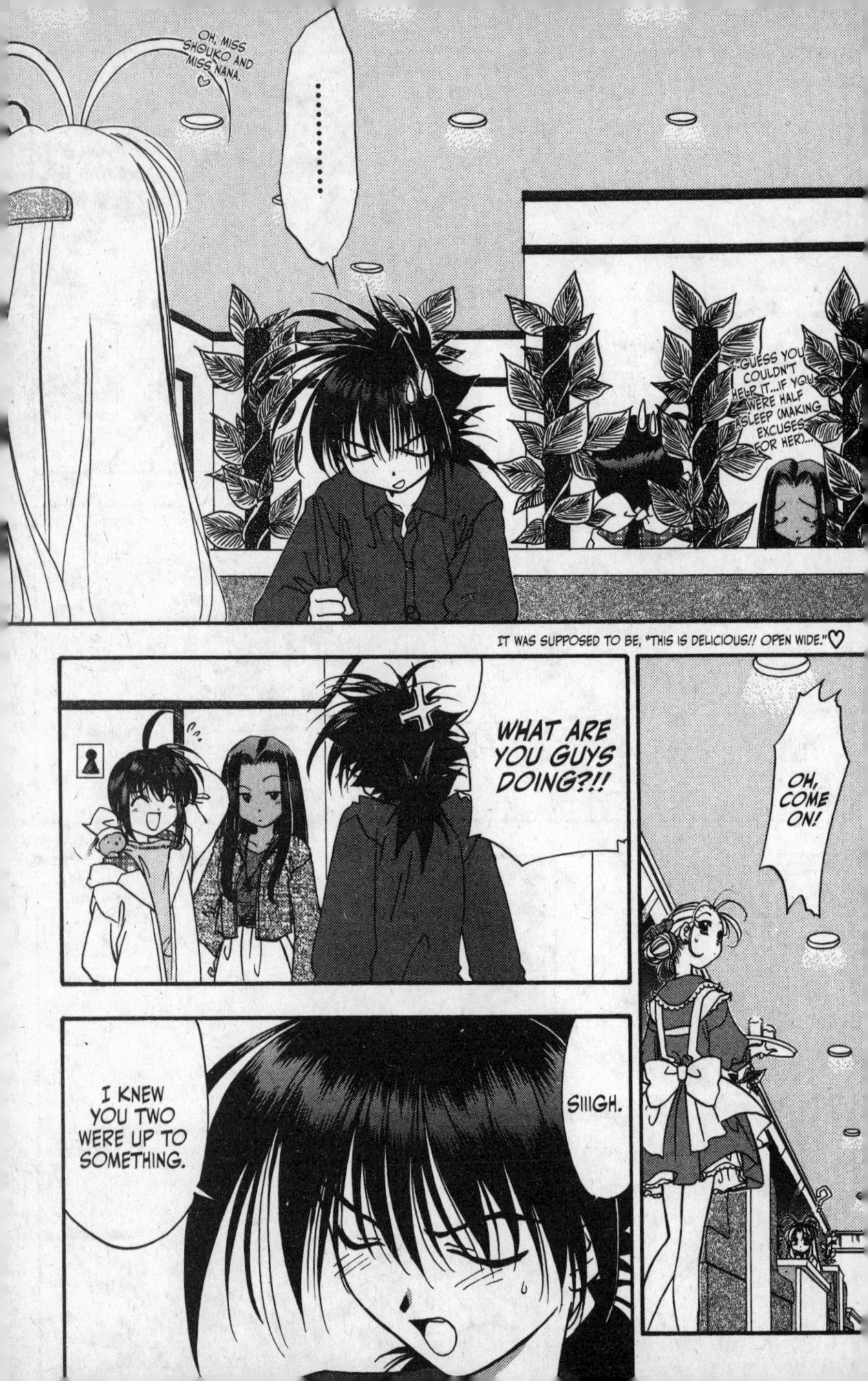
I GUESS YOU COULDN'T HELP IT...IF YOU WERE HALF ASLEEP (MAKING EXCUSES FOR HER)...
......
OH, MISS SHOUKO AND MISS NANA. ♡
IT WAS SUPPOSED TO BE, "THIS IS DELICIOUS!! OPEN WIDE." ♡
OH, COME ON!
WHAT ARE YOU GUYS DOING?!!
SIIIGH.
I KNEW YOU TWO WERE UP TO SOMETHING.

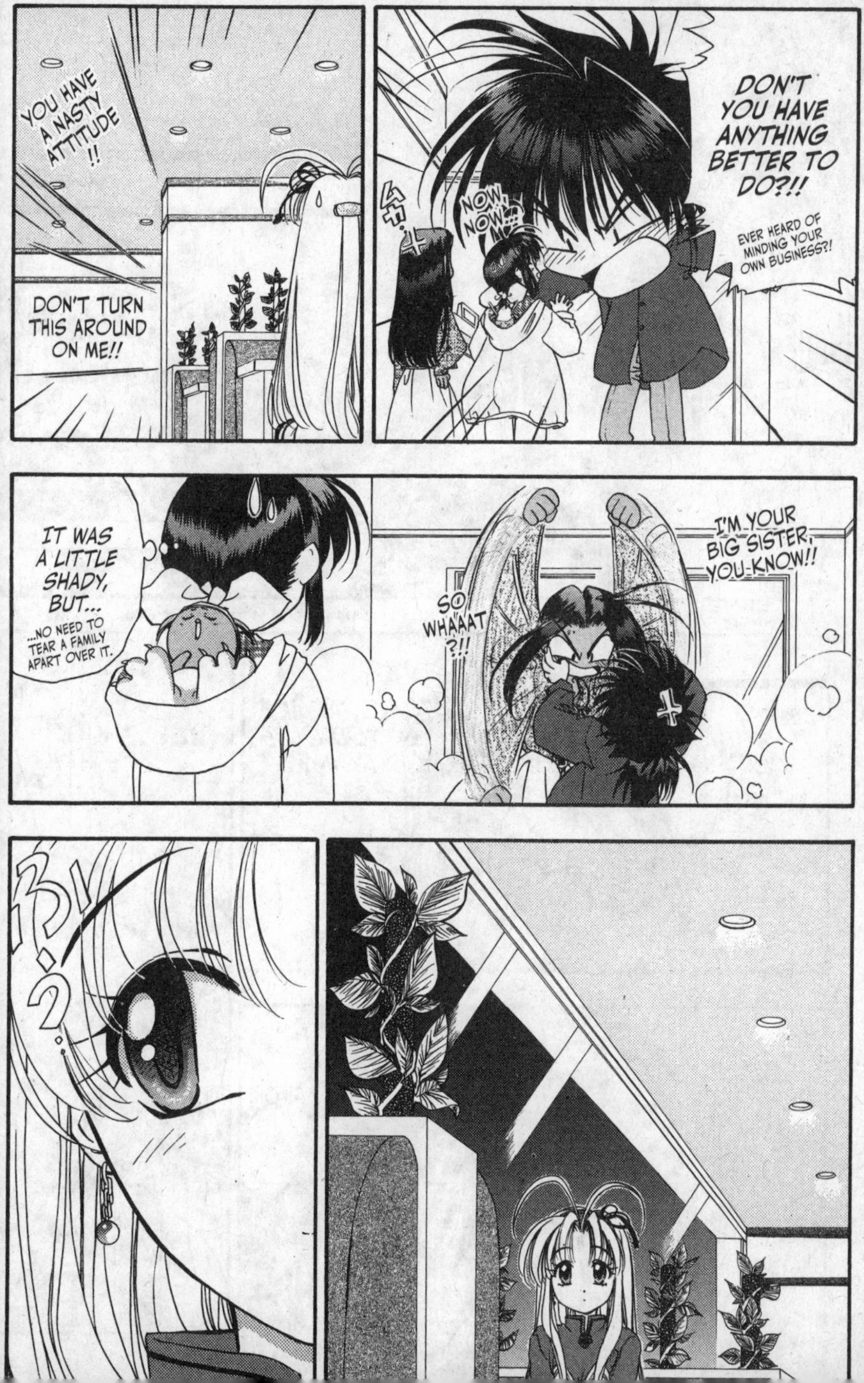
DON'T YOU HAVE ANYTHING BETTER TO DO?!!
EVER HEARD OF MINDING YOUR OWN BUSINESS?!
NOW, NOW...!!
ムカ
YOU HAVE A NASTY ATTITUDE !!
DON'T TURN THIS AROUND ON ME!!
I'M YOUR BIG SISTER, YOU KNOW!!
SO WHAAAT ?!!
IT WAS A LITTLE SHADY, BUT...
...NO NEED TO TEAR A FAMILY APART OVER IT.

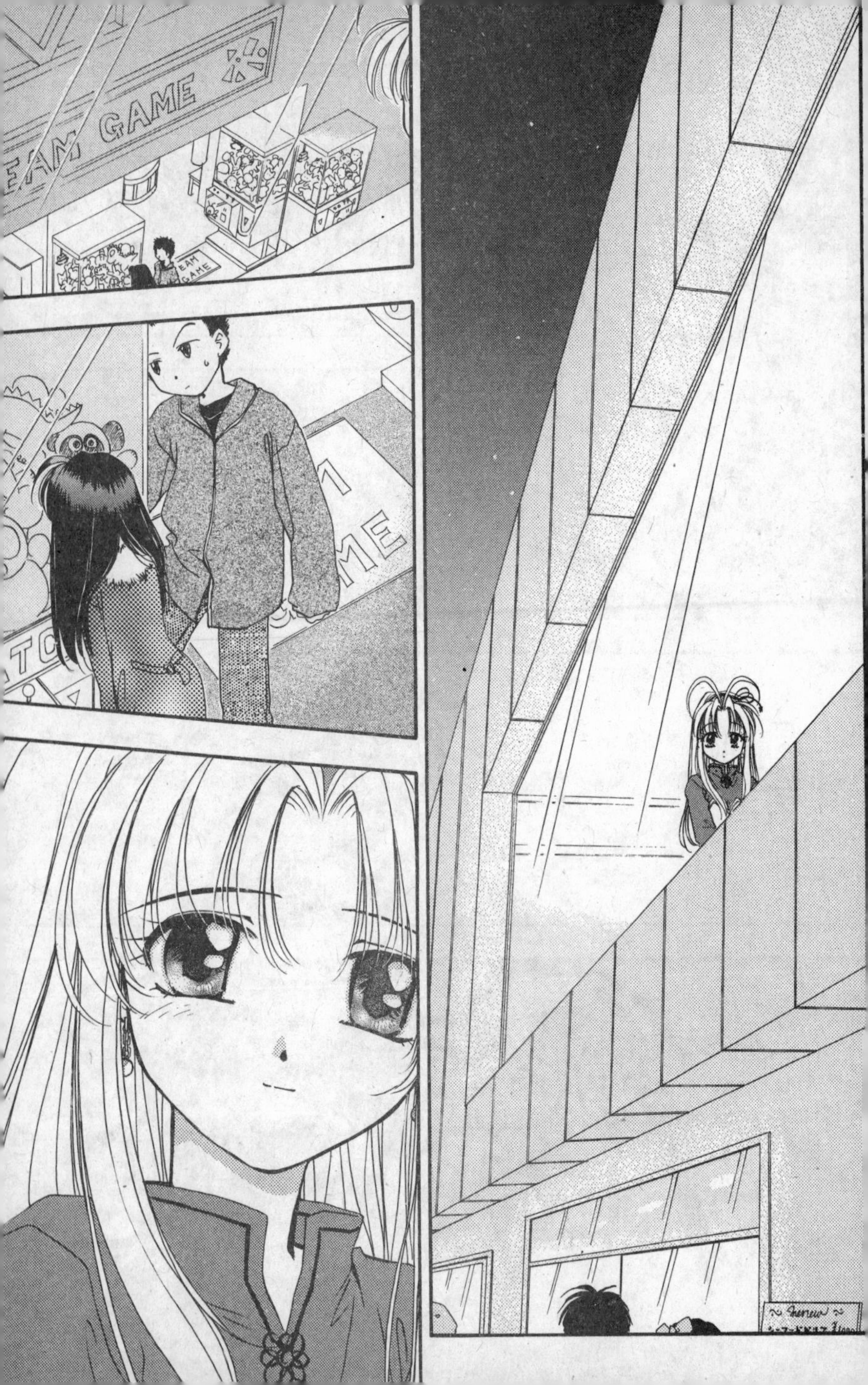
EAM GAME
EAM GAME
ME
ATC

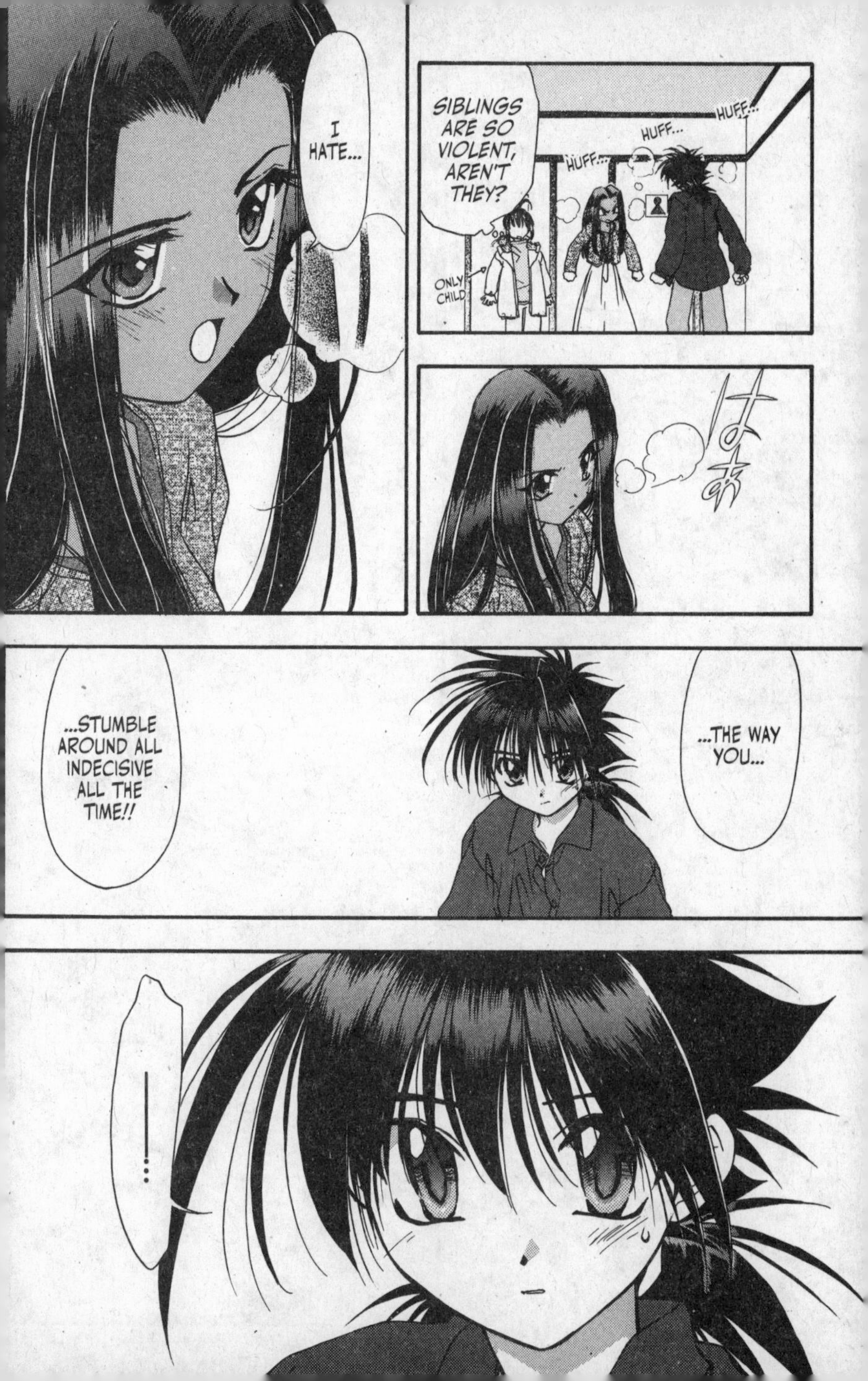
HUFF...
HUFF...
HUFF...
SIBLINGS ARE SO VIOLENT, AREN'T THEY?
ONLY CHILD
はあ
I HATE...
...THE WAY YOU...
...STUMBLE AROUND ALL INDECISIVE ALL THE TIME!!

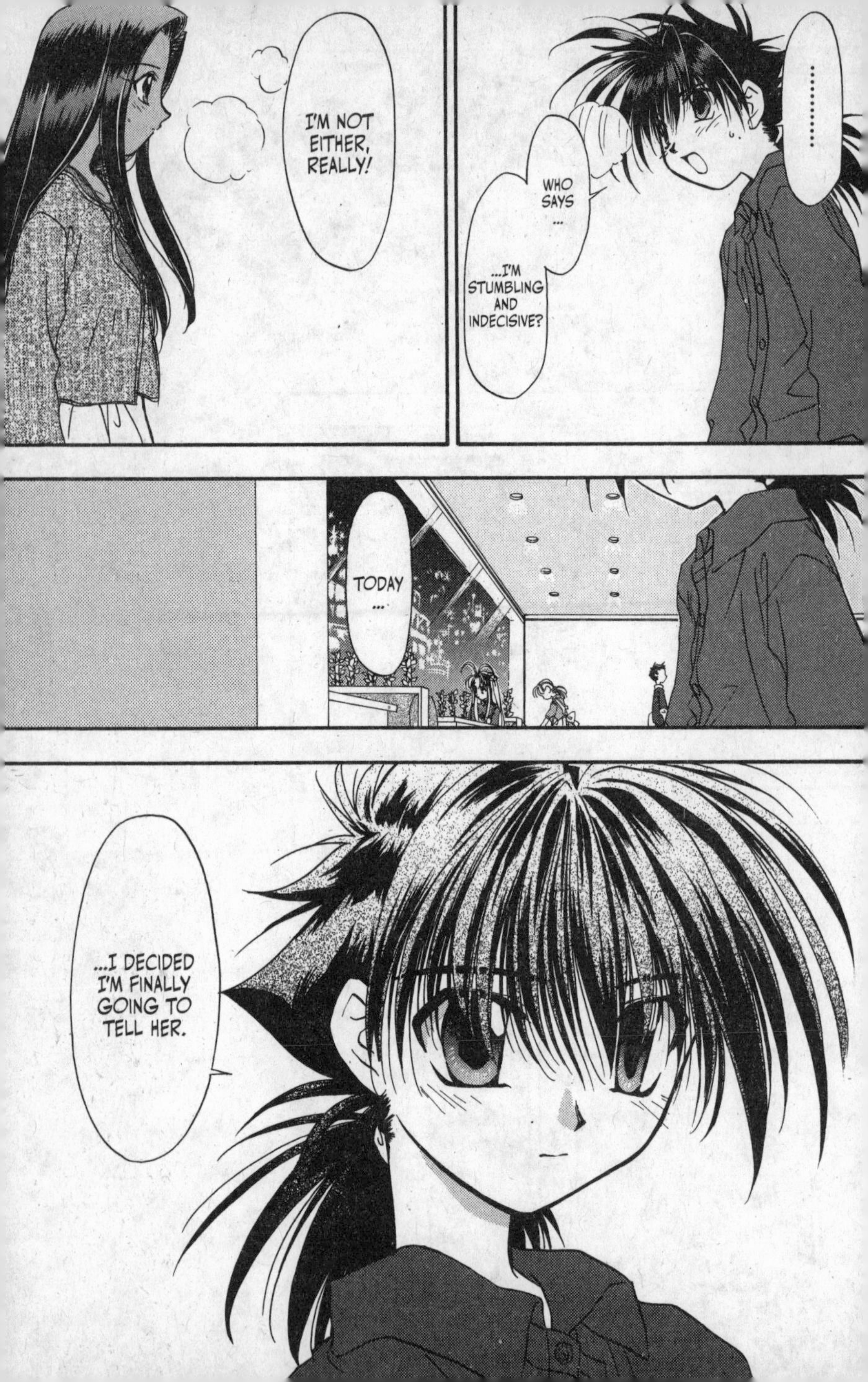

......
WHO SAYS ...
...I'M STUMBLING AND INDECISIVE?
I'M NOT EITHER, REALLY!
TODAY ...
...I DECIDED I'M FINALLY GOING TO TELL HER.

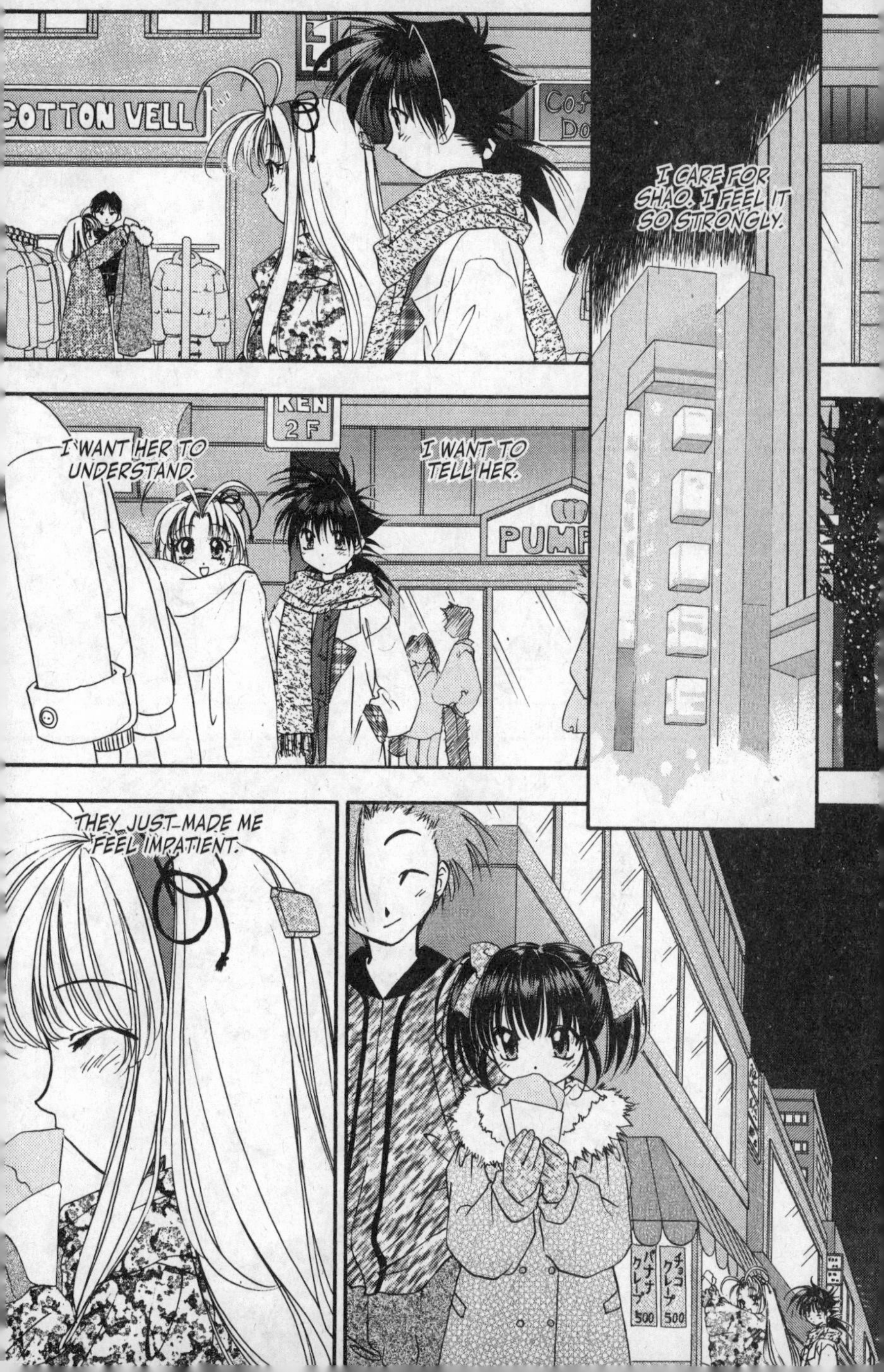

I CARE FOR SHAO. I FEEL IT SO STRONGLY.
COTTON VELL
KEN
2 F
I WANT TO TELL HER.
I WANT HER TO UNDERSTAND.
PUMP
チョコクレープ 500
バナナクレープ 500
THEY JUST MADE ME FEEL IMPATIENT.

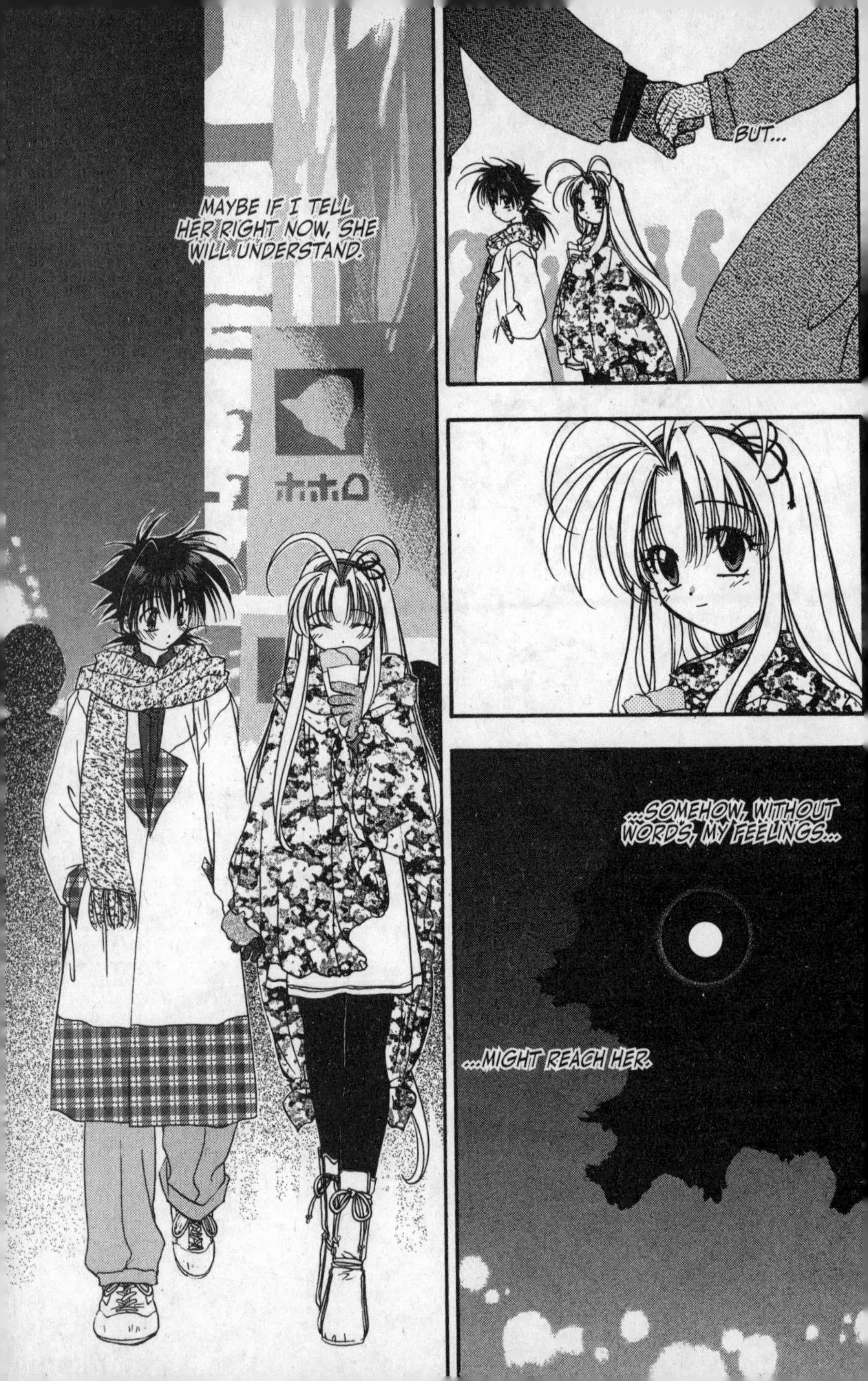
MAYBE IF I TELL HER RIGHT NOW, SHE WILL UNDERSTAND.
ホホロ
BUT...
...SOMEHOW, WITHOUT WORDS, MY FEELINGS...
...MIGHT REACH HER.

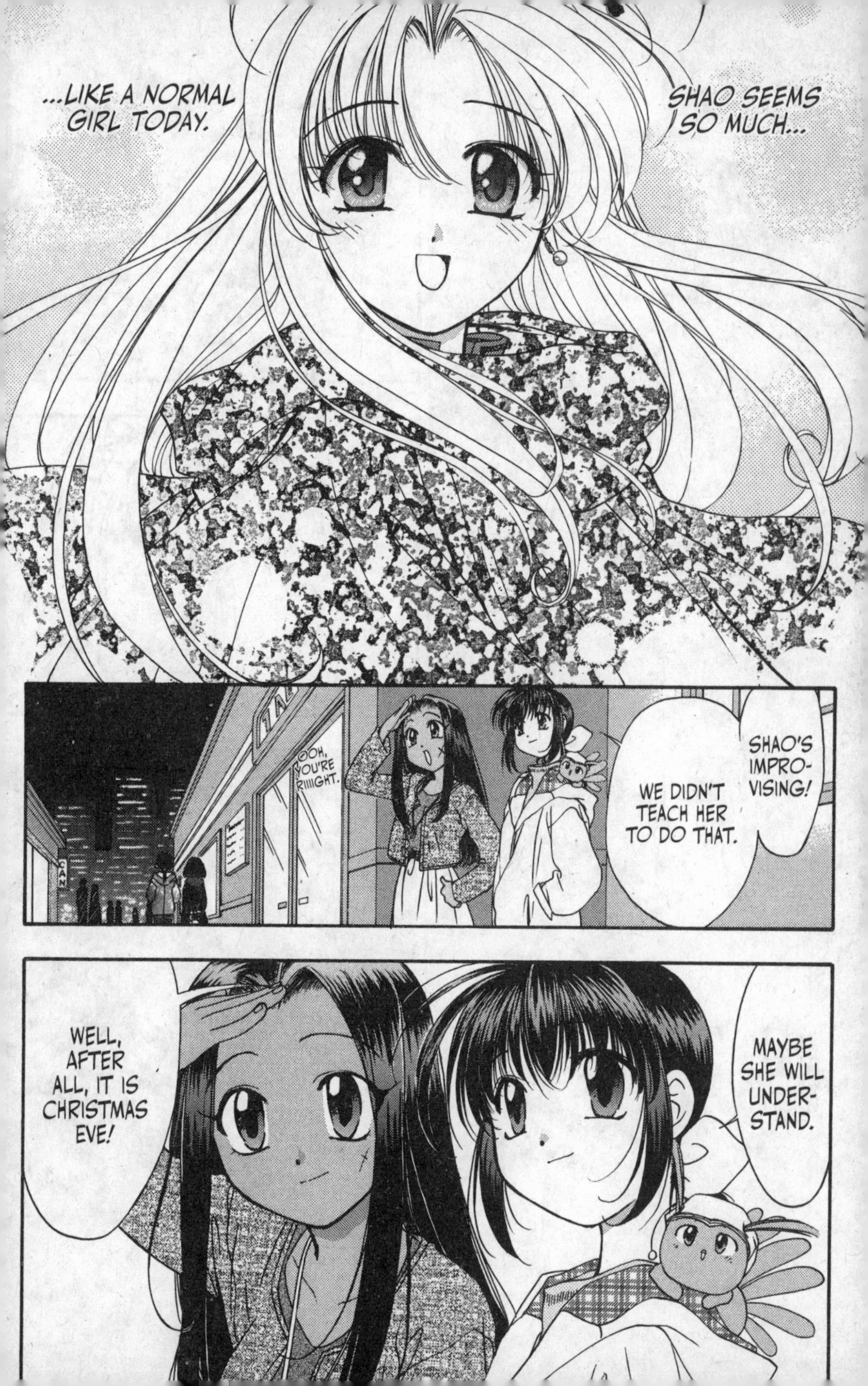
SHAO SEEMS SO MUCH...
...LIKE A NORMAL GIRL TODAY.
SHAO'S IMPROVISING!
WE DIDN'T TEACH HER TO DO THAT.
OOH, YOU'RE RIIIIGHT.
MAYBE SHE WILL UNDERSTAND.
WELL, AFTER ALL, IT IS CHRISTMAS EVE!

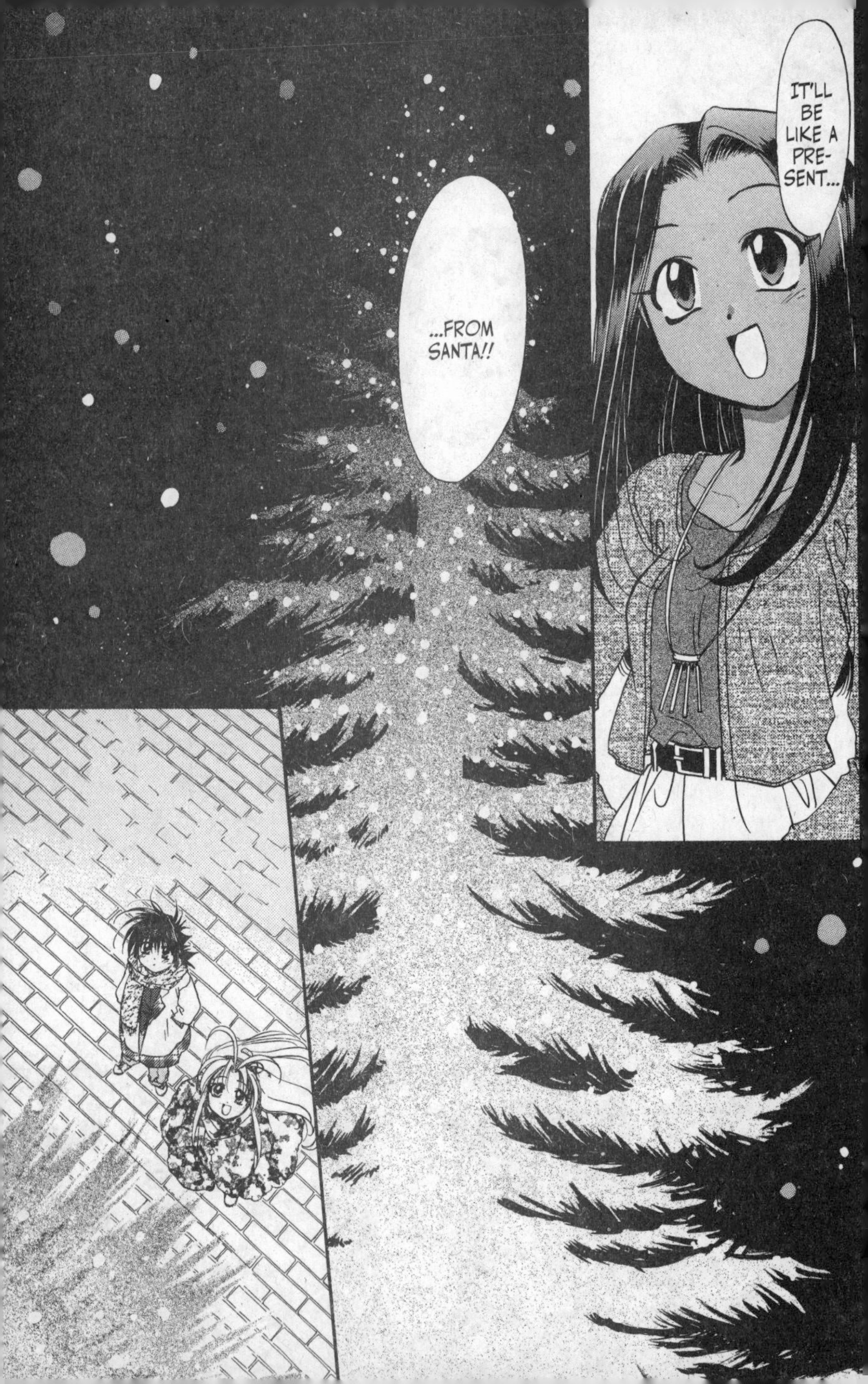
IT'LL BE LIKE A PRESENT...
...FROM SANTA!!

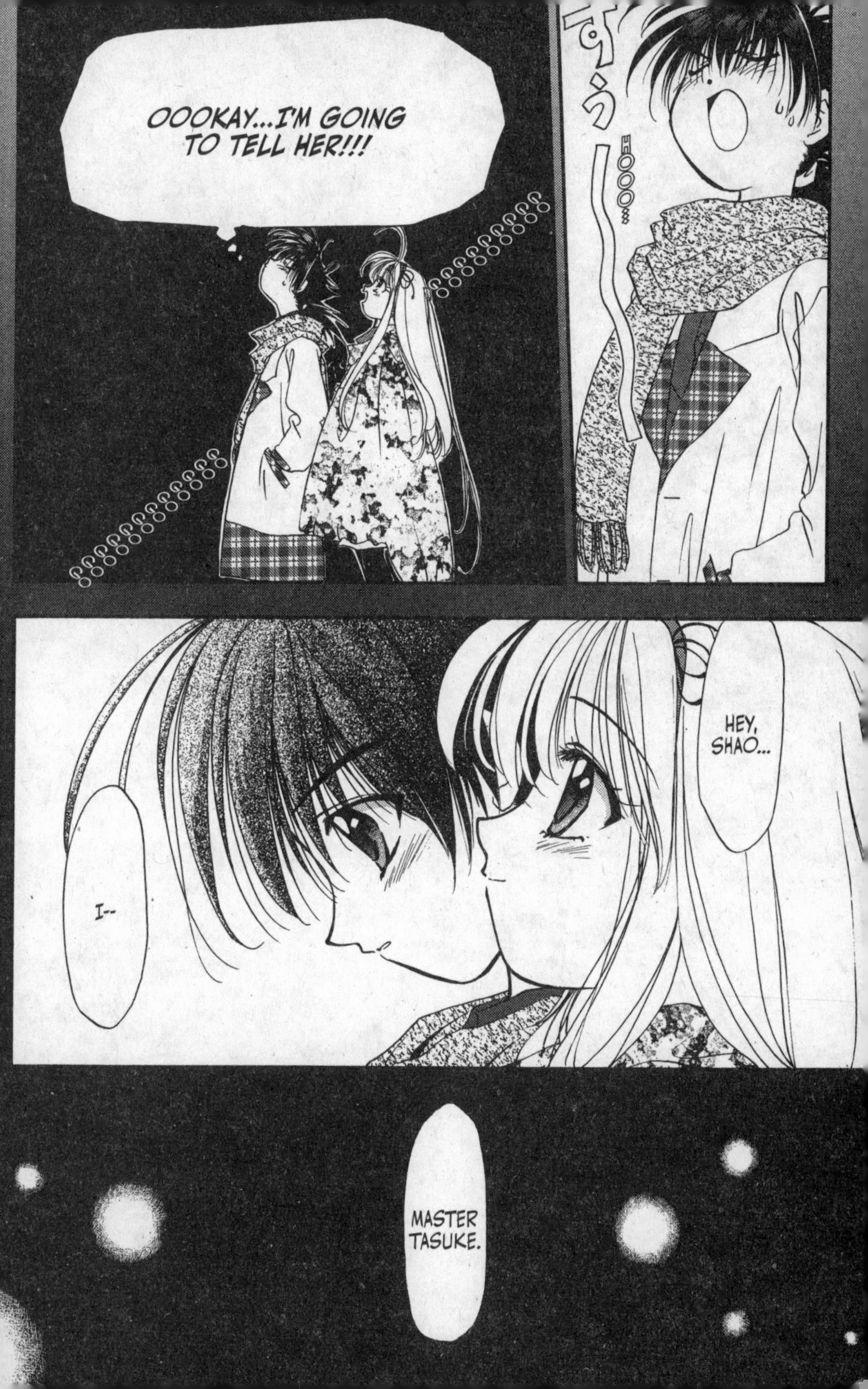
すぅー
HOOOO...
OOOKAY...I'M GOING TO TELL HER!!!
HEY, SHAO...
I--
MASTER TASUKE.

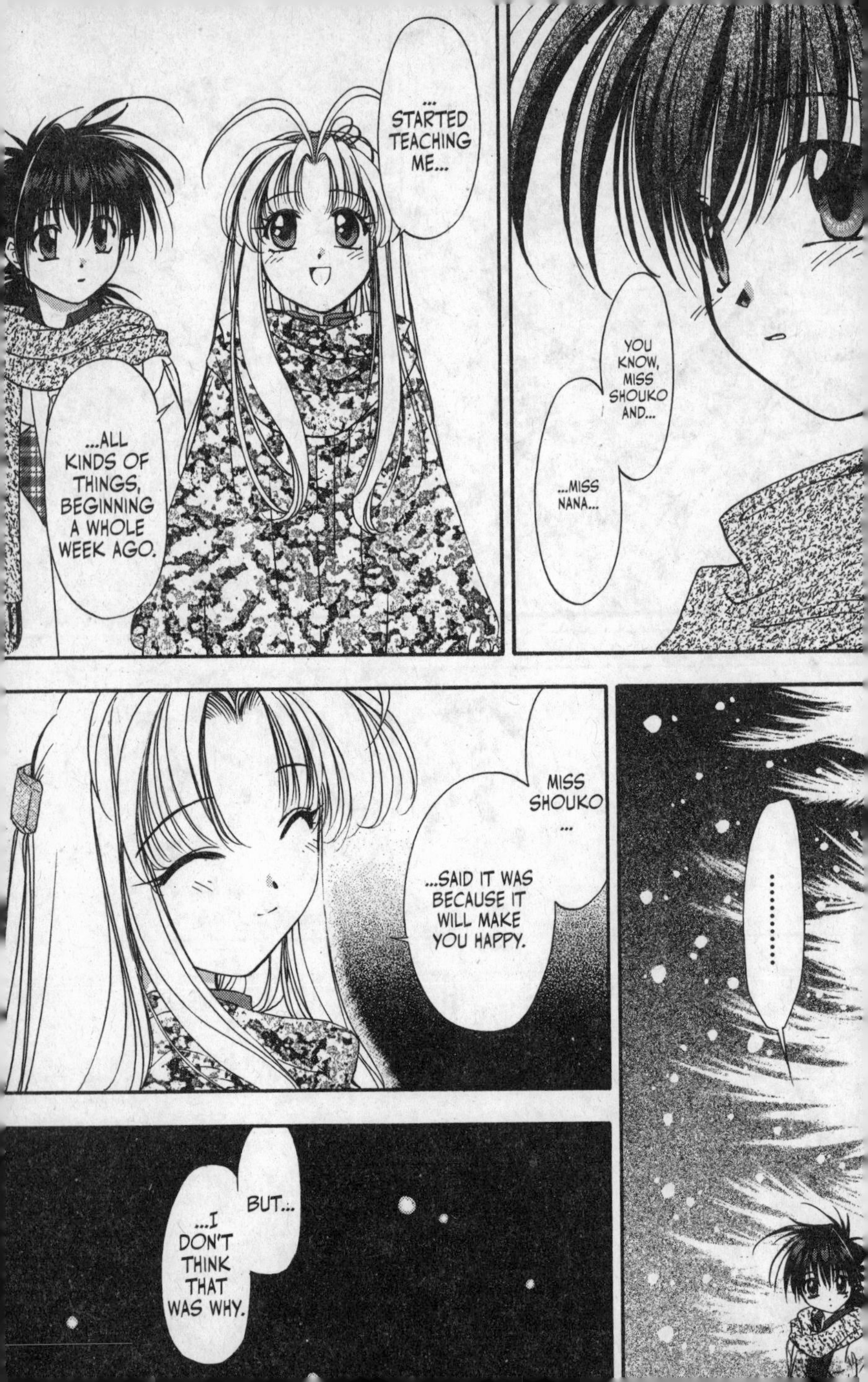

YOU KNOW, MISS SHOUKO AND...
...MISS NANA...
...STARTED TEACHING ME...
...ALL KINDS OF THINGS, BEGINNING A WHOLE WEEK AGO.
......
MISS SHOUKO ...
...SAID IT WAS BECAUSE IT WILL MAKE YOU HAPPY.
BUT...
...I DON'T THINK THAT WAS WHY.

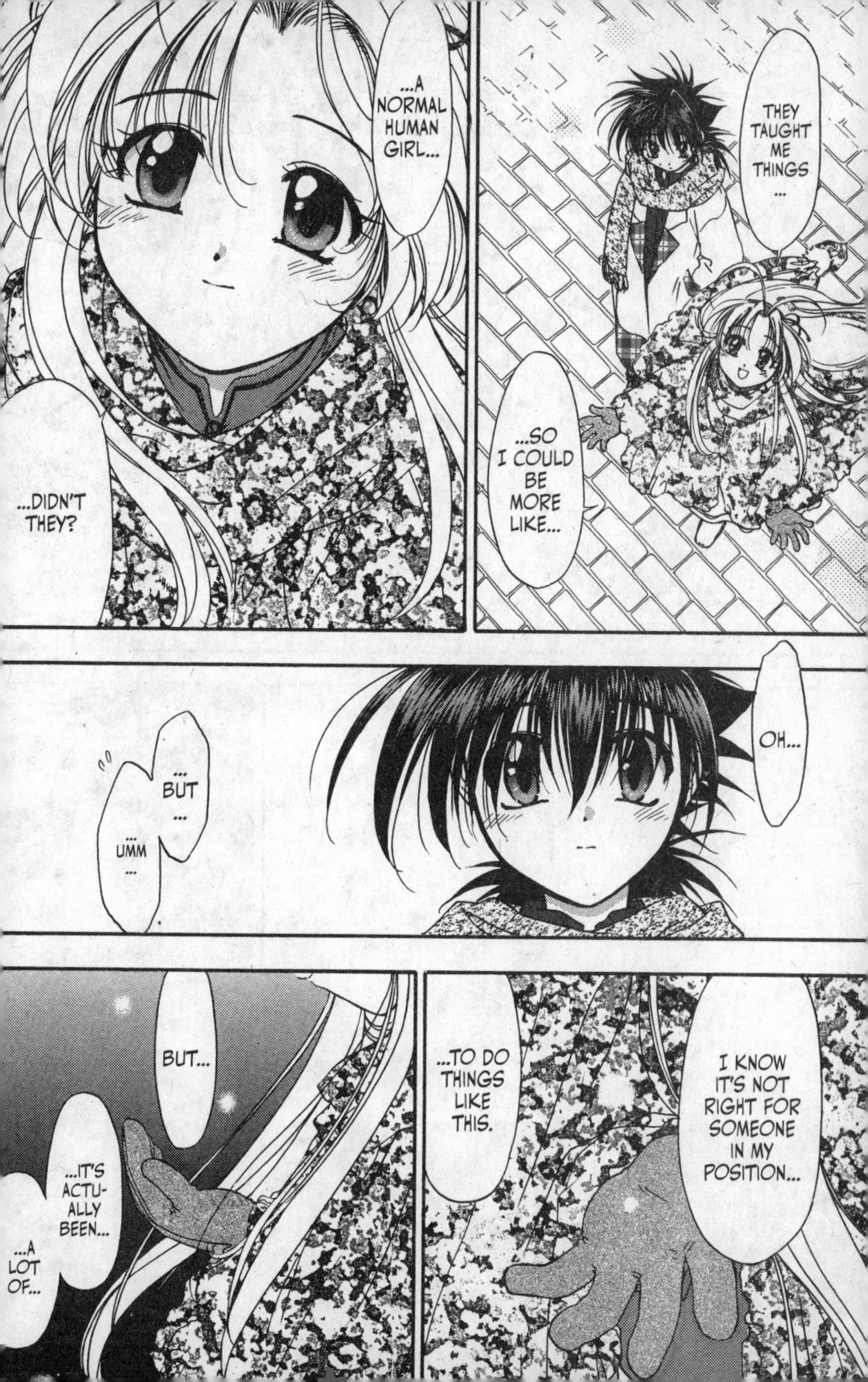
THEY TAUGHT ME THINGS ...
...SO I COULD BE MORE LIKE...
...A NORMAL HUMAN GIRL...
...DIDN'T THEY?
OH...
... BUT ... ... UMM ...
I KNOW IT'S NOT RIGHT FOR SOMEONE IN MY POSITION...
...TO DO THINGS LIKE THIS.
BUT...
...IT'S ACTU-ALLY BEEN...
...A LOT OF...

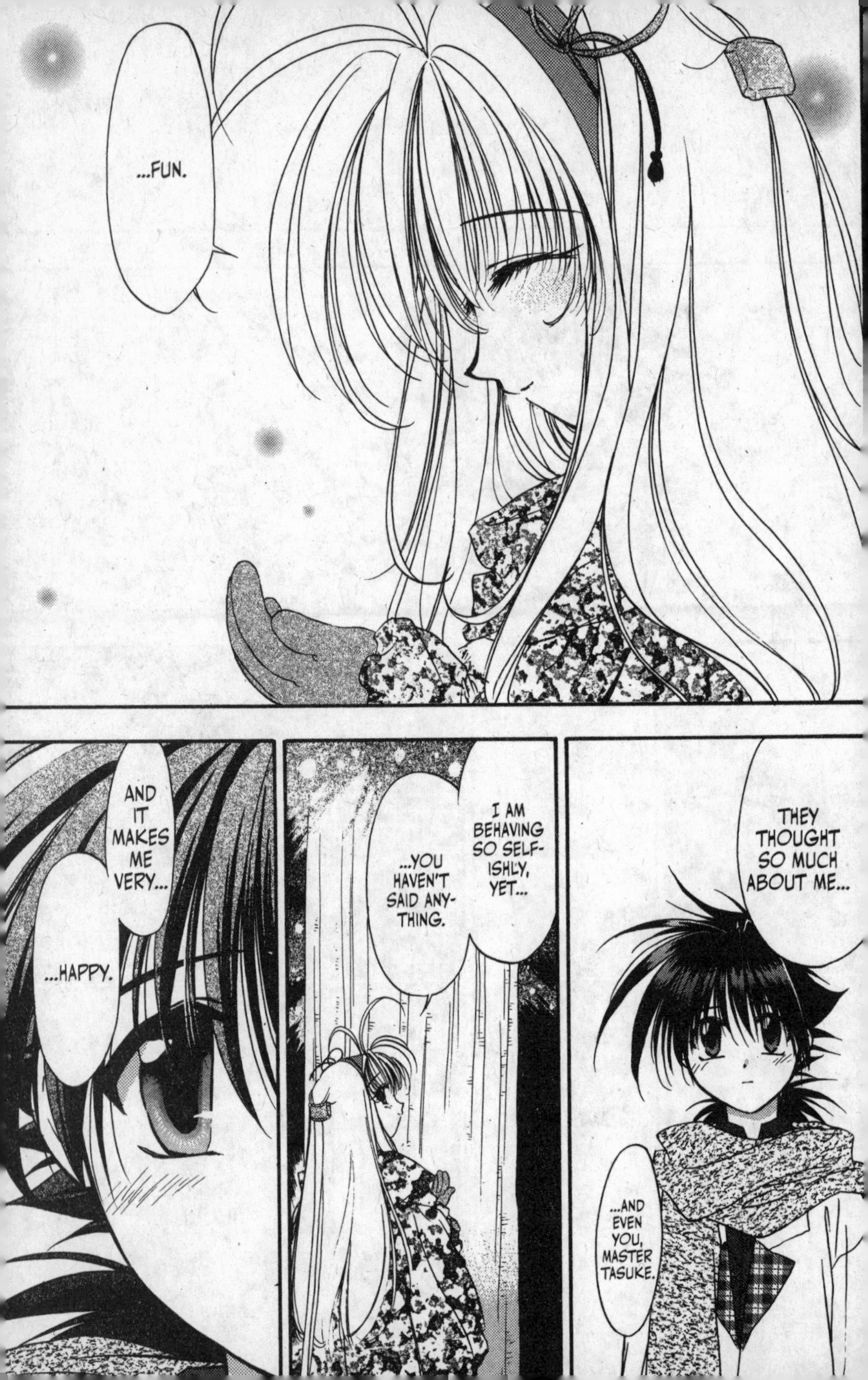
...FUN.
THEY THOUGHT SO MUCH ABOUT ME...
...AND EVEN YOU, MASTER TASUKE.
I AM BEHAVING SO SELF-ISHLY, YET...
...YOU HAVEN'T SAID ANY-THING.
AND IT MAKES ME VERY...
...HAPPY.

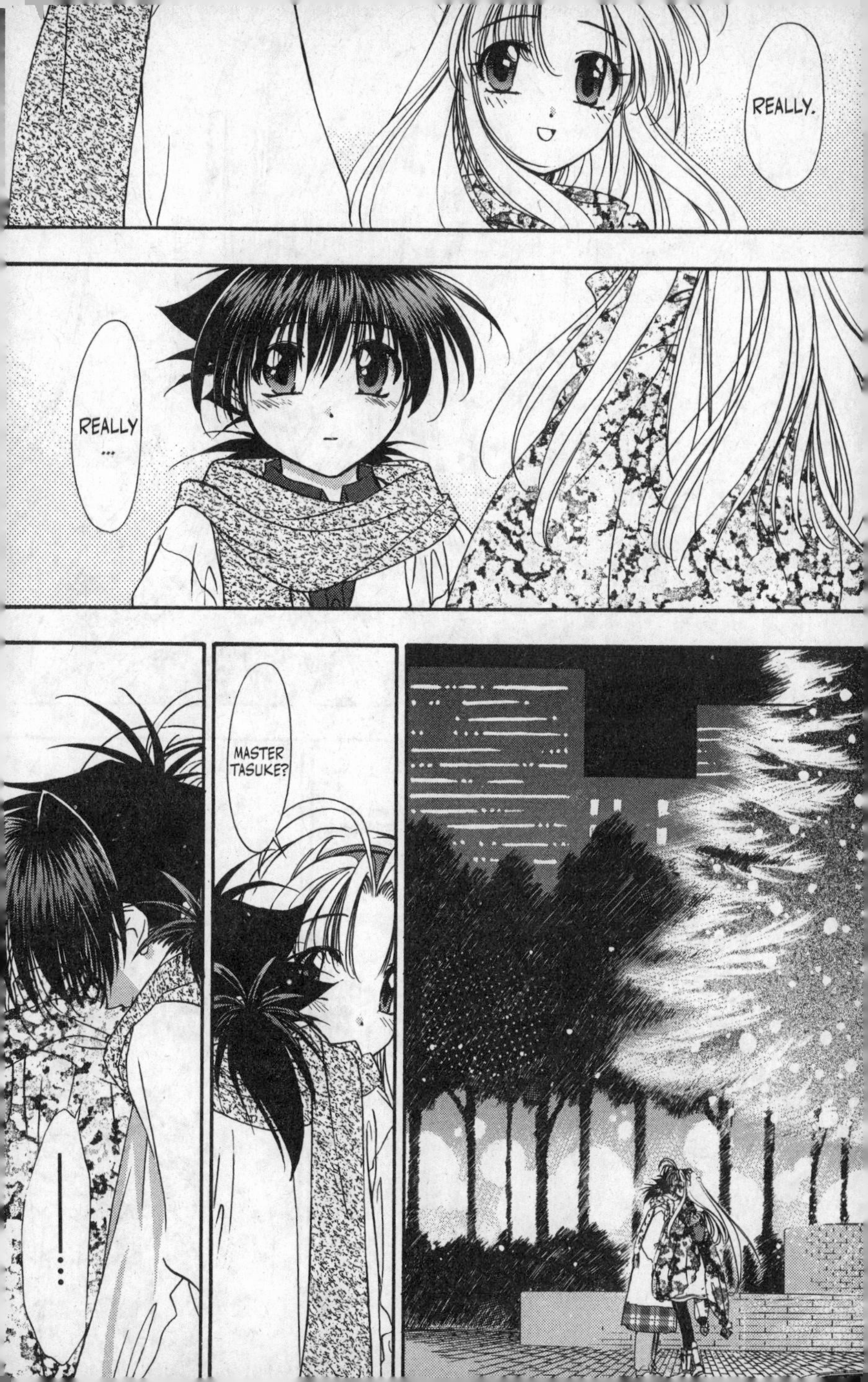
REALLY.
REALLY ...
MASTER TASUKE?

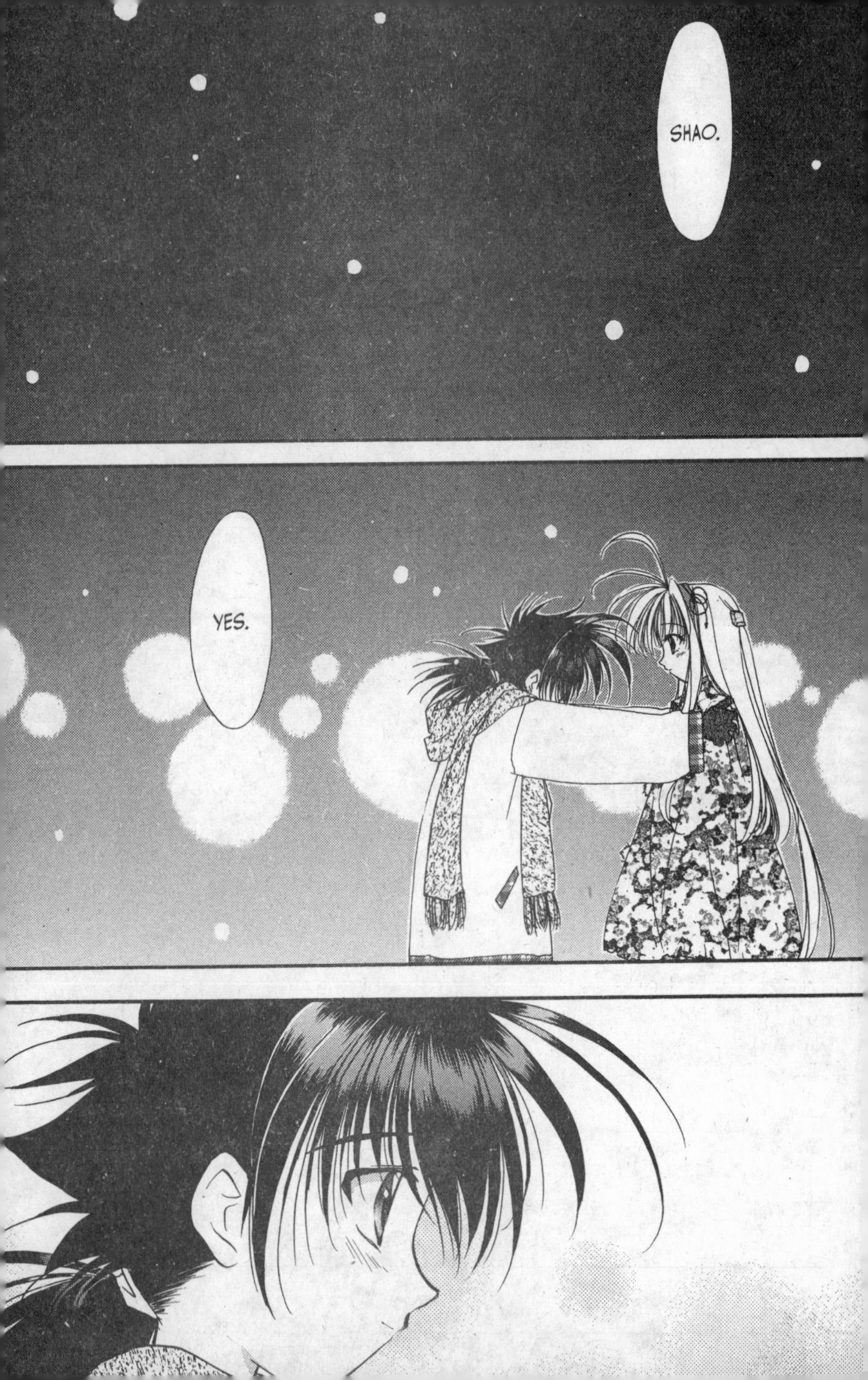
SHAO.
YES.

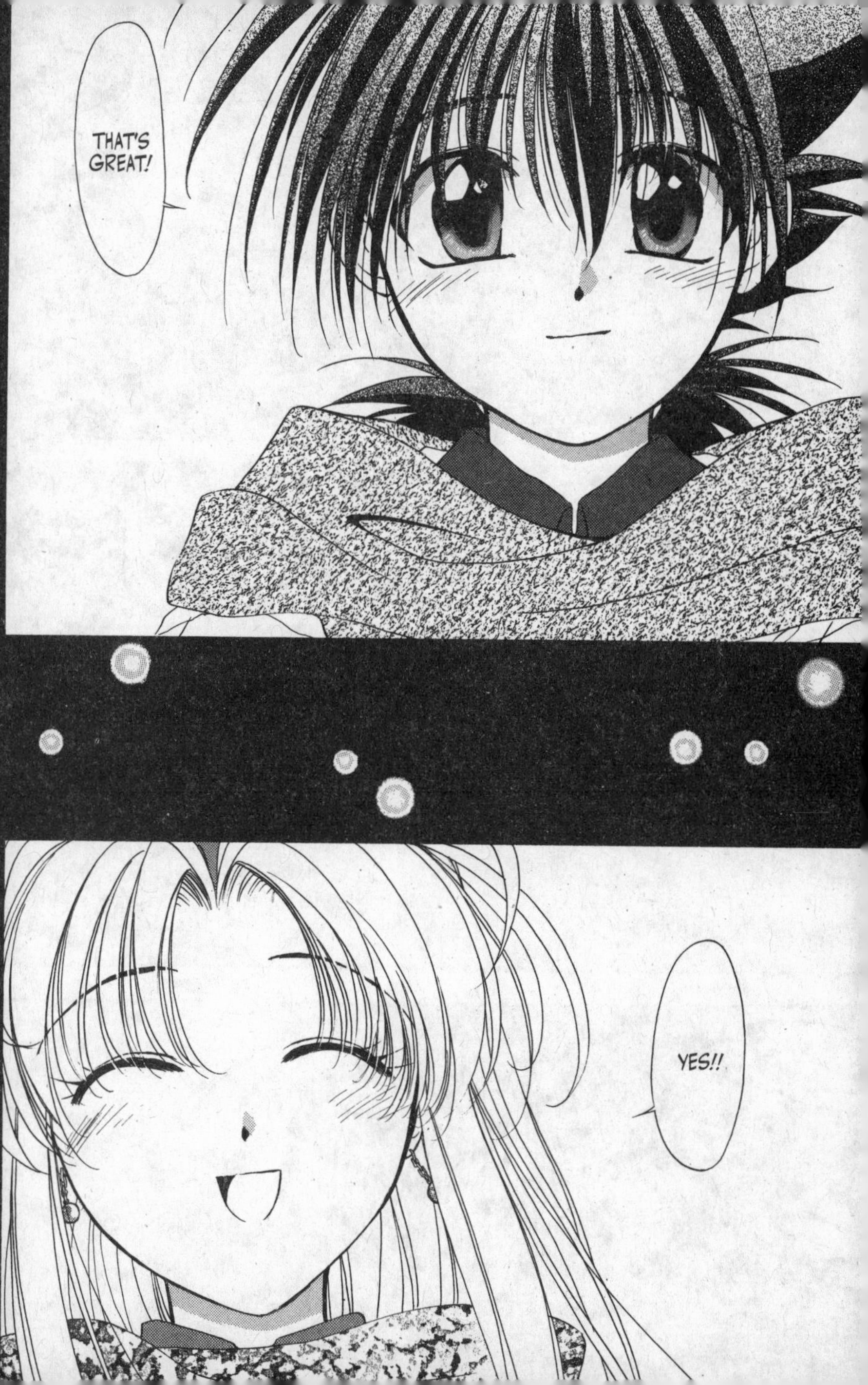
THAT'S GREAT!
YES!!

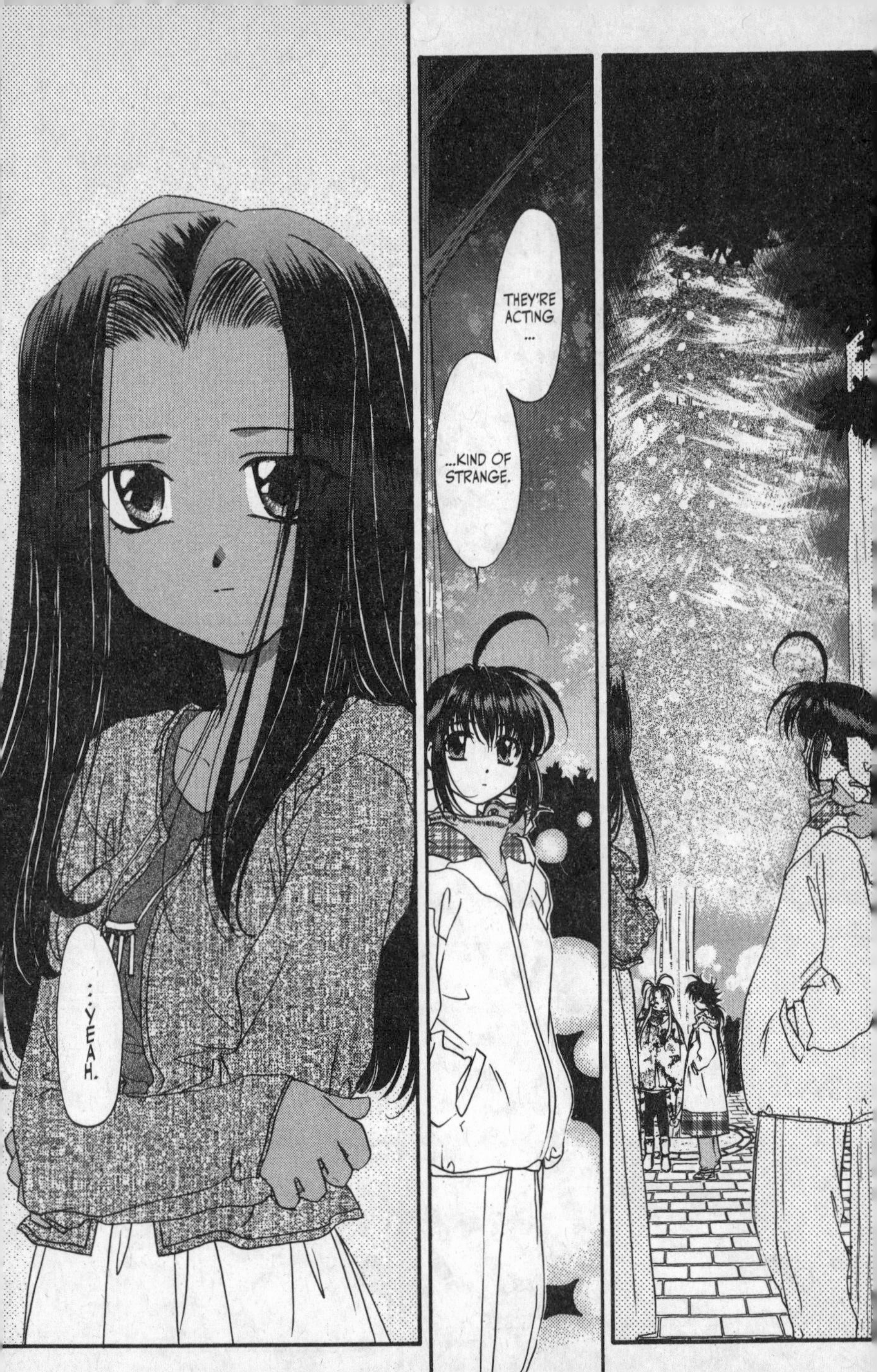
THEY'RE ACTING ...
...KIND OF STRANGE.
...YEAH.

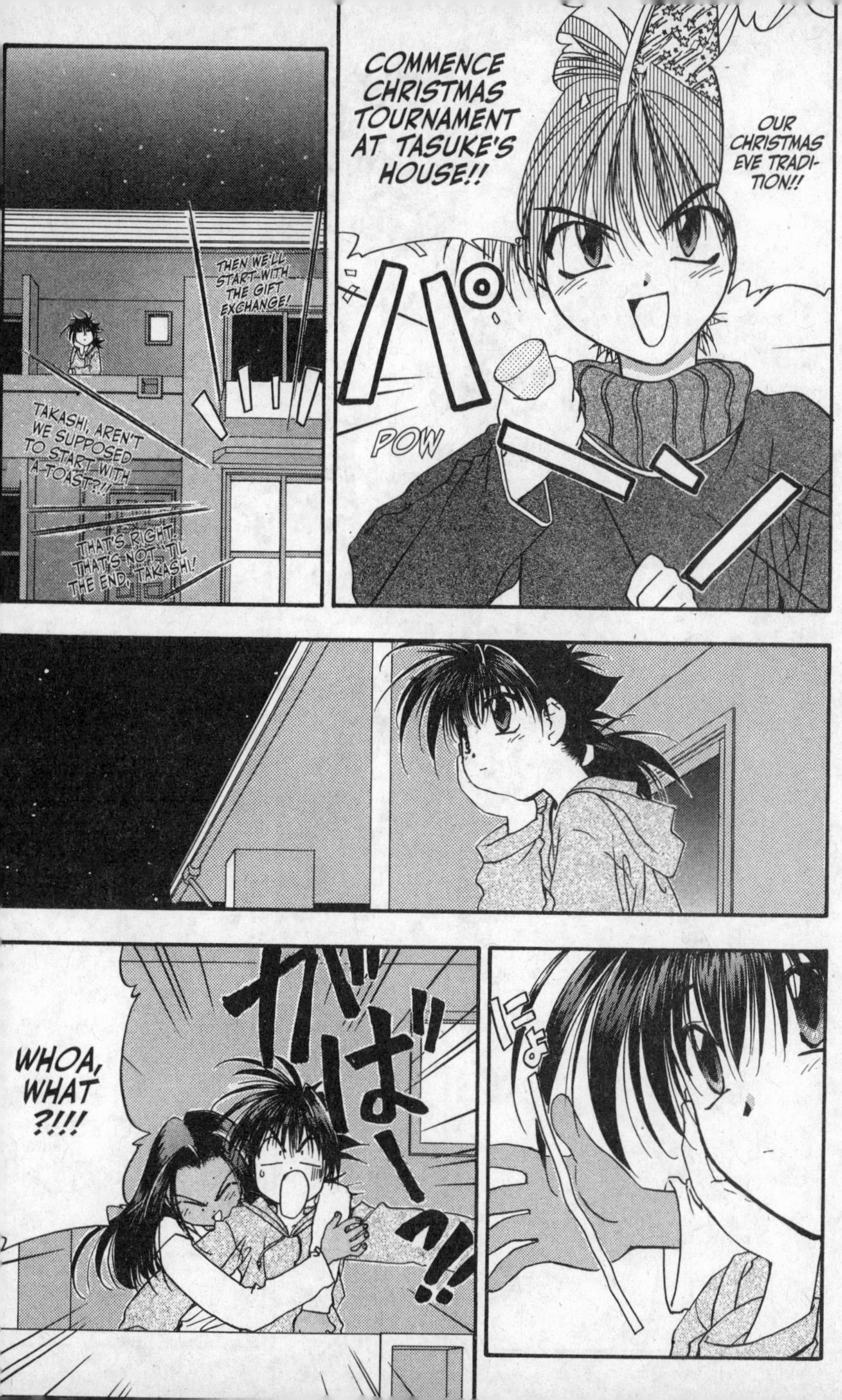
COMMENCE CHRISTMAS TOURNAMENT AT TASUKE'S HOUSE!!
OUR CHRISTMAS EVE TRADI-TION!!
POW
THEN WE'LL START WITH THE GIFT EXCHANGE!
TAKASHI, AREN'T WE SUPPOSED TO START WITH A TOAST?!!
THAT'S RIGHT. THAT'S NOT 'TIL THE END, TAKASHI!
WHOA, WHAT ?!!!

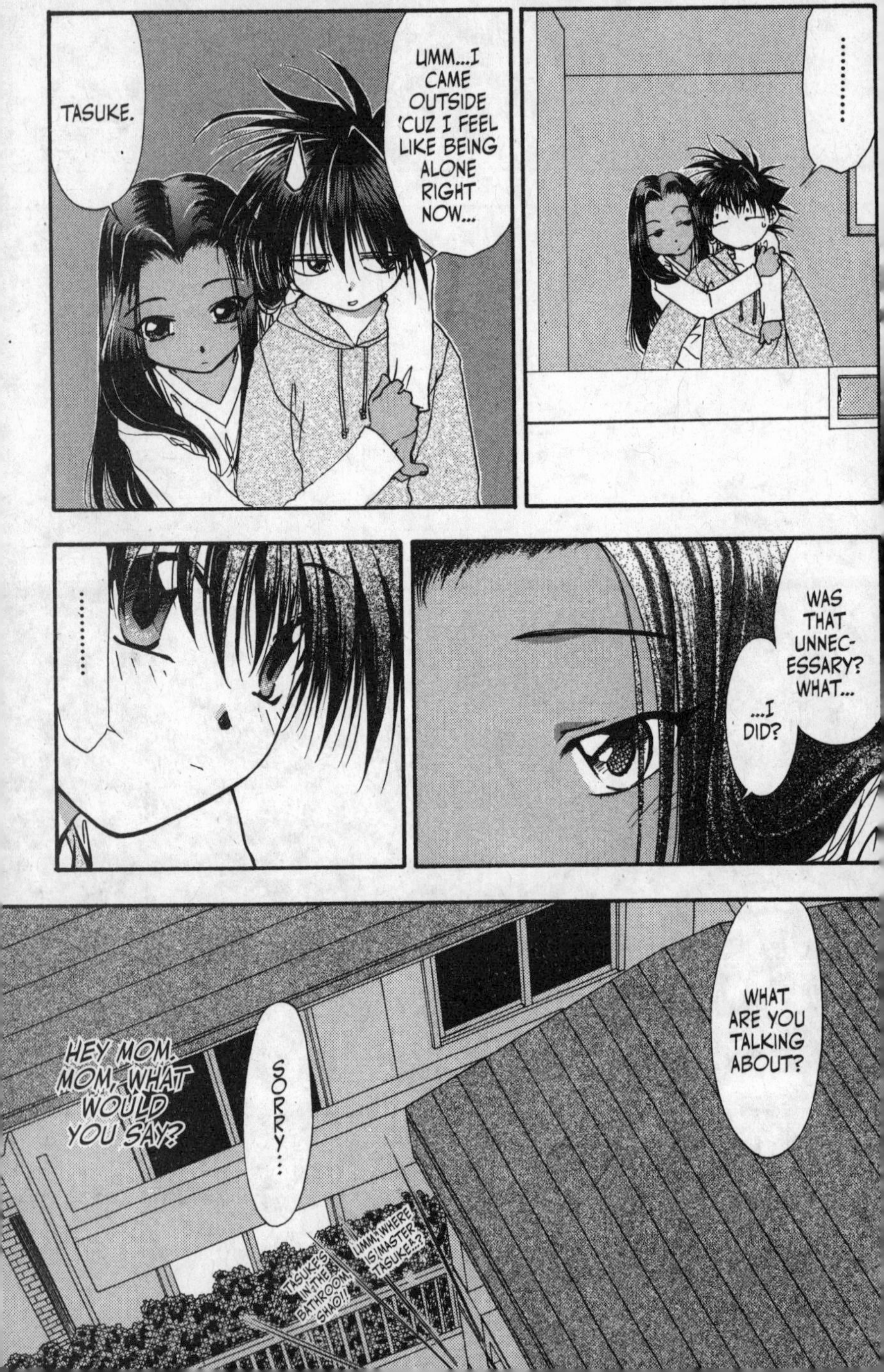
....
UMM...I CAME OUTSIDE 'CUZ I FEEL LIKE BEING ALONE RIGHT NOW...
TASUKE.
WAS THAT UNNEC-ESSARY? WHAT...
...I DID?
....
WHAT ARE YOU TALKING ABOUT?
SORRY...
HEY MOM. MOM, WHAT WOULD YOU SAY?
UMM, WHERE IS MASTER TASUKE...?
TASUKE'S IN THE BATHROOM, SHAO!!

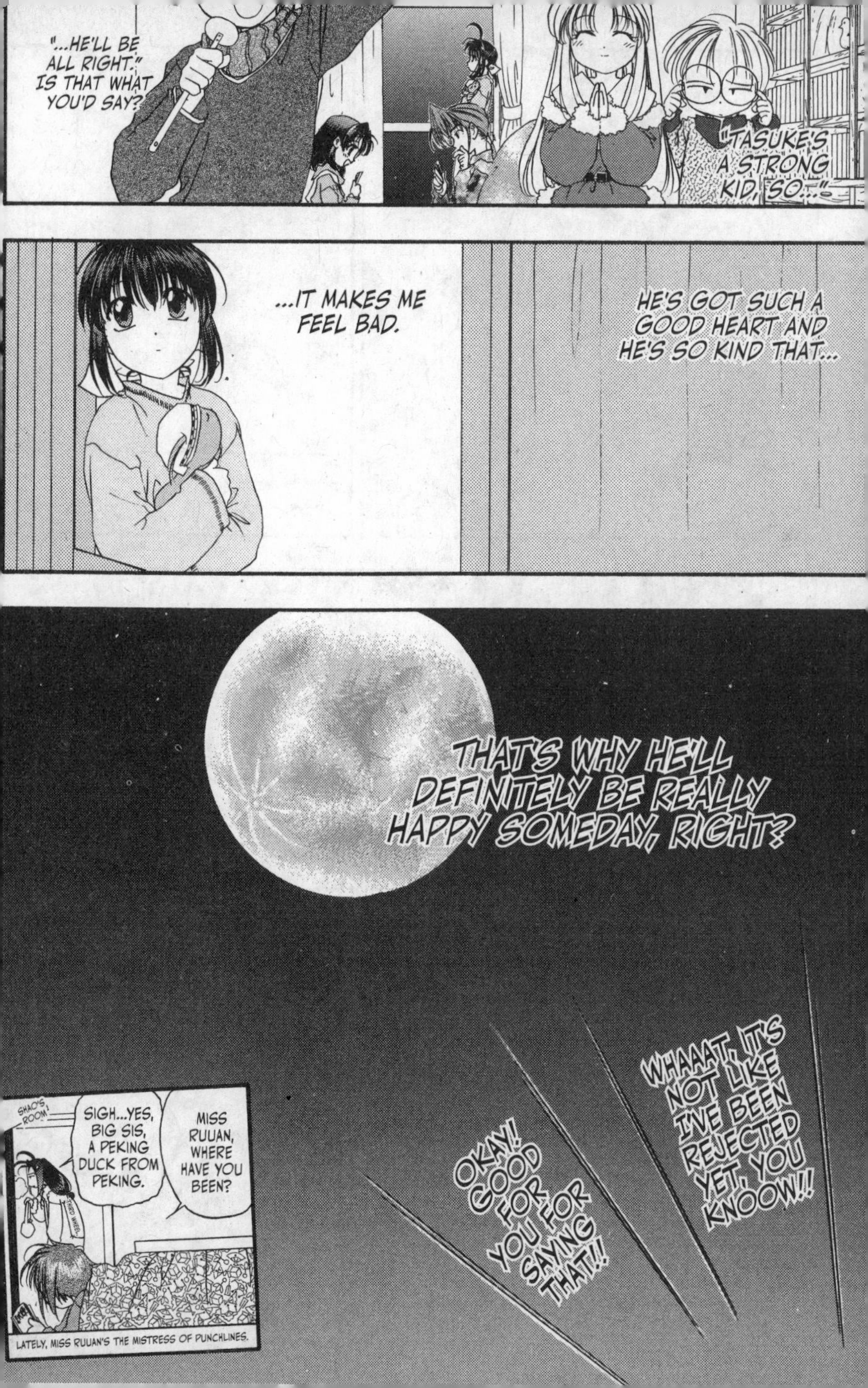
"TASUKE'S A STRONG KID, SO..."
"...HE'LL BE ALL RIGHT." IS THAT WHAT YOU'D SAY?
HE'S GOT SUCH A GOOD HEART AND HE'S SO KIND THAT...
...IT MAKES ME FEEL BAD.
THAT'S WHY HE'LL DEFINITELY BE REALLY HAPPY SOMEDAY, RIGHT?
WHAAAT, IT'S NOT LIKE I'VE BEEN REJECTED YET, YOU KNOOW!!
OKAY! GOOD FOR YOU FOR SAYING THAT!!
SHAO'S ROOM
MISS RUUAN, WHERE HAVE YOU BEEN?
SIGH...YES, BIG SIS, A PEKING DUCK FROM PEKING.
THIRD WHEEL
LATELY, MISS RUUAN'S THE MISTRESS OF PUNCHLINES.

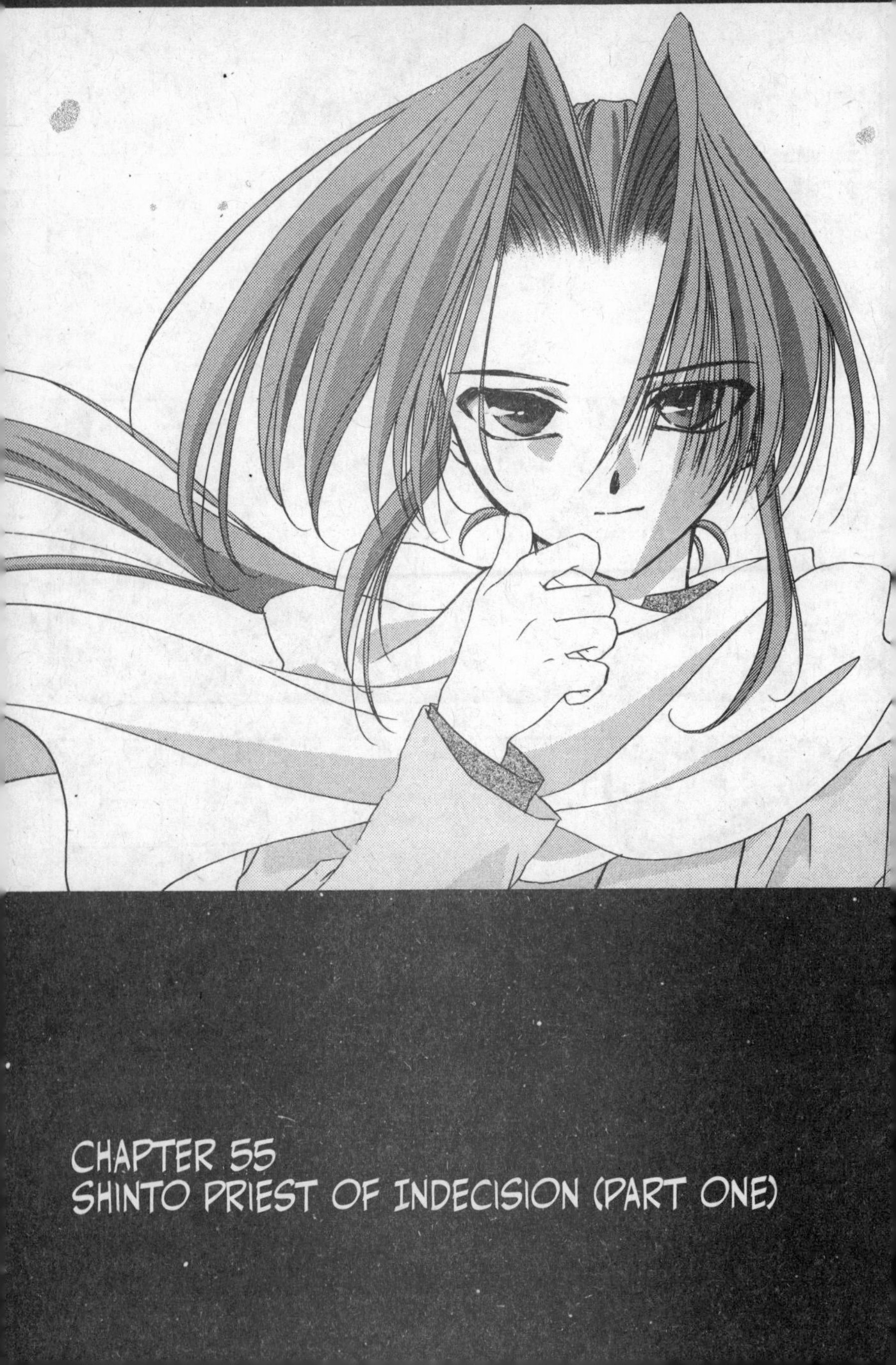

CHAPTER 55
SHINTO PRIEST OF INDECISION (PART ONE)

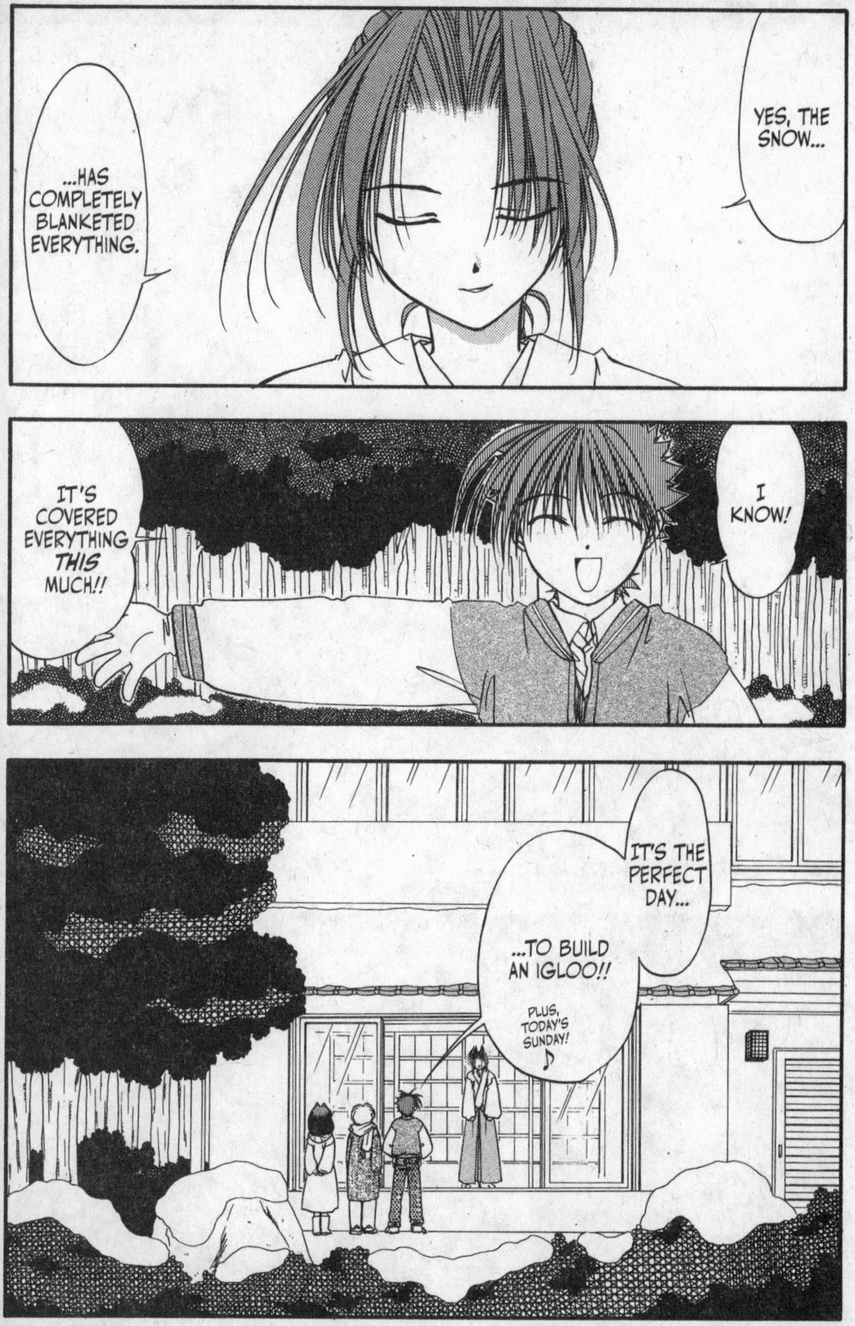
YES, THE SNOW...
...HAS COMPLETELY BLANKETED EVERYTHING.
I KNOW!
IT'S COVERED EVERYTHING *THIS* MUCH!!
IT'S THE PERFECT DAY...
...TO BUILD AN IGLOO!!
PLUS, TODAY'S SUNDAY! ♪

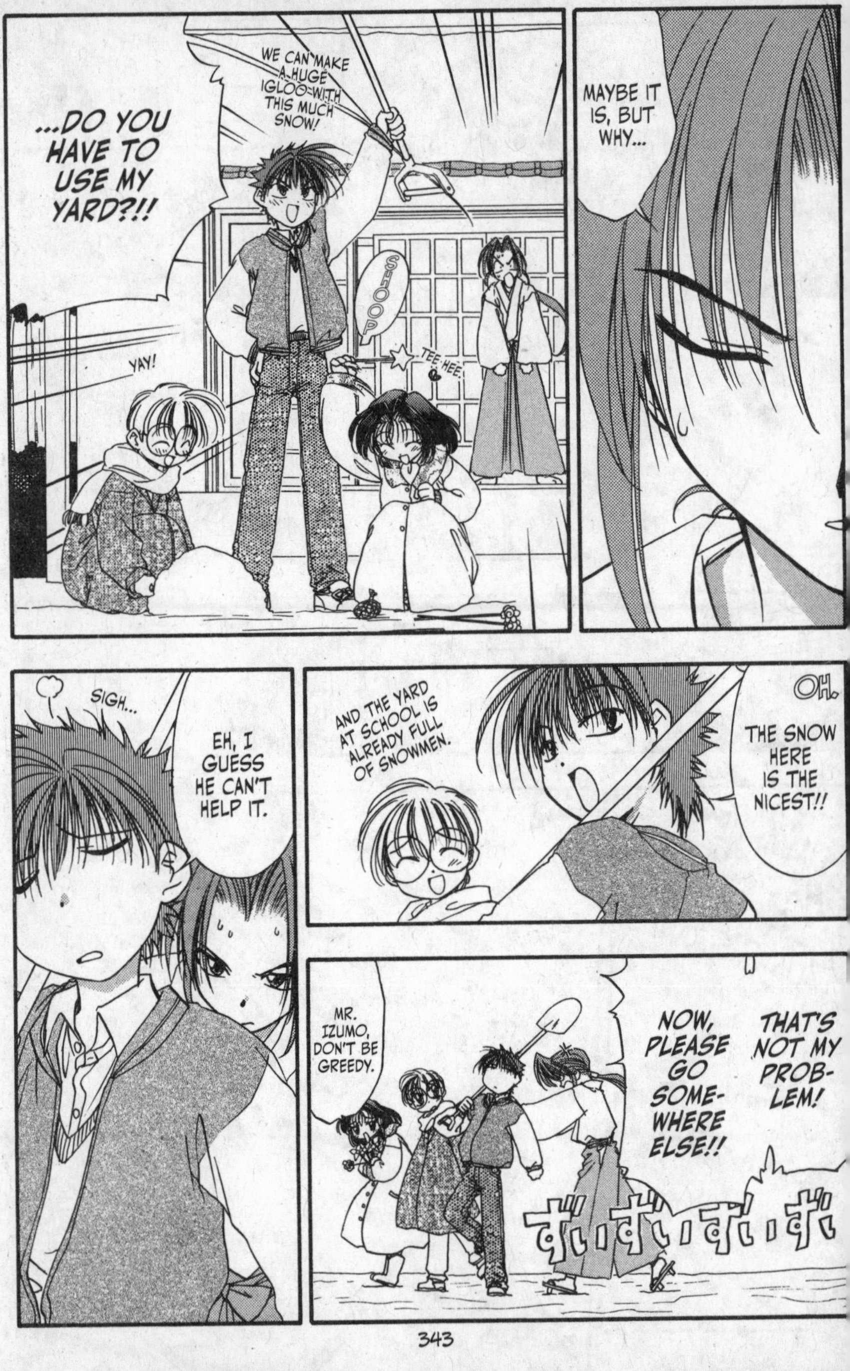
MAYBE IT IS, BUT WHY...
WE CAN MAKE A HUGE IGLOO WITH THIS MUCH SNOW!
...DO YOU HAVE TO USE MY YARD?!!
SHOOP
TEE HEE
YAY!
OH.
THE SNOW HERE IS THE NICEST!!
AND THE YARD AT SCHOOL IS ALREADY FULL OF SNOWMEN.
THAT'S NOT MY PROB-LEM!
NOW, PLEASE GO SOME-WHERE ELSE!!
MR. IZUMO, DON'T BE GREEDY.
ずぃずぃずぃず
SIGH...
EH, I GUESS HE CAN'T HELP IT.

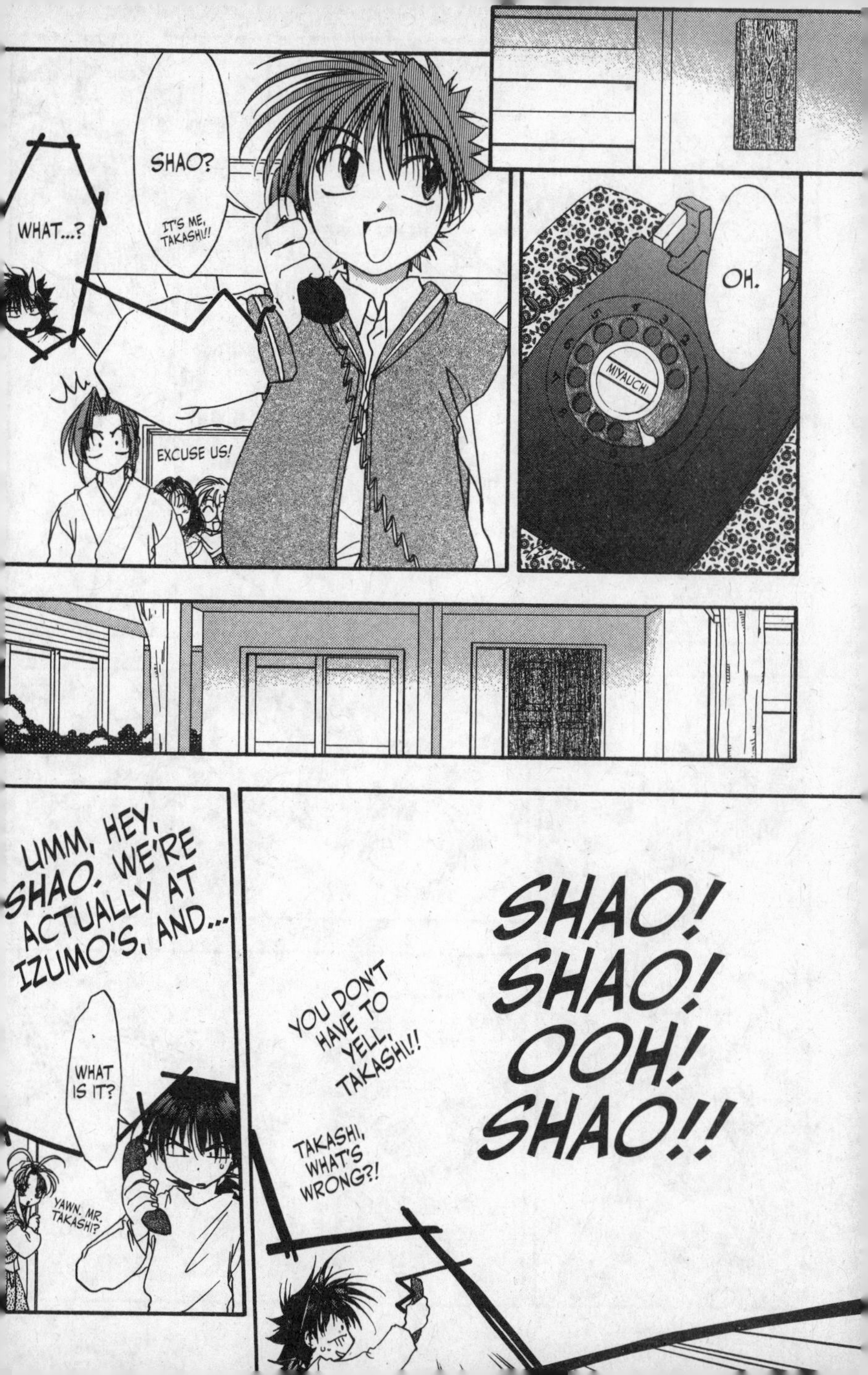
MIYAUCHI
OH.
MIYAUCHI
SHAO?
IT'S ME, TAKASHI!!
WHAT...?
EXCUSE US!
SHAO! SHAO! OOH! SHAO!!
YOU DON'T HAVE TO YELL, TAKASHI!!
TAKASHI, WHAT'S WRONG?!
UMM, HEY, SHAO. WE'RE ACTUALLY AT IZUMO'S, AND...
WHAT IS IT?
YAWN. MR. TAKASHI?

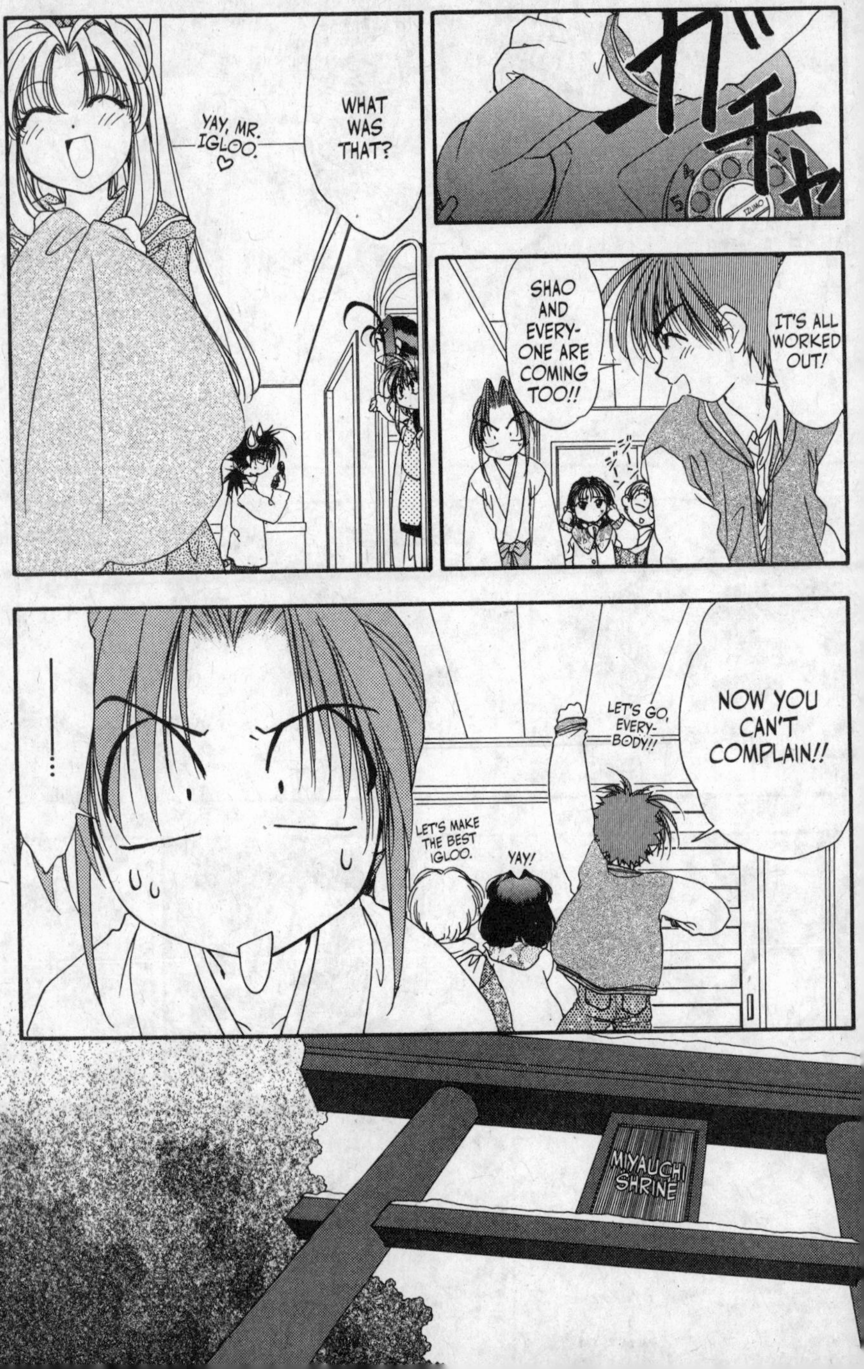
ガチャ
IZUMO
IT'S ALL WORKED OUT!
SHAO AND EVERYONE ARE COMING TOO!!
WHAT WAS THAT?
YAY, MR. IGLOO. ♡
NOW YOU CAN'T COMPLAIN!!
LET'S GO, EVERYBODY!!
YAY!
LET'S MAKE THE BEST IGLOO.
......
MIYAUCHI SHRINE

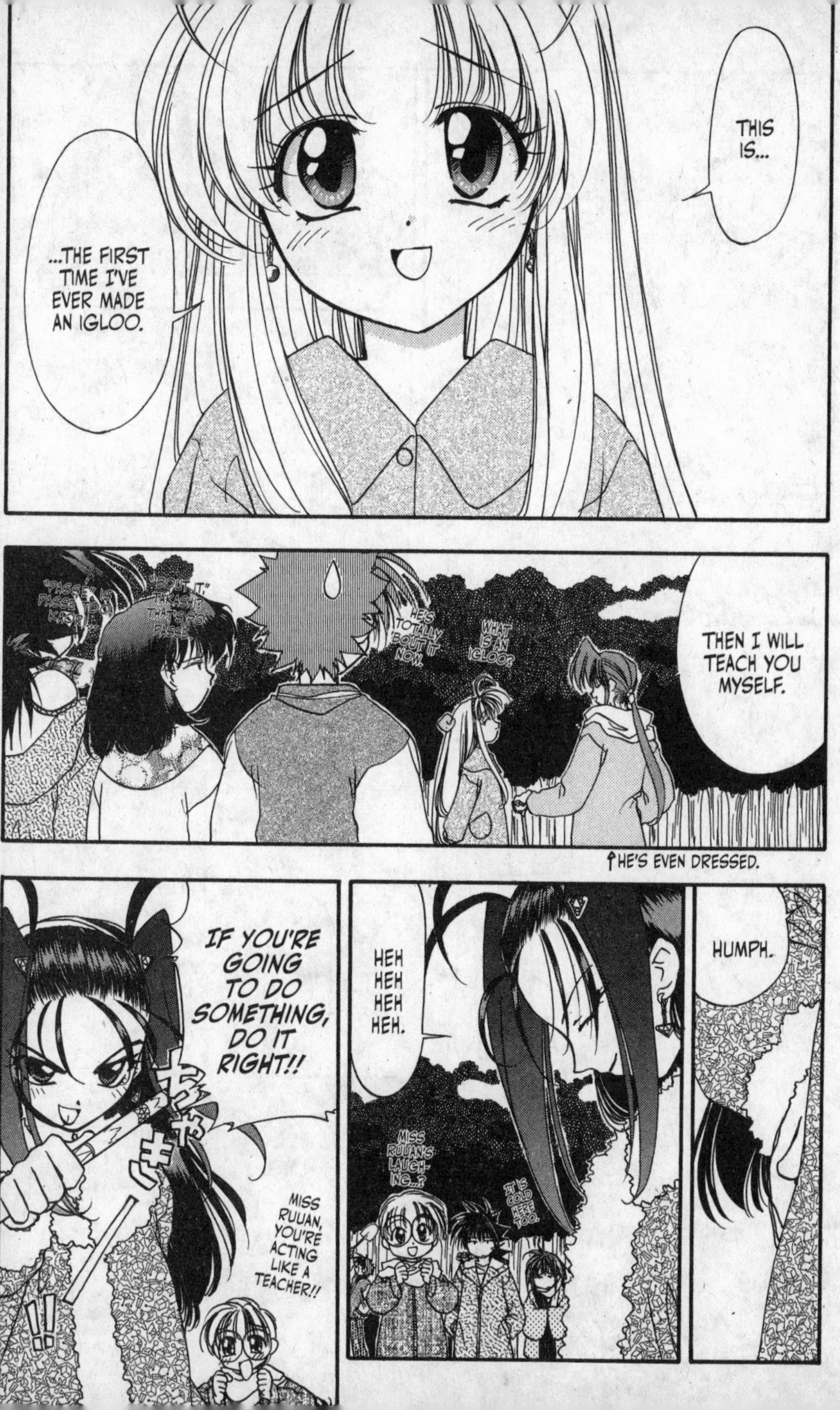
THIS IS...
...THE FIRST TIME I'VE EVER MADE AN IGLOO.
THEN I WILL TEACH YOU MYSELF.
WHAT IS AN IGLOO?
HE'S TOTALLY 'BOUT IT NOW.
"'BOUT IT," TAKASHI? THAT'S SO PASSE.
"PASSE" IS PASSE TOO, KAORI...
↑HE'S EVEN DRESSED.
HUMPH.
HEH HEH HEH HEH.
IT IS COLD HERE TOO.
MISS RUUAN'S LAUGHING...?
IF YOU'RE GOING TO DO SOMETHING, DO IT RIGHT!!
MISS RUUAN, YOU'RE ACTING LIKE A TEACHER!!

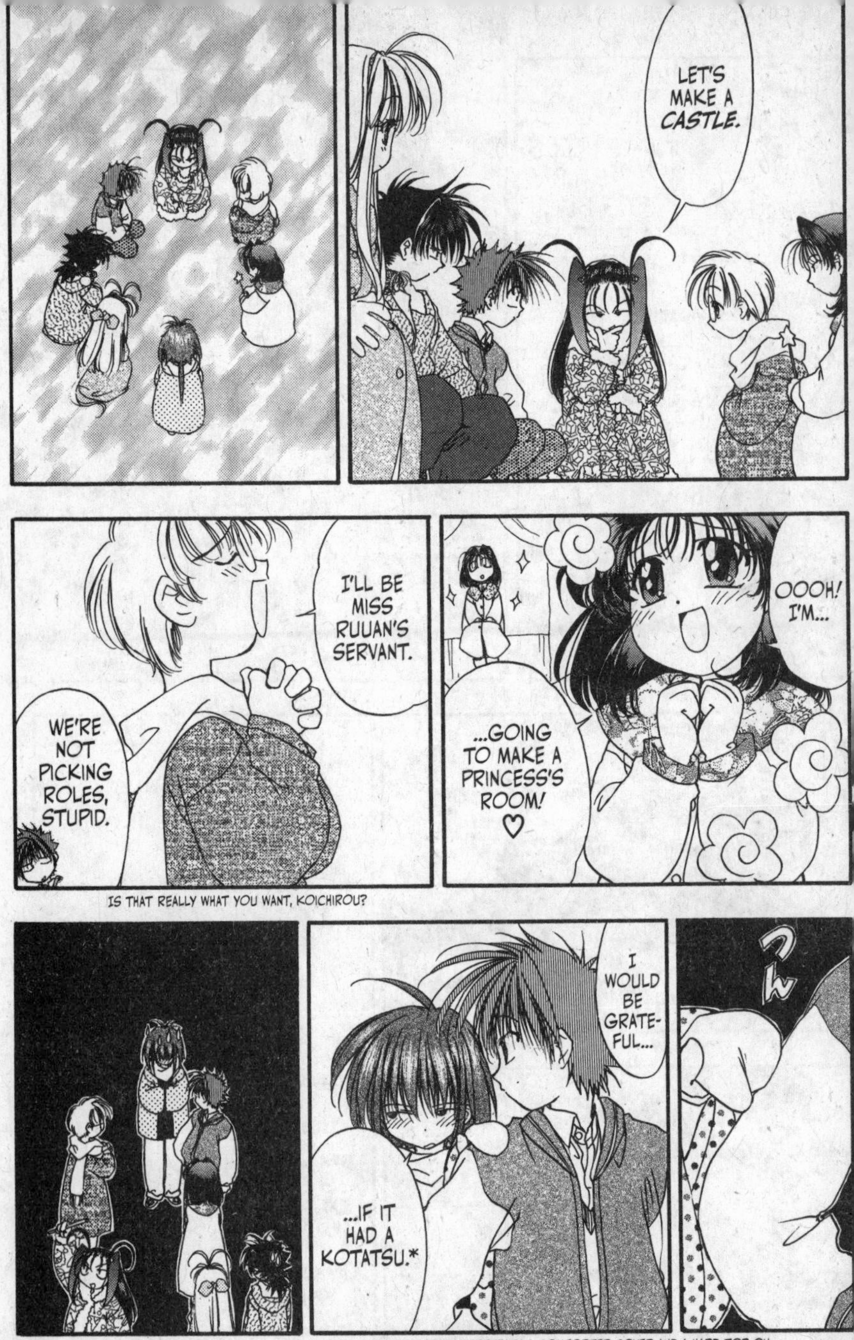
LET'S MAKE A CASTLE.
OOOH! I'M...
...GOING TO MAKE A PRINCESS'S ROOM! ♡
I'LL BE MISS RUUAN'S SERVANT.
WE'RE NOT PICKING ROLES, STUPID.
IS THAT REALLY WHAT YOU WANT, KOICHIROU?
I WOULD BE GRATE-FUL...
...IF IT HAD A KOTATSU.*

* A TABLE WITH A HEATER UNDERNEATH A COMFORTER COVER AND A HARD TOP ON TOP. IT KEEPS YOU WARM WHEN YOU SIT WITH YOUR LEGS IN THE COMFORTER.

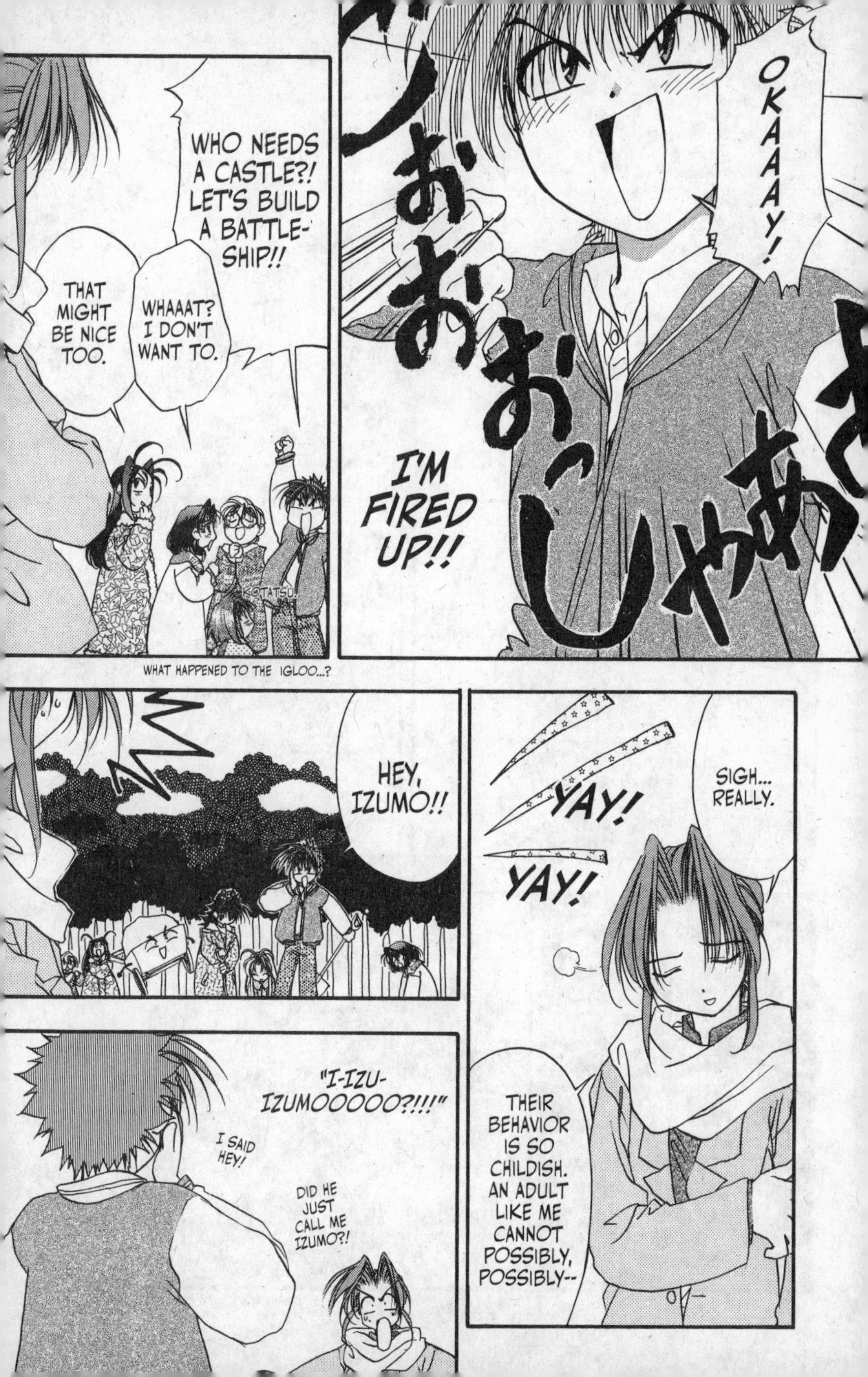
OKAAAY!
おおっしゃあ
I'M FIRED UP!!
WHO NEEDS A CASTLE?! LET'S BUILD A BATTLE-SHIP!!
WHAAAT? I DON'T WANT TO.
THAT MIGHT BE NICE TOO.
KOTATSU
WHAT HAPPENED TO THE IGLOO...?
SIGH... REALLY.
YAY!
YAY!
THEIR BEHAVIOR IS SO CHILDISH. AN ADULT LIKE ME CANNOT POSSIBLY, POSSIBLY--
HEY, IZUMO!!
"I-IZU-IZUMOOOOO?!!!"
I SAID HEY!
DID HE JUST CALL ME IZUMO?!

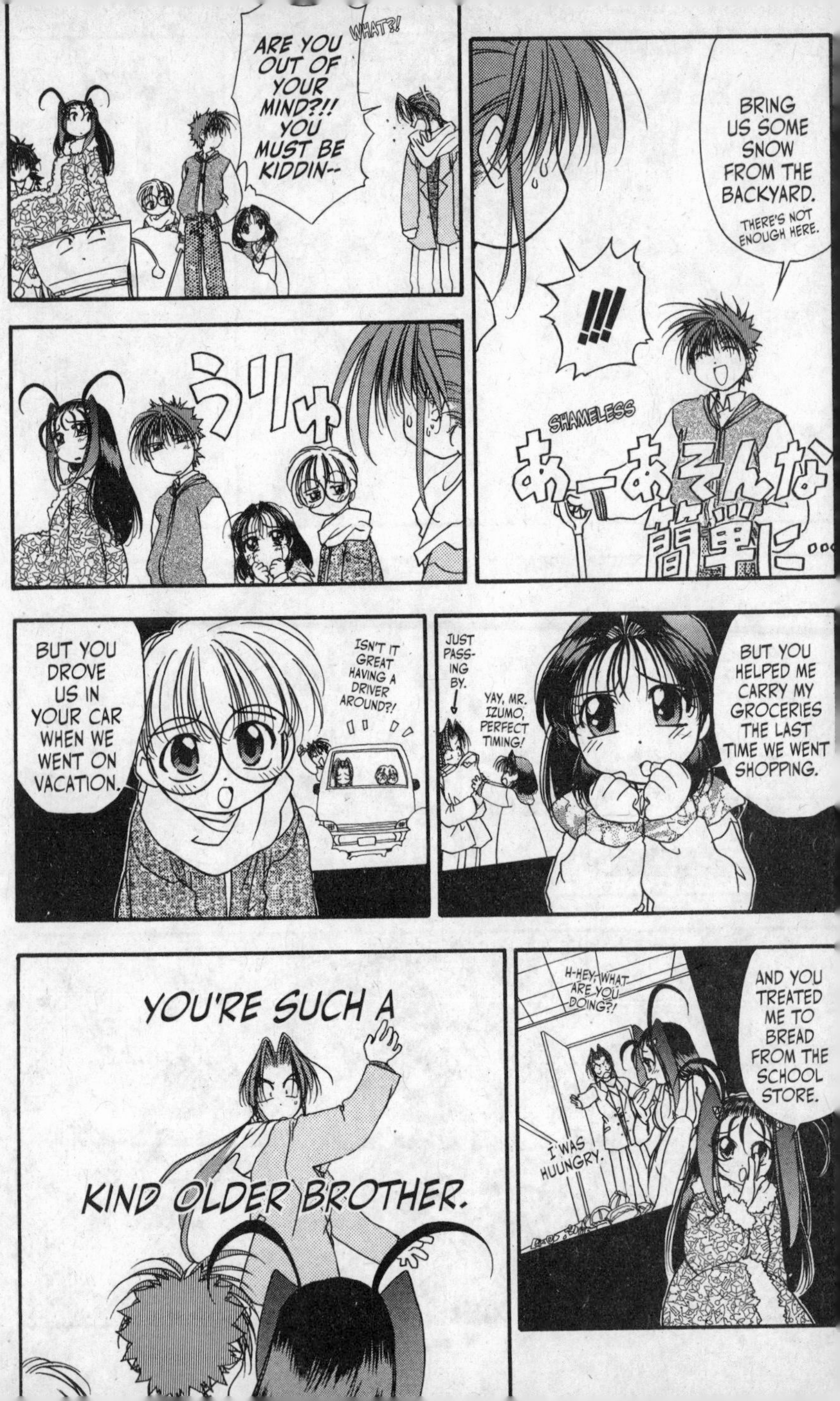
BRING US SOME SNOW FROM THE BACKYARD.
THERE'S NOT ENOUGH HERE.
!!!!
SHAMELESS
あーあそんな簡単に…
WHAT?!
ARE YOU OUT OF YOUR MIND?!! YOU MUST BE KIDDIN--
うりゅ
BUT YOU HELPED ME CARRY MY GROCERIES THE LAST TIME WE WENT SHOPPING.
JUST PASSING BY.
YAY, MR. IZUMO, PERFECT TIMING!
BUT YOU DROVE US IN YOUR CAR WHEN WE WENT ON VACATION.
ISN'T IT GREAT HAVING A DRIVER AROUND?!
AND YOU TREATED ME TO BREAD FROM THE SCHOOL STORE.
H-HEY, WHAT ARE YOU DOING?!
I WAS HUUNGRY.
YOU'RE SUCH A
KIND OLDER BROTHER.

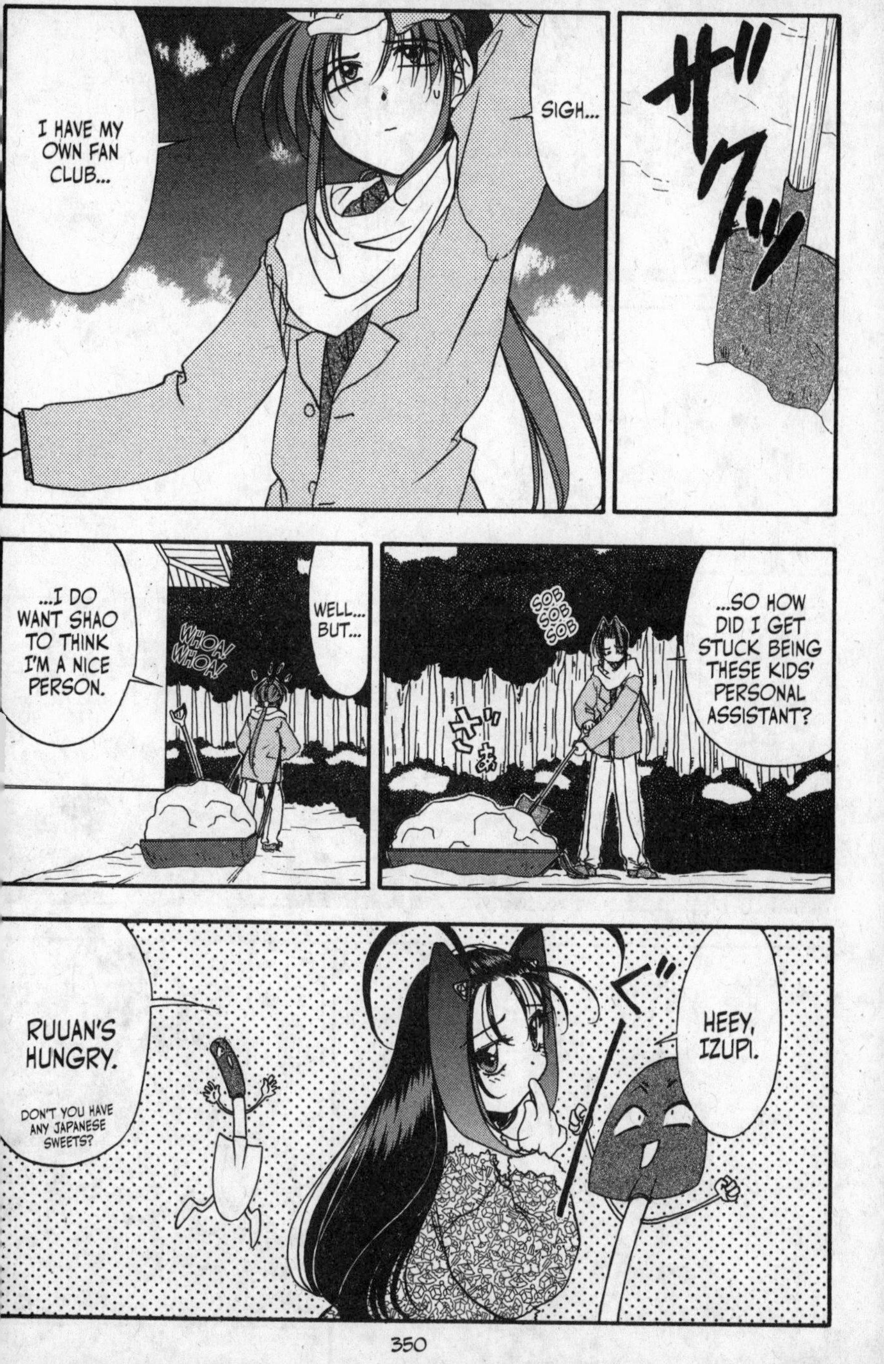
SIGH...
I HAVE MY OWN FAN CLUB...
...SO HOW DID I GET STUCK BEING THESE KIDS' PERSONAL ASSISTANT?
SOB SOB SOB
WELL... BUT...
...I DO WANT SHAO TO THINK I'M A NICE PERSON.
WHOA! WHOA!
HEEY, IZUPI.
RUUAN'S HUNGRY.
DON'T YOU HAVE ANY JAPANESE SWEETS?

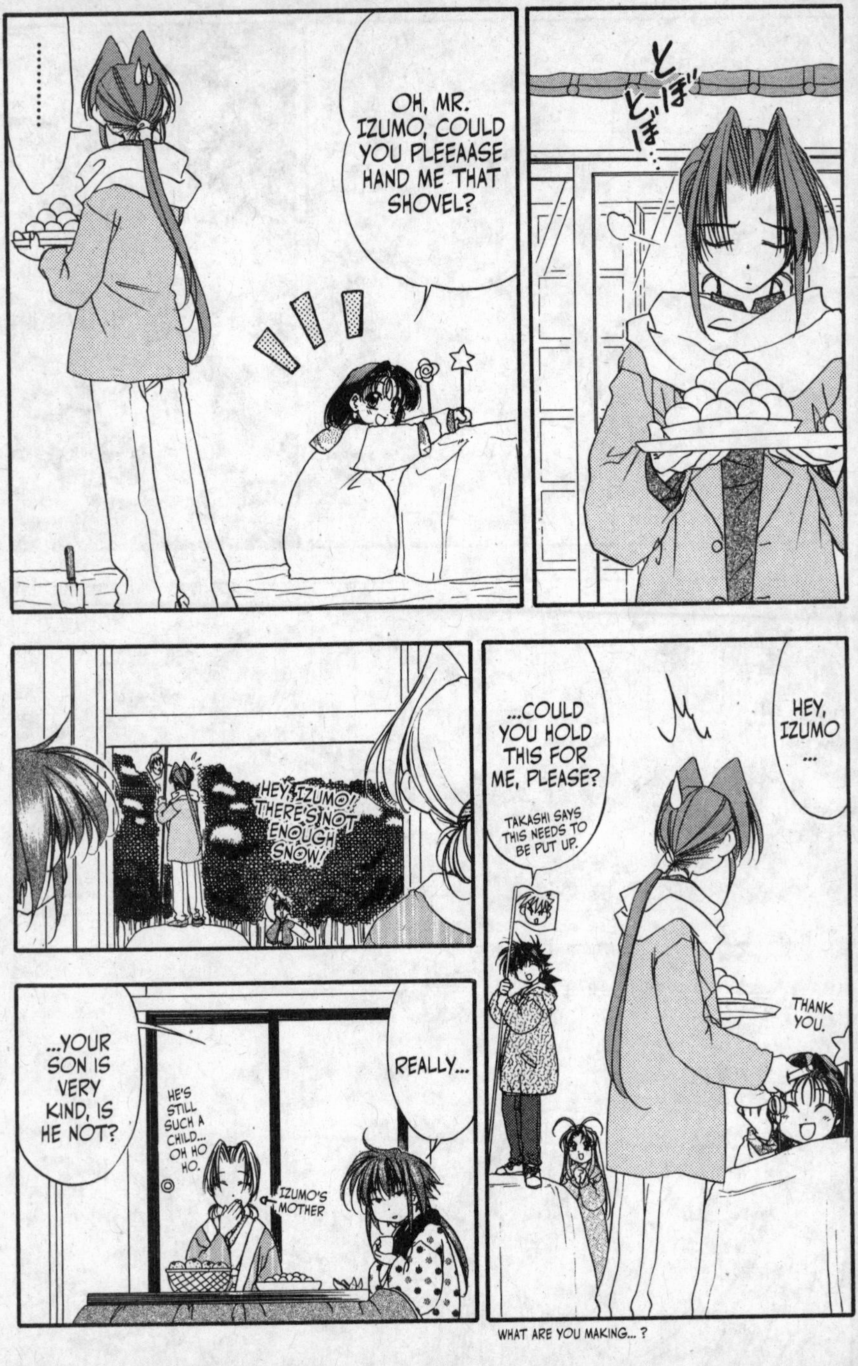
とぼとぼ…
OH, MR. IZUMO, COULD YOU PLEEAASE HAND ME THAT SHOVEL?
......
HEY, IZUMO...
...COULD YOU HOLD THIS FOR ME, PLEASE?
TAKASHI SAYS THIS NEEDS TO BE PUT UP.
THANK YOU.
HEY, IZUMO!! THERE'S NOT ENOUGH SNOW!
REALLY...
...YOUR SON IS VERY KIND, IS HE NOT?
HE'S STILL SUCH A CHILD... OH HO HO.
IZUMO'S MOTHER
WHAT ARE YOU MAKING... ?

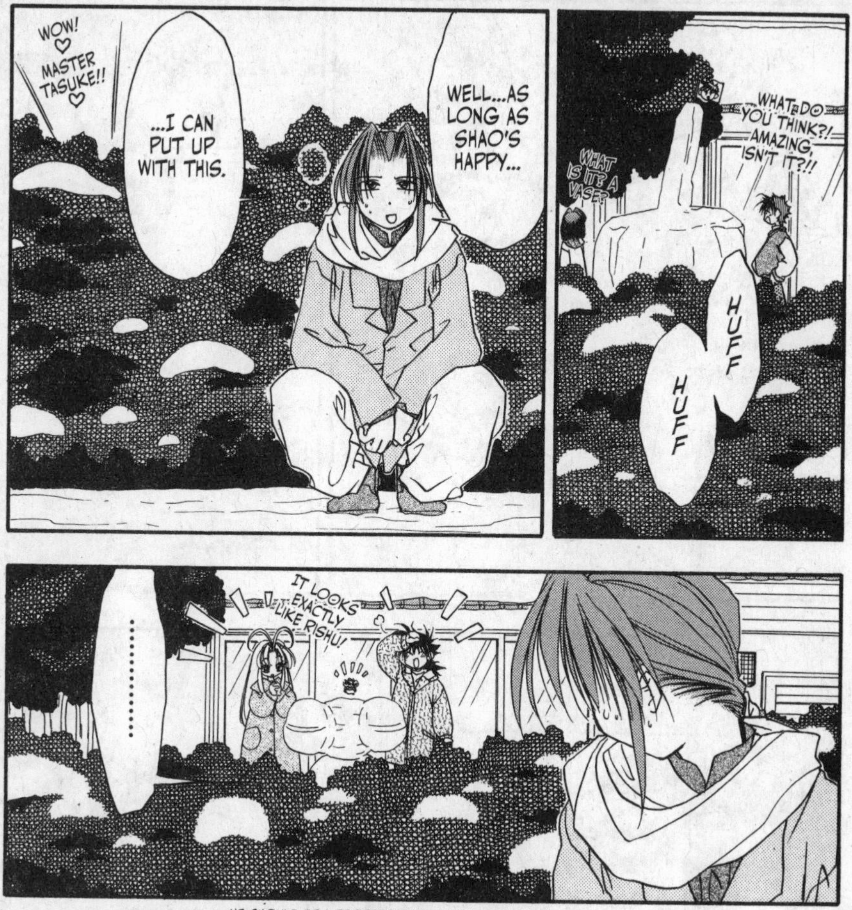
WHAT DO YOU THINK?! AMAZING, ISN'T IT?!!
WHAT IS IT? A VASE?
HUFF
HUFF
WELL...AS LONG AS SHAO'S HAPPY...
...I CAN PUT UP WITH THIS.
WOW! ♡ MASTER TASUKE!! ♡
IT LOOKS EXACTLY LIKE RISHU!
......

HE SHOULD BE A PROFESSIONAL SNOW SCULPTOR.

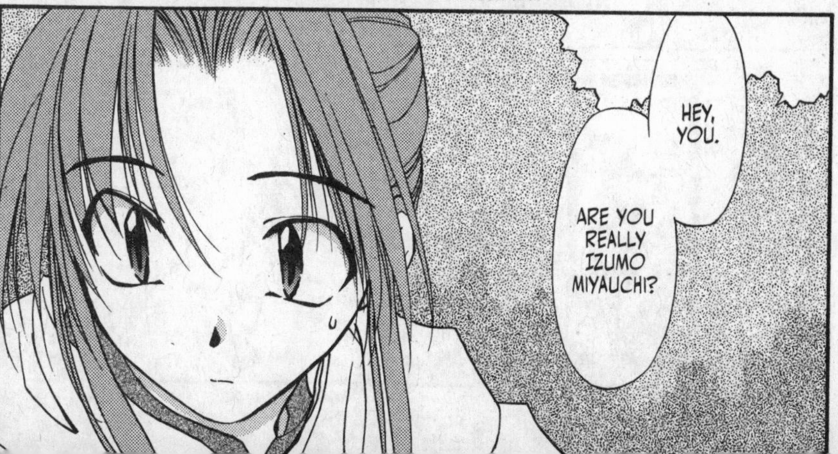
HEY, YOU.
ARE YOU REALLY IZUMO MIYAUCHI?

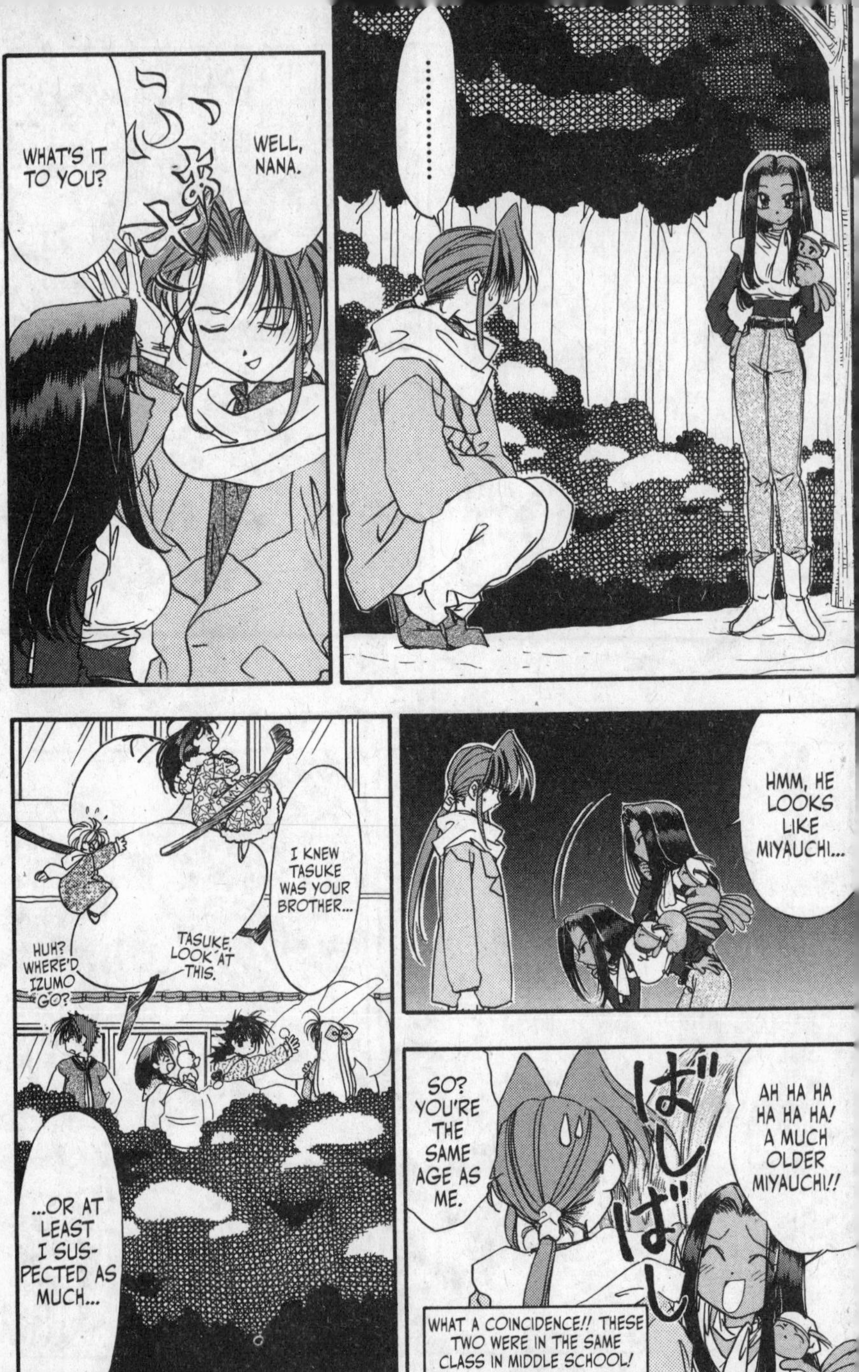
......
WELL, NANA.
WHAT'S IT TO YOU?
HMM, HE LOOKS LIKE MIYAUCHI...
AH HA HA HA HA HA! A MUCH OLDER MIYAUCHI!!
ばしばし
SO? YOU'RE THE SAME AGE AS ME.
WHAT A COINCIDENCE!! THESE TWO WERE IN THE SAME CLASS IN MIDDLE SCHOOL!
I KNEW TASUKE WAS YOUR BROTHER...
TASUKE, LOOK AT THIS.
HUH? WHERE'D IZUMO GO?
...OR AT LEAST I SUSPECTED AS MUCH...

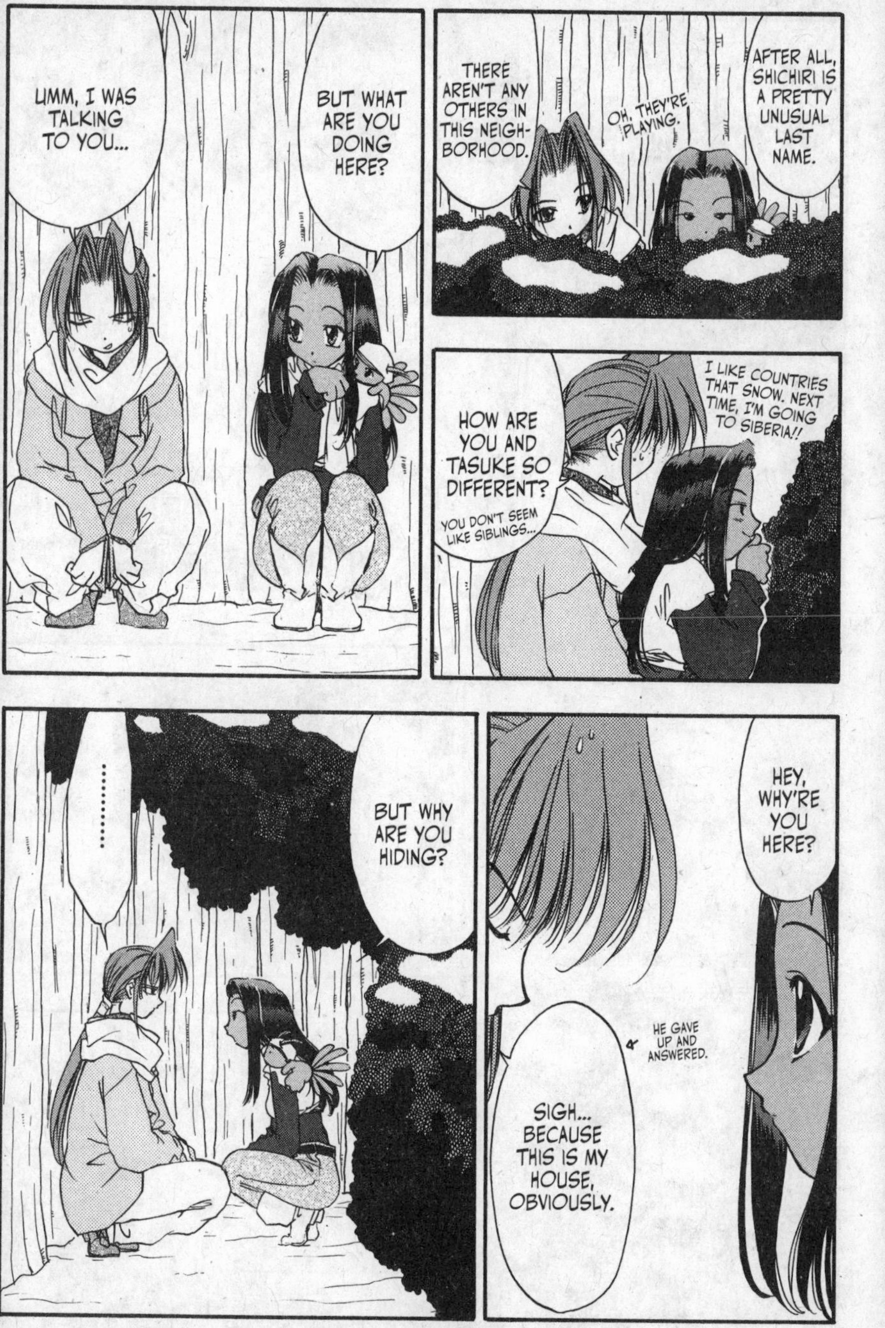
AFTER ALL, SHICHIRI IS A PRETTY UNUSUAL LAST NAME.
OH, THEY'RE PLAYING.
THERE AREN'T ANY OTHERS IN THIS NEIGHBORHOOD.
I LIKE COUNTRIES THAT SNOW. NEXT TIME, I'M GOING TO SIBERIA!!
HOW ARE YOU AND TASUKE SO DIFFERENT?
YOU DON'T SEEM LIKE SIBLINGS...
BUT WHAT ARE YOU DOING HERE?
UMM, I WAS TALKING TO YOU...
HEY, WHY'RE YOU HERE?
HE GAVE UP AND ANSWERED.
SIGH... BECAUSE THIS IS MY HOUSE, OBVIOUSLY.
BUT WHY ARE YOU HIDING?
....

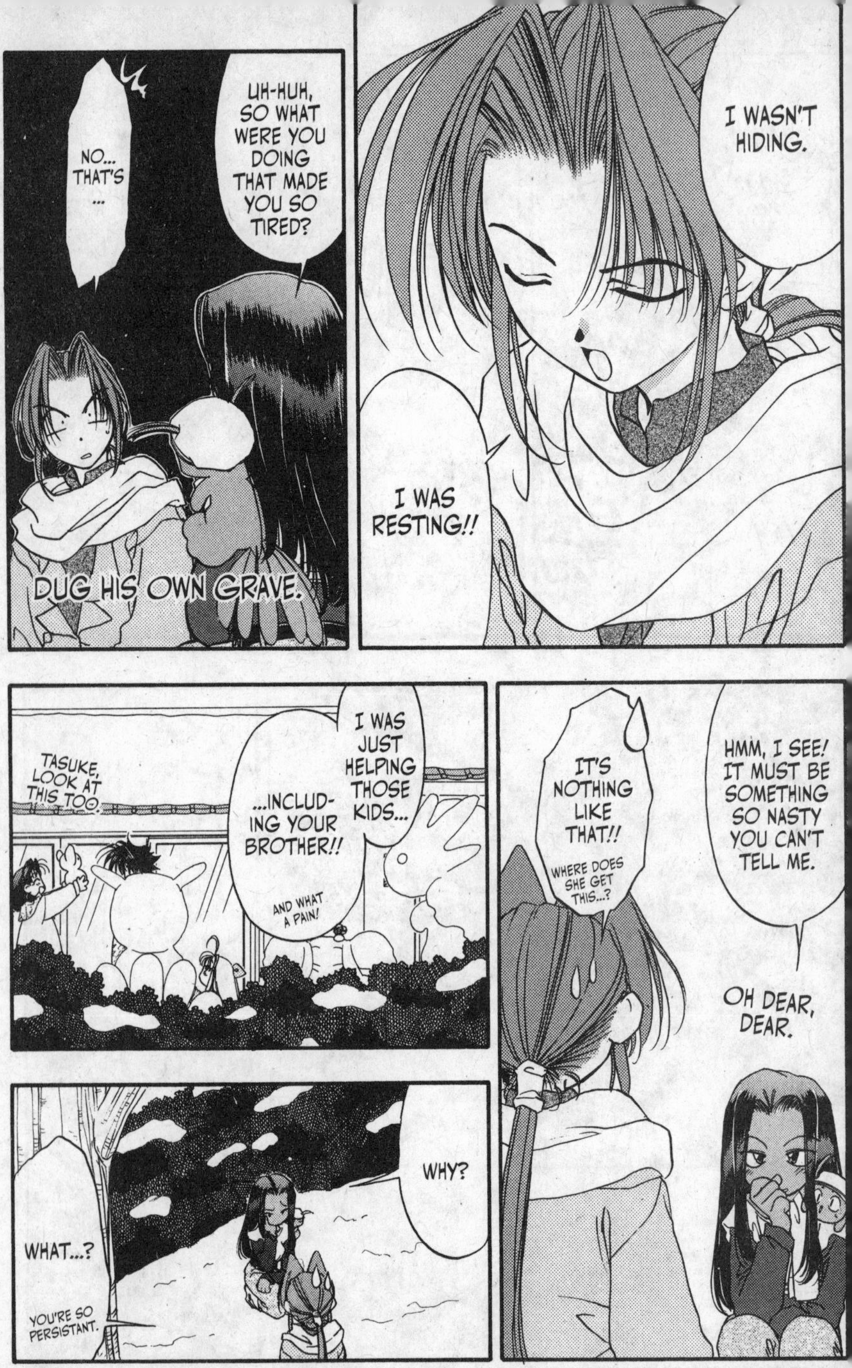
I WASN'T HIDING.
I WAS RESTING!!
UH-HUH, SO WHAT WERE YOU DOING THAT MADE YOU SO TIRED?
NO... THAT'S ...
DUG HIS OWN GRAVE.
HMM, I SEE! IT MUST BE SOMETHING SO NASTY YOU CAN'T TELL ME.
IT'S NOTHING LIKE THAT!!
WHERE DOES SHE GET THIS...?
OH DEAR, DEAR.
I WAS JUST HELPING THOSE KIDS...
...INCLUD-ING YOUR BROTHER!!
AND WHAT A PAIN!
TASUKE, LOOK AT THIS TOO.
WHY?
WHAT...?
YOU'RE SO PERSISTANT.

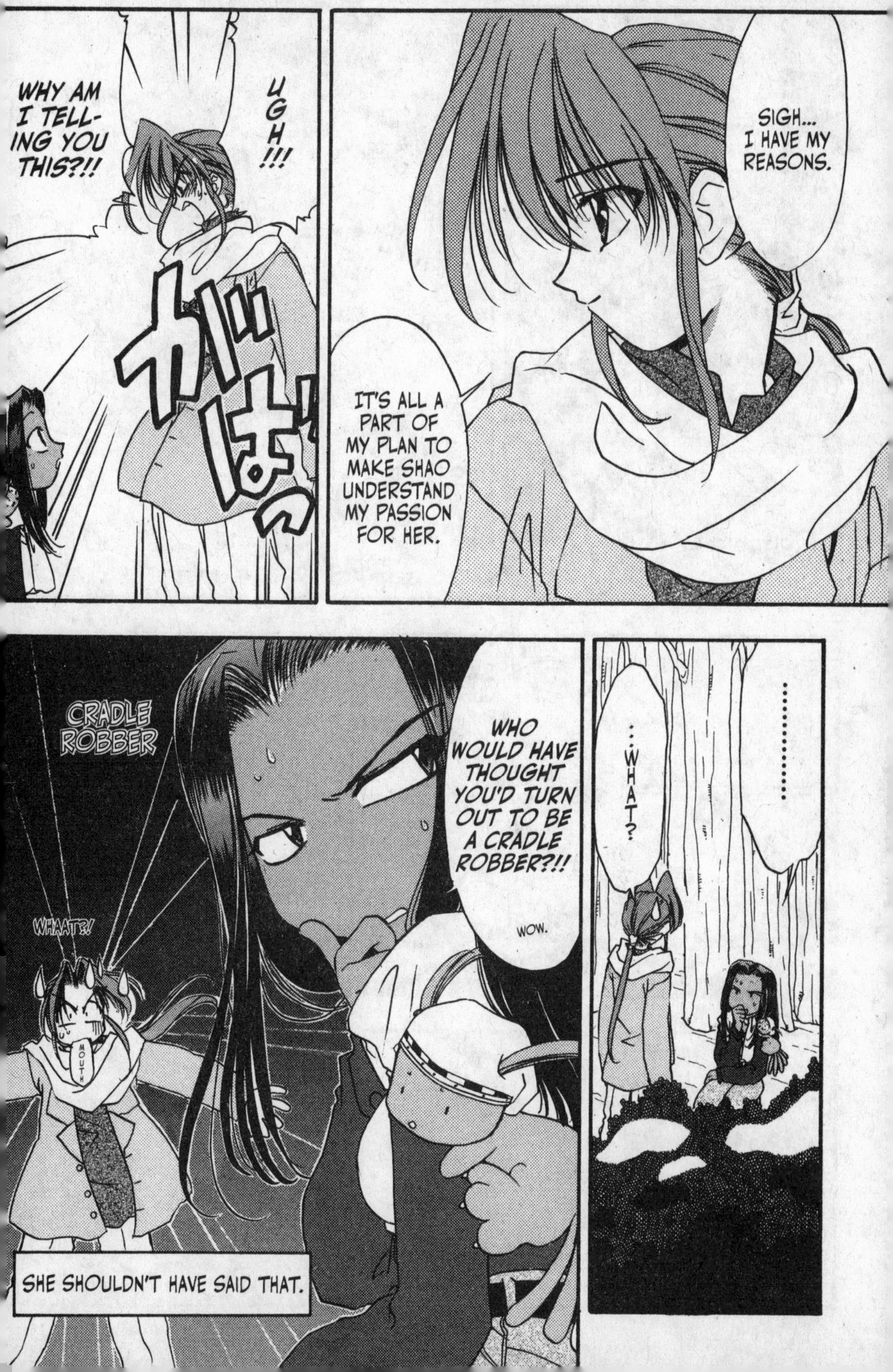

SIGH... I HAVE MY REASONS.
IT'S ALL A PART OF MY PLAN TO MAKE SHAO UNDERSTAND MY PASSION FOR HER.
UGH!!!
WHY AM I TELL-ING YOU THIS?!!
ガばっ
......
...WHAT?
WHO WOULD HAVE THOUGHT YOU'D TURN OUT TO BE A CRADLE ROBBER?!!
WOW.
CRADLE ROBBER
WHAAT?!
MOUTH
SHE SHOULDN'T HAVE SAID THAT.

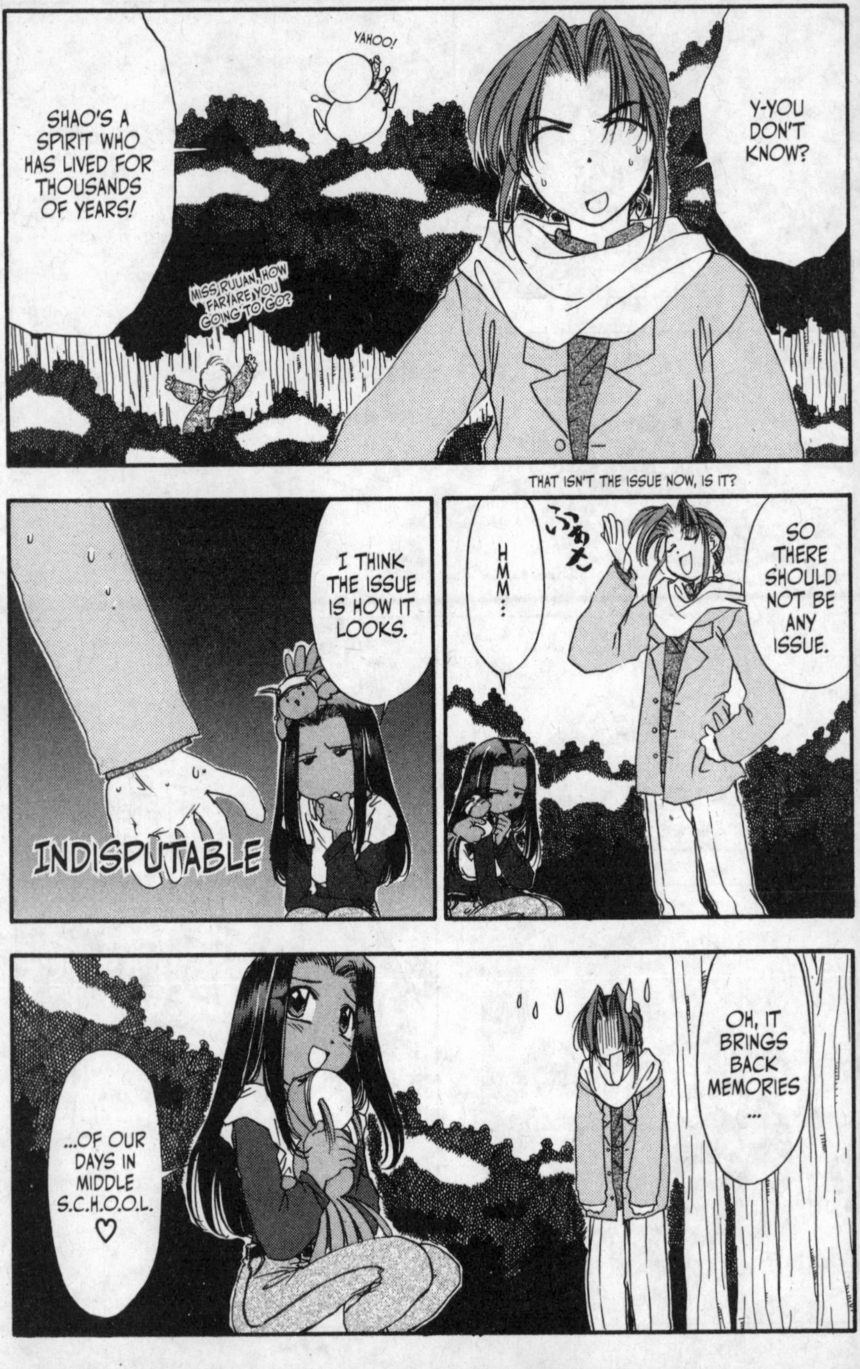
Y-YOU DON'T KNOW?
YAHOO!
SHAO'S A SPIRIT WHO HAS LIVED FOR THOUSANDS OF YEARS!
MISS RUUAN, HOW FAR ARE YOU GOING TO GO?
THAT ISN'T THE ISSUE NOW, IS IT?
SO THERE SHOULD NOT BE ANY ISSUE.
HMM...
I THINK THE ISSUE IS HOW IT LOOKS.
INDISPUTABLE
OH, IT BRINGS BACK MEMORIES ...
...OF OUR DAYS IN MIDDLE S.C.H.O.O.L. ♡

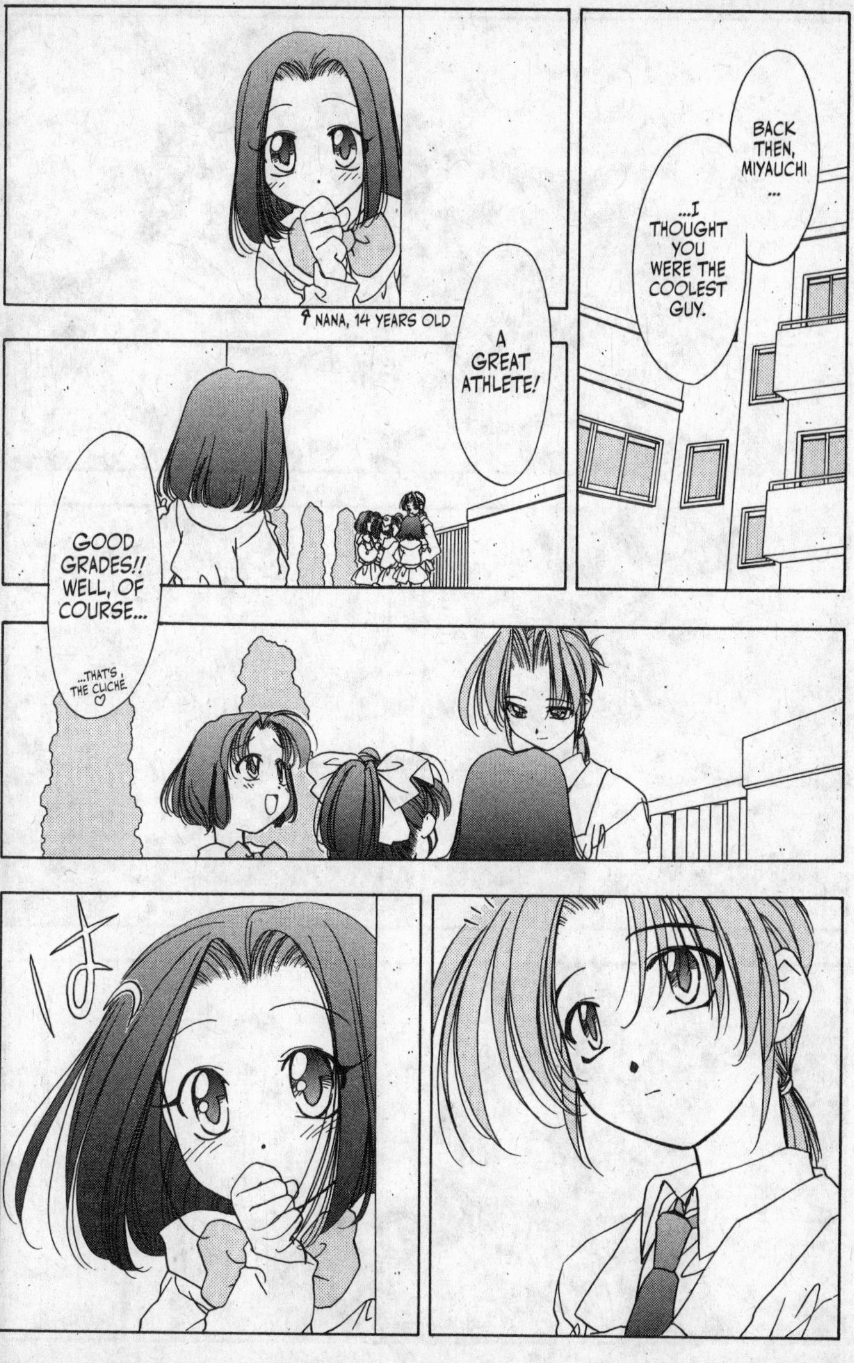
BACK THEN, MIYAUCHI ...
...I THOUGHT YOU WERE THE COOLEST GUY.
A GREAT ATHLETE!
NANA, 14 YEARS OLD
GOOD GRADES!! WELL, OF COURSE...
...THAT'S THE CLICHÉ ♡
は

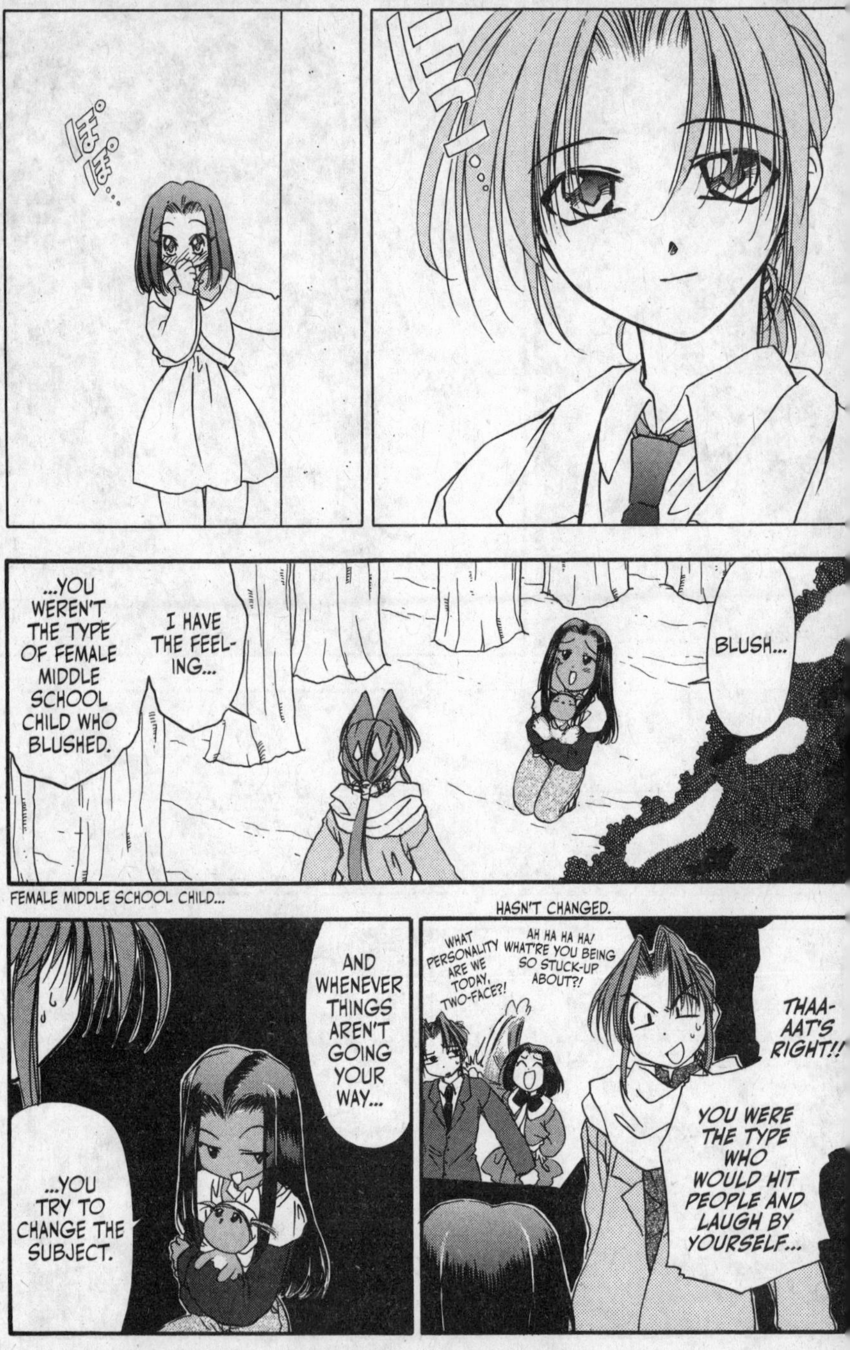

ニコー
ぽぽ...
BLUSH...
I HAVE THE FEEL-ING...
...YOU WEREN'T THE TYPE OF FEMALE MIDDLE SCHOOL CHILD WHO BLUSHED.
FEMALE MIDDLE SCHOOL CHILD...
HASN'T CHANGED.
THAA-AAT'S RIGHT!!
AH HA HA HA! WHAT'RE YOU BEING SO STUCK-UP ABOUT?!
WHAT PERSONALITY ARE WE TODAY, TWO-FACE?!
YOU WERE THE TYPE WHO WOULD HIT PEOPLE AND LAUGH BY YOURSELF...
AND WHENEVER THINGS AREN'T GOING YOUR WAY...
...YOU TRY TO CHANGE THE SUBJECT.

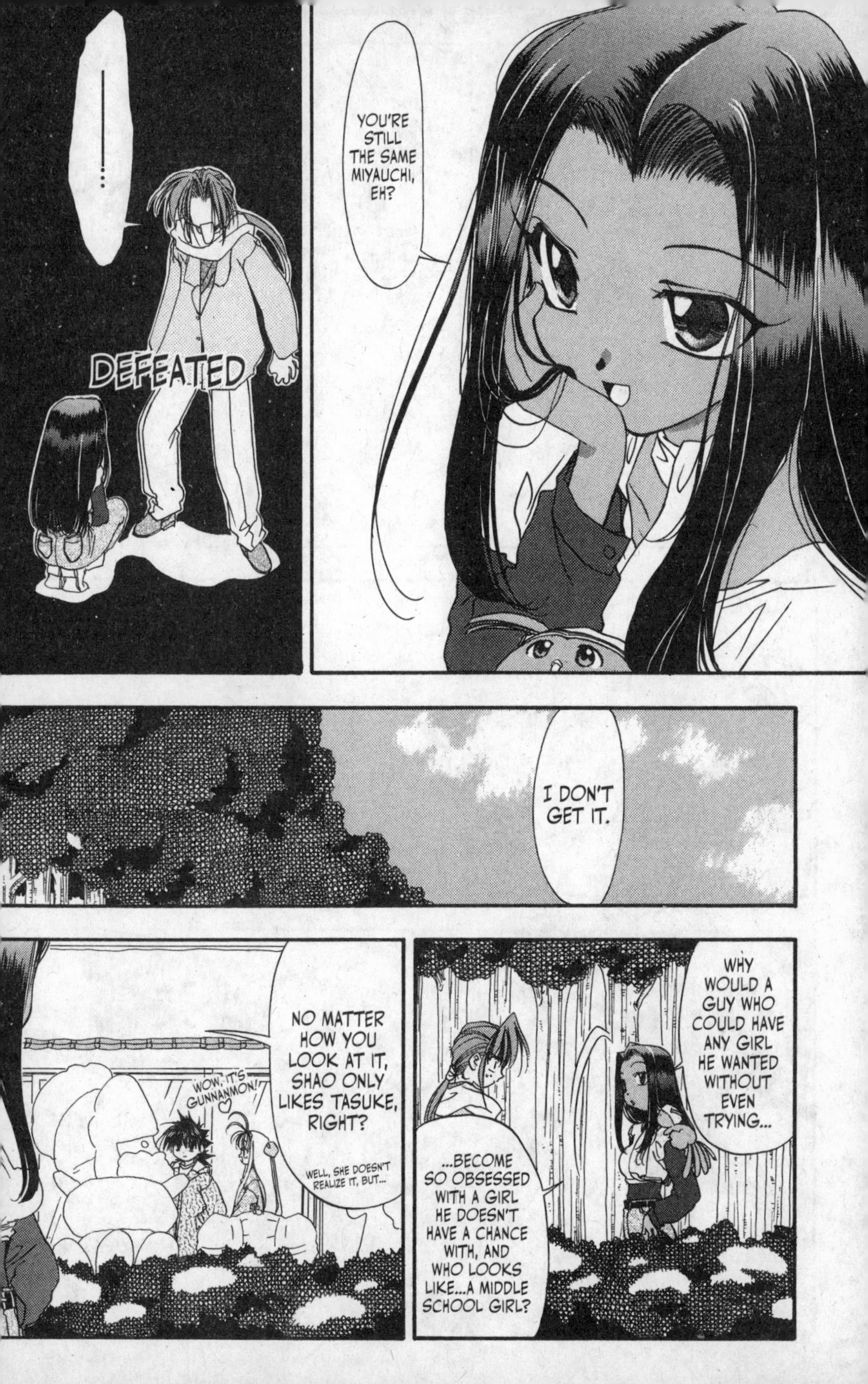
YOU'RE STILL THE SAME MIYAUCHI, EH?
......
DEFEATED
I DON'T GET IT.
WHY WOULD A GUY WHO COULD HAVE ANY GIRL HE WANTED WITHOUT EVEN TRYING...
...BECOME SO OBSESSED WITH A GIRL HE DOESN'T HAVE A CHANCE WITH, AND WHO LOOKS LIKE...A MIDDLE SCHOOL GIRL?
NO MATTER HOW YOU LOOK AT IT, SHAO ONLY LIKES TASUKE, RIGHT?
WOW, IT'S GUNNANMON!
WELL, SHE DOESN'T REALIZE IT, BUT...

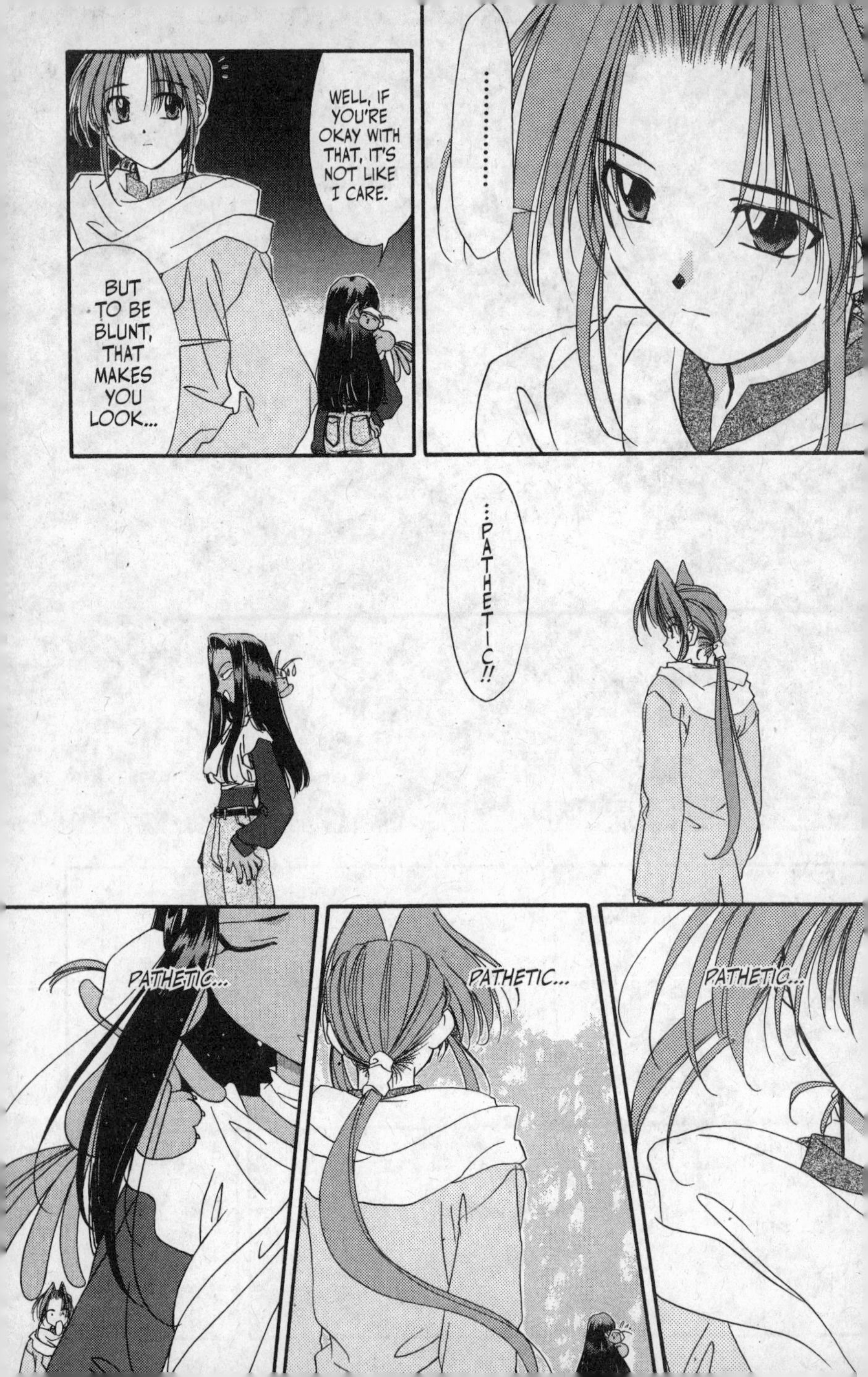
....
WELL, IF YOU'RE OKAY WITH THAT, IT'S NOT LIKE I CARE.
BUT TO BE BLUNT, THAT MAKES YOU LOOK...
...PATHETIC!!
PATHETIC...
PATHETIC...
PATHETIC...

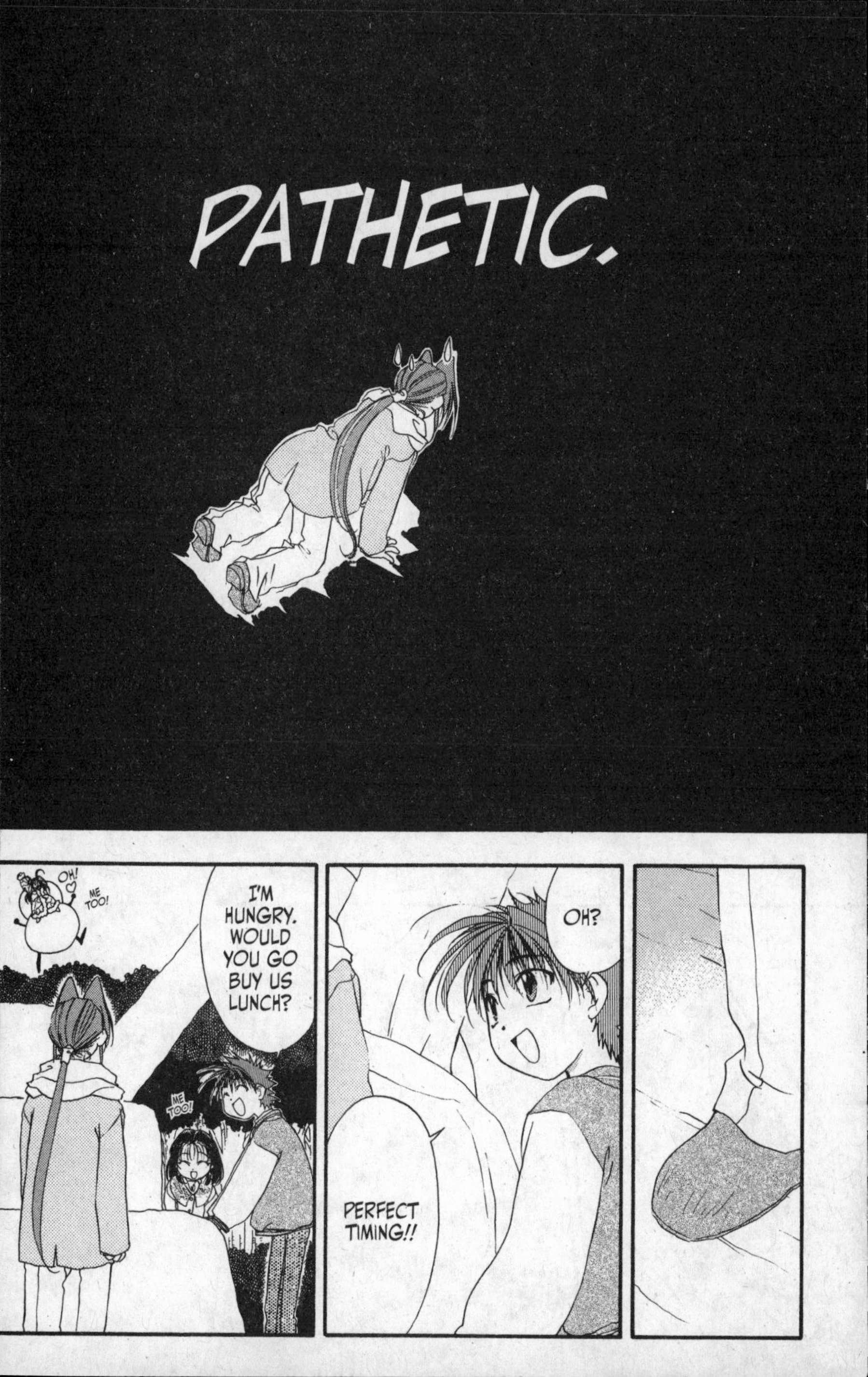
PATHETIC.
OH?
PERFECT TIMING!!
I'M HUNGRY. WOULD YOU GO BUY US LUNCH?
OH! ♥
ME TOO!
ME TOO!

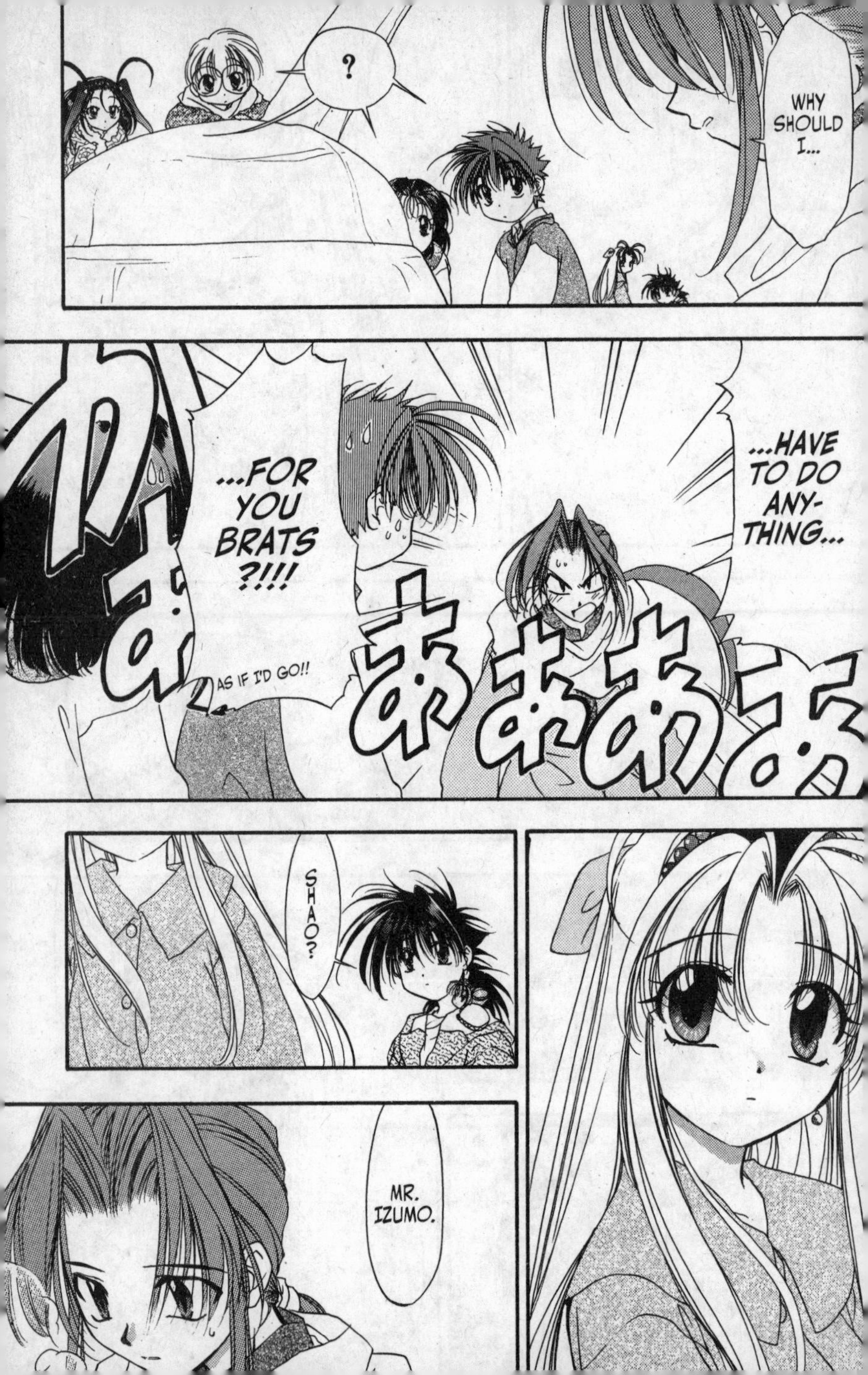
WHY SHOULD I...
?
...HAVE TO DO ANY-THING...
...FOR YOU BRATS?!!!
AS IF I'D GO!!
SHAO?
MR. IZUMO.

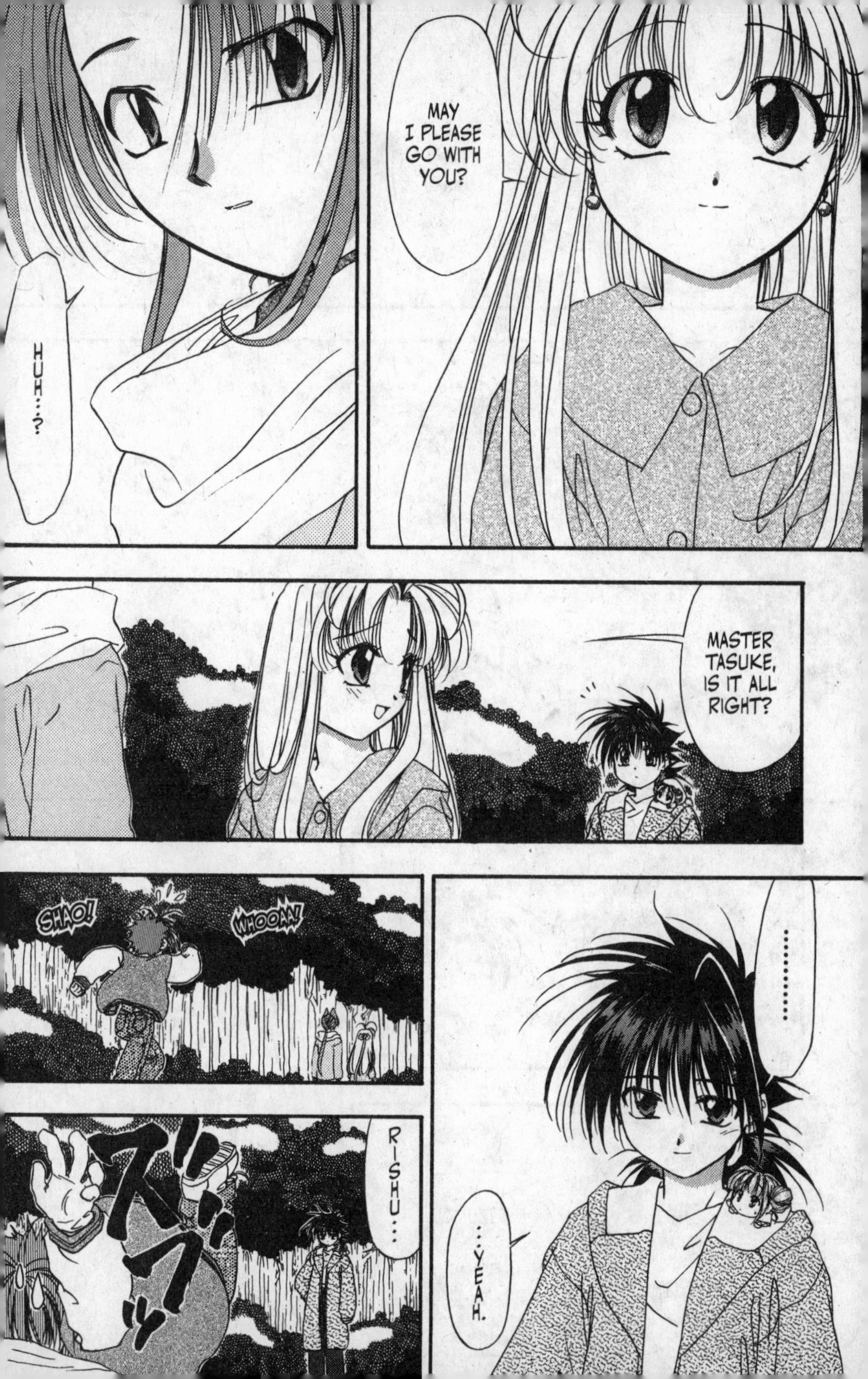
MAY I PLEASE GO WITH YOU?
HUH...?
MASTER TASUKE, IS IT ALL RIGHT?
......
...YEAH.
WHOOAA!
SHAO!
RISHU...

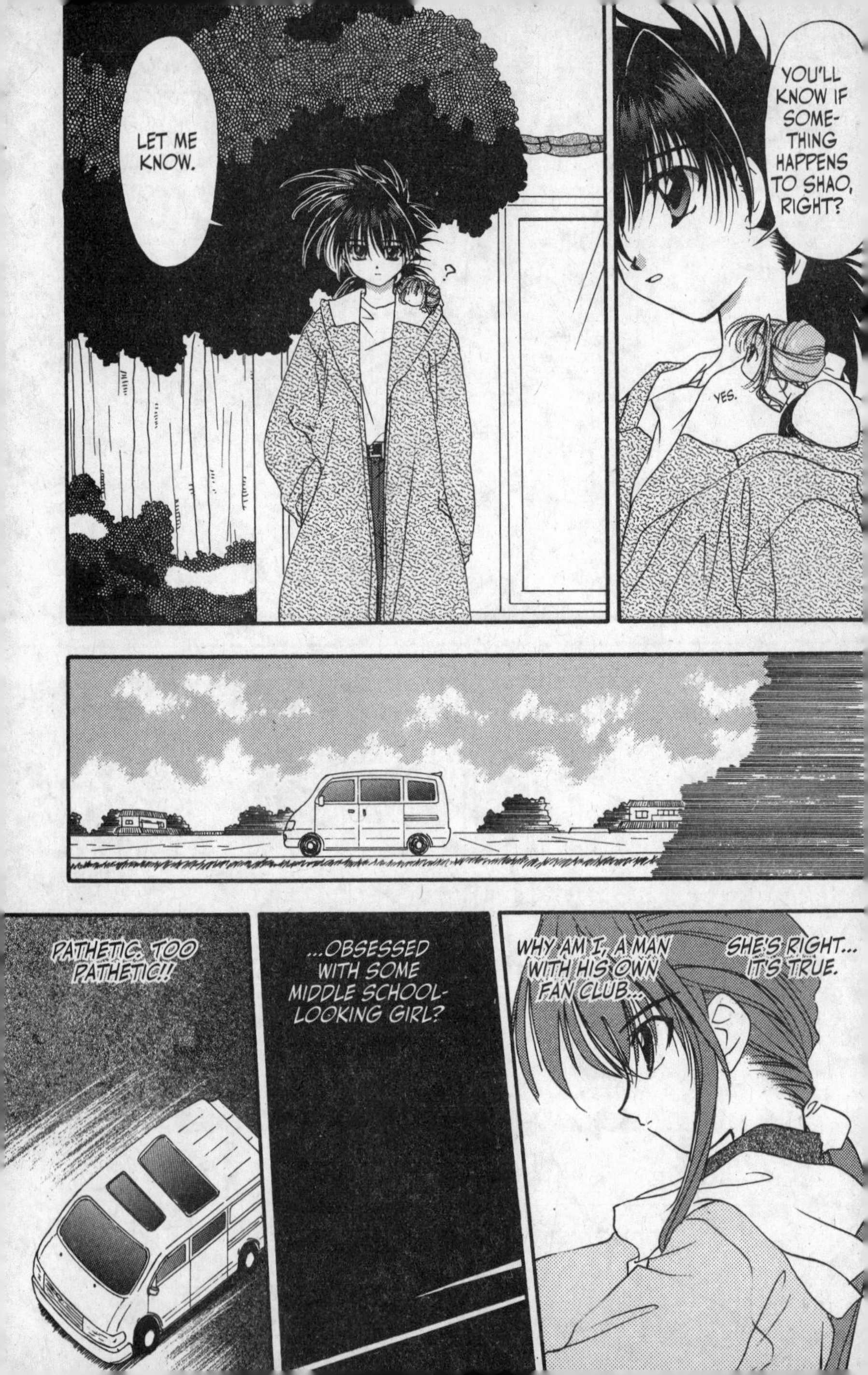
YOU'LL KNOW IF SOME-THING HAPPENS TO SHAO, RIGHT?
YES.
LET ME KNOW.
SHE'S RIGHT... IT'S TRUE.
WHY AM I, A MAN WITH HIS OWN FAN CLUB...
...OBSESSED WITH SOME MIDDLE SCHOOL-LOOKING GIRL?
PATHETIC. TOO PATHETIC!!

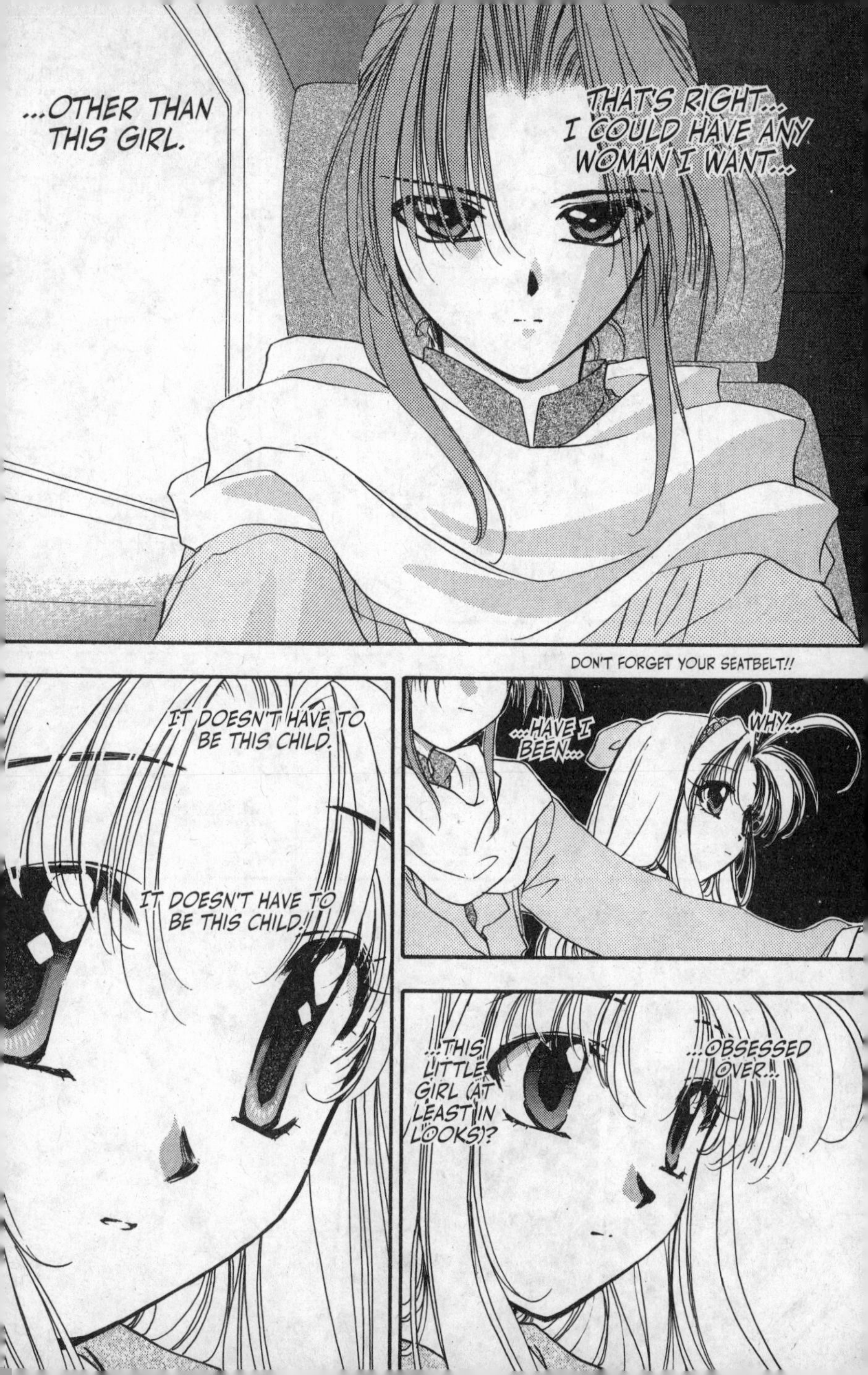
THAT'S RIGHT... I COULD HAVE ANY WOMAN I WANT...
...OTHER THAN THIS GIRL.
DON'T FORGET YOUR SEATBELT!!
WHY...
...HAVE I BEEN...
...OBSESSED OVER...
...THIS LITTLE GIRL (AT LEAST IN LOOKS)?
IT DOESN'T HAVE TO BE THIS CHILD.
IT DOESN'T HAVE TO BE THIS CHILD!!

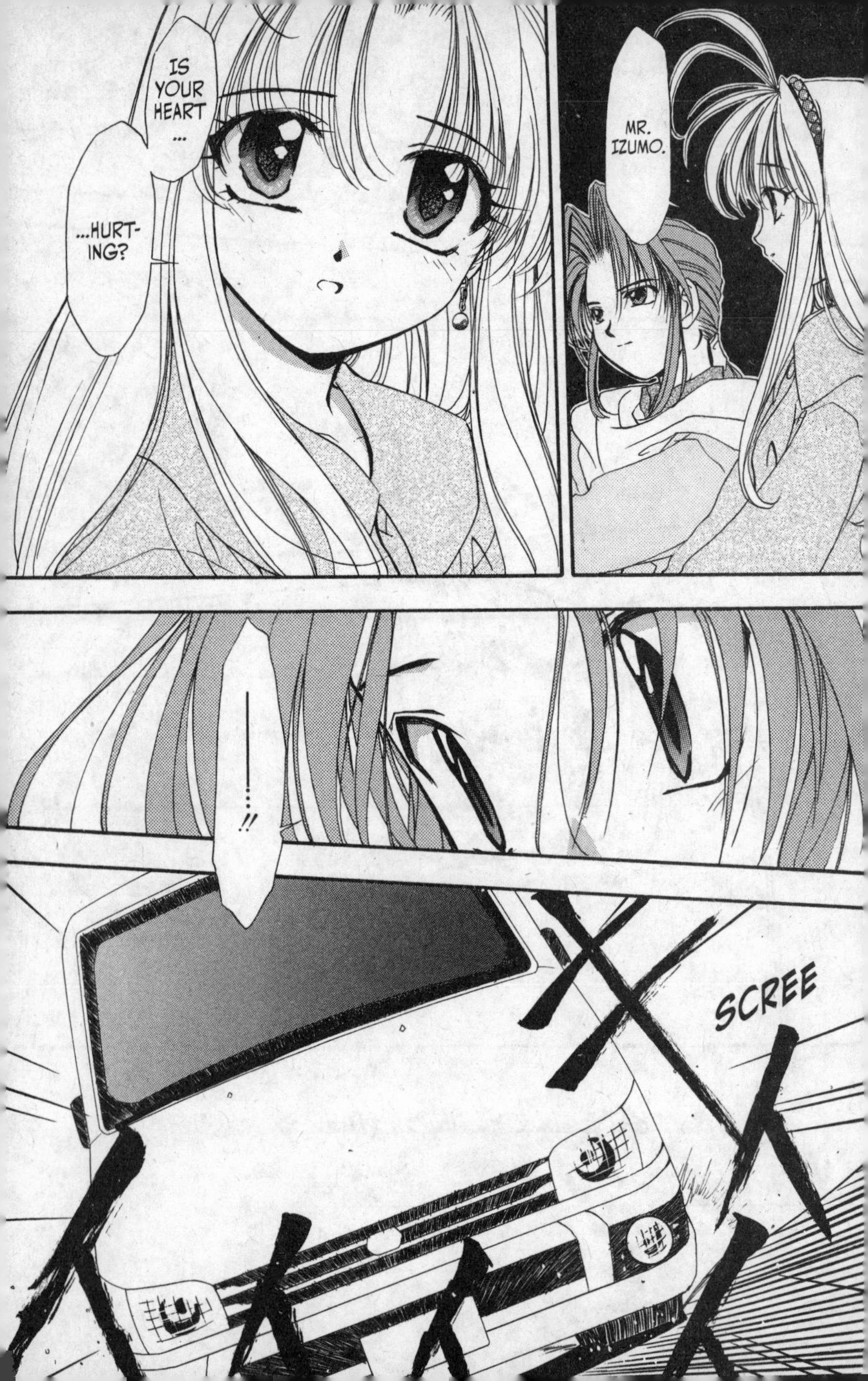
MR. IZUMO.
IS YOUR HEART ...
...HURTING?
......!!
SCREE

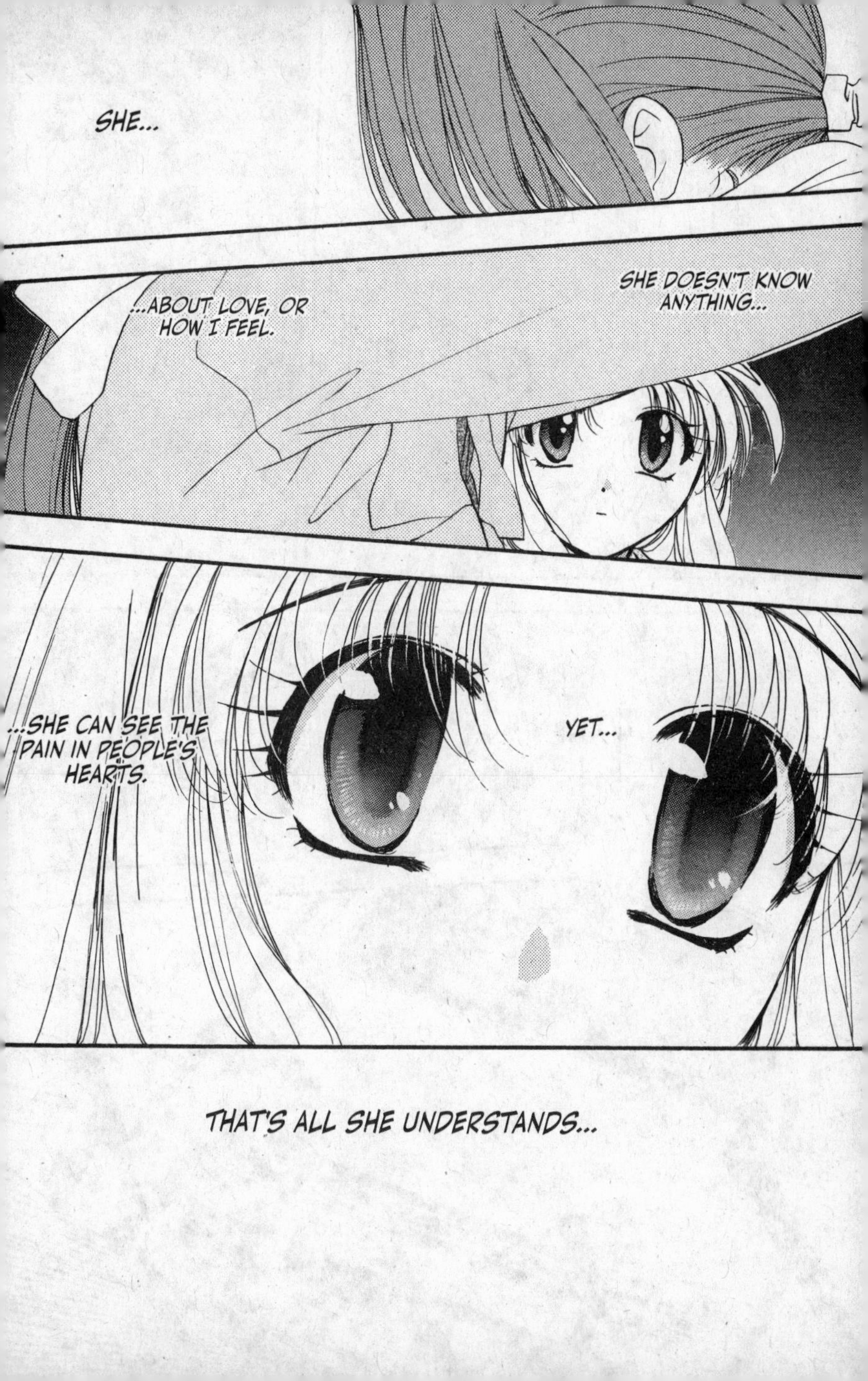
SHE...
SHE DOESN'T KNOW ANYTHING...
...ABOUT LOVE, OR HOW I FEEL.
YET...
...SHE CAN SEE THE PAIN IN PEOPLE'S HEARTS.
THAT'S ALL SHE UNDERSTANDS...

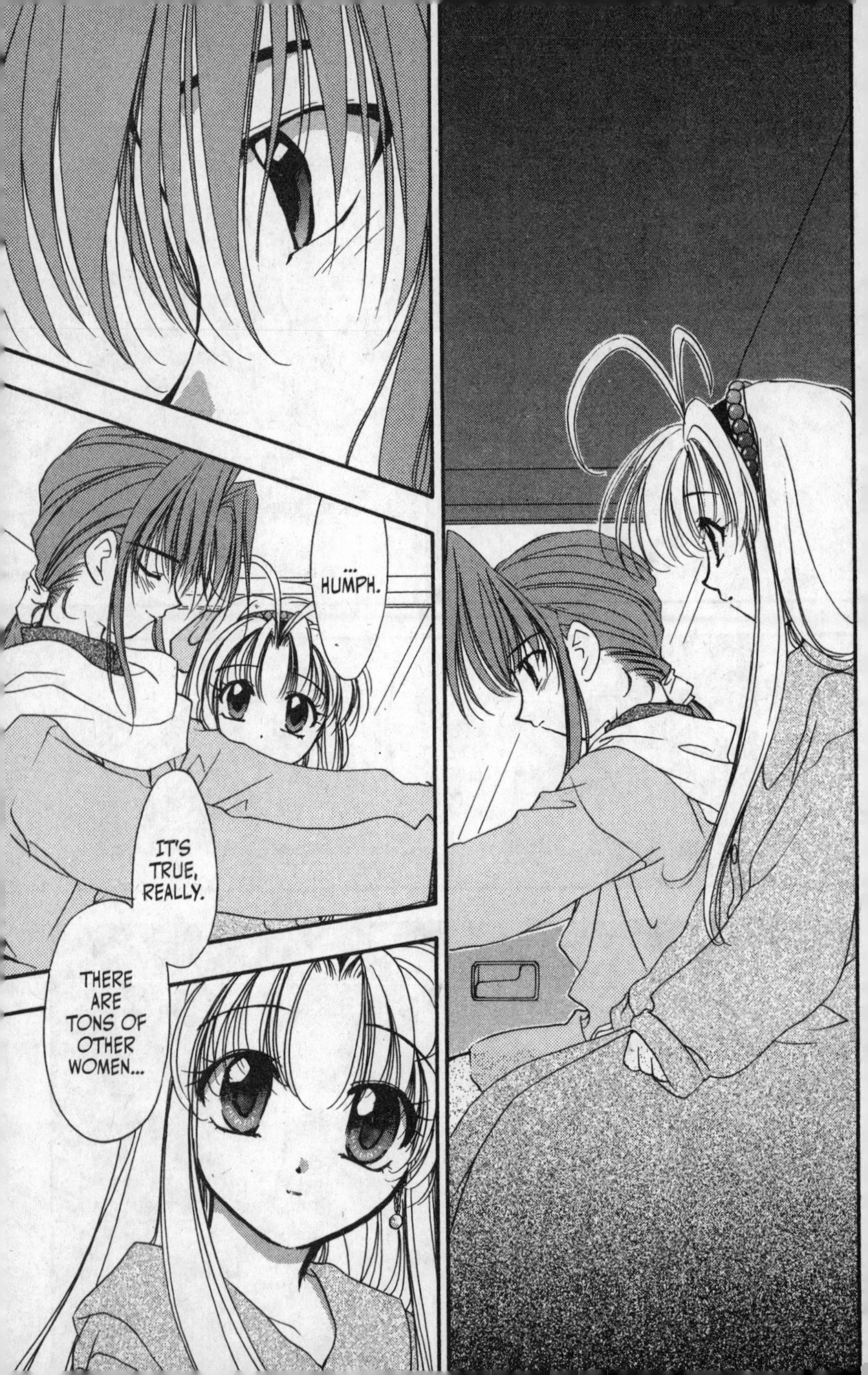
...HUMPH.
IT'S TRUE, REALLY.
THERE ARE TONS OF OTHER WOMEN...

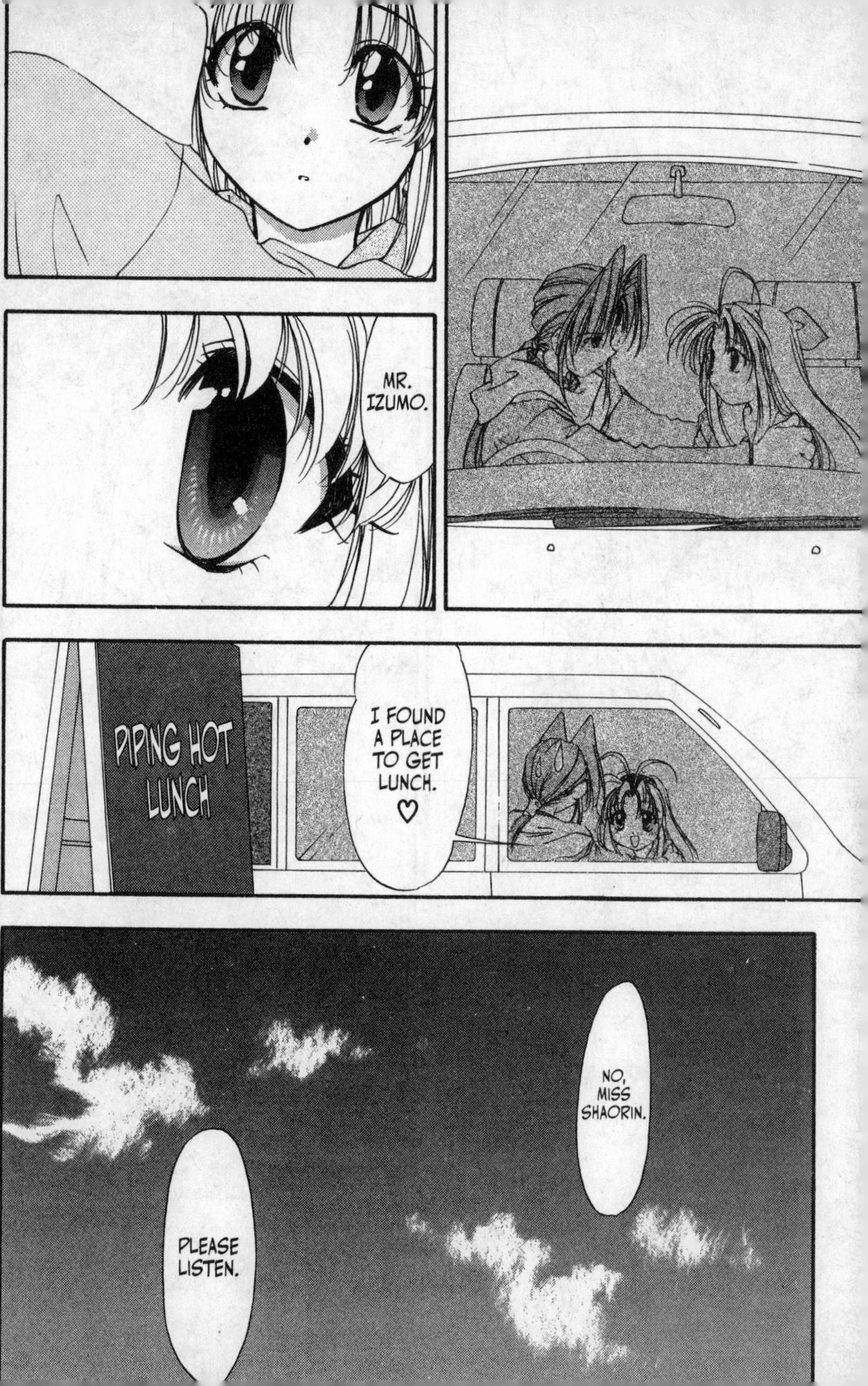
MR. IZUMO.
I FOUND A PLACE TO GET LUNCH. ♡
PIPING HOT LUNCH
NO, MISS SHAORIN.
PLEASE LISTEN.

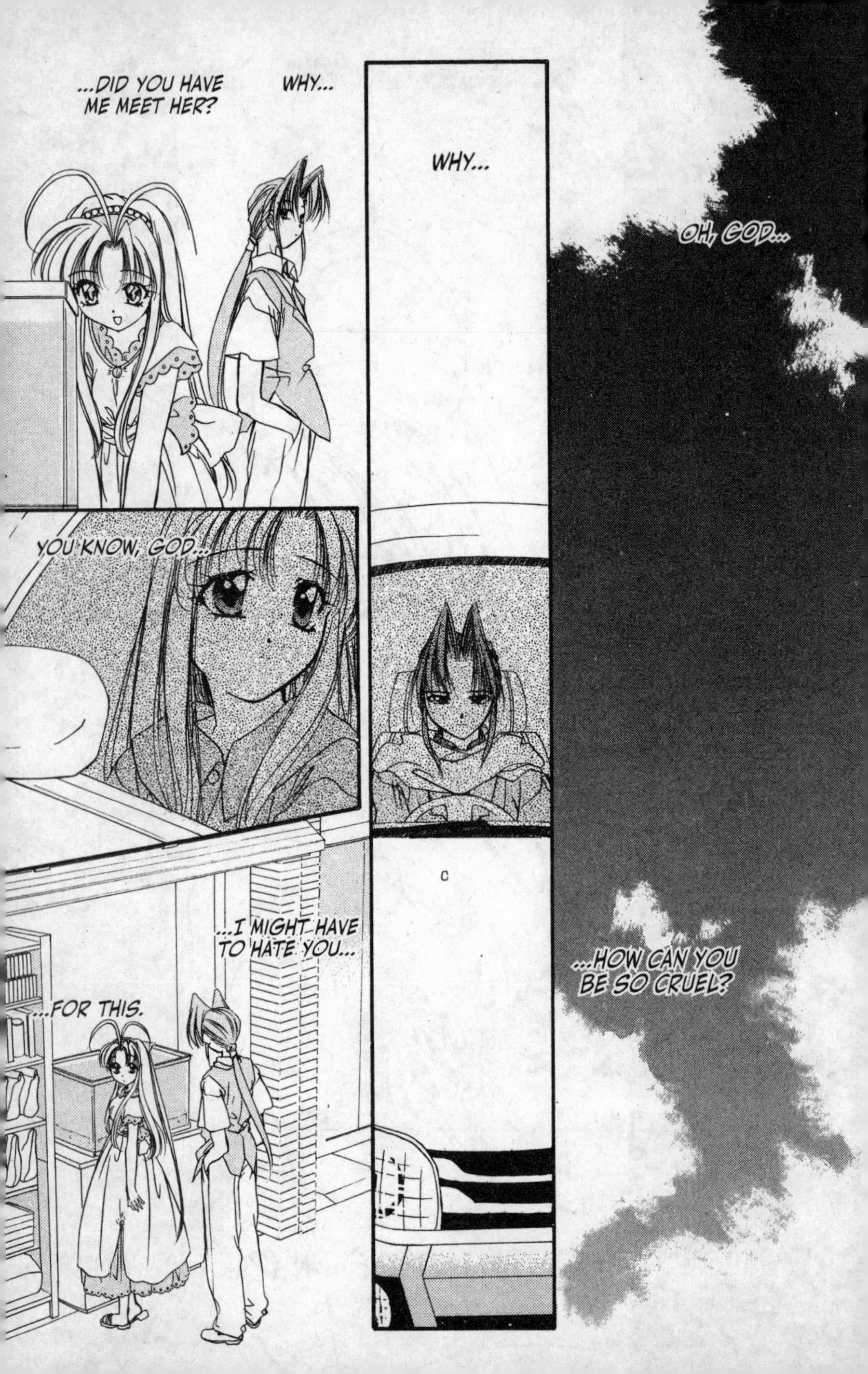
OH, GOD...
...HOW CAN YOU BE SO CRUEL?
WHY...
WHY...
...DID YOU HAVE ME MEET HER?
YOU KNOW, GOD...
...I MIGHT HAVE TO HATE YOU...
...FOR THIS.

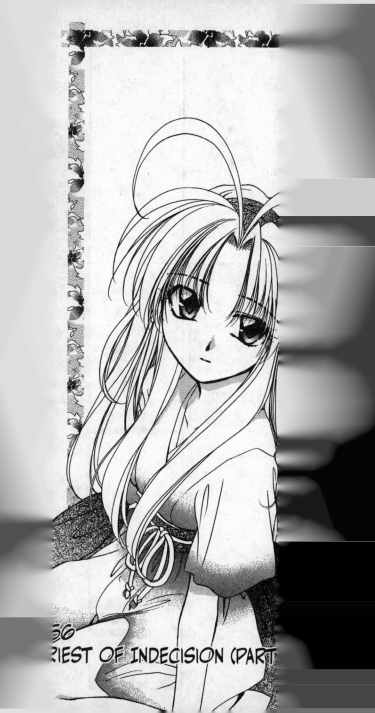

56
RIEST OF INDECISION (PART

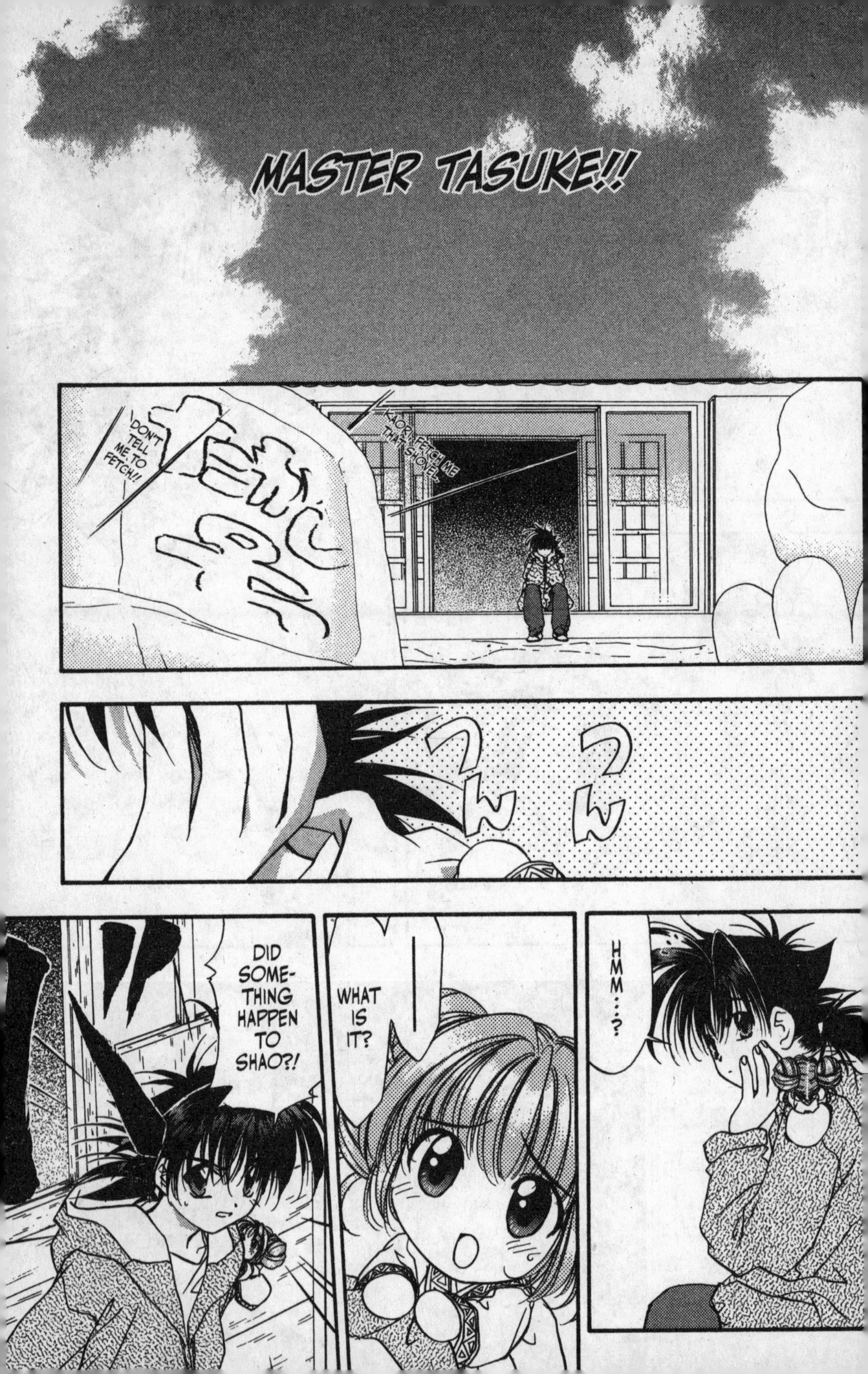
MASTER TASUKE!!
KAORI, FETCH ME THAT SHOVEL.
DON'T TELL ME TO FETCH!!
HMM...?
WHAT IS IT?
DID SOME-THING HAPPEN TO SHAO?!

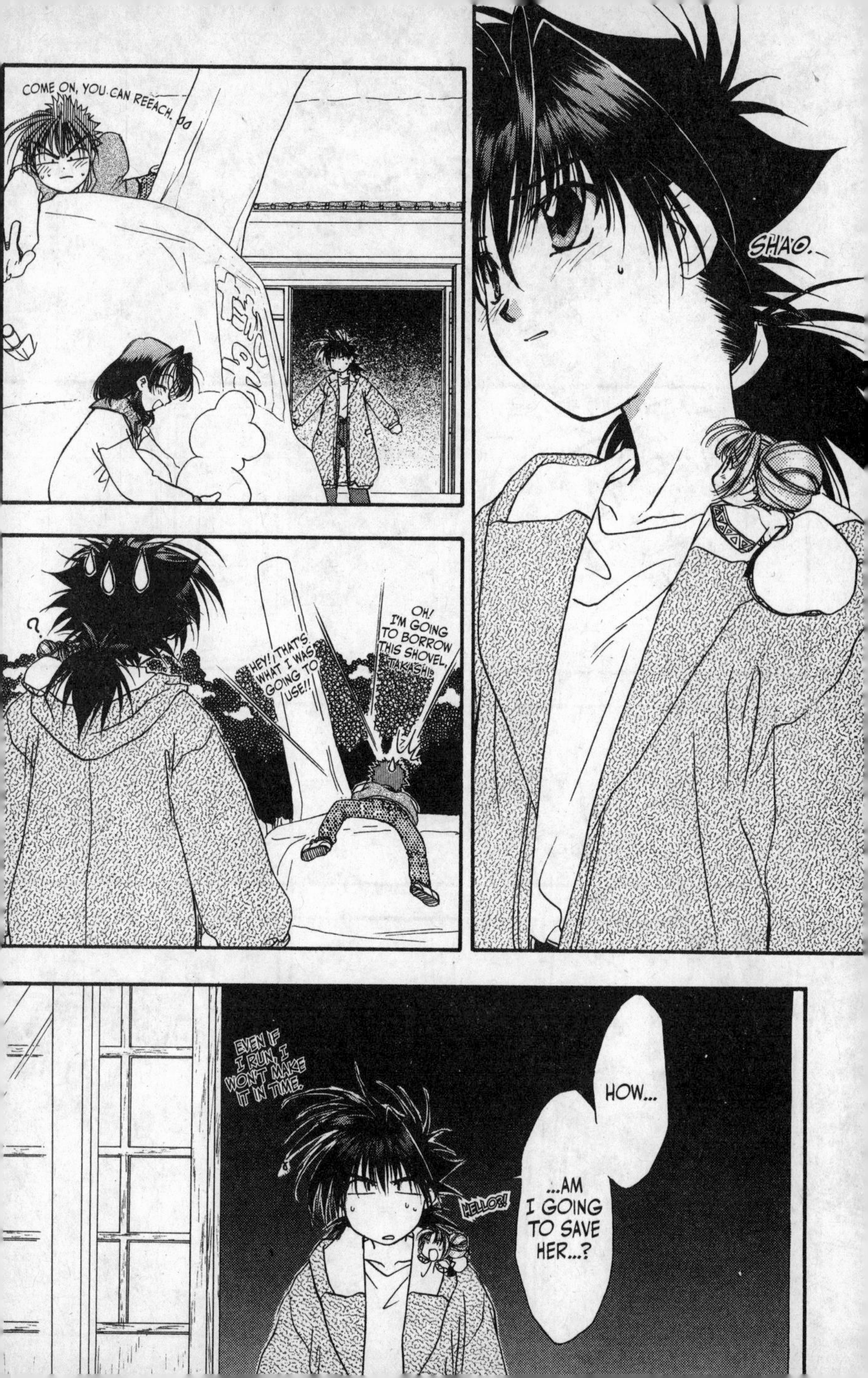
SHAO.
COME ON, YOU CAN REEACH.
OH! I'M GOING TO BORROW THIS SHOVEL, TAKASHI!!
HEY!! THAT'S WHAT I WAS GOING TO USE!!
?
HOW...
...AM I GOING TO SAVE HER...?
HELLO?!
EVEN IF I RUN, I WON'T MAKE IT IN TIME.

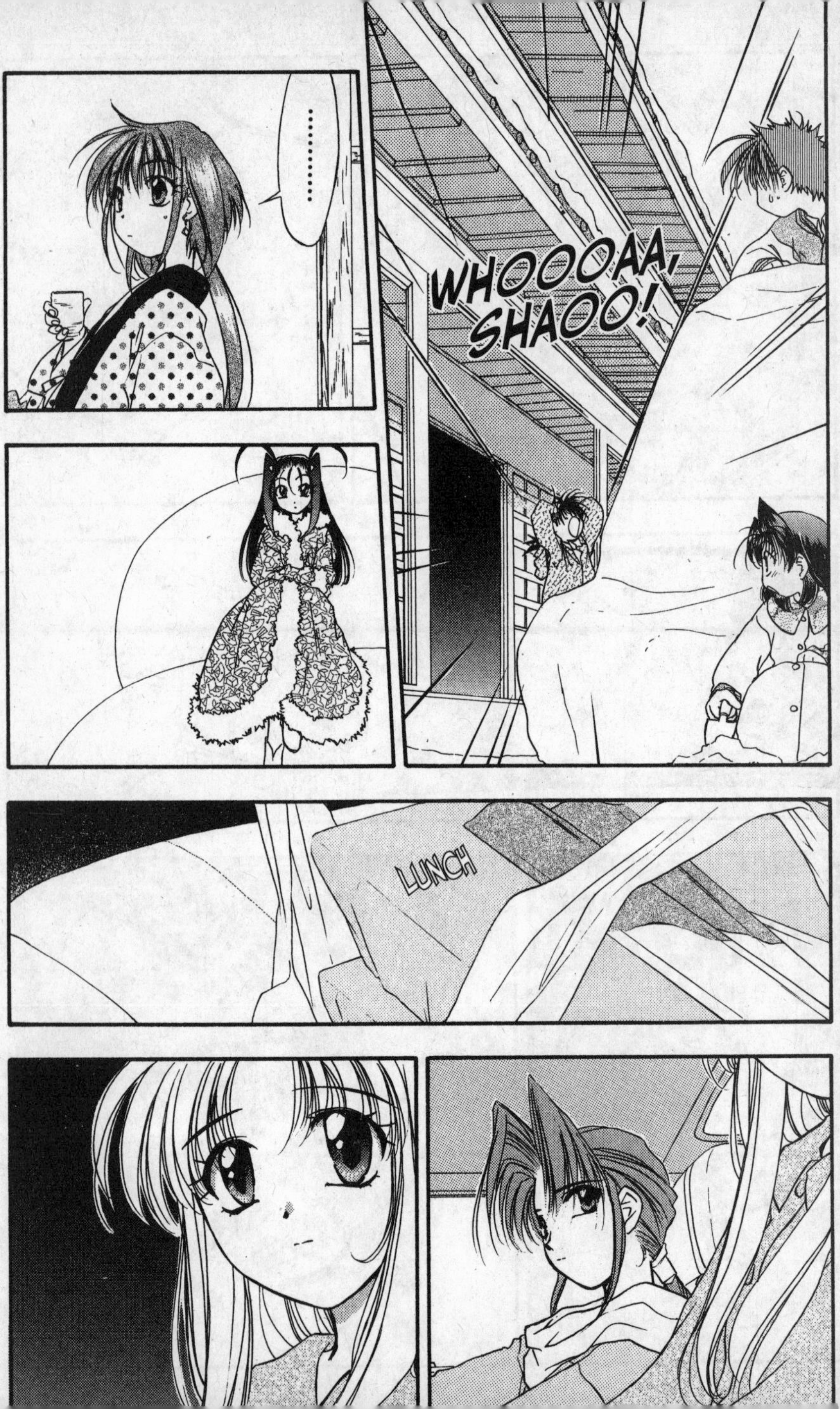
WHOOOAA, SHAOO!
......
LUNCH

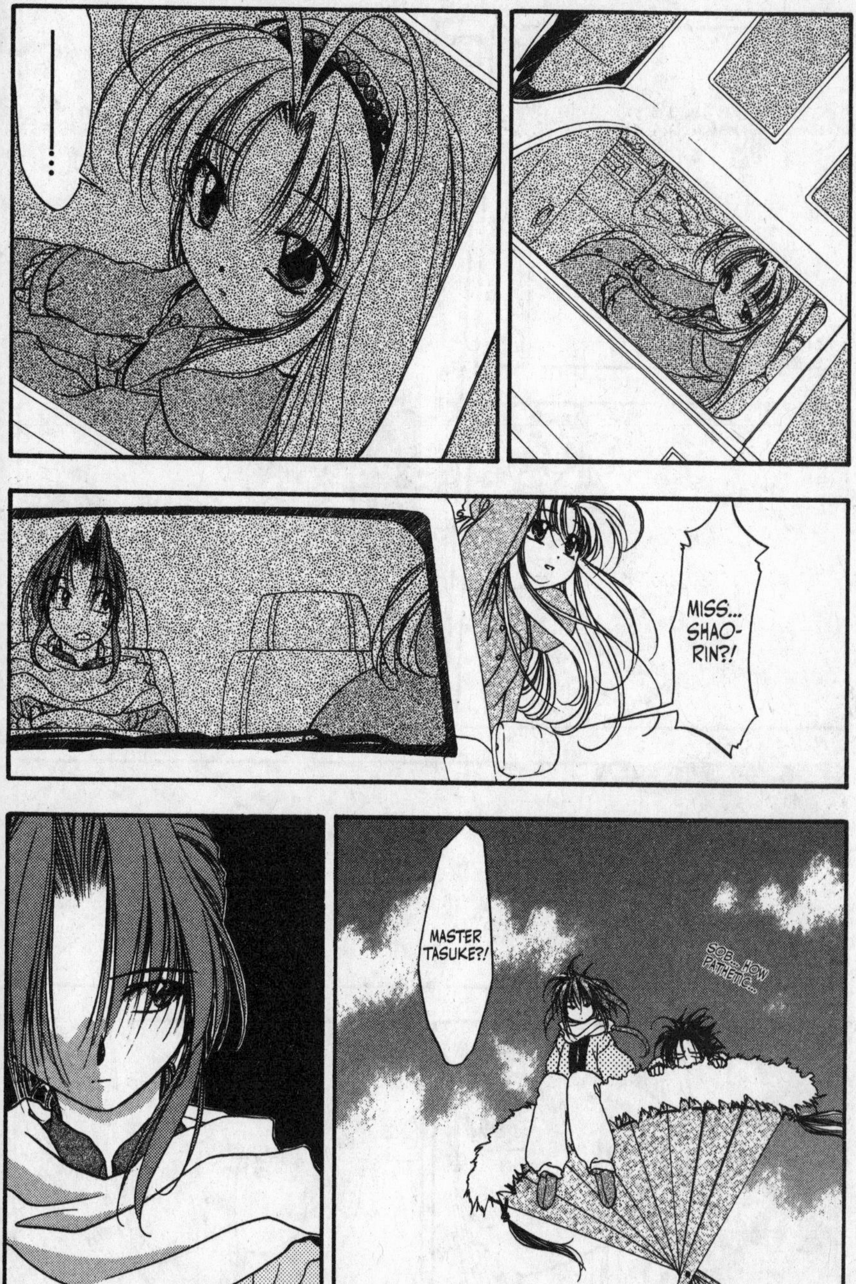
......
MISS... SHAO-RIN?!
MASTER TASUKE?!
SOB... HOW PATHETIC...

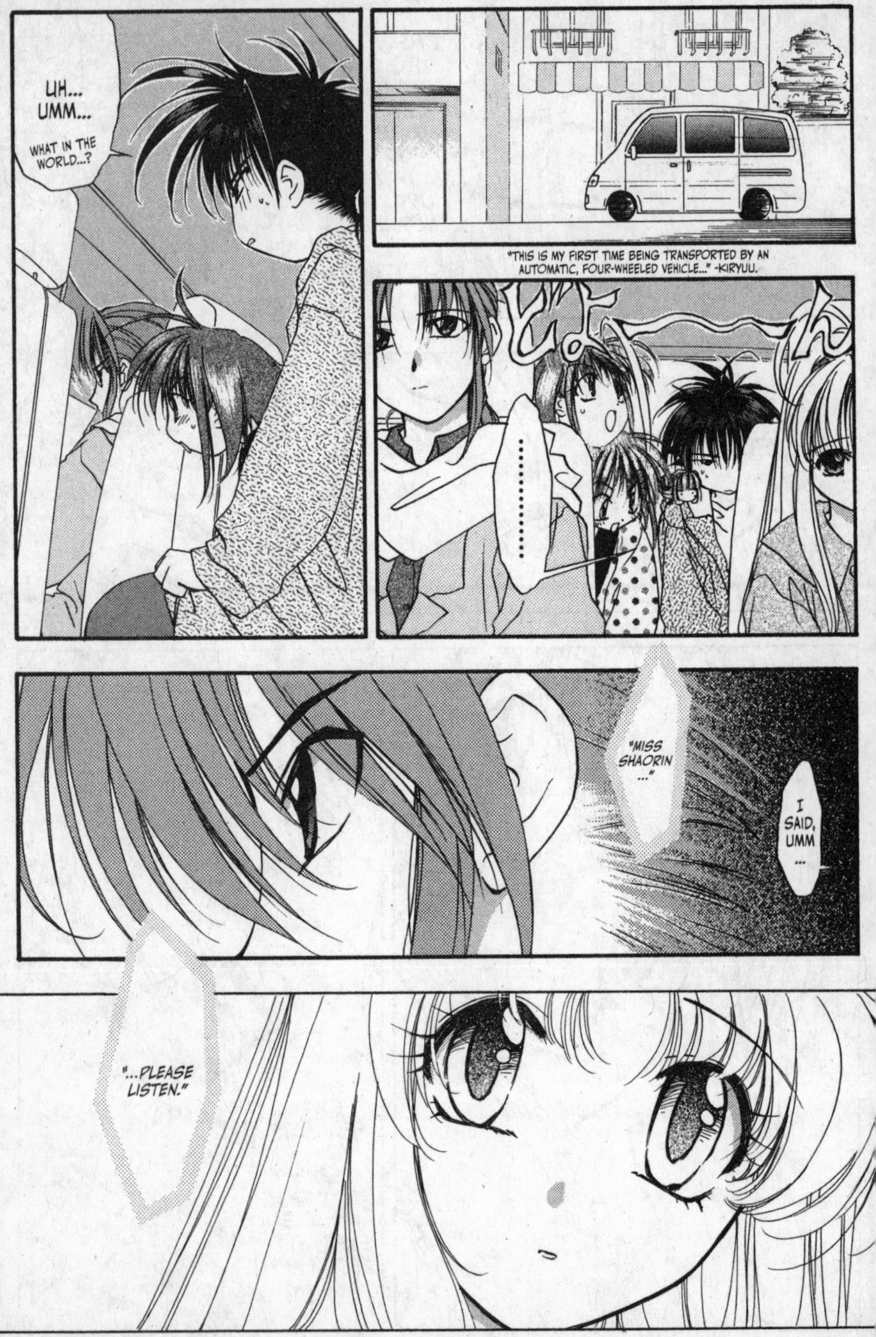
"THIS IS MY FIRST TIME BEING TRANSPORTED BY AN AUTOMATIC, FOUR-WHEELED VEHICLE..." -KIRYUU.
......
UH... UMM...
WHAT IN THE WORLD...?
I SAID, UMM ...
"MISS SHAORIN ..."
"...PLEASE LISTEN."

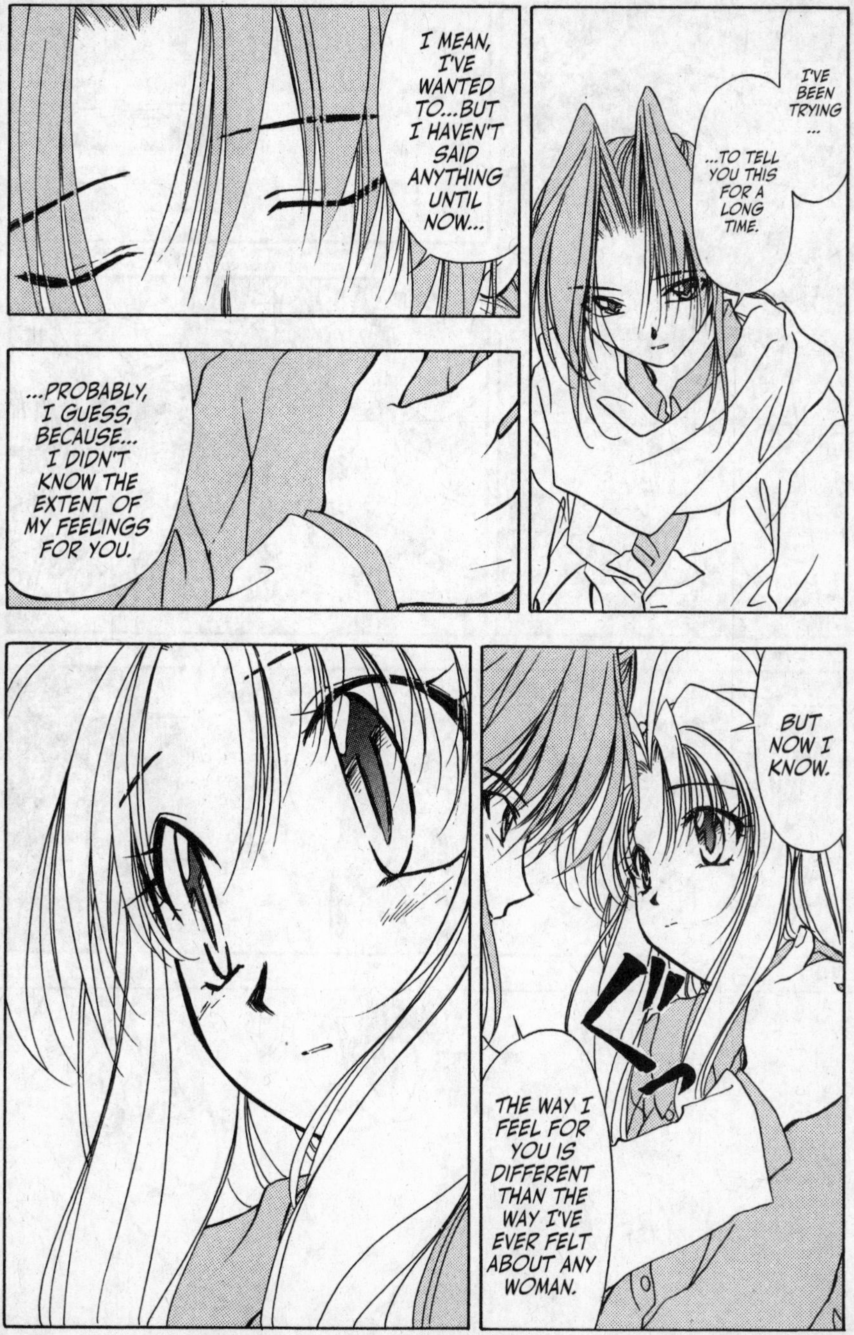
I'VE BEEN TRYING ...
...TO TELL YOU THIS FOR A LONG TIME.
I MEAN, I'VE WANTED TO...BUT I HAVEN'T SAID ANYTHING UNTIL NOW...
...PROBABLY, I GUESS, BECAUSE... I DIDN'T KNOW THE EXTENT OF MY FEELINGS FOR YOU.
BUT NOW I KNOW.
THE WAY I FEEL FOR YOU IS DIFFERENT THAN THE WAY I'VE EVER FELT ABOUT ANY WOMAN.

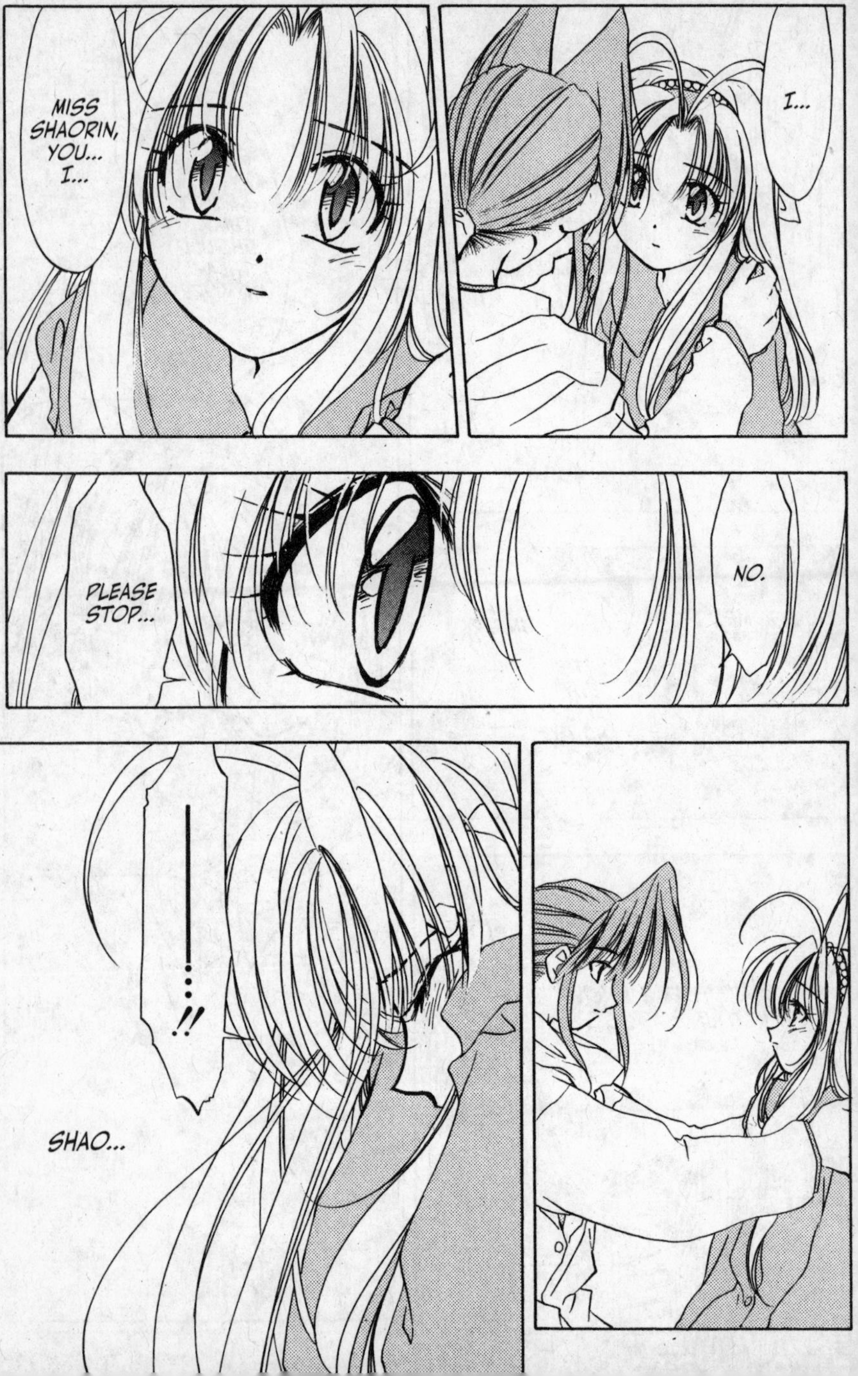
I...
MISS SHAORIN, YOU... I...
NO.
PLEASE STOP...
—...!!
SHAO...

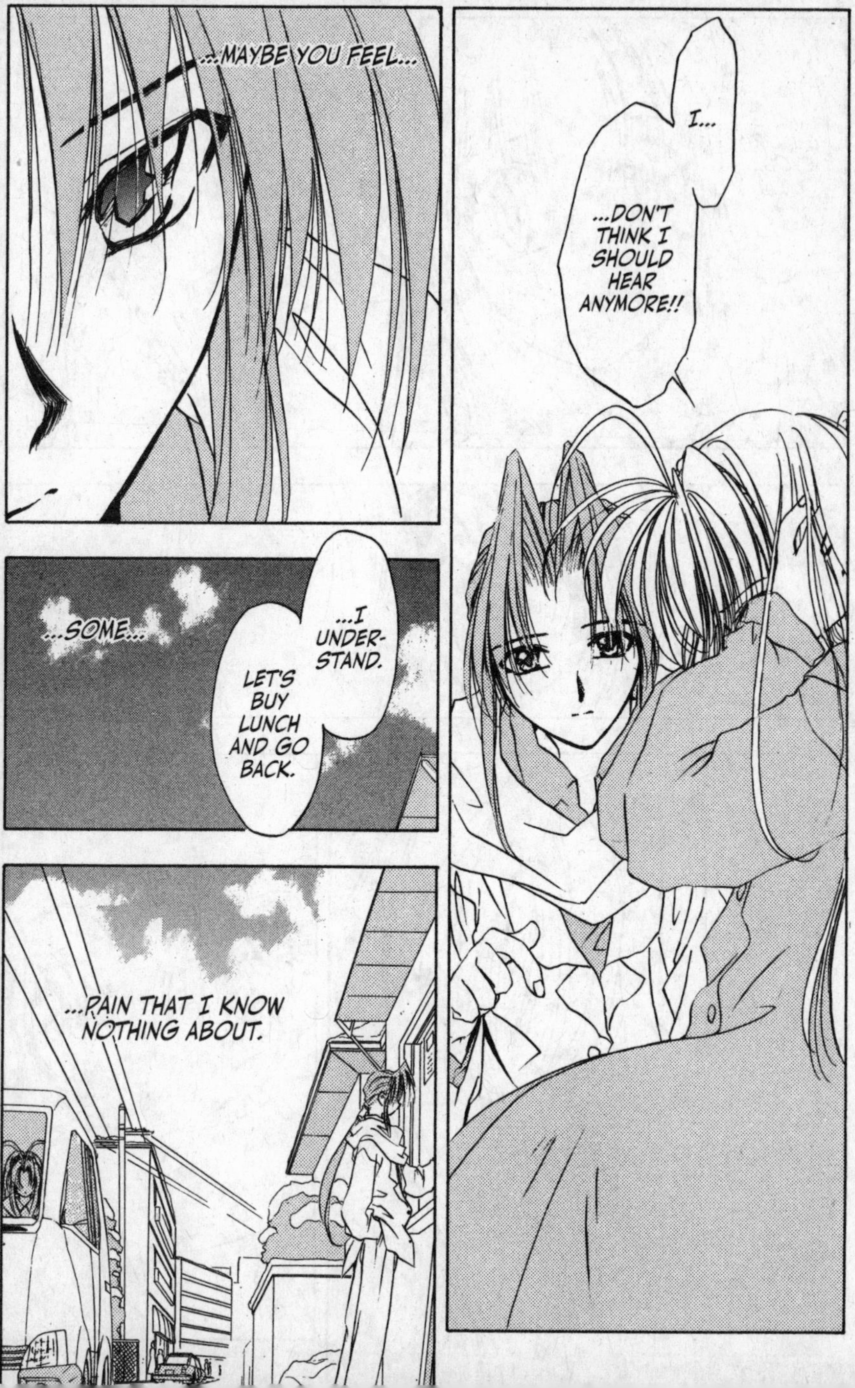
I...
...DON'T THINK I SHOULD HEAR ANYMORE!!
...MAYBE YOU FEEL...
...I UNDERSTAND. LET'S BUY LUNCH AND GO BACK.
...SOME...
...PAIN THAT I KNOW NOTHING ABOUT.

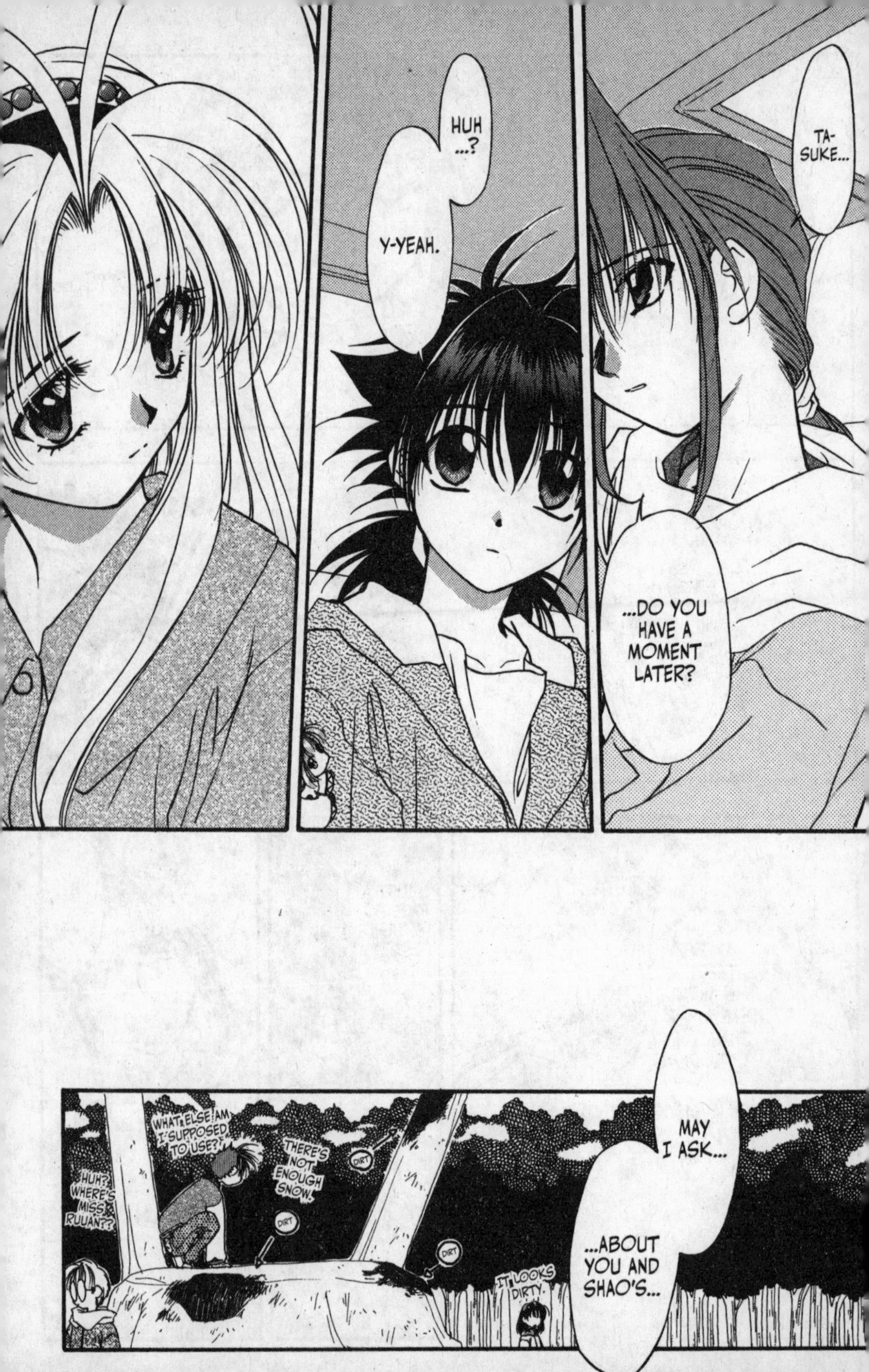
TA-SUKE...
...DO YOU HAVE A MOMENT LATER?
HUH ...?
Y-YEAH.
MAY I ASK...
...ABOUT YOU AND SHAO'S...
DIRT
THERE'S NOT ENOUGH SNOW.
WHAT ELSE AM I SUPPOSED TO USE?
DIRT
IT LOOKS DIRTY.
DIRT
HUH? WHERE'S MISS RUUAN??

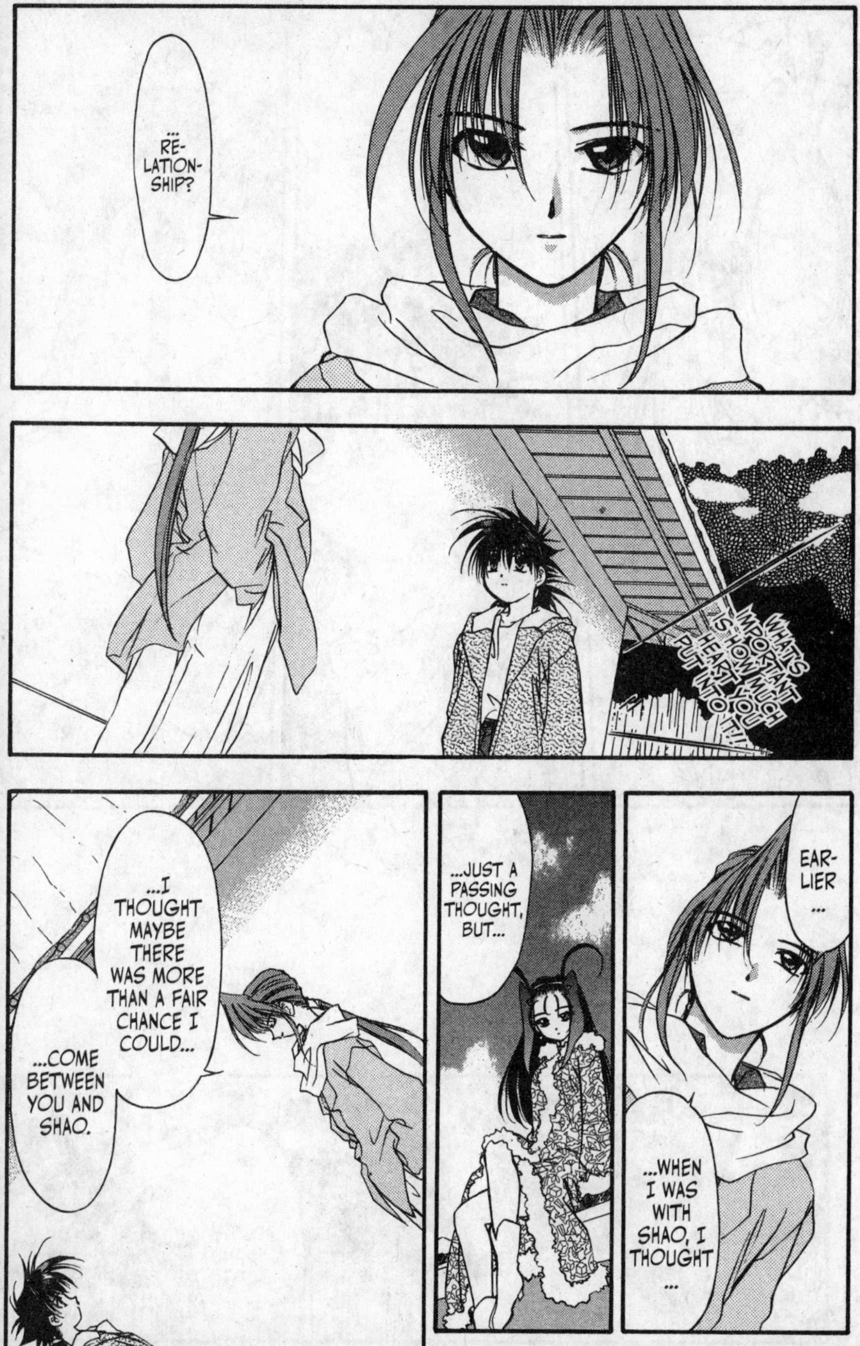
...RE-LATION-SHIP?
WHAT'S IMPORTANT IS HOW MUCH HEART YOU PUT INTO IT!!
EAR-LIER ...
...WHEN I WAS WITH SHAO, I THOUGHT ...
...JUST A PASSING THOUGHT, BUT...
...I THOUGHT MAYBE THERE WAS MORE THAN A FAIR CHANCE I COULD...
...COME BETWEEN YOU AND SHAO.

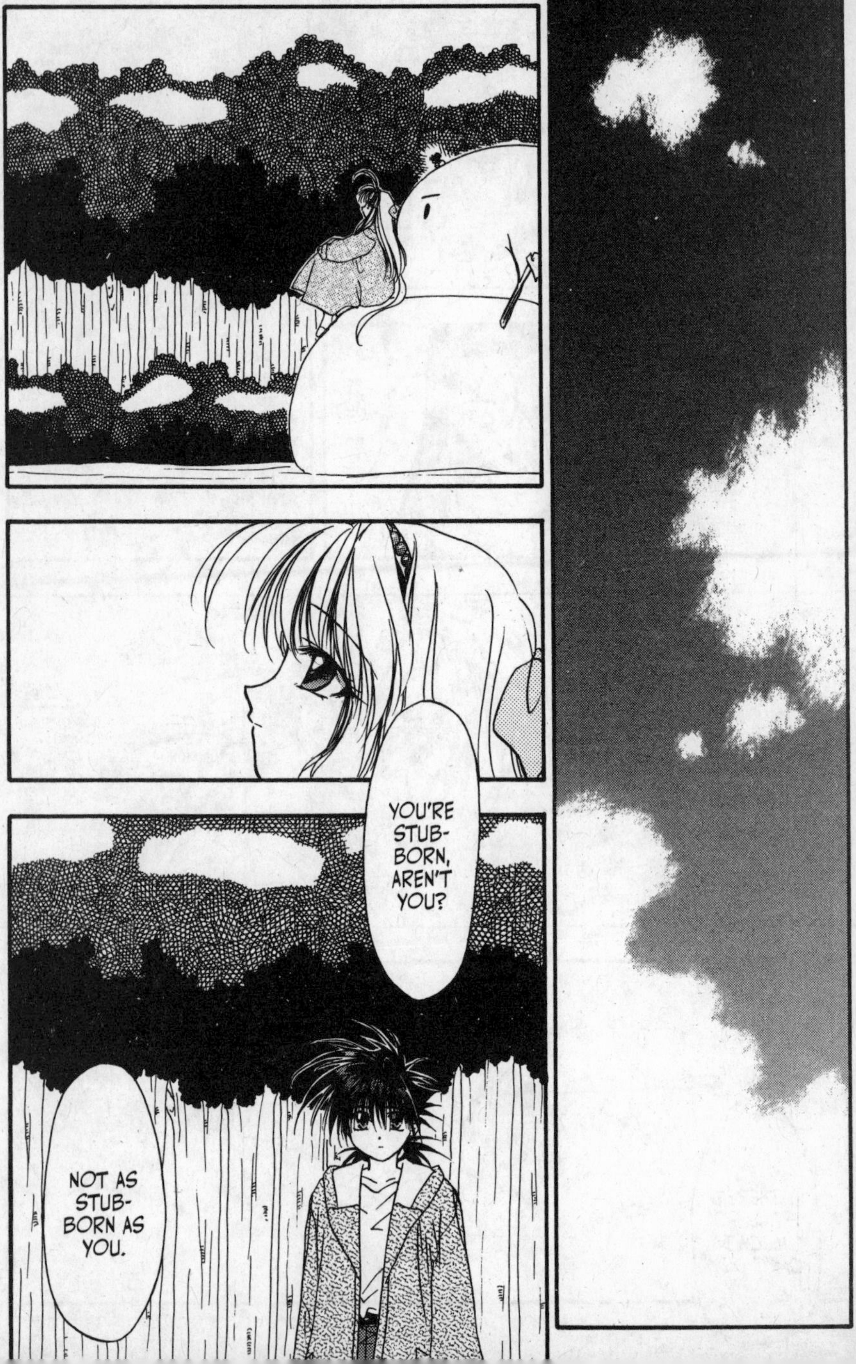
YOU'RE STUB-BORN, AREN'T YOU?
NOT AS STUB-BORN AS YOU.

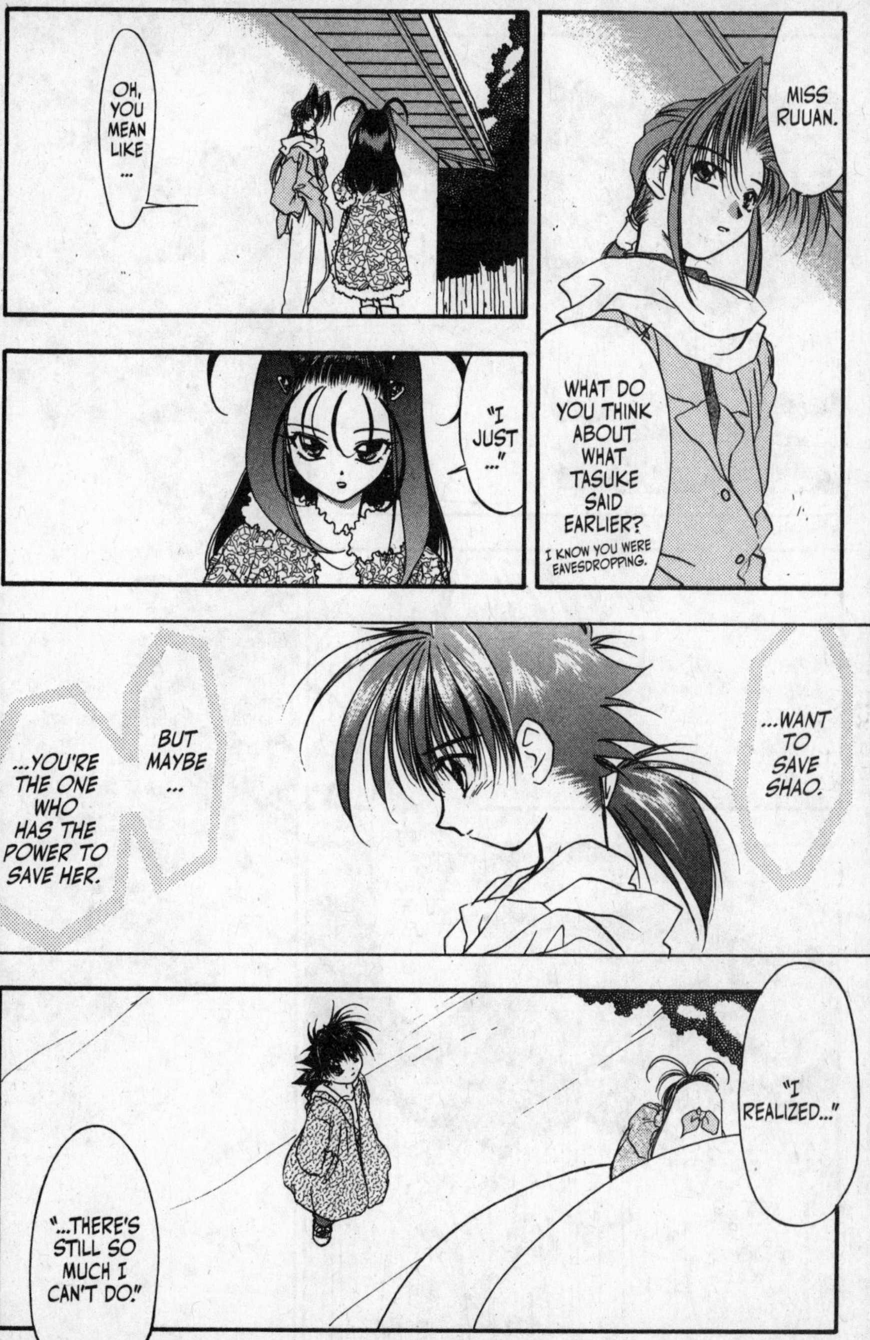
MISS RUUAN.
WHAT DO YOU THINK ABOUT WHAT TASUKE SAID EARLIER?
I KNOW YOU WERE EAVESDROPPING.
OH, YOU MEAN LIKE ...
"I JUST ..."
...WANT TO SAVE SHAO.
BUT MAYBE ...
...YOU'RE THE ONE WHO HAS THE POWER TO SAVE HER.
"I REALIZED..."
"...THERE'S STILL SO MUCH I CAN'T DO."

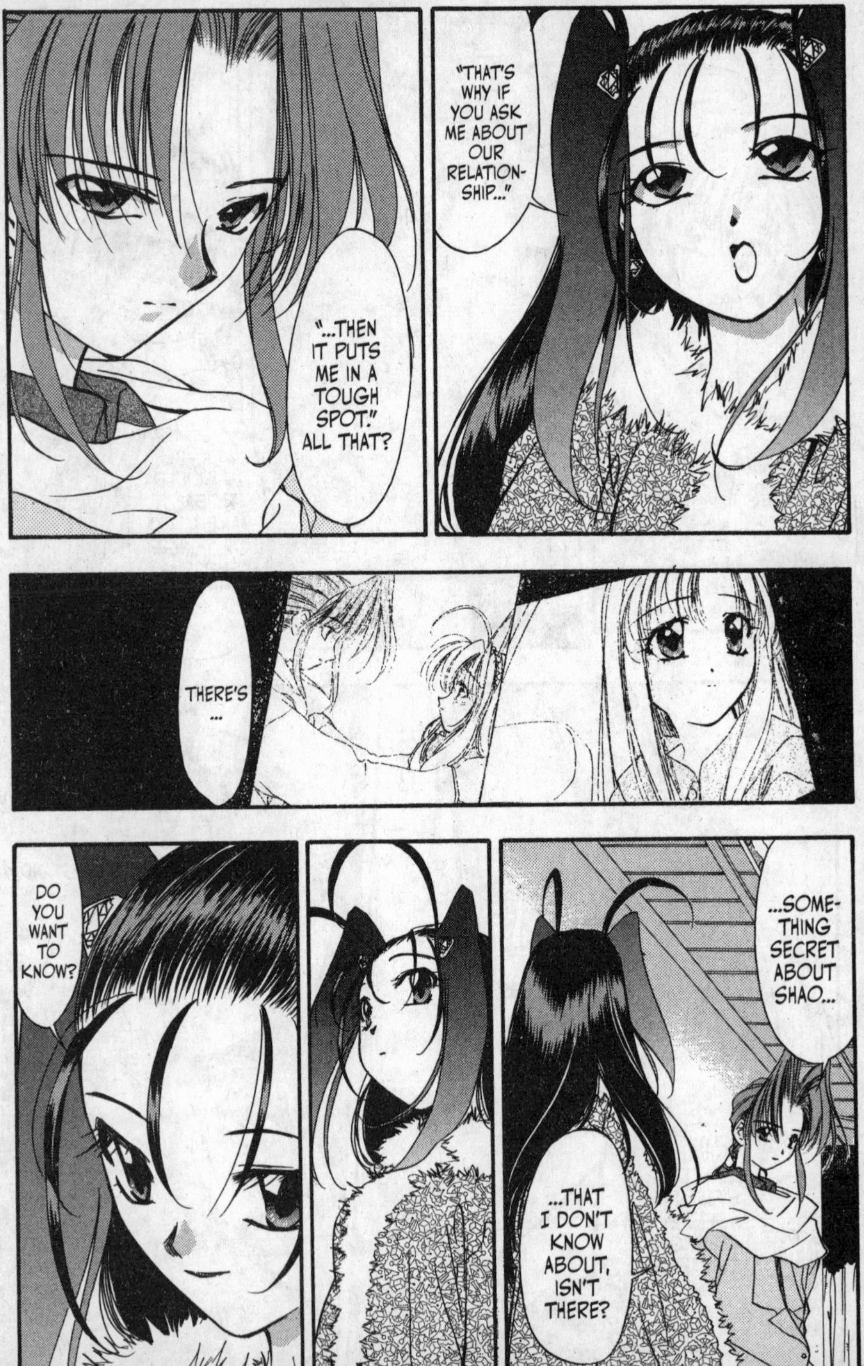
"THAT'S WHY IF YOU ASK ME ABOUT OUR RELATION-SHIP..."
"...THEN IT PUTS ME IN A TOUGH SPOT." ALL THAT?
THERE'S ...
...SOME-THING SECRET ABOUT SHAO...
...THAT I DON'T KNOW ABOUT, ISN'T THERE?
DO YOU WANT TO KNOW?

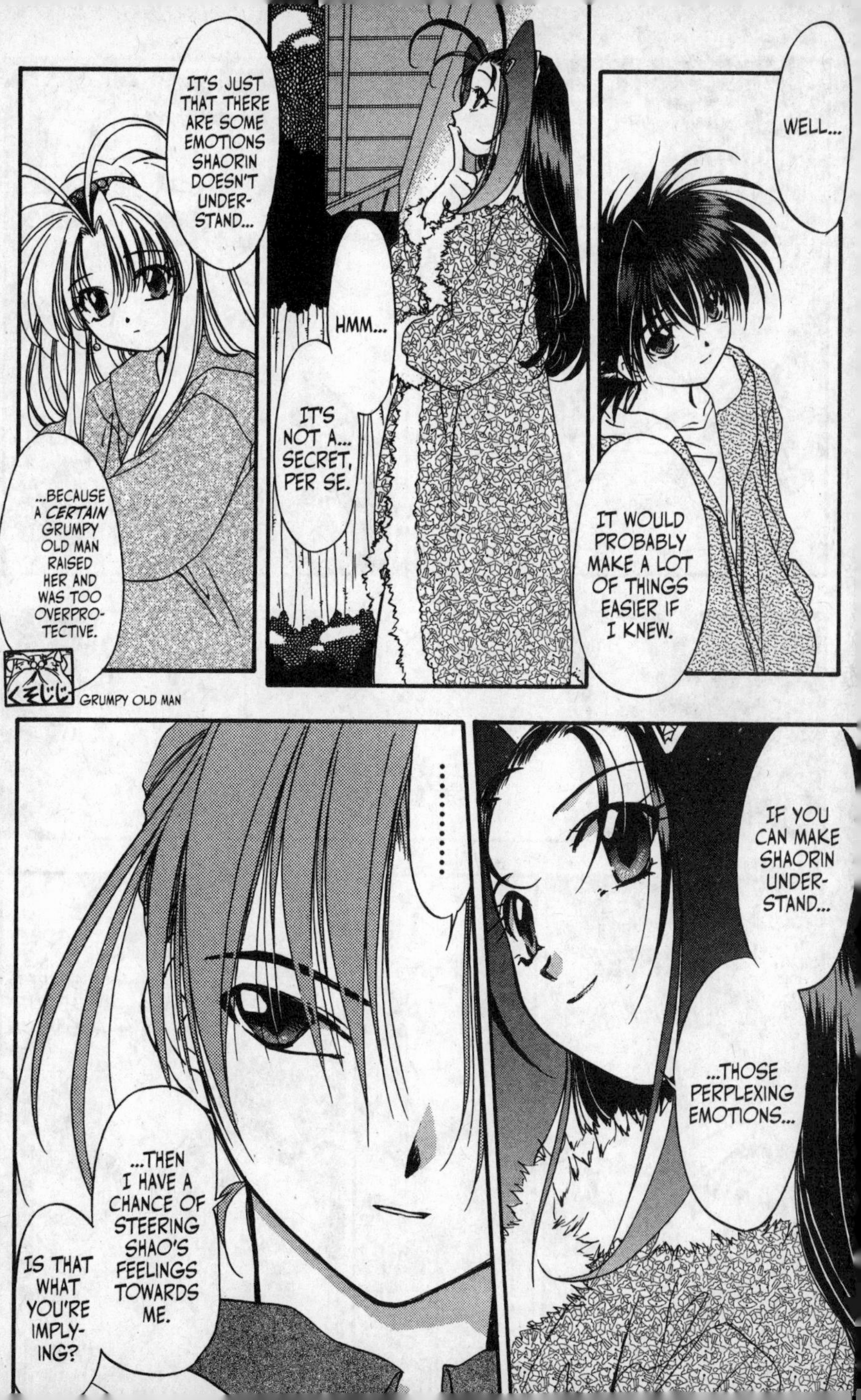
WELL...
IT WOULD PROBABLY MAKE A LOT OF THINGS EASIER IF I KNEW.
HMM...
IT'S NOT A... SECRET, PER SE.
IT'S JUST THAT THERE ARE SOME EMOTIONS SHAORIN DOESN'T UNDER-STAND...
...BECAUSE A *CERTAIN* GRUMPY OLD MAN RAISED HER AND WAS TOO OVERPRO-TECTIVE.
くそじじ GRUMPY OLD MAN
IF YOU CAN MAKE SHAORIN UNDER-STAND...
...THOSE PERPLEXING EMOTIONS...
......
...THEN I HAVE A CHANCE OF STEERING SHAO'S FEELINGS TOWARDS ME.
IS THAT WHAT YOU'RE IMPLY-ING?

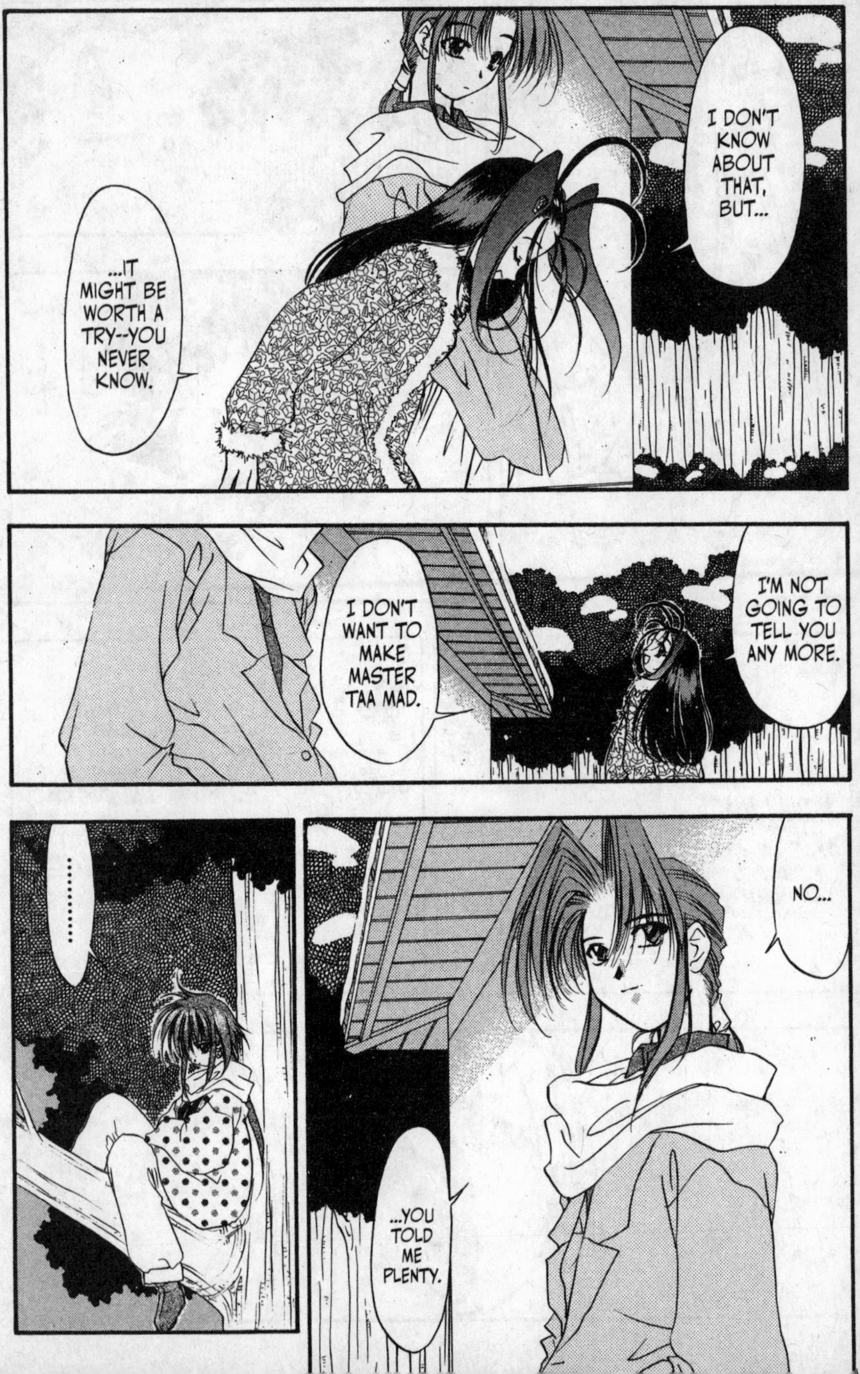
I DON'T KNOW ABOUT THAT, BUT...
...IT MIGHT BE WORTH A TRY--YOU NEVER KNOW.
I'M NOT GOING TO TELL YOU ANY MORE.
I DON'T WANT TO MAKE MASTER TAA MAD.
NO...
...YOU TOLD ME PLENTY.
......

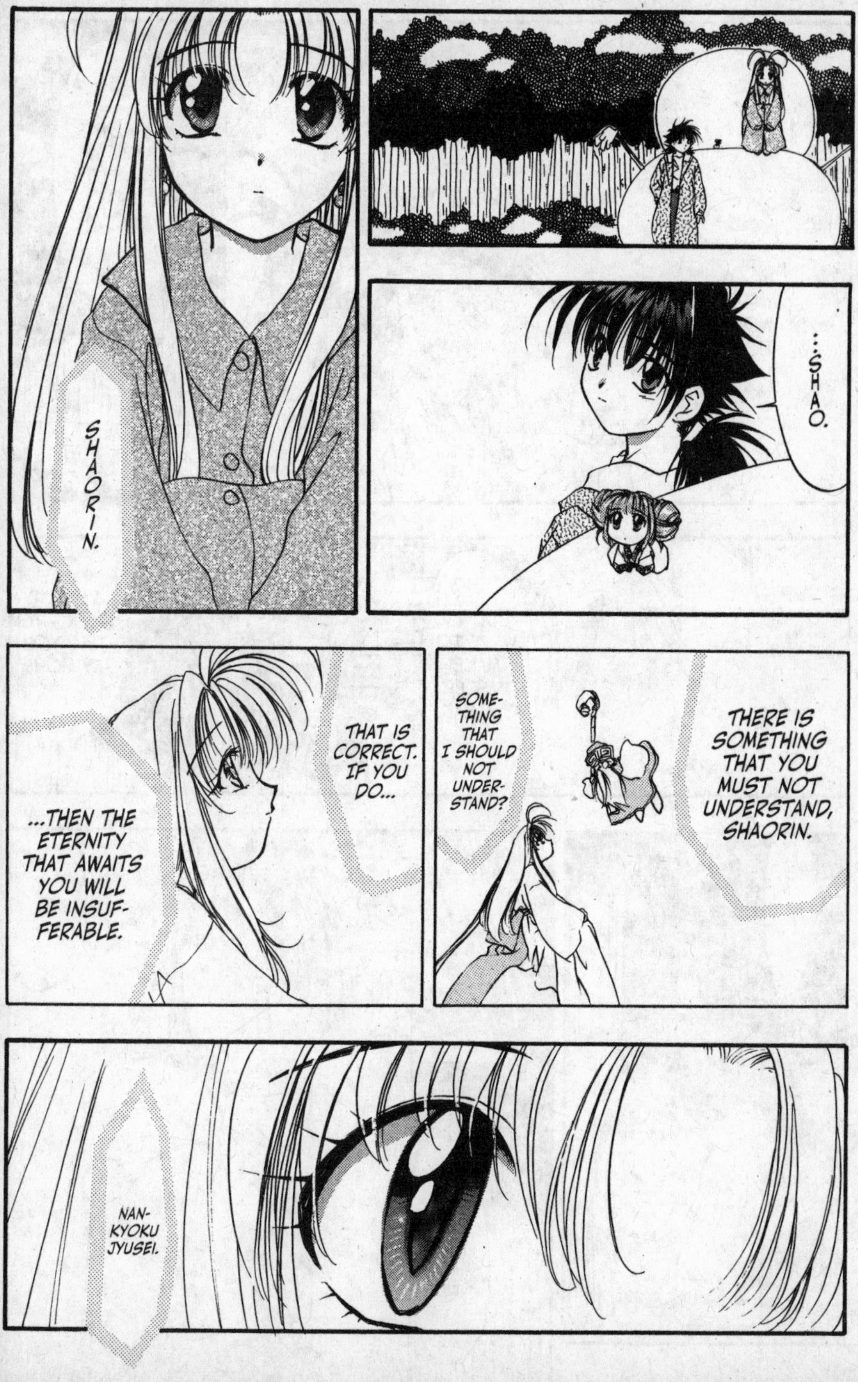
...SHAO.
SHAORIN.
THERE IS SOMETHING THAT YOU MUST NOT UNDERSTAND, SHAORIN.
SOMETHING THAT I SHOULD NOT UNDERSTAND?
THAT IS CORRECT. IF YOU DO...
...THEN THE ETERNITY THAT AWAITS YOU WILL BE INSUFFERABLE.
NANKYOKU JYUSEI.

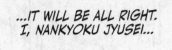

IS IT A HARD-SHIP?
BUT SHAO-RIN...
IT IS VERY, VERY MUCH A HARD-SHIP.
...IT WILL BE ALL RIGHT. I, NANKYOKU JYUSEI...
...WILL PROTECT YOU FOREVER.
SHAO.
UMM...

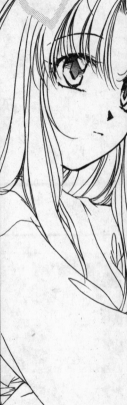

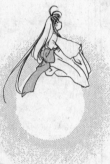

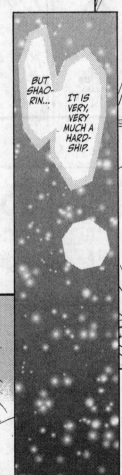

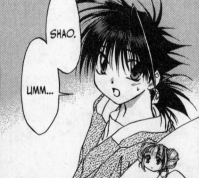

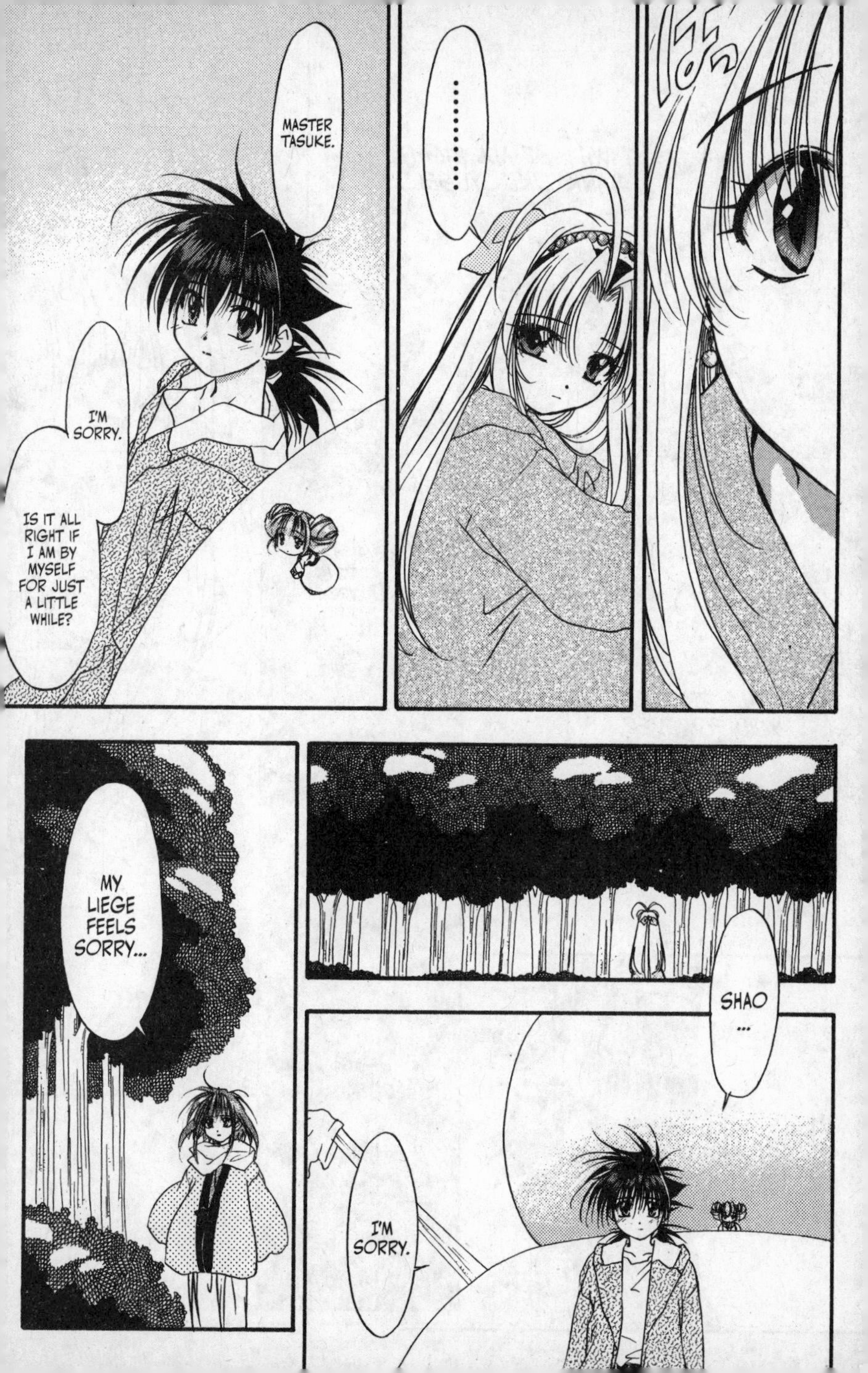
......
MASTER TASUKE.
I'M SORRY.
IS IT ALL RIGHT IF I AM BY MYSELF FOR JUST A LITTLE WHILE?
SHAO ...
I'M SORRY.
MY LIEGE FEELS SORRY...

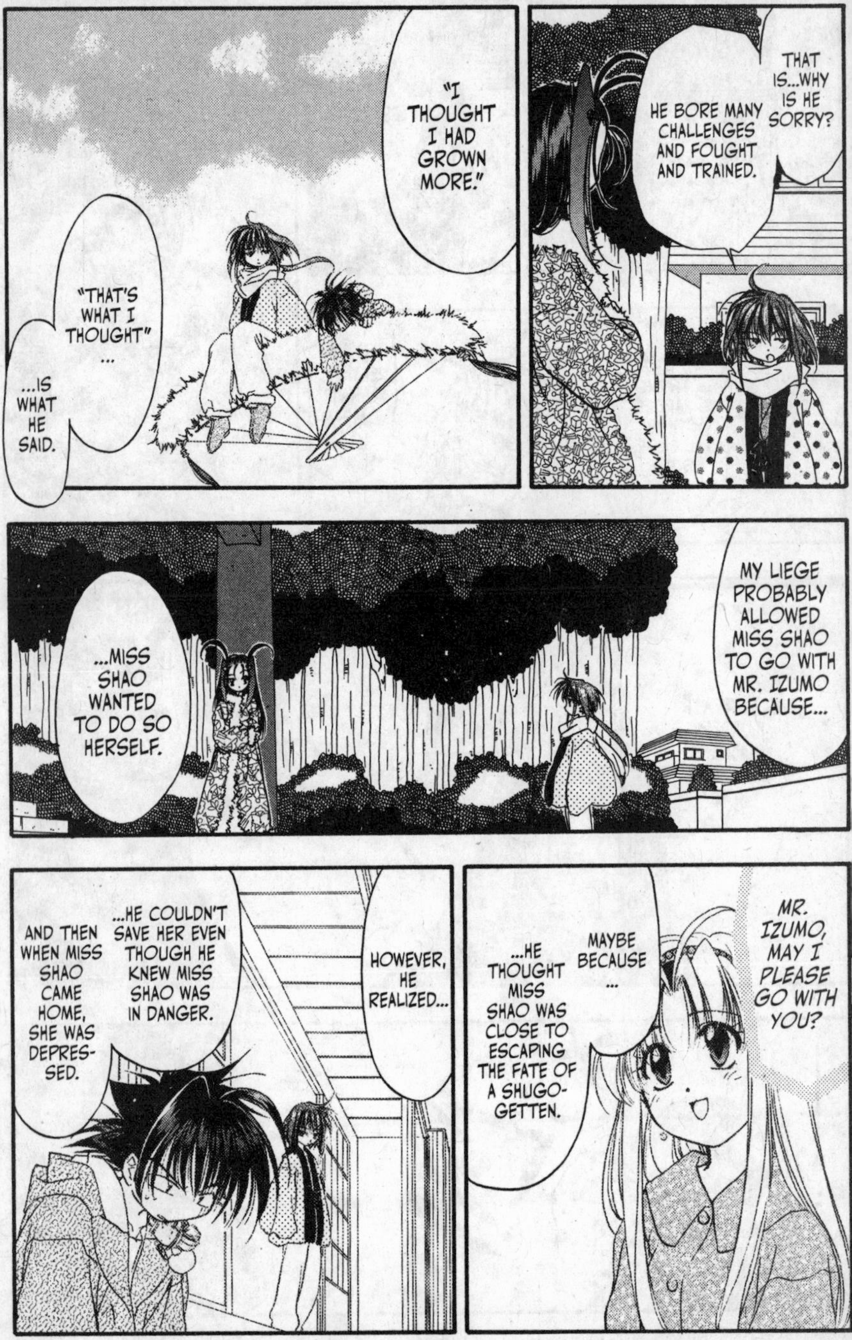
THAT IS...WHY IS HE SORRY?
HE BORE MANY CHALLENGES AND FOUGHT AND TRAINED.
"I THOUGHT I HAD GROWN MORE."
"THAT'S WHAT I THOUGHT" ...
...IS WHAT HE SAID.
MY LIEGE PROBABLY ALLOWED MISS SHAO TO GO WITH MR. IZUMO BECAUSE...
...MISS SHAO WANTED TO DO SO HERSELF.
MR. IZUMO, MAY I PLEASE GO WITH YOU?
MAYBE BECAUSE ...
...HE THOUGHT MISS SHAO WAS CLOSE TO ESCAPING THE FATE OF A SHUGO-GETTEN.
HOWEVER, HE REALIZED...
...HE COULDN'T SAVE HER EVEN THOUGH HE KNEW MISS SHAO WAS IN DANGER.
AND THEN WHEN MISS SHAO CAME HOME, SHE WAS DEPRES-SED.

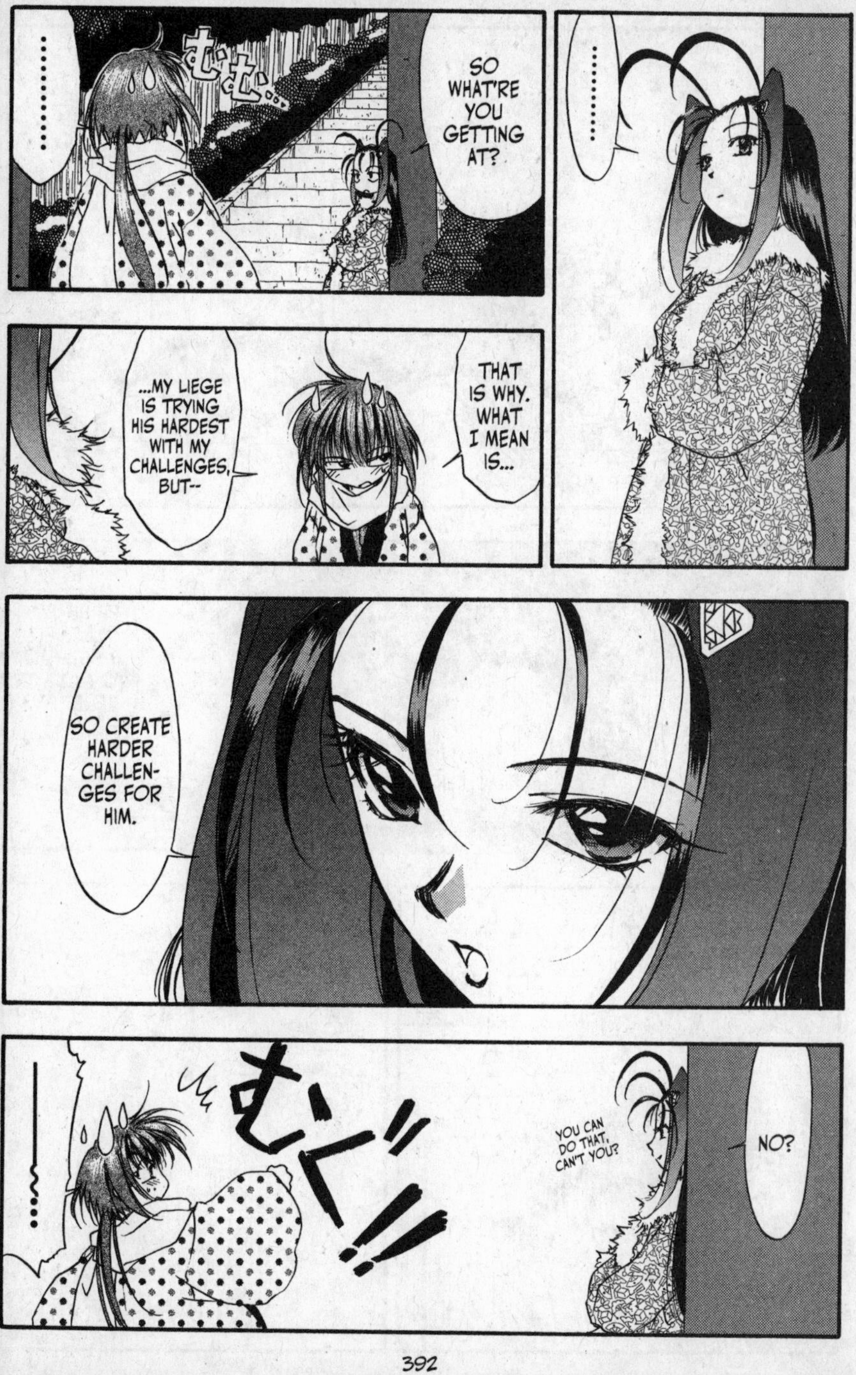
......
SO WHAT'RE YOU GETTING AT?
......
THAT IS WHY. WHAT I MEAN IS...
...MY LIEGE IS TRYING HIS HARDEST WITH MY CHALLENGES, BUT--
SO CREATE HARDER CHALLENGES FOR HIM.
NO?
YOU CAN DO THAT, CAN'T YOU?
......

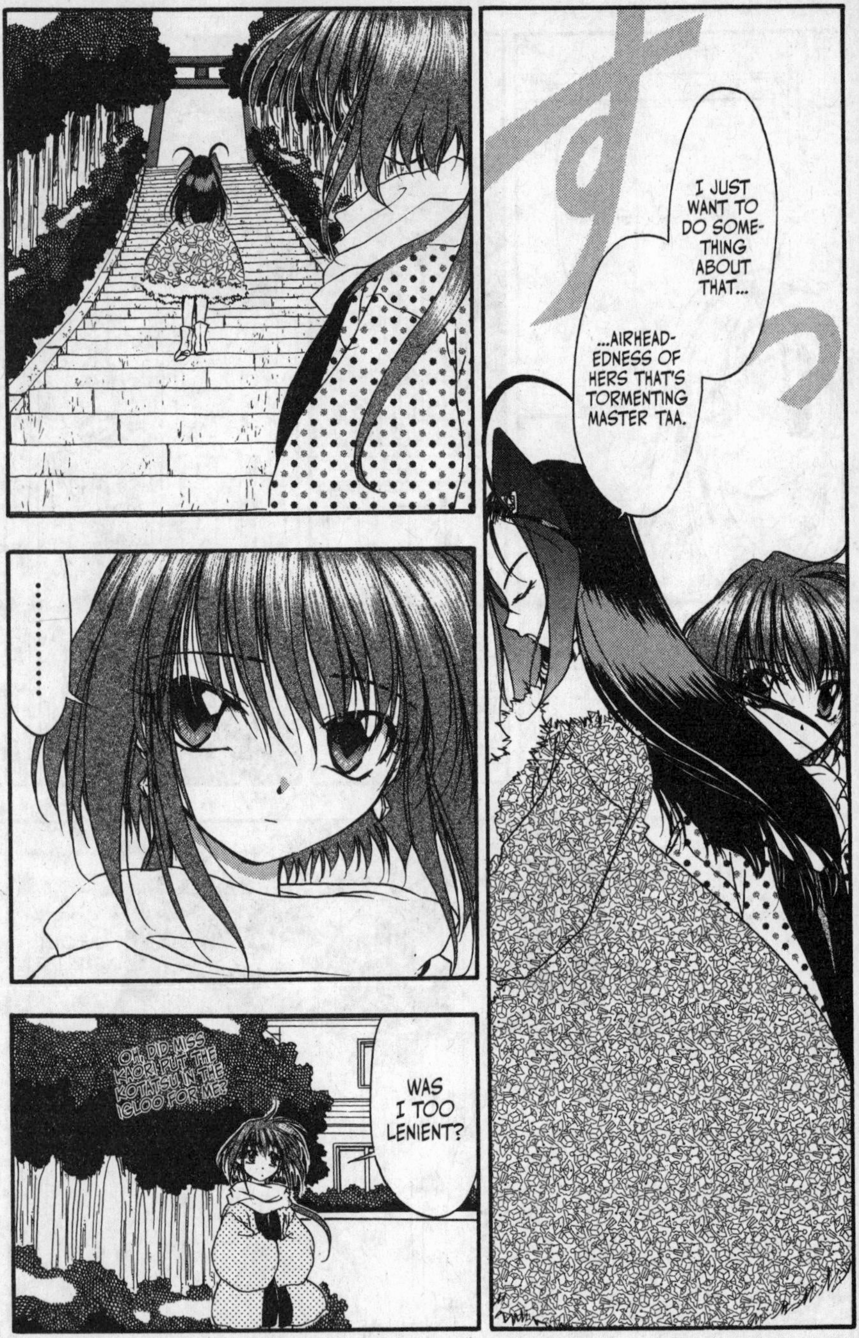
すっ
I JUST WANT TO DO SOME-THING ABOUT THAT...
...AIRHEAD-EDNESS OF HERS THAT'S TORMENTING MASTER TAA.
......
WAS I TOO LENIENT?
OH, DID MISS KAORI PUT THE KOTATSU IN THE IGLOO FOR ME?

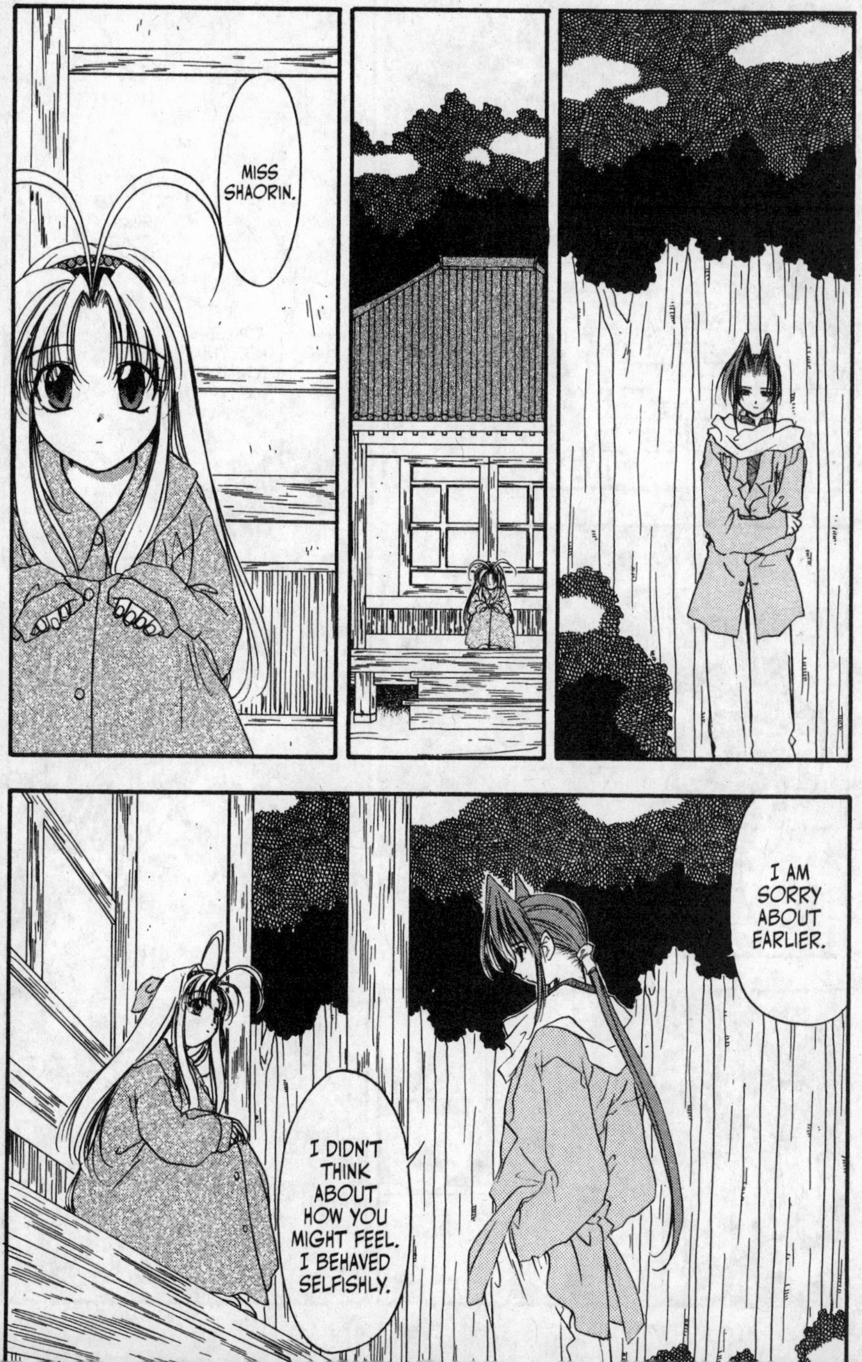
MISS SHAORIN.
I AM SORRY ABOUT EARLIER.
I DIDN'T THINK ABOUT HOW YOU MIGHT FEEL. I BEHAVED SELFISHLY.

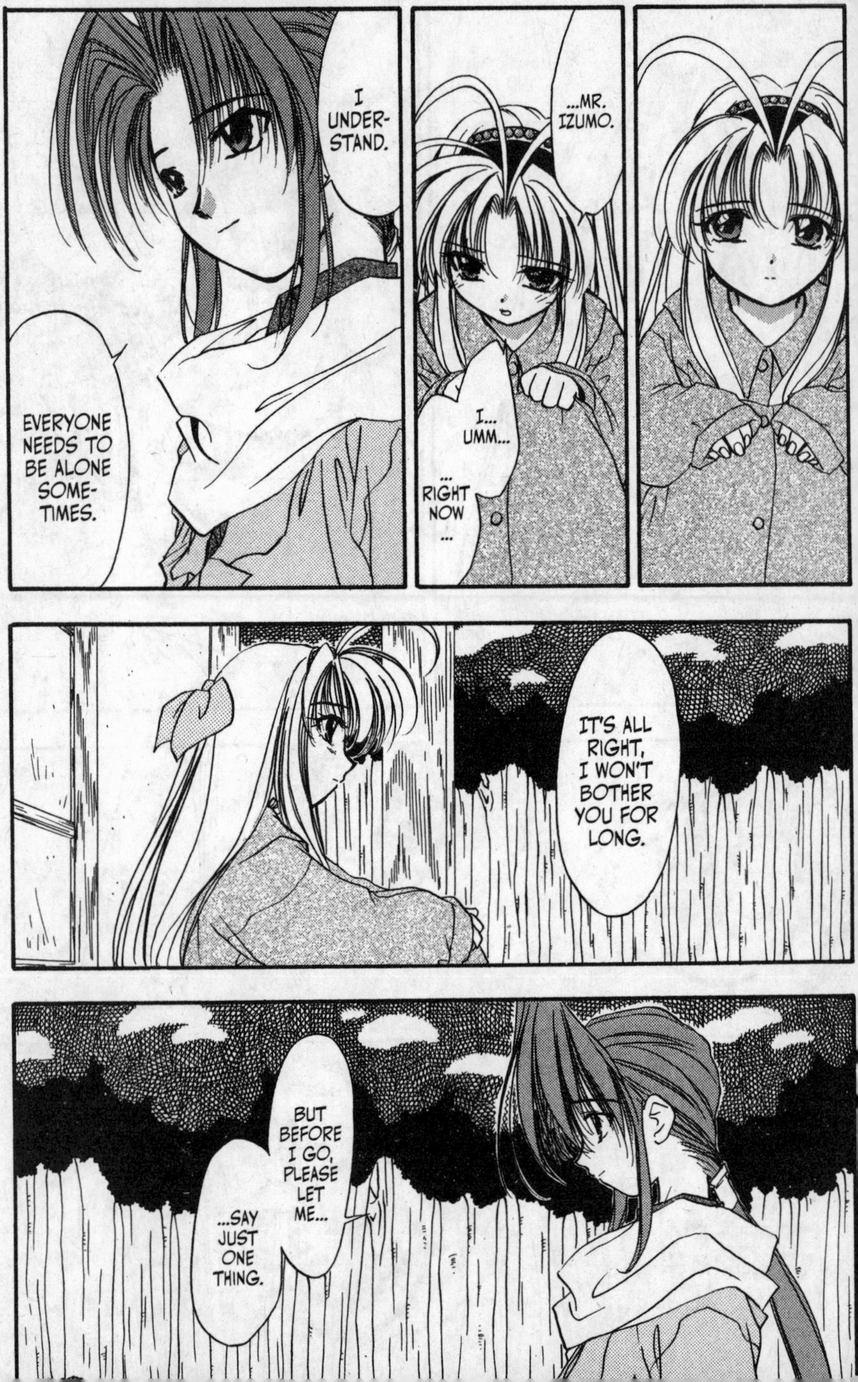
...MR. IZUMO.
I... UMM...
... RIGHT NOW ...
I UNDER-STAND.
EVERYONE NEEDS TO BE ALONE SOME-TIMES.
IT'S ALL RIGHT, I WON'T BOTHER YOU FOR LONG.
BUT BEFORE I GO, PLEASE LET ME...
...SAY JUST ONE THING.

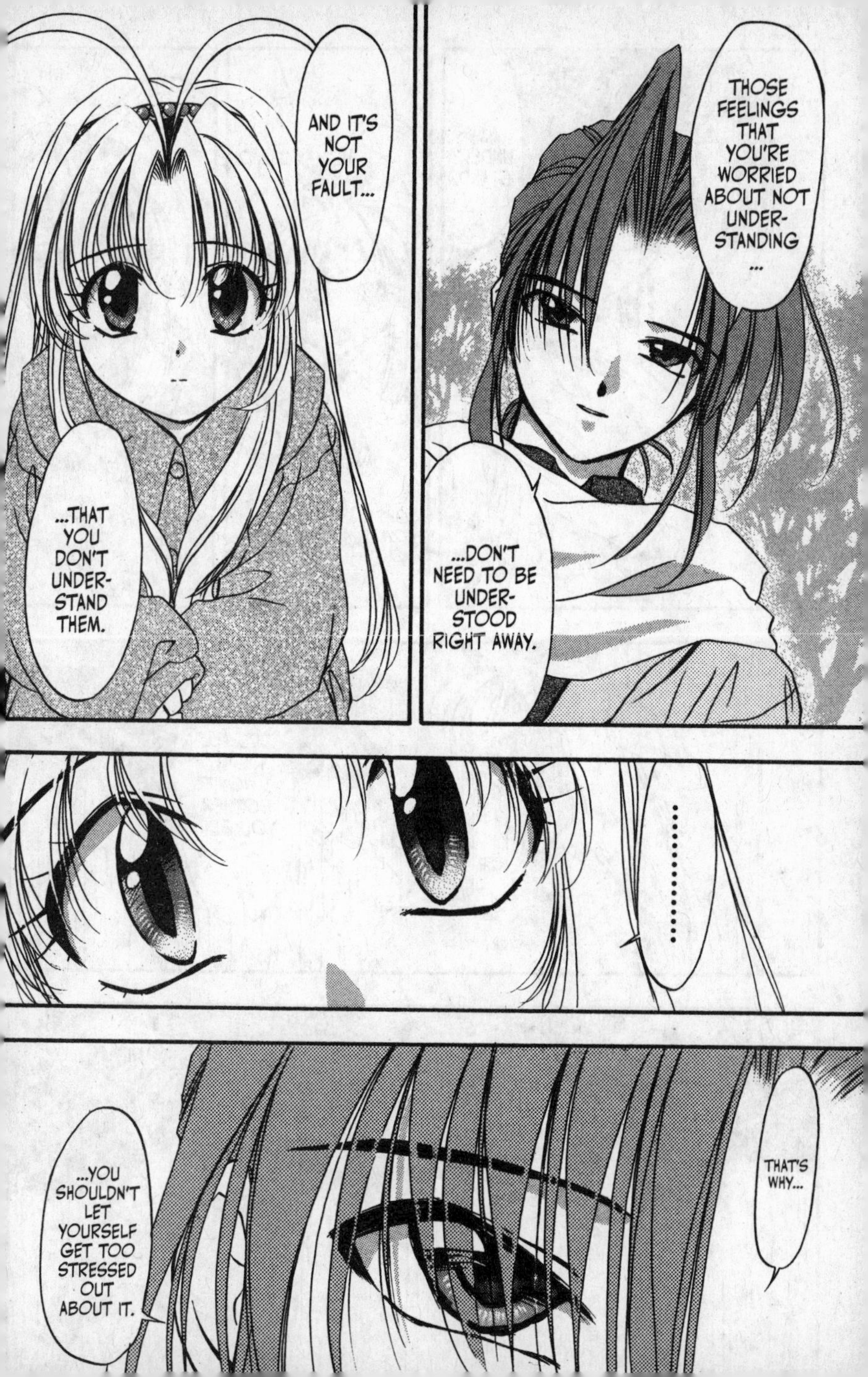
THOSE FEELINGS THAT YOU'RE WORRIED ABOUT NOT UNDER-STANDING ...
...DON'T NEED TO BE UNDER-STOOD RIGHT AWAY.
AND IT'S NOT YOUR FAULT...
...THAT YOU DON'T UNDER-STAND THEM.
....
THAT'S WHY...
...YOU SHOULDN'T LET YOURSELF GET TOO STRESSED OUT ABOUT IT.

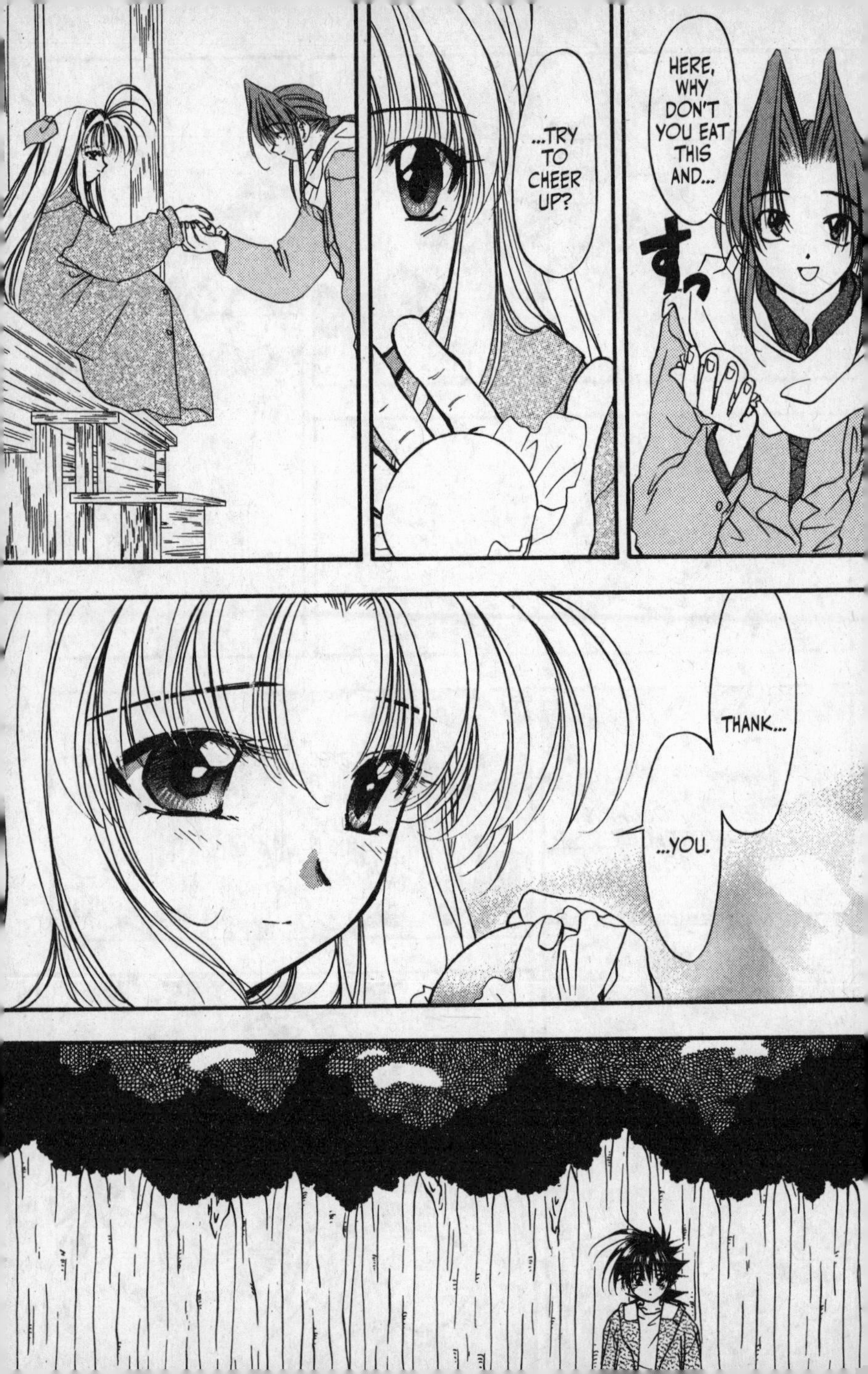
HERE, WHY DON'T YOU EAT THIS AND...
すっ
...TRY TO CHEER UP?
THANK...
...YOU.

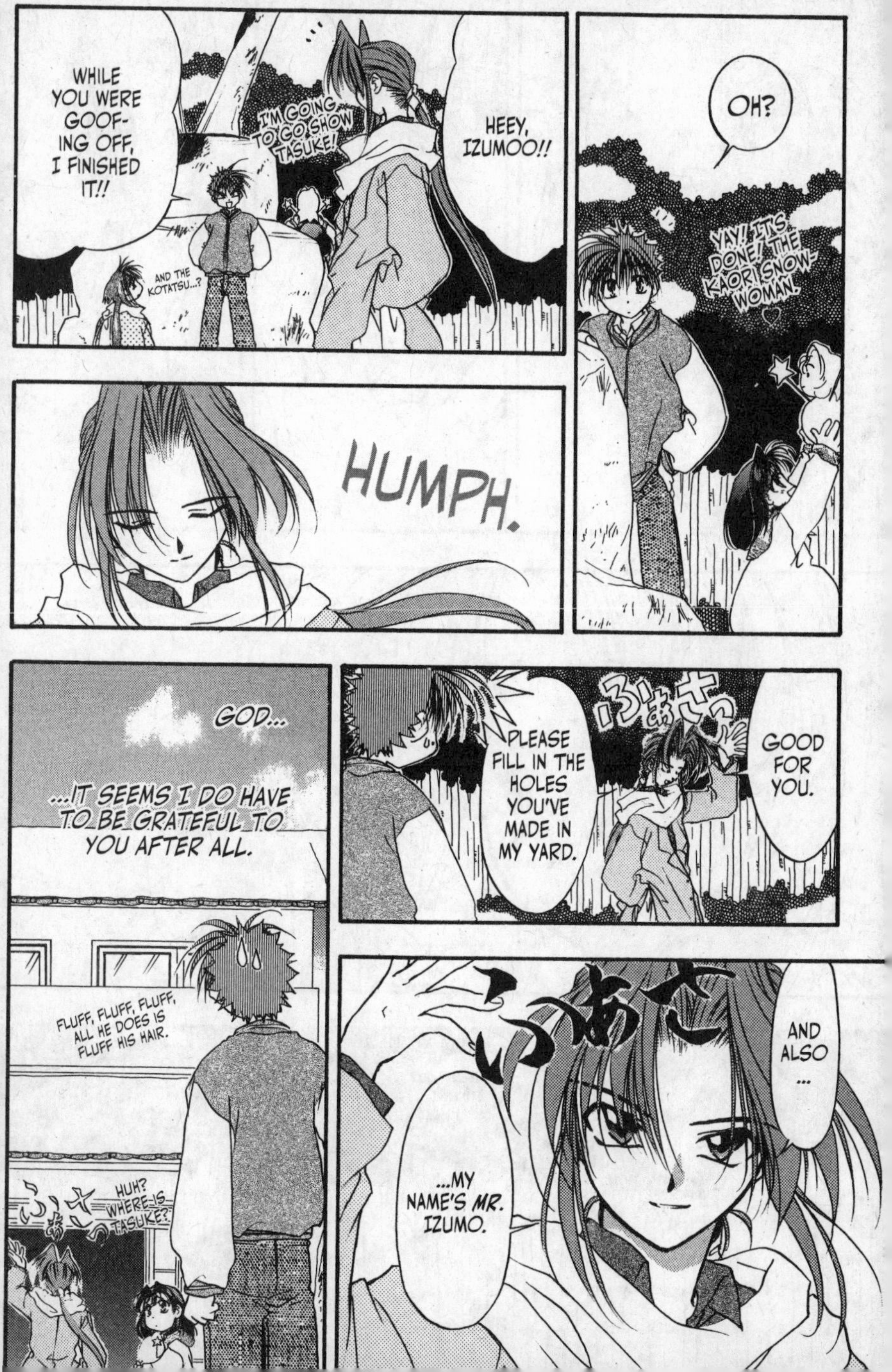
OH?
YAY! IT'S DONE! THE KAORI SNOW-WOMAN. ♡
HEEY, IZUMOO!!
I'M GOING TO GO SHOW TASUKE!
WHILE YOU WERE GOOF-ING OFF, I FINISHED IT!!
AND THE KOTATSU...?
HUMPH.
GOOD FOR YOU.
ふぁさっ
PLEASE FILL IN THE HOLES YOU'VE MADE IN MY YARD.
GOD...
...IT SEEMS I DO HAVE TO BE GRATEFUL TO YOU AFTER ALL.
AND ALSO ...
ふぁさ
...MY NAME'S MR. IZUMO.
FLUFF, FLUFF, FLUFF, ALL HE DOES IS FLUFF HIS HAIR.
HUH? WHERE IS TASUKE?

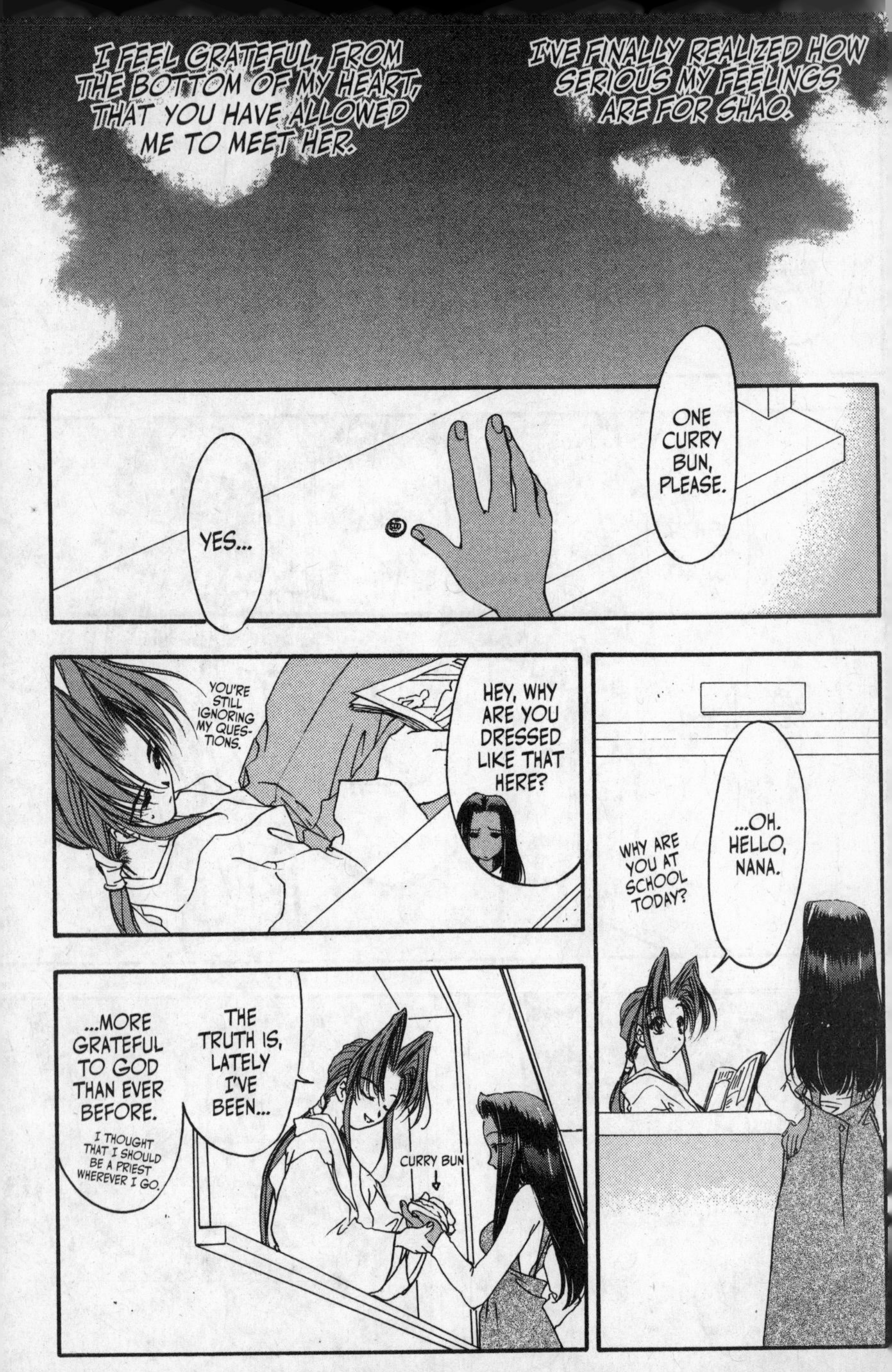
I'VE FINALLY REALIZED HOW SERIOUS MY FEELINGS ARE FOR SHAO.
I FEEL GRATEFUL, FROM THE BOTTOM OF MY HEART, THAT YOU HAVE ALLOWED ME TO MEET HER.
ONE CURRY BUN, PLEASE.
YES...
...OH. HELLO, NANA.
WHY ARE YOU AT SCHOOL TODAY?
HEY, WHY ARE YOU DRESSED LIKE THAT HERE?
YOU'RE STILL IGNORING MY QUESTIONS.
THE TRUTH IS, LATELY I'VE BEEN...
...MORE GRATEFUL TO GOD THAN EVER BEFORE.
I THOUGHT THAT I SHOULD BE A PRIEST WHEREVER I GO.
CURRY BUN

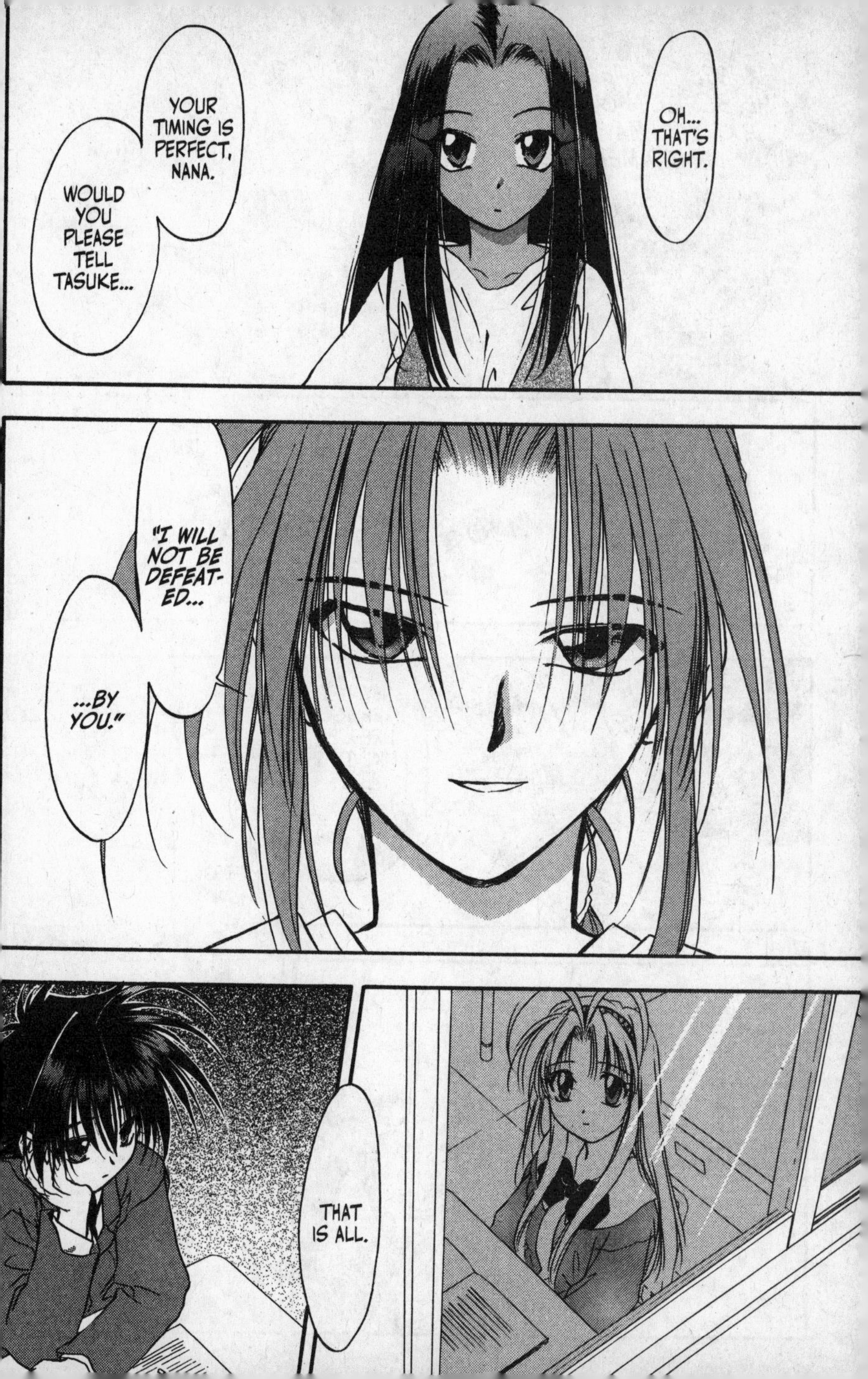
OH... THAT'S RIGHT.
YOUR TIMING IS PERFECT, NANA.
WOULD YOU PLEASE TELL TASUKE...
"I WILL NOT BE DEFEAT-ED...
...BY YOU."
THAT IS ALL.

SPECIAL SIDE STORIES

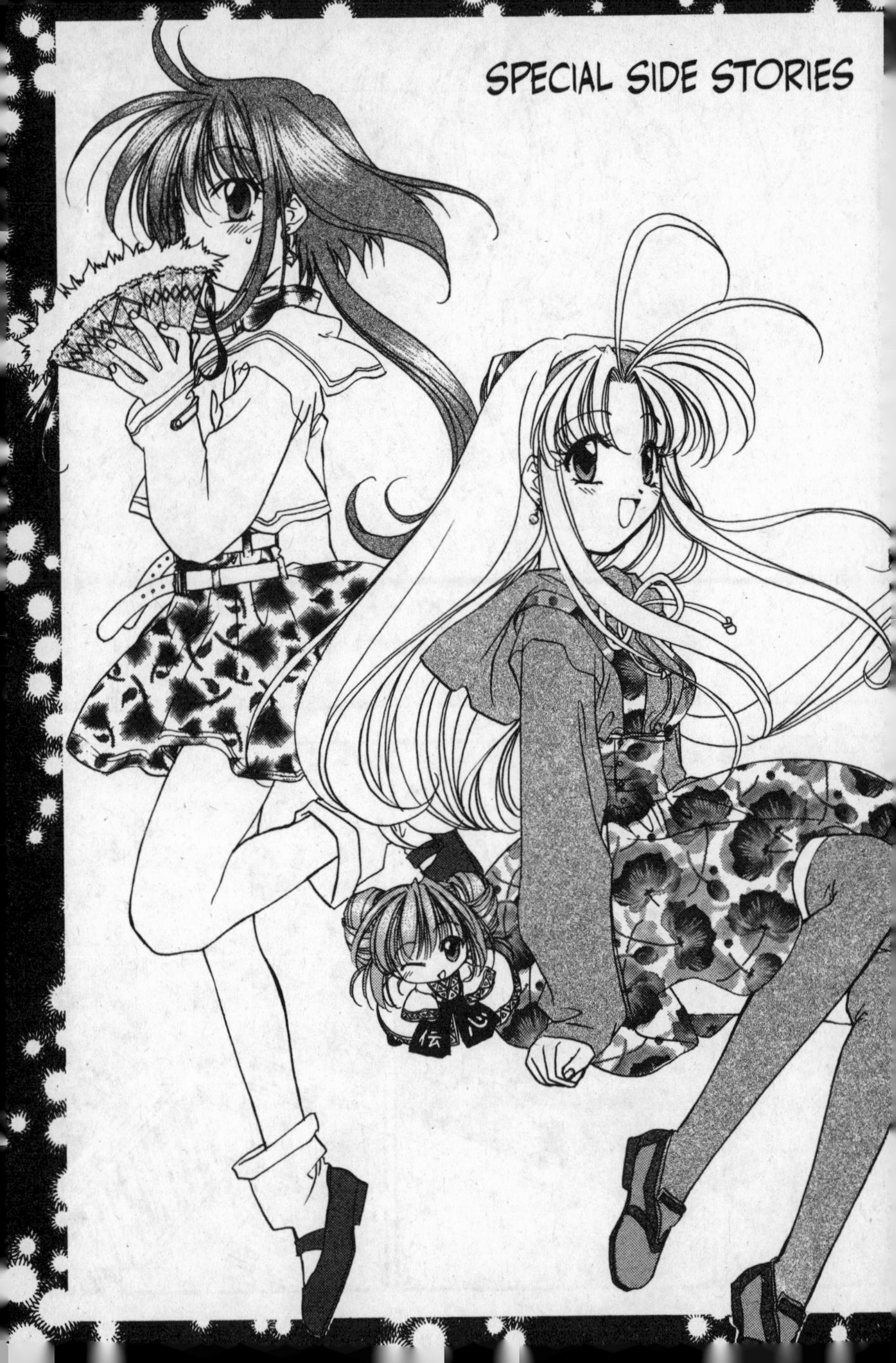

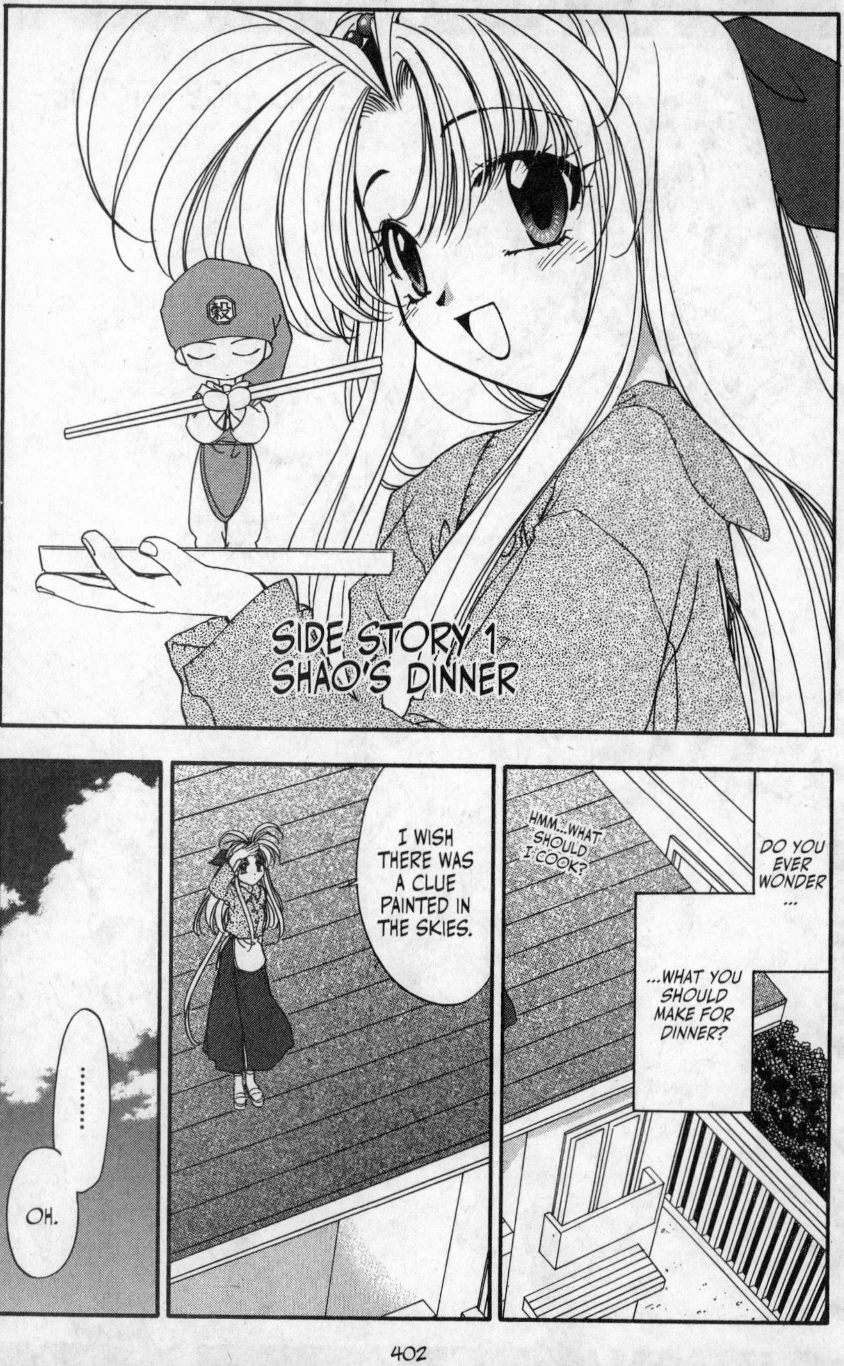
SIDE STORY 1
SHAO'S DINNER
DO YOU EVER WONDER ...
HMM...WHAT SHOULD I COOK?
...WHAT YOU SHOULD MAKE FOR DINNER?
I WISH THERE WAS A CLUE PAINTED IN THE SKIES.
......
OH.

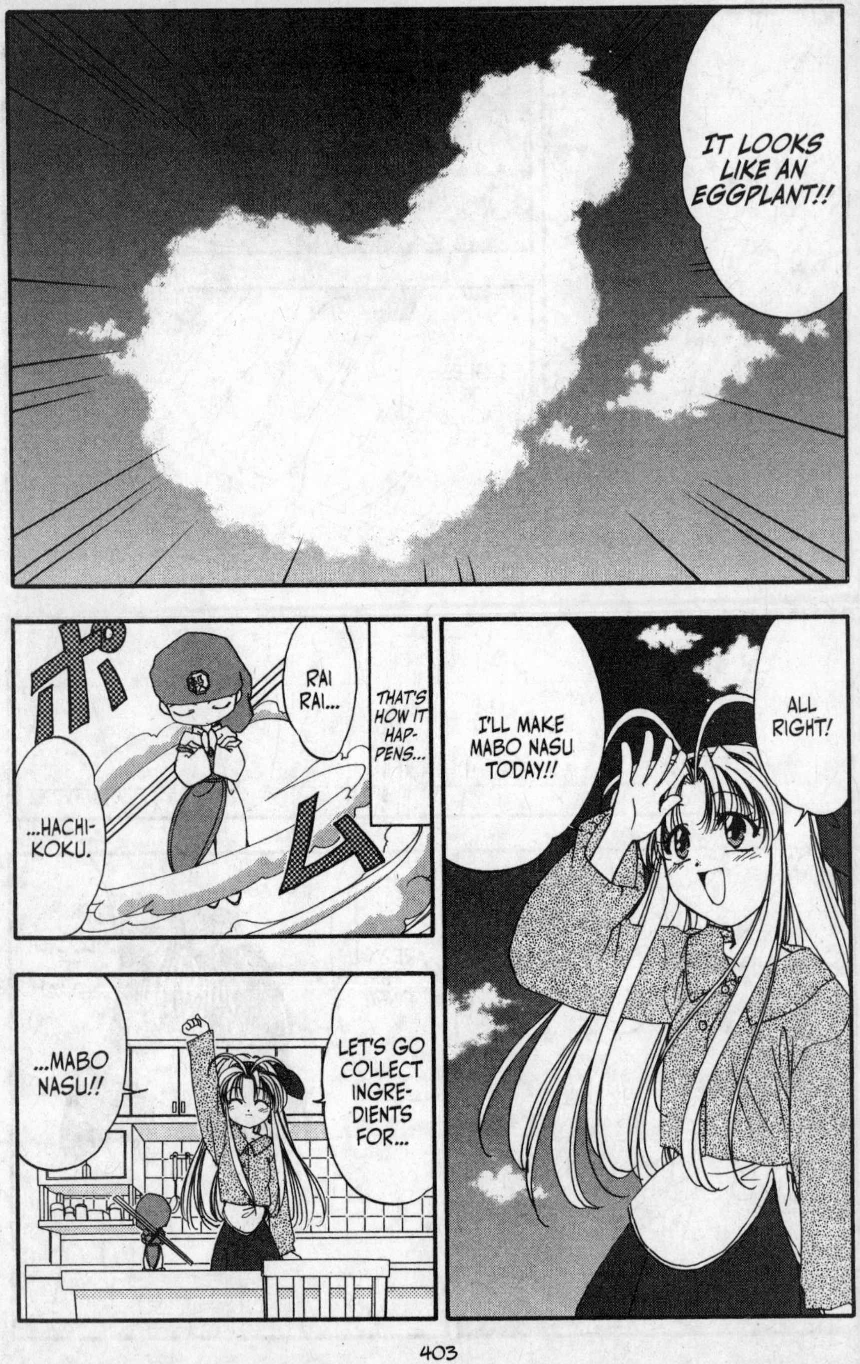
IT LOOKS LIKE AN EGGPLANT!!
ALL RIGHT!
I'LL MAKE MABO NASU TODAY!!
THAT'S HOW IT HAP-PENS...
RAI RAI...
...HACHI-KOKU.
ポム
LET'S GO COLLECT INGRE-DIENTS FOR...
...MABO NASU!!

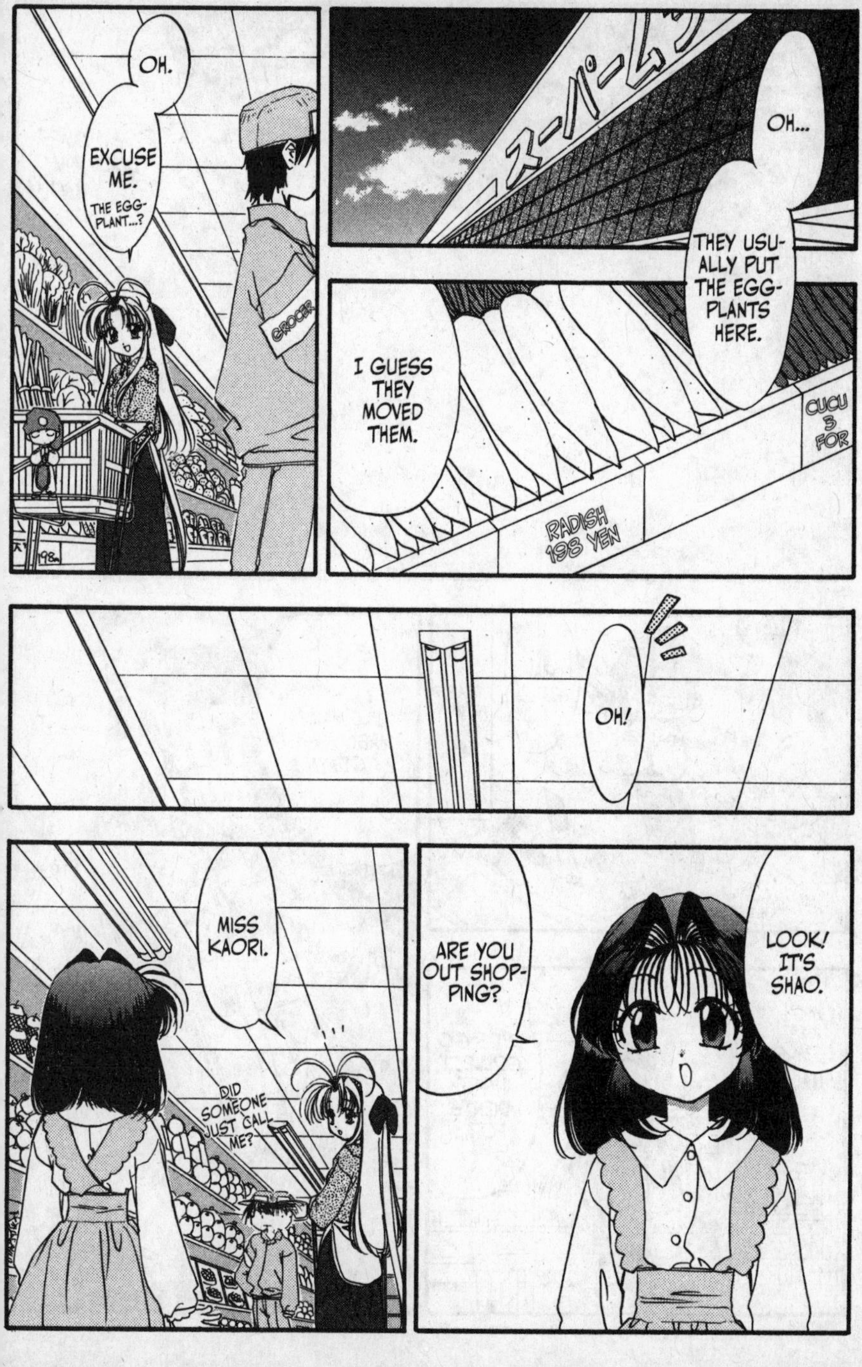
スーパーム
OH...
THEY USU-
ALLY PUT
THE EGG-
PLANTS
HERE.
I GUESS THEY MOVED THEM.
CUCU 3 FOR
RADISH 198 YEN
OH.
EXCUSE ME.
THE EGG-PLANT...?
GROCER
OH!
LOOK! IT'S SHAO.
ARE YOU OUT SHOP-PING?
MISS KAORI.
DID SOMEONE JUST CALL ME?

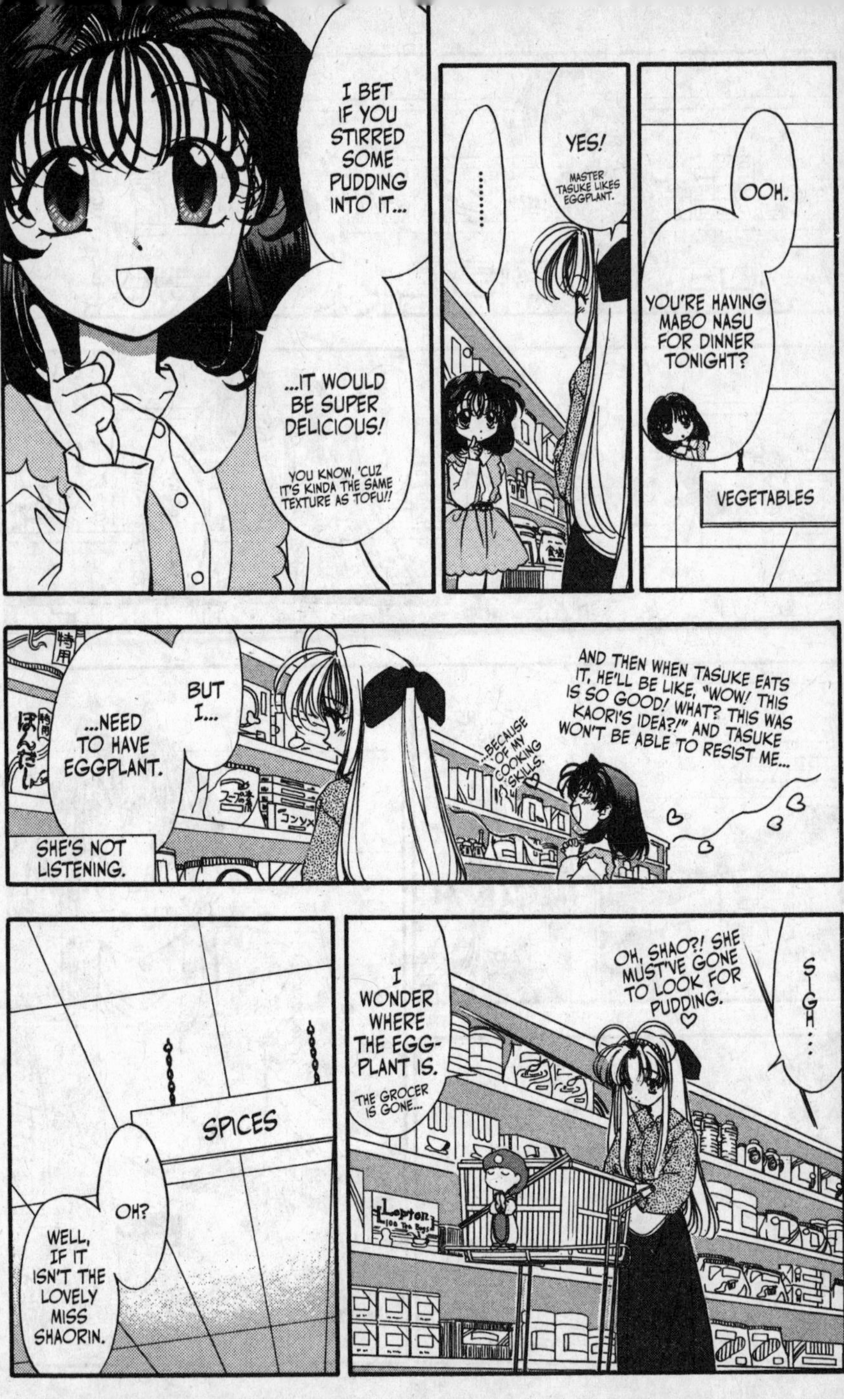
OOH.
YOU'RE HAVING MABO NASU FOR DINNER TONIGHT?
VEGETABLES
YES!
MASTER TASUKE LIKES EGGPLANT.
......
I BET IF YOU STIRRED SOME PUDDING INTO IT...
...IT WOULD BE SUPER DELICIOUS!
YOU KNOW, 'CUZ IT'S KINDA THE SAME TEXTURE AS TOFU!!
AND THEN WHEN TASUKE EATS IT, HE'LL BE LIKE, "WOW! THIS IS SO GOOD! WHAT? THIS WAS KAORI'S IDEA?!" AND TASUKE WON'T BE ABLE TO RESIST ME...
...BECAUSE OF MY COOKING SKILLS.
BUT I...
...NEED TO HAVE EGGPLANT.
SHE'S NOT LISTENING.
SIGH...
OH, SHAO?! SHE MUST'VE GONE TO LOOK FOR PUDDING.
I WONDER WHERE THE EGG-PLANT IS.
THE GROCER IS GONE...
SPICES
OH?
WELL, IF IT ISN'T THE LOVELY MISS SHAORIN.

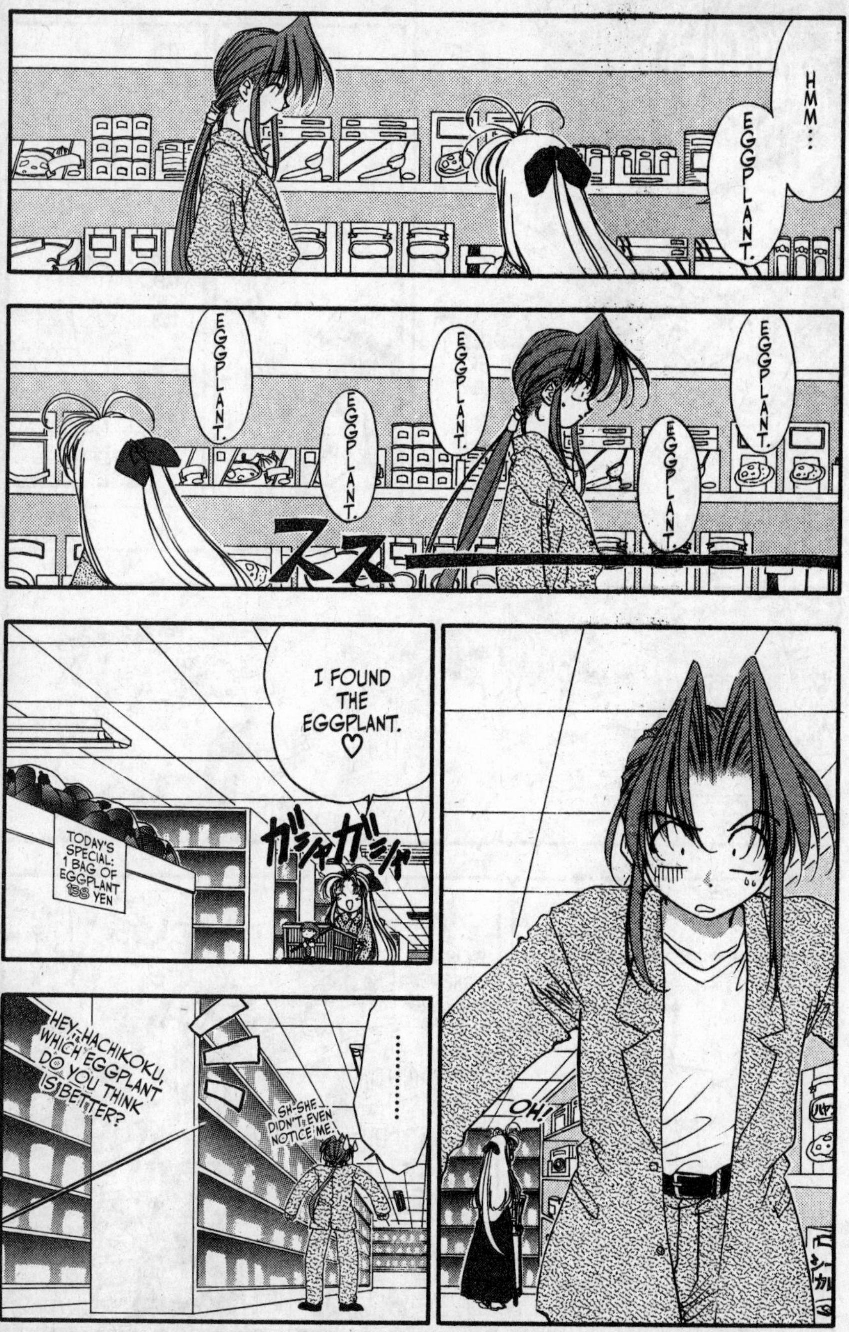
HMM... EGGPLANT.
EGGPLANT.
EGGPLANT.
EGGPLANT.
EGGPLANT.
EGGPLANT.
スス
OH!
I FOUND THE EGGPLANT. ♡
TODAY'S SPECIAL: 1 BAG OF EGGPLANT 138 YEN
ガシャガシャ
......
SH-SHE DIDN'T EVEN NOTICE ME.
HEY, HACHIKOKU, WHICH EGGPLANT DO YOU THINK IS BETTER?

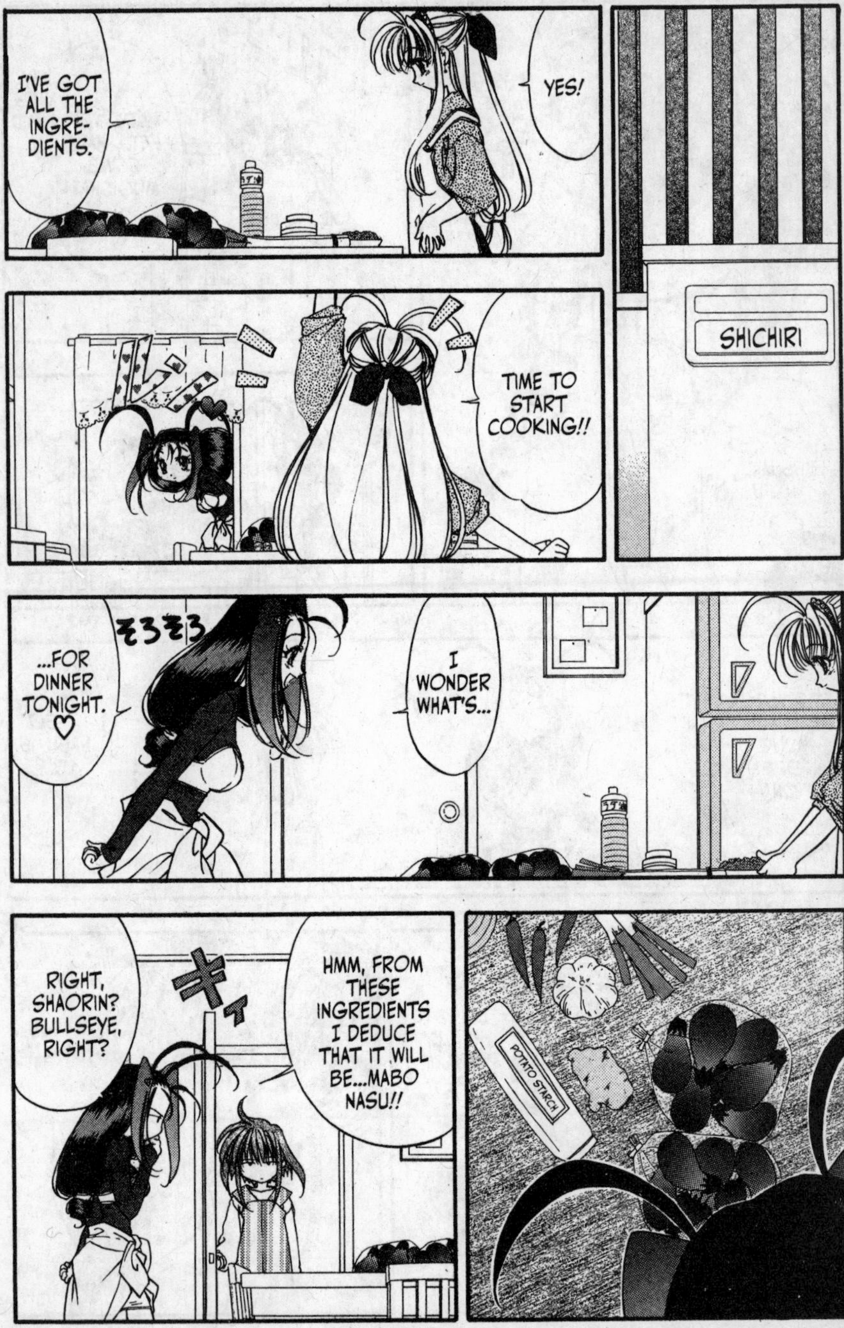
SHICHIRI
YES!
I'VE GOT ALL THE INGREDIENTS.
TIME TO START COOKING!!
I WONDER WHAT'S...
そろそろ
...FOR DINNER TONIGHT. ♡
POTATO STARCH
HMM, FROM THESE INGREDIENTS I DEDUCE THAT IT WILL BE...MABO NASU!!
キィ
RIGHT, SHAORIN? BULLSEYE, RIGHT?

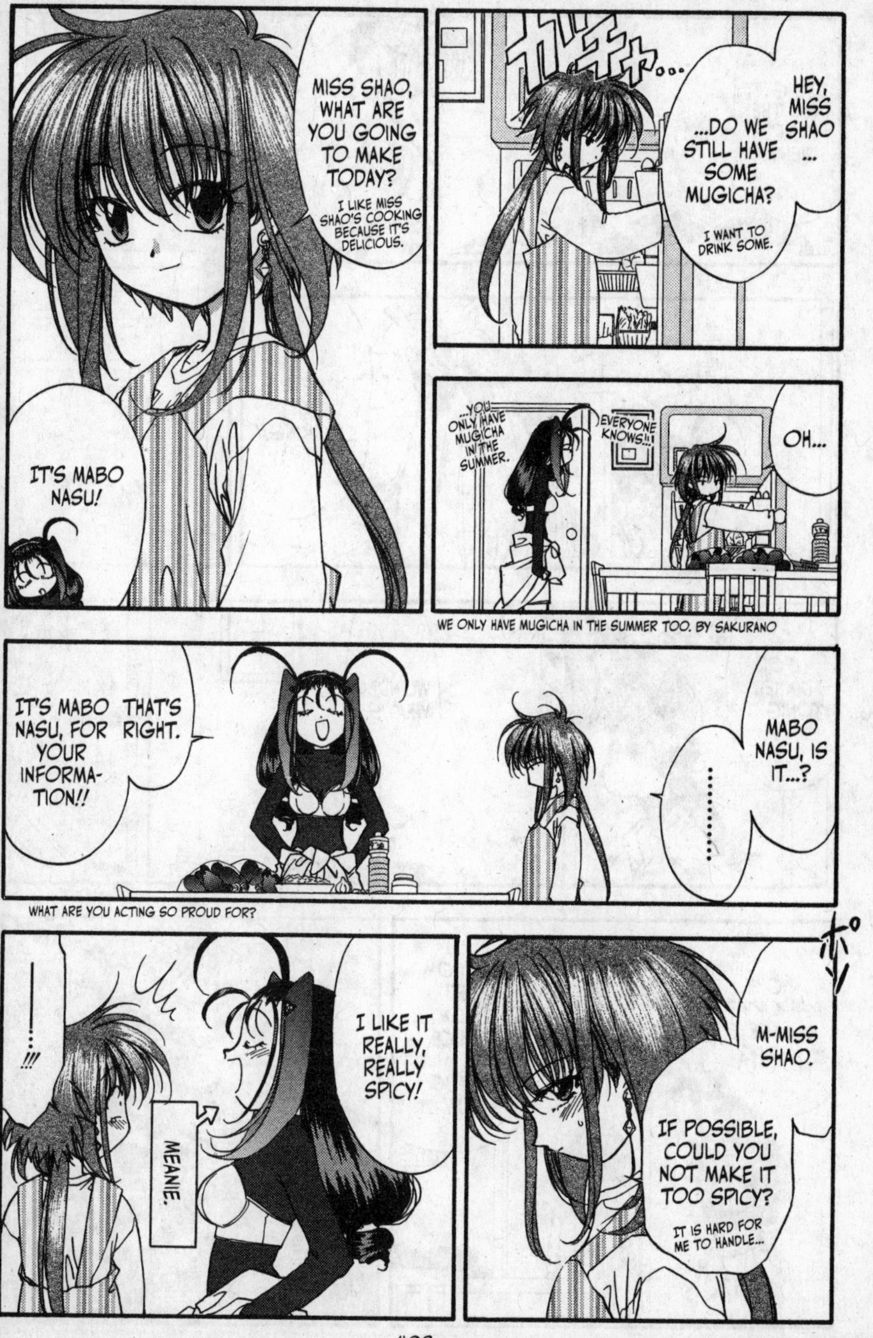

ガチャ...
HEY, MISS SHAO ...
...DO WE STILL HAVE SOME MUGICHA?
I WANT TO DRINK SOME.
OH...
EVERYONE KNOWS!!
...YOU ONLY HAVE MUGICHA IN THE SUMMER.
MISS SHAO, WHAT ARE YOU GOING TO MAKE TODAY?
I LIKE MISS SHAO'S COOKING BECAUSE IT'S DELICIOUS.
IT'S MABO NASU!
WE ONLY HAVE MUGICHA IN THE SUMMER TOO. BY SAKURANO
MABO NASU, IS IT...?
....
THAT'S RIGHT.
IT'S MABO NASU, FOR YOUR INFORMATION!!
WHAT ARE YOU ACTING SO PROUD FOR?
ポッ
M-MISS SHAO.
IF POSSIBLE, COULD YOU NOT MAKE IT TOO SPICY?
IT IS HARD FOR ME TO HANDLE...
I LIKE IT REALLY, REALLY SPICY!
MEANIE.
...!!!

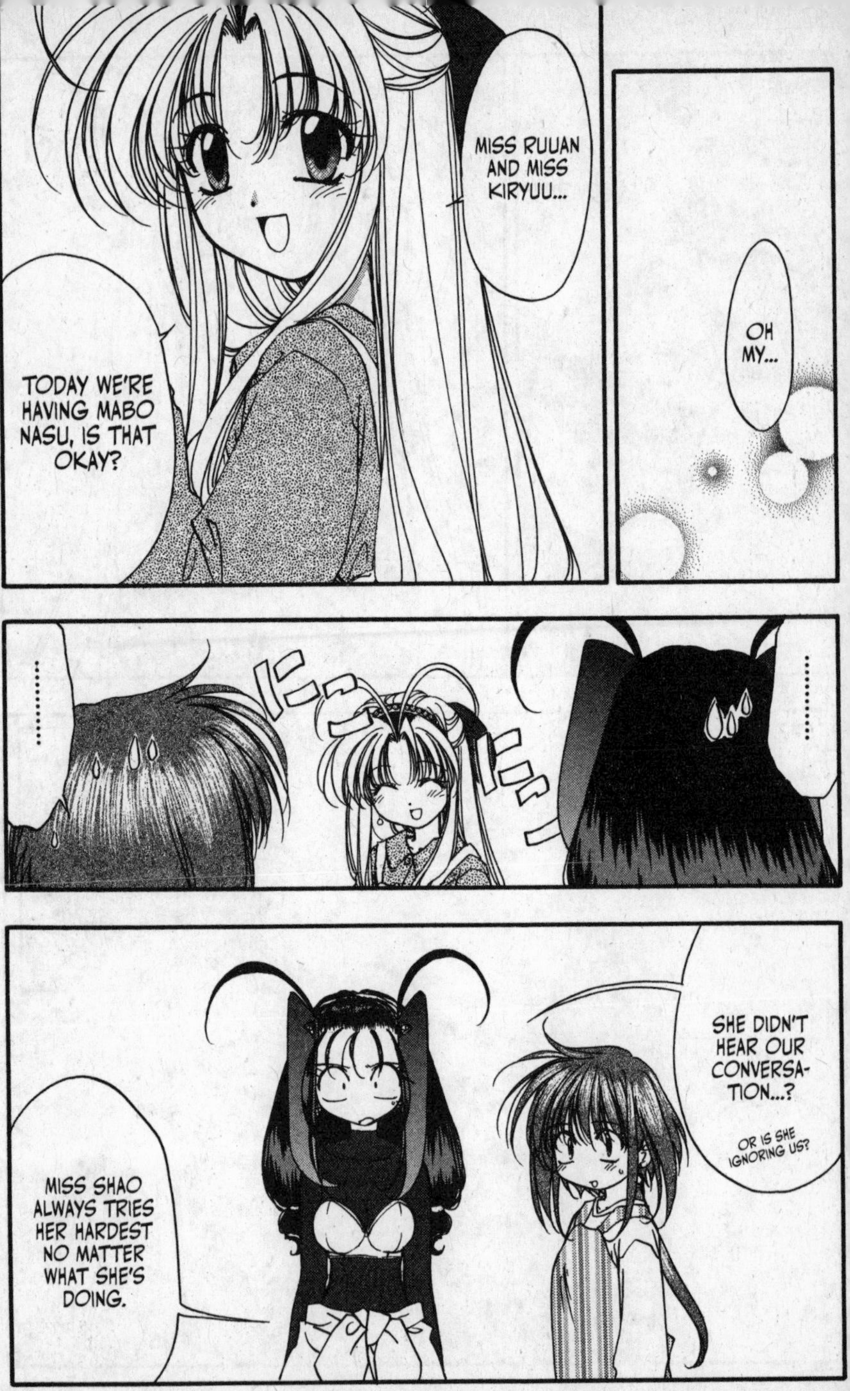
OH MY...
MISS RUUAN AND MISS KIRYUU...
TODAY WE'RE HAVING MABO NASU, IS THAT OKAY?
......
......
SHE DIDN'T HEAR OUR CONVERSA-TION...?
OR IS SHE IGNORING US?
MISS SHAO ALWAYS TRIES HER HARDEST NO MATTER WHAT SHE'S DOING.

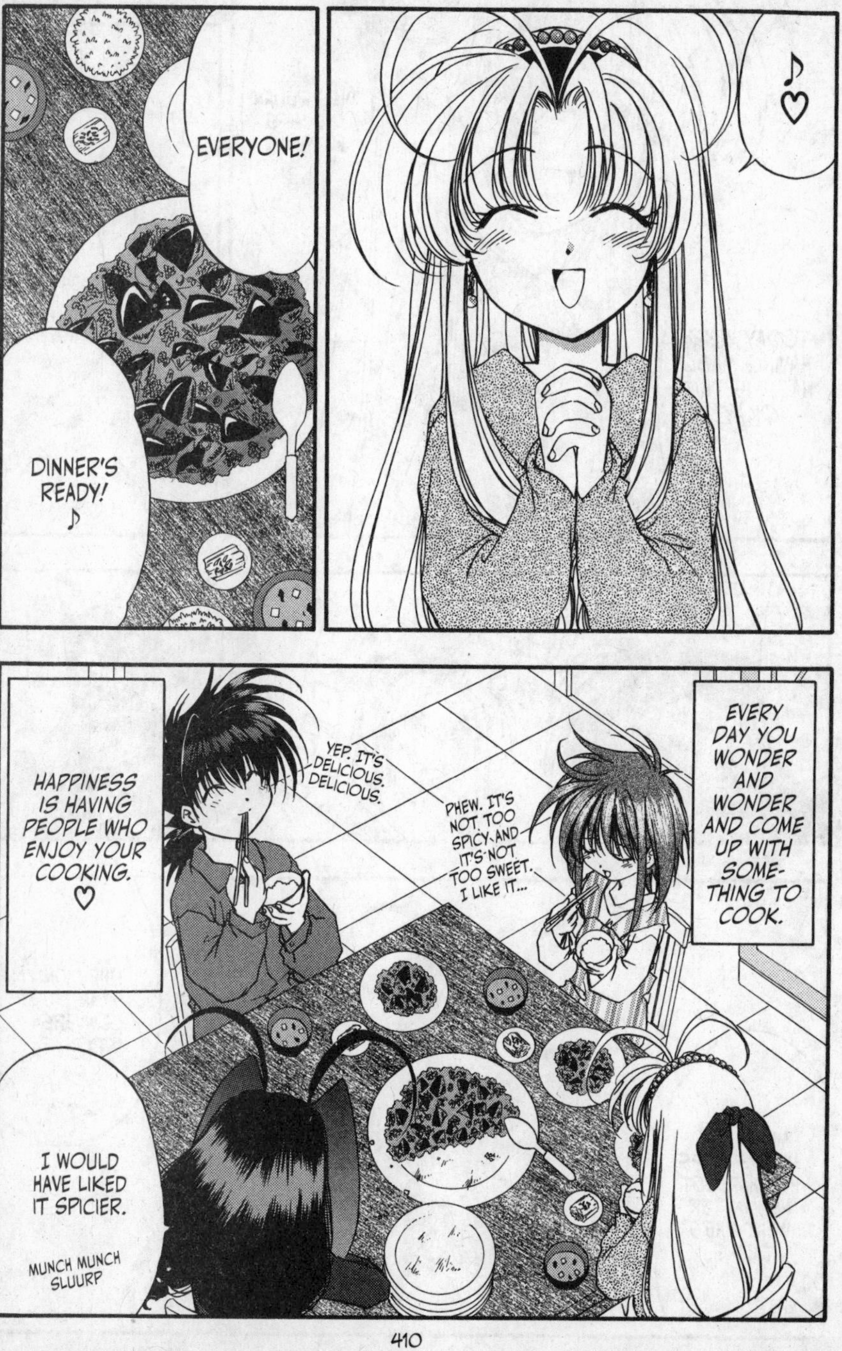
♪ ♡
EVERYONE!
DINNER'S READY! ♪
EVERY DAY YOU WONDER AND WONDER AND COME UP WITH SOME-THING TO COOK.
PHEW. IT'S NOT TOO SPICY, AND IT'S NOT TOO SWEET. I LIKE IT...
YEP. IT'S DELICIOUS. DELICIOUS.
HAPPINESS IS HAVING PEOPLE WHO ENJOY YOUR COOKING. ♡
I WOULD HAVE LIKED IT SPICIER.
MUNCH MUNCH SLUURP

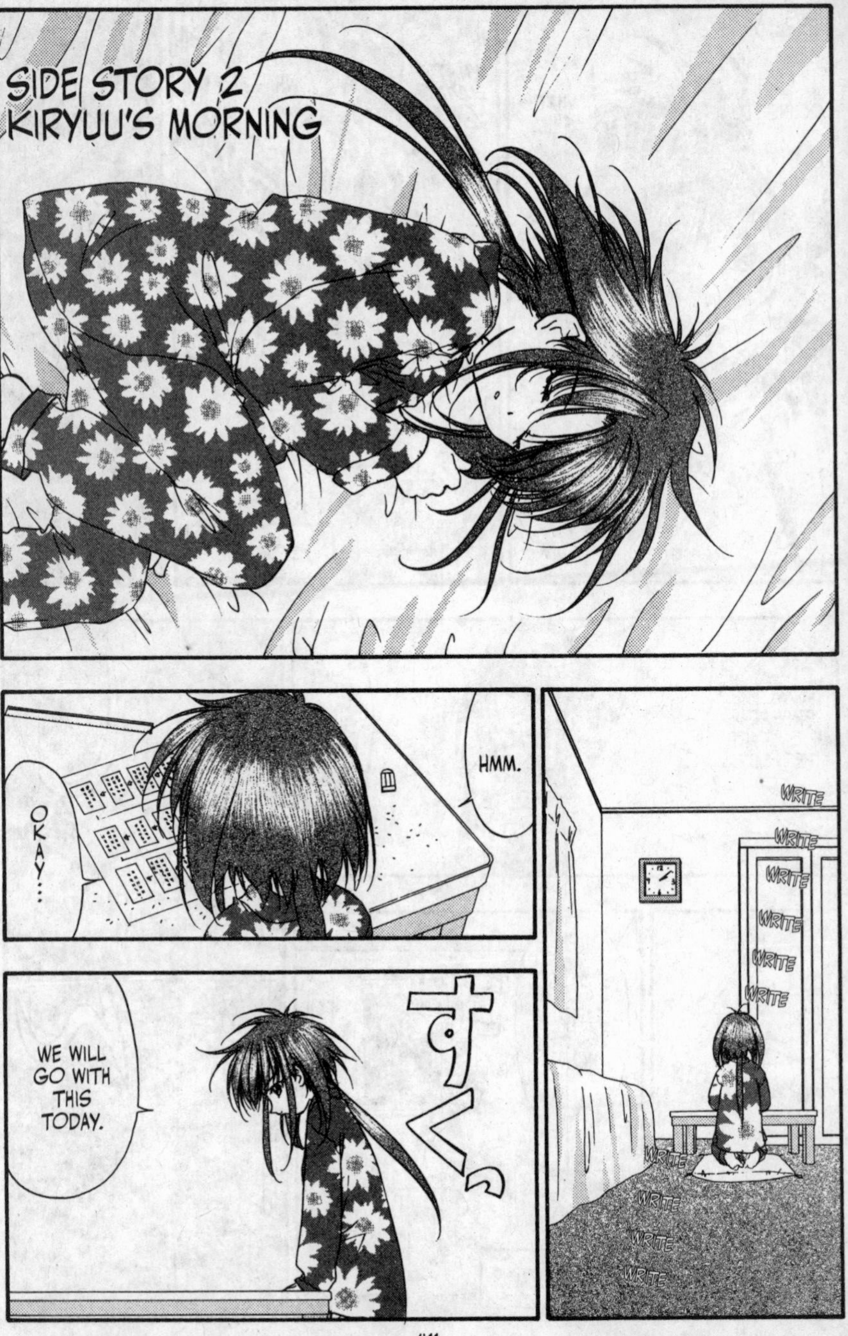
SIDE STORY 2
KIRYUU'S MORNING
WRITE WRITE WRITE WRITE WRITE WRITE
WRITE WRITE WRITE WRITE
HMM.
OKAY...
WE WILL GO WITH THIS TODAY.

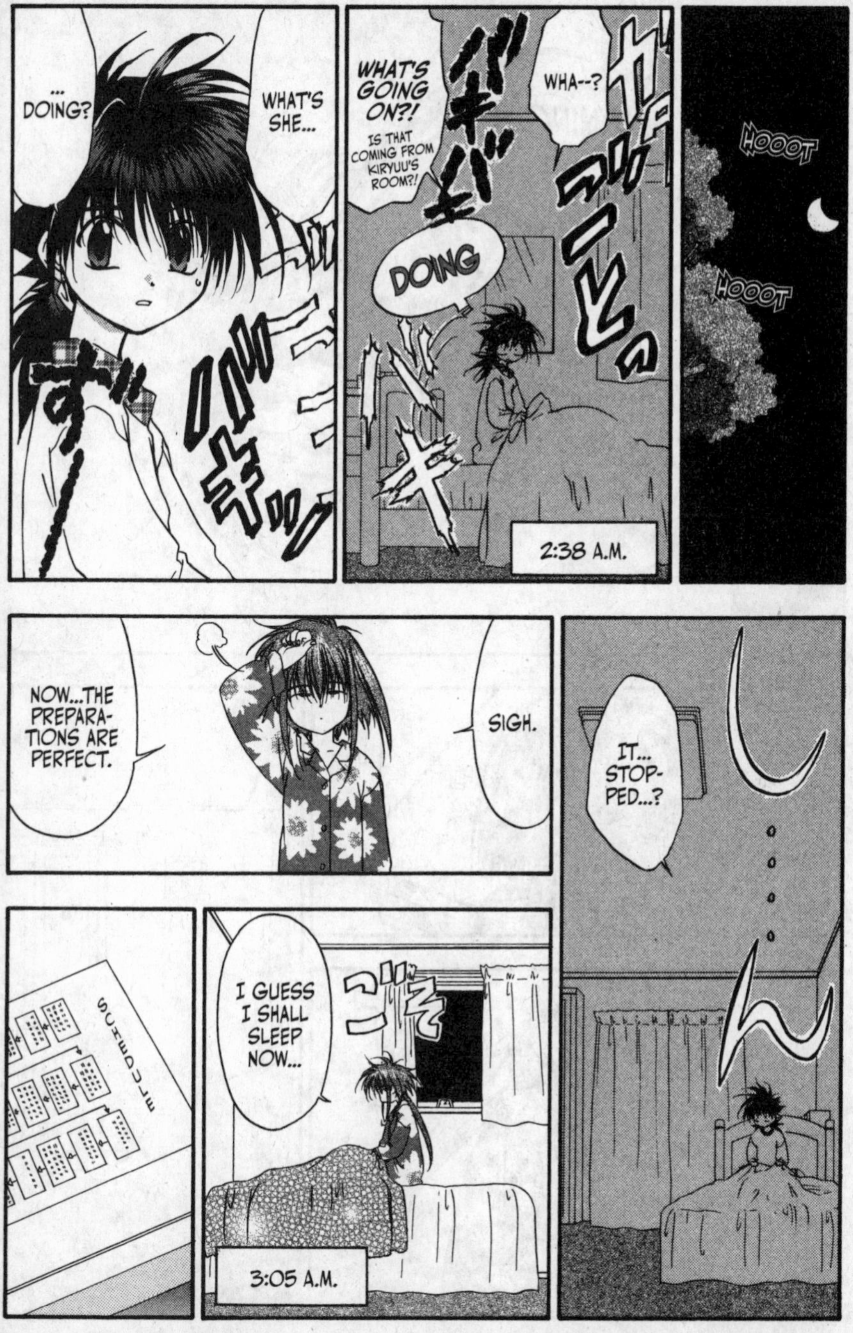
HOOOT
HOOOT
WHA--?
2:38 A.M.
WHAT'S GOING ON?!
IS THAT COMING FROM KIRYUU'S ROOM?!
DOING
WHAT'S SHE...
... DOING?
IT... STOPPED...?
SIGH.
NOW...THE PREPARATIONS ARE PERFECT.
I GUESS I SHALL SLEEP NOW...
3:05 A.M.
SCHEDULE

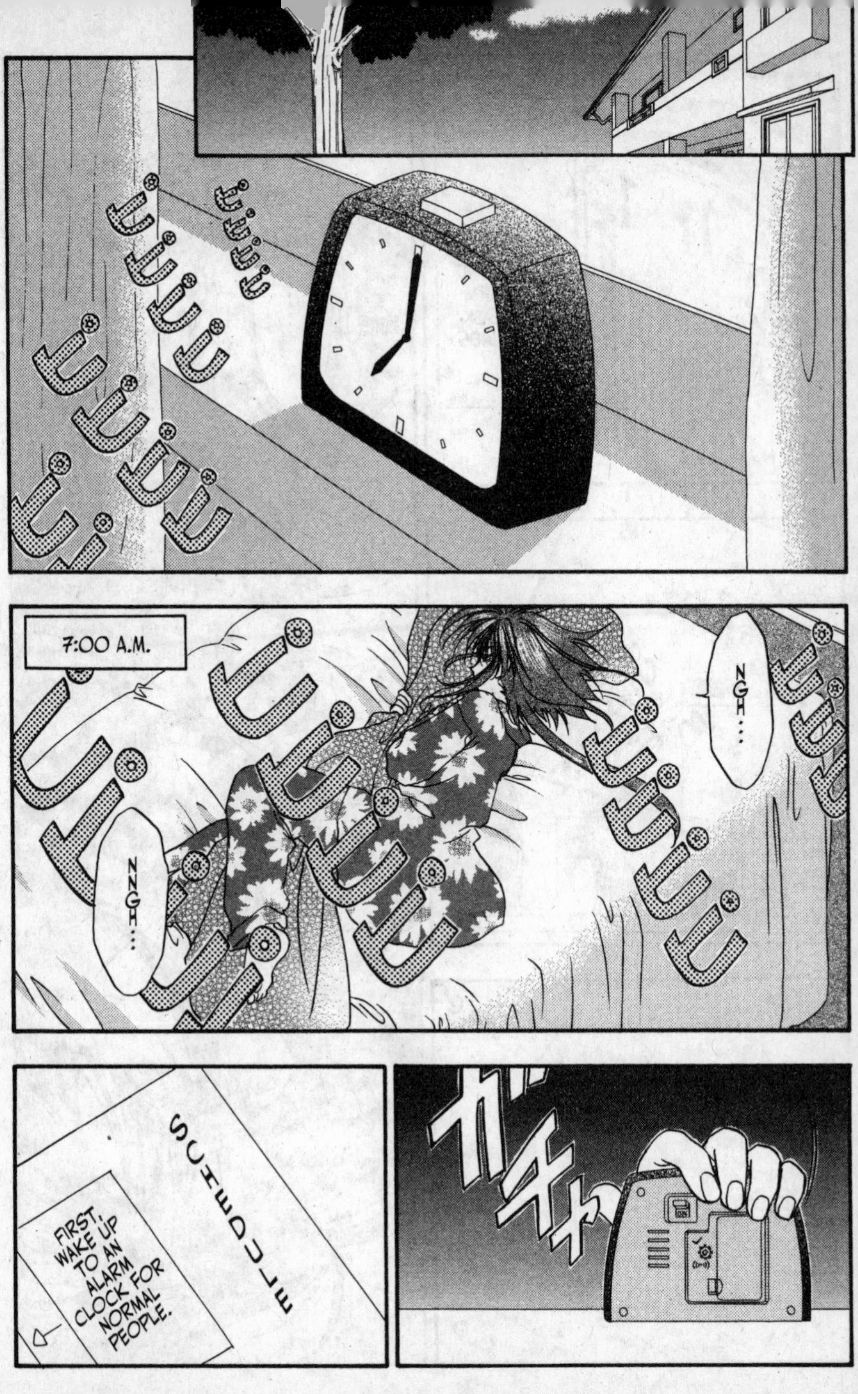

ピピピピ
ピピピピ
ピピピピ
ピピピピ
NGH...
7:00 A.M.
ピピピピ
ピピピピ
NNGH...
ガチャ
SCHEDULE
FIRST, WAKE UP TO AN ALARM CLOCK FOR NORMAL PEOPLE.

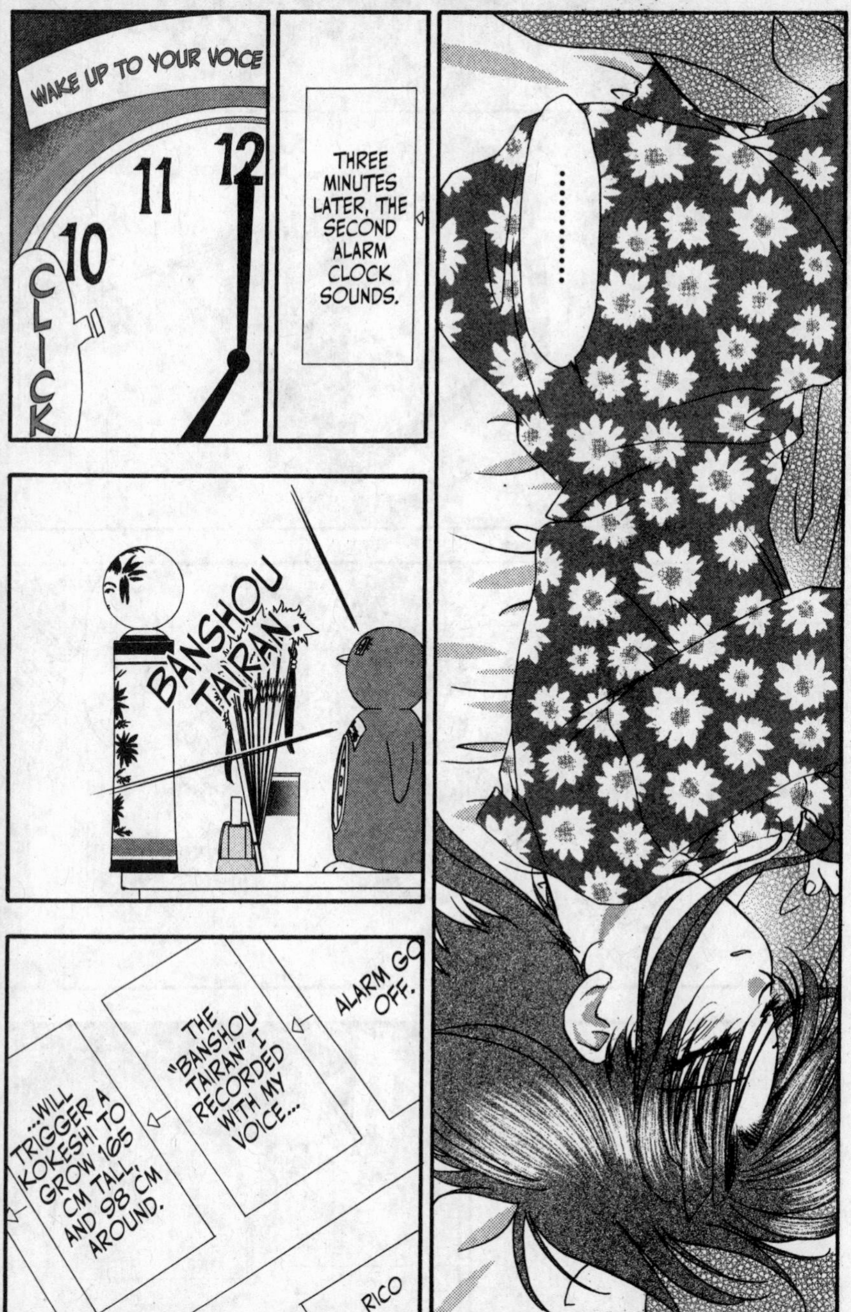
......
THREE MINUTES LATER, THE SECOND ALARM CLOCK SOUNDS.
WAKE UP TO YOUR VOICE
12
11
10
CLICK
BANSHOU TAIRAN.
ALARM GO OFF.
THE "BANSHOU TAIRAN" I RECORDED WITH MY VOICE...
...WILL TRIGGER A KOKESHI TO GROW 165 CM TALL, AND 98 CM AROUND.
RICO

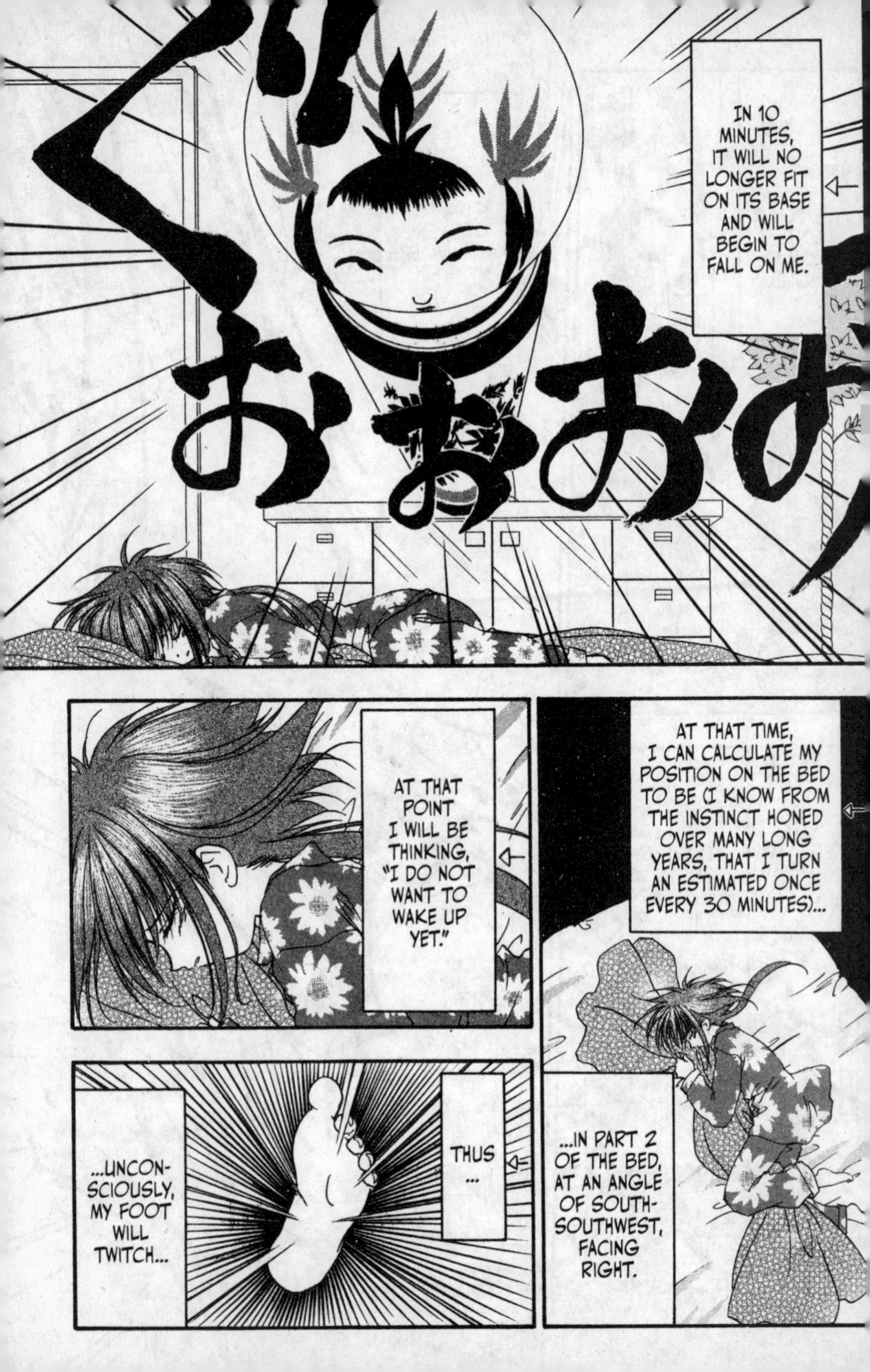
IN 10 MINUTES, IT WILL NO LONGER FIT ON ITS BASE AND WILL BEGIN TO FALL ON ME.
AT THAT TIME, I CAN CALCULATE MY POSITION ON THE BED TO BE (I KNOW FROM THE INSTINCT HONED OVER MANY LONG YEARS, THAT I TURN AN ESTIMATED ONCE EVERY 30 MINUTES)...
...IN PART 2 OF THE BED, AT AN ANGLE OF SOUTH-SOUTHWEST, FACING RIGHT.
AT THAT POINT I WILL BE THINKING, "I DO NOT WANT TO WAKE UP YET."
THUS ...
...UNCONSCIOUSLY, MY FOOT WILL TWITCH...

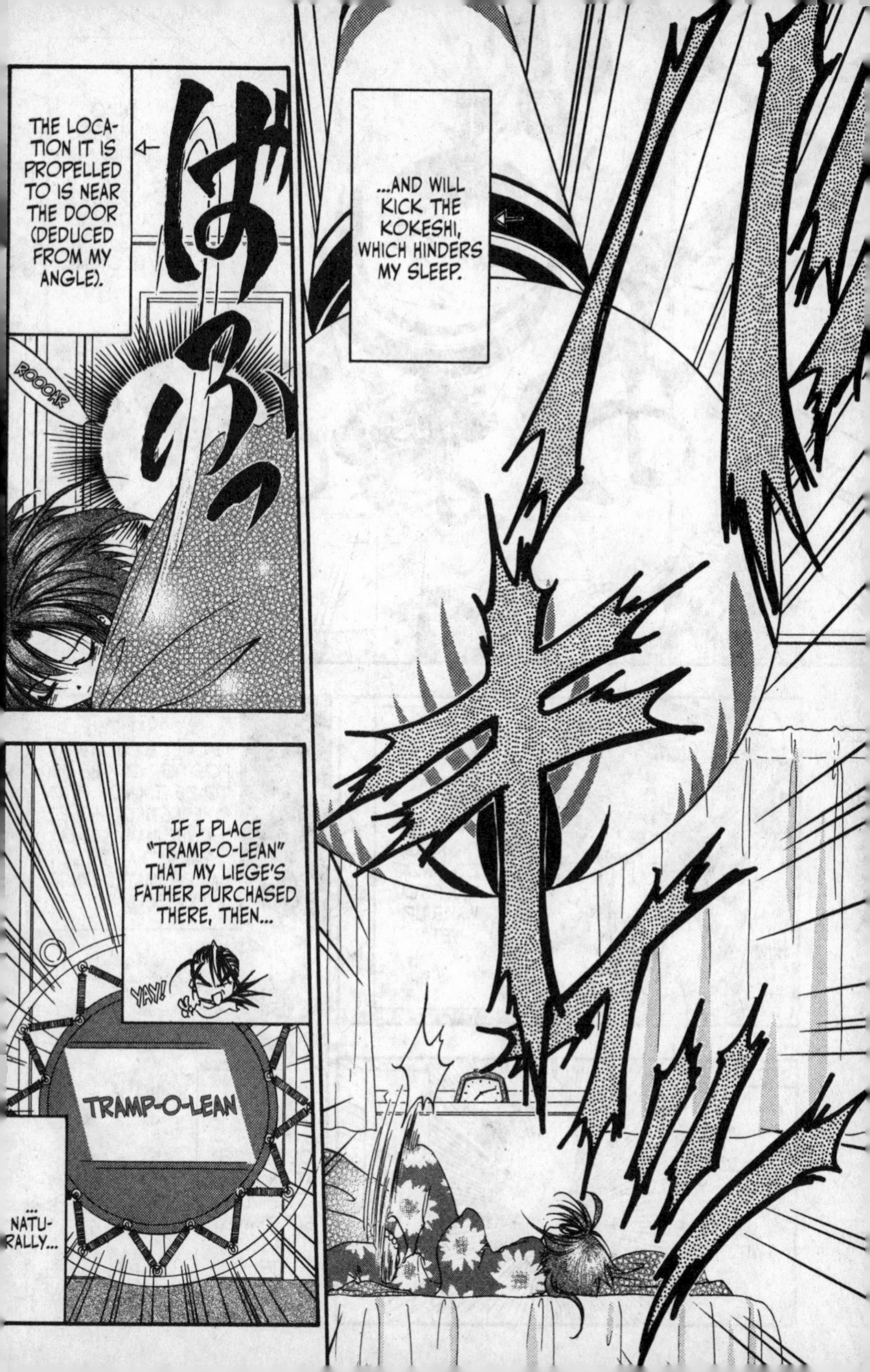
THE LOCATION IT IS PROPELLED TO IS NEAR THE DOOR (DEDUCED FROM MY ANGLE).
ROOOAR
IF I PLACE "TRAMP-O-LEAN" THAT MY LIEGE'S FATHER PURCHASED THERE, THEN...
YAY!
TRAMP-O-LEAN
... NATURALLY...
...AND WILL KICK THE KOKESHI, WHICH HINDERS MY SLEEP.

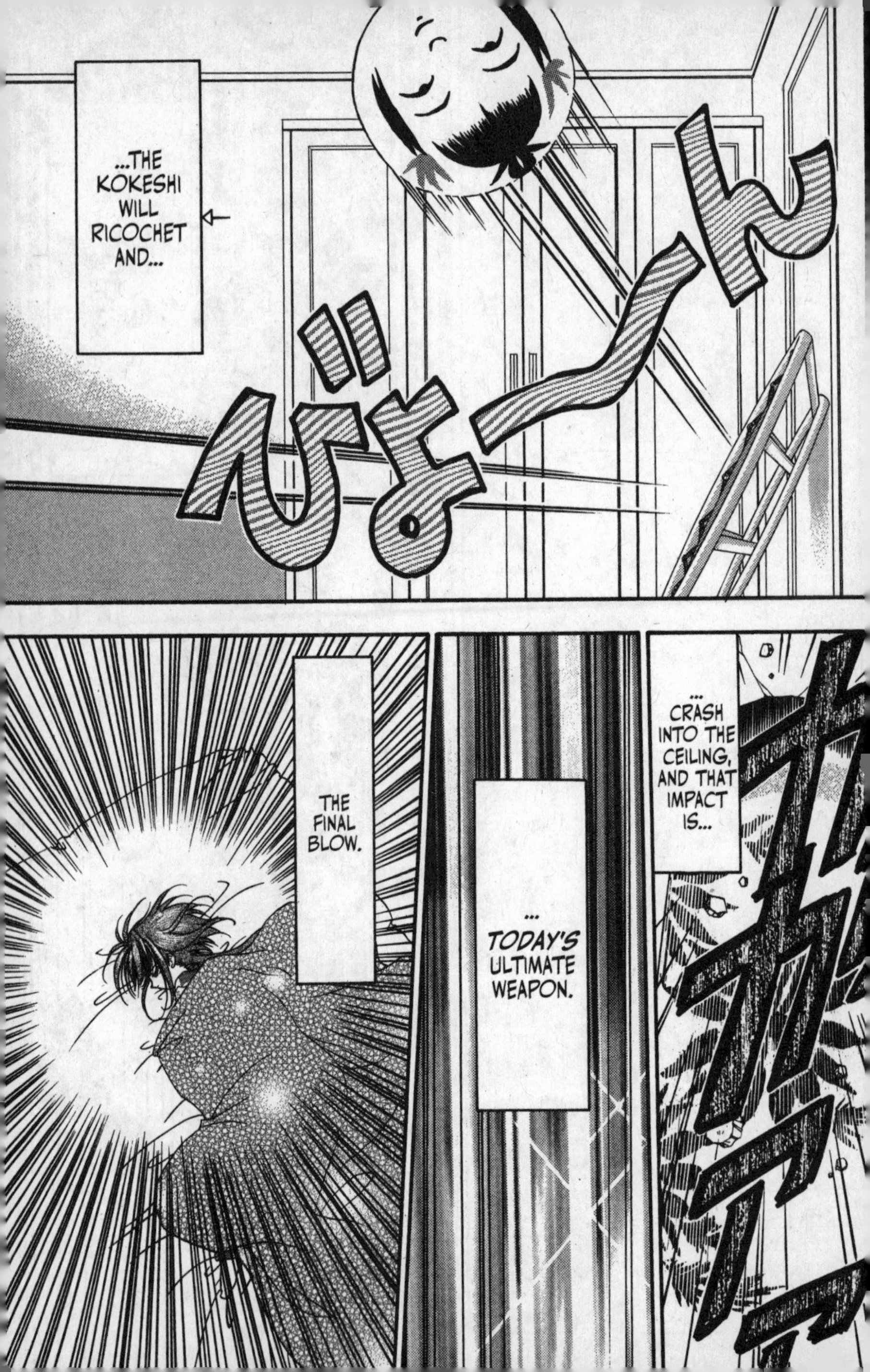
...THE KOKESHI WILL RICOCHET AND...
びよーん
...CRASH INTO THE CEILING, AND THAT IMPACT IS...
... TODAY'S ULTIMATE WEAPON.
THE FINAL BLOW.

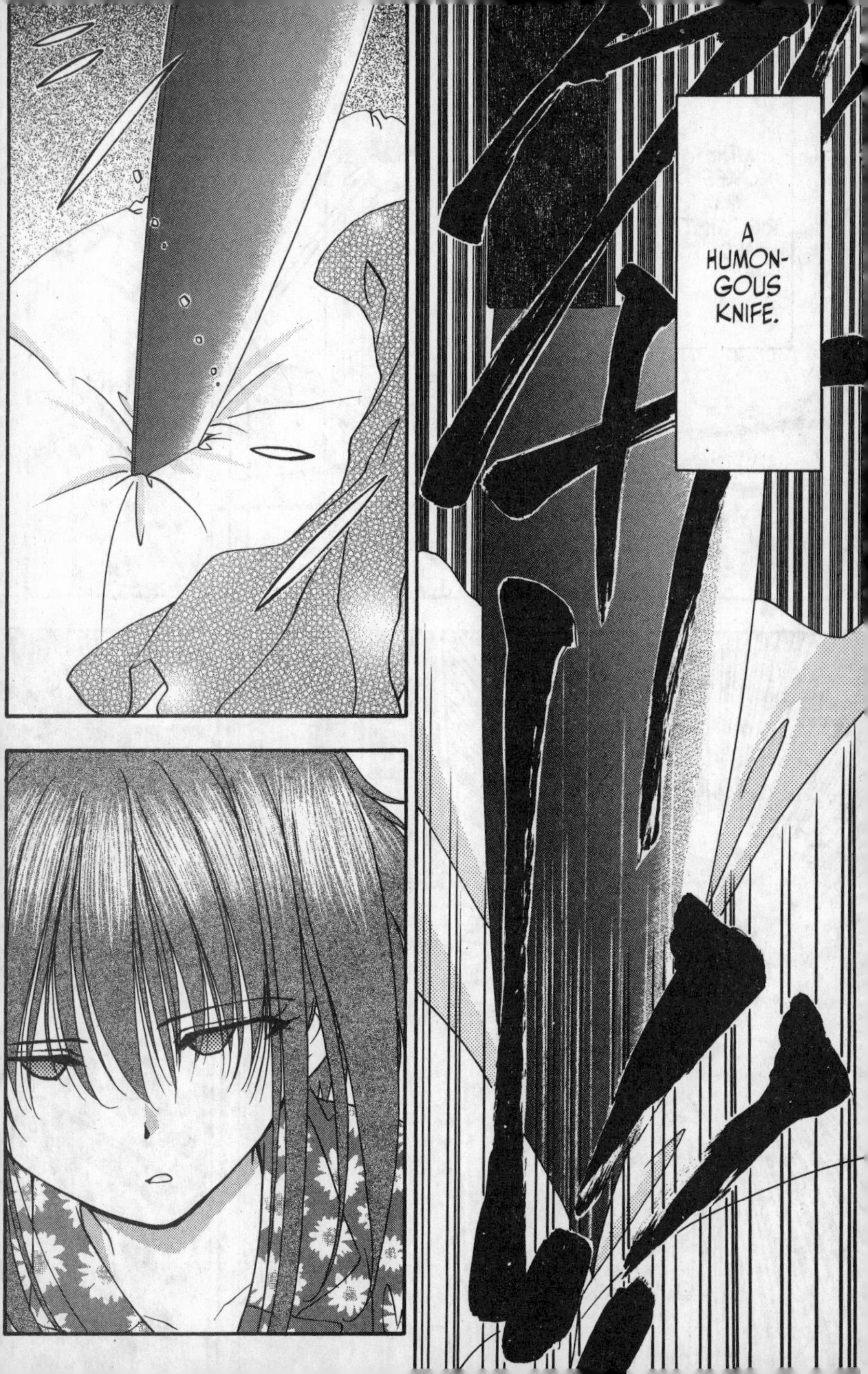
A HUMON-
GOUS
KNIFE.

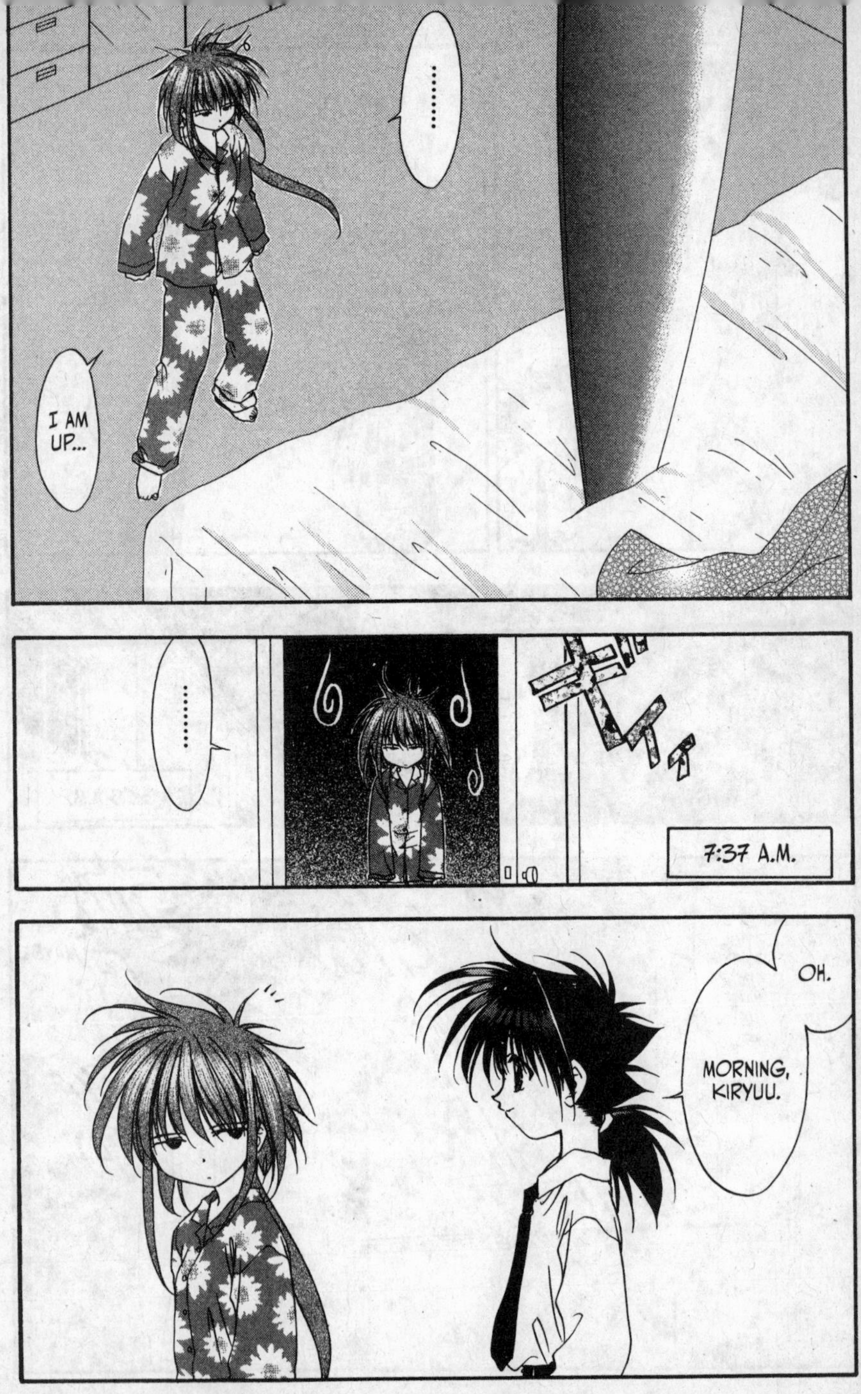
......
I AM UP...
7:37 A.M.
......
OH.
MORNING, KIRYUU.

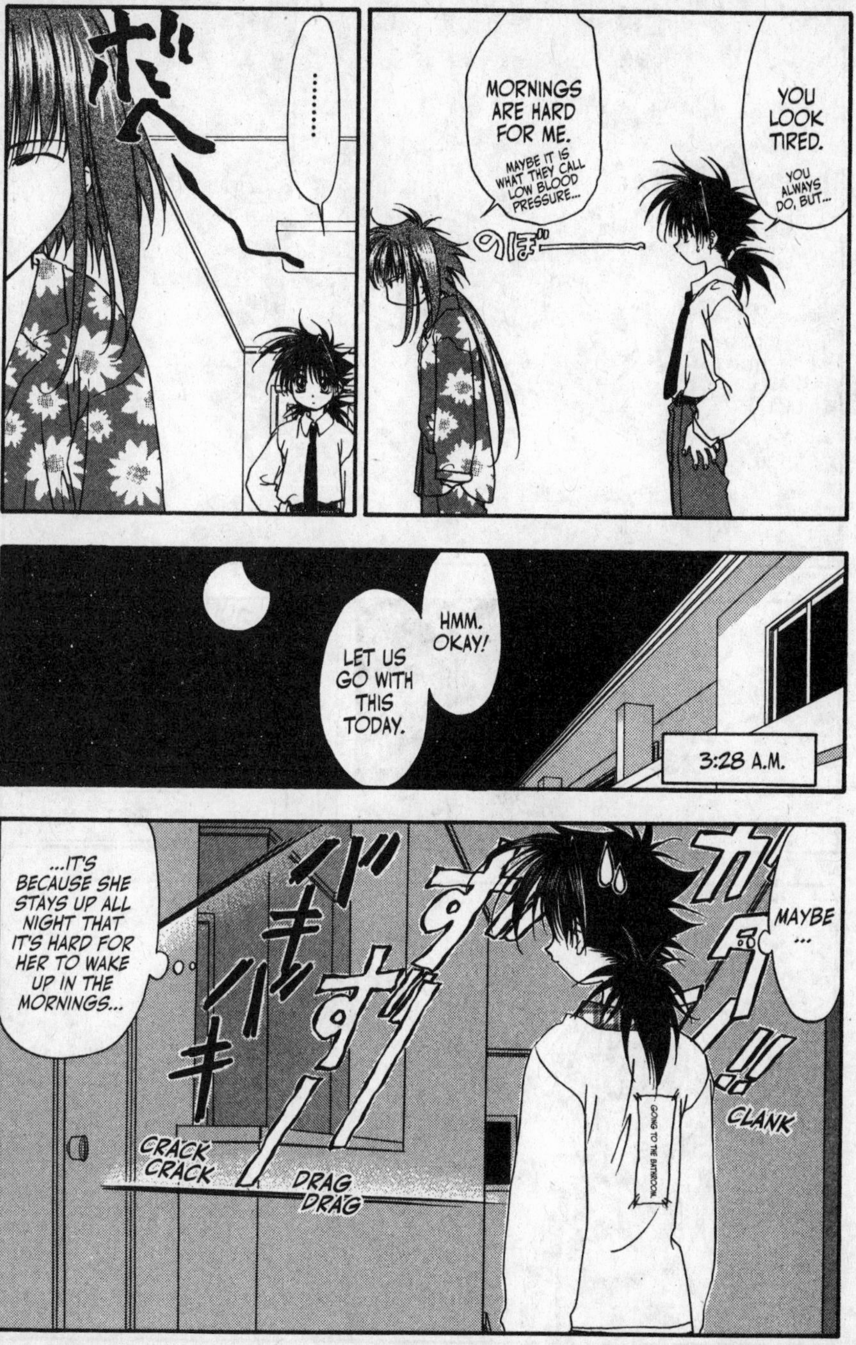
YOU LOOK TIRED.
YOU ALWAYS DO, BUT...
MORNINGS ARE HARD FOR ME.
MAYBE IT IS WHAT THEY CALL LOW BLOOD PRESSURE...
......
3:28 A.M.
HMM. OKAY!
LET US GO WITH THIS TODAY.
MAYBE ...
CLANK
GOING TO THE BATHROOM.
...IT'S BECAUSE SHE STAYS UP ALL NIGHT THAT IT'S HARD FOR HER TO WAKE UP IN THE MORNINGS...
DRAG DRAG
CRACK CRACK

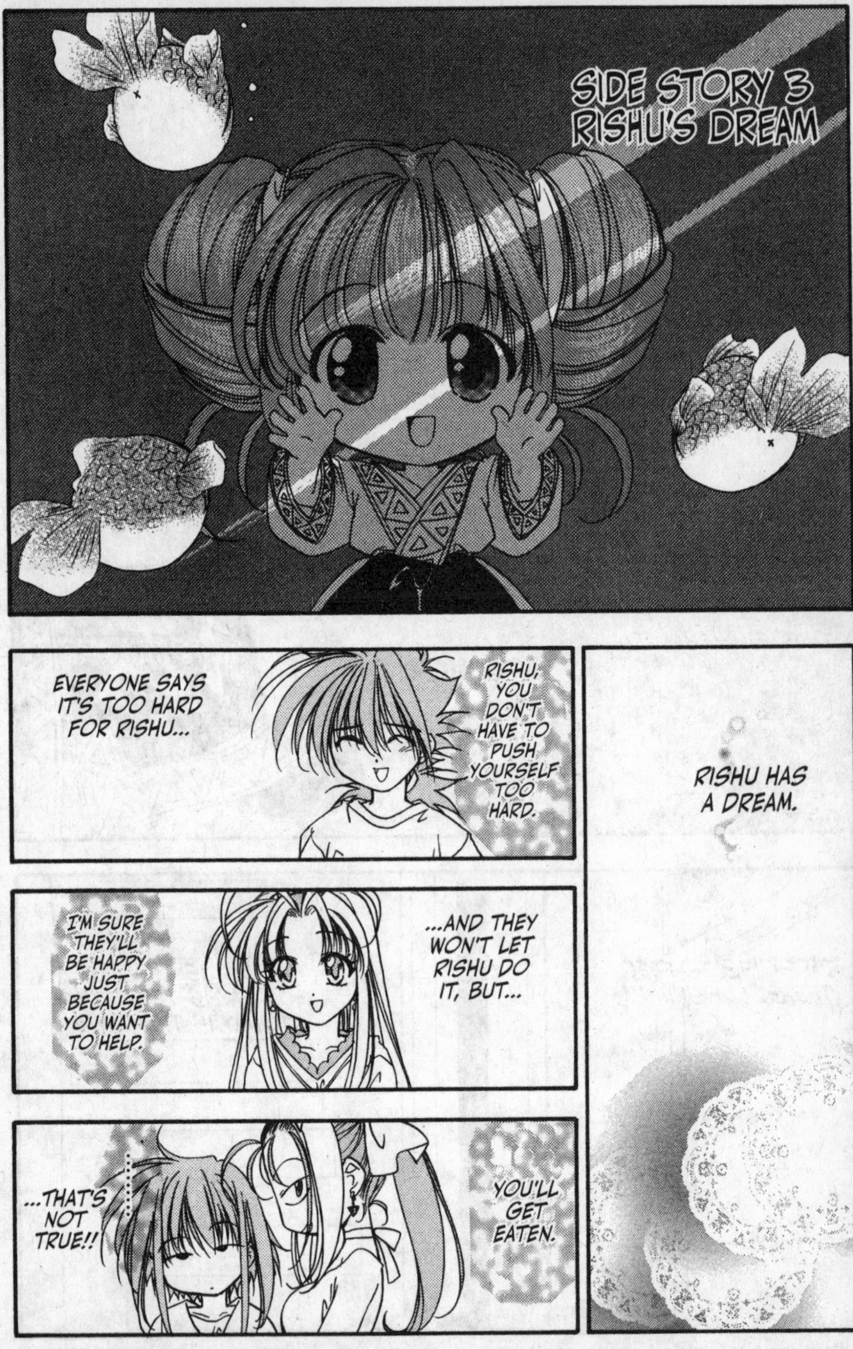
SIDE STORY 3
RISHU'S DREAM
RISHU HAS A DREAM.
RISHU, YOU DON'T HAVE TO PUSH YOURSELF TOO HARD.
EVERYONE SAYS IT'S TOO HARD FOR RISHU...
...AND THEY WON'T LET RISHU DO IT, BUT...
I'M SURE THEY'LL BE HAPPY JUST BECAUSE YOU WANT TO HELP.
YOU'LL GET EATEN.
...THAT'S NOT TRUE!!

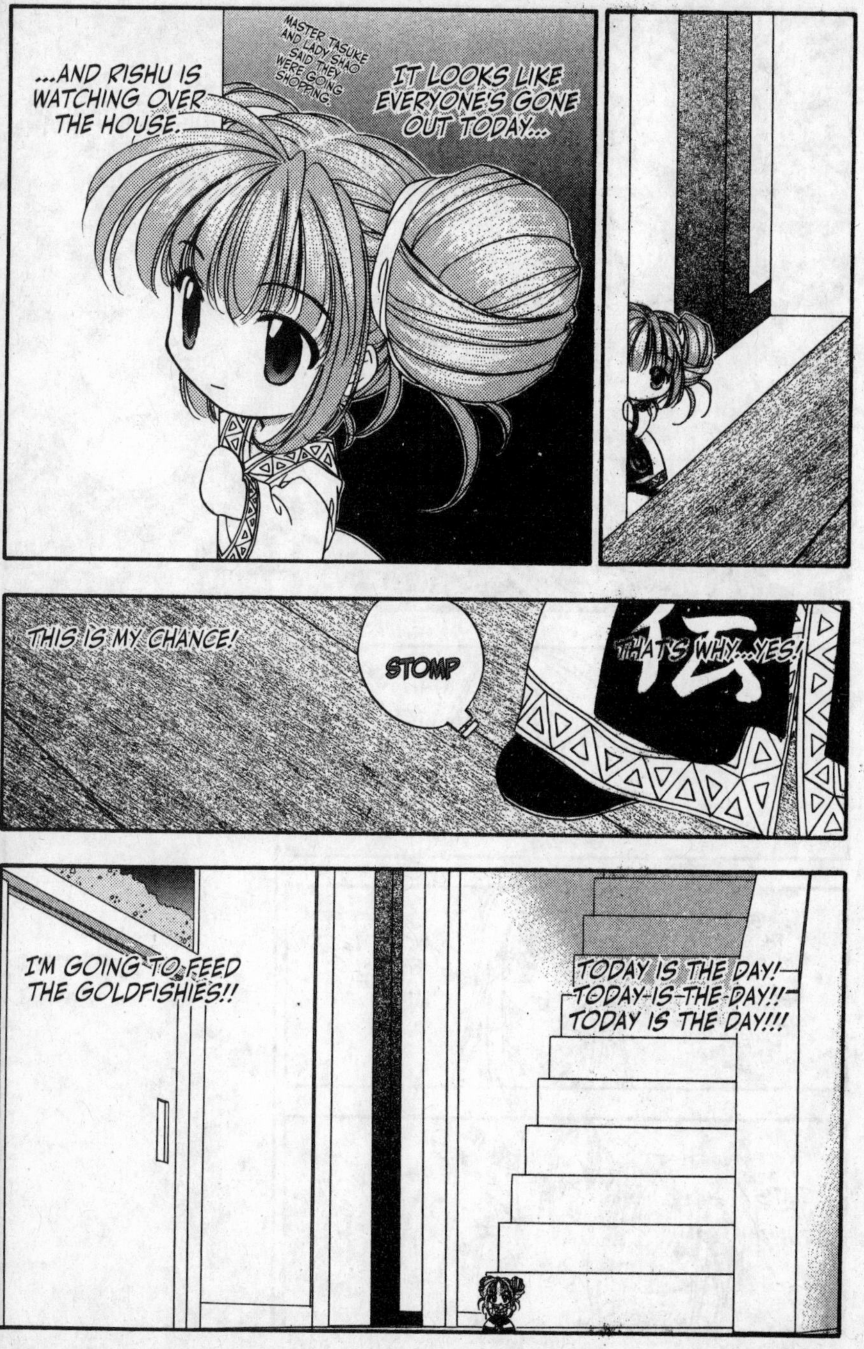
MASTER TASUKE AND LADY SHAO SAID THEY WERE GOING SHOPPING.
IT LOOKS LIKE EVERYONE'S GONE OUT TODAY...
...AND RISHU IS WATCHING OVER THE HOUSE.
THAT'S WHY...YES!
STOMP
THIS IS MY CHANCE!
TODAY IS THE DAY! TODAY IS THE DAY!! TODAY IS THE DAY!!!
I'M GOING TO FEED THE GOLDFISHIES!!

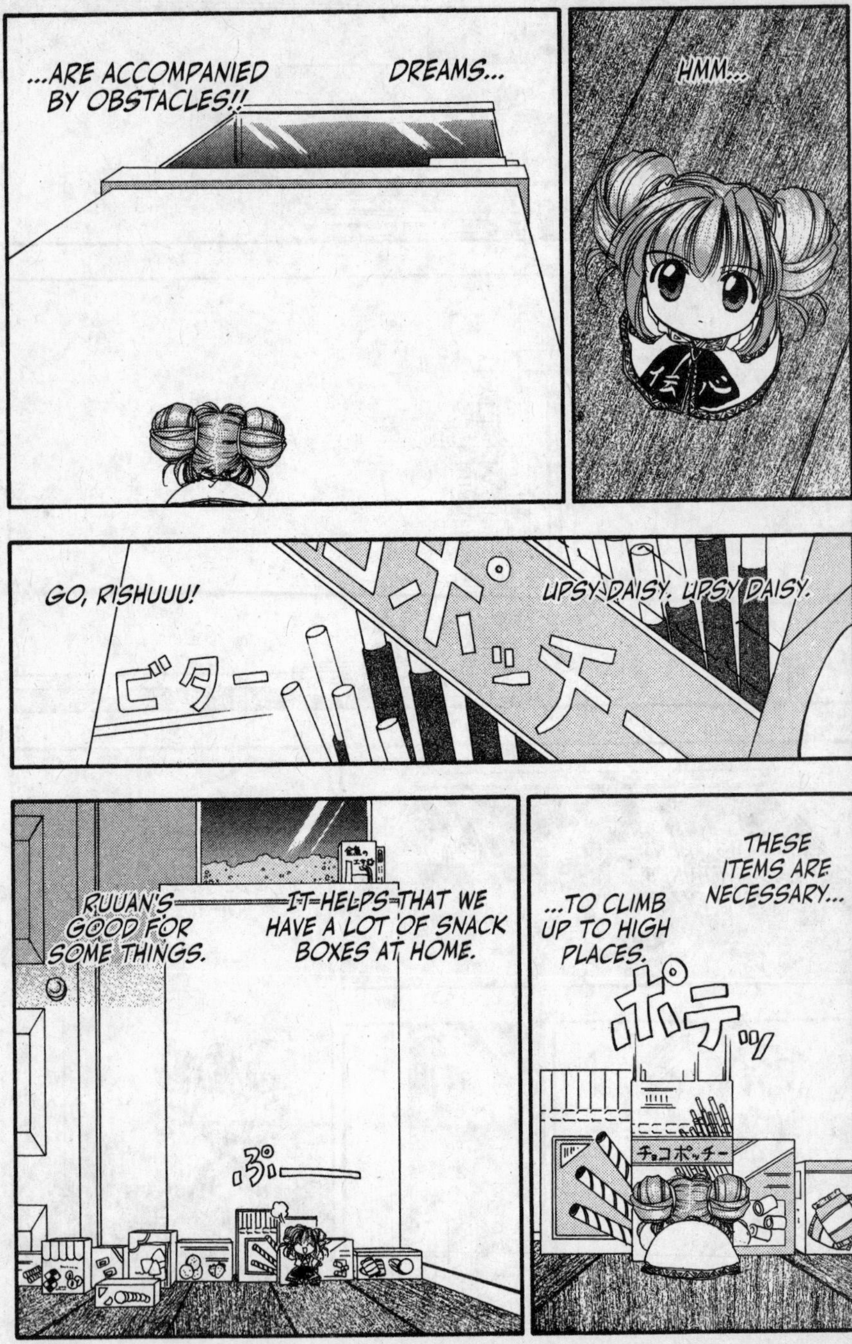
HMM...
DREAMS...
...ARE ACCOMPANIED BY OBSTACLES!!
UPSY-DAISY. UPSY DAISY.
GO, RISHUUU!
ビター
THESE ITEMS ARE NECESSARY...
...TO CLIMB UP TO HIGH PLACES.
ポテッ
チョコポッチー
IT HELPS THAT WE HAVE A LOT OF SNACK BOXES AT HOME.
RUUAN'S GOOD FOR SOME THINGS.
ぷー

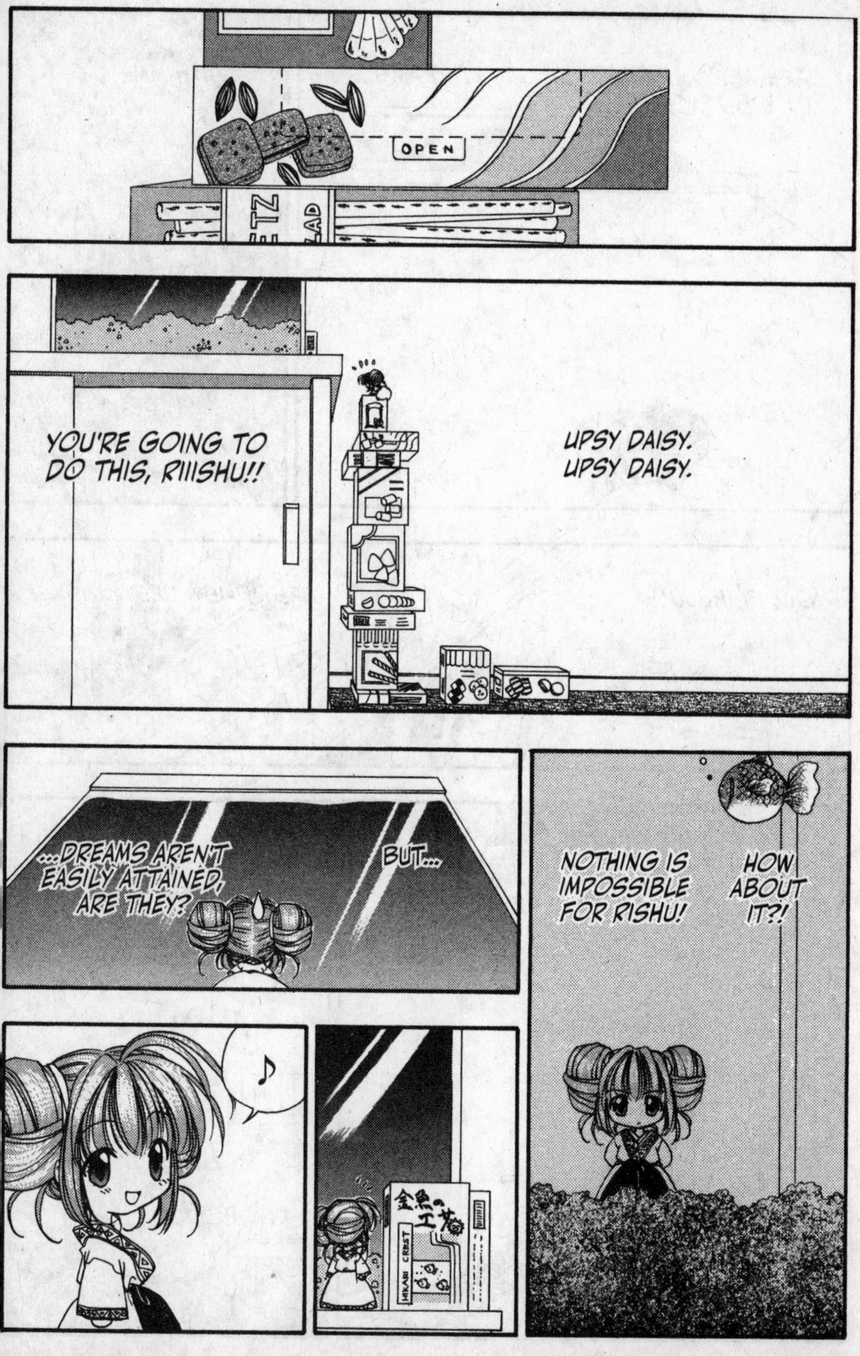
OPEN
UPSY DAISY. UPSY DAISY.
YOU'RE GOING TO DO THIS, RIIISHU!!
HOW ABOUT IT?!
NOTHING IS IMPOSSIBLE FOR RISHU!
BUT...
...DREAMS AREN'T EASILY ATTAINED, ARE THEY?
HIKARI CREST
♪

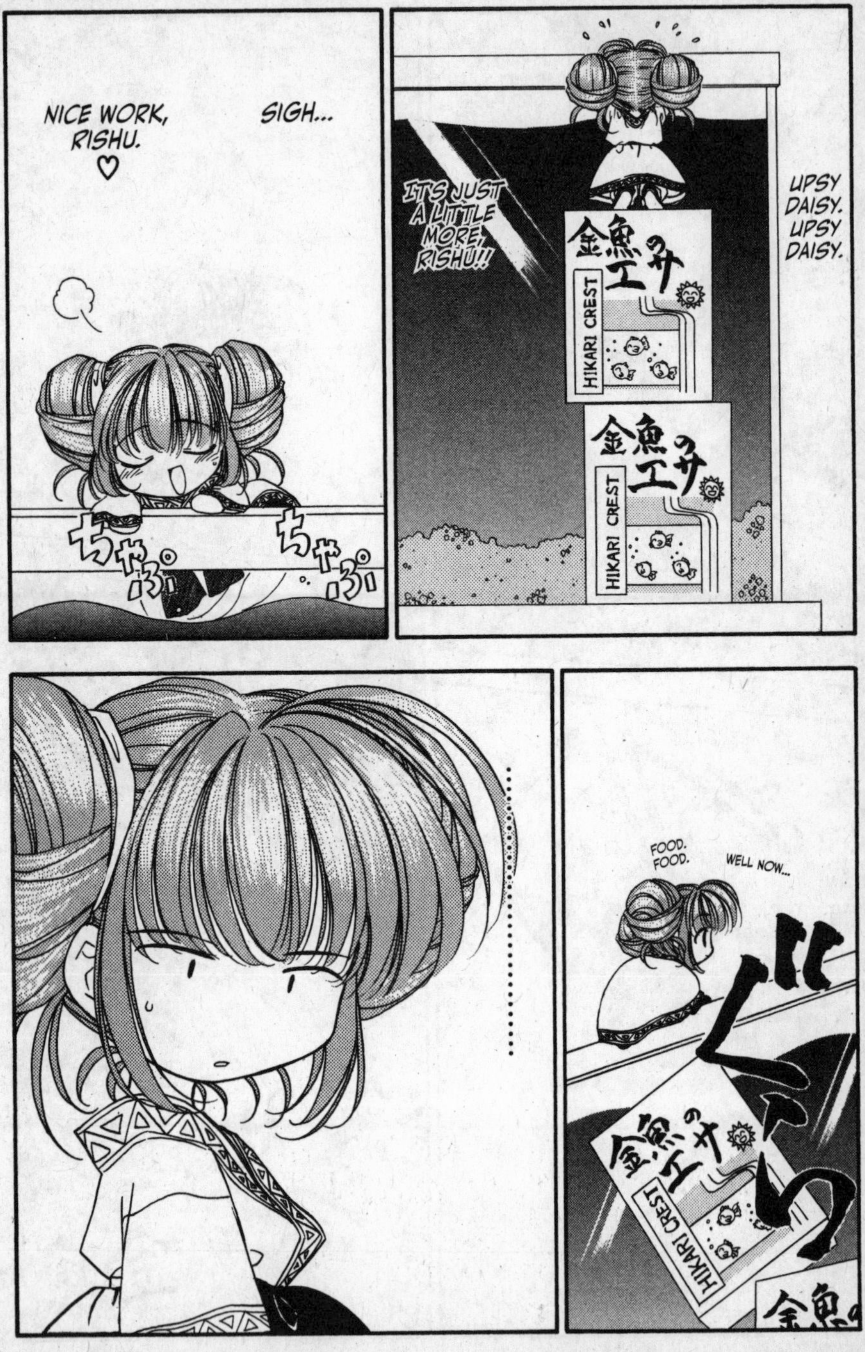
UPSY DAISY. UPSY DAISY.
IT'S JUST A LITTLE MORE, RISHU!!
金魚のエサ
HIKARI CREST
SIGH...
NICE WORK, RISHU. ♡
ちゃぷ ちゃぷ
WELL NOW...
FOOD. FOOD.
......

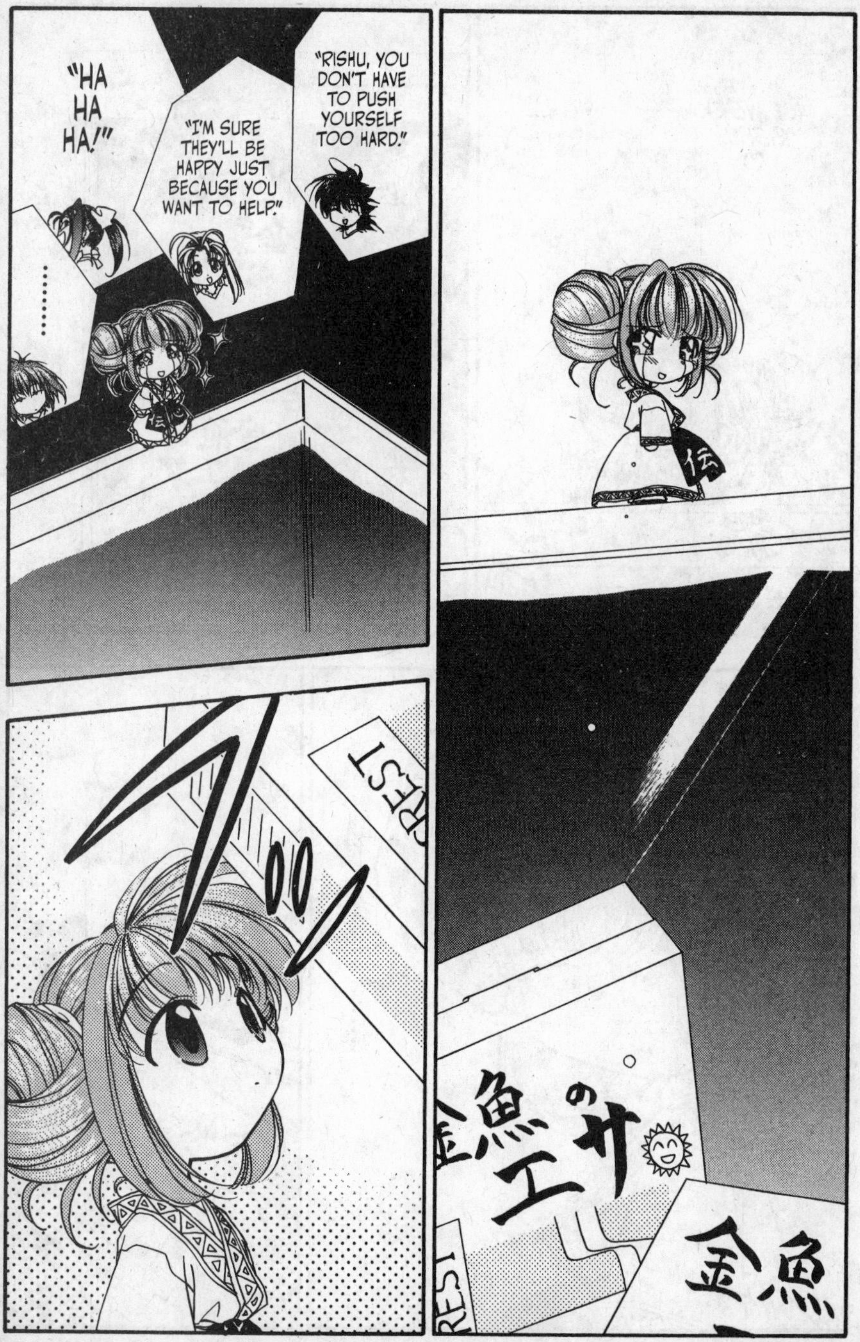
金魚のエサ
金魚
REST
"RISHU, YOU DON'T HAVE TO PUSH YOURSELF TOO HARD."
"I'M SURE THEY'LL BE HAPPY JUST BECAUSE YOU WANT TO HELP."
"HA HA HA!"
……
REST

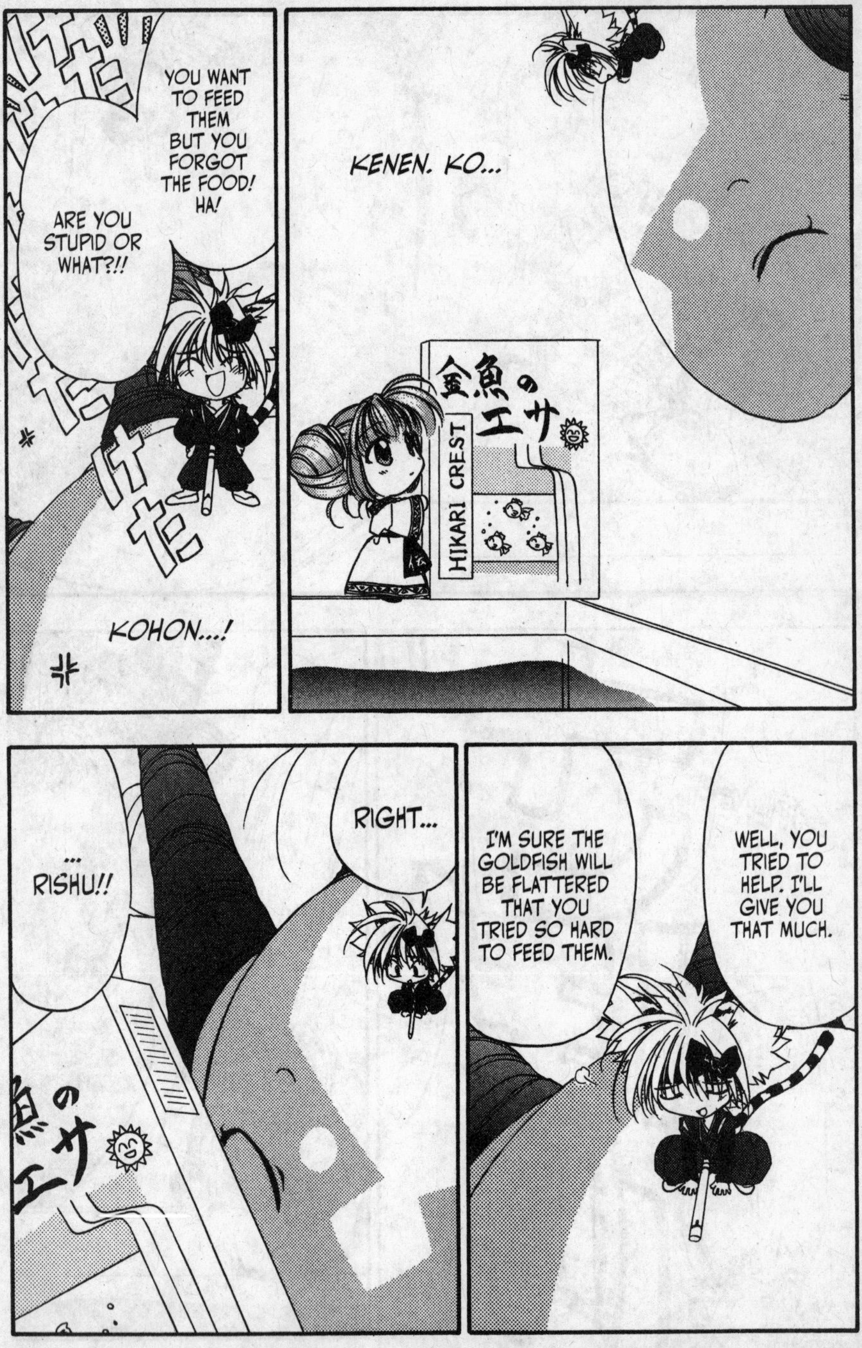
金魚のエサ
HIKARI CREST
KENEN. KO...
YOU WANT TO FEED THEM BUT YOU FORGOT THE FOOD! HA!
ARE YOU STUPID OR WHAT?!!
KOHON...!
WELL, YOU TRIED TO HELP. I'LL GIVE YOU THAT MUCH.
I'M SURE THE GOLDFISH WILL BE FLATTERED THAT YOU TRIED SO HARD TO FEED THEM.
RIGHT...
... RISHU!!

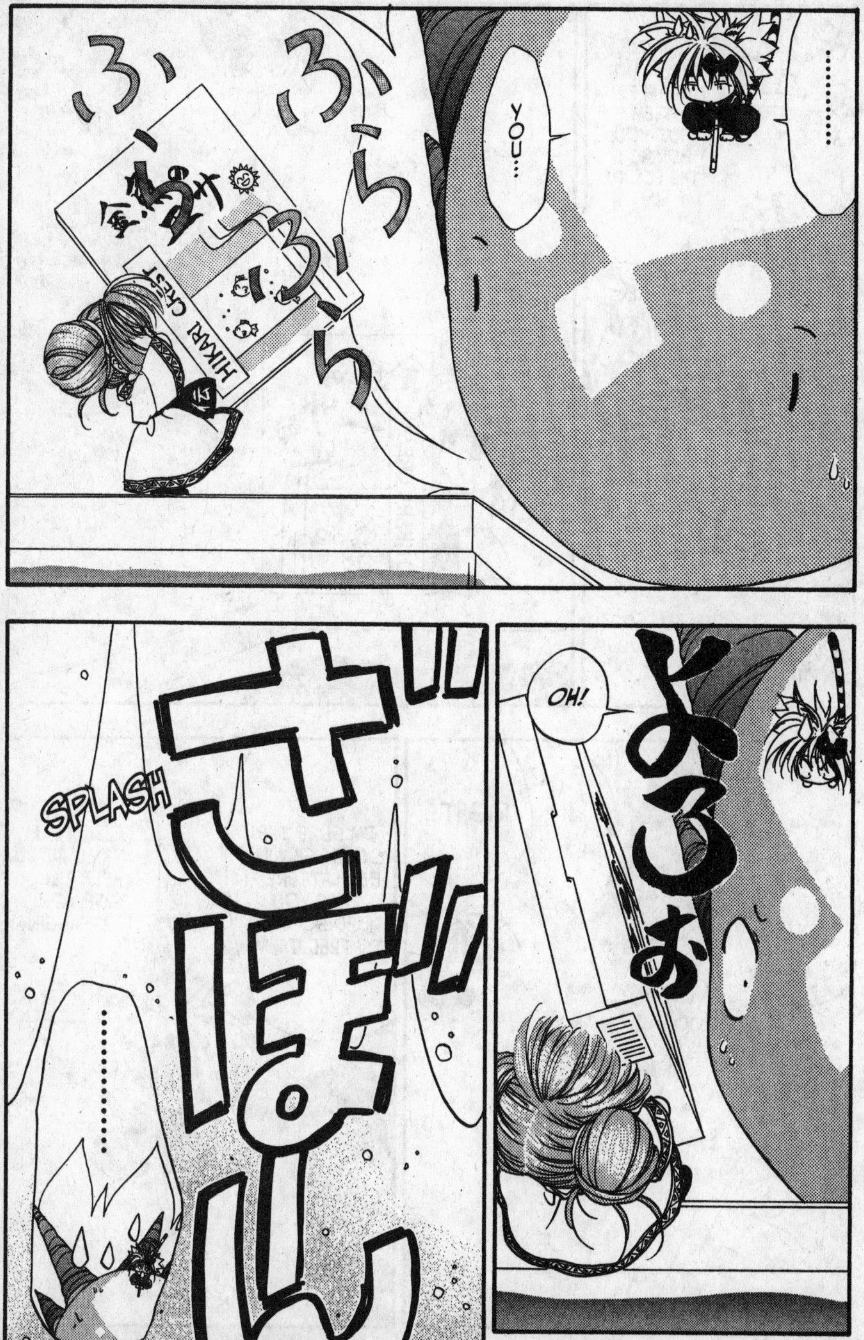

......
YOU...
ふらふら
ふらふら
HIKARI CREST
よろしお
OH!
ざっぽーん
SPLASH
......

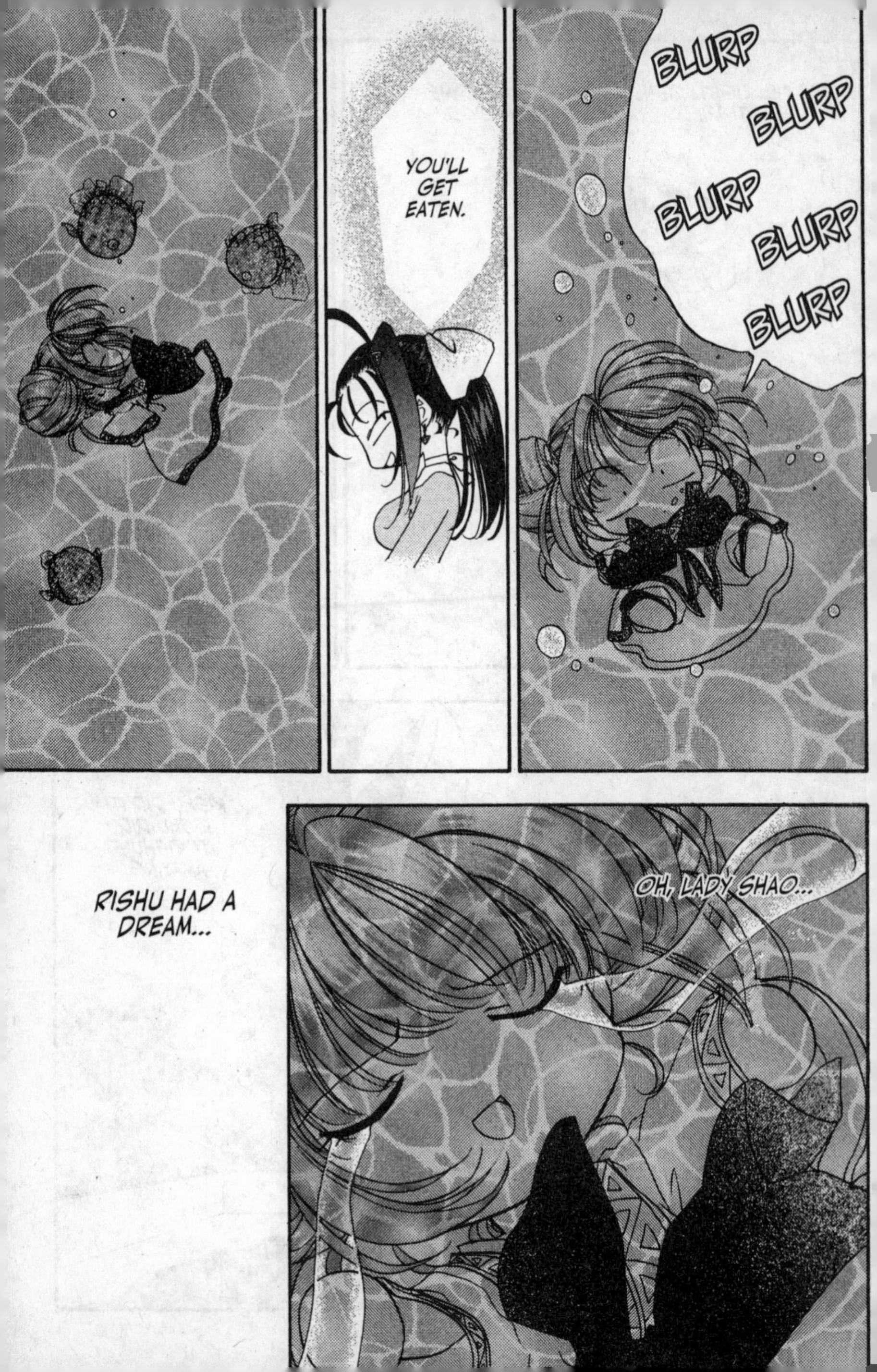
BLURP
BLURP
BLURP
BLURP
BLURP
YOU'LL GET EATEN.
OH, LADY SHAO...
RISHU HAD A DREAM...

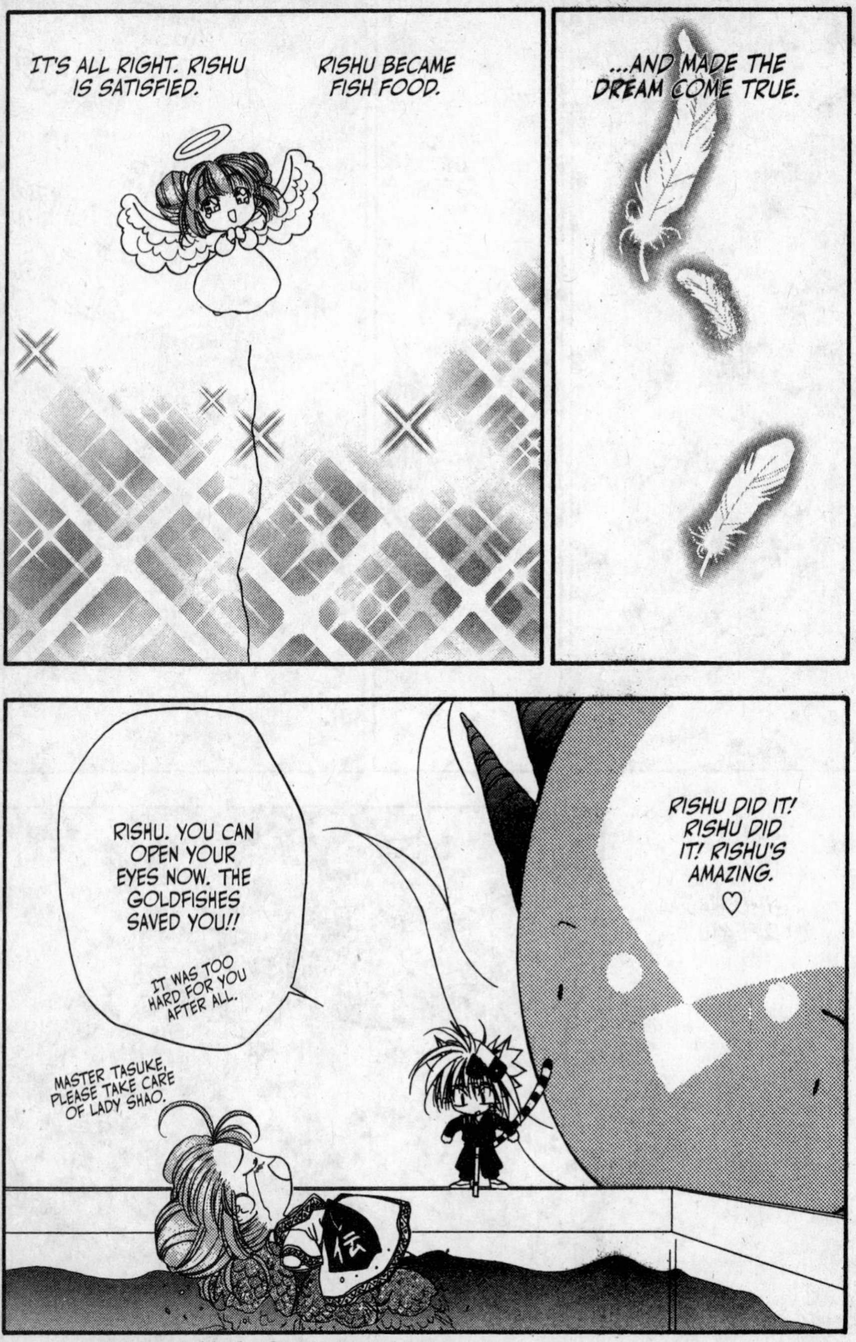
...AND MADE THE DREAM COME TRUE.
RISHU BECAME FISH FOOD.
IT'S ALL RIGHT. RISHU IS SATISFIED.
RISHU DID IT! RISHU DID IT! RISHU'S AMAZING. ♡
RISHU. YOU CAN OPEN YOUR EYES NOW. THE GOLDFISHES SAVED YOU!!
IT WAS TOO HARD FOR YOU AFTER ALL.
MASTER TASUKE, PLEASE TAKE CARE OF LADY SHAO.

MAMOTTE SHUGOGETTEN 8 THE END

IF YOU'RE PURE OF HEART YOU
SEE THIS NEXT VOLUME PREVIE

AFTER MANY BRUTAL PHYSICAL
TRIALS, KIRYUU DECIDES TO CHALLEN
TASUKE'S EMOTIONAL ABILITIES. SH
IS DELIBERATELY SENT TO STAY A
IZUMO'S HOUSE WHILE TASUKE STE
OVER THE POSSIBILITIES OF TH
PRIEST MOVING IN ON THE NAIVE A
UNSUSPECTING SHUGOGETTEN.
IT CERTAINLY DOESN'T HELP THAT
OLD NANKYOKU JYUSEI RETURNS
TAKE HIS LITTLE GIRL BACK A
WILL TASUKE AND SHAO'S LOVE
TO FRUITION IN THIS FINAL VO
OF *MAMOTTE SHUGOGETTE*
WILL SHAO GO BACK TO SHIT
TO AWAIT ANOTHER MASTE

STOP!

This is the back of the book.

uldn't want to spoil a great ending!

printed "manga-style," in the authentic Japanese right-to-left
e none of the artwork has been flipped or altered, readers
ence the story just as the creator intended. You've been
so TOKYOPOP® delivered: authentic, hot-off-the-press,
fun!

DIRECTIONS

1
2
5
6

If this is your first time reading manga-style, here's a quick guide to help you understand how it works.

It's easy... just start in the top right panel and follow the numbers. Have fun, and look for more 100% authentic manga from TOKYOPOP®!

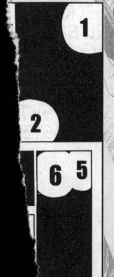

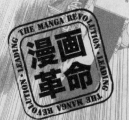